ESSAYS

ON THE

SCOTTISH REFORMATION

1513 — 1625

MARY, QUEEN OF SCOTS.

ESSAYS

ON THE

SCOTTISH
REFORMATION
1513-1625

Edited by

DAVID McROBERTS

BURNS

GLASGOW

1962

FIRST PUBLISHED . . . 1962

INDEXED IN EGLI

Printed in Scotland
by JOHN S. BURNS & SONS, 25 Finlas Street,
Glasgow, N.2.

Foreword

In 1959, when preparations were afoot for marking the fourth centenary of the protestant reformation in Scotland, *The Innes Review* devoted two issues to a series of essays by various scholars, dealing with aspects of ecclesiastical life in Scotland in the sixteenth century. The authors of the different articles tackled their subjects individually with little or no collaboration. Their independent investigations have brought to light facts overlooked by earlier writers and, very often, they have suggested a new analysis of situations and have produced unexpected estimates of motives and characters. In fact, there was so much new research material and so much fresh assessment of already known documents, incidents and personalities that it seemed desirable to re-issue these essays in one volume. The essays have been reprinted practically as they appeared in *The Innes Review*, with all their repetitions, some contradictions and inconsistencies, all of which have been allowed to stand, since they illustrate diverse aspects of subjects and diverse possible opinions. In addition to this reprinted matter, there has been added a lengthy essay on the religious orders, some primary documents and a series of illustrations with brief comments.

The remarkable feature of this enterprise has been that a group of scholars working independently on quite distinct aspects of sixteenth-century life in Scotland have produced the outline of a coherent account of events in Scotland between the years 1513 and 1625.

The history presented in these essays is somewhat different from the simple " traditional " stories which have long been accepted by one side or another in the writing of Scottish ecclesiastical history. Those " traditional " accounts were very largely based on the propaganda literature of one or other of the parties actually involved in the sixteenth-century struggle. No great movement in human history is simple or straightforward: the religious revolution in sixteenth-century Scotland least of all. The essays which follow show some of the complex influences which led to the revolution and disclose some of the mixed motives of those who played a part in the drama. The story which emerges from the following pages is much more involved, much more human, exciting and real, and therefore much more credible, than the uncomplicated and ingenuous tales of our grandfathers.

Much help from scholars, especially on the staffs of Scottish universities and major libraries, has assisted the production of this book. It is impossible to acknowledge individually the generosity of these and of others at home and furth of Scotland. We can only hope that the result of our united effort will be sufficiently valuable as a contribution to the further study of Scottish history to make them feel that their effort has not been wasted. And finally, we may be allowed to hope that the ungrudging help given to this work by protestant and catholic scholars alike is convincing proof that the " auld Parisiane kyndnes," which sometimes lightened sixteenth-century controversy, is still very much alive.

DAVID McROBERTS.

CONTENTS

LIST OF ILLUSTRATIONS

WITH NOTES THEREON

MARY, QUEEN OF SCOTS - - - - - *Frontispiece*

Mary, Queen of Scots, was at least nominal head of the Scottish
state during the whole critical period of the religious revolution.
Sooner or later, in discussing the Scottish reformation, the student
will meet problems, which make it necessary to form some estimate of Mary's enigmatic character. Historians will, for example,
continue to debate her part in the Kirk o' Field tragedy and, in
this matter, her character will remain till Judgment Day tarnished
by the peculiarly Scottish verdict " Not proven." Whatever her
innocence or guilt, the last eighteen years of her life provide a
spectacle of great endurance and steadfastness of purpose, and the
courage and regal serenity of her death give her an undying place
in European history. This " memorial portrait," now at Blairs
College, Aberdeen, was commissioned by her faithful retainers
and was preserved, down to the French Revolution, in the Scots
College at Douay. The portrait depicts Mary as a martyr for the
catholic faith and as foundress and patron of the Scots College
in Douay.

From the picture in Blairs College, Aberdeen.

PLATE I. JAMES V AND MARY OF GUISE - *facing p.* 16

The lives of James V and his second queen, Mary of Guise, span
the final decades of the decline of the medieval church in Scotland. Few leaders contributed more to the decay of the Scottish
church than these two politiques who, though devout catholics
according to the ideas of the time, consistently subordinated the
church to the exigencies of their own political schemes.

*From the portrait at Blair Castle, reproduced by kind permission
of His Grace the Duke of Atholl.*

ix

sists only of a choir and unfinished transept. As the middle ages drew to a close, the piety of kings, bishops, nobles and burghs found expression, not in establishing new monastic houses, but in the foundation of these collegiate kirks, where a group of clergy, organised on the lines of a cathedral chapter, performed the liturgy with considerable solemnity, carrying out the functions of a chantry foundation, as at Roslin or Biggar, or providing an important centre of education, as at King's College, Aberdeen, or St. Salvator's, at St. Andrews, or forming an influential centre of music, such as the Chapel Royal in the castle of Stirling.

PLATE V. DETAIL OF THE SIXTEENTH-CENTURY CHOIR
SCREEN, KING'S COLLEGE, ABERDEEN - *facing p.* 80

The only pre-reformation church in Scotland to retain its medieval choir stalls and screen in fairly complete form is Bishop Elphinstone's chapel in King's College, Aberdeen. The stalls, made in the early years of the sixteenth century, possibly by " Johne Fendour, wrycht," who made the stalls of the parish church of St. Nicholas in New Aberdeen, are in the richest style of the Gothic tradition and display all the varied detail and superb craftsmanship of the period. Few examples of Scottish pre-reformation ecclesiastical woodwork survive, but, if we may judge from the King's College stalls and the Beaton Panels from Arbroath, some Scottish medieval churches were as well furnished in this respect as any comparable churches in christendom.

From the photograph by Alexander Cain, A.R.P.S.

PLATE VI. PANEL OF THE TRINITY COLLEGE ALTAR-
PIECE - - - - - - - *facing p.* 81

Trinity College Kirk, founded by Mary of Gueldres, in 1462, on the outskirts of the city of Edinburgh, was in possession of a tabernacle, or altarpiece, painted by the famous Flemish artist, Hugo van der Goes. Two double panels of the altarpiece survive, displaying portraits of King James III and Queen Margaret of Denmark and it has been suggested that the picture was a memorial of the royal marriage, which took place at Holyrood in 1469. The panel shown in the illustration depicts Sir Edward Boncle, provost of Trinity College Kirk from 1462 to 1496: he wears his choir habit, a long linen surplice, and over his arm hangs his furred almuce. In the background is an organ of fifteenth-century type, such as was common enough in the larger churches of medieval Scotland.

*From the picture in the National Gallery of Scotland, reproduced
by gracious permission of Her Majesty the Queen.*

This manuscript choir book from the abbey of Scone contains a dozen polyphonic settings for the Ordinary of the Mass, some thirty motets, six settings for the *Magnificat* and two for the *Salve Regina* and many of these compositions are by Robert Carver, canon of Scone, and written between the years 1513 and 1546. The illustration shows the opening page of Carver's ten-part mass, where Carver records that he wrote the mass in honour of St. Michael, patron of the abbey, in the year 1513, when he was twenty-two years of age. A surviving manuscript such as this, taken in conjunction with Court and burgh records, makes it clear that, in the greater churches of late medieval Scotland, music of very high quality was performed and some proportion of the music was the work of native composers.

From the Manuscript in the National Library of Scotland.

This late medieval processional banner was preserved for the past century at the catholic church of Fetternear in Aberdeenshire. From its heraldry and decoration one can deduce that this banner (which is in an unfinished state) was being made, about the year 1521, for the confraternity of the Holy Blood in the collegiate kirk of St. Giles in Edinburgh and the embroidering of the banner was stopped because of the exile and unexpected death, in London in 1522, of Gavin Douglas, bishop of Dunkeld and provost of the college kirk of St. Giles. The decorative motifs of the banner—rosary, confraternity cords, passion symbolism and the Image of Pity—show that the devotional imagery prevalent in northern Europe was familiar in sixteenth-century Edinburgh.

From the original in the National Museum of Antiquities of Scotland: reproduced by permission of the Bishop of Aberdeen.

There appear to have been well over one hundred hospitals, founded in connection with the medieval church in Scotland. These hospitals provided social services, catering for the needs of the sick, pilgrims, lepers, poor, aged and infirm of all kinds. While they varied in size the bulk of them were small institutions and they were founded both by ecclesiastics and layfolk: Dunbar's Hospital in Old Aberdeen, for example, was founded by Bishop Gavin Dunbar in 1531 and Trinity Hospital in Edinburgh was the foundation, in 1460, of Mary of Gueldres, queen of James II.

The illustration of Dunbar's Hospital, Aberdeen, is from the original picture in Aberdeen University Library, by kind permission of the Librarian.

PLATE X. THE SACRAMENT OF EXTREME UNCTION

This fifteenth-century bas-relief represents the administration of the Sacrament of Extreme Unction. It was found in Edinburgh in 1859, when the foundations of an old house in Mary King's Close were being cleared away. The carving has formed part of a fifteenth-century retable, representing the Seven Sacraments which, no doubt, adorned the altar of some church or chapel in Edinburgh. The scene depicted in the carving would be very familiar in the parochial life of medieval Scotland. The sick man lies in bed; the priest, at the head of the bed, holds the oil stock (somewhat weathered); beside the priest stands the parish clerk, vested in surplice and holding the " holy water styk and stop." The third figure, at the foot of the bed, is an acolyte, dressed in surplice, holding a lighted candle (rather broken) and a book for the responses. The sick man's children kneel here and there in the room, praying for their father's recovery, and the physician, at the window, prepares some potion. Historians who think that it is sufficient to repeat Sir David Lindsay's anti-clerical gibes about " umest clayis " or the " best cow " are perpetuating a caricature and they fail to appreciate another aspect of medieval ministry, the deep religious consolation and spiritual peace that the Last Sacraments brought not only to the sick but also to their families.

From the original in the National Museum of Antiquities of Scotland.

PLATE XI. TITLE-PAGE OF ARCHIBALD HAY'S ADDRESS, PROPOSING THE FOUNDATION OF ST. MARY'S COLLEGE, ST. ANDREWS - - - - *facing p.* 144

Scotland, which was a small kingdom, had a disproportionate number of its ecclesiastics trained partially or completely abroad: this meant that the higher ecclesiastical ranks of the pre-reformation church in Scotland were very strongly influenced by all the changing ideas and tendencies of the larger European community. Here we have Archibald Hay, a nephew of Archbishop James Beaton of St. Andrews, while still at the university of Paris in 1538, proposing to his uncle the foundation of a very modern college at St. Andrews, where Greek and Hebrew, as well as Latin, should be taught (together with Arabic and Chaldaic if possible) and medicine should be included in the curriculum. The proposed college should also have a well stocked library and a printing press. Archibald Hay's later *Gratulatorius Panegyricus,* addressed to Cardinal David Beaton of St. Andrews, suggests that the cardinal was vigorously planning to realise the sort of college proposed by his humanist cousin and eventually St. Mary's College at St. Andrews became, in some respects, the outcome of these humanist dreams.

Library of the Dean and Chapter of York Minster.

This illustration shows the surviving sixteenth-century wing of St. Mary's College at St. Andrews, founded by Archbishop James Beaton, in 1539, as part of a drive to improve the efficiency of the *Studium Generale* of St. Andrews and to raise the level of scholarship of the diocesan clergy. St. Leonard's College at St. Andrews, founded a quarter of a century earlier, in 1512, by Prior John Hepburn of St. Andrews, had a similar purpose and illustrates the concern with higher standards of learning among the religious orders.

Picture by courtesy of the Royal Commission on Ancient and Historical Monuments of Scotland.

Scots religious, at the close of the middle ages, played their part in the internal reformation of the church that had been gradually gathering momentum since the fifteenth century. Scots Carmelite friars are to be found, for example, among the leaders of the reform movement which produced the reformed Carmelite Congregation of Albi, in France. The rejuvenation of the Franciscan order in Scotland is marked by the foundation of Observant friaries in Scotland, in the reigns of James IV and James V. The regimes of Abbots Chrystall and Reid at Kinloss, Abbot Walter Malin at Glenluce or Abbot Mylne at Cambuskenneth show the new leaven at work among the older orders of monks and canons. Scots names appear prominently too among the new counter-reformation orders of Jesuits and Capuchins. The illustration shows a copy, made by Alexander Makneill, notary, of a bull of indulgence, granted by Pope Leo X on 5th June, 1518, to the reformed Scottish Dominicans. The bull mentions that their provincial, Friar John Adamson, had lately journeyed to Rome for the chapter-general of the whole order (where he was considered for election as master general of the order in succession to Cardinal Cajetan) and that, in the reform of the Scottish province begun by Adamson, a closer following of the rule was being inculcated, more friars were taking up the study of theology and a new revival of interest in the liturgy was evident.

From the original in the National Library of Scotland.

This work on the immortality of the soul was written by the Italian humanist, Pico della Mirandola, and edited, in 1541, by Giovanni Ferreri, an Italian scholar living in France, who had been engaged by the abbot to give lessons to the monks at Kinloss. While in Scotland, Ferreri's contacts had not been restricted to Kinloss Abbey and, on his return to Paris he corresponded with prominent Scots ecclesiastics. This is his presentation copy to Henry Sinclair, who later became bishop of Ross. The evidence for the soul's immortality was widely questioned in the sixteenth century, so much so that the Scots provincial council of 1549 was moved to legislate " against those who deny the immortality of the soul."

Edinburgh University Library.

This panoramic view, published in Lyon's *History of St. Andrews,* is based on an early drawing, which must date to about the year 1530. It shows the city of St. Andrews—the ecclesiastical metropolis of medieval Scotland—as it appeared before it was shorn of its glory in the religious revolution. Conspicuous on the sea front is the archbishop's castle or palace, which, a few years later, would be the scene of Cardinal Beaton's murder. The metropolitan cathedral (drawn with strange lack of perspective), with the adjacent priory and the church of St. Rule, are all enclosed within the great precinct wall, recently built by Priors John and Patrick Hepburn. The collegiate church of St. Mary of the Rock overlooks the harbour: the collegiate establishments of St. Salvator, St. Mary and St. Leonard are all indicated by name: the parish church of the Holy Trinity is easily picked out and the houses of the Blackfriars and Greyfriars are as yet undamaged by the followers of Norman Leslie or John Knox.

This portrait of Cardinal David Beaton came originally from the Scots College in Rome (which may have inherited it from the earlier Scots Hospice in Rome) and it is now preserved in Blairs College, Aberdeen. Beaton, the outstanding statesman of the Scottish church in the sixteenth century, is typical of the ecclesiastical careerist of his time; a man of lax morals, who through the influence first of his uncle, Archbishop James Beaton, and later of his own diplomacy at the Scots and French Courts, attained to the highest position possible in the Scottish church—archbishop of St.

Andrews and primate, legate *a latere* of the Holy See and cardinal priest of the Holy Roman Church. Beaton's patriotism and statesmanship made him the greatest obstacle to the political schemes of Henry VIII in Scotland: the assassination plot, fostered by the English king, combined with other local and personal vendettas to result in the brutal murder of the cardinal in the castle of St. Andrews on the 29th May, 1546, an event which proved to be a major disaster to the cause of the catholic religion in Scotland.

From the picture in Blairs College, Aberdeen.

Even the ill-documented diocese of the Isles was not without its contacts with the renaissance learning of Europe. The author of the work from which this title-page comes is Roderick Maclean, firstly archdeacon, then bishop of the Isles. It consists of Latin verses in praise of St. Columba, the patron of his diocese. Roderick Maclean describes himself here as " Son of Hector " and a " Scottish Gael," and, as " Roderick, son of Hector, Irishman." Maclean had previously matriculated at Luther's university of Wittenberg. By 1549 he had returned to the faith of his ancestors and he published this work at Rome with the famous renaissance printer, Blado. On this title-page are some Greek verses by James Thornton, subdean of Ross, addressing the man who likes to be at odds with his fellows.

Aberdeen University Library.

In the first half of the sixteenth century in Scotland, a twofold liturgical revival was in progress. The earlier revival was centred in Aberdeen and is associated with the scholars of Bishop Elphinstone's *Studium Generale*. This aimed at expurgating and revising the medieval Sarum liturgical books, which were in use, and the publication of a standard Scottish version of the Sarum Use for the whole kingdom. The most important surviving product of this movement is the *Aberdeen Breviary* sponsored by Bishop Elphinstone. A somewhat later Scottish liturgical movement turned to the more radical revision of the Roman liturgical books, effected on the continent by the Spanish Cardinal Quignones. About twenty of these Quignonian books—breviaries and missals—survive from sixteenth-century Scotland: these books are associated with the names of well known ecclesiastics, who were striving for an internal reformation of the church, such as Robert Reid, bishop of Orkney. The illustration shows the title-page of a Quignonian breviary, published at Lyons in 1546, which belonged successively to John Greenlaw, prebendary of Corstorphine, and John Watson, canon of Aberdeen, thus proving a link of friendship between two churchmen, who are both known to have been active on behalf of the internal reformation of the church.

Library of St. Gregory's Church, Preshome, Banffshire.

The unique copy of this book on the mass is preserved in the British Museum. It was published at Mainz, in 1544, and it was written in Germany by Robert Wauchope, a Scots theologian, who was sent by Pope Paul III, along with some other catholic reforming priests into Lutheran-infected territories. The appointment of Wauchope to a post in Scotland was resisted by James V, but the pope appointed him Archbishop of Armagh and he was active, in that capacity, in many discussions during the early stages of the Council of Trent. In this book, Wauchope vigorously defended the sacrificial character of the mass against those who attacked it and he also argues that it is unnecessary to allow the chalice to the laity. He may have acted as a liaison officer between the Scottish prelates and Trent: he certainly interested himself in Scottish relations with Trent.

By kind permission of the Director and Trustees of the British Museum.

The illustration shows the title-page, from the unique copy in the British Museum, of *An Comfortable Exhortation* by John Johnsone, who refers to himself as a humble professor of divinity, but who has not otherwise been identified. The author was undoubtedly a Scot and a witness of the death of Patrick Hamilton who, in 1528, was the first Scot to suffer for Lutheranism. The book was addressed to the " Christian brethren " in Scotland, that is to the Lutherans. The title-page gives the place of printing as Paris, but this is a false imprint. The book was actually printed, in 1535, by Hoochstraten, who also printed Patrick Hamilton's *Places* and the Lutheran catechism of John Gau. Hoochstraten's secret press travelled from the Low Countries to what was then Denmark and back. This work was probably printed by him in Antwerp and secretly exported from there to Scotland, part of the inflow of heretical works, which the Scottish Parliament attempted to halt by legislation on several occasions in the early sixteenth century.

By kind permission of the Director and Trustees of the British Museum.

The little town of Dundee, which probably had fewer than 5,000 inhabitants in the sixteenth century, was one of the principal ports of the realm, trading with the Low Countries and the Hanseatic cities. Being a commercial centre, it was open to all continental influences and its burgesses were in direct contact with the Lutheran ideas of the north German and Scandinavian states. Dundee became early a stronghold of Lutheran doctrines and it became the port of entry and departure for many religious idealists and refugees: protestants like Alexander Alane escaped by way of Dundee in 1530, and John Wedderburn in 1538: later, catholics like Father John Hay, the Jesuit, in 1579, or George Strachan, in 1602, found the port of Dundee equally suitable for their travelling arrangements. This view of Dundee was drawn by Captain Slezer, about the year 1680, for his *Theatrum Scotiae*, but Dundee had changed little in appearance from the early sixteenth century. The great tower of the burgh church of St. Mary is the prominent landmark: the steeples of the friars' churches had already disappeared by the time the *Gude and Godly Ballads* were written.

James Stewart, the eldest of James V's illegitimate sons, provided to the wealthy priory of St. Andrews at the tender age of seven, became the political leader of the protestant reformers in Scotland. As early as 1553, the prior seems to have been of the protestant faction since Marcus Wagner, visiting Scotland in that year with letters of commendation from protestants abroad, was entertained to a meal in the priory of St. Andrews by Lord James and the Laird of Dun. Despite his deacon's orders, he married, in 1562, Agnes Keith, daughter of the Earl Marischal. His dubious loyalty to his half-sister, Mary, during her personal reign as Queen of Scots, issued, at least on one occasion, in active rebellion and he was declared by the papal nuncio, Vincenzo Laureo, to be " the head and principal author of Huguenotism in Scotland." After Mary's forced abdication, he became regent of the kingdom and, on 23rd January, 1570, he was assassinated at Linlithgow as a result of a combination of personal and public vendettas, not unlike what had led to the murder of Cardinal Beaton a quarter of a century earlier.

*From the picture at Darnaway Castle, reproduced by kind permission
of the Right Hon. the Earl of Moray.*

On 3rd December, 1557, several of the protestant leaders, Argyll,
Glencairn, Morton, Erskine of Dun and others, signed the
" Common Band," binding themselves to maintain and forward,
with all their might, the most blessed word of God and His Congregation and to forsake and renounce the Congregation of Satan.
These phrases gave the party the name by which they were known
henceforward. The Band gave the protestant faction coherence
and it has been described as a document than which " nothing
could be plainer as a manifesto of revolution."

From the original in the National Library of Scotland.

From the time, in 1547, when William Cecil accompanied the
Protector Somerset on his expedition into Scotland and helped
William Patten to write up the published account of the campaign,
he must have been interested in the solution of the problem of
Anglo-Scottish relationship. Cecil's personal religious convictions
were possibly not very deep-rooted for, during the reign of Mary
Tudor, he is described as having " frequented Masses, said litanies
with the priest, laboured a great pair of beads, which he continually carried, preached to his parishioners at Stamford and asked
pardon for his errors in King Edward's time." After Elizabeth's
accession, however, he substituted the Prayer Book for the rosary
and, in due course, when he became the queen's very capable
secretary, he was the chief foreign support of the protestant revolution in Scotland. The Treaty of Edinburgh, in July, 1560, was
the triumph of Cecil's diplomacy and statesmanship as regards
Scotland; it ensured the elimination of French political and
military influence in Scotland and created the situation which
made possible the ultimate victory of the Lords of the Congregation.

From the picture in the Bodleian Library.

John Winram is an excellent example of an able man without any
specific religious convictions, who was intent on making his career
in the church, be it catholic or Calvinist. Born in the last decade

xix

of the fifteenth century of the family of Winram of Ratho, he studied in the university of St. Andrews and became a canon of the great Augustinian priory in the city. He became sub-prior in 1536 and, as vicar-general of the archbishop, he was deeply involved in the proceedings against Lutheranism and Calvinism. He preached at the trial of George Wishart and was engaged in the proceedings against Walter Myln in 1558, though Knox is curiously silent about this fact. Winram attended the Parliament of 1560 and, in December of the same year, was approved for the ministry by the first General Assembly: in April of the following year, he was elected Superintendent of Fife, Fothrick and Strathearn—*Episcopus Fifanorum,* as the inscription on his monument once read. Those who had fought and suffered for the new kirk often seem to have deeply resented Winram's easy promotion and to have suspected his sincerity. He summoned one such critic, in 1561, to answer before the session of St. Andrews for having described him as a " fals, dissaitfull, gredy and dissimblit smayk, for he wes ane of tham that maist oppressed, smored and held down the Word of God and now he is cumin to it and professis the same for gredines of gayr lurkand and watchand quhill he maye se ane other tym." He died at an advanced age in 1582, having been less disturbed by the changes that had taken place than almost any man in Scotland. He had begun his career in St. Andrews as a poor scholar, achieved position and influence before the reformation, then added to these a wife and an increase of income and was honoured by this monument in St. Leonard's collegiate kirk after his decease.

PLATE XXVI. PUBLICISTS OF THE PROTESTANT PARTY
facing p. 321

Both Buchanan and Knox displayed a genius for what is now called " mass communication." Buchanan, humanist poet and scholar, provided a political ideology for the Scottish protestants in his *De Iure Regni* and an official history which skilfully presented their view of the contemporary struggle to the educated classes in European society. Knox, known chiefly in his lifetime as a powerful and inspiring preacher, left unpublished at his death that *History of the Reformation in Scotland* whose dramatic sweep and intense vigour have eclipsed Buchanan and have given Knox himself a posthumous fame greater than he had in his lifetime. The two portraits are taken from the *Icones* of Theodore Beza, itself an example of the skilful use of the printing press to create a popular image of the protestant movement.

The pages reproduced here are from books which belonged to Ninian Winzet (and later to John Greenlaw) and to the Dominican friar, John Black. The first is the title-page of a concise concordance to the bible; the second is a page from the commentary of Aquinas on the Epistle of St. James. They remind us that both sides in the reformation crisis appealed to sacred scripture in support of their teaching. The underlinings and marginal notes on the second page stress the importance of the virtue of mercy and the necessity of showing the reality of faith by good works. We catch a glimpse here of Friar John Black, a defender of the old faith, studying scripture, with the current controversy in mind: he was murdered at Holyrood in 1565, having recovered from an earlier attempt on his life by members of the protestant kirk in Edinburgh.

In the north-east of Scotland, which would seem to have largely escaped the initial iconoclastic phase of the religious revolution, a number of medieval sacrament houses (or wall cupboards for the reservation of the Eucharist) still survive. The decoration of these sacrament houses proves that there existed generally, in late medieval Scotland, that same intense popular devotion to the Blessed Sacrament, which was widespread in the Low Countries and Germany. Benefactors apparently continued to gift these elaborate shrines for the Holy Eucharist to parish churches right up to the very eve of the reformation, thereby showing that, in some areas at any rate, the downfall of the old faith was not anticipated. The illustration shows the sacrament house in the now dismantled parish church of Deskford in Banffshire. This sacrament house was erected in 1551, the gift of Alexander Ogilvie of that Ilk and his wife Elizabeth Gordon, whose coats of arms are carved upon it. A feature of these sacrament houses of the final decade are the scriptural texts relating to the Eucharist from the sixth chapter of St. John's Gospel, showing clearly that that generation of catholic men felt the need of re-asserting the scriptural basis of their devotional life.

SOME DOCUMENTS OF THE SCOTTISH REFORMATION.

PLATE XXIX. ABBOT QUINTIN KENNEDY ON THE MASS

facing p. 400

Quintin Kennedy, commendatory abbot of Crossraguel, and Ninian Winzet, schoolmaster of Linlithgow and later abbot of St. James in Ratisbon, are the best known of the catholic apologists who challenged the Scottish protestant spokesmen. Kennedy was especially concerned to defend the mass against their attacks. In the treatise, illustrated here, which apparently circulated in manuscript, he sets out to show, " conforme to the scripturis of almytie god," that the mass was instituted by Jesus Christ in the Last Supper and is not, as his opponents affirm, "inventit be the brayne of man." It is addressed to the general reader but particularly " to Knox, Willock, Wynrame, Gudeman, Dowglas, Hereot, Spottiswod, Athenis (i.e. Gordon, titular archbishop of Athens), and all the laif of the famows precheouris to the congregatioun," and is dated 1561. The original is now in Blairs College, Aberdeen.

PLATE XXX. BAS-RELIEF IN KINKELL CHURCH, ABERDEENSHIRE - - - - - - - *facing p.* 401

This bas-relief in the ruined church of Kinkell, Aberdeenshire, represents pictorially the propitiatory character of the sacrifice of the mass. The central figure is Christ on the cross—the once and forever sacrifice for our redemption. Below the cross is the altar on which rests the chalice and, alongside the altar, stands the much worn figure of a priest in eucharistic vestments. The combination of images is intended to illustrate that the liturgical action of the mass is the application of the unique sacrifice of Calvary to the church. On the right of the crucifix is a figure of our Lady to complete the picture of Calvary, where

> " Stabat mater dolorosa
> Juxta crucem lachrymosa
> Dum pendebat Filius."

To the left of the crucifix an angel holds a chalice to receive the blood from the wounds of Christ, an image which recalls the words of the Canon of the Mass: " Jube haec perferri per manus sancti angeli tui in sublime altare tuum Domine." Below the angel, in an order still reminiscent of the Canon of the Mass are four heads (between which is a label, bearing a now erased inscription, which was variously read as *Purgatorium* or *Preces Sanctorum*). These represent the souls in purgatory who are being cleansed from the dregs of their sins by the salvific blood of the Redeemer applied to them in the mass. The whole panel would, of course, be brightly coloured: the heads in the lower left hand corner of the carving would be surrounded by the painted flames of purgatory. The lead sockets still remain to show that three separate copper wires (presumably gilded or coloured red) stretched from the wounded side of Christ, one each to the chalice on the altar, to the chalice in the angel's hand, and to the souls in purgatory, thus bringing home vividly to the onlooker that it is the one sacrifice of Calvary that is re-presented for the church in the mass and applied to the final cleansing of the souls in purgatory. The initials A. G., depicted on the frontal of the altar, and repeated elsewhere in this carved panel, together with the date 1525, show that the monument was set up by Alexander Galloway, rector of Kinkell and canon of Aberdeen, one of the most influential ecclesiastics in north-east Scotland in the sixteenth century. The handsome sacrament houses which Galloway presented to many churches in Aberdeen diocese and his denunciation of Patrick Hamilton's anti-eucharistic theology to his friend Jacobus Latomus, rector of Standonck's college, in 1528, shows that he was deeply devoted to promoting devotion to the Blessed Sacrament and alert to the need for defending the theological ideas, expressed in this bas-relief, which he set up in his church of Kinkell.

Block by courtesy of the Aberdeen University Press.

PLATE XXXI. TOMB OF NINIAN WINZET AT RATISBON

facing p. 416

Ninian Winzet disclaimed possession of any but very ordinary learning: but if his writings are the product of an ordinary grammar school teacher, then standards must have been higher among pre-reformation Scottish teachers than has been usually suggested. His books were suppressed by the Scottish protestant authorities and he himself narrowly escaped arrest. After further study abroad, he became a Benedictine monk and, as abbot of St. James in Ratisbon, worked to establish a Scottish monastic community which would serve as a base for counter-reformation activity in Scotland. Ninian Winzet died at Ratisbon on the 21st September, 1592, in the 74th year of his age, and his monument stands in the abbey-church of St. James.

PLATE XXXII. FRAGMENTS OF MEDIEVAL GLASS IN MAGDALENE CHAPEL, EDINBURGH - *facing p.* 417

For a variety of reasons, but mainly because Scotland throughout the reformation period lacked any leader sufficiently strong and sufficiently zealous for religion, whether catholic or protestant, and also because the small Scottish population was intimately bound together by ties of kinship which on occasion could prove stronger than religious antagonism, the religious revolution in Scotland was far less costly in terms of human life than was the case in England or any other country of Europe. On the other hand, the wholesale destruction in Scotland of medieval works of religious art is unparalleled in christendom. The destruction of medieval stained glass, for example, is practically complete: there was extensive destruction of it in the populous districts affected by the initial impact of the reformation and, in other districts, during the next few decades, the medieval stained glass would fall into disrepair and, because of Calvinist aversion to the images of the saints, it would not be maintained. Of all "that ancient braverye" of stained glass that adorned the cathedrals, abbeys, burgh churches and even some of the rural churches of Scotland in the middle ages, there remain (apart from broken fragments) only these four roundels of glass in the Magdalene Chapel in Edinburgh. These roundels date from about the year 1545 and show the royal arms of Scotland, the coat of arms of the queen regent, Mary of Guise, the coat of arms of Michael Macqueen (a wealthy citizen of Edinburgh who refounded the Maison Dieu as the Magdalene Hospital) and the arms of his wife, Janet Rynd, impaled with those of her husband.

The ruined abbey of Melrose illustrates more than one point in the ecclesiastical history of Scotland. The surviving ruins of the monastic church and cloister date from a fourteenth-century reconstruction of the abbey and they display a great amount of beautifully sculptured decoration. This feature shows how far the fourteenth-century community of Melrose had departed from the early austerity of Cistercian architecture and incidentally the wealth that the community had derived from their progressive farming and wool trade. The buildings were attacked in the English forays of 1544 and 1545. The efforts of the monks to keep buildings in repair were consistently thwarted by the commenda-tory lay-abbot James Stewart, illegitimate son of James V. The church seems to have been dismantled by a party of the Congrega-tion in 1559, but the greater part of the demolition of walls, which the visitor sees to-day is due to four causes: the thieving of Sir Walter Scott of Branxholm, who was brought before the Court of Session, in 1573, for his activities: the quarrying of wrought stone from the building for the enlargement of the abbot's lodging to form a mansion house for the last commendator, James Douglas who became Earl of Morton: the construction of a new parish church out of the ruins in 1618: and the wholesale removal of dressed stone during the next hundred years for building houses and walls in and about the town of Melrose. Even in ruin the abbey kirk of Melrose is impressive by reason of its size and great beauty and when one reflects that this is only one out of over fifty medieval abbey or priory churches (not to mention cathedrals, college kirks, friaries and large burgh churches), one stands amazed at the extraordinary number of large churches built and maintained as an expression of their religious devotion by the comparatively small medieval population of Scotland.

Crown copyright reserved. Reproduced by permission of the Ministry of Works.

This poem by Sir Richard Maitland of Lethington appears in that fine example of sixteenth-century penmanship, the Maitland Quarto Manuscript. Maitland was a moderate, critical of old and new kirkmen alike, but he is one of the many witnesses to the social distress of his period, already acute before 1560, but intensified after it. The feuing of kirk lands was one of the chief causes of distress, as we are reminded by the legislation of Queen Mary's parliament of 1563, many old-established tenants being forced to move. Maitland's picture of a general decline is confirmed by one of the most interesting of the early protestant ministers, William Lauder, first minister of Forgandenny, who wrote

> " The Mes that Idoll, praysit be God is past,
> Bot Covatyce, the quhilk is cum in last,
> Is the worst Idoll of the twa be far."

In a poem entitled *The Lamentation of the Pure* he says that the pity papists have on those who beg from door to door will accuse his own co-religionists on Doomsday, and he continues

> " Yit Papistis bearis ilk ane to uther
> More liberall luife, I am moste sure,
> Nor dois sum Minister to his Brother,
> How lang Lord wyll this warld indure."

That was in 1568: more bitter experience lay ahead when people would look back, perhaps with exaggerated appreciation, to the " auld kyndnes " and the " blyithnes " lamented by Lauder and Maitland.

Archbishop Hamilton was hanged at Stirling in 1571, partly at least in revenge for the assassination of the Regent Moray. A contemporary witness reports that he exhorted the people to remain constant in the catholic faith, " for swa termit he the papistrie," and died " as he had lived, ane obstinat papist." The illustration shows an entry in the calendar of the Paisley Missal which records the death of the archbishop, who was also abbot of Paisley. Although a commendatory abbot, Hamilton had been a good superior to the Benedictine community at Paisley, which long remained a centre of catholic resistance, and it seems likely that the monk of Paisley who noted the day of his death in the calendar of the missal may have looked upon him as a martyr, as one who had atoned by his constancy unto death for the admitted scandals in his life.

This page from a seventeenth-century Flemish Franciscan martyrology represents Father John Gray being slain in his cell at Brussels in 1579. He was a Scottish exile who was probably a secular priest before joining the Franciscans abroad. The story of Father Gray is a reminder that exile did not necessarily mean ease and security. Another Scottish priest, a native of Edinburgh, who died for his religion furth of Scotland was the Venerable George Douglas, hanged and drawn at York in 1587.

Scattered here and there in the churches of continental Europe are to be found traces of the Scottish catholicism that went into exile as a result of the religious revolution. The illustration shows the tablet, erected in the church of the Premonstratensian canons at Grimbergen in Brabant, by a nephew of John Leslie, the last catholic bishop of Ross, recording the foundation, in 1597, of an anniversary mass, in the abbey church, for the soul of his uncle, who had died at Brussels the previous year.

In the later middle ages, probably from the Jubilee Year of 1450, the Scots nation held the ancient church of Sant' Andrea delle Fratte as their national church in Rome and, alongside the church was the national hospice, which was the common resort of all Scots pilgrims and residents in the Eternal City. The church and the hospice can be seen (T.S. Andree delle fratte) in the centre of this detail from Antonio Tempesta's panoramic map of Rome, dated 1593. During the last decades of the sixteenth century, the national hospice was little frequented and continuous efforts were made to have the hospice and its revenues devoted to the now more urgent task of educating Scots youths, who might return to Scotland as priests and help in the work of preserving the catholic faith among the faithful remnant that still existed throughout the kingdom. This transformation was achieved when, on the 5th December, 1600, Pope Clement VIII published the bull *In supremo militantis ecclesiae,* establishing the Scots College in Rome and annexing to the new college the property and revenues of the medieval hospice, together with some of its obligations. The Scots College in Rome, which still flourishes, played an important part in the preservation of the catholic religion in Scotland and it provided Scottish catholics with an important centre in Rome in immediate contact with the central administration of the church.

When Archbishop James Beaton II of Glasgow left Scotland in the wake of the French army in 1560 and settled down in Paris for forty years or more as the ambassador successively of Mary Queen of Scots and her son James VI, his behaviour might be termed unheroic, but his presence in Paris did provide a necessary and respected leader for the Scots catholics who found themselves living in exile after 1560. Beaton co-ordinated much of the activity of this expatriated Scottish catholicism and, in particular, he took under his patronage the scholars of the old Scots foundation in the university of Paris, gave them, in 1569, a house in the Rue des Amandiers and, on his death, bequeathed a substantial fortune to them thereby becoming the " second founder " of the Scots College in Paris, as the " memorial portrait " from the college, here illustrated, declares. When Archbishop Beaton died in Paris in 1603, at the advanced age of 86, the catholic hierarchy of medieval Scotland came to an end but, by his work, Beaton had helped to ensure the survival of catholicism in his native land for throughout the seventeenth and eighteenth centuries, his college in Paris supplied missionary priests to work among the catholics of Scotland and became in effect the G.H.Q. of Scottish catholicism both at home and abroad.

The Scots catholic exiles on the continent realised early the need for some institution where young men could be trained as priests to work in Scotland and take the place of the pre-reformation clergy, who were gradually dying out, and thus ensure the continued ministration of the sacraments to those who remained faithful to the old religion. The Scots College, which eventually settled at Douay, then in the Spanish Netherlands, was the first of the Scots Colleges to be founded for this purpose. Its foundation seems to have been the work of several Scots exiled priests and its first superior was James Cheyne, parson of Aboyne and canon of Aberdeen. Queen Mary, from her English prison gave liberally to what she called " Cheyne's seminary " (the " memorial portrait," which is the frontispiece of this book, actually calls her the foundress). Pope Gregory XIII also helped and there were many other benefactors. The College was forced by political and other circumstances to move about a great deal in its early years— Douay, Tournai, Pont-à-Mousson, Louvain and Antwerp all received it in turn and finally, in 1612, it settled permanently at Douay. The illustration shows the establishment as it existed in 1627: it is a detail taken from the unique panoramic view of the city preserved in the town hall at Douay. Down to the time of the French Revolution, which worked havoc among these institutions, the Scots colleges at Douay, Paris, Rome and Madrid and the Scots Benedictine monasteries in the Holy Roman Empire provided the means by which the catholic church managed to survive in Scotland after the disastrous defeat in the sixteenth century and maintain itself through the difficult period of the penal laws down into modern times.

THE POLITICAL BACKGROUND OF THE
REFORMATION, 1513-1625[1]

by

J. H. BURNS

Centenary commemorations seem in some ways inappropriate to the Scottish reformation. The date 1560 marked neither an end nor a beginning in its development. The work of the "Reformation Parliament" was of doubtful legality and uncertain permanence. In part, the achievements of 1560 were merely transitional; in part, they were no more than a skeleton of principles, never to be clothed in actual flesh. Not for another generation did Scottish protestantism acquire fully its characteristic presbyterian government, and not for another century after that was the kirk secure in either its constitution or its doctrine. A beginning is still harder to locate than an end. The burning of Patrick Hamilton in 1528 was a portent, no doubt; but the 1525 act against Lutheran books suggests that Hamilton's death was itself a climax rather than a beginning. And in those early years, sixteenth-century protestantism seems to have mingled with the last traces of fifteenth-century Lollardy. Yet the significance of 1560 escapes these reflections. The medieval catholic church in Scotland did not, in fact, recover from the blows struck by the " Reformation Parliament ". Even at the time the events of 1559-1560 were evidently revolutionary. This is particularly important in the present context; for it was the overthrow of the established temporal authority, the seizure of political power, and the use of that power to bring down the church that made these years revolutionary. Protestant and catholic were alike aware of this.[2] The reformation was a revolution, dependent for its success on the wielding of political power. The politics, moreover, must be external as well as internal. Scotland was a small but integral part of the European states system. Allied to catholic France, neighboured by the England in which Elizabeth's accession brought about the decisive overthrow of catholicism, Scotland moved with limited freedom in a dangerous world.[3]

The political world, domestic and foreign, in which the Scottish reformation took place, was governed by forces that had little to do with theological controversies. It is true that in the sixteenth century politics and religion interacted in a way that is hard to understand in a secular age such as our own; and it is important to avoid the solecism of talking as though religious considerations had no independent effect on political actions but were merely a mask for material interests. But it is at least as important to remember that religion never dominated politics to the

1. This essay is an attempt to indicate and illustrate the main political factors in Scottish history between 1513 and 1625, and to suggest how politics affected religious developments. Though mainly chronological in form, it is not intended as a compressed narrative history of the period. Footnotes are given to elucidate the text, not to indicate authorities.

2. For protestant awareness, see, e.g., Knox's letters of June-July, 1559 (*Works*, ed. Laing, vi, pp. 23-36), where he tries to disclaim political objectives for the Congregation. For a catholic view, see Ninian Winzet's *Buke of Four Scoir Thre Questionis* (Antwerp, 1563), qq. 29-31 (*Certain Tractates*, ed. J. K. Hewison, Scottish Text Society, i, pp. 94-97), insisting on the political implications of protestant teaching.

3. In what follows, reference is made chiefly to the " triangle " of Scotland, England, and France, with some mention of Spain and the Empire. This, of course, over-simplifies Scotland's foreign relations. Other connections were important—e.g., relations with Denmark in the reign of James V and later; but it seems fair to assume that the relations here analysed were the most important.

I

exclusion or even to the subordination of ordinary political motives. Forces were at work in the world of politics by which the religious leaders might gain or lose, but which they could do little to control. To understand these forces, it is necessary to understand the nature of Scottish politics before the complications of the religious struggle. To this end an examination of the reign of James V is a useful means.

I

The years of James V's minority (1513-1528) are particularly revealing because, in the absence of effective government, the permanent forces in Scottish political life had free rein and can thus be studied in their fullness. None of Scotland's needs after Flodden (September, 1513) could be met without firm direction of her policies. The battle had left the country not merely with the too familiar problems of a royal minority but also deprived of an experienced ruling class. The struggle for power round the infant king was complicated by being carried on largely by untried and imprudent men, whose fathers had died at Flodden. Nor was there a native-born " natural " regent to assume power. Things might have been different had either Margaret Tudor, the queen dowager, or John Duke of Albany, the young king's senior male relative,[4] been other than they were. Margaret had the passionate nature of her family without its political skill. Albany, French by birth and education, lacked the concentration which later enabled another French regent, Mary of Guise, to persevere in the government of Scotland till her death.

Yet Albany's task might well have been too much for a more skilful and determined statesman. The diplomatic situation delayed his arrival in Scotland until May, 1515, and by then rival interests had had free play for over a year and a half. Margaret had forfeited such claim to authority as she might have had by her marriage, in August, 1514, to the young Earl of Angus[5]—a marriage that allied her to the powerful house of Douglas but alienated many other nobles. Major rivalries like that between the Douglases and the house of Hamilton (whose head, James, first Earl of Arran, was next heir to the crown after Albany himself[6]) were intertwined with innumerable lesser conflicts. The church, after the death of Elphinstone in October, 1514, seemed for the moment to do no more that afford fresh matters for dispute—the see of St. Andrews itself being the chief instance. Andrew Forman, who eventually obtained St. Andrews, and James Beaton, Archbishop of Glasgow, were men of ability and, at least on occasion, of good will; but they lacked the moral authority of statesmen like Kennedy and Elphinstone.

In these unpromising conditions Albany made a firm and not unsuccessful start. He had one advantage: the country was free from the fear of invasion now that peace had been made with England. But Albany's successes against his domestic rivals imperilled his international position. Margaret and her husband, together with Home[7] and Arran,

---

4. See Genealogical Table A.

5. Archibald Douglas, sixth Earl of Angus (?1489-1557). Succeeded 1513.

6. This is true after the death of James V's posthumously-born brother at the end of 1515: see Genealogical Table A. Arran (d. 1529) received his earldom in August, 1503, on the occasion of James IV's marriage to Margaret Tudor.

7. Alexander Home, third Lord Home (d. 1516). Succeeded 1506. He was one of the few important leaders to survive Flodden.

suffered reverses; and Henry VIII and Wolsey faced the prospect of Scotland's achieving internal peace under a Francophile regent. This they were determined to prevent. Henry demanded that Albany should return to France; and when this was refused by the Scottish Estates, the English agents who had already been fomenting trouble in Scotland redoubled their efforts. Despite this, Albany maintained his position and, indeed, consolidated it by executing Home and his brother for treason in the autumn of 1516. But the impending Hapsburg-Valois conflict, which was to dominate European politics for forty years, soon had its effect on Scottish affairs. Francis I of France now wished to maintain good relations with England, and the Scottish regency was part of the price he was willing to pay. When Albany returned to France in the summer of 1517 and remained there for four years, his own tastes were no doubt gratified. But politically his withdrawal meant the appeasement of England by France. The Auld Alliance might be renewed (Treaty of Rouen, August, 1517), with provision for a French marriage in due course for the young King of Scots; but the government Scotland needed was denied. " Cleanse the Causeway " symbolises the anarchy of these years, when Angus might have won supremacy out of disorder (as he did seven years later) had he not by then quarrelled irreconcilably with his wife. Margaret's influence was now exerted in favour of Albany's return and the French connection. But not till deteriorating Anglo-French relations made it diplomatically tolerable did Albany at last return in November, 1521.

A latent pattern in Scottish politics now declared itself. The government was committed to the French alliance, the opposition was associated with the English interest. There was hardly, perhaps, an English " party " in any true sense. But the opposition to France cannot be dismissed as merely the product of selfish and treasonable intrigues. Men whose goodwill and patriotism are not in doubt looked to an ultimate union with England as the best security for Scotland's future.[8] Nor were the motives of the French party those of unalloyed patriotism. Yet, both in interest and in sentiment, the French policy had the stronger basis. The emotional basis was at times unsteady, for the French were never uniformly or universally popular in Scotland. But contemporary observers were struck by the expression of pro-French feeling in Scotland after Francis I's disaster at Pavia in 1525, and it is still impressive evidence that the Auld Alliance was no mere marriage of convenience. As for interest, the simple truth was that, as long as English policy combined with Scots resentment to make a permanent honourable settlement between the two countries impossible (and few men did more to that end than Henry VIII), the French alliance was Scotland's only available support against her far more powerful neighbour.

The French alliance, however, bound the Scots to a country still more disproportionately powerful than England. This potential threat to Scotland's interests and integrity could be resented and resisted by men who had no inclination for intrigue with England. Events during Albany's second residence in Scotland illustrate this point. The Scots were willing enough to muster and march against England when Henry

---

8. This is well illustrated by the theologian John Major, whose *Historia Majoris Britanniae*, published in 1521, reads at times like a propagandist plea for a matrimonial union of England and Scotland. Major, as an East Lothian man, had Douglas loyalties: Gavin Douglas, bishop of Dunkeld, was one of his patrons. But it is hard to believe that Major's views were merely a rationalisation of the Douglas intrigues with Henry VIII.

VIII renewed his imperious demand for the regent's dismissal. But the commanders, led by Huntly,[9] did not construe the obligations of allies as meaning needless aggression over the border, and they frustrated Albany's military designs in the autumn of 1522. But the sequel also reveals an essential weakness in Scotland's position at this time. The expedition being abandoned, the feudal army dispersed. When the English attacked the border counties in the spring and summer of 1523, no defence was available. Albany, who had again been in France, returned with auxiliary forces and besieged Wark Castle. This too was abortive, and it was Albany's last attempt at action in Scotland. He left in May, 1524, and never returned.[10]

This time Henry VIII succeeded in preventing the establishment of a strong regency. With his support, Margaret and Arran procured the " erection " of the twelve-year-old James V—i.e., his proclamation as *de facto* sovereign. In fact, of course, even the pretence of government disappeared: nothing was left but rival factions. The real beneficiary was Angus. Returning from exile in September, 1524, he began another attempt to make himself supreme. His success this time was assisted by the international situation. The French defeat at Pavia (February, 1525) was followed by an Anglo-French *rapprochement*, and this had its counter-part in a three years' truce between England and Scotland from October, 1525. Next year Angus won, at least for a time, the support of James Beaton, now Archbishop of St. Andrews and hitherto a leader of the " French party ". In June, 1526, Angus had the Estates declare that the young king, now fourteen, should personally assume his prerogatives. All delegated authority was thus revoked, and Angus, controlling the young king's person, disposed of the effective power. Arran accepted defeat[11], and even allied himself with Angus, playing a large part in defeating attempts by Lennox[12] to challenge the new order. But " order " is hardly an apt term for the Douglas despotism which dominated but did not govern Scotland for the next two years. The moral and political decline which had begun at Flodden now reached its nadir. Yet in the very nature of Angus's power there lay the hope of better things. His tyranny was in part tolerated because it was exercised in the name of the crown. If he lost control of the king, he lost much of his strength. When James, by then sixteen, escaped from Angus in the summer of 1528, only a short struggle was needed to drive Angus and his brother, George Douglas,[13] once more from the realm as forfeited traitors. There was once more a king in more than name in Scotland.

II

There are grounds for holding that the Stewart kings had something like a traditional policy. Externally, this policy aimed at the preservation of Scotland's independence, with the French alliance as the principal and

---

9. Alexander Gordon, third Earl of Huntly (d. 1524). Succeeded 1501.

10. Albany, however, described himself as " Governor of Scotland " until 1528, and till then and even later there were schemes for his return. He also took part in James V's matrimonial diplomacy between 1529 and 1536.

11. Margaret did not: she turned again to Albany, and diplomatic gossip revived the earlier rumour of a liaison between them. Margaret's attempts to obtain a divorce from Angus fostered this notion; but when (with Albany's aid) she succeeded in 1527, she married Henry Stewart (?1495-1552), created first Lord Methven in 1528. (See R. K. Hannay, *The Letters of James V*, ed. Denys Hay, Edinburgh, 1954, esp. p. 136 n.)

12. John Stewart, third Earl of Lennox (d. 1526). Succeeded 1513. See Genealogical Table A.

13. Sir George Douglas of Pittendriech (?1492-1552). His was the moving spirit in much of the Douglas manoeuvring at this period. He was the father of James, fourth Earl of Morton, later regent.

normal means, though not the only one. Internally, the policy was to impose order and justice in a community where there were many insolent and clamorous rivals to the royal power. Alliances were possible here too, at least in theory. The support of the church and the commons could in principle be invoked against the feudal anarchy of the nobles. But it may be doubted whether, even apart from the recurrent misfortune of royal minorities, there was much hope of success for such policies. Abroad, it was clear that the French alliance was far more important to Scotland than the Scottish alliance was to France, while no adequate and lasting alternative could be found elsewhere. At home, for reasons to be indicated later, there was no coherent, independent entity called " the church " capable of allying itself with " the crown ". As for the commons, the burgesses in Scotland were not strong enough to lend really powerful aid to a vigorous monarchy. The " lesser barons " or gentry in this period were, it is true, developing rapidly, and later in the century their influence was to be of great importance. But they were not sufficiently independent of the great feudal houses to form a separate centre of effective power.[14] Above all, the Scottish crown lacked the machinery of strong government. There had been conciliar and judicial development since the latter part of the fifteenth century; James V was himself to take an important step in 1532 by establishing the College of Justice; and during his reign it seems that the royal secretariate began to develop into an effective instrument of policy. But, even allowing for the disparity between the two realms, Scotland had little to compare with the fabric of Tudor government under Henry VII and Henry VIII.[15] James V, like his predecessors, undertook a task for which he had neither the material nor the means.

The sixteen-year-old king began vigorously. A five years' truce with England was agreed in December, 1528. James put down the worst excesses of the border chiefs,[16] and then turned his attention to the highlands. During his minority little or nothing had been done about this vast intractable region. It was yet another weakness of the Scottish crown that it had to govern what were in effect two countries, one even less governable than the other. Yet even in the highlands James had some success, superseding the quasi-viceregal power of the Earl of Argyll[17] and entering into direct relations with the chiefs. But this affront to a leading magnate did not improve relations with the nobility, of whom James's boyhood experiences had given him a natural suspicion. There was a good deal of disaffection in 1531 and 1532, amounting in at least one case—the Earl of Bothwell[18]—to treason with England. James, however, survived these troubles and pursued a number of constructive policies. The century-old commercial treaty with the Low Countries

---

14. The failure of a representative system like the English " knights of the shire " to develop in Scotland is significant here. The right of the " lesser barons " to representation in parliament was not securely established till near the end of the sixteenth century. On social classes generally, James VI's analysis in *Basilicon Doron*, though it refers to a period two generations after the reign of James V, is relevant for the whole century as a unique picture of the social situation as it appeared from the throne.

15. If Mr. G. R. Elton's comment in a recent general survey of " The Age of the Reformation "—" Scotland had to wait for Knox before drawing a line under its messy medieval politics " (*New Cambridge Modern History*, ii, Cambridge, 1958, p. 8)—seems open to criticism, it is because it implies that the line *was* drawn at the reformation and that Knox had a significant part in its drawing. Both suggestions are debatable. That Scottish politics throughout the sixteenth century were " messy " in a " medieval " way can hardly be gainsaid.

16. One episode is immortalised in the ballad of Johnnie Armstrong.

17. Archibald Campbell, fourth Earl of Argyll (d. 1558). He succeeded in 1529-30 and was married to Helen Hamilton, daughter of the first Earl of Arran and sister to the second earl, later regent.

18. Patrick Hepburn, third Earl of Bothwell (?1512-1556). Succeeded 1513. He was again in trouble at the end of the decade, and was banished in December, 1540.

was renewed; the College of Justice was established; and there was some attempt to introduce ecclesiastical reforms. But relations with the church require special notice.

James is conventionally represented as a monarch who supported the church in the conflict with protestantism, partly, no doubt, from conviction, but partly because he leaned heavily on clerical support in the conduct of his government. There is some truth in this, but it is unduly simplified. James's " support " for the church was quite compatible with shameless exploitation of its benefices on behalf of his bastards and favourites.[19] And clerical support for the king was by no means unqualified. Royal relations with Archbishop James Beaton, for example, were far from harmonious: the archbishop was detained on a treason charge for a long period in 1532-33, when hostilities with England had been renewed; no complete reconciliation seems to have taken place till the summer of 1535. Despite such tensions, however, and despite James's determination to maintain royal rights in ecclesiastical appointments, he was orthodox enough in his attitude towards heresy. Several heretics were burnt in August, 1534. But more serious than heresy at home was the existence of the now schismatic power of Henry VIII in England. This introduced a new factor into Anglo-Scottish relations and it calls for some consideration of James V's foreign policy in the early years of his reign.[20]

These were years of comparative but rather deceptive calm. The Hapsburg-Valois conflict subsided for a time with the peace of Cambrai (August, 1529), and Henry VIII's energies were absorbed largely by the conflict with Rome. Wolsey's fall in the autumn of 1529 was soon followed by the first session of the Reformation Parliament, whose Act of Supremacy in 1534 made absolute England's breach with the papacy. All this (and Henry's divorce and re-marriage) took place without foreign interference. Neither Francis I nor Charles V wished to antagonize England; and the pope himself, at odds with the emperor since the sack of Rome in 1527, lacked both freedom of manoeuvre and the support of the powers. All this affected James V's diplomacy, mainly concerned at this period with his marriage.[21] The French match envisaged in the Treaty of Rouen (1517) meant English hostility which Francis was now unwilling to incur: James's demands for the hand of Francis's daughter Madeleine were therefore resisted. Charles V was willing enough to detach Scotland from the French alliance, and several imperial

---

19. The effrontery with which this policy was pursued is well illustrated in a letter addressed by James to Clement VII in 1533: " Holy Father . . . as I have three illegitimate sons, I am obliged to confess to Your Holiness . . . that the fault is my own, and I acknowledge the error of human weakness. Yet out of fatherly affection for their welfare . . . we beg Your Holiness . . . to dispense our sons . . . so that they may be promoted to Holy Orders . . . so that they may hold any Church dignities whatsoever, even two, three, or four benefices together . . . and so that when they attain their twentieth year, they may be able to be promoted to Archiepiscopal, Primatial, and Episcopal dignities " (27th February, 1533. Translation based on text given by A. Theiner, *Vetera Monumenta Hibernorum et Scotorum Historiam Illustrantia*, Rome, 1864, p. 599; but cf. Hannay, *Letters of James V*, p. 235, for a summary based on the text in the Caprington MS.).

20. Two points about ecclesiastical affairs must be borne in mind. First, building on earlier foundations, James vindicated against the papacy a wide measure of control over appointments to prelacies. Second, to quote R. K. Hannay: " By 1542 the secularisation of the leading abbacies had gone so far as to be entirely beyond papal control " (*Acts of the Lords of Council in Public Affairs*, 1501-1554, Edinburgh, 1932, Introduction, p. liv: see generally pp. xlv-lviii). This does not of itself mean that religious life had come to a standstill in the monasteries concerned: it does mean that James had less motive to imitate Henry VIII's policy than he might otherwise have had.

21. A brief account must foreshorten and oversimplify this diplomacy. Not enough attention, perhaps, has been paid to the lucid and well documented account by Edmond Bapst, *Les Mariages de Jacques V* (Paris, 1889). A good deal of the documentary evidence can now be conveniently followed in Hannay, *Letters of James V*, especially the documents from the Tyninghame MS. for the years 1529-1532 (pp. 153-233 *passim*).

brides were considered, some, no doubt, merely in order to put pressure on France, but some with serious intentions. By 1535, with James in his twenty-third year, the matter was assuming some urgency after six years of fruitless diplomacy. At this point Henry VIII began his prolonged attempt to draw his nephew into alliance and schism. He offered James the hand of Mary Tudor and proposed a personal meeting to discuss the ecclesiastical problem. James refused the marriage offer, as he was then about to accept Francis I's proposal of the Bourbon princess Marie de Vendôme instead of Madeleine. But he was ready to temporise about the suggested meeting till the late summer of 1536. Then, having entertained for a time the notion of marrying his mistress, Margaret Erskine, Lady Lochleven,[22] he resolved to go to France himself to press the negotiations there to a conclusion. The result of this visit is well-known: the dropping of the marriage-treaty with Marie de Vendôme and the winning of the long-sought marriage with Madeleine. This was a diplomatic triumph all the more remarkable in that Francis I was now again at war with the emperor, so that England's benevolent neutrality was important to him.[23]

Neutrality in the continental struggle did not affect Henry's attitude to Scotland. While James was in France (he did not return till May, 1537), the old alliance of English intrigue and Douglas ambition was stirring up disorder. Plots aimed at the king's life were discovered at a time when James had just suffered the loss of his young wife on 7th July. In the middle of that month, Angus's sister, Janet, Lady Glamis[24] and her son-in-law, the Master of Forbes,[25] were arrested for complicity in the plots. James hastened to form a new matrimonial alliance with France. In August an embassy, led by David Beaton, was sent; and by the turn of the year a treaty was negotiated which, in June, 1538, brought to Scotland a woman destined to play a critical part in the country's history—Mary, daughter of the first Duke of Guise. Henry VIII was also a suitor for Mary's hand, and the marriage cannot have improved relations between the two kings.[26]

A formidable but short-lived coalition was forming against the schismatic king of England. Francis I and Charles V made peace in June, 1538, and accepted for the moment Pope Paul III's scheme for joint action against the enemies of the faith—the Turks, the Lutherans, and the English. It was important to prevent Scotland following England's schismatic example, and from the start of his pontificate Paul had courted James's goodwill.[27] In December, 1538 (when David Beaton received

---

22. Daughter of John, fifth Lord Erskine; sister of John, first Earl of Mar (regent, 1571-72); wife of Sir Robert Douglas of Lochleven. Her son by James V (born 1531) was James Stewart, later Earl of Moray and regent. Her marriage to Douglas had been annulled, but the annulment was not upheld at Rome.

23. The romantic accounts of James's amorous preference of Madeleine to Marie may well be true; but in view of his repeated attempts to obtain Madeleine's hand before ever setting eyes on her, it is natural to see the marriage as a diplomatic and not just as a romantic triumph.

24. Widow of John Lyon, sixth Lord Glamis (?1491-1528), and usually referred to as Lady Glamis, though by 1535 she had married Archibald Campbell of Skipnish, uncle of the Earl of Argyll. Her husband was imprisoned along with her and killed when trying to escape.

25. Son of John Forbes, sixth Lord Forbes. He is sometimes said to have married another sister of Angus; but his wife was, in fact, a daughter of Janet, Lady Glamis, so that he was Angus's nephew by marriage, not his brother-in-law.

26. Henry's third wife, Jane Seymour, died in October, 1537, soon after the birth of her son (later Edward VI). Henry's agents were investigating the possibility of a marriage with Mary of Guise very shortly afterwards.

27. Symbolically, this was shown by the presentation to James of the cap and sword blessed by the pope at Christmas, 1536 (*Letters of James V*, p. 328). A more substantial token was the extension from eight to twelve months of the period during which the king might propose names for vacant benefices of more than 200 gold florins in value, meanwhile enjoying the temporalities (Bull of 7th March, 1535: *op. cit.*, p. 285).

his cardinal's hat), the bull excommunicating Henry VIII, drafted in 1535, was put in execution. But Henry survived the crisis of 1539 with no worse consequence than the politic marriage with Anne of Cleves negotiated by Thomas Cromwell. Yet so long as the possibility of joint action by Francis and Charles remained, Henry felt the need of precautions on his northern border. This is the background to Sir Ralph Sadler's Scottish mission early in 1540.

Scotland afforded few grounds for English optimism. Ecclesiastical influence seemed paramount, with David Beaton, Archbishop of St. Andrews since the previous spring, as the king's chief adviser. Strong action against heresy in 1539 was followed in 1540 by a strengthening of the law against it, together with provisions for reform within the church. Events might prove that severity was a two-edged weapon; they certainly proved that the movement for reform from within lacked adequate strength. But, meanwhile, orthodoxy was in the ascendant. James was deaf to Sadler's persuasions on church matters, though he still did not rule out the possibility of meeting his uncle. All the signs seemed to indicate a strong and confident monarch: James's circumnavigation of his realm, during which he achieved a considerable pacification of the remoter areas; the annexation to the crown of the Lordship of the Isles; the confirmation of James's revocation (in 1537 when he was in France) of all grants made during his minority; the granting of an amnesty for all past crimes and treasons (the Douglases excepted). But before long James's strength and confidence were seriously sapped.

In the spring of 1541 James's two infant sons died, leaving him again without a direct heir.[28] Abroad, the transitory coalition of France and the Empire was breaking up as Charles provocatively made his son Philip Duke of Milan. Henry VIII again sought to strengthen his northern border, renewing his invitation to James to meet him at York. While Beaton was absent in France, James accepted; but his advisers convinced him of the impolicy of such a meeting, and he failed to appear. English forces were mustering in the north even before the proposed meeting, and James's non-appearance, together with the renewal of open war between Francis I and Charles V, made an English attack on Scotland in 1542 almost inevitable. The attack, preceded by a revival of the old English claim to suzerainty, came in the late summer and autumn. With it came the disaster of Solway Moss, followed in December by the king's death, just after the birth of his daughter, Mary, now Queen of Scots.

The king's death, like the bungling strategy that led to Solway Moss, was an accidental misfortune. But the calamitous end of James's reign has deeper under-currents. A persistent dilemma of the Scottish monarchy had reappeared. The king had governed largely without, and even against, the magnates in time of peace; but in war he needed the support of the magnates, who controlled virtually all the nation's armed strength. The disaffection of the nobility, evinced before and—disastrously—at Solway Moss, was the inevitable reaction to James's strong government in the 1530's. And to the old feudal jealousy of royal power and the

---

28. Albany had died, withou tissue, in 1536. From then till the birth of James's first son in 1540, and again after the death of the two baby princes in the spring of 1541, the heir presumptive was James Hamilton, second Earl of Arran (d. 1575), who had succeeded his father in 1529. See Genealogical Table A.

stubborn malignity of the Douglases there was now added a factor later to be of capital importance. How far protestantism in any real sense had begun to win converts among the Scottish nobility is hard to gauge. There had certainly been an intensification of anti-clerical feeling, and Henry VIII's methods of redistributing church property, if rejected by James (satisfied, no doubt, with his *modus vivendi* with the papacy), might still attract some of his nobles. It is clear too that one element in the disaffection of 1542 was fear lest Beaton should invoke ecclesiastical sanctions against suspected heretics among the magnates. Henceforward, if resentful nobles turned to England for support, their resentment was likely to be directed against church as well as state. At the same time, the church now had a powerful motive for supporting the traditional anti-English, pro-French policy. The lines of something more like a dispute between parties than anything so far seen in Scotland were being drawn as the country was plunged once more into the uncertainties of a royal minority.

III

At the beginning of 1543, the nominal sovereign of Scotland was a tiny child, whose brothers had died in infancy. The heir presumptive was the weak but ambitious James Hamilton, second Earl of Arran.[29] The queen dowager was a young Frenchwoman with less than five years' experience of the country. The leading statesman was an able and forceful prelate, whose power had already aroused the suspicion of the nobility. The country had just suffered a humiliating defeat in battle. A number of its leading men were prisoners in England. There, not only the enmity of Henry VIII but the rancour of the exiled Douglases menaced Scotland. Abroad, the Hapsburg-Valois conflict raged once more: England was not yet involved, and it was not in France's interest to give provocation by assisting the Scots. James V's deathbed cry, reported by Knox, seems apt enough: "All is lost!"

Nothing, it seemed, could prevent the triumph of English influence and with it of schism, if not heresy. Arran, proclaimed regent by a Convention of Estates on 3rd January, took two Dominicans of dubious orthodoxy as his chaplains and showed marked favour to the protestants. Beaton was soon in custody. Angus was back in Scotland with his brother George; and with them came the Solway Moss prisoners, now the "Assured Scots", pledged to further England's interest. Of the policies involved in this, the most defensible was the proposed marriage between the baby queen and Henry's son, Edward; but some at least of the assured lords had gone far beyond this, undertaking to promote Henry's claim to direct suzerainty, and perhaps even to kidnap the infant queen. In March a full parliament confirmed Arran's appointment, named ambassadors to treat for the English marriage, and authorised the use of the vernacular bible.

The direction of events changed with astonishing rapidity when Beaton regained his liberty and two important persons came back to Scotland from France. One was Matthew Stewart, fourth Earl of Lennox, Arran's nearest rival in the royal succession and indeed, if

---

29. See preceding and following notes. Arran was connected by marriage with the Douglases, his wife being a daughter of James Douglas, third Earl of Morton. But he also had family connections with Beaton, for his mother was the cardinal's cousin.

Arran's birth were regarded (as it might be) as illegitimate, himself heir presumptive to the throne.[30] The other was Arran's illegitimate brother, John Hamilton, abbot of Paisley (later Archbishop of St. Andrews). France itself was stirring. Francis might not wish to provoke Henry, but a complete triumph of English policy in Scotland was as unacceptable to the French king now as a similar triumph of French influence had been to Henry twenty-five years earlier. A French fleet appeared off the Scottish coast. When, early in July, the English marriage was agreed in the Treaty of Greenwich, the terms were already in jeopardy. Arran was yielding to his opponents before the end of the month; and though he ratified the treaty on 25th August, less than a fortnight later he was doing penance for his apostasy and had agreed to govern with a council including both Beaton and the queen dowager. In the ensuing struggle, Lennox changed sides and joined the English party. But by midwinter Beaton was winning: parliament, in December, voided the Greenwich treaty, renewed the French alliance, and made Beaton chancellor. For the last two and a half years of his life, Beaton dominated the Scottish scene.

Beaton had many faults, but it was not by his fault that these years were among the most wretched in Scottish history. Henry VIII's aggressive policy, a desperate attempt to enforce a treaty which even his own agents told him was quite unacceptable in Scotland, lacked even the justification of success. The "rough wooing" of Hertford's onslaught not only destroyed the marriage treaty it was intended to impose, it destroyed for the time being any possibility of creating in Scotland an English party that was not a party of treason. Any chance of success for Henry's policy vanished when, in the summer of 1544, in pursuance of an agreement with Charles V, he attacked France. This brought French aid to Scotland in the summer of 1545. In the direct Anglo-Scottish fighting, this may not have greatly mattered; but the war on two fronts strained Henry's resources and made a decisive victory in Scotland impossible. England had been isolated by the peace of Crespy between France and the emperor in September, 1544; and when Henry at last made peace with Francis I at Camp in June, 1546, Scotland was to be "comprehended", as in 1515. During the struggle, however, much had happened in Scotland itself.

Some degree of unity was produced by the English attack, but it was neither immediate nor complete. Lennox continued the struggle against Arran and the cardinal till he was driven, in August, 1544, into an English exile of over twenty years. Hertford's indiscriminate devastation in the spring and summer of that year did not spare the Douglases or Henry's other supporters. There was a revulsion of feeling. But it led, not to support for Arran, but to an attempt to set up an alternative government under Mary of Guise. Military disaster commonly produces a desire for a new government; but unless the change is made swiftly and decisively, the results are apt to be unfortunate. In Scotland the upshot was a futile struggle during the later months of 1544, at the end of which Arran and the cardinal were still in power—a not unremarkable

---

30. The question of Arran's legitimacy turned on the validity of the divorce of James, first Earl of Arran, from his first wife, Elizabeth Home. If this were held invalid, the subsequent marriage to Janet Beaton (niece of Archbishop James Beaton and cousin to the cardinal) was null, James, second Earl of Arran, was illegitimate, and Lennox (1516-1571), who succeeded his father in 1526, was next heir to the crown. See Genealogical Table A.

fact, for most of the nobles and several prominent churchmen, led by Archbishop Gavin Dunbar of Glasgow,[31] had joined the opposition. Some unity was restored at the end of the year; and in February, 1545, Arran and Angus won their joint victory at Ancrum Moor. But Douglas duplicity persisted. In the summer, when French troops had arrived, a joint invasion of England was frustrated by the Douglases. A disastrous autumn followed. Hertford attacked again with appalling severity; Lennox and Glencairn[32] concerted with the chiefs of the Isles an onslaught on the west coast; and the Maxwell strongholds of Caerlaverock, Lochmaben, and Threave were placed at England's disposal. Yet Arran and Beaton vindicated their authority. They defeated the western attack and, in November, they regained the Maxwell castles.

The cardinal was evidently the greatest single obstacle to Henry's success. He was also an object of envy to many Scottish nobles, and of hatred and fear to the small but growing group of protestants. The English and protestant parties were not yet identical, but some of Henry's most prominent supporters—Glencairn, Cassilis,[33] and the Earl Marischal,[34] Lord Maxwell[35] and Lord Somerville[36]—now professed protestantism or inclined towards it. The Scottish protestants at this time acquired their first outstanding preacher, George Wishart, who had returned from England in 1543. In this situation a conspiracy against Beaton was built up. It first took shape in April, 1544, and was given substance, with discreet encouragement from England, in the summer of 1545. The plot hung fire, however—partly, perhaps, because there was good hope of a more direct success for English policy. The conspiracy again gathered momentum in the spring of 1546; but by then the conditions had been transformed by the burning of Wishart as a heretic in March. When Beaton was assassinated on 29th May, the motivation was complex: revenge for Wishart's death, the long-matured policy of the English party, and also a personal property dispute between Beaton and Norman Leslie, Master of Rothes.[37] Important in itself, the episode also epitomises the varied forces by which events were produced.

For Henry VIII the murder of Beaton came too late; for the Scottish protestants the crisis it gave rise to came too soon. Only a few extremists rallied to the murderers in the castle of St. Andrews. In July and August the " Castilians " were first denounced as traitors and then besieged. The peace treaty limited for the moment their hope of English aid (though it also deprived the government, for the moment, of the French aid without which, as things turned out, the castle could not be reduced). Once again a degree of unity had been superficially produced among the Scottish leaders, and the Castilians had no hope of really influential support. But before anything decisive had been achieved either way, the situation was changed by the deaths of some outstanding figures.

Henry VIII died on 28th January, 1547. Edward VI was a minor,

---

31. Dunbar (d. 1547) had been ousted by Beaton from the chancellorship which he had held since 1528. The rivalry between the two archbishops was notorious and seems at this period to have led Dunbar closer to the English party than he had been in the 1530's when he upheld the French alliance. His political activities in the 1540's merit closer examination than they have received.
32. William Cunningham, third Earl of Glencairn (d. 1548). Succeeded 1540-1541.
33. Gilbert Kennedy, third Earl of Cassilis (1515-1558). Succeeded 1527.
34. William Keith, fourth Earl Marischal (d. 1581). Succeeded 1527.
35. Robert Maxwell, fifth Lord Maxwell (d. 1546). Succeeded 1513.
36. Hugh Somerville, fourth Lord Somerville (1486-1549). Succeeded 1522.
37. Eldest son of George Leslie, fourth Earl of Rothes. He died in 1554.

and Hertford, his uncle, became protector as Duke of Somerset. The death of Francis I followed on 31st March. His successor was Henry II, whose ambitious policy was a potential threat to the insecure new regime in England. The spring saw busy intercourse between Scotland and France, between the Castilians and England. When the papal absolution for Beaton's murderers (the basis of the interim truce in December) arrived in April, they rejected it. But their hopes of relief were disappointed. A French fleet arrived and the castle surrendered at the end of July. The inmates, John Knox among them, became French prisoners. Meanwhile, old differences were reappearing. Documents found at St. Andrews showed that many Scots lords had again bound themselves to England. The rivalry between Arran and Mary of Guise, long restrained by Beaton, broke out irrepressibly. The queen dowager's family, the Guises, won a dominant position at the French court, and Scotland played a large part in their schemes.

In these circumstances it was a mercy for Scotland that, when the next English blow fell at Pinkie on 10th September, 1547, it was guided by a hand less resolute than Henry VIII's. Somerset was prevented by insecurity at home from following up what might have been a decisive victory. As it was, Pinkie drove Scotland into dependence on France. More was at stake now than a renewal of the Auld Alliance. It was still easier for a patriotic Scotsman to turn to France than to England. But misgivings about the French alliance were now more than ever justified. The sovereign was a girl, who must eventually marry; and any marriage must represent some kind of victory for the house into which the queen married. The English match was now repugnant to all but the hired agents of England. But a French marriage must mean some degree of subjection—how much was unknown—of Scotland to France. The only available alternative—the marriage to Arran's son which the regent had vainly sought for some years—meant yielding to the ambitions of a house whose pretensions far outran their abilities, and whose victory must mean almost certain civil strife. It is hardly surprising that the French match was preferred. It ran along the lines of traditional loyalties. It implied the maintenance of the church, to which most Scotsmen still adhered. And (at the lowest reckoning) it was the price that must be paid for the military and diplomatic aid without which the prostrate country could not recover.

French aid began to reach Scotland late in 1547 and was substantial by the following summer. In July, 1548, the price was paid: the young queen was to go to France and, in due course, marry the dauphin. Eighteen months more of bitter fighting followed; but when England and France made peace at Boulogne in March, 1550, the English had been expelled from most of the strongholds seized after Pinkie. The long war of the " Rough Wooing " was over.

Peace came at a moment of transition. The era of the reformation was yielding to that of the counter-reformation. The great and lasting territorial victories of continental protestantism—in Germany and northern Europe—were largely past, and the catholic reconquests were being prepared for by the rise and progress of the Jesuits and by other forces. The last great age of the Empire was ending; Spain was soon to dominate Europe and much of the world beyond. Scotland, in this changing world, needed leadership more than ever. The recent war had combined many of the worst features of civil and international conflict. An instrument of government more effective than a largely paralysed feudal monarchy was plainly required. The ancient church would have to move more freely with the new currents of catholic reform if its destruction was to be averted. Of all this, there was little sign and little hope. The strongest personality in the country was a Frenchwoman and a member of one of the most ambitious houses in Europe: Mary of Guise was to do some good in Scotland and to attempt more, but she depended on France—and, in 1550, she still had four years of manoeuvre and intrigue between her and the regency. The hierarchy of the church was headed by John Hamilton, who, even if he had had no other faults, suffered, in many eyes, from the ineradicable fault of being a Hamilton. It was one of the church's many misfortunes at this time to be led by a kinsman of the queen dowager's chief rival. Neither church nor state afforded much inspiration to a demoralised people.

The Guises were quick to concert their plans. Mary went to France in September, 1550, with a train that included leading protestant sympathisers such as Glencairn,[38] Cassilis, and the Earl Marischal. By the time she returned from the French court, in November, 1551, there had been war between France and the Empire for two months. England was not now the formidable power she had been four or five years earlier, and did not constitute a threat to Scottish interests. The border had been settled by the Treaty of Norham in the summer of 1551, and Scotland was not to be drawn in the old way into France's wars. Even the queen dowager's attempt, more than a year after her return, to raise an official expeditionary force to fight on the continent was frustrated. Arran, meanwhile (or Châtelherault as he may now be called, from the French duchy conferred on him at the time of the marriage treaty with France), held on stubbornly to power. But he was in the end no match for Mary of Guise in skill or resolution. Fortune, too, favoured the more vigorous contender: in July, 1553, Edward VI died and, after a brief period of uncertainty, Mary Tudor succeeded him. There had been signs that Châtelherault might turn again to the protestants and look for English support. That possibility vanished with a catholic queen on the English throne. By April, 1554, when the Queen of Scots' twelfth birthday was approaching, with the accompanying danger of a hostile scrutiny of the regent's stewardship, Châtelherault gave up the struggle. On 12th April the Estates appointed Mary of Guise to succeed him.

Mary of Guise faced a complex task: to govern an intractable realm so as to conserve her daughter's inheritance and, at the same time, to serve the interests of France and the ambitions of her house. The religious issue, important as it was to be, was but one factor in her problem. It would be a travesty to suggest that the preservation of catholicism was a paramount consideration in the queen regent's mind. Even in a century of so-called religious wars, there was no such simple relationship between religious belief and political action. The Most Christian King of France was at this very time supporting the heretical princes of Germany against the Holy Roman Emperor—whose own troops had sacked Rome itself in 1527. Alike of the catholic church and of the new protestant communions, it was true that they could not survive without the support of political power, while those who wielded that power often seemed indifferent to their survival. Events in Scotland in the 1550's are incomprehen-

---

38. Alexander Cunningham, fourth Earl of Glencairn (d. 1575). Succeeded 1548.

sible if it is assumed that Mary of Guise was committed to a " catholic " policy.

The accession of Mary Tudor in England meant, diplomatically, much more than the replacement of a protestant by a catholic sovereign. It meant the accession of a queen who was half Spanish herself and who, less than three months after her succession was secured, was promised in marriage to the emperor's son, Philip of Spain. The marriage took place in the July following Mary of Guise's Scottish triumph. Now, so long as Mary Tudor was childless, Mary Queen of Scots was, in catholic eyes, the legitimate heir to the English throne.[39] To Henry II and the Guises, she would naturally be a far more acceptable Queen of England than Mary Tudor, now sharing her throne with the son of Henry's rival, Charles V. The prospect of securing for the dauphin, Francis, the three kingdoms of France, England and Scotland need not have seemed unreal in the age when Charles V still, after nearly forty years, held together his extraordinary assemblage of realms and territories.[40] With such possibilities in view, Scotland must be firmly held, and this was Mary of Guise's task.

The new regent made what was perhaps an over-confident start. She filled the great offices with French advisers—de Rubay became keeper of the Great Seal (and even, after the disgrace of Huntly[41] and Argyll following the failure of their highland campaign, chancellor). Villemore was comptroller, Bonot governor of Orkney. The influence of d'Oysel, the French ambassador, was always great. This might be defended on account of the proved unreliability of so many Scottish magnates.[42] But it could not be a popular policy, and anti-French feeling grew, with no English threat to offset it. Then, in the autumn of 1555, John Knox returned to Scotland. He had been an obscure figure when he left for the French galleys eight years earlier. Now he had behind him his English experience and the authority of Calvin's Geneva, where he had been chosen minister by the English congregation. His preaching in Scotland in 1555-1556 proved to be " the end of the beginning " of the Scottish reformation. In May, 1556, it brought Knox an ecclesiastical summons to Edinburgh; but, in his own words, " that dyet held nott." The reason why his condemnation was postponed until he had returned to his Genevan flock was almost certainly the queen regent's intervention to protect him. Her policy towards the protestants throughout this period was one of careful moderation. She did not associate many Scotsmen with her government, but she was not partisan in her limited choice. Cassilis replaced Archbishop Hamilton as treasurer when she took office; he and Glencairn were members of the justiciary commission of May, 1555; in 1556 the surviving " Castilians " had their forfeitures revoked. The comparatively conciliatory tone of Knox's *Letter to the Queen Regent*, written this summer, fits into this context. It was politics, not religion, that embroiled the regent with the magnates.

---

39. See Genealogical Table B.

40. Professor Denys Hay has recently pointed out that the sixteenth century saw a great development of the dynastic concept of politics, in which matrimonial alliances played an essential part (*New Cambridge Modern History*, i, Cambridge, 1957, pp. 9-10).

41. George Gordon, fourth Earl of Huntly (d. 1562). Succeeded 1524. He had become chancellor after Beaton's death.

42. Mary of Guise had good reason to know the stuff of which the Scottish magnates were made, for she had herself played upon their interested motives in her quest for power (see *The Scottish Correspondence of Mary of Lorraine*, ed. A. I. Cameron, Edinburgh, Scottish History Society, 1927, esp. pp. 325 ff.).

The European scene was changing again. Charles V abdicated and his inheritance was divided. Mary Tudor's husband, denied the crown matrimonial in England, became Philip II of Spain. His wife was barren and in poor health: the English succession was a vital factor in European politics. Papal policy, meanwhile, was unhampered by overmuch concern for catholic unity. Cardinal Caraffa had been one of the great figures of the counter-reformation; but as Pope Paul IV (from May, 1555), his primary political aim was to expel Spanish power from Naples. He allied himself with France (still the ally of the Turks and the refuge and support of the heretical enemies of Mary Tudor). In September, 1556, Philip attacked the Papal States. French policy called for a Scottish attack on England, the domain of Philip's wife. But the Scots were no more inclined to attack England in the interest of France than were the English to attack France in the interest of Spain. The queen regent had vainly tried, in the summer of 1556, to free her government from dependence on feudal levies by proposing a standing army financed out of taxation. But this was not to be borne. Significantly, the opposition was led, not by the great lords—some of whom, according to Lesley, supported the proposal—but by " the baronnis and gentill men ", the lesser nobility or gentry. And of the two spokesmen they sent to the regent, one (Sandilands of Calder[43]) was a protestant, while the other (Wemyss of that Ilk[44]) later supported both the regent and her daughter against the Congregation. More than partisan opposition was being aroused, and the regent found great difficulty in imposing a war policy. England was drawn into the continental struggle in the spring and summer of 1557, but in July a renewal of peace between England and Scotland was negotiated. Only in November was the regent able to take advantage of border affrays to muster forces for an invasion. Even then she suffered a sharp reverse when the Scottish commanders refused point blank to attack. Those who thus challenged Mary's authority included some protestant supporters—Cassilis and (a more recent convert) Argyll; but with them they had Huntly—an opportunist, no doubt, but no protestant—and Châtelherault, who was—Châtelherault. It was the last name that made Knox so suspicious of this " contradictioun maid to the Auctoritie ". He feared the contamination of the emergent Congregation by the dynastic ambitions of the turncoat Hamilton.

The resistance to the regent did not come from a protestant party. But the protestants were becoming stronger, more influential, and bolder. Lord James Stewart, bastard son of James V, and later Earl of Moray and regent, soon to prove the strongest man in the country, signed the letter of March, 1557, inviting Knox to return (an event that was, in fact, postponed for over two years). When the Congregation acquired coherent form by the " Common Band " of 3rd December, 1557, it had among its leaders Glencairn, Argyll and his son,[45] and James Douglas, Earl of Morton.[46] But the protestant hope was still to win concessions by demonstrating their potential strength. No open breach was precipitated.

---

43. Sir James Sandilands of Calder (?1482-1562). Succeeded c. 1505.
44. Sir John Wemyss of Wemyss (?1513-1571). Succeeded 1544.
45. Archibald Campbell, Lord Lorne (?1538-1573). Succeeded his father as fifth Earl of Argyll in 1558.
46. James Douglas (?1516-1581), younger son of Sir George Douglas of Pittendriech. He acquired the Earldom of Morton by marriage, succeeding his father-in-law, the third earl, in 1550. His uncle, Archibald, sixth Earl of Angus, died in January, 1557, and was succeeded by Morton's elder brother, David, as seventh earl. He, in turn, died in June, 1557, and the Earldom of Angus passed to his infant son, Archibald, the eighth earl (1555-1588). Morton became tutor to the young earl and thus controlled the Angus estates, as well as those of Morton, for many years.

When, also in December, 1557, the regent moved for fulfilment of the marriage contract between her daughter and the dauphin, she had protestant support. The embassy appointed by the Estates included not only Cassilis and Lord James but also Erskine of Dun, one of the staunchest protestants of all. Protestant support was essential to the regent; but it was just as essential for the protestants to court her favour. They had no other resource—Henry II of France might help English protestant rebels against Mary Tudor, but Mary Tudor herself was no such Machiavel; and without English aid the Scottish government could not be brought down. It must, therefore, be propitiated.

On the other hand, it was vital for France to secure Scotland by the royal marriage, especially after her defeat by Spain (with English help) at St. Quentin in August, 1557. The balance was somewhat redressed when the Duke of Guise captured Calais at the turn of the year. But the French position was still uncertain. In fact (though this could not yet be known), both sides in the long Hapsburg-Valois struggle were becoming exhausted. In the autumn of 1558, on the pretext of uniting against heresy, steps were taken (under Guise auspices) towards the peace eventually made by the Treaty of Cateau-Cambrésis in April, 1559. But a year earlier Mary Queen of Scots had married the dauphin under a treaty providing for a union of the two crowns, Francis becoming King of Scots and the eldest son of the marriage being destined to reign in both realms. By secret agreements, signed by the young queen but unknown to the Scots commissioners, Scotland was handed over to the French king should the marriage be childless. The ambassadors returned in the autumn, four of them dying mysteriously on the way. In December the Estates ratified the treaty and granted the dauphin the crown matrimonial. The Guise triumph seemed complete.

But the radical instability of political affairs soon intervened. In November, 1558, Mary Tudor died and Elizabeth succeeded to the English throne. From the outset, even before its full implications were plain, this implied the possibility of renewed English support for disaffection in Scotland. During 1558, the fortunes of the Scottish protestants had varied. There were signs of more decisive action by the church authorities; but the most decisive thing actually done—the burning of the aged Walter Milne in April—probably strengthened the protestants by its harshness. By the autumn it was becoming apparent that the attack on the church was linking up with social unrest in the lower orders. Churchmen may not have been alone in their alarm at this. The explosive blend of religious and social revolt was disagreeably familiar to all members of the sixteenth-century " Establishment ", lay and clerical, protestant and catholic alike. For the time being the lords of the Congregation held to a cautious course. They voiced, but did not press, certain demands in the parliament of November-December, 1558. They sought to clarify their position, as the threat of violence mounted, by blaming any " tumult or uproar " caused by the religious conflict on those who refused orderly reform. The pamphlets written by Knox in the spring and summer[47] must by now have been adding to the latent violence of the situation; but the storm did not fully break for another five or six months.

---

47. *The First Blast of the Trumpet against the Monstrous Regiment of Women*; *Letter to the Queen Regent* (with additions to the 1556 text); *The Appellation*; *Letter to the Commonalty of Scotland*. All were published in Geneva.

PLATE I.

JAMES V
AND
MARY
OF GUISE.

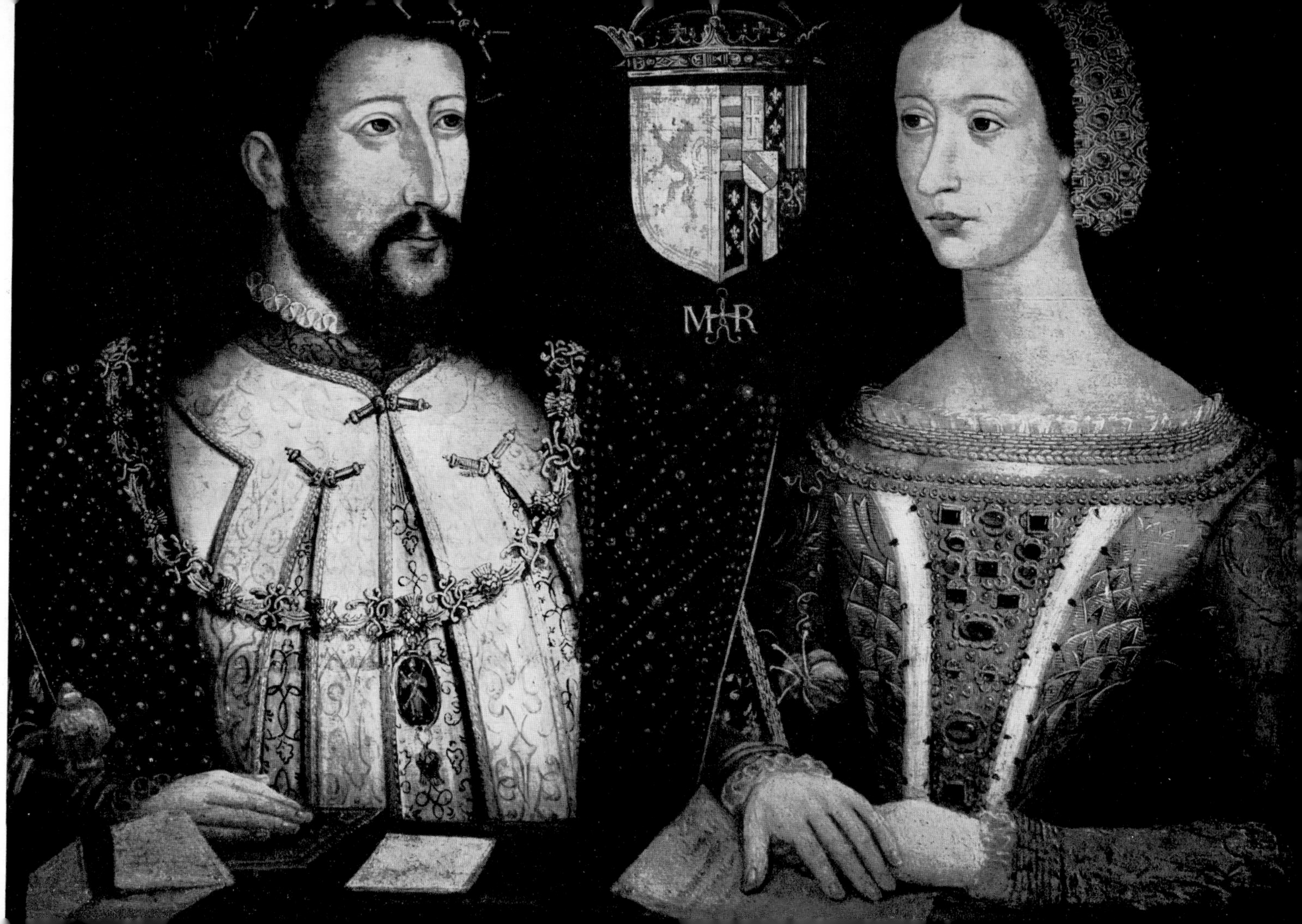

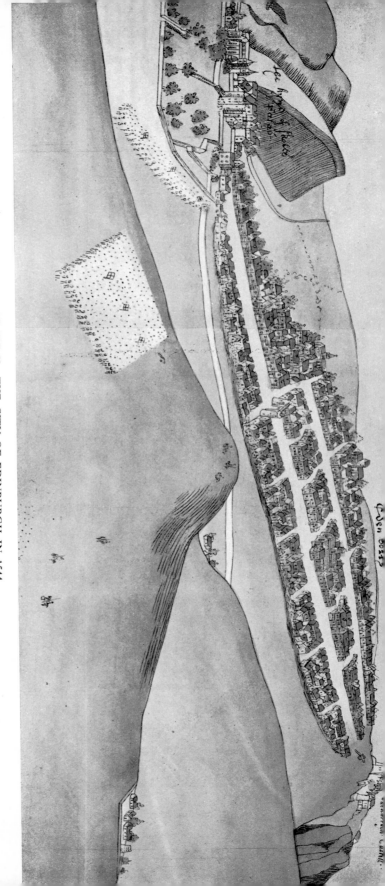

PLATE II. THE CITY OF EDINBURGH IN 1544.

By March, 1559, when the last provincial council of the medieval Scottish church met, the Franco-Spanish negotiations were about to succeed, while the chance of a continued alliance between England and Spain had dwindled. In April, Cateau-Cambrésis ended the Hapsburg-Valois conflict. For England the treaty confirmed the loss of Calais and made any faint hope of its recovery depend on non-intervention in France—and Scotland. Against this background Mary of Guise now took vigorous action against the Congregation. In May (which saw Knox's final return to Scotland) the " uproar for religion " and the Wars of the Congregation began. Initial protestant successes (culminating in the occupation of Edinburgh at the end of June) were not sustained. Evacuating the capital by the Appointment of Leith (24th July), the lords recognised their need of English aid; and, reluctantly, that aid was given. The reluctance had several sources: Elizabeth's treaty obligations, her dislike of rebels, her caution, and her parsimony, all contributed. But the Acts of Supremacy and Uniformity in May had proclaimed the direction of her religious policy; and the accidental death of Henry II in July had brought Francis and Mary to the throne of France as well as Scotland. Their armorial quarterings announced their intention of adding England too, so that the defeat of French influence in Scotland became vital to Elizabeth. Meanwhile, the Congregation acquired a kind of dynastic respectability when Châtelherault joined the lords in September. With English financial help, they again occupied Edinburgh in October and declared the queen regent deposed. Their manifestoes had become steadily more political and less religious in tone. National dislike of French control, feudal dislike of any control, the dynastic ambitions of the Hamiltons, the diplomatic schemes of Maitland of Lethington[48] and Lord James Stewart, all played a part; militant protestantism was, for the moment, in the background. But another defeat in November showed that the Congregation's army could not match the regent's French troops, whose reinforcement, moreover, they could not prevent. Naval intervention by England at the turn of the year frustrated the regent's offensive in Fife, while bad weather defrauded her of French reinforcements. By the end of February, 1560, the Treaty of Berwick embodied a full alliance between Elizabeth and the Congregation. France was beset by internal difficulties, the conspiracy of Amboise declaring itself in March. English troops entered Scotland and joined the army of the Congregation in besieging Leith in April. But negotiations had already begun. The military operations were mismanaged and almost irrelevant. And Mary of Guise was dying. Her death on 10th June, soon after Cecil had arrived in Scotland to hasten the negotiations, was followed in less than a month by the Treaty of Edinburgh, which destroyed all she had fought for. The " Reformation Parliament " in August adopted legislation purporting to replace catholicism by a nation-wide protestant church. The Congregation had won.

In the perspective of Scottish politics from 1513 to 1560 the Congregation's victory is seen to be at once more and less than a protestant triumph. That it could not have been what it was without protestantism is quite clear, however much dispute there may be as to the extent to which the Scottish people had abandoned catholicism at this date. But no one can

---

48. William Maitland (?1525-1573), son of Sir Richard Maitland of Lethington. Secretary to Mary of Guise, he joined the Congregation in 1559, succeeding John Knox as their secretary. After Mary Queen of Scots returned in 1561, he served her in the same capacity.

read the statements of the protestant leaders themselves, or study the terms of the settlement of 1560, without seeing that this was also a victory for the feudal magnates in their long struggle with the crown. Involved in this was the usual disedifying tangle of personal rivalry and ambition. But the feudal victory had more respectable associations. With it there went genuine national feeling among those who were impatient of the French hegemony with which Mary of Guise's government had become identified. It was one paradox among many that this " nationalism " could triumph only by the help of an older enemy than the Guises—the English.

IV

The summer of 1560 ought, by all appearances, to mark a period. In fact, there were many loose ends. Elizabeth rejected the proposal of marriage with Châtelherault's son, Arran,[49] which would have put her alliance with the Congregation on a firm dynastic footing. The relations between the absent sovereigns who reigned in Scotland and the protestant lords who ruled there were ambiguous. Francis and Mary withheld their assent to the legislation of the " Reformation Parliament " and their ratification of the Treaty of Edinburgh. But it was a quite unlooked for event in December that threw all into confusion—the death of Francis. This reduced Mary to the status of queen dowager in France, while her Guise relatives lost their preponderance when Catherine de' Medici became regent during the minority of her son, Charles IX. (The dwindling possibility of a renewed French attempt in Scotland vanished in the spring of 1562 when religious dissension in France exploded in the first religious war.) And for the first time in her life Mary Queen of Scots became a personal factor in the politics of her realm. Many calculations collapsed before the fact that Mary would soon return to Scotland. It became the policy of Lord James and Lethington, the leading statesmen of the Congregation, to achieve a working arrangement with the queen whereby, in exchange for her acceptance of the religious settlement of 1560, they would support her claim to the English succession. This meant the abrogation or modification of the Treaty of Edinburgh; and in the end Elizabeth was no more willing to alter the treaty than Mary was to accept it as it stood. But hope was very much alive when Mary reached Scotland in August, 1561.

The personal reign of Mary Stewart (1561-1567) has almost obsessively preoccupied writers of all sorts—controversialists, historians, biographers, novelists—for nearly four centuries. Here only the main political threads in a familiar pattern need be indicated. One principal clue lies in the very phrase " personal reign ". A legitimate sovereign once more occupied the throne in person. This would have been important even if the sovereign had not been Mary with her peculiar gift for attracting loyalty. To resist the queen was a very different matter from resisting a regency backed by foreign troops. The forces that had won the Congregation's victory in 1560 would never again have the unity that had made that victory possible; yet there would likewise never be a concentration of opposite forces sufficient to reverse the verdict of 1560. Some external pressure was needed to tip the balance, and England provided it; but much was to depend on the way in which the pressure was exerted.

---

49. James Hamilton, third Earl of Arran (1537/38-1609). Insane from 1562 until his death.

The two main phases of Mary's reign in Scotland are divided by her marriage to Darnley in the summer of 1565. During the four years before that, Scottish policy ran along lines largely determined by Lord James Stewart and Maitland of Lethington, and its aim was an amicable settlement with England whereby Elizabeth would recognise Mary as her successor. To think of Mary as a " catholic " ruler in this period is quite misleading. She herself, together with those under her protection, practised the faith at court. But her proclamation of August, 1561, forbade any attempt to change the settlement of 1560 till parliament had taken order in the matter. Financial arrangements were made which conferred a kind of state recognition on the protestant ministers (while leaving most ecclesiastical wealth to the lay lords who had acquired it). Huntly, the nominal leader of the catholic nobility, fell foul of Mary's government and was firmly put down in the campaign which ended at Corrichie (September, 1562). The papal nuncio, de Gouda, was not officially acknowledged, and Mary sent no representatives to the final session of the Council of Trent. But if policy was not " catholic ", it was hardly " protestant ". Lethington and Lord James (Earl of Mar in February, 1562; Earl of Moray about the time of Huntly's fall, from which he gained substantially[50]) held Knox and the other zealots at arm's length when the ministers denounced the " idolatry " of the queen's mass. They promoted a policy which deprived the protestant ministry of adequate financial resources. Like Mary's, their aims were essentially diplomatic and dynastic. The English succession and the ultimate union of the two realms were their political goals.

Till the summer of 1562, the prospects of an agreed settlement seemed fair, if not bright. A meeting between the two queens was all but arranged when the dangerous situation in France, where the first religious war had begun in the spring, convinced Elizabeth's advisers that the meeting must be postponed. But the new situation in France also forced Catherine de' Medici into alliance with the Guises, and in this way a project she had previously opposed became practical politics. This was the marriage of Mary to Don Carlos, son of Philip of Spain; and it was actively discussed in 1562-63. The negotiations were conducted by Lethington, with at least the acquiescence of Moray, despite the obvious dangers of such a marriage from a protestant point of view. There was, indeed, sharp disunity among the protestants at this time, and a prolonged estrangement between Moray and Knox. In the summer of 1563 Moray refused to press Mary for a parliamentary settlement of the religious question. This, Knox alleged, was owing to the earl's selfish eagerness to secure royal confirmation of his Moray title and lands. And personal motives might also have weighed with Moray in regard to the Spanish marriage. Such a marriage might have taken Mary out of Scotland again, leaving Moray to enjoy the viceregal position he had hoped for before the death of Francis II brought the queen unexpectedly home. In any event the Spanish project came to nothing, being virtually ended by the prince's serious illness in the autumn of 1563.

In one way the Spanish marriage policy had done its work, by

---

50. Lord James was created Earl of Mar in February, 1562, on the occasion of his marriage to Agnes Keith, daughter of the Earl Marischal. But there seems already to have been some idea of giving him the Earldom of Moray, held by Huntly since the death of the last earl (bastard son of James IV) in 1544. Lord James publicly assumed the title Earl of Moray in September, not long before the Gordons were defeated at Corrichie. His other gains included the sheriffdoms of Elgin and Inverness. The Earldom of Mar passed in 1565 to Moray's uncle, John Erskine, sixth Lord Erskine.

arousing Elizabeth's alarmed opposition. She began to hint at an English husband for Mary. This proposal was slow to crystallise; and when it did, it took the surprising form of a suggestion that Mary might marry the English queen's own lover, Robert Dudley (created Earl of Leicester that year). Mary and her advisers treated this remarkable proposal with politic care. How soon its hollowness was apparent to them is uncertain: Moray and Lethington were certainly despondent and anxious by the end of the year. Probably, however, Elizabeth was not alone in her temporising. Mary, too, had an alternative matrimonial policy, which hinged on the return to Scotland of Matthew Stewart, Earl of Lennox, exiled in England since 1544. Such a move in itself was unwelcome in several quarters. The Hamiltons, already checked by the measures taken against them in 1562 after the crazy activities of Arran[51] (now hopelessly insane), could not but see it as a threat to their dynastic interests. Morton, too—soon to be a central figure—was threatened, since Lennox's wife (Margaret Douglas, daughter of the sixth Earl of Angus) might challenge his claim to control the Angus estates of his nine-year-old nephew, the eighth earl.[52] But Mary was looking beyond Lennox to his son by Margaret Douglas (herself the daughter of Margaret Tudor). Henry Stewart, Lord Darnley, was, after Mary herself and his own mother, next in succession to the English throne.[53] (His mother was regarded by English catholics as their leader, and both his parents had been in trouble with Elizabeth on this account.) A marriage between Mary and Darnley would confront Elizabeth with a conjunction of the two best claims to her inheritance, a conjunction with a special appeal for her catholic subjects. Elizabeth cannot have wished for such a match; but she allowed first Lennox (in September, 1564) and then his son (in February, 1565) to go to Scotland. Then, in March, 1565, she exasperated Mary and drove Moray and Lethington almost to desperation by making it clear that the preposterous Leicester marriage would not affect her attitude to the succession. Mary moved rapidly towards the marriage with Darnley, which took place on 29th July, 1565, despite Elizabeth's opposition and the alienation of Moray, who, reconciled with Knox, was plotting rebellion with Châtelherault and Argyll. The first phase was decisively over.

The wider context of these events is important. The preparatory phase of the counter-reformation was ending. Pius IV confirmed the Tridentine decrees in January, 1564; soon he and Philip of Spain were canvassing the idea of a catholic league against heresy. In the summer of Mary's marriage the meeting at Bayonne of Catherine de' Medici, Charles IX, his sister, the Queen of Spain, and Alva, seemed to indicate a new development in catholic organisation, though no league, in fact, materialised. There were grounds for protestant alarm. But the events of the autumn in Scotland showed how times had changed since 1559. Moray and his associates launched their rebellion in the expectation of English aid and Scottish support. Neither was forthcoming in sufficient measure, and the affair (the Chaseabout Raid) was an almost ludicrous failure. Mary appeared to have emerged triumphant.

---

51. Late in March, 1562, Arran had accused Bothwell of betraying a plot between them to capture the queen and kill Lord James and Lethington. He subsequently claimed to be married to Mary and said he had been bewitched. He remained hopelessly mad for the last forty-seven years of his life

52. See n. 46 above.

53. See Genealogical Table B.

The victory of 1565 proved, in fact, to be only the prelude to the series of disasters in which Mary's reign ended. Her marriage was a failure, and her husband's ineptitude drove her into ever greater reliance on the Italian secretary, Riccio, who had taken Lethington's place in her confidence. Riccio became the symbol of a policy to which formidable opposition developed—a policy which might conceivably have led to a serious endeavour, with papal and Spanish support, to restore catholicism The policy, however, was opposed on narrower grounds than those of religion. On the one hand, Moray and the other rebels of 1565 (apart from Châtelherault, who was pardoned on condition that he remained out of Scotland for five years) were threatened with forfeiture at a parliament summoned for March, 1566. On the other, Darnley, denied the crown matrimonial, resented Riccio's ascendancy and harboured real or factitious suspicions that the Italian was his wife's lover. The improbable allies joined forces. Darnley undertook to procure the rebels' pardon, Moray and his associates promised to support Darnley's claim to the crown matrimonial; both sides agreed to uphold the religious settlement of 1560. A second agreement, instrumental to the first, was made between Darnley and a group of conspirators in Scotland—led by Morton, Ruthven,[54] and Lindsay[55]—for the murder of Riccio. The murder took place on 9th March, and Moray returned to Edinburgh on the following day. So far as he and his friends were concerned the plot succeeded: their forfeiture was forestalled and their pardon eventually secured. But the queen parried any more complete *coup d'état*, winning back Darnley, escaping from Edinburgh to join forces with Huntly[56] and Bothwell,[57] and returning in triumph to the capital on 18th March. Morton, Ruthven, and Lindsay, and the many other plotters, were driven to England. But the attempt to rule without Moray had failed. In April he returned to the council, along with Argyll and Glencairn; and though his position was not wholly secure during the early summer, he was firmly enough in favour by September to induce Mary to allow Lethington to return.[58]

There were by now new factors in the situation. Mary's son had been born on 19th June, and her dislike for Darnley, intensified by his share in the Riccio murder, was now fostered by growing affection for Bothwell. Except for the provision of an heir, the Darnley marriage had failed completely, and it was to seek an " outgait " from it that the famous Craigmillar " conference " took place in late November or early December. It seems clear that the participants—Moray, Lethington, Bothwell, Huntly, and Argyll—discussed among themselves, and with the queen, the possibility of a divorce. This was rejected lest it endanger the prince's legitimacy. The only other way out was Darnley's death: this must have been apparent to both Mary and Moray, whatever the degree of their subsequent complicity.

Events moved swiftly. Late in December Mary pardoned Morton

---

54. Patrick Ruthven, third Lord Ruthven (?1520-1566). Succeeded 1552. He had opposed Mary of Guise as Provost of Perth in 1559. He died in exile in England after the Riccio murder.
55. Patrick Lindsay, sixth Lord Lindsay of the Byres (d. 1589). Succeeded 1563.
56. George Gordon, fifth Earl of Huntly (d. 1576). He became chancellor in 1566 before the formal revocation, in 1567, of the forfeiture imposed after Corrichie. He married Anne Hamilton, Châtelherault's third daughter.
57. James Hepburn, fourth Earl of Bothwell, Duke of Orkney (?1535-1578). Succeeded 1556. His first wife was Jane Gordon, daughter of George, fourth Earl, and sister of George, fifth Earl of Huntly.
58. Lethington's precise part in the Riccio conspiracy is rather obscure, but his complicity was certain and Mary was reluctant to readmit him to her favour.

and most of the other Riccio plotters. She restored Archbishop Hamilton's consistorial jurisdiction—a curiously isolated act, unless it was a preparation for Bothwell's divorce. When Morton returned to Scotland in January, 1567, there was an unsuccessful attempt to involve him in Darnley's murder. The actual signatories of the murder band seem to have been Bothwell, Huntly, Argyll, Lethington, and Balfour of Pittendriech.[59] At the end of January came Mary's somewhat sudden tenderness for her husband, then lying sick at Glasgow. She brought him to Edinburgh and saw him lodged in the house where he met his death in the early hours of 10th February, 1567.

For all the centuries of controversy, the essence of what happened in the next six months lies in Mary's passionate irresponsibility. Her conduct had few defenders at the time, and would have had few since had it not been for her twenty years in prison and her death on the scaffold. By her failure to prosecute the murderers effectively; by her persistent favouring of Bothwell, whose guilt was hardly in doubt; above all, by her marriage to him (by protestant rites) on 15th May after what was manifestly his contrived divorce[60]—by all this she alienated her friends and delivered herself up to her enemies. Her ruin destroyed any faint hope of a speedy catholic restoration in Scotland. Such a restoration had never, indeed, been more than secondary in Mary's plans. But those plans were now shattered. The pope disowned her. France even considered an alliance with those who overthrew her. At home, a broadly-based confederacy forced her surrender at Carberry Hill on 15th June. Popular opinion, worked upon by Knox and his colleagues, was (if at times fickle) predominantly hostile. Yet Mary might still have saved something from the ruin of her fortunes if she had had any freedom of action. The coalition which had ruined Bothwell and imprisoned the queen was soon divided against itself. Argyll and Huntly joined the Hamiltons in a meeting at Dumbarton a fortnight after Carberry Hill, and this faction, led by Archbishop Hamilton, was soon in touch with France. So, however, was the dominant party, uncertain (with good cause) of Elizabeth's attitude to their drastic proceedings. Moray himself was in France, still unsatisfied that what had been done in his absence was justified, still regarded as a possible ally for France. Elizabeth heartily disliked the principle implied in Mary's imprisonment, but policy forbade her to weaken the protestant cause in Scotland. The protestant zealots had exacted from the confederate lords a religious settlement which, at least in its property aspect, cannot have pleased many of the lay leaders. And the preachers demanded Mary's execution, which most of the lords reckoned an impolitic excess. In the end they resisted both this extremity and the queen's restoration proposed by Elizabeth through her ambassador, Throckmorton. Armed with the Casket Letters,[61] they induced Mary to avoid a public trial and almost certain death by abdicating on 24th July in favour of her son and appointing Moray regent.

The finality of the abdication, however, was not at once evident. The baby King James VI was crowned on 29th July; Moray, returning

59. Sir James Balfour of Pittendriech (d. ?1583). Son of Sir Michael Balfour of Montquhanie. With two of his brothers, he was among the St. Andrews "Castilians". He subsequently became Official of Lothian, a lord of session, clerk register, and lord president.

60. The "divorce" was in reality a dual process—a decree of nullity in Archbishop Hamilton's consistorial court, followed by a divorce in the protestant commissary court.

61. These had been in the hands of the confederate lords since 20th June.

to Edinburgh on 11th August, saw his sister four days later, extracted a personal surrender from her, and accepted the regency. He was proclaimed regent on 22nd August, almost exactly six years after welcoming Mary at Leith. But much was still uncertain. Elizabeth was angrier than ever at the seditious proceedings in Scotland. The Hamiltons, ambitious and unreliable as usual, might have been ready to see Mary executed on their own terms, but could not be regarded as likely supporters of the new order. European opinion had, no doubt, been shocked by Mary's behaviour, but it could not be expected to regard that behaviour as justifying what had now been done. In the event, European opinion mattered less than might have been expected, because the main powers were preoccupied with their own troubles—Spain in the Netherlands, France in the third religious war. Yet Moray's situation was uneasy enough. With some skill he avoided serious trouble and, in part, consolidated his position for over eight months. Then came Mary's escape from Lochleven on 2nd May, 1568.

In a week Mary had an army of six thousand men and the support of a formidable " band " of nobles and churchmen. But Moray's resolution and decisiveness were equal to the occasion. Intercepting the queen's army on its way from Hamilton to Dumbarton at Langside, he routed it on 13th May. Three days later Mary crossed into England. It was a fatal miscalculation. She could not know that it would mean nineteen years in prison with the block at the end; but she might have realised that what hope she had of restoring her fortunes lay in Scotland, where she could at least act, not abroad, where she could do no more than intrigue. Her conduct is understandable enough in human terms, but the episode illustrates again how much depended on purely personal factors.

V

If Langside was an end, it was also a beginning—the beginning of an intermittent civil war from which Scotland did not emerge finally till 1573, after a " fugue of regency "[62] in which four men ruled the country and three of them died while doing so. The sources of this conflict were many. Moray's policy had somewhat patched up the edifice of Scottish government, but he had opened new cracks as well. His policy was vigorously protestant, so that catholic magnates, such as Atholl,[63] Eglinton,[64] and Montrose,[65] who had been willing enough to oppose Bothwell, could not support Moray. His ecclesiastical policy was also unwelcome to those who found the new kirk discipline irksome and those who were reluctant to disgorge even part of their acquired riches to sustain the ministers. His failure to prosecute Bothwell's accomplices in the Darnley murder, though readily understandable in one who had at least " looked through his fingers " at the crime, was censured by some; his rigorous policy towards the queen by others. And behind all this, older forces were at work—the dynastic rivalry of the Hamiltons and the Lennoxes, and the old anarchic resentment of a government which, whatever its faults, tried to enforce justice against wrongdoers.

---

62. The phrase is Dr. Agnes Mure Mackenzie's.
63. John Stewart, fourth Earl of Atholl (d. 1579). Succeeded 1542.
64. Hugh Montgomerie, third Earl of Eglinton (?1530-1585). Succeeded 1546.
65. William Graham, second Earl of Montrose (d. 1571). Succeeded 1513.

Moray's position was thus in many ways weak when he left Scotland for the " conference " summoned to determine the issue between Mary and her opponents which met at York in October, 1568. But the other participants in the involved proceedings at York and subsequently at Westminster were little better off. The difficulties of Mary's party need no emphasis. Lethington, whose policy of moderation and, if possible, the restoration of the queen soon alienated him finally from Moray, was committed to a series of dangerous intrigues with Mary and the Duke of Norfolk.[66] Norfolk himself shared those dangers, aggravated in his case by lack of resolution. Even Elizabeth and her advisers were far from happy, for Mary's arrival in England had placed them in a number of seemingly insoluble dilemmas[67]: abroad, relations with both Spain and France were bad; at home, the conspiracy and rebellion of 1569 were already in the making. Elizabeth's policy was to avoid, as far as possible, any definite commitment on the Scottish issue, but, at the same time, to elicit from Moray so damaging an attack on Mary that no reconciliation between brother and sister would be possible, while Moray would be left dependent on English goodwill for the survival of his regency. In this she was successful; but the ambiguous outcome of the conference left Elizabeth with what proved to be the dangerous liability of the captive Queen of Scots. The danger was the greater because the manifest unfairness of the proceedings at York and Westminster had, by reaction, begun somewhat to restore Mary's reputation.

In Scotland too, as Moray found when he returned in February, 1569, Mary's strength was growing. The split in the confederacy which had deposed the queen widened irreparably when Mary at last agreed to give up Bothwell. Châtelherault returned to Scotland soon after Moray himself, having failed to win Elizabeth's support for his claim to the regency and having then accepted a commission from Mary as her lieutenant. A combination of the Hamilton faction and the forces of Huntly and Argyll might have been formidable, but no effective combination took place. At the convention held at Perth in July, Moray secured a decisive rejection of Mary's proposal that her divorce from Bothwell be procured. More dangerous to Moray at this time than the Scottish opposition was the ambitious conspiracy which turned upon the projected marriage of Mary and Norfolk. Lethington was deeply engaged in this scheme, and Moray and Morton countered his influence by charging him, in September, 1569, with complicity in the Darnley murder. But the trial, fixed for 22nd November, was postponed when it became clear that to proceed with it would mean civil war. Meanwhile, in England the Norfolk plot and the northern rebellion had been defeated, and Moray was called upon to assist in mopping-up operations against fugitives who had crossed the border. His chief success in these operations, the capture of the Earl of Northumberland, proved costly; for it provoked a violent reaction both among the borderers, whose code it violated, and among Mary's supporters. Full-scale civil war, averted when Lethington's trial was postponed, was again imminent when Moray was assassinated by Hamilton of Bothwellhaugh in Linlithgow on 23rd January, 1570.

66. Thomas Howard, fourth Duke of Norfolk (1536-1572). He commanded the English forces in Scotland in 1560. Later, though still a protestant, he came to be regarded by English catholics as their leader.
67. This is well illustrated by a paper in Cecil's hand, dated May, 1568, and entitled " Memoriall of things to be considered upon the Q. of Scottes coming into the realme " (*Cal. Scot. Pap.*, ii, 1563-1569, p. 679). It has sections headed " Dangers if she pass to France ", " Dangers if she remain in England ", and " Dangers if she return to rule as before in Scotland ".

The " Good Regent " of legend had, in fact, been a maladroit and unfortunate politician, and the chaotic Scotland he left at his death was no inappropriate monument to the indecision and mixed motivation that had marked his career. Moray's death was followed by open war between the Marians and the party now led by Morton and Mar.[68] The alliance of Mary's supporters and the English rebels provoked a sharp border attack by Elizabeth's forces. But the persistently critical state of England's international position (worsened in May by the publication of Pius V's bull excommunicating and deposing Elizabeth) induced a more moderate policy towards Scotland. Elizabeth's candidate for the regency, Lennox, was appointed in July, and a truce in the civil war followed in September. The truce, it is true, did not last long. The regencies of Lennox (July, 1570, to September, 1571) and Mar (September, 1571, to October, 1572) and the earlier part of Morton's (till the capture of Edinburgh Castle in May, 1573) were taken up by a bitter conflict, ending with the final defeat of the queen's cause.

The course of that conflict need not be described. What is needed here is an assessment of the forces on each side and an indication of the international setting of the civil war. The first task is far from easy, and such assessments as historians have made tend to be little more than bare and conflicting assertions.[69] Some points are clear. Only a minority of the magnates, led by Morton, Mar, Lennox, and Glencairn, supported the king's party. The Marians had either the active or the passive support of the other great lords, prominent on that side being Châtelherault, Huntly, Argyll, Atholl, and Sutherland.[70] With this aristocratic preponderance went a considerable body of support from the gentry; and these two elements together must have carried at least the acquiescence of a large part of the common people, especially in the rural areas. In the towns the situation is less easily assessed, but it was certainly more favourable to the king's party. Some towns, like Dundee, were overwhelmingly protestant. Others, including the capital, were much less dependable from the protestant point of view. The substantial burgesses seem, in general, to have been protestants and king's men; but that in itself might lead the lower orders in the towns governed by the burgesses into opposition. With such a distribution of forces, there could be no easy victory for the government. The best they could look for in the near future was a stalemate, unless outside pressure was brought to bear upon the situation.

The pressure came primarily from England. It was now more than ever England's interest to have a stable and reliable regime north of the border. England's situation around 1570 was one of unenviable isolation, and a troubled Scotland offered too easy an access for Spanish or French hostility. Elizabeth tried first to achieve a solution by arranging for Mary's return under strict guarantees, including an Anglo-Scots alliance and the surrender of James VI as a hostage. But no guarantees were enough to satisfy the king's party in Scotland of their safety if the queen returned, and the scheme fell through (March, 1571). France, too, had

---

68. John Erskine, sixth Lord Erskine (d. 1572). Created Earl of Mar in 1565. His sister was Moray's mother.

69. For example, Hume Brown (*History of Scotland*, Cambridge, 1902, ii, p. 144) says: " The strength of the King's party lay in the Protestant clergy and the mass of the commons." W. L. Mathieson (*Politics and Religion*, Glasgow, 1902, i, p. 160) says: " On the other (*scil.* the Queen's) side . . . were . . . the bulk of the aristocracy . . . and the mass of the commons."

70. Alexander, eleventh Earl of Sutherland (1552-1594). Succeeded 1567.

opposed this settlement, and English policy now turned, on this ground among others, towards a *rapprochement* with France. The moment was opportune: Charles IX had reached an accommodation with the Huguenots and was seeking defensive and offensive alliances against Spain. The Ridolfi plot, though it was a fiasco which proved fatal to Norfolk and most damaging to Mary, intensified English anxiety about Spain's purposes and made the French alliance all the more desirable. The false start of the proposed marriage between Elizabeth and Charles's brother, Anjou, delayed matters; but at last, in April, 1572, the Treaty of Blois bound England and France to terms which included the virtual abandonment of Mary Queen of Scots by France and provided for an Anglo-French attempt to pacify Scotland.

The pacification duly took place; but its context was radically altered by the sequence of events inaugurated by the Netherlands' revolt against Spain a few weeks before the Anglo-French treaty was concluded. French intervention aroused English anxieties which expressed themselves in Sir Humphrey Gilbert's expedition to Flushing. Meanwhile, Charles IX found that his forward policy was leading directly to a single-handed war with Spain, in which, whatever else happened, the Huguenots were likely to make large gains in France. The ensuing political struggle in France issued in the massacre of protestants on St. Bartholomew's Day (24th August, 1572). If English interests had been threatened by French actions in the Low Countries, English opinion was appalled by the massacre. The new alliance was shaken to its foundations. But in the end neither side was ready to give up its diplomatic advantages. Though few of its intended purposes were realised, the Scottish settlement was among those few. But it was hardly the joint enterprise envisaged at Blois. Elizabeth's agent, Killigrew, brought about the Pacification of Perth (February, 1573) which made peace between Morton's government and Huntly and the Hamiltons. The queen's men in Edinburgh Castle, led by Kirkcaldy of Grange and by Lethington (now crippled by disease), were less tractable: only a bombardment by English siege-guns induced them to surrender on 28th May, 1573.

The events of 1573 upheld the verdict of 1567, as that in turn had endorsed the verdict of 1560. But the situation now was very different from the situation in the 1560's. For the first time in Scotland there was effectively in power a government decisively committed to protestantism. The second stage of the reformation, led by Andrew Melville, took place under very different auspices from the first stage, led by Knox (whose death, in November, 1572, also serves to mark a period[71]). And it was in this second period that Scottish protestantism acquired many of the features that were later to be most characteristic of it. Together with presbyterian government, based on the parity of ministers and the rejection of episcopacy, there emerged the doctrine of the " two kingdoms ", laden with possibilities of conflict between church and state. But the conflict which raged intermittently for a century and more after Andrew Melville's return to Scotland in 1574 arose from an argument as to what kind of protestantism was to be established in Scotland. The conflict over protestantism as such was not yet over: the basis for a powerful catholic party still existed in Scotland. But this conflict was

---

71. By the mid-1570's almost all the leading figures of Mary's personal reign were either dead or otherwise out of action. By 1575, besides Moray, Knox, Lennox, and Mar, the following were also dead: Chatelherault (1575), Archbishop Hamilton (1571), Lethington (1573), Argyll (1573), Glencairn (1575). Huntly died in 1576. Arran was a lunatic and Bothwell was to die in a Danish prison in 1578.

increasingly carried on by means of influence and intrigue, relying ultimately on the dwindling hope of foreign intervention.[72] For this reason, the remainder of James VI's minority and his personal reign can be dealt with more briefly than earlier stages in the struggle.

Morton's assured supremacy as regent lasted for just short of five years. During that period he governed with a combination of strength, rapacity, and disregard of the hostility he aroused that may inspire a certain reluctant admiration for this least attractive of all the unattractive men who ruled or sought to rule Scotland in the age of the reformation. The hostility was real and widespread, and one of its most significant elements was the kirk's dislike of Morton's greedy Erastianism. But his dismissal from the regency in March, 1578, was the work of forces some of which were little to the kirk's liking. The movement of opposition was headed by Atholl, the leading catholic magnate, and the new Earl of Argyll, who had succeeded his half-brother in 1573.[73] Atholl became chancellor and hopes ran high among Scottish catholics both at home and in exile. But the hopes were disappointed. Morton turned the formal ending of James's minority to his advantage (much as his uncle, the sixth Earl of Angus, had done forty-five years before when another boy king was on the throne), seized the king's person through the instrumentality of the young Earl of Mar,[74] and regained his place on the council and with it, before long, his predominance. The surviving leaders of the Hamiltons[75] were driven into exile in May, 1579, a month after Atholl's death had removed one of the chiefs of the party that had brought Morton down a year before.

Abroad, a great trial of strength between protestantism and the counter-reformation was imminent, and Scotland was to be drawn into the struggle. Spain achieved a partial pacification in the Low Countries in May, 1579, and was soon to receive an accession of strength when, in 1580, Philip ascended the Portuguese throne (vacant since August, 1578). The persistent religious conflict in France had enhanced the power of the Guises and the Catholic League. Gregory XIII had renewed Pius V's bull against Elizabeth, and her government had been challenged in Ireland. It was in these circumstances that James VI's cousin, Esmé Stuart, Seigneur d'Aubigné, arrived in Scotland in September, 1579, as an emissary of the Guises.[76] His favour with the young king grew so

---

72. A parallel can to some extent be drawn between the position of the catholic party in Scotland after 1573 and that of the protestants before 1560. Both parties were excluded from power, and each sought at least toleration, at most domination. Both found that the conversion of the established authorities was impossible, and both turned to foreign sources of support to redress the balance—the protestants to England, the catholics to France and, increasingly, Spain.

73. Colin Campbell, sixth Earl of Argyll (d. 1584).

74. John Erskine, Earl of Mar (?1562-1634). Succeeded his grandfather, the regent, in 1572.

75. Lord John Hamilton (?1542-1604), third son of Châtelherault, Commendator of Arbroath since 1551, created Marquess of Hamilton in 1599; and Lord Claud Hamilton (?1546-1621), Commendator of Paisley, who (unlike his brother) remained a catholic. He became Lord Paisley in 1587, when his commendatorship was erected into a temporal lordship. Lord John, it should be noted, was (leaving aside his insane elder brother, Arran) heir presumptive to the throne from the death of his father in 1575 till the birth of James VI's first son in 1594. By then the position of heir presumptive had been occupied by the head of the house of Hamilton ever since Albany's death in 1536, except for brief periods, amounting together to little more than two years (1540-41 and 1566-67). See Genealogical Table A.

76. He was the only son of John Stewart, Seigneur d'Aubigné, younger brother of the Regent Lennox, and had been born about 1542. The Lennox Earldom, which d'Aubigné soon received from James, had passed to the king himself on the death of his grandfather, the regent, in 1571. In 1572, however, it was conferred on the king's uncle, Darnley's younger brother, Charles Stewart, sixth Earl of Lennox. He died in 1576, and the earldom passed to another brother of the Regent Lennox, Robert Stewart, bishop of Caithness (?1517-1586), created seventh Earl of Lennox in 1578. He resigned it in d'Aubigné's favour and became Earl of March instead. Meanwhile, the Lennox claim to the Scottish throne, after James himself (who united the direct and the Lennox claims) had passed to the king's cousin, Arbella Stuart (1575-1615), daughter of Charles, the sixth earl; she also inherited from her grandmother, Margaret Douglas (d. 1578), a claim to the English succession.

rapidly that within a matter of months he was Earl of Lennox (by which title it will be convenient to refer to him), commendator of Arbroath, lord high chamberlain, and captain of Dumbarton. Morton, the kirk, and Elizabeth all recognised Lennox as their enemy; but he contrived the fall of Morton by the end of 1580 (Morton was executed for complicity in the Darnley murder in June, 1581) and parried the hostility of the kirk by professing himself a convert to protestantism. Elizabeth's attempts to dislodge him were unavailing, and his favour with the king was confirmed when, in August, 1581, he was created Duke of Lennox.

A scheme to make Scotland the springboard for the " enterprise of England "—the catholic re-conquest backed by Spain, the pope, and the Guise faction in France—now developed, with Lennox as its principal artificer in Scotland and Jesuit emissaries (including the Scots William Crichton and Edmund Hay) as its channels of communication. The scheme rested on estimates of the political and military possibilities which were enthusiastic rather than realistic; and what little chance of success it had was destroyed by the Raid of Ruthven in August, 1582. The old combination of English influence, protestant anxiety, and the desire of a rival group of magnates to oust the ruling faction, brought about the seizure of the king and his detention for ten months in the castle of Ruthven. The leaders were Gowrie,[77] Angus,[78] Mar, and Glencairn,[79] and their victory was eagerly welcomed both in the kirk, whose authority was much restored by the new regime, and in England. By the end of the year Lennox had left Scotland; he died in May, 1583.

The government of the Ruthven lords, however, proved no more stable than its predecessor. The new leaders found, like others before them, that Elizabeth's support was an uncertain resource. Counter-intrigues inspired from France and backed by James himself were soon at work, and by the end of June, 1583, the king was free. The next few months saw the virtual destruction of the English party: their attempted recovery in the spring of 1584 was defeated; and on 2nd May, 1584, the last act of the Ruthven episode ended with Gowrie's execution for treason.

James VI's minority is a period whose end escapes easy definition. The formal termination of the regency is worse than meaningless in terms of actual power. Morton's fall left the real direction of affairs in the hands of Lennox, not of the king, still only in his fifteenth year. Even after the final defeat of the Ruthven faction, James, who was now eighteen, remained very much under the influence of other minds and, as will be seen, of one mind in particular. But it seems fair to say that from the summer of 1584 onwards the king himself became an increasingly important factor in determining policy; and it is, therefore, appropriate to end here the present part of the analysis.

The years from 1568 to 1584 reveal both change and continuity in Scottish politics. The changes are obvious—the firmer establishment of protestantism, the yielding of the Auld Alliance with France to a new alliance with England. But there are striking elements of continuity, which can perhaps best be seen if we compare the minority of James VI

77. William Ruthven, first Earl of Gowrie (d. 1584), was the second son of Patrick, third Lord Ruthven, and had joined his father in the plot to murder Riccio. His earldom was conferred on him in August, 1581, being erected out of the abbey lands of Scone.
78. Archibald Douglas, eighth Earl of Angus (?1555-1588). Succeeded 1557: see n. 46 above.
79. James Cunningham sixth Earl of Glencairn (d. 1631). Succeeded 1580.

with that of James V two generations earlier. Both minorities reveal the essential weakness of the Scottish polity—its lack of a continuing " state " capable of surviving the demise of royal authority. In both cases a royal minority means a squabble of factions about the royal person (the existence in the later period of a second royal person—the exiled queen— complicates but does not substantially change the situation). Both minorities show how many issues—political, diplomatic, religious— depended on the shifting distribution of power among magnates whose own interests as often as not had little or nothing to do with those issues. Again, both at the beginning of the sixteenth century and at its close, Scotland, weakened by this uneasy balance of power among rival nobles and by the lack of effective government, enjoyed only a limited autonomy. External influence repeatedly came in to determine the direction of Scottish policy. In the reign of James V the dominant influence had been French, with England as the disturbing factor. In James VI's time the dominance had passed to England, and the intervening forces were those of France, Spain, and the papacy, acting through the Jesuits. But the similarity of pattern is there. It is easy for us to say after the event that Scotland, throughout this period, was moving towards the inevitable union with England. But no statesman at the time dared assume that the union was, within any measurable time, inevitable; nor could it be known in advance under what conditions the union would come if it came at all. There were large and vital uncertainties as James VI began to assume personal authority.

VI

The difficulty of drawing a clear line between James VI's minority and his personal rule is well illustrated by developments after the second defeat of the Ruthven lords in 1584. The policies adopted were evidently wholly to the king's taste. This is most notably true of the anti-presbyterian policy of the so-called " Black Acts " of the parliament which met in June, 1584. Yet the government was conducted not by James but by the man who had now succeeded Lennox in royal favour—James Stewart, Earl of Arran.[80] Arran was resolute and unscrupulous, and he had dominated James ever since the king's escape, in June, 1583, from the Ruthven faction. During this year's predominance his foreign policy had been intricate, involving conciliatory approaches to the Guises, to Spain, even to the pope. But now, in the summer of 1584, Arran and James became convinced that a *rapprochement* with England was needed. This conviction was in part owing to the increasing influence of Patrick, Master of Gray,[81] who had originally returned to Scotland as a catholic convert and an agent of Mary, but now regarded the catholic enterprise as futile. It was Gray who, in August, 1584, went to London to negotiate on James's behalf. But he also sought to oust Arran by persuading Elizabeth to allow the exiled leaders of the former Ruthven faction to return to Scotland. The catholic threat soon assumed a new form in the scheme (March, 1585) to exclude the protestant Henry of Navarre from

---

80. He was the second son of Andrew Stewart, second Lord Ochiltree (himself descended, though in a line of dubious legitimacy, from James Hamilton, first Earl of Arran, and also notable as the father of John Knox's second wife). He was made Earl of Arran in April, 1581, notwithstanding the fact that the mad earl, Châtelherault's eldest son, was still alive: Stewart, indeed, had been appointed his curator. He died in 1595.

81. Eldest son of Patrick Gray, fifth Lord Gray. He succeeded his father as sixth Lord Gray in 1608 and died in 1612.

the French succession; Philip of Spain was deeply involved, and the protestant world as a whole took alarm. Elizabeth sent Sir Edward Wotton to the Scottish court, and an Anglo-Scottish league for the defence of religion was negotiated amid a baffling series of intrigues which defies summary. In the end the knot was violently cut. Gray contrived the release by Elizabeth of the banished protestant lords, and the ministers who had gone into exile after the " Black Acts " also returned. Arran fled before his assembled enemies, to end his life in obscurity. Soon after his defeat, which took place early in November, 1585, the defensive league with England was concluded.

The new situation was not a simple reversal. The returned exiles had no exclusive predominance, for at the same time the banished Hamiltons came back to Scotland, while influential advisers, such as Gray, Maitland (the chancellor),[82] and Bellenden (the justice clerk),[83] remained in power. Former Ruthven lords like Angus and Mar sat once more in the council; but so did the catholic earls of Huntly,[84] Montrose,[85] and Crawford.[86] This situation gave James greater freedom of action than he had had hitherto, and his policy soon showed the fruits of independence. The alliance with England was confirmed by the treaty proclaimed at Berwick on 5th July, 1586; but there was no yielding to the extreme protestant party at home. The " Black Acts " were upheld, and James successfully defended episcopacy in the person of Archbishop Adamson of St. Andrews, whose excommunication by the Synod of Fife he caused to be revoked. Soon, however, James was faced with a bigger crisis than had yet occurred since his emancipation.

In August, 1586, Mary Queen of Scots was charged with complicity in the Babington plot against Elizabeth, and the train of events began which ended at Fotheringay on 8th February, 1587. James's conduct during the months when his mother's life hung in the balance reflects more credit on his prudence than on his sense of honour. That he had little cause to love a mother of whom he can have had no personal recollection and who had shown no special concern for him in her political schemes is perfectly true; but it is also irrelevant. Given the assumptions of the time, Mary's death was an affront to James's personal honour and to the honour of his country which ought to have been resisted and prevented by any means in his power. Contemporary evidence shows that this was the view of almost all his advisers. But James preferred to preserve the English alliance and with it his hope of the English crown by acquiescing in what was done.

The crisis over Mary's death was the prelude to a still sharper crisis: for catholic indignation against Elizabeth touched off the long-meditated " enterprise of England ". The success of the Armada must, at the lowest reckoning, bar James from the English succession, and it might well mean far more than that for protestantism and for Scottish independence. The Anglo-Scottish alliance—all but destroyed at Fotheringay, despite James's pusillanimity—now regained its strength, and preparations to resist Spain went forward on both sides of the border which had

---

82. John Maitland (1548-1595), younger brother of Lethington, the secretary. He became chancellor after Arran's fall, and was created Lord Thirlestane in 1590.
83. Sir Lewis Bellenden (d. 1591) had succeeded his father as justice clerk in 1577.
84. George Gordon, sixth Earl of Huntly (d. 1636). Succeeded 1576; created Marquess of Huntly in 1599.
85. John Graham, third Earl of Montrose (1548-1608). Succeeded 1571.
86. David Lindsay, eleventh Earl of Crawford (1552-1607). Succeeded 1573.

lately seen a revival of the old savage raiding. The " enterprise " failed. But the defeat of the Armada, important as it was, is one of those events that look more decisive to posterity than they seemed at the time—the more so because the historian has at his disposal evidence to show that the foundations of Spanish predominance were already crumbling. In Scotland, 1588 brought relief, but no final delivery from protestant fears. In 1589, Elizabeth revealed to James treasonable correspondence with Spain by Huntly, Errol,[87] and other catholic lords. Four years later the catholic conspiracy associated with the " Spanish Blanks " caused fresh alarm. When it is recalled that these were also the years of the extravagant activities of Francis Stewart, Earl of Bothwell,[88] and of the feud between Huntly and Moray[89] which ended in the slaying of the " Bonnie Earl " commemorated in one of the finest of Scots ballads, it will be clear that the failure of the " enterprise " brought little peace to Scotland.

The persistent threat from Spain might have been expected to attach James more closely to the English alliance. But his policy was less straightforward than this. English goodwill he certainly desired. But he would not commit himself to a protestant policy so decided as to deliver him into the power of the " left-wing " faction in the kirk. His idea seems to have been to hold a balance between protestant and catholic in a country still deeply divided between the two parties, and thus to vindicate a greater measure of independence for royal policy than could be afforded by reliance on either side. This was a policy which a strong, energetic monarch, properly equipped, might have carried to success. But James was neither strong nor energetic, and his equipment remained largely that of feudal monarchy. Important attempts were made at this period, thanks largely to John Maitland, Lord Thirlestane, the chancellor, to modernise the machinery of government in Scotland. But no rapid progress was possible.[90] In fact, the early 1590's revealed in their anarchy the contemptible weakness of James's authority. So weak was he at one point that he had to make a concession, if not a surrender, to the presbyterian party. This was in 1592, after Huntly had killed Moray, and it took the form of the act whereby the presbyterian hierarchy of courts, already in practical existence over most of the country, was given parliamentary authority. At the same time, however, the 1584 assertion of royal authority was upheld and James was no more disposed than before to yield to the extreme left wing.

The king's reactions to the affair of the " Spanish Blanks " showed that he still hoped to hold a balance between protestant and catholic. He was even, it seems, prepared to weigh seriously the possible advantages of yet another scheme for a Spanish attack on England through Scotland. But the possibilities of such policies, always slight, were running out. When Bothwell, in the last stage of his extraordinary career, attempted (in part as Elizabeth's agent) the kind of *coup de main* by which Scottish politics had so often been determined in the past (July, 1593), he unwit-

---

87. Francis Hay, ninth Earl of Errol (d. 1631). Succeeded 1585.

88. Only son of Lord John Stewart (?1532-1563), bastard son of James V, and Jean Hepburn, sister of the Earl of Bothwell who married Queen Mary. Born in 1563, he became Earl of Bothwell in 1581, three years after his uncle's death in Denmark. He lived in exile from 1595 till his death in 1612.

89. James Stewart (d. 1592), son of Sir James Stewart (created Lord Doune in 1581). He married Elizabeth, eldest daughter of the regent Moray, and assumed the Moray title in virtue of this marriage in 1580.

90. Maitland was a reforming statesman in some ways, but he was also much involved in the feudal politics of his time, and he made many enemies. He took part in the plot which ended in the slaying of Moray, his object being a substantial share in the lands of the young Earl of Argyll. Thus, for all his ability, he cannot be regarded as a far-seeing statesman who rose above the level of his own age.

tingly prepared the way for developments which make the mid-1590's something of a watershed in Scottish history. James's defeat of Bothwell (not complete until April, 1595) depended on allies who would not support him unless he abandoned the catholic earls; and this he was constrained to do. Huntly and Errol went into exile in the spring of 1595; and though their exile was not prolonged and the king's inclination to temporise with catholic power both at home and abroad survived this crisis, there is a sense in which the events just noted mark the beginning of the end of the old feudal politics of Scotland. Material prosperity was growing, and with it there grew a middle class of burgesses and lairds on whose support royal power could largely depend. This middle class was by no means composed of extreme presbyterians, but it had become solidly protestant in the generation since the civil war following the deposition of James's mother, and its members were little inclined to look with favour or indulgence upon the turbulence of the magnates, from which they were often the chief sufferers. Besides this, James was able gradually to buy support among the nobility and gentry, largely by means of temporal lordships erected out of former church lands.[91] Neither material interests nor feudal power were now so likely to upset the established order as had once been the case. From the end of the sixteenth century onwards the return of Scotland to the ancient church must depend on forces other than those which had commonly been deployed in the past.

This is not to say that peace and order descended on Scotland once and for all in 1595. For many years traces of the old anarchy lingered on, to mingle with the new conflicts that distracted the country in the new century. But for the moment it was court intrigue rather than the methods of Cleanse-the-Causeway that prevailed. There was ample violence in reserve, and the king could be as violent as his subjects: the tragedy at Gowrie House in August, 1600, proved this beyond question. But as a description of the tendencies of the period what has been said can be defended. It was in these years between 1595 and his succession to the English crown in 1603 that James, seconded by an able group of advisers,[92] and in some respects building on foundations laid by the chancellor, Maitland, fashioned an instrument of government for Scotland which later enabled him, after he had gone to England, to do (as he boasted) with his pen what his ancestors could not do with their swords. That achievement, still remarkable, will seem less miraculous if the preparatory work of the 1590's is borne in mind, together with the fact that this work was itself made easier by changing economic and social conditions.

91. The fate of the pre-reformation church lands lies near the heart of Scottish politics throughout this period. In the present context, a cardinal event is the Act of Annexation in 1587, whereby ecclesiastical property, with certain specified exceptions, was declared to be annexed to the crown. (James subsequently regretted this act because of its effect on his plans for an episcopal system of church government.) See the discussion by D. Masson, *Register of the Privy Council of Scotland*, 2nd series, ii, 1625-27, Edinburgh, 1899, Introduction, pp. cxvi-clxxvi. This includes (pp. cxliv-clxlvii) a list, prepared by Maitland Thomson, showing the disposition in temporal lordships of the principal monastic lands. For reasons stated at the end of the list, however, it gives a less than complete notion of the number of persons who benefited from the policy of erection.

92. Chief among these advisers were the following: Walter Stewart, Commendator of Blantyre (Lord Blantyre, 1606; d. 1617), who was treasurer from 1596 to 1599; George Seton, Lord Urquhart (1555-1622; Lord Fyvie, 1587; Earl of Dunfermline, 1605), who was lord president and became chancellor in 1604; John Lindsay, second son of David Lindsay, ninth Earl of Crawford (lord of session with the title of Menmuir, 1581), who was secretary from 1596 till 1598, the year of his death; James Elphinstone, third son of Robert, third Lord Elphinstone (1557-1612; Lord Balmerino, 1603), who was secretary from 1598 to 1609; and Thomas Hamilton—"Tam o' the Cowgate" (Lord Binning, 1613; Earl of Melrose, 1619; Earl of Haddington, 1627), who was lord advocate from 1596 to 1612, secretary from 1612 to 1627, lord president from 1616 to 1627, and lord privy seal from 1627 till his death in 1637.

PLATE III. THE MEDIEVAL PRECINCT OF GLASGOW CATHEDRAL.

PLATE IV. THE COLLEGIATE KIRK OF ROSLIN.

James was never more skilful or more successful than in those final years of his personal government in Scotland. Some of his most notable—if least durable—successes were in the field of ecclesiastical policy. Adroitly turning successive crises to his own advantage, he achieved a degree of control over the kirk which would have seemed impossible ten years earlier, and which left him some considerable freedom of manoeuvre in relation both to his catholic subjects and to the catholic world generally. This freedom was important to James because of his overmastering preoccupation with the English succession. So far as the protestant powers of northern Europe were concerned, James's succession was accepted as desirable and even necessary to their security. But most of the political power of Europe was still in catholic hands: Spain was still formidable and seemed more so than she truly was; in France, soon to be clearly the most powerful state of all, events had shown that only a king prepared to accept catholicism could reign. James's secret diplomacy aimed at securing his title on the catholic as well as on the protestant side, by professing his willingness to extend toleration to the English catholics and posing as a possible, even a probable, convert to catholicism himself. He made some progress because the catholic world again lacked even the semblance of unity. France and Spain were inevitably at odds, and the papacy, too, was suspicious of Spain's policy. From France and Rome alike, as well as from some Italian states, James received discreet, cautious, and shrewdly sceptical encouragement. But it may be doubted whether all his perilous manoeuvring contributed much to the eventual ease with which the English crown came to him in 1603. Far more important was the conversion of Robert Cecil[93] to the view that James's succession was the best course for England.

The twenty-two years of James's " pen-government " in Scotland are dominated by his endeavours to assimilate the kirk to the church of England, first in government, then in faith and practice. His considerable, though impermanent, success was based on an approach to absolute power in church and state alike such as no Scottish ruler before him had ever enjoyed. As far as the conflict between catholicism and pro-testantism was concerned, these years are only an epilogue to the main story examined here. In Scotland, as in England, the alarm of the Gunpowder Treason in 1605 led James to abandon whatever tolerant intentions he may have had towards his catholic subjects, who were thereafter harried with a vigour which might have satisfied the protestant extremists had they not been alienated by the king's imposition of prelacy and what they regarded as papistical practices. The death of John Ogilvie in 1615 was the outstanding episode in this phase of protestant-catholic relations. But catholic numbers were still too great and catholic power too substantial for the repression to be more than partial. It is remarkable that the chancellor of Scotland was himself a catholic at this period[94]; and catholic nobles, such as Huntly and Errol, Home[95] and Herries,[96] could still protect their dependants in the practice of their

---

93. Later first Earl of Salisbury (?1563-1612). He became Elizabeth's secretary in 1596, two years before the death of his father, William Cecil, Lord Burghley, lord treasurer of England since 1572 and, before that, Elizabeth's secretary from the beginning of her reign.
94. George Seton, Earl of Dunfermline: see n. 92 above.
95. Alexander Home, sixth Lord Home (1557-1619; restored—his father (d. 1575) having been forfeited in 1573—in 1578), created Earl of Home in 1605.
96. John Maxwell, sixth Lord Herries of Terregles (d. 1631). Succeeded 1604.

faith. There were whole counties where the old religion still prevailed; and these were not merely in the far north and west, for Dumfries and Kirkcudbright must be reckoned among them. There were even towns where catholics were numerous enough to alarm the protestant authorities. But though the catastrophic decline which reduced Scots catholics to a tiny minority in the eighteenth century had not yet taken place, there was little real basis for the panic fear which repeatedly seized protestants at this period. The pattern of European politics was changing: the age of religious wars (which had never been purely religious) was passing, and less than a quarter of a century after James VI's death the Peace of Westphalia drew confessional frontiers which were not thereafter to be altered by the shifts of political power. In the new world of the seventeenth century Scottish catholicism could no longer play a decisive part.

* * *

When James IV died at Flodden, Scotland was part of catholic christendom, part of the Europe of the renaissance—soon, indeed, to be the Europe of the reformation, but, so far as Scotland was concerned, catholic Europe still for another generation and more. The small Scottish realm was inextricably involved in the relationships of European politics: the most powerful link was with France, but relations with England, whether hostile or, as they at times were, warily amicable, had the strength afforded by propinquity. Already, wise as well as selfish and ambitious men looked to a union with England as the natural destiny of the Scottish nation. But no basis for such a union had yet been laid, though the dynastic consequences of James IV's marriage to Margaret Tudor were in the end to bring it about. Meanwhile, Scotland must make her own way, hampered in her movements by many restricting factors. Chief among these was the radical instability of a feudal monarchy in which the strength of " over-mighty subjects " was repeatedly enhanced by the effects of prolonged royal minorities. Government, when government was possible, was carried on with inadequate machinery in a country where, despite the progress of the fifteenth century, material resources were poor and ill-developed and where poor communications confronted massive geographical obstacles. In a society where unity was still largely to seek, spiritual and intellectual leadership were little better than political control. The church shared fully in the ecclesiastical weaknesses of the age, and less than fully in the new movements seeking to remedy those weaknesses. Ecclesiastical wealth was to an overwhelming extent exploited by the crown and the nobility for secular purposes. Scotland entered upon one of the decisive centuries of European history poorly equipped for the exigencies of the time.

A very different picture appears at the death of James VI one hundred and twelve years later. The union with England had been achieved and, against all the odds, it had been achieved by the accession of a Scots king to the English throne and not *vice versa*. But this historical accident could not prevent Scotland's being the junior partner in the union, and indeed the evolution of Anglo-Scottish relations in the sixteenth century had shown that Scotland, subjected to the immense pull of her powerful neighbour, must tend to became a satellite. Union with England had come, then; the link with catholic Europe had gone (though it is unfair to argue, as is sometimes done, that Scotland lost all her European contacts as a result of the reformation and the Union). This was inevitable because the catholic Scotland of 1513 had become a protestant Scotland. In retrospect, it must seem a matter of necessity that the politico-religious destiny of Scotland should be bound up with that of England. Yet for a time in the middle years of the sixteenth century there seemed to be a possibility that Scotland would preserve catholicism along with the French alliance. What might have happened if an enlightened catholic ruler had used the French alliance for the defence of the church, instead of sacrificing everything, as Mary of Guise did, to the political interest of France, must remain an unanswerable speculative question. But it is permissible to be sceptical of any enduring solution to the problem which left Scotland and England on opposite sides of the fence which was dividing Europe. The modern critic may too readily condemn the catholic schemers of the late sixteenth century for seeking, as it seems, to solve the religious problem of winning back Scotland and England for the faith by the political weapons of plotting and assassination, dynastic diplomacy and armed force. It is true that motives were always mixed and that the admixture of non-religious ambition and power-politics was always large. It is true that the methods adopted were often morally reprehensible. It is also true that many, if not all, of the schemes were ill-conceived and worse executed. Yet the devious intriguers and adventurers who risked the torture-chamber and the shambles of a sixteenth-century treason execution to further these crack-brained plans were at least right in their basic presupposition. This was that the politico-religious destinies of Scotland and England were inseparable, that there could be no secure victory for catholicism in one realm which did not rest upon a parallel victory in the other. In Scotland fortune favoured the protestant party, in that there was at the critical moments—in 1559-60, in 1567, in 1573—a momentary balance of political forces sufficient to decide the issue against the catholics and their allies. The state of religious policy in England was throughout, of course, an essential element in this balance. But had the decision in Scotland gone the other way, there can be no certainty that this in turn might not have been decisive in England.

The situation just examined was not merely an international situation. It was in part an internal Scottish situation. Here the essential point is that the unruliness of the magnates was a standing challenge to royal power, while it was not until the end of the period that the crown could find in other social elements any firm foundation for its authority. The feudal nobility were able to take advantage of the religious upheaval to continue their hereditary feuds with one another and their old struggle with the crown. In so doing, they were also able to profit largely from the plunder of ecclesiastical property and thus acquire a motive for defending the new religious settlement which, in many cases, had little to do with religious convictions. In some ways, however, the furious anarchy of post-reformation politics in Scotland is deceptive. The event showed that this kind of thing was burning itself out; and though the ashes remained unpleasantly hot for many decades, a new situation had arisen, in which first the crown and later the burgesses and gentry could take over. The period surveyed here ends with the crown in the ascendant as it had never been in Scottish history. One important fact about this royal ascendancy should be emphasised. If the new power of the crown was built in part upon the exhaustion of the magnates, in part upon the growing prosperity of the middle classes, and in part upon improvements in the machinery of government which went on intermittently during James VI's personal reign, it must not be forgotten that the peace in which royal authority grew (by no means an unbroken peace) was also a purchased tranquillity. It was purchased largely by the granting of temporal lordships carved out of the old church lands. The new Scotland of the seventeenth century was fed from the material body of the medieval church. There is a certain irony in the fact that, different as the circumstances were, James VI, like James V and James IV before him, lived by the exploitation of endowed ecclesiastical wealth. The old system of exploitation and the new differed in many ways, but in at least one way the two were similar: in both the cause of religion suffered. David I may have been a " sair sanct for the Croun "; but if so, the balance was amply redressed: for, whether before or after the reformation, and whether the church were catholic or protestant, those who wore the Scottish crown were no true friends to the church.

GENEALOGICAL TABLE — A

THE SCOTTISH SUCCESSION

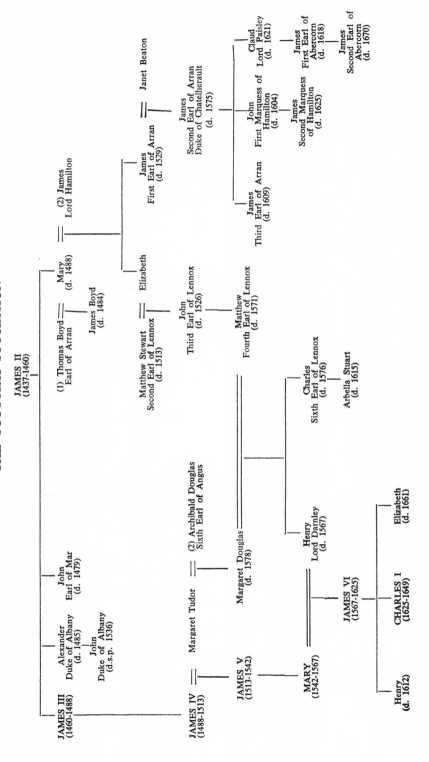

GENEALOGICAL TABLE — B
THE ENGLISH SUCCESSION

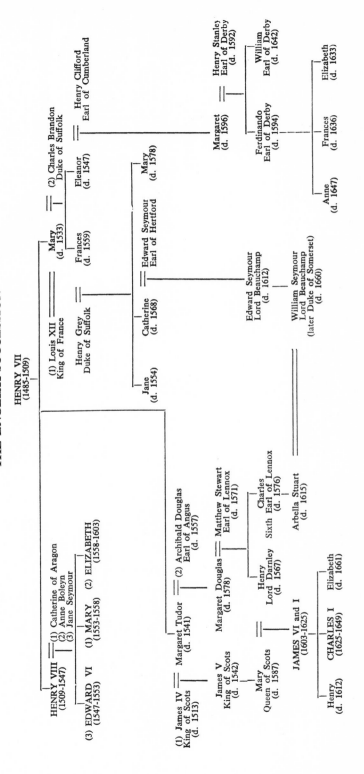

THE SCOTTISH HIERARCHY, 1513-1565

by

MATTHEW MAHONEY

The collapse of catholicism in Scotland at the reformation, has been attributed to the failings of the hierarchy. Such was the judgment of Ninian Winzet and Nicholas de Gouda, which has been endorsed by historians. In their opinion, the success of the reformers was due to the misappropriation of benefices, to the indifference and immorality of the prelates and the consequent ignorance of the faithful.[1] Of clerical delinquency there is ample evidence in various acts of parliament, in the statutes of provincial councils, held immediately prior to the reformation, and in the records of legitimations under the Great Seal and the Privy Seal. "Nowhere else," it has been observed, "would the pious champions of the church be compelled to say so much that was evil of those who should have been their pastors."

The weight of this evidence seems to have inhibited a detailed assessment of the composition and functions of the hierarchy during this period. Yet there are indications that this interpretation is inadequate. The legislation of the provincial councils which condemned clerical corruption, also provides evidence of a movement within the hierarchy, for disciplinary reform in accordance with the decrees of the Council of Trent. More noteworthy is the absence from Winzet's Tractate and from the report of the papal nuncio, of any criticism of the actions of the Scottish crown. If there were unworthy bishops, responsibility lay with those who had exercised the crown right of nomination.

In default of such a detailed assessment it is proposed here to deal only with a few restricted but pertinent aspects. In the first instance, we are concerned with the occupants of the thirteen Scottish sees, to the exclusion of the heads of the greater religious houses, who, with the bishops constituted the First Estate of the realm. Of the bishops, our interest in the main will be limited to the method of their appointment, to their failings and achievements, to the circumstances in which they governed the church and attempted reform and lastly to their conduct during the religious revolution.

It is significant that in January, 1560, the Cardinal of Guise, on behalf of Francis II and Mary Queen of Scots, attempted to disclaim responsibility for the very obvious misuse of the right of nomination.[2] The greatest culprit in this respect was James V, whose example was followed by the Regent Arran and Mary of Lorraine. Such were his nominations and the effects of his clerical taxation that the traditional description of his policy as pro-clerical, is very much a travesty. There were also occasions when baronial interests were paramount, and sons of the greater nobles swept into the richer benefices, with similarly disastrous results to the church. Spiritual interests were not a primary consideration in episcopal appointments and the good bishops received

1. Ninian Winzet; *Certain Tractates*, edit. J. K. Hewison, Scottish Text Society, i, pp. 3-14. J. H. Pollen *Papal Negotiations with Mary Queen of Scots*, Scottish History Society, pp. 129-139. Extracts in *Source Book of Scottish History*, edit. W. C. Dickinson, G. Donaldson, I. A. Milne, second edition, 1958, ii, pp. 152-155.

2. Pollen, *op. cit.*, p. 29, note.

promotion because of their administrative ability or for equally secular reasons.

Secularisation of church appointments naturally resulted in worldly prelates. James IV, James V, who had at least nine illegitimate children, and Arran, were unlikely to have viewed this irregularity as an impediment to ecclesiastical preferment. All three sought benefices for their illegitimate sons, but when James IV embarked on this policy, he could invoke the example of Innocent VIII and Alexander VI. The age in which Margaret of Navarre, a crypto-protestant, wrote the Heptameron as a " vehicle of evangelical instruction," was not greatly scandalised by incelibate clerics. Luther's visit to renaissance Rome, in 1510, did not cause the reformation and Knox's attack on catholicism was not based on the scandalous lives of Scottish prelates, but on the allegation that the mass is idolatrous.

No protestant critic of clerical immorality was more severe than Abbot Quintin Kennedy or Ninian Winzet, two catholic apologists. A tentative survey of episcopal legitimations and similar evidence confirms the association of immorality and secularisation. Some of the bishops had already erred in that respect before their nomination: such were Cardinal Beaton and Patrick Hepburn of Moray. It is also evident that the incidence of immorality is very much higher among the baronial bishops, the sons of the greater nobles.

Appreciation of the difficulties of the Scottish episcopate, has been hampered by inadequate analysis of the religious policies of James V and Mary or Lorraine. Although James V refused to follow the example of his uncle, Henry VIII, he gravely weakened the church by his nominations and clerical taxation while patronising Sir David Lindsay, who is reputed to have " broken the keys of Rome " by his anti-clerical satire. Similarly, to describe the pro-French policy of Mary of Lorraine as in the catholic interest, is dangerously akin to accepting the propaganda of the lords of the Congregation. In one of their proclamations they accused the queen regent of acting as an agent-provocateur; her policy of tolerating the reformers was to induce their persecution as heretics. On the contrary, her antagonism to Archbishop Hamilton and her conciliation of leading protestants, led directly to the emergence of the aggressive Calvinist minority.

The revolutionary character of the Scottish reformation can be best appreciated by comparison with the French wars of religion. Apart from the many similarities, there is the advantage that protestant failure in France, prevented the canonisation of a Huguenot interpretation of history. Thus Condé's alliance with Elizabeth in 1562 and the consequent English occupation of Havre, have not received the salute, which has been accorded to the Treaty of Berwick and English intervention at Leith. The French lesser nobility, the " Storm-troopers of the Huguenot movement," were in many ways similar to the lairds, who crowded into the "Reformation Parliament" in August, 1560. The strictures, passed in this instance, on some aspects of Calvin's ethic are more applicable to the revolutionary manifestoes of Knox; " a monstrous confusion of morality and law: the sort of confusion which, in a minor degree perhaps, the contemporary totalitarian state has made."[3]

---

3.   J. E. Neale, *The Age of Catherine de Medici*, p. 21.

Criticism of the faithful bishops' conduct in the "Reformation Parliament" would seem at times to forget that the religious revolution had been achieved. The act inflicting the death penalty for a third offence of saying mass, was only a parliamentary ratification of the actions of the reformers; celebration of mass was forbidden under penalty of death at Perth, in May, 1559. The act explains—"And presentilie notwithstanding the reformatioun already maid according to Goddis word yit nottheless thair is sum of the same papis kirk that stubburnlie perseveris in thair wickit idolatrie sayand mess and baptizand conforme to the papis kirk. . . ."[4]

The medieval bishop was not simply an ecclesiastical official; he displayed the characteristics of what has been called a "sacral" as opposed to a secular age. There was then no complete differentiation of church and state. The underlying theory was in accordance with the best tradition. Thus "St. Thomas does not conceive of a relation between two different societies, between state and church in any modern sense but of a distinction of functions (gubernationes, regimina, ministeria, potestates). We are entirely on the lines of what historians have called the Gelasian doctrine of the distinction and interrelation of the two great spheres of human life within one single society—the christian society, the respublica christiana."[5]

In practice the distinction between the two powers of sacerdotium and regnum became blurred. In addition to his spiritual office as successor of the apostles, the medieval bishop was also in Scotland, a feudal magnate with a baronial court, a member of the First Estate and perhaps also a crown official, an ambassador, a member of the king's council or even chancellor. Langland's description of the secular pursuits of English clerics in the prologue to the Vision of Piers Plowman could also be applied to Scotland.[6]

> " Some serve the king and his silver count
> In Chequer and Chancery courts making claims for his debts
> Of wards and wardmotes waifs and estrays.
> And some serve as servants to lords and ladies,
> And instead of stewards sit in session to judge.
> Their mass and their matins their canonical hours
> Are said undevoutly."

Cardinal Wolsey was not the only cleric whose service to Caesar excelled what he owed to God.

Henry VIII took advantage of this confusion to justify his actions by denying the Gelasian doctrine. The preamble to the Act of Restraint of Appeals, 1533, stated that there was a logical distinction and thus implicitly denied any real distinction between the temporal and spiritual powers. "This realm of England is an empire . . . governed by one supreme head and king . . . unto whom a body politic . . . divided in terms and by names of spirituality and temporality. . . ."[7] When he attempted to persuade his nephew James V to follow his example he was reminded of traditional catholic doctrine; " By my troth there are two

---

4. Source Book, p. 186.
5. A. P. D'Entreves, Aquinas—Selected Political Writings: Introd., p. xxi.
6. Everyman edition, p. 3, translated into Modern English by Donald and Rachel Attwater.
7. H. Bettenson, Documents of the Christian Church, p. 307.

laws, the spiritual law and the temporal. The cure of the one pertaineith to the pope's holiness and the spirituality; the other to the king's power and the temporality."[8]

This confused situation was derived not from any lack of clarity in the Gelasian doctrine, but from ecclesiastical tenure of land in a feudal age. It was only by such tenure that the church could exist as an institution and maintain its independence. Land tenure, however, entailed secular obligations and the more dangerous evils of wealth. Throughout the middle ages there had been a renewal of the ideas of apostolic poverty, in the Cluniac reform, by St. Bernard of Clairvaux and by St. Francis of Assisi. Towards the end of the period there was a general decline from these ideals when misuse of ecclesiastical wealth aroused bitter and justifiable criticism. Dante had previously traced the scandals to what was for long known as the donation of the Emperor Constantine;

> " Ah, Constantine ! to how much ill gave birth,
> not thy conversion, but that dower which the
> first rich father took from thee."

Sir David Lindsay paraphrased these lines on a number of occasions but it was more usual in Scotland to blame David I the " sair sanct " who built and endowed fifteen abbeys and left the crown " in povertie."

It has been estimated that the revenue of the church in Scotland on the eve of the reformation exceeded £300,000 when the patrimony of the crown amounted to only £17,500.[9] The comparison can be misleading, if it is not explained, that the crown had been impoverished by land grants to nobles, and maladministration during regencies. The church also maintained many of the services now undertaken by the welfare state. These figures do indicate, however, why the Scottish crown found it desirable to finance government administration and to increase the royal income at the expense of the church. A major factor, which has not until recently received adequate attention, was the policy of clerical taxation initiated by James V, which has been considered analagous to the dissolution of the English monasteries.[10]

Clerics were frequently in arrears in paying these taxes and were occasionally distrained for debt. It was difficult to raise large sums of money when at least half of their income was in kind. Consequently, they resorted to feu-farming, a peculiarly Scottish usage whereby heritable tenure was granted on payment of a single fixed sum and certain yearly feu-duties. Feuing of church property was on so extensive a scale in that period, that with the contemporary practice of granting monasteries *in commendam*, there resulted a dissolution of ecclesiastical property, even before the reformation.[11]

Similar considerations are apparent in ecclesiastical appointments, although there were other influences in the recruitment of a civil service. It was only from the ranks of the clergy that a sufficient number of educated men could be obtained. Such is the testimony of hostile

---

8.   *Sadler Papers*, edit. Clifford, i, p. 27.

9.   Gordon Donaldson, *Thirds of Benefices*, 1561-1572, Scot. Hist. Soc., Introd., p. xv.

10. W. Stanford Reid; *Clerical Taxation: the Scottish alternative to dissolution of the monasteries*, 1530-1560: Catholic Historical Review, xxxv, 1948.

11. Cf. D. E. Easson, *Medieval Religious Houses—Scotland*, 1957, p. 29. W. Stanford Reid: *op. cit.*, R. K. Hannay, *Church Lands at the Reformation*, Scot. Hist. Rev., xvi, *A Study in Reformation History*, Scot. Hist. Rev., xxiii.

English contemporaries and John Major noted as a fault of the Scottish nobility, a failure to educate their children in letters and morals. In these circumstances as the Scots parliament indicated to the Holy See, it was impossible to employ prelates effectively in government, unless the crown had a say in their promotion. Thus was the way open for the misuse of the crown right of nomination to bishoprics and monasteries.

The pre-reformation church in Scotland was organised into thirteen bishoprics. St. Andrews, which was made a metropolitan see in 1472 by Sixtus IV, had eight suffragans, Dunblane, Dunkeld, Brechin, Aberdeen, Moray, Ross, Caithness and Orkney. Glasgow, raised to a similar status twenty years later, by Innocent VIII, had finally three suffragans, Galloway (Whithorn or Candida Casa), Argyll or Lismore and the Isles. For three centuries, the archbishops of York had opposed the erection of an archiepiscopal see in Scotland, on the grounds that they had metropolitan jurisdiction " *usque ad extremos Scotiae fines* "; a claim last renewed by Henry VIII after Flodden. Before 1472, the bishoprics of Orkney and the Isles were subject to the Norwegian see of Trondhjem and Galloway to York.

There were conflicts over jurisdiction between St. Andrews and Glasgow, which are considered to have prevented the calling of a provincial council for over fifty years.[12] James III, parliament and most of the Scottish bishops objected when St. Andrews was erected into a metropolitan see. The granting of a similar status to Glasgow resulted from a petition, claiming that Glasgow had been recognised as the " Special Daughter of the Roman Church," since the twelfth century. Exemption from the jurisdiction of St. Andrews was at first granted only for the lifetime of Bishop Blacader, but his successors, James Beaton (I) and Gavin Dunbar received similar rights. The conflict was not settled until Archbishop James Beaton (II) obtained perpetual exemption from all primatial and legatine jurisdiction of the archbishops of St. Andrews.[13] Unfortunately, this rivalry degenerated at times, into what was almost a clan feud, between the adherents of the two sees. On one occasion there was a riot in Glasgow cathedral in the presence of Cardinal Beaton and Archbishop Dunbar. The crossbearers of the two prelates came to blows and occasioned a general melée, which inspired a celebrated passage in Knox's history.

To Knox, however, the incident was simply an exhibition of pride by the cardinal and " *folie de grandeur* " on the part of Archbishop Dunbar. There was thus the implication that the conflict over jurisdiction can be interpreted solely in terms of personal animus or ambition. Apart from belittling the prelates, it also illustrates that *simpliste* approach to the Scottish reformation, which views the hierarchy as a homogeneous group, wherein personal or ecclesiastical rivalry was the sole disruptive agent.

II

Episcopal appointments were definitively effected by papal confirmation, but by the end of the fifteenth century, chapter election in Scotland had been replaced by royal nomination. In 1487, Innocent VIII,

---

12.   J. Robertson, *Concilia Scotiae*, i, p. cxxxiv.
13.   J. Dowden; *The Medieval Church in Scotland*, p. 17.

granted by indult to James III, the privilege of virtually nominating to bishoprics and monasteries with an income of more than two hundred florins, up to eight months after the vacancy.[14] The crown was to enjoy the temporalities until the vacancies had been filled. Provision to these vacancies was delayed for that period, to allow for consideration of royal supplications. the result was " a practical compromise whereby the chapters were excluded, the crown sought to make all its nominations decisive in all elective benefices, while the papacy was able to reserve the provisions and levy the promotion taxes."[15] Although the two succeeding popes, Alexander VI and Julius II, did not renew the indult, the Scottish kings considered the privilege perpetual and extended it to all elective benefices.

Leo X adopted a different policy and provided to St. Andrews, Cardinal Cibo, his nephew and a grandson of Innocent VIII.[16] The previous archbishop-elect had been killed at Flodden. The Scots had invaded England in opposition to papal policy and this had probably influenced the appointment. The campaign, which occasioned the excommunication and death of James IV, had resulted from an alliance with France against Henry VIII, then a papal ally and a member of the Holy League. Mainly as a consequence of this provision, which was later withdrawn, the Duke of Albany, as regent, insisted on a renewal of the indult of Innocent VIII.[17] Apparently, it had been proposed in Scotland to renounce papal authority, except in matters of faith.[18] The policies of the two Medici popes, Leo X (1513-1521) and Clement VII (1523-1534) engendered similar reactions throughout Europe. In 1519, Leo X confirmed the indult in perpetuity and declared any infringement to be null and void.[19] It was apparently later extended to all cases where the privilege of nomination was involved. Until this had been achieved, Albany had persistently omitted to make the formal act of obedience to Leo, which was required from all catholic sovereigns on the election of a pope.[20]

The final stage was reached in 1535, when Paul III explicitly recognised the Scottish right of nomination—" *ius nominandi.*"[21] The period of delay was extended to twelve months, during which the Crown could enjoy the temporalities. These privileges exceeded the concessions which Leo X made to Francis I of France, in the Concordat of Bologna, 1516. The papacy then recognised the royal control over church appointments, which French monarchs had exercised for almost a century, in accordance with the Gallican Pragmatic Sanction of Bourges. The concordat allowed a period of six months for nomination.[22]

Significance attaches to the date of this grant to James V. The English Act of Supremacy of the previous year had made Henry VIII supreme head of the church in England. For a number of years his

14. *Source Book*, p. 88-9.
15. R. K. Hannay; *Acts of the Lords of the Council*, 1501-1554, Introd. p. xlix. Cf. Hannay; *The Scottish Crown and the Papacy*, 1424-1560, Hist. Assoc. of Scotland, 1931.
16. J. Herkless and R. K. Hannay; *The Archbishops of St. Andrews*, ii, pp. 83 seq.
17. *Letters of James V*, collected and calendared by R. K. Hannay, edited by D. Hay. 1954, pp. 41, 49-51.
18. *Letters and Papers of Henry VIII*, xiv, part 1, no. 843.
19. *Letters of James V*, p. 68.
20. A few weeks after Albany had offered filial obedience to Leo X, a papal bull was issued, June 1, 1520, confirming Albany's administration by apostolic authority. *Ibid.*, p. 79.
21. *Ibid.*, p. 285.
22. S. Z. Ehler and J. B. Morral, *Church and State through the Centuries*, p. 139.

nephew had exploited the difficulties of Clement VII, in order to obtain papal approval for his policy of clerical taxation. The schismatic actions of Henry VIII thus benefited James V. Royal control over ecclesiastical appointments had also been strengthened by various acts of parliament. In the reign of James I, the offence of " barratry," for which the penalty was exile, had been defined as unlawful and unauthorised pursuit of promotions or emoluments by " purchase." Papal promotions without crown license were thus illegal, since payment of the usual promotion tax was, by statutory definition, " purchase."[23]

The Scottish crown did not hesitate to exploit this control at times even in defiance of papal wishes. James V refused to entertain a provision to Dryburgh by Paul III, of Robert Wauchope, a Scottish theologian of European repute, who later as Archbishop of Armagh, attended the Council of Trent.[24] The example of the papal nepotists, Sixtus IV, Innocent VIII and Alexander VI had not passed unnoticed in Scotland. Generally, ecclesiastical benefices came to be regarded as sources of income, divorced from spiritual office, to be appropriated by the crown, or granted as marks of favour, as pension for past service, as expense accounts for civil servants and even as scholarships. Of the evils which resulted, there is a contemporary description by John Major of the scandals attending the system of holding religious houses *in commendam;* " Behold then here what may happen to religion from the possession of great wealth ! By open flattery do the worthless sons of our nobility get the governance of convents *in commendam*—the wealth of these foundations is set before them like a mark before a poor bowman—and they covet these ample revenues, not for the good help that they might thence render to their brethren, but solely for the high position that these places might offer, that they might have the direction of them and out of them may have the chance to fill their own pockets."[25]

It has recently been claimed that before 1560, the crown had turned its power of nomination into a power of appointment. The case is quoted of the gift in 1548, of the priory of Eccles to Marion Hamilton, of spirituality and temporality, without reference to Rome.[26] There is no evidence in the printed records of nomination to Rome, but there is an eighteenth-century transcript in the Blairs Archives, of a letter, in the name of Mary to Paul III, nominating Marion Hamilton to Eccles.[27] There are also letters of nomination after that date, and before 1560, in the printed records. It is, therefore, incorrect to suggest that there was a tendency in practice, to deny papal jurisdiction in Scotland, before the reformation.

Bishoprics could not be granted *in commendam*, but James IV made two nominations to St. Andrews, which virtually came within that category. In 1497, he nominated his brother, James, Duke of Ross, then aged eighteen to that see. There were various motives for the appointment, but there is no doubt that it resulted in material advantage to the crown. As the archbishop-elect was nominated first to Holyrood and later to Dunfermline and Arbroath, there was a progressive resignation to the crown of the ducal lands of Ross.[28] The duke was never conse-

23. *Source Book*, p. 85.
24. *Letters of James V*, pp. 392-4, 398, 400, 405, 410-411.
25. Major, *History of Greater Britain*, trans. A. Constable, Scot. Hist. Soc., pp. 136-7.
26. *Registrum Secreti Sigilli*, v, Introd. pp. iii-iv.
27. MSS. Royal Letters, 1524-1548, Letter no. 118, fol 143, Mary to Paul III, 16 Kal. Feb., 1548-9.
28. Herkless and Hannay, *op. cit.*, i, p. 198.

crated and was, in fact, only administrator. When he died in 1504, scandal was further aggravated by the appointment of James IV's illegitimate son, Alexander Stewart, then aged nine. When James IV thanked Julius II in 1505, he promised that the see would be administered with special care.[29] Yet revenues from the archbishopric and the archdeaconry of St. Andrews, also held by Alexander, who fell unconsecrated at Flodden, were diverted to the royal treasury.[30]

Most of the other appointments of this reign betray the desire of James IV, either to reward crown servants or to provide them with expense accounts. Andrew Forman who became bishop of Moray in 1501, was a noted diplomat, who negotiated the marriage of James IV and Margaret Tudor.[31] Robert Cockburn was described as being in the royal service when he was nominated to Ross in 1507.[32] Abbot George Hepburn of Arbroath, brother of the first earl of Bothwell, was treasurer when he became bishop of the Isles in 1511.[33] When David Arnot was promoted to Galloway in 1509, he made way for the promotion of Andrew McBrek, a royal chaplain, to Cambuskenneth.[34] More spectacular was the rise to prominence of James Beaton (I) who succeeded as treasurer on the death of his brother, Sir David, in 1505. In the previous year he had obtained Dunfermline *in commendam* for two years and had, apparently, failed to convert the benefice *ad vitam*. In 1506, James recommended that Beaton should be appointed to Dunkeld as coadjutor, with the right of succession, but the request did not receive papal confirmation. In 1508 he was recommended to the vacant see of Galloway, with the monasteries of Restennot and Inchmahome as well as the provostry of Lincluden. Less than a year later, on the death of Archbishop Blacader, he was translated to Glasgow. He was ordained and consecrated, *ordinatus et consecratus* on April 15, 1509.[35] The *Diurnal of Occurents* states that James IV, without the advice of the clergy, " gav all the benefices that vaikit in his time to his familiaris . . . whereof came great skaith on this realm." The exaggeration can be forgiven when we review the episcopal appointments of his reign.

Insufficient attention has been given to the effects of succeeding episcopal appointments which may be considered in six groups;

1. The appointments after Flodden, when the interests of the church were sacrificed to a rapacious nobility. Apart from the strongly disputed appointment to St. Andrews, all went to relatives of the more powerful barons.

2. The nominations of the Duke of Albany, perhaps the least disreputable, between 1518 and 1524.

3. The nominations of 1525 and 1526 when the house of Douglas was rising to supreme power.

4. The appointments of the personal rule of James V, when the dominant aim was exploitation of the church, for the financial benefit of the crown.

29. *Letters of James IV*, 1505-1513, calendared by R. K. Hannay, edit. R. L. Mackie and A. Spilman, Scot. Hist. Soc., 1953, no. 20.
30. Herkless and Hannay, *op. cit.*, i, p. 230.
31. *Ibid.*, ii, pp. 13 seq.
32. *Letters of James IV*, no. 88. Dowden; *The Bishops of Scotland*, p. 224.
33. Dowden, *op. cit.*, p. 291.
34. *Letters of James IV*, nos. 233-4.
35. Herkless and Hannay, iii, pp. 9 seq.

5. The appointments during the regency of Arran, who attempted to make the church the appanage of the Hamiltons.

6. The nominations of Mary of Lorraine, which reflect her desire to obtain support for the Franco-Scottish alliance.

1. *The Appointments after Flodden.*

What Major wrote of commendatory abbots might have been inspired by the scramble for benefices after Flodden, in which Alexander Stewart, archbishop-elect of St. Andrews, Bishop George Hepburn and a number of abbots were killed.[36] Within the next four years as many bishops died; William Elphinstone of Aberdeen in 1514, George Brown of Dunkeld in 1515, William Meldrum of Brechin in 1516, and Andrew Stewart of Caithness in 1517. Alexander Gordon (I) was forced on the chapter of Aberdeen by his cousin, the earl of Huntly.[37] Gavin Douglas, son of Archibald " Bell the Cat," the earl of Angus, was provided to Dunkeld.[38] He had attempted with the help of Henry VIII to get St. Andrews. Andrew Stewart, though not even in major orders, had been elected to Dunkeld through the influence of his brother, the earl of Atholl: he was later recommended for Caithness.[39] John Hepburn, son of the first earl of Bothwell, was appointed to Brechin and another Hepburn, James, was provided to Moray, which had been vacated by Bishop Forman on his translation to St. Andrews.[40]

This had been the chief prize, for which at various times there had been six candidates.[41] Prior John Hepburn, who had acted as vicar general for the royal archbishops-elect, was elected by the chapter. He withdrew in favour of the aged Bishop Elphinstone who died shortly afterwards. Prior Hepburn was again elected and he then proceeded to besiege the Castle of St. Andrews, held by another candidate, Gavin Douglas. The latter had been nominated by the queen mother and recommended to the pope by her brother, Henry VIII. Queen Margaret married Gavin's nephew, the sixth earl of Angus, in 1514. Meanwhile Leo X had provided Cardinal Cibo. This provision was withdrawn as the result of strong opposition; the cardinal's procurator was not allowed to enter Scotland.[42] Bishop Forman was then provided on his resigning to the cardinal, the archbishopric of Bourges.

The appointment was finally effected by Archbishop Forman surrendering nearly all his benefices, as well as those of his friends; he was allowed to retain only Dunfermline. The archbishopric of Bourges had been ceded to Cardinal Cibo: Prior John Hepburn received a pension from the revenues of St. Andrews: another Hepburn succeeded Archbishop Forman in Moray and James Ogilvy was appointed to Dryburgh. The archbishop's brother, Robert Forman, who had obtained a papal provision to Aberdeen, had to withdraw in favour of Alexander Gordon

36. Henry VIII explained to Leo X, that the Scottish prelates, who had been killed in battle, had not worn distinctive clerical dress—" *absque ullo conspicuo sacerdotali habitu occisos fuisse.*" Theiner, *Vetera Monumenta Hibernorum et Scotorum*, pp. 510-511.
37. Dowden, *op. cit.*, p. 135.
38. *Ibid.* pp. 82-3.
39. Myln, *Vitae Episcoporum Dunkeldensium*, trans. R. K. Hannay, *Rentale Dunlekdense*, Scot. Hist. Soc., pp. 331-4. Dowden, pp. 82 and 248.
40. Dowden, *op., cit.*, pp. 167 and 189.
41. Herkless and Hannay, ii, pp. 82 seq.
42. Theiner, *op. cit.*, pp. 513-4.

and John Forman had to surrender Kilwinning to Archbishop Beaton, who had also been a candidate for St. Andrews.[43] In the questionable exchange of St. Andrews for Bourges, Leo X, who made six of his relatives cardinals, cannot be considered blameless.

To this unseemly distribution of benefices without regard for the moral and intellectual qualifications of the candidates, Bishop Lesley, ascribed the main cause of the spread of the " fiery flame of heresy." It was at this time that Patrick Hamilton, later executed for heresy, was appointed abbot of Fearn, at the age of thirteen. It is significant that no attempt was made to fill the poor see of the Isles, which remained vacant for many years. It has been alleged that clerics attained an inordinate political influence, as a result of the heavy deathroll of lay barons at Flodden. There is no doubt that the nobility obtained a disproportionate and disastrous hold on the higher appointments of the church.

2. *Albany's Nominations.*

The Duke of Albany spent less than three years in Scotland as regent, but he maintained control over episcopal appointments in the nine years from 1515 until 1524. The nominations after 1518 appear to have been based on some regard for the suitability of the candidates. They suggest that in the troubled years after Flodden, Albany played the part of " honest broker ", in the midst of a rapacious nobility. Of the six appointments after 1518, none went to a member of the nobility. In the majority there was a reversion to the policy of James IV—the exploitation of church benefices for the reward of crown servants. Gavin Dunbar (I), provided to Aberdeen in 1518, was Clerk of the Rolls and the Register.[44] Archbishop James Beaton (I) of Glasgow, translated to St. Andrews in 1522, had been Chancellor since 1513.[45] Robert Cockburn of Ross, who was translated to Dunkeld in 1522, had been employed on a number of embassies and at the time of his translation, was on a mission to the English Court.[46] Gavin Dunbar (II), nephew of his namesake of Aberdeen, was tutor of James V, when he was promoted to Glasgow in 1524.[47]

3. *The Nominations of 1525 and 1526.*

In 1524 James V was proclaimed king at the age of twelve. Albany was dismissed from the regency and the pope was asked to ignore any recommendations that he might make to ecclesiastical benefices.[48] There followed a period of intrigue, during which, an English faction with specific aims, first appeared among the nobility. The queen mother returned to prominence and her husband, the earl of Angus, returned from England, pledged to carry out Cardinal Wolsey's instructions. His return did not have Margaret's approval, who shortly afterwards, on the annulment of their marriage, married Henry Stewart. Archbishop Beaton and Bishop Dunbar of Aberdeen were imprisoned as supporters of Albany, but after their release they joined Queen Margaret's party. In June, 1526, the king, who was in the hands of Angus, was declared to have royal authority. In the following month, Archbishop Beaton was removed from the chancellorship, which was taken over by Angus, who

43. *Letters of James V*, pp. 28, 30, 46, 61-2. Herkless and Hannay, ii, pp. 141 seq.
44. Dowden, *op. cit.*, p. 137.
45. Herkless and Hannay, *op. cit.*, iii, pp. 17 seq.
46. *Letters of James V*, p. 104, Dowden, p. 86.
47. D. E. Easson, *Gavin Dunbar*, p. 4.
48. *Letters of James V*, p. 106.

thus achieved supreme power, when " none durst strive with a Douglas nor yet with a Douglas's man."

The *Complaynt of Schir David Lyndesay to the Kingis Grace* thus describes the abuses of the period;

> " Thay lordis tuke no more regaird
> But quho mycht purches best rewaird;
> Sum to thair friendis gat benefyceis,
> And uther sum gat Byschopreis."

Some of the bishops appointed between January, 1525, and June, 1526, may come within this category and it is possible that these and other appointments violated the crown right of nomination. At least it was for that reason that an act of parliament, in 1526, enacted that those who entered upon such benefices without crown licence were guilty of treason. The more probable explanation is that these nominations were made in order to forestall Angus, who shortly afterwards filled the chief political offices with his supporters.

Two abbots who, according to Dr. Magnus the English agent in Scotland, were regarded as " good Englishmen " were then promoted to bishoprics.[49] Abbot Shaw of Paisley was recommended for Moray, and in the same letter the pope was asked to appoint as his successor in Paisley John Hamilton, aged fourteen, an illegitimate son of the earl of Arran.[50] The latter at that time was a supporter of Queen Margaret. The other " good Englishman," Abbot George Crichton of Holyrood, was provided to Dunkeld in 1526.[51] Two bishops, who at different times were members of the regency council, took the opportunity of resigning their sees in favour of relatives. Bishop James Chisholm of Dunblane resigned in favour of his brother, William, but he retained the fruits of the see, the collation of benefices and the right of regress.[52] Bishop Arnot of Galloway resigned in favour of Henry Wemyss, who was probably his nephew: his mother was an Arnot. In this instance half of the fruits and the right of regress were retained.[53] Two other appointments were less reputable. Robert Montgomery, son of the earl of Eglinton, was provided to Argyll. Two dispensations were required; one for age, he was twenty-four, and another for homicide. It was explained that he did not commit the crime " *manibus suis.*"[54] In the same year " *Magister Robertus Mungumry, postulatus de Argyll,*" was a student in the paedagogium at St. Andrews.[55] Probably about the same time John Campbell, son of Sir Duncan Campbell of Glenurchy, was provided to the see of the Isles which had been vacant since 1513. He did not take up the appointment: it was later alleged that he found the annate and expenses excessive.[56]

---

49.   *Letters and Papers of Henry VIII,* iv, no. 1372.
50.   *Letters of James V,* p. 113.
51.   Dowden, *op. cit.,* p. 87. Clement VII had previously been requested to appoint Abbot Crichton, coadjutor and successor to Robert Cockburn of Dunkeld with the right to retain Holyrood. *Letters of James V,* p. 117.
52.   Dowden, *op. cit.,* p. 207.
53.   *Ibid.,* p. 372. Bishop Arnot refused to give up the *commenda* of Tongland to his successor and James V requested Clement VII to grant it to William Stewart, later bishop of Aberdeen. *Letters of James V,* pp. 153-4.
54.   Dowden, p. 291. In 1532 it was proposed that Robert Montgomery should resign in favour of David Beaton, then abbot of Arbroath, and receive a pension. *Letters of James V,* p. 223.
55.   *Early Records of the University of St. Andrews,* p. 222.j
56.   Dowden, p. 291. John Campbell apparently did not take up the appointment but resigned in favour of Ferquhard McCachane who was duly provided. James V, however, on November 1, 1529, nominated James Ogilvy, abbot of Dryburgh. *Letters of James V,* pp. 162-3.

4. *The Appointments of James V.*

James V escaped from the custody of Angus in May, 1528, and the first episcopal appointment of his personal rule marks the change. A previous recommendation for a Douglas was withdrawn in favour of Alexander Stewart, a half-brother of the Duke of Albany.[57] He already possessed Inchaffray and Scone *in commendam* and on his appointment to Moray he was allowed to retain the deanery of Brechin.[58] In 1532 the treasurer, William Stewart, who supported James's policy of clerical taxation, was promoted to Aberdeen.[59] In the following year the king addressed a remarkable letter to Clement VII, which is thus summarised: " James has three illegitimate sons and confesses his lapse. Yet he has paternal feelings—if he had not, he would be less than human—and he asks the pope to dispense with the defect of birth, so that the boys may be promoted to holy orders with some relaxation as to age and, after having assumed the clerical character, minority and defect of birth notwithstanding, they may be able to hold any secular or regular benefices in title or *commenda*—two, three, four or more incompatibles—and the greater dignities in collegiate churches, also abbacies and conventual priories, coadjutors being deputed until mature age; further, that they might have indult not to mention defect of birth in impetrations at the Apostolic See, and on reaching their twentieth year may be eligible for archiepiscopal, primatial and episcopal promotion. This request makes heavy demands upon the pope's clemency, which nevertheless James expects a pope named Clement to grant."[60]

That such a letter was addressed to the Holy See is explained by reference to the cold war which Henry VIII had been waging against Clement VII since 1530. Its arrival in Rome probably coincided with reports of the enactment in early March, 1533, of the Act of Restraint of Appeals. The dispensation was granted in August, 1534, after papal authority had been abolished in England, and less than a year later, Paul III explicitly recognised the Scottish crown right of nomination. As a result of this crude but successful blackmail, James V, between 1535 and 1541, nominated four of his infant illegitimate sons to five of the largest monasteries in Scotland; James Stewart " senior " to Melrose and Kelso, James " *secundus*," later the earl of Moray, to St. Andrews, Robert to Holyrood and John to Coldingham. A fifth, Adam, became prior of the Charterhouse of Perth. With the exception of James Stewart " senior " who died in 1557, all became protestants.

To effect these promotions, two abbots and a prior were made bishops. James V, who later criticised episcopal abuses after seeing Lindsay's Satire, apparently saw no scandal in the promotion of a prior and an abbot, whose children had previously been legitimated. When James nominated Prior Patrick Hepburn to Moray in March, 1538, there was significantly no reference to the prior's moral character. There was " none with a stronger claim than Patrick of St. Andrews, who has not only birth and letters to recommend him, but a record of wise, just and

---

57. Henry VIII had recommended Alexander Douglas for Moray on May 31, 1528. *Letters of James V*, p. 145.
58. Dowden, p. 169.
59. *Letters of James V*, p. 217. Dowden, p. 139.
60. *Letters of James V*, p. 237-8. *Source Book*, pp. 91-2.

high minded administration in the priory for many years."[61] Similarly, there was no reference to the moral character of Abbot Cairncross when he was nominated to Ross, in 1538. "Robert, abbot of Holyrood, at once occurred to the king as a sound man with an excellent record in the business of the realm."[62] A similar scandal attended the promotion of David Beaton. Six years prior to his nomination as coadjutor to his uncle, three of his children were legitimated under the Privy Seal. Thus three clerics, officially known to have led immoral lives, were promoted to the episcopate in this period. Much has been made of James V's criticism of clerical immorality and of his threat to send six of the proudest bishops to his uncle, Henry VIII, but as Abbot Quintin Kennedy later observed, those who profited by putting bairns in charge of five thousand souls, were the first to decry the vices of clerics.

Of the other episcopal appointments, two went to the sons of nobles. William Cunningham, son of the earl of Glencairn, was nominated to Argyll in 1539, at the age of twenty-six.[63] He was apparently never consecrated, but resigned the see in 1553 to make way for James Hamilton and became dean of Brechin. Robert Stewart, son of the earl of Lennox, was promoted to Caithness in 1542, at the age of twenty.[64] A pension from the see was sought for a "James Steward." Robert Stewart was never consecrated but was in exile for a number of years, because of the treasonable action of his brother, the earl of Lennox. The best appointment was that of Robert Reid, abbot of Kinloss, to Orkney, in 1541. Even this was marred by a transaction which was later condemned as simony by Archbishop Hamilton's Catechism. The see was burdened by a pension of eight hundred marks to John Stewart, an illegitimate son of James V.[65]

5. *The Appointments of Arran's Regency.*

The first months of Arran's regency were characterised by a pro-English policy. Cardinal Beaton was imprisoned and an act of parliament allowed the reading of the bible in the vernacular. (An English statute a fortnight previously had restricted the reading of the bible on the grounds that it had been "disputed, rhymed and jangled in every alehouse and tavern.") This phase lasted for only a few months and the reversal of policy has been attributed at least in part to the regent's half-brother, Abbot John Hamilton. It has been stated that the abbot had previously favoured reformed opinions, but at this stage of his career he was militantly catholic, though it has been suggested that this resulted from a promise of Cardinal Beaton to support his nomination to Dunkeld.[66] Shortly after the death of Bishop George Crichton, the abbot was elected to that see. Two pensions were granted, fifty ducats to Robert Wauchope and one thousand pounds to Alexander Campbell, brother of the earl of Argyll, who had opposed Arran's pro-English

---

61. *Letters of James V*, pp. 342-3. The prior was also to get Scone in perpetual *commenda*.
62. *Ibid.*, p. 356. Robert Cairncross was also to have a life pension of five hundred merks from the teinds of the parish churches of Falkirk and Livingstone and the lands of Brochtoun, which belonged to Holyrood.
63. *Letters of James V*, p. 364. Dowden p. 390.
64. *Letters of James V*, p. 370, 432-3. Dowden, p. 249.
65. *Letters of James V*, p. 423. Dowden, p. 265.
66. Herkless and Hannay, v, pp. 10-11.

policy.[67] The cardinal had been released from imprisonment and the regent publicly recanted his errors in the Franciscan church in Stirling.

Arran's policy in regard to episcopal appointments seems to have been governed by a desire to advance the interests of his family, tempered by the necessity of conciliating his chief rivals, Huntly and Argyll. Alexander Gordon (II), Huntly's brother and a member of Mary of Lorraine's party, was promised the see of Caithness; it was proposed to remove the bishop-elect, Robert Stewart. The earl of Huntly undertook to support the regent's scheme for the marriage of a Hamilton to Queen Mary.[68] Negotiations for this promotion were still in progress when Huntly's uncle, William Gordon, was nominated to Aberdeen.[69] On this occasion a pension was granted to John Hamilton, son of the regent and then five years of age. Another pension was granted to the secretary, David Paniter, who was nominated shortly afterwards to Ross.[70]

Cardinal Beaton was murdered on May 29, 1549, and two days later Bishop John Hamilton was admitted to the temporalities of St. Andrews. (Norman Leslie, one of the cardinal's murderers was a half-brother of Bishop Paniter.) Abbot Donald Campbell, son of the second earl of Argyll, was nominated to Dunkeld but after lengthy litigation Robert Crichton, nephew of Bishop George Crichton, was finally provided.[71] Meanwhile, the papal bulls for the provisions to St. Andrews and Ross had been withheld, because of Arran's attitude to Dunkeld and Glasgow, vacant by the death of Archbishop Dunbar in April, 1547.[72] Arran had nominated to Glasgow another half-brother, James Hamilton, with a request for pensions for two sons, David and Claude.[73] Thus Hamiltons were to have the two archbishoprics. This nomination was naturally rejected and Donald Campbell who had failed to get Dunkeld was then proposed. In the meantime, Alexander Gordon was provided to Glasgow, apparently on his plea that the crown had not made a suitable nomination within the stipulated period.[74] He was consecrated at Rome. Arran opposed this appointment and Mary of Lorraine, who wished to obtain his agreement to her assumption of the regency, then intervened. She wrote to Henry II of France, asking him to indicate to the pope that the provision prejudiced the right of nomination. She also asked that the Archbishop of St. Andrews be made legate a latere and that a coadjutor should be appointed.[75]

Finally, four interrelated appointments were made on September 4, 1551. James Beaton (II) was promoted from Arbroath to Glasgow. James Hamilton, a son of the regent was provided to Arbroath. Alexander Gordon resigned Glasgow, became archbishop of Athens in partibus and was granted Inchaffray in commendam. Gavin Hamilton, a cousin of the primate, became coadjutor with right of succession to St. Andrews. The powers of legate a latere were not granted until the following year. The

67. Dowden, p. 89.
68. Herkless and Hannay, pp. 21-2.
69. Dowden, p. 141.
70. *Ibid.*, p. 226.
71. *Ibid.*, pp. 91-2
72. R. K. Hannay, *Some Papal Bulls Among the Hamilton Papers*, Scot. Hist. Rev., xxii, p. 40.
73. Dowden, p. 349.
74. Hannay, *Acts of the Lords of the Council*, Introd. p. liv.
75. *Balcarres Papers*, Scot. Hist. Soc., ii, pp. 68-70.

papal bulls of the provision to Arbroath were not released until Arran had agreed to resign the regency.[76]

At this stage, Henry II had intervened to exploit ecclesiastical appointments in Scotland, in the interests of the Franco-Scottish alliance. The bulls for the appointments to St. Andrews and Ross were released after Arran had accepted the Treaty of Haddington, 1548, whereby Queen Mary was to marry the dauphin.[77] Arran received the French duchy of Châtelherault and his eldest son went to France as a hostage, but with the promise of a French bride. Two episcopal appointments of 1553 reflect the same policy. James Hamilton exchanged benefices with William Cunningham, bishop-elect of Argyll, and in the same year Alexander Gordon, archbishop of Athens, was nominated to the Isles.[78]

6. The Appointments of Mary of Lorraine.

Before her assumption of the regency in 1554, Mary of Lorraine had exploited the crown right of nomination in the interests of the French alliance. This was the main object of her policy, to which all other considerations were subordinated. Queen Mary, before her marriage to the dauphin, had been induced to sign three documents, whereby in the event of her death without heirs the kingdom of Scotland was to be granted as a gift to the king of France.[79] In such a situation religious considerations were unlikely to be paramount. Henry II, although, suppressing heresy in France, had not hesitated to make two incongruous alliances against the Emperor, Charles V. In 1551, he allied with the German Lutheran princes and two years later he confirmed a treaty with the Sultan, Suleiman I. It is against this background that we should view the policy of Mary of Lorraine. Until the Scottish parliament had ratified the granting of the crown matrimonial to the dauphin in November, 1558, she displayed a conciliatory attitude towards the reformers. Similarly, her episcopal appointments betray an attempt to win adherents for her policy. Abbot Donald Campbell of Coupar, who had failed to get Glasgow, was nominated to Brechin and his nephew, the earl of Argyll, was granted the temporalities of the see, a month before he signed the " Godlie Band."[80] Donald Campbell did not receive a papal provision; his son, Archibald, had been legitimated in 1552.[81] Alexander Gordon was nominated to Galloway, but again papal confirmation was not granted.[82] Adam Bothwell, son of a provost of Edinburgh, was nominated to Orkney, duly provided and consecrated.[83] All three, Campbell, Gordon and Bothwell, joined the reformers.

Despite these unsuitable nominations, Mary of Lorraine informed Henry II in June, 1559, that it was due to the negligence of the prelates that she had not been informed of the spread of the so-called evangelical doctrines. Henry then complained to Paul IV that most of the prelates,

---

76. Hannay, *Some Papal Bulls Among the Hamilton Papers*, pp. 25 seq.
77. *Ibid.*, p. 40.
78. *Ibid.* and Dowden, pp. 292, 391.
79. *Source Book*, p. 159-60.
80. Dowden, p. 190-1.
81. *R.S.S.*, iv, no. 1800.
82. Dowden, p. 374.
83. *Ibid.*, p. 267. The Orcadians would not accept Adam Bothwell's " mutation off religion." The bishop closed the doors of his church and would not allow mass to be said. A priest, however, celebrated mass at the request of the islanders. Spottiswoode, *History of the Church of Scotland*, ii, p. 73.

dissolute in life had joined the new sects.[84] Six months later, an attempt was made to disclaim responsibility for the very obvious misuse of the right of nomination. The cardinal of Guise, at the instance of Francis II and Queen Mary, instructed the French ambassador at Rome to ask the pope to revoke all papal provisions made without royal approval and to abstain from such appointments in the future. The reasons for this request provide an ironic commentary on the actions of the Scottish crown: " Those who have been provided to those benefices are unworthy persons, and ought to be deprived, seeing that they are now foremost in Scotland in sustaining and maintaining errors and false doctrine against our holy faith and religion, and who, as far as they can, favour the rebels and heretics, who are raising trouble in that kingdom against their king and queen."[85]

The cardinal of Guise was remarkably ill-informed; the two bishops, the three bishops-elect, Lord James, commendator of St. Andrews, and the other commendatory abbots who joined the reformers, had all received royal nomination. Shortly after this request had been made to Paul IV, James Thornton, the Scottish agent in Rome, informed the regent that express letters were required explicitly declaring the royal nominees free from all suspicion of heresy.[86] Donald Campbell and Alexander Gordon could hardly be described as orthodox, since both joined the reformers in the previous year. In May, 1559, John Row had also written from Rome to Donald Campbell, explaining that there were impediments to his promotion to Brechin.[87]

The necessity of a guarantee of orthodoxy explains the delay in two provisions which were not effected until 1561. Henry Sinclair, president of the College of Justice, was appointed to Ross and William Chisholm (II) was appointed coadjutor to his uncle and namesake of Dunblane.[88] Later in the reign of Mary Queen of Scots, two further papal appointments were made. John Sinclair, dean of Restalrig, who had succeeded his brother as president of the College of Justice, was provided to Brechin in 1565.[89] John Lesley may have received papal provision to Ross in 1567; if so, he was provided for a second time, in April, 1575.[90]

These appointments cannot be accepted as typical of the occasionally dubious religious policy of Queen Mary. On the death of John Sinclair, in 1565, the pope was asked to provide Alexander Campbell, then aged sixteen.[91] In March, 1567, John Carswell, superintendent of the Isles, was appointed to that see by the crown, naturally without reference to Rome.[92]

---

84. Pollen, *op. cit.*, pp. xxviii and 18.
85. *Ibid.*, p. 29, note.
86. *Ibid.*, p. 30.
87. Row's *History of the Church of Scotland*, pp. lvii-lviii. The survival of this letter casts doubt on the traditional story, that John Row arrived in Scotland as papal nuncio in September, 1558, and did not return to Rome. Row later co-operated in drawing up the *First Book of Discipline* and the *Confession of Faith.*
88. Dowden, pp. 207, 228.
89. Pollen, pp. 512-6. Dowden, p. 191.
90. F. M. Powicke, *Handbook of British Chronology*, p. 233. Father Pollen, however, states that forma succession was not expedited until 1575. *Op. cit.*, p. 332, note.
91. Dowden, p. 192.
92. Powick, *op. cit.*, p. 227. It would appear that the appointment had been made in January, 1565. Cf. *R.S.S.*, v, no. 1885.

III

The supplication addressed to parliament by the reformers in 1560, is marred by a vehemence of expression which has occasioned regret. It alleged that clerics were the most corrupt in life and manners in the realm, and that there was not one lawful minister in the " rabble of the clergy." The manifesto continued—" We further offer ourselves to prove them all thieves and murderers, yea, rebels and traitors to the lawful authority of emperors, kings and princes and therefore unworthy to be suffered in any commonwealth." These allegations were specifically aimed at the bishops and other prelates and a demand was made for their exclusion from parliament.

The sectarian extravagance of this passage has shocked and puzzled historians, not least because the six Johns—Knox, Willock, Spottiswoode, Douglas, Winram and Row—who drew up the *First Book of Discipline* and the *Confession of Faith*, had all been members of the " clerical rabble.' A possible influence may be traced in the language of Marcourt's placards against the mass which appeared in Paris in October, 1534. The aim of these placards was identical with the fundamental tenet of Knox's polemic—that the mass is idolatrous. The vituperative terms there applied to priests and the catholic hierarchy are similar to those of the supplication: " *meurtriers des ames . . . faux-temoins . . . traistres.*"[93] Reference to these placards helps to clarify the terminological ambivalence which has occasioned confusion in the historiography of the Scottish reformation. Allegations against the pre-reformation clergy are sometimes referred to immorality and, on occasion, in identical terms, to belief in such doctrines as were rejected by the reformers.

Knox on a number of occasions referred to clerical immorality, but he quite clearly did not consider this the sole, or even the main, charge against the prelates. In the *Appellation* of 1558 against his condemnation by a spiritual court, the main indictment against the bishops was their support of false doctrines. The nobles were asked to consider the religious controversy and compel the bishops to answer various accusations— " but principally for the false and deceivable doctrine which is taught by their false prophets, flattering friars and other such venomous locusts." Clerical immorality, when mentioned, was a supplementary proof that the catholic church was " nothing but idolatry," " false, damnable and diabolical " and " so corrupt and vain that no true servant of God can communicate with it, because that, in so doing, he should manifestly deny Christ Jesus and his eternal verity." The *Proclamation of the Congregation* in 1559, to the " Generation of Anti-Christ, the pestilent Prelates and their Shavelings within Scotland," was equally explicit. " Yea, we shall begin that same war which God commandeth Israel to execute against the Canaanites; that is contract of peace shall never be made till ye desert from your open idolatry and cruel persecution of God's children."

That the reformers were not deeply incensed by prelatical scandal seems obvious from their attempts to win over that notorious offender, Patrick Hepburn of Moray. Alexander Gordon, who co-operated with Knox in 1559, and acted as commissioner of Galloway from 1562 until 1568, had lived in concubinage for seventeen years before the reformation.

---

93. Kidd, *Documents of the Continental Reformation*, p. 529.

It is also apparent that in spite of their abhorrence of " bloody persecutors," they welcomed the adherence of prelates who had taken part in the trial of Walter Miln in 1558, Robert Stewart of Caithness, Alexander Gordon, Donald Campbell of Coupar, John Winram, sub-prior of St. Andrews, and John Grierson, the provincial of the Dominicans.[94] Knox, for obvious reasons, did not give the names of those present at the trial, but on different occasions blamed Archbishop Hamilton and Patrick Hepburn.

There were unquestionably grave irregularities which are amply documented in contemporary records. The provincial council of 1549 described the causes of heresy as " the corruption of moral and profane lewdness of life in churchmen of almost all ranks, together with crass ignorance of literature and of all the liberal arts." The works of Sir David Lindsay provide evidence of anti-clerical feeling, occasioned by the scandalous lives of many clerics: an anti-clericalism, not necessarily heretical, which was later mobilised and directed by the aggressive Calvinist minority.

The complaint, *clerici clericaliter non viventes*, was not unusual throughout the middle ages, but it was not peculiar to that era. In the third century, before the alleged secularisation of the church by the Emperor Constantine, there had been worldly bishops.[95] The pre-reformation church in Scotland, however, has been singled out as providing one of the worst examples of clerical ignorance and laxity—" of the churchmen's neglect of catholic doctrine, ignorance of it, indifference to their ignorance, and of their assumption that the doctrine must somehow continue present to men's minds and function in their lives."[96] Less sympathetic historians have concentrated on this aspect to the exclusion of other features. In particular, there has been emphasis on moral laxity as illustrated by the number of clerics who had illegitimate offspring.

It is not always explained that these scandals were mainly due to the appointment of commendatory abbots and to the promotion of civil servants in minor orders. Such clerics had not taken a vow of chastity, but marriage entailed resignation of their benefices and some in consequence contracted irregular unions. Many of the commendatory abbots were younger sons of nobles, and in that age when life was often short and death violent, they may have been reluctant to accept major orders, which would have hindered return to secular life in the event of their succession. John Erskine, a third son and commendator of Dryburgh and Inchmahome, resigned his benefices on the death of his elder brothers and became sixth Lord Erskine in 1555.[97] Later, as the Regent Mar, he appointed " tulchan bishops " in the reformed church of Scotland.

Of the clerical civil servants, one of the most prominent was Patrick Paniter, secretary of James IV and father of Bishop David Paniter. There is no evidence that he was ever in major orders, yet, at various times, he held the following benefices; the rectory of Fetteresso, the vicarage of Kilmany, the chancellorship of Dunkeld, the archdeaconry of Moray and the rectory of Tannadice, together with the abbey of Cambuskenneth. He served in the artillery at Flodden and, in consequence, solicited papal

---

94. Calderwood, *History of the Kirk of Scotland*, i, p. 338, quoting Foxe.
95. Cf. J. Lebreton and J. Zeiller, *The History of the Primitive Church*, English translation, iv, p. 1035 seq.
96. Philip Hughes, *A Popular History of the Reformation*, p. 324.
97. *Scots Peerage*, v, p. 612.

absolution.[98]. It is, therefore, inadvisable to accept such titles as rector, vicar or abbot as evidence of priestly status or religious profession, a precaution not always observed in interpreting the lists of clerical legitimations.[99] Apart from such considerations, there was a tendency to delay ordination to the priesthood. Reginald Pole, whose moral integrity cannot be impugned, was ordained priest two days before his consecration as archbishop of Canterbury and twenty years after he became a cardinal.

The brief survey of the episcopal nominations indicates promotion of unworthy prelates, in some cases after the legitimation of their children. About half of the incelibate bishops belonged to that influential, but generally unepiscopal, group who were sons of the greater nobles. Of seventeen of these bishops, twelve had illegitimate offspring; four of the two bishops and the three bishops-elect who defected were also of the same group. It may have been considered equitable that the nobility should have been strongly represented in the hierarchy, but such churchmen had usually little regard for the duties of the clerical state. There are other important features which differentiate this group. Most of these bishops were appointed when the nobles had control, or under a weak regency which found it necessary to acquire baronial support and only a few of these prelates held important offices of state.

About one-third of those nominated to bishoprics in this period can be included in this baronial group: generally a much higher proportion than in England and probably lower than in most countries on the Continent. It may have been desirable in that unsettled period to have prelates capable of protecting church property. It was with this plea that the chapter of Dunkeld justified the election of Andrew Stewart in 1515. There is no doubt that such protection was necessary. Bishop Brown, even when escorted by forty horsemen of his household, was attacked by a neighbouring landowner.[100] Bishop Stewart of Aberdeen was attacked and robbed of the cathedral plate in 1544; it was returned in a damaged state after the assailant had received a plough-gate of land.[101] There was also the " Tragedy of the Cardinal." These professional risks were not always appreciated by contemporaries: John Major, perhaps too doctrinaire, thought that bishops should be content with twelve or fourteen servants. Archbishop James Beaton (I) was not exceptional in requiring the protection of a steel corslet. The cheap gibe of " clattering conscience " occasioned by that unclerical attire, was hardly appropriate from Bishop Gavin Douglas, whose nephew seized Coldingham, after a brother-in-law had murdered the prior.

There were the four Hepburns, who displayed the temperament of a Border family rather than ecclesiastical virtues. George Hepburn, abbot of Arbroath, bishop of the Isles and brother of the first earl of Bothwell, was killed at Flodden. His cousin James was nominated to Moray in 1516. Another cousin, Patrick, who had succeeded to the priory of St. Andrews on the death of his uncle, John Hepburn, became bishop of the same see in 1538. A nephew, John, son of the first earl of

98. R. L. Mackie, *Letters of James IV*, Introd. pp. xxviii-xxxiv. *Letters of James V*, pp. 8-9.
99. D. Hay Fleming, *The Reformation in Scotland*, Appendix B.
100. Myln, *op. cit.*, trans. Hannay, p. 306.
101. *Registrum Episcopatus Aberdonensis*, i, p. lvii.

Bothwell, was provided to Brechin in 1517, with a dispensation for defect of age. Three of these bishops, James, Patrick and John, had children legitimated. John had at least five sons, one of whom was not legitimated.[102] Of the incelibate bishops of that period, Patrick Hepburn was the most scandalous. It is certain that he had at least eleven children by a number of mistresses and to some of these children he feued the lands of Moray and Scone, which he held *in commendam*.[103] Two of his sons were legitimated under the Great Seal on December 18, 1533, almost five years before his nomination to Moray.[104] James V was then more concerned with obtaining the priory of St. Andrews for his own illegitimate son, James Stewart. Patrick Hepburn was the guardian of the fourth earl of Bothwell, who married Queen Mary. In 1559, he is stated to have promised to join the lords of the Congregation, but he changed his mind after the abbey of Scone had been reformed by a " rascal multitude " from Dundee. In this instance, Knox, the earl of Argyll and Lord James Stewart, prior of St. Andrews, who apparently valued the adherence of this prelate, attempted in vain to stay the fury of the mob.[105]

There were three Gordons: Alexander (I) of Aberdeen was a cousin of the third early of Huntly, William, also of Aberdeen, and Alexander (II) of Glasgow, Athens, the Isles and Galloway, were respectively, son and grandson of the same earl. Alexander (I) was forced on the chapter of Aberdeen by his cousin, Huntly, after the death of Bishop Elphinstone in 1514. William Gordon was nominated in 1545 as a result of his father's support of Arran and Alexander (II), with the bizarre ecclesiastical career, was a member of Mary of Lorraine's party. After the archbishop joined the reformers, he married Barbara Logie, and thereby publicly acknowledged a liaison of seventeen years. He had six sons, of whom the eldest John was born about 1544, and one daughter.[106] Alexander (I) had a son, David, who was not legitimated.[107] William Gordon had three sons and three daughters and it is probable that the chapter of Aberdeen was referring to their mother when they advised the bishop, in 1559, to avoid the company of the " gentill woman be whom he is gretely sclanderit."[108]

The three Hamiltons were illegitimate. David, an illegitimate son of Lord James Hamilton and half-brother of the first earl of Arran, was commendator of Dryburgh and bishop of Argyll, to which he was provided in 1497.[109] His nephew, John, an illegitimate son of the same earl, was nominated to Paisley at the age of fourteen, to Dunkeld in 1544, and to St. Andrews on the death of Cardinal Beaton. Two of his sons were legitimated before his translation to St. Andrews. He had three sons and three daughters, by Grissel Sempill, formerly the wife of James Hamilton of Stanehouse.[110] James Hamilton, bishop-elect of Argyll, was also an illegitimate son of the first earl of Arran, and on his provision in July,

102. *R.S.S.*, iii, no. 75; v, no. 1478.
103. *Register of the Privy Council*, i, p. 465. *R.M.S.*, v, no. 681.
104. *R.M.S.*, iii, no. 1329.
105. Calderwood, *op. cit.*, i, p. 472.
106. Gordon Donaldson, *Alexander Gordon, Bishop of Galloway, 1559-1575, and his work in the Reformed Church.* Transactions of the Dumfries-shire and Galloway Natural History and Antiquarian Society. Third Series, xxiv, p. 115.
107. *R.S.S.*, v, no. 1102.
108. *R.S.S.*, iv, no. 2430; v, no. 2890. Dowden, p. 142, note.
109. Dowden, pp. 387-9.
110. *R.S.S.*, iii. nos. 2122, 2977. Herkless and Hannay, v, pp. 246-7.

1553, he was described as sub-dean of Glasgow, a benefice which he held until his death in 1580.[111] On March 10, 1554, four sons and a daughter of Mr. James Hamilton, dean of Brechin and sub-dean of Glasgow, were legitimated.[112]

The conduct of the Stewarts was no more edifying. Andrew, son of John, the first earl of Atholl, in spite of his brother's support, did not obtain Dunkeld but was later provided to Caithness. Alexander Stewart, bishop of Moray, was the son of Alexander, duke of Albany by his first wife, Catherine Sinclair, and on the annulment of this marriage, was declared illegitimate. Before his provision to Moray in 1529, he had been granted Inchaffray and Scone *in commendam*. On a number of occasions, James V asked the pope to make Alexander Stewart, legate *a latere* and cardinal.[113] This bishop had at least two sons and a daughter.[114] Robert Stewart of Caithness, who joined the reformers, was a son of the third earl of Lennox and uncle of Henry Darnley, who married Queen Mary. After his brother's treason, he spent much time in England, where he was appointed to a prebend of Canterbury. He was never consecrated and was probably not in major orders.[115]

Gavin Douglas, Bishop of Dunkeld, was the youngest son of the fifth earl of Angus. He is of renown as a poet, but as a bishop he was disreputable: Scott's description in Marmion is obviously fictive:

> " A noble lord of Douglas blood,
>   With mitre sheen and roquet white.
>   Yet showed his meek and thoughtful eye
>   But little pride of prelacy;
>   More pleased that, in a barbarous age,
>   He gave rude Scotland Virgil's page
>   Than that beneath his rule he held
>   The bishopric of fair Dunkeld."

He died in London in 1522, an exile for treason: he left an illegitimate daughter.[116] Robert Montgomery of Argyll, son of the first earl of Eglinton, had three, perhaps four, illegitimate sons.[117] Donald Campbell, son of the second earl of Argyll, abbot of Coupar and bishop-elect of Brechin, had five illegitimate sons.[118] William Cunningham, bishop-elect of Argyll, was a brother of that prominent reformer, Alexander, the fifth earl of Glencairn. He was never consecrated but resigned the see in 1553 and apparently exchanged benefices with his successor, James Hamilton, dean of Brechin. When Cunningham was vicar general of Brechin, *sede vacante*, John Erskine of Dun was appointed bailie of the temporalities of the see in May, 1557. Six months later, these were granted in gift to the earl of Argyll.[119] In December of the same year, Glencairn, Erskine and Argyll signed the " Godlie Band." There is thus the suspicion, that Cunningham was closely associated with the leading reformers.

---

111. Dowden, p. 391.
112. *R.S.S.*, iv, no. 2523.
113. *Letters of James V*, pp. 138, 164.
114. *Scots Peerage*, i, pp. 152-3.
115. Dowden, pp. 248-251.
116. *Ibid.*, p. 85, note.
117. *Scots Peerage*, iii, p. 437 and *R.S.S.*, iv, no. 2402.
118. *Ibid.*, i, p. 336.
119. Dowden, p. 190.

Broadly speaking, there was no great social contrast within the hierarchy: traditionally the greater nobles had considered the prelates as their rivals in wealth and influence. Most of the other bishops of this period were sons of lairds and might be described as belonging to the lesser landed gentry. Such were the Beatons, the Chisholms, the Crichtons and the Dunbars. Many were distinguished servants of the crown; William Elphinstone, James Beaton (I), Cardinal Beaton and Gavin Dunbar held the office of chancellor, Robert Reid and the two Sinclairs were presidents of the College of Justice. In contrast, there was a very definite social differentiation between the prelates and the parochial clergy, which may partly explain the bitter language of Ninian Winzet. His *Tractatis* were written " at the desire and in the name of the afflictit catholiks and inferiour ordour of clergie and layit men in Scotland." One of the major causes of the decline in the church in this period was the poverty of the parochial clergy, in contrast to the pluralism and misuse of ecclesiastical wealth, prevalent among the prelates. A very high proportion of the parish churches of Scotland were appropriated to monastic houses, cathedrals and collegiate churches: rectories were sometimes granted to civil servants and teinds or tithes were often feued to laymen. As a result of the diversion of parish church revenues, poorly remunerated priests were appointed as vicars and chaplains. This in turn led to many abuses such as the dilapidation of church property and a tendency to augment income by rigid insistence on fees and mortuary dues. More grave was the decline in public esteem for sacerdotal function and the priestly status; hence the gibe of Sir David Lindsay;

> " And with ane plak to buy ane Messe,
> Fra Drounkin Schir Jhone Latyneless."

Ten at least of these bishops had illegitimate children, but probably at least six, had thus occasioned scandal before nomination. Cardinal Beaton's private life was irregular and as a prelate he did not adorn the spiritual estate. He had at least eight children, which Knox celebrated with vindictive relish in the epithets, " carnal Cardinal " and " graceless Grace." Contemporary catholic apologists explained that he had contracted an " uncanonical marriage," which terminated on his ordination to the priesthood. Two daughters and a son were legitimated when he was abbot of Arbroath, six years before his provision to the episcopate.[120] Three sons were legitimated a year before he became a cardinal and another four sons were legitimated in 1545.[121] In two instances there may be duplication: there is thus definite evidence for the legitimation of eight children. William Chisholm (I) of Dunblane had certainly four children.[122] When Robert Cairncross was abbot of Holyrood and eighteen months before his provision to Ross, two of his sons and a daughter were legitimated.[123] John Lesley, who was nominated to Ross by Mary Queen of Scots, had three illegitimate daughters.[124] James Hay had a son and a daughter and Henry Wemyss of Galloway had two sons.[125] Archbishop Forman, James Chisholm of Dunblane,

---

120. *R.S.S.*, ii, no. 843.
121. *Ibid.*, ii, no. 3200; iii, no. 1263.
122. *R.S.S.*, iv, no. 764; Dowden, p. 207.
123. *R.S.S.*, ii, no. 2366.
124. Dowden, p. 231.
125. *R.S.S.*, iv, no. 1488; Dowden, p. 225. *R.S.S.*, iv, no. 1780.

William Stewart and Gavin Dunbar of Aberdeen had each, at least, one illegitimate child.

Three of the bishops, William Elphinstone, David Paniter and John Lesley, were the sons of clerics. Apart from further indicating clerical immorality, this also suggests nepotism, of which there are more obvious examples. There were the three Beatons, James (I), his nephew, the Cardinal, and his nephew James (II). Andrew Durie of Galloway was a cousin of the cardinal. The brothers, James and William Chisholm and their nephew William (II), held the see of Dunblane for over a century. Archbishop Gavin Dunbar was a nephew of his namesake of Aberdeen. George Crichton and his nephew Robert were bishops of Dunkeld. Nepotism was a failing of even the virtuous popes of that period, but the influence of this example may have been reinforced by other considerations. Most of these prelates proved their ability before their promotion and they were definitely not the worst appointments; some were provided as a result of resignations *in favorem* which were generally considered reprehensible.

Some of these bishops had social ambitions for their daughters. Ninian Winzet remarked on their " solicitude be marriage efter to haif brocht the baronis to be impis of their posteritie." When Margaret Beaton, daughter of the cardinal, married David Lindsay, later the tenth earl of Crawford, she had a dowry of four thousand marks. Jane Chisholm, a daughter of William Chisholm (I), had a dowry of £1,000 when she married Sir James Stirling of Keir, and Jane Forman received from her father, the archbishop, a similar sum on her marriage to Alexander Oliphant of Kellie. It was this scandal which inspired the Complaint of Temporalitie in Lindsay's Satire, that ample provision was now required for their daughters;

> " For quhy ? the markit raisit bene sa hie,
> That prelats Dochtours of this Natioun
> Ar maryit with sic superfluitie;
> Thay will nocht spair to gif twa thowsand pound,
> With thair dochtours to an nobill man."

To summarise, briefly, the much quoted episcopal legitimations and similar evidence, approximately two out of five bishops in this period were incelibate. Twenty-two had illegitimate offspring: eighteen were either baronial bishops or had occasioned scandal, before nomination to the episcopate. At most, these figures illustrate the misuse of the right of nomination and the secularisation of the church by the nobility.

Before considering other aspects it is opportune to recall what medieval Scotland owed to its hierarchy. The institution of bishoprics and diocesan organisation were paramount factors in the two formative centuries before the war of independence, when Scotland became a nation. There may be some doubt concerning the role of the regular clergy in that war, but the strongest allies of Wallace and Bruce were Bishop Lamberton of St. Andrews and Bishop Wishart of Glasgow. The Declaration of Arbroath, " one of the masterpieces of political rhetoric of all time," was drawn up by Bishop Bernard de Linton, when he was abbot of Arbroath. The political services of Bishop Kennedy and Bishop Elphinstone in a later period further illustrate the unquestioned loyalty of the hierarchy to the Scottish crown. In contrast, their betrayal by the crown in the sixteenth century was the most potent cause of their decline and ultimate destruction. Of other services, it can only be mentioned that all four universities owe their foundation wholly or in part to bishops: Bishop Wardlaw at St. Andrews, Bishop Turnbull at Glasgow and Bishop Elphinstone at Aberdeen. Edinburgh University, founded after the reformation, owed its institution to money left for that purpose by Bishop Reid of Orkney.

The tradition of political service and scholastic endowment continued up to the reformation. To mention only the more prominent, James Beaton (I) whose only fault has been limited to persecution of heretics, rendered outstanding political service as chancellor from 1513 to 1526. Archbishop Gavin Dunbar was chancellor from 1528 until 1543: in marked contrast to Knox's unflattering references, there is the celebrated epigram of George Buchanan expressing admiration for the archbishop. There was much in the career of Cardinal Beaton that is to be regretted, but like Wolsey and Richelieu, he was primarily a servant of the crown and of his services as chancellor and patriot there should be no question. He has been criticised for what some would describe as anglophobia and a reckless policy of aggression towards England, which led to Solway Moss. Yet, while the cardinal was in France in 1541 and 1542, he attempted to bring about a change in papal policy in regard to England. He suggested to the papal nuncio in Paris that Charles V should form an alliance with England, sue for the hand of Princess Mary and thus bring back Henry VIII to papal obedience. The nuncio thought that the proposal indicated the speech of a cardinal, rather than a partisan of Scotland and France.[126] It was not the policy of a reckless anglophobe.

There has been a tendency to view the bishops as forming a homogeneous group with unanimous and consistent political aims. The traditional anti-English policy of the Scottish clergy, reinforced by dislike of the English reformation, has generally been considered as a major influence in this period. Of their patriotism, there is evidence in the large number of clerics in the Scottish forces at Flodden and Pinkie. Yet this does not prove the prevalence of a rabid anglophobia. Apart from the anglophil Gavin Douglas and Robert Stewart, who were exiled for treason, there were a number of prominent clerics who displayed a less nationalist attitude.

Bishop Elphinstone opposed the French alliance which led to Flodden. John Major, in his significantly titled *History of Greater Britain*, published in 1521, advocated a union of England and Scotland. Archbishop Forman was a member of the pro-English Douglas party. In 1533, Archbishop James Beaton (I) was imprisoned on a charge of treason. It would seem that he had written to Henry VIII, in an attempt to circumvent the agressive policy, which James V was then considering, under the influence of Clement VII and Charles V.[127] Similarly, Archbishop Gavin Dunbar opposed the anti-English policy which led to Solway Moss.[128] In 1544, four bishops supported an attempt to oust Arran from the regency. Ostensibly, the motive was that Arran had broken the Treaty of Greenwich with England, on the advice of Cardinal Beaton. During the crucial period 1553 to 1558, when England was governed by the catholic Mary Tudor, there was no religious advantage in the Scottish clergy

126. Herkless and Hannay, iv, p. 62.
127. *Ibid.*, iii, pp. 223-4.
128. D. E. Easson, *Gavin Dunbar*, p. 76.

following an anti-English policy. On the contrary, it was the protestant party which was then pro-French.

Much has been made of the complaint of " crass ignorance of literature and of all the liberal arts—*bonarum literarum et artium omnium crassa inscitia,*" with reference to the humanist connotation of the phrase.[129] The term " *bonae literae,*" describes the cause for which Erasmus and " his partisans battled."[130] Some of those present at the provincial council of 1549 are known to have been interested in the humanist movement; such were Bishop Reid or Orkney, Abbot Quintin Kennedy of Cross-raguel, John Winram, sub-prior of St. Andrews and John Stevenston, precentor of Glasgow. In addition, the following possessed works by Erasmus, Bishop William Gordon of Aberdeen, James Stewart, commendator of St. Andrews, John Grierson, provincial of the Dominicans and Alexander Anderson, sub-principal of Aberdeen University.[131] There was unquestionably clerical ignorance, but not to the unrelieved extent so often assumed.

Throughout this period, the Scottish hierarchy attempted to further education by legislation and endowment. Bishop Elphinstone, who founded Aberdeen University in 1495, is generally considered responsible for the education act of the following year, whereby the eldest sons of " barronis and frehaldaris " were to attend grammar schools and spend three years at a university. The bishop was also instrumental in the establishment of the first printing press in Scotland by Chepman and Millar in 1507, " for imprenting within our realme of the bukis of our lawis, actis of parliament, croniclis, mess bukis and portuus (breviaries)." One of the first productions of this press was the Aberdeen Breviary in two volumes, 1509-10.[132] St. Leonard's College at St. Andrews was founded in 1512 by Prior John Hepburn and the archbishop-elect, Alexander Stewart, who was a pupil of Erasmus. The synodal constitution (1516-1521), of Archbishop Forman, enacted that monks from certain monasteries were to attend St. Andrews, that the "*Alma Universitas* may flourish in the number of scholars and students." A decree of the provincial council of 1549 extended this measure to the major religious houses throughout the country.[133] St. Mary's College at St. Andrews was founded in 1538 by Archbishop James Beaton (I): its organisation was completed by Archbishop Hamilton in 1554. Bishop William Stewart is reputed to have founded the library of King's College, Aberdeen. Bishop Robert Reid, who left eight thousand marks for the endowment of a university at Edinburgh, had been a patron of the Italian scholar, Giovanni Ferreri, when abbot of Kinloss: they continued the work of Abbot Chrystall who had refounded the library.[134] There should also be mentioned the eminent lawyers, Henry and John Sinclair, of whose

---

129. The synodal constitutions of Archbishop Forman, employ the terms, *scientiae* and *literae*, Patrick, *op. cit.*, p. 277, note.
130. J. Huizinga, *Erasmus of Rotterdam*, p. 103.
131. Cf. " Early Scottish Libraries " *Innes Review*, ix.
132. *Source Book*, pp. 122-4.
133. Patrick, *op. cit.*, pp. 106-7, 276-7.
134. J. Durkan, " The Beginnings of Humanism in Scotland " and Appendix II, " Kinloss Abbey Library," *Innes Review*, iv.

libraries we now have catalogues; that of the former is outstanding.[135] Robert Cockburn of Ross and Dunkeld was a patron of the French humanist, Symphorien Champier.[136] Gavin Douglas of Dunkeld has an honoured reputation as poet and translator of Virgil and Bishop Lesley of Ross provided a valuable history of sixteenth-century Scotland.

Against the alleged indifference of the bishops, there may be cited the decrees of the provincial councils of 1549 and later, which are more often considered as evidence of scandal than of an attempt at reform. Delay in calling such a council has been ascribed to rivalry between the archbishops, but this would appear inadequate. Of greater influence were the secular considerations evident in episcopal nominations and the political confusion during regencies. Archbishop Forman, probably in accordance with the decrees of the fifth Council of the Lateran (1512-1517), drew up his synodal constitutions on his promotion to St. Andrews.[137] In addition to the regulations already mentioned, dealing with education, they were concerned with the general conduct of clerics, the duties of beneficed clergymen and other matters, such as the registration of wills and the prohibition of clandestine marriages.

More important were the disciplinary reforms of the provincial councils. The legislation of 1549 consisted of a series of ordinances, including canons of the fifth and seventh sessions of the Council of Trent. They deal with clerical immorality, the education of the clergy, the appointment of preachers and professors of canon law and theology, as well as with reform of the consistorial courts.[138] The council of 1552 explained that " owing to troublous times and their manifold embarassments," certain statutes of 1549 had not been carried into effect. It was also claimed that " many frightful heresies have run riot in many diverse parts of this realm, but have now at last been checked by the providence of All-good and Almighty God, the singular goodwill of princes and the vigilance and zeal of prelates for the Catholic faith and seem almost extinguished." This council also ordered the publication of a catechism, " that is, a plain and easy statement and explanation of the rudiments of the faith." Passages were to be read in all parish churches on Sundays and Holidays of Obligation, unless a sermon was given. Penalties were enacted for breach of this regulation. Priests were warned to prepare themselves by " constant, frequent and daily rehearsal of the lesson to be read, lest they expose themselves to the ridicule of their hearers, when through want of preparation they stammer and stumble in mid-course of reading."

It has been claimed that the disciplinary legislation was ineffective, even that it could not be effective. In support of this view, reference is made to certain articles submitted to Mary of Lorraine by some " Iemporall Lordis and Barronis " and considered by the provincial council, in 1559. After mentioning previous legislation, it was alleged that

---

135. " Early Scottish Libraries," *Innes Review,* ix.
136. J. Durkan, *op. cit.,* p. 9.
137. Patrick, pp. 260-278.
138. *Ibid.,* pp. 84, 134.

" thar hes folowit nan or litill fruict as yitt, bot rather the said (spiritual) Estate is deteriorate, nor emends be ony sic persuasion as hes bene hidertill usit."[139] Before considering the circumstances which hindered reform, it may be noted that the Tridentine legislation, applied by the provincial council in 1549, was effective on the continent and it is to the credit of the Scottish hierarchy that they adopted these disciplinary decrees within three years of their promulgation.

Archbishop Hamilton's catechism has been praised for its eirenic tone and for the lack of any polemical references to the reformers. It consists of four sections, dealing with the commandments, the creed, sacraments, and, finally, an exposition of the Our Father and the Hail Mary.[140] The preface states that the aim in matters of controversy was exposition in agreement with the decisions and definitions of general councils, " lawfully gathered in the Holy Spirit for the corroboration of our faith." It was also explained that when the faithful were instructed in the catechism, they would more easily understand " higher doctrine contained in the Gospels and Epistles " and explained by preachers. The catechism, however, has been criticised for its omissions and for divergence from Tridentine teaching. Briefly, there is no distinct section upon the mass as a sacrifice, papal authority is ignored and its exposition of the role of faith in justification, does not follow the decree on that doctrine, published five years previously at Trent.

These defects have been magnified and analysed without reference to their historical context. The provincial council which ordered the publication of the catechism met within a few days of the reception of protestant envoys at Trent in January, 1552. Discussion of the mass and of the sacrament of Holy Order which had been proposed in that session, were postponed to allow a hearing of the Lutheran proposals. Four years previously, Charles V had attempted to impose religious unity by the Interim of Augsburg, a studiously vague statement of catholic doctrine with modification, among other things, of the Tridentine teaching on justification. The Lutheran envoys asked that doctrines previously determined by the council, should be re-considered and that the pope should be subject to conciliar decisions. The council was adjourned in April as a result of the second Schmalkaldic war, in which Henry II of France, who had opposed the re-opening of the Council of Trent, was an ally of the German Lutheran princes. The situation in Scotland was further complicated at this juncture, by the efforts of Mary of Lorraine, to fulfill an " unwritten bond " with Henry II, whereby " French interests should prevail in Scotland."[141]

Criticism of the catechism's exposition of faith generally ignores these circumstances and would seem in some cases to be made without reference to the Tridentine definition—" We may be said to be justified by faith because faith is the beginning of all salvation—the basis and root of justification: for without it, it is impossible to please God and attain his adoption." The Council of Trent had been adjourned while considering the proposals of the Lutheran envoys, and it would appear that the

139. *Source Book*, p. 163.
140. There are two modern editions; a facsimile, with a preface by the Rev. Professor Mitchell, 1882, and T. G. Law's edition, with a preface by W. E. Gladstone, 1884.
141. *Scottish Correspondence of Mary of Lorraine*, edit. A. I. Cameron, Scot. Hist. Soc., p. 334.

compilers of the Catechism accepted this as a warrant for giving an exposition of faith which, in some respects, approaches that in the Interim of Augsburg.[142] The absence of a distinct section on the mass as a sacrifice can be explained by the postponement of consideration of that doctrine at Trent; indulgences, similarly ignored in the Catechism, were not considered at Trent until 1563.

The lack of any reference to papal authority, however, has been held to be in accordance with a practice of ignoring the papacy before 1560, in appointments to major benefices.[143] It is incorrect to suggest that there was such a practice before the reformation and the absence of reference cannot be interpreted as a denial of papal authority. Such an interpretation is contradicted by the preface of the Catechism, which opens as follows: " John, be the Mercie of God, Archbischop of Sanct Androus, Metropolitan and primat of the hail kirk of Scotland, and of seit Apostolyck Legatnait (*legatus natus* of the Apostolic See)." The council of 1559 also ignored papal authority in its instructions for preachers but it also sent " supplicatory letters . . . to our most holy lord the Pope," regarding provisions to prelacies, and inquisitors into episcopal morals, appointed by the council, were instructed, if necessary, " to inform and notify his holiness, our lord the pope, without delay or foreclosing of the case."[144]

The omission can be explained by the confusion caused by the survival of the conciliar theory, which considered the pope to be subject to a general council.[145] The Lutheran envoys had made this proposal at Trent. John Major, the leading Scottish theologian of that period, had defended this theory against Cardinal Cajetan.[146] There are also indications of a preoccupation with this topic in Scotland in this period.[147] The Council of Florence had defined papal primacy over the whole church in 1439, and William Hay had expounded that doctrine in his lectures in King's College, Aberdeen, given about 1535.[148] Florence, however, had not been recognised as a general council by the French monarchy, and Henry II took up a similar attitude to the Council of Trent, in 1551.

---

142. Two statements in the catechism, to which objection has been made, appear to be paralleled in the *Interim of Augsburg*. " This (special) faith obtains to us the abundant grace of the Holy Spirit which pours into our hearts, the true love of God and of our neighbour "; would seem to be an expansion of " *ea namque fides impetrat donum Spiritus Sancti, quo diffunditur caritas in cordibus nostris.*" " This (special) faith is always joined with hope and charity and works through love," would seem to be a very free rendering of "*Haec enim justitia fide, spe ac caritate ita constat ut si aliquam harum justitiae huic subtraxeris, eandum ipsam mancam plane reliqueris.*"

   (Archbishop Hamilton's *Catechism*, fol. xciii and xciv. For the text of the Interim of Augsburg, cf. Le Plat; *Monumentorum ad historiam Concilii Tridentini potissimum illustrandum spectantium amplissima collectio*, iv, pp. 38–9.) The catechism also uses the terms " general faith " and " special faith ", employed by catholic " mediating theologians " and by Melancthon. The circumstances of the catechism's compilation also explain the use of language, reminiscent of the Edwardian *Homily on Faith* and the incorporation of a passage, " though not of theological importance " from Luther's *Larger Catechism*: this passage could be from a common source.

143. *Source Book*, p. 146, note. See above.

144. Patrick, *op. cit.*, pp. 164, 177.

145. H. Jedin, *A History of the Council of Trent*, trans. Dom Ernest Graf, O.S.B., i, chapters I, II, V and page 384.

146. *Ibid.*, p. 34, 144, note.

147. " Early Scottish Libraries," *Innes Review*, ix, pp. 14-15.

148. After citing all grades of bishops up to the patriarch of Constantinople, there follows: " *Super omnes istos est papa Petri successor et vicarius Christi, habens plenitudinem potestatis qui habet illam potestatem in alium derivare quod videtur sibi. Et dicitur papa quia pater patrum. Et per hoc stat unitas ecclesiae. Quia omnia membra sunt sub uno capite. Quare illi qui hanc potestatem negant sunt schismatici et unitatis ecclesie divisores.*" MSS. Aberdeen University Library, for the transcript of which thanks are due to the Rev. John Barry.

IV

The traditional description of James V's policy in the 1530's as pro-clerical needs considerable revision. His reputation as an orthodox sovereign derives from his refusal to follow the policy of Henry VIII in dissolving the monasteries, and from the number of heresy trials during his reign. To view his policy in these terms is to ignore the role of financial interest and it is relevant to note the difference, which appreciation of such factors has necessitated in the interpretation of the last decade of the reign of Henry VIII. " If, instead, we look at it from the economic and social standpoint, the pattern undergoes a marked change: what was a mere appendage, now becomes the focal point of a new dis-position."[149] A cursory survey of the episcopal appointments indicates that such an approach to the policy of James V is not unwarranted. If we accept as a focal point the financial problems of the Scottish crown in the face of severe inflation, the religious policy of James V acquires a less puzzling aspect and a more mundane significance.

The chronic poverty of the Scottish crown in this period was due to a number of causes, which still await detailed examination, royal extra-vagance, maladministration during the regencies and the breakdown of the feudal system.[150] In addition, during the sixteenth century, Scotland in common with most countries in Western Europe underwent severe inflation as a result of the price revolution. Over the century, the Scots pound depreciated in terms of sterling from five shilling to one shilling and eight pence, but in the same period the general level of prices in England rose by over five hundred per cent.[151] James IV's nominations to St. Andrews provide evidence of an attempt to solve this problem, by tapping the wealth of the church. The appointment of two royal arch-bishops-elect deprived the church of the guidance of a metropolitan for almost twenty years, and absence of archiepiscopal control led to a number of abuses which Archbishop Forman attempted to remove, by his synodal constitutions. In spite of the very obvious harm to the church, James V continued this policy by exploiting the danger of Lutheran infiltration and the example of his uncle, Henry VIII. For political reasons, a dissolution of the monasteries was impracticable in Scotland, since James needed the support of the clergy. Apart from their traditional opposition to the crown, the nobility had been alienated by various acts of the king. There was the fear that an attack was intended on their estates, since an Act of Revocation, issued by James in 1537 and ratified by parliament in 1540, enabled him to revoke grants which they had received. This solution had its dangers and James continued the more profitable policy of clerical taxation and exploitation of the right of nomination.

It is now apparent that the institution of the College of Justice, for long regarded as the " most memorable legislative act " of the reign, was an afterthought, proposed in justification of a permanent tax on the clergy. "A fund to maintain the civil judges was made the pretext for imposing upon the Scottish prelates a perpetual subsidy, of which it soon became evident that the king would devote as little as possible to the

---

149. S. T. Bindoff, *Tudor England*, 1950, p. 112.
150. Cf. W. Stanford Reid, *op. cit.*
151. For the economic history of England in this period see Bindoff *op. cit.* and G. R. Elton, *England Under the Tudors*, 1955, chapter ix, " England during the Price Revolution."

ostensible purpose,"[152] Archbishop Gavin Dunbar, as chancellor, was associated with the scheme in so far as it was a legal reform, but he was very probably unaware of the financial implications, which the Duke of Albany, as James's representative, negotiated in Rome.[153] Archbishop James Beaton (I) strenuously opposed this taxation, more particularly when the money was diverted to the account of the Master of Works, to be spent on building operations at the royal palaces. These accounts show that in the period 1535-1541 sums were received from four taxes on the clergy, the Old Tax, a statutory contribution to government finances: the Tax of the Three Teinds, authorised by Clement VII on July 17, 1531: the Great Tax, ostensibly for the support of the College of Justice, and a fourth, voted in 1535, to pay for the expenses of James V and his ambassadors, during the negotiations for his marriage to Madeleine de Valois.[154]

The timing of legislation against heretics and of the heresy trials betrays a similar opportunism. When papal approval was granted for the institution of the College of Justice, a papal nuncio, Sylvester Dario, arrived in Scotland to ensure a more active repression of heresy. He returned to Rome with an official extract of a declaration, made by James in parliament, to maintain the authority and freedom of the church.[155] The heresy trials of the next two years can be related to specific concessions, which James hoped to obtain from Clement VII.[156] This was expressly admitted in a letter of November 5, 1534, in which James V congratulated Paul III on his election. John Lauder had been sent to the late pope, " to testify to (James's) zeal and regard for the papacy, and to ask the pope to acquiesce in certain proposals in view of that devotion." James hoped that Paul III would confirm the favours which had been granted, but not expedited, by Clement VII.[157] These favours included the dispensations for the ecclesiastical preferment of the king's illegitimate sons, granted in March, 1534: the recognition and the extension of the crown right of nomination and papal incorporation of the College of Justice. Two bulls granting these favours were issued in March, 1535. In the following June, parliament passed acts for the repression of heresy. The granting of these concessions coincided with a halt in official action against heretics, but it was renewed in 1538, when further favours were desired from the papacy.[158] Paul III was petitioned in August of that year, for the promotion to the Sacred College, with powers of a legate *a latere*, of David Beaton, then Bishop of Mirepoix and coadjutor to St. Andrews.[159] In December, 1538, David Beaton was made cardinal but without the powers of legate, for which James continued to supplicate for the next two and a half years.[160]

---

152. R. K. Hannay, *The College of Justice*, p. x.
153. D. E. Easson, *Gavin Dunbar*, p. 44.
154. *Accounts of the Masters of Works*, 1529-1615, i, p. xiv.
155. R. K. Hannay, *The College of Justice*, pp. 55-6.
156. David Stratoun and Norman Gourlay were among those executed for heresy in the period, 1532-34. John Willock and George Wishart fled to England about this time.
157. *Letters of James V*, pp. 279-80.
158. In 1539, Beverage and Keillor, two Dominicans, and Thomas Forret, vicar of Dollar, were among those executed. George Buchanan escaped from imprisonment and fled from Scotland.
159. *Letters of James V*, p. 349.
160. *Ibid.*, pp. 358, 377, 384, 400, 405, 422.

There seems little doubt that the presence of a legate *a latere* in Scotland was required for financial reasons, in particular to avoid referring to Rome for confirmation of the feuing of church lands.[161] The Great Tax for the support of the College of Justice entailed the payment by the clergy of £72,000 over four years. It was difficult to raise such a sum when about half of ecclesiastical revenue was in kind. From this date there was a considerable increase in the feuing of church property, but papal confirmation was required, since it was a form of alienation forbidden by canon law. It was within the power of a legate *a latere* to confirm such transactions and these faculties were granted to Archbishop Hamilton, when he was appointed legate by Julius III, in 1552.[162] James V had prevented the granting of such powers to Archbishop Beaton, who opposed the policy of clerical taxation and had suggested that Archbishop Gavin Dunbar be made legate. The latter does not seem to have been aware of this proposal, since James asked the pope not to inform the archbishop that there had been a royal supplication.[163] Paul III, however, seems to have appreciated the effects of James's policy, since Cardinal Beaton did not receive the long-coveted legateship until after the king's death.[164]

Similarly, the legislation of March, 1541, for the repression of heresy, can be associated with a fresh demand for a permanent tax on the clergy, although the enactment of the death penalty for the denial of papal authority may have been for the benefit of Henry VIII, who had again attempted to suborn his nephew. In the following month, James informed Paul III that he was astonished that papal approval had not been granted for the voluntary gift, which the clergy had made because of his services in repressing heresy.[165] This, however, was a travesty of the transaction; the grant had, apparently, been extorted as the price for not keeping a rendezvous with Henry VIII at York. An annual tax of 10,000 crowns was at first demanded and the clergy offered a voluntary gift of £5,000, which was paid with reluctance. The clergy resisted the king's original demand by protestation at Rome.[166] A few days before this letter had been sent to Paul III, the Court of Session issued an order to distrain upon the temporal lands of Cardinal Beaton, for arrears of payment of the tax for the support of the College of Justice.[167]

In the same parliament, a statute was passed for the " reforming of kirks and kirkmen." After referring to the negligence of divine service and the lack of " reparatioun " to the honour of God, to the Blessed Sacrament and the Virgin Mary and the Saints, it stated that the main cause of the church and clerics being " lychlit and contempnit," was the " unhonestie and misreul of kirkmen baith in witt, knawledge and maners."[168] Yet for this unhappy state of affairs James V was mainly and directly responsible. His episcopal nominations, the provision of his infant illegitimate sons to monastic houses, and his policy of clerical

161. R. K. Hannay, *Rentale Sancti Andree*, p. xxvi.
162. *Warrender Papers*, edit. A. I. Cameron, Scot. Hist. Soc., i, pp. 28-9.
163. *Letters of James V*, p. 183.
164. Hannay, *Rentale Sancti Andree*, pp. xxvi-xxvii.
165. *Letters of James V*, p. 424.
166. Hannay, *Rentale Sancti Andree*, p. xxii.
167. Herkless and Hannay, v, p. 58.
168. *Source Book*, pp. 99-100.

taxation, secularised the church, weakened the hierarchy and provided occasion for criticism and contempt, when the expression of anti-clerical views had royal toleration and approval. Taxation also forced the clergy to insist on the laity meeting their financial obligation towards the church at a time when the payment of ecclesiastical dues was most unpopular. One of the charges against David Stratoun in a heresy trial in 1534, was the refusal to pay teinds to the prior of St. Andrews. The unpopularity of the mortuary offerings, the " corps presentes," is a recurring theme in the works of Sir David Lindsay. James V may have proposed the abolition of such dues at the provincial council of 1536, but the clergy could hardly be sympathetic, when the main object of the council was to ratify the financial arrangements for the support of the College of Justice.[169]

The clergy apparently suggested to James that it would be more appropriate to raise money by confiscating the estates of heretics. Sir James Hamilton of Finnart was appointed to investigate this proposal. It is stated that the appointment was agreeable to the clergy, but there is the further consideration that Hamilton was then Master of Works, to whom the clerical taxes were diverted. There are puzzling aspects in what followed. His cousin, a brother of the heretic, Patrick Hamilton, accused Hamilton of Finnart of complicity in an old plot for the murder of the king. Kirkcaldy of Grange, Learmonth of Dairsie and Lord Erskine, urged instant action and Hamilton of Finnart was executed on August 16, 1540.[170] Kirkcaldy and Learmonth were then protestants and Erskine may have been disappointed that his son's nomination to Dryburgh was then countered by papal preference for Robert Wauchope.

It is possible, on this basis, to provide a more reasonable interpretation of James's apparently inconsistent policy. The traditional view of the orthodox, pro-clerical monarch and persecutor of heretics, who imprisoned Archbishop Beaton, inspired Buchanan to attack the Franciscans and approved of Sir David Lindsay's anti-clerical lampoons, is barely credible. While neither attempting the hazardous task of analysing James's character, nor denying the sincerity of his catholicism, it can be stated that he was, in some respects, a cynical opportunist. For material reasons, he represented himself to the papacy, as a staunch upholder of orthodoxy, while obtaining financial favours by a form of blackmail. By his support of anti-clericalism, he attempted to force the clergy into meeting his demands for taxation.

After the death of James V, in 1542, the protestant and pro-English party achieved control. The " assured lords," captured at Solway Moss, were released on the understanding that they would carry out the instructions of Henry VIII. Cardinal Beaton was imprisoned: the story of the forged will, first circulated some months after the king's death, was not seriously considered by the cardinal, whose enemies either feared, or were unable, to make a formal accusation. In spite of the protests of Archbishop Dunbar, parliament passed an act allowing the circulation of the bible in the vernacular. Arran, then governor, agreed to the English marriage alliance and engaged as chaplains two ex-Dominicans,

---

169. Herkless and Hannay, iii, pp. 233-7.
170. Herkless and Hannay, iv, pp. 54-5. Cf. Andrew Lang, *History of Scotland*, i, Appendix G, *The Tragedy of Finnart*, pp. 504-6.

John Rough and Thomas Williams. The abbey of Lindores and the friaries of Dundee and Perth were sacked. Within a few months, Arran was reconciled with the cardinal and recanted his errors.

A reversal of policy did not bring financial relief to the Spiritual Estate. Cardinal Beaton and Archbishop Dunbar confirmed the support of many nobles by the granting of feus on a large scale. Argyll, Huntly and Seton received grants from the cardinal at this time: so many grants were made that a new rental book was prepared for the lands of St Andrews on September 3, 1545.[171] Rejection of the English marriage alliance had also been occasioned by the excessive demands of Henry VIII, who insisted on having the custody of the queen and the succession to the Scottish throne in the event of her death. He then attempted to persuade the Scots by the " Rough Wooing," the invasions of 1544 and 1545. The earl of Hertford was instructed to destroy Edinburgh, Leith and St. Andrews: no quarter was to be granted to the relatives and supporters of the cardinal.[172] In these and later English invasions, churches and monasteries were targets for destruction, while heretical books were imported by the cartload. The clergy, however, had to meet the major cost of national defence. The main object of the conventions of the clergy, convoked by the cardinal in May, 1543, and January, 1546, was to discuss and ratify clerical subsidies. Between 1543 and 1545, the clergy had to meet new taxation amounting to £13,000.[173]

Cardinal Grimani had been sent as papal legate, to supervise the collection of the tax solicited by James V, shortly before his death, and to arrange for the liberation of Cardinal Beaton. He reported that the latter and the dowager were financially exhausted; that there was so much heresy that Scotland was likely to follow the example of England.[174] The legate had arrived in Scotland with French ambassadors bringing money and munitions, which were seized by the earl of Lennox, who had joined the English party. Shortly afterwards Mary of Lorraine, supported by some nobles and four bishops, attempted to remove the cardinal and Arran from the government. On June 10, 1544, this group suspended Arran from the regency because he had followed the advice of the cardinal in breaking the Treaties of Greenwich with England. The bishops, who supported this action, were Gavin Dunbar of Glasgow, Robert Reid of Orkney, William Chisholm of Dunblane and Patrick Hepburn of Moray. Sir George Douglas, a noted traitor, claimed credit for the scheme, but the queen dowager seems to have been the prime mover. She was then more concerned with achieving her personal ambitions than with the national cause. Throughout the crisis the one stable factor was the unselfish patriotism of the cardinal, who was prepared to co-operate with Mary of Lorraine, but not to be subservient to her aims.[175]

By November, the two factions had been reconciled, but shortly afterwards the scheme was broached for the marriage of James Hamilton to the queen. It has been suggested that the cardinal first proposed this

171. Hannay, *Rentale Sancti Andree*, p. xxviii.
172. *Source Book*, pp. 132-3.
173. *Rentale Sancti Andree*, p. xxvii. To the taxes mentioned by Hannay, there should be added, half of the £16,000 levied by parliament in October, 1545. Cf. W. Stanford Reid, *op. cit.*
174. Cf. R. K. Hannay, *Letters of the Papal Legate in Scotland*, 1543, Scot. Hist. Rev., xi, pp. 1-26.
175. *Scottish Correspondence of Mary of Lorraine*, pp. 60-65.

scheme, but it was reported to Mary of Lorraine that he would never consider it.[176] James Hamilton went to the castle of St. Andrews, which was then being strongly fortified, and it was reported that the cardinal hoped to get custody of the queen. The fracas in Glasgow Cathedral, which took place in 1545, indicates that the two archbishops had not yet been fully reconciled and it may have been hoped to remove the divisions in the hierarchy at the provincial council, which was summoned in 1546. Apparently the chief object of this council was to obtain clerical support for the cardinal's policy and the speedy collection of a subsidy of £13,000. It is possible that his policy was not then generally accepted as being in the best interests of the church.[177] At one or other of these meetings convened by the cardinal, it was also enacted that prelates should assign benefices for the support of professors of theology and preachers.[178] This was again enacted in the provincial council held by Archbishop Hamilton in 1547.[179]

Wishart had returned to Scotland, probably in July, 1543, in the company of the English commissioners. He preached in Montrose and in Dundee, where his opinions may have occasioned the attacks on the friaries, in Ayrshire and finally in East Lothian. He was in close association with Crichton of Brunston, Kirkcaldy of Grange, Norman Leslie, Sir George Douglas and the earl of Cassillis, who at various times were implicated in plots for the murder of the cardinal, details of which had been submitted to England for approval. In April, 1544, a " Scottishman called Wysshert " took details of such a plan to London, where he was received by Henry VIII. There is no direct proof that this was George Wishart, the heretic. The evidence is circumstantial, but the rebuttal depends mainly on *ex-parte* estimates of Wishart's character; to Knox he was an " innocent lamb."

Cardinal Beaton was murdered three months after the execution of George Wishart and some of the assassins had been concerned in the earlier plots. Knox relates an improbable speech by James Melville, who, incidentally, like Wishart, was " a man of nature most gentle and most modest ": he claimed to revenge that " notable instrument of God, Master George Wishart." There is no doubt that Norman Leslie and some of the others had a private quarrel with the cardinal, and if Henry VIII did not directly inspire the deed, he rewarded those who undertook the " Godly work." Arran, apparently, had no doubt that it was due to private quarrels and the guile of Henry VIII—" *per privatas injurias et dolo angli regis.*"[180]

The clergy offered a subsidy of £3,000 a month for the siege of the castle of St. Andrews, which was held by the murderers of the cardinal and their supporters. Arran, however, was more concerned with the safety of his son, held as a hostage by the castilians, who had demanded a papal absolution as the condition of their surrender. When it arrived they considered it insufficient and sent (to London) Henry Balnaves, who is stated to have returned with money and the best gunner in

176. *Balcarres Papers*, edit. M. Wood, Scot. Hist. Soc., i, pp. 246-7.
177. *Rentale Sancti Andree*, pp. xlix-l.
178. Blairs MSS. Royal Letters, 1524-1548.
179. Robertson, *Statuta*, vol. i, p. cxlvi.
180. Blairs MSS. Royal Letters, 1524-1548.

England.[181] John Knox entered the castle at this time, after the arrival of the papal absolution and before the departure of Balnaves for England. His action may have been dictated by the request made to Arran by a provincial council held in March, 1547, for the enforcement of the laws against heretics. The castle was surrendered on July 31, 1547, fourteen months after the cardinal's murder. Six weeks later, Hertford invaded Scotland and inflicted a crushing defeat at Pinkie. Archbishop Hamilton was, apparently, in the field and many clerics were killed in battle. An act of parliament had previously granted to the next of kin the presentation, provision and collation of the benefices of those clergymen who fell in action.[182]

The supremacy of French interests in Scotland was achieved by the Treaty of Haddington in July, 1548, and the removal of Arran from the regency was a question of time. The queen and James Hamilton were sent to France. Military disaster had resulted in a decline in the influence of Arran and Archbishop Hamilton, who was treasurer. When peace was made with England, Mary of Lorraine went to France accompanied by most of the nobles, who were likely to cause trouble, and after a year's stay she managed to retrieve her financial position by subsidies from the revenues of Guienne and Brittany. Meanwhile, Archbishop Hamilton had initiated the programme of reform through the legislation of the provincial council of 1549.

It is to the credit of the archbishop that this policy was initiated, but he can hardly be described as typifying the reforming spirit of Trent. His translation from Dunkeld to St. Andrews could not have been welcome in Rome and it was not effected until after the battle of Pinkie. The delay was probably due to dislike of Arran's ecclesiastical policy and disapproval of the archbishop's irregular life. It would appear that the chapter of St. Andrews put forward Archbishop James Beaton (II) of Glasgow, a more suitable choice. News of the English victory and the danger of Arran resuming a pro-English and protestant policy, if his nomination were rejected, probably determined the papal provision.[183]

It is significant that the archbishop's main efforts at reform, the councils of 1549 and 1552, the publication of his catechism and the re-organisation of St. Mary's College, took place under the regency of Arran. The latter was forced to resign in 1554, for by then he had only two supporters, the primate and Lord Livingstone. The archbishop was removed from the treasurership and replaced by the earl of Cassillis, a protestant, who had been involved in one of the plots to murder Cardinal Beaton. Disciplinary reform of the church required the co-operation of the primate and the crown authority, which was conspicuously absent throughout the greater part of Mary of Lorraine's regency. The archbishop, as a Hamilton was opposed to the regent's policy. He is stated to have been against the resignation of the regency by Arran and at a later date, most of the clergy, under the archbishop's influence, are reputed to have opposed the taking of the crown-matrimonial to France.[184]

181. *Scottish Correspondence of Mary of Lorraine*, p. 184.
182. *Source Book*, pp. 142-4.
183. Herkless and Hannay, v, p. 42 and note.
184. *Ibid.*, v, pp. 57 and 88.

Evidence of the regent's dislike of the primate is provided by the letter of Cardinal Sermoneta to Paul IV in 1566.[185] After mentioning some of the scandals and abuses in Scotland, the names are given of those prelates considered as most capable of executing reforms and most acceptable to the regent. Archbishop Hamilton is not mentioned and no mention is made of his efforts at reform, by the provincial councils of 1549 and 1552. The omission of his name can hardly be due to the irregularity of his private life, as the list includes two bishops who, in that respect, had a similar reputation: Patrick Hepburn of Moray and William Chisholm (I) of Dunblane. The latter apparently lent the regent £4,400 in 1555.[186]

Mary of Lorraine seems to have been more interested in clerical taxation than in disciplinary reform. In 1555 and 1556, she asked Paul IV for a subsidy of two-tenths, in order to rebuild fortifications.[187] Yet a year later she informed her brother, the cardinal of Lorraine, that she would not meddle with the forts since she could not garrison them.[188] In 1556, she asked permission for the appropriation of a quarter of ecclesiastical revenues, to be spent on the restoration of churches and monasteries.[189] It might have been a coincidence that most of the " ruinous " parish churches in the Merse, inspected by Archbishop Hamilton in 1555, were appropriated to Kelso and Coldingham, which were held by royal commendators.[190] Henry II, in 1559, asked that up to fifty per cent of ecclesiastical income should be appropriated for the support of a criminal court, similar apparently to his " Chambre Ardente," and for the payment of a French garrison.[191] The regent, however, was not always scrupulously concerned with the use of clerical wealth. When she nominated her brother, the cardinal of Guise, to Kelso in 1558, she had originally suggested that a pension of £900 be granted to a son of that eminent reformer, the earl of Glencairn. The petition for this pension was later withdrawn.[192]

Mary of Lorraine's pre-occupation with financial matters may also throw some light on Cardinal Sermoneta's letter. Apart from the dilapidation and feuing of church property, the main complaint against the clerics and the prelates was that they engaged in trade. This, however, was the complaint of the merchants, whose support the regent was then attempting to acquire. The same letter has a much quoted section on the immoralities of Scottish nuns which has some puzzling features.[193] The letter complains of the over great revenues of monks which seems to be the cause of this unbridled license. The only license mentioned is that of nuns and it is curious that this should be ascribed to the wealth of monks. At the same time nothing is said of the immoralities of clerics, monks and prelates, of which there is ample evidence. In view of the regent's ambivalent policy, it is permissible to seek some other explanation for this

185. Pollen, *op. cit.*, pp. 528-30.
186. *Balcarres Papers*, ii, p. xlix.
187. Pollen, *op. cit.*, pp. 522 seq.
188. *Ibid.*, p. 429.
189. *Ibid.*, p. 530.
190. *Source Book*, pp. 151-2.
191. Pollen, p. 19.
192. *Ibid.*, p. 30.
193. *Source Book*, p. 150-1.

complaint. In July, 1555, an Edinburgh merchant, James Henrison, very probably a protestant, offered to increase the crown revenues by £30,000, without " ony sic danger, grudge or murmour of the pepill as there is now."[194] Unfortunately, we are not given details, but there is a relevant passage in the 1554 version of Lindsay's Satyre of the Thrie Estaits, which was performed in August of that year, in Edinburgh, before Mary of Lorraine.

> " Thir wantoun Nunnis ar na way necessair
> Till Common weill nor zit to the glorie
> of Christis Kirk. . . .
>
> . . . .
>
> Thair rents usit till ane better fyne
> For Commonweil of all this regioun."

Lindsay then goes on to suggest that the revenues of the nunneries be used to provide salaries for judges.[195] Mary of Lorraine was chronically short of money; she cannot be considered scrupulous in regard to ecclesiastical wealth and she had a keen interest in social legislation. It is not, therefore, improbable that she had some sympathy for Lindsay's suggestion.

Mary of Lorraine also conciliated the protestant party; since England was then catholic under the rule of Mary Tudor, they were no longer anglophil. This was not an entirely new venture, as many of the protestant leaders had supported her attempt to oust Arran from the regency in 1544. The first public acknowledgement of this policy was the revocation of the forfeitures of Cardinal Beaton's murderers and their associates. Henry Balnaves expressed his gratitude by offering the regent his services.[196] It has generally been ascribed to the leniency of Mary of Lorraine that John Knox was able to preach with impunity, for almost ten months, after his return in the autumn of 1555. In May, 1556, he was summoned to appear in the church of the Blackfriars in Edinburgh, but that " diet held not." The regent, who had alienated almost all the Scots nobles and depended on French officials, was then tolerant of protestants.[197] This policy won their support, and although the reformers objected to the Franco-Scottish alliance after Elizabeth succeeded to the English throne, it was only through their support that it was achieved.

In 1557, when Châtelherault, the former regent, Huntly, Cassillis and Argyll, refused to invade England in support of the French alliance, leading protestants, Lord James Stewart and Kirkcaldy of Grange as well as Maitland of Lethington, sided with the regent.[198] The protestant party supported the French marriage alliance and of the nine commissioners sent to France in 1558, three, Lord James Stewart, Cassillis and Erskine of Dun, were protestants. In the parliament of November, 1558, that party supported the granting of the crown-matrimonial to the dauphin, while most of the clergy, under the influence of Archbishop Hamilton, are stated to have opposed this action. Lord James and another protestant, the earl of Argyll, were commissioned to take the crown to France.

---

194. *Scottish Correspondence of Mary of Lorraine*, p. 403 and note.
195. *Works of Sir David Lyndsay*, Scottish Text Society, ii, p. 349. Cf. R. K. Hannay, *The College of Justice*, p. 80.
196. *The Scottish Correspondence of Mary of Lorraine*, pp. 404-6.
197. *Ibid.*, p. 375.
198. Tytler, *History of Scotland*, vi, p. 67.

This political alignment had elicited conciliatory measures on the part of the regent. In March, 1557, John Knox had been invited to return to Scotland by Lord James and others, because the " friars were daily in less estimation with the Queen Regent and the rest of the nobility "; the invitation was later withdrawn. In December of the same year the " Godlie Band " was drawn up and shortly afterwards a petition was presented to Mary of Lorraine by Sandilands of Calder, which asked for communion under both kinds and the celebration of the Lord's Supper in the vernacular. To this she apparently replied that the protestants could worship as they pleased, until parliament decided on the religious question, provided there were no public assemblies in Leith and Edinburgh. In April, 1558, Walter Miln, an elderly priest who had married, was executed for heresy; he denied the Real Presence. Mary of Lorraine disclaimed responsibility for the execution and protestant preachers taught openly in Leith and Edinburgh. Their sermons led to iconoclasm, which occasioned the demand of the " temporall Lordis and Barronis " in their articles, " that na manner of persons be sa bald as to burn, spuilie, or destroy kirks, chappels or religious places, and ornaments tharof, nor attempt ony thing be way of deid to the hurt and injuring thairof, or for deforming or innovating the lovable ceremonies and rites tharof usit in Haly Kirk."[199] On September 1, 1558, the procession in honour of St. Giles in Edinburgh was rabbled by a protestant mob: the statue was smashed but the regent took no action. Another protestant petition was presented to Mary of Lorraine in November, and she is then reported to have replied that she would remember all that had been said, and that she would deal with the religious controversy later. The regent spent that winter in " sumpteous and magnifique banqueting," in the hope that the lords " would stay their enterprises."[200] The Beggars' Summons appeared on January 1, 1559, and threatened appropriation of the friaries before Whitsunday. Archbishop Hamilton then summoned a number of protestant preachers to appear at St. Andrews, but the regent requested that the trial should be postponed. In March, the provincial council met in Edinburgh and since parliament had ratified the French marriage alliance, Mary of Lorraine ceased to conciliate the protestant party.

Her change of policy was too late. Conciliatory measures had only strengthened the aggressive Calvinist party, which inspired iconoclastic mobs to attack churches and disturb religious services. Archbishop Hamilton's policy of disciplinary reform could hardly be effective in a church under physical attack. When it was alleged that the " Spiritual Estate was deteriorate," it was not explained that the regent was greatly to blame. The provincial council replied to this criticism by appointing inquisitors into episcopal morals and by a request to Mary of Lorraine to nominate to bishoprics and other benefices, only those whose morals, learning and age enabled them to fulfil their spiritual duties. Of her nominations to the episcopate, four defected and of these, three, Alexander Gordon, James Hamilton and Donald Campbell, very obviously did not meet the requirements laid down by the council. There was clearly a deterioration when such clerics were considered worthy to succeed the

---

199. *Source Book*, p. 167.
200. Lesley, *Historie of Scotland*, Bannatyne Club, p. 269.

three bishops who died in the autumn of 1558, Robert Reid of Orkney, David Paniter of Ross and Andrew Durie of Galloway. It would be then more accurate to say that disciplinary reform was hindered and nullified, rather than ineffective.

V.

The Beggars' Summons, which was apparently based on the English Supplication of Beggars of 1529, heralded the religious revolution.[201] No reference was made to monastic and other church property, which had by then largely passed out of the control of the clergy as a result of commendation and feuing: a process which the provincial council of 1559 attempted to reverse. The council of 1549 had forbidden the feuing of church glebes by rectors and vicars, but that of 1559 prohibited " any archbishop, bishop, abbot, prior, etc." from granting long or short leases of any church lands in their benefices, except to tenants and those who farmed such property. Leases which had been made in contravention of this measure were " *ipso iure* null and invalid on the passing of an irritant decree."[202] This legislation undoubtedly influenced many of those who later joined the Congregation, either with the aim of retaining their hold on church property, or in the hope of further acquisitions. The prevalence of such motives would seem patent, from the refusal of parliament to ratify the First Book of Discipline, which contained a scheme for the endowment of the reformed church. Those with little sympathy for the religious ideas of the reformers may also have been prompted by events in England. When Mary Tudor restored catholicism, a statutory guarantee was made that there would be no attempt to dispossess the owners of ecclesiastical property. It is by no means improbable that many justified their support of the Congregation in the hope of a similar arrangement in Scotland.

Knox returned to Scotland in early May and by the end of the month, after the iconoclasm at Perth, the Congregation began the war against the " Canaanite " bishops. It is now generally accepted that Knox's account of this period is in the main a party pamphlet, with the object of refuting the charges made by Mary of Lorraine. He was concerned to prove that the Congregation was not seditious, that the Congregation was not responsible for the destruction of churches, and that there had been no negotiations with England. Unfortunately, Mary of Lorraine, in her policy of conciliation, had not realised that Knox diverged from both Luther and Calvin, in advocating resistance on religious grounds to the civil authorities. The mass was idolatrous because it was invented by man: in the Old Testament the penalty for idolatry was death: finally, from the same source, it was alleged that such punishment could be inflicted by the " whole body " of the people and " every member of the same."[203] The policy of the regent's French advisers at this time was definitely conciliatory. Against the hearsay evidence, transmitted by Throckmorton, that Bishop Pellevé advised Mary of Lorraine to order

201. *Source Book*, pp. 168-9.
202. Patrick, *op. cit.*, pp. 97-8, 179-82.
203. Cf. J. W. Allen, *A History of Political Thought in the Sixteenth Century*, second edition, 1941, pp. 106-116. " But who was to be the judge of false religion and whether Knox himself was a true preacher or false? Always in the 16th century controversies, we come down to the same question: and always from the Calvinists we get the same absurd answer. The whole of Knox's case rested on the assumption that the true religion was ' manifestly known '." P. 114.

a wholesale massacre of protestants, there is the close examination by Father Pollen, of the records of the diplomatic missions of Melville, Bethencourt and Pellevé, which reveal a conciliatory attitude.[204]

This was obviously an attempt to reconcile incompatibles. The regent, however, did attempt to carry out this policy. After the lords of the Congregation seized Edinburgh at the end of June, she proposed terms which were, in fact, a capitulation to their demands. They were to have liberty of religious profession, on the condition that mass could be celebrated and there was to be no preaching of the reformed religion, wherever the regent was residing. The offer was rejected because of the conditions. On July 24th, the dowager's troops, led by D'Oysel and Châtelherault, recaptured Leith and forced the Congregation to accept a truce, which in spite of their military defeat was again conciliatory. They were to leave Edinburgh within twenty-four hours and give up the minting dies which they had seized. The capital was to have the religion it chose. Catholics and protestants were to have religious freedom and neither side was to molest the other. Knox gave a false account of these terms, so that they could later accuse the regent of breaking the truce. The preachers refused to give up the Edinburgh churches, and the protestant members of the town council opposed the taking of a vote to decide the religion of the capital.[205] Mary of Lorraine acquiesced in this breach of the treaty; the insurgents who had lost the war definitely won the truce.

To understand the second phase of the war which began in October, it is necessary to refer to English advice and aid. In August, 1559, Cecil, after receiving a number of pleas for aid, drew up a memorandum, which became the blue-print of the revolutionary programme. A committee, appointed by the Three Estates, was to rule Scotland in the name of the queen; Scotland was to be free from idolatry: there was to be peace between the two countries and Scotland was not to be subject to France. If the French king, Francis II, Mary's husband, objected, then the government of the country was to be committed to the next heir, the duke of Châtelherault.[206] This solution was complicated by the absence from Scotland of Châtelherault's heir, the earl of Arran, who had been sent to France after the Treaty of Haddington. On August 28, Arran arrived in Cecil's house, having been smuggled out of France by a " fine piece of secret service work " on the part of Throckmorton.[207] Meanwhile, he had become a protestant and according to the diplomatic gossip of that period, his conversion resulted from despair at seeing Queen Mary wed to Francis.[208] He arrived in Scotland on September 8. Three weeks later, Archbishop Hamilton informed the regent that he had failed to prevent his half-brother, Châtelherault, from joining the Congregation. In another letter of the following day, he also informed her of the new twist in the propaganda of the Congregation, which was in accordance with Cecil's instructions. The earl of Argyll was spreading reports that the French intended to occupy the kingdom and expel the inhabitants.[209]

204. Pollen, pp. xxxi-xxxviii and xliii-xlv. *Calendar of State Papers, Elizabeth, Foreign*, iii, 344.
205. Andrew Lang, *John Knox and the Reformation*, pp. 140-148.
206. *Sadler Papers*, i, pp. 375-7: *Calendar of State Papers, Scotland*, i, no. 537. *Calendar of State Papers, Elizabeth, Foreign*, i, pp. 518-9.
207. J. E. Neale, *Elizabeth*, p. 94.
208. R. K. Hannay, *The Earl of Arran and Queen Mary*, Scot. Hist. Rev., xviii, p. 263.
209. *The Scottish Correspondence of Mary of Lorraine*, pp. 424-8.

On October 16, Châtelherault and the Congregation entered Edinburgh and falsely accused the regent of breaking the truce by fortifying Leith. When she refused to desist, Cecil's plan was put into operation: she was deposed from the regency and a committee was formed to govern the country. To finance their operations they seized the rents of Archbishop Hamilton and appointed factors in the sees of Ross, Dunkeld, Dunblane and Glasgow. Bishop William Chisholm (I) was kidnapped; he was held until Christmas and was forced to pay the expenses of his captors.[210] The Congregation issued proclamation in the name of Francis and Mary, signed by a forged seal.[211] Within a month they had to abandon their artillery and flee from Edinburgh, to the jeers of the townsfolk. Archbishop Hamilton reconsecrated St. Giles. The canons regular were restored in Holyrood and some members of the Congregation, including Robert Stewart, commendator of Holyrood, and Lord Ruthven, submitted to the regent.[212] By Christmas, the Congregation was expelled from Stirling; the regent's French troops were within reach of St. Andrews when an English fleet appeared in the Forth on January 23. A few weeks later they intercepted Bishop Adam Bothwell who had embarked in a small ship in an attempt to return to Orkney; he was taken to St. Andrews.[213]

English military intervention, which marks the third phase of the revolution, resulted from the tortuous diplomacy of Cecil. As a signatory of the treaty of Cateau-Cambrésis of 1559, the English government had undertaken not to help Scottish rebels. To circumvent this treaty and hoodwink Philip II of Spain, who was then displaying an interest in Scottish affairs, Cecil turned to subterfuge. Less than a week after the Congregation's flight from Edinburgh, he gave instructions outlining the proposals, which the Congregation were to put forward to obtain English military aid. " It is thought meet for divers respects that the nobility of Scotland should in their distress conceive and direct their suit to the Queen's majesty upon these articles following, the enlarging thereof is to be left to their considerations."[214] Elizabeth and many members of her council opposed active intervention, but she was forced into authorising this policy, by Cecil's threat of resignation.[215]

The terms of the Treaty of Berwick, February 27, 1560, between the representatives of Elizabeth and those of Châtelherault, followed the instructions outlined by Cecil.[216] Nothing was said about religion: Elizabeth took Scotland under her protection and promised military aid in the expulsion of the French, only for the preservation of Scottish freedom and liberty, during the marriage of Queen Mary to the king of France, and for one year afterwards. The Scots, while denying any intention of withdrawing allegiance from Mary, proceeded to do so by making a military alliance with England. Cecil had correctly assessed the risks involved, since Throckmorton had informed him in December of the Huguenot plot, which resulted in the Tumult of Amboise in

---

210. *Report by De la Brosse and D'Oysel on Conditions in Scotland.* Miscellany of Scot. Hist. Soc., ix, p. 103.
211. *Ibid.*, pp. 93 and 124.
212. Pollen, p. 417-8.
213. *Two Missions of Jacques de la Brosse*, Scot. Hist. Soc., p. 74.
214. *Sadler Papers*, i, p. 569. Calendar of State Papers, Foreign, p. 103-6.
215. Neale, *Elizabeth*, pp. 99-100.
216. *Source Book*, pp. 169-71.

March, and immobilised French aid on a large scale.[217] Among those who signed the Treaty of Berwick were Archbishop Alexander Gordon, Gavin Hamilton, abbot of Kilwinning and coadjutor of St. Andrews, and the earl of Huntly. The English army entered Scotland at the beginning of April, but attempts were made to arrive at a peaceful settlement, which were wrecked by the insistence of the Hamiltons on the demolition of Leith.[218]

A combined Anglo-Scots attack on Leith on May 7 was repulsed with heavy losses; the English wounded were left untended in the streets of Edinburgh. Five weeks later Mary of Lorraine died, and on July 7 the Treaty of Edinburgh ended hostilities. A clause of this treaty expressly stated that the question of religion was to be remitted to the king and queen. For this clause Cecil provided an explanation. He found the question of religion " too hot to meddle with " : he complained of the religious intransigence of the Scottish nobles and expressed the fear that their " folly would hazard all."[219] This clause was a dead letter as far as the Congregation was concerned; five superintendents had been nominated by the lords of the council, in accordance with the First Book of Discipline, which had been drawn up in May. The Reformation was accomplished before parliament met in the following August and the celebration of mass was forbidden wherever the Congregation had control.

Throughout the revolution there were only seven sees with bishops in full possession. The bishopric of the Isles was vacant: Caithness and Argyll were held by bishops-elect and papal confirmation was awaited for Ross, Brechin and Galloway. Of the seven bishops in full possession of their sees, one, Adam Bothwell of Orkney, defected. He had been nominated by Mary of Lorraine and seems to have been of very pliable character. He is considered to have been very much under the influence of his uncle, Sir John Bellenden, the Justice-Clerk, who later " probably extroted " the bishop's services, for the marriage of Mary Queen of Scots and the earl of Bothwell.[220] It is probable that Adam Bothwell's defection was due to the influence exerted by Lord James Stewart and other leaders of the Congregation, when the bishop was taken to St. Andrews in 1560. Alexander Gordon, who had been consecrated as archbishop of Athens *in partibus*, owed his ecclesiastical promotion to his support of Mary of Lorraine. The archbishop, like two of the bishops-elect, James Hamilton and Donald Campbell, who also defected, had a number of illegitimate offspring. Their action lends credence to the explanation of Bishop Lesley, that the statutes of the provincial council of 1559, led a number of clerics to join the rebels.[221] Robert Stewart, bishop-elect of Caithness, who had been nominated by James V and was probably never in major orders, was considered " simple and of lyttle action or accomte."[222]

Of the six bishops who remained faithful to the church, there were only two, James Beaton (II) of Glasgow and Robert Crichton of Dunkeld, whose episcopal status had not been weakened by scandal or family connection. The exchange of letters between Archbishop Hamilton and

---

217. Neale, *Elizabeth*, pp. 99 and 103. *The Age of Catherine de Medici*, pp. 47-8.
218. *Two Missions of Jacques de la Brosse*, p. 125.
219. *Cecil MSS., Hist. MSS. Comm.*, part i, pp. 241 and 247.
220. Spottiswoode, *The History of the Church of Scotland*, ii, p. 73.
221. Lesley, *op. cit.*, p. 271.
222. *Scots Peerage*, v, p. 355.

PLATE V. DETAIL OF THE SIXTEENTH-CENTURY CHOIR SCREEN,
KING'S COLLEGE, ABERDEEN.

the earl of Argyll, occasioned by the latter's appointment of a protestant preacher, illustrates the difficulties of a baronial primate of irregular life.[223] His position was further aggravated when his half-brother, Châtelherault, took over the leadership of the Congregation. Bishop William Gordon, also of scandalous life, was further compromised when his nephew, the earl of Huntly, joined the Congregation. The defection of Patrick Hepburn of Moray, which at one time seemed probable, would not have resulted in a great loss. William Chisholm (I) of Dunblane likewise incelibate, had been incapacited by illness since early 1559[224] Archbishop Beaton went to France after the death of Mary of Lorraine and was Scottish ambassador in Paris until his death in 1603. Robert Crichton of Dunkeld, whose provision had been opposed by Arran and Mary of Lorraine, was the only bishop with sufficient courage to interview the papal nuncio, Nicolas de Gouda, in 1562.

Patrick Hepburn of Moray, whose nephew, the earl of Bothwell, had supported the regent, and William Gordon of Aberdeen, probably under the influence of Huntly, did not attend the "Reformation Parliament" in August. There is no question that the parliament was illegal and its composition and procedure were equally unusual. There was a departure from established practice in the large numbers of lesser barons or lairds who were present. They probably attended as a result of a summons from the protestant Privy Council, which no doubt was addressed only to those who were assured supporters of the reformers. The spiritual members of the committee of the Lords of the Articles were elected mainly from those clerics who had defected. The only exception was Gavin Hamilton, coadjutor to St. Andrews, who occupied a dubious position. He signed the Treaty of Berwick, but Archbishop Hamilton stated that he opposed the adoption of the Confession of Faith.[225] The Lords of the Articles by established practice, formed a committee which normally carried out the business of parliament.

Apart from those who defected, only three bishops attended, Archbishop Hamilton, William Chisholm (I) of Dunblane and Robert Crichton of Dunkeld. Attempts had been made to force the adherence of the first two. Bishop Crichton seems to have been ignored; he may have been considered to be without influence or unlikely to accept reformed opinions. All three refused to accept the Confession of Faith, but they have been strongly criticized for not displaying more energetic opposition.[226] Archbishop Hamilton in particular, because of the reported pusillanimity of his attitude, has been considered a crypto-protestant.[227] Generally there has been an unfavourable comparison with the conduct of the English hierarchy in 1559.[228] With the exception of that episcopal " vicar of Bray," Anthony Kitchin of Llandaff, all the English bishops refused to take the Oath of Supremacy. Archbishop Heath of York and Bishop Scott of Chester vigorously denounced the bill to restore the royal supremacy, in the House of Lords.

---

223. Herkless and Hannay, v, pp. 89-92.
224. *Scottish Correspondence of Mary of Lorraine*, pp. 415 and 423.
225. Letter to Archbishop Beaton, Keith, *History of Affairs of Church and State in Scotland*, iii, pp. 4-7.
226. Bellesheim, *History of the Catholic Church of Scotland*, trans. Hunter Blair, ii, p. 302 seq.
227. Herkless and Hannay, v, p. 128.
228. Cf. C. G. Mortimer, " The Scottish Hierarchy in 1560," *The Clergy Review*, xii, pp. 422-450.

There were, however, very significant differences between the two hierarchies. Most of the English bishops were distinguished theologians and lawyers, who had been promoted to the episcopal bench, almost exclusively, as a reward for loyal service to the crown, usually over a long period. They were recruited mainly from the squirearchy and, generally, were not sons of the greater nobles. There were no baronial bishops such as the Hamiltons, the Hepburns or the Gordons.[229] More important, the catholic restoration under Mary Tudor had resulted in a reconstituted hierarchy.

Comparison with the specifically parliamentary procedure of the Elizabethan religious settlement, also ignores the peculiar status of the Scottish " Reformation Parliament." It must have been obvious to the Scottish prelates that in dealing with the religious question, parliament was contravening the Treaty of Edinburgh: it was also equally apparent that the reformation had already been accomplished in fact. The acts of parliament then passed explicitly make that admission.[230] Why then did the bishops attend ? The explanation may be found in clause thirteen of the concession made to the Scots in the Treaty of Edinburgh. Bishops, abbots and other clerics, who complained that they had received " any harm either in person or goods . . . and such reparation shall be appointed as to the said estates shall appear to be reasonable."[231]

This clause was probably due to Archbishop Hamilton, who had sent a memorandum to the Bishop of Valence, representing Francis II and Mary in the negotiations, which led to the treaty.[232] In addition to the request for the return of their property, and guarantees of personal safety, he had recommended that a commissioner be sent from France to hold the parliament and control legislation. His advice was not accepted and the most reasonable interpretation of the archbishop's subsequent actions, is that he attempted to use his influence to cause delay and minimise religious differences. Thus a restoration of catholicism would be less difficult. His letter of August 18, to Archbishop Beaton in Paris, confirms that such was his hope; " I neither can nor will I think that our sovereign will let all this country be oppressed wrongously by subjects: but I will not judge until I see the uttermost."

This is a more adequate explanation than those based on the most sinister interpretations of some of the archbishop's actions. To his half-brother, Châtelherault, he expressed his determination to die a catholic and he refused to assent to the Treaty of Edinburgh. Yet in the " Reformation Parliament," he expressed approval of a scheme for the marriage of the earl of Arran to Queen Elizabeth. He had expressed his readiness to obey Châtelherault in everything except matters of conscience.[233] He was thus conciliatory but opposed to compromise in matters of faith and his attitude on other occasions should, therefore, be interpreted in that light.

---

229. Lacy Baldwin Smith, *Tudor Prelates and Politics*, 1953, chapters i-iii.
230. *Source Book*, p. 186. See above.
231. *Ibid.*, p. 184. This clause was ignored. Cf. Letter of Thomas Archibald, Chamberlain of the Archbishopric of Glasgow, August 28, 1560. Keith, iii, pp. 7-10.
232. Keith, iii, pp. 2-3.
233. Herkless and Hannay, v, pp. 131-2.

Spottiswoode relates that the archbishop sent a canon regular of Holyrood to ask John Knox to retain the " old polity." His advocacy of episcopacy in this instance has been interpreted as displaying an ambiguous attitude. The primate on that occasion, however, explained his motives. " The multitude, that beast with many heads, should just be so dealt with."[234] There is no reason for doubting the sincerity of this explanation and Archbishop Hamilton was not exceptional in holding such views. The Anabaptist aberrations at Munster, in 1534, when polygamy was justified by an appeal to the Old Testament, were still fresh in the minds of that generation. When Archbishop Parker of Canterbury heard of the Scottish reformation, his comment was—" God keep us from such a visitation as Knox has attempted in Scotland, the people to be orderers of things." The excesses of the Peasants' Wars in Germany probably occasioned the advice of Cardinal Wolsey from his deathbed in Leicester Abbey. Heresy was to be suppressed because it led to civil disorder: " there is no trust in routs, or unlawful assemblies of the common people: for when the riotous multitude be assembled, there is among them no mercy or consideration of their bounden duty."[235] It is not improbable that Knox and his brethren were aware of such fears when they roused the " rascal multitude."

The prelates, apparently, hoped to delay parliamentary ratification of the religious revolution, as they asked for time to consider the Confession of Faith. They may have hoped for the arrival of a French commissioner, as requested by Archbishop Hamilton, to control legislation. For a report of their attitude in parliament, we are dependent mainly on Maitland of Lethington, who cannot be considered disinterested. Similarly, John Brand who delivered the primate's message to John Knox, was later a minister of the reformed church. The catholic prelates who attended the reformation parliament are stated to have admitted the need for reform, to have expressed their willingness to abolish abuses contrary to scripture and to agree with all that might stand with God's Word. To interpret this as an acceptance of the protestant principle of an appeal to the bible in matters of faith, is to read abuses only in a protestant sense and to ignore catholic doctrine of the living word.[236]

The establishment of the reformed church was achieved as a result of the collapse of royal authority, English intervention and the land-hunger of the Scottish nobility. The " rascal multitude," apparently so prone to iconoclasm, could not be persuaded to fight for the Congregation at Leith, hence national consciousness was less effective than we are sometimes led to believe. Throughout the revolution, the hierarchy was divided and had little religious or political influence. Of the eleven bishops and bishops-elect, seven were baronial prelates, John and James Hamilton, William and Alexander Gordon, Patrick Hepburn, Donald Campbell and Robert Stewart. With the possible exception of Robert Stewart, all had been incelibate and of the seven, four defected. William Chisholm (I) of Dunblane might almost be included in this group: he had a number of illegitimate off-spring and apparently indulged that landhunger, which was characteristic of the nobility. Of the others,

---

234. Spottiswoode, *op. cit.*, i, p. 372.
235. Cavendish, *Life of Wolsey*, Temple Classics, p. 245 seq.
236. Cf. G. H. Tavard, *Holy Writ or Holy Church*, chapter xii. The Council of Trent, esp. p. 208.

Adam Bothwell defected and James Beaton (II) went, some would say fled, to France in July, 1560. It is significant that the provision of the courageous and truly episcopal Robert Crichton had been opposed by the crown authorities.

If the role of the Scottish hierarchy throughout the revolution cannot be considered glorious, the explanation must be sought in the actions of the crown. For a period of thirty years before the reformation, there was a deliberate and persistent misuse of the right of nomination, of which the composition of the hierarchy in 1560 provides sombre testimony. In the exercise of their spiritual duties, the bishops were also impeded by the mercenary and mundane policies of James V, Arran and Mary of Lorraine. The myth that the hierarchy was primarily to blame for the decline and destruction of the pre-reformation church had its origin in the attempts of Mary of Lorraine, and the French Monarchy, to disclaim responsibility and to divert attention from their bankrupt policy of conciliation.

PARISH LIFE IN SCOTLAND,

1500-1560

by

DENIS McKAY

The life of the parish was integrated at this period. There was no sharp division between church life on one hand and social and economic life on the other. The morning peal of the church bell at five in summer and six in winter was at once a signal to the chaplain for the turn to come forth to say " morrow mass ", and a notice to the guildsman to take up his tools for the day's work: the " aucht houris " bell in the evening was not only the curfew but a signal for prayer. The parish clergy had many civic duties not directly connected with the cure of souls. It was the duty of the parish priest, for example, to warn mothers and nurses not to overlie infants.[1] It was he, with his parish clerk, who was to be summoned to provide a list of parishioners for the census which the Lords of the Articles proposed to hold in 1556.[2] The parish church, too, was used for many purposes other than divine service. Often the only building of suitable size in the parish, it served as the common meeting place and news centre of the people and was used for purposes now answered by a public hall. Courts both civil and ecclesiastical were held in the parish church: parliament sometimes met in a great parish church: it was used as a bank and an exchange with money payments made on a specified altar as an essential part of the transaction.[3] It was also used as a prison and a mortuary.[4] This unification of the secular and religious life had good results, but it also encouraged evil practices. It was admirable, for example, that craftsmen should combine in guilds not solely, or even primarily, for their own industrial and commercial advantage, but also as fraternities bound to the practice of religion and the exercise of charity. On the other hand, the familiar use of the parish church for secular purposes led to a grave lack of reverence for the building which provoked official condemnation of " carreling and wanton synging in the kirk ", and of those people who " beand in the kirk in the tyme of Goddis word or service, occupies thameself in vaine, evil or ony warldly talking, lauchhing, scorning or ony siclik doingis."[5] It was also thought necessary to warn the clergy against irreverent behaviour in church.[6]

Who were the parish clergy at this time? Andrew Forman, Archbishop of St. Andrews (1516-1521), in synodal constitutions, enumerated the parish clergy as rectors, vicars perpetual, portioner and pensioner, chaplains with or without cure, and parish clerks.[7] To the rector (or parson, as he was usually known) fell the rule and cure of souls in the parish. It was his duty to see to the due celebration of mass and the administration of the sacraments. Yet the parishioners of many churches

---

1. *Statutes of the Scottish Church*, pp. 273-4.
2. *Acts of Parliament of Scotland*, ii, p. 614.
3. *Protocol Book of Gavin Ros*, no. 173.
4. J. P. Lawson, *Book of Perth*, p. 59. But Fittis (*Ecclesiastical Annals of Perth*, p. 37) claims that this was a post-reformation use of Halkerston's Tower at St. John's Kirk in Perth.
5. *Archbishop Hamilton's Catechism*, ed. Mitchell, fol. xxxvi.
6. *Statutes of the Scottish Church*, pp. 260-1.
7. *Ibid.*, p. 260.

never saw their rector. It is estimated that, of the thousand-odd parish churches which served the country, over nine hundred were appropriated that is to say, they had been gifted to a monastery, or cathedral, or collegiate church, which was then regarded as the rector and served the parish cure by appointing a vicar and sharing the teinds of the parish with him. For example, when a parish was appropriated to a prebendal stall in a cathedral, the canon or prebendary of the cathedral who drew his allowance (prebenda) from the fruits of the parish church was absolved through his duties in the major church from direct service in the parish church of which he was rector or vicar plenary. Thus, on 1st June, 1555, William Tunno, schoolmaster at Peebles, was appointed to the parish church of Menar, one of the churches appropriated to the *personatus* of the archdeacon of Glasgow, the most important member of the bishop's *familia*. Alexander Dick, the archdeacon, nominated Tunno who was known as vicar pensioner or curate of Menar, allowing him a pension of twenty-four marks, as well as the small casual offerings of the parishioners, which he was to enjoy, together with a manse and glebe.[8]

Two other methods of sharing the fruits of the parish between rector and vicar were practised. Firstly, the vicar, and not the rector, collected the whole income of the parish and paid the rector a pension: Sir George Mason, curate of Campsie, made this kind of arrangement with his rector (in 1506)[9]: and secondly, the third and oldest method of division was for the vicar to receive the smaller or vicarage teinds of hay and flax, and the yearly produce of stock animals, lambs, calves, foals, geese, etc., as well as offerings from the people (e.g., the Pasch fines, paid at Easter), while the rector received the great teinds or teind sheaves levied upon all grain, wheat, oats, barley, etc., the chief source of teind income.

In those parishes in which the rector claimed the great teinds, he had the duty of " leading and uplifting " the teind sheaves from the fields on notice from the parishioner that they were ready, the fair division of the crop (nominally one-tenth to the rector) being assessed by witnesses.[10] But by the first half of the sixteenth century the rector had in many cases disembarrassed himself, not only of the task of having the teind sheaves uplifted, but also of the trouble of collecting the money payment which had in some cases been arranged in commutation.[11] A parochial middleman, the tacksman of the teind, collected the fruits of the parish and paid the rector a rent, a suitable arrangement for the rector if the parish were distant. The tacksman also paid the pensions of the parish clergy. In 1537 the rectorial and vicarage teinds of the churches of Roskene and Slamannan were farmed out to a layman, Robert Hamilton of Briggis, who had the duty of paying the parish chaplain.[12] In 1558, at Bendochy, a lay tacksman paid the " just and usual salary " of the parish priest and the parish clerk.[13]

Even when the rector was not a member of a corporate body he might still be absent from his parish on royal business: he might be studying at a university[14]: he might be a minor or a layman not able to act in the

---

8. *Cartularium Glasguense*, transcribed, J. Dillon, ii, pp. 1546-1549.
9. *Diocesan Registers of Glasgow*, no. 184.
10. *Protocol Book of Dominus Thomas Johnsoun*, no. 344; *Protocol Book of James Foulis*, no. 185.
11. *Chartulary of Lindores Abbey*, no. cxxiii.
12. *Protocol Book of Dominus Thomas Johnsoun*, nos. 121, 222.
13. *Register of the Great Seal*, 1546-1580, no. 1779.
14. *St. Andrews Formulare*, i, no. 15.

cure[15]: he might be a pluralist holding more than one benefice: or he might be living on his rectory as a retirement pension in his old age.[16]

A non-resident rector might still take an active interest in his parish. Even if the rector had farmed out his church to a tacksman he still had to see that the parish clergy received their pensions. In 1540, the rector of Slamannan issued a warrant to his tacksman to pay the pension of eight pounds due to a chaplain.[17] William Muir found many examples of a rector supervising the work of his vicar.[18] He outlines the attention paid to the church of Dysart by Robert Danielston, a notable pluralist, who combined his rectory of Dysart with that of Ayr, as well as a canonry in the Chapel Royal, Stirling.[19] The vicar of Dysart, George Strachan, who was appointed to an altar in St. Serf's church, Dysart, while he was vicar of Channelkirk, later rising to be parish priest of Dysart, appointed a parish chaplain to do his work in St. Serf's parish, without consulting the rector. Danielston protested in 1551 against this action of Strachan, but the latter continued in his vicarage and added another chaplainry to his appointments. In 1553, the rector went to the parish church of Dysart on the " vigil of the holy pasch " and, finding Strachan absent from duty, took out a notarial instrument stating that, since the vicar did not officiate in the cure, the rector had no need to pay him his pension.[20] Strachan, however, survived the attention of the rector and the changes at the reformation to die as the bachelor vicar of Dysart in 1587.

Examples can also be found of an active interest in parochial affairs of an abbot whose convent held a rectory. Although the abbey of Lindores had contracted out of the maintenance of the choir of St. Mary's, Dundee, in 1443, abbot John made generous grants of money to repair the damage done to the choir by " our auld enemies of England " when they burned the greater part of Dundee in 1548.[21] Abbots are found taking an active part in the election of parish clerks. The abbot of Paisley, as rector of Neilston, personally attended the appointment of Gavin Maxwell of Breidland as parish clerk of Neilston in 1552.[22] At the election of the clerk at Mauchline, in 1524, the abbot of Melrose made necessary and apparently successful intervention to preserve his rights of patronage in the church against local interests which were challenging them.[23] There is no doubt, however, that the well-accepted medieval principle—*qui facit per alium facit per se*—worked to the disadvantage of the parishioners. Absent rectors were tempted to have the job of parish priest done for as little cost as possible, sometimes appointing a stipendiary, the parish chaplain, with no security of tenure, and possibly failing to pay him his due.[24] But precepts from Rome and local synodal statutes[25] had

---

15. *Protocol Book of Mark Carruthers*, no. 1.
16. *St. Andrews Formulare*, i, no. 112.
17. *Protocol Book of Dominus Thomas Johnsoun*, no. 222.
18. William Muir, *Antiquities of Dysart*, p. 16.
19. *Fasti Ecclesiae Scoticanae*, 8, p. 424.
20. *Antiquities of Dysart*, p. 16.
21. Maxwell, *Old Dundee*, pp. 125-126.
22. Hutton, Collections of the Shires, ii, 25.
23. *Protocol Book of Gavin Ros*, no. 725; cf. no. 975.
24. *Protocol Book of John Cristisone*, no. 415.
25. " Quod quelibet ecclesia parochialis proprium rectorem habeat seu vicarium perpetuum in loco residentem " (*Reg. Epis. Aberd.*, i, p. 77).

made this chaplain irremovable by the rector, once he had been collated by the bishop.[26] He had become the perpetual vicar pensioner.

Parish clergy described as perpetual, for instance, a perpetual chaplain or a perpetual parish clerk, were appointed for life. The creation of a class of parish priest known as perpetual vicar did not end the appointment of parish chaplains with no fixity of tenure. A mere stipendiary removable at the will of the rector could still be appointed with the consent of the bishop.[27] In many cases, too, the vicar pensioner himself appointed a parish chaplain to do his work or to help him, as in the case at Dysart mentioned above. The terms " portioner " and " pensioner " refer to the method of paying the vicar and not to his tenure, which was perpetual. The portion of the revenue of the parish church received by a vicar portioner was perhaps one half,[28] while the fixed pension paid to a vicar would be much less. For example, in 1542, the whole fruits of the rectory and vicarage of Alveth, Banffshire, came to eighty pounds approximately, of which the vicar pensioner received ten pounds, along with his manse and glebe.[29] In this case he was also exempted from paying the " synodal ", a small honorific payment to the bishop and " procurations ", a payment of money made to the bishop to cover the cost of the hospitable entertainment which the bishop could claim for himself and his train on visitations. A vicar had also the right to make a collection on an " alms board " or dish.[30]

Chaplain was a general term for priest. The parish chaplain (*capellanus parochialis*) was the parish priest or curate. He assisted or deputised for the rector or vicar at the high altar of the parish church, where, in the absence of his principal, he celebrated the parish mass and administered the sacraments to the people. The vicar of Dundee and his parish chaplain were jointly responsible for the cure of souls of St. Mary's parish, Dundee.[31] Parish chaplains were *capellani curati*. The great majority of chaplains were without parochial cure. To this class of priest belonged a chaplain attached to the service of an individual, " the chaplain of the Stewart ", for example, celebrating mass in a chapel and possibly performing secretarial duties and instructing the children of the family: a chaplain employed in an institution, such as the chaplain of St. Michael's chapel in Rothesay Castle: a chaplain attached to a guild with the duty of serving the altar maintained by the guild in the parish church, and possibly helping with confessions[32]: a " chantry " chaplain celebrating requiem masses according to the terms of a foundation in a chapel or college, or at one of the side altars ranged round the walls and pillars of a burgh church: or a priest in charge of a side chapel, such as the chapel of the Blessed Virgin at the east end of the town of Linlithgow.[33]

A chaplain without cure was appointed by a patron from the ranks of the chantry priests: by a nobleman choosing a family chaplain: by a member of the family which founded the chaplainry, in this case " a

26. Dowden, *Medieval Church*, p. 64.
27. Dowden, *Medieval Church*, p. 124.
28. Ducange, *s.v.* portionarius.
29. Dowden, *Medieval Church*, p. 124.
30. Liber Sententiarum Officialis Sanctiandree, f. 19.r; Ayr Burgh Court Book, i, f. 60v.
31. *Reg. Epis. Brechin.*, i, p. 155.
32. *Registrum Cartarum S. Egidii*, p. 216.
33. *Protocol Book of Dominus Thomas Johnsoun*, no. 10.

chaplain of my own kindred and blood ",[34] if possible, even if it meant appointing a minor with a vicar to serve the altar for him[35]: by a craft guild, by a group of parishioners,[36] or by the burgh council appointing a chaplain to one of the altars which they maintained in the parish church, and paying him out of the common good.

The commonest method of paying chaplains was from rents raised on a ground annual. A tenement was given in endowment of an altar and the chaplain of the altar for the time, or his representative, was given sasine at the site of the ground or building by accepting " earth and stane ", or a penny, or both, from the donor through a bailie.[37] In 1542, Bernard Carngyll, perpetual vicar of Banff and Innerboyndie, was able to purchase an annual rent of ten merks for two hundred pounds Scots. This annual rent was to be given to a chaplain in Aberdeen Cathedral.[38] At the foundation of a chaplainry, the lands producing the rents for the upkeep of the chaplain were specified in the charter of foundation. In addition to the income from ground annuals, chaplains could count on money offered for prayers, and on a share in the donations for the many requiem masses provided for in wills, which sometimes called for the services of thirty or more chaplains, some celebrating a mass, some making responses to another, and some merely attending and adding to the dignity of the service. In some cases, a chaplain, particularly a guild chaplain, was paid in kind, receiving his meals at the houses of the craftsmen. An appointment to an altar at Elgin, made by the town council, provided " honest board " in the houses of eight and, at the most, fourteen neighbours.[39] A chaplain chorister, whose duty it was to sing in the choir at St. Nicholas's, Aberdeen, had a weekly rota of houses, where he could have his meals, dining at the provost's house on Mondays and with other burgesses for the rest of the week, except Friday, when he dined with the parish priest,[40] probably on good red fish, coarse bread and wine or beer. When his annual rents were not paid, as sometimes happened, a chaplain might foolishly take the law into his own hands, like Sir John Hay of Stirling, who seized a brazen pot in distraint,[41] but he could always count on the help of the town sergeants to help him collect his dues.

The poorest of the chaplains had a very modest living. Some made up for the smallness of their rewards by holding two or more chaplainries or other office. Some added to their income by trading. Sir William Corstorphine was granted the Lady Service at the college of Crail in 1553 on the understanding that he gave up trading, under the penalty of a fine of one hundred pounds.[42] Although a priest might help to till his glebe (a chaplain at Dunglas was charged to keep his garden well[43]), he was forbidden to engage in trade.[44] Evasion of this ban on trading was

34. *Muniments of the Royal Burgh of Irvine*, i, p. 177.
35. *Protocol Book of Gilbert Grote*, nos. 152, 153.
36. *Protocol Book of John Foular*, ii, no. 3.
37. *Protocol Book of Dominus Thomas Johnsoun*, no. 238.
38. Cramond, *Annals of Banff*, ii, p. 14.
39. Cramond, *Records of Elgin*, i, p. 87.
40. *Cart. S. Nich. Aberd.*, ii, pp. 354-5.
41. *Scottish Antiquary*, x, p. 168.
42. Beveridge, *Churchyard Memorials of Crail*, p. 27.
43. *MSS. of the Duke of Athole*, p. 125.
44. *Statutes of the Scottish Church*, nos. 22, 23, 63.

common and persistent enough to provoke fresh prohibitions at the provincial councils held in 1549[45] and 1559[46].

It was forbidden to sell for profit, fish, salt, butter and other foodstuffs, as well as wool and other merchandise. Another example of a trader chaplain is found at Ayr, where Sir William Reid engaged in the important salt trade selling twenty bolls for ten pounds in November, 1518.[47] Some of the salt he sold may have been produced at the saltpans of Prestwick,[48] but he also imported salt. In May, 1519, he and a layman partner purchased one-third share of a cargo of salt, wine and iron due to be discharged at Ayr.[49] Sir William Reid was among the richer chaplains. So also were those who were able to lend money. Sir John Polwart, who held altars at Linlithgow and Torphichen, was able to make a loan of twenty shillings and eightpence, apparently free of interest.[50] Sir John was a good manager of his affairs. He was wise enough in his generation to survive the changes of 1560 in comfort. In December, 1568, he was able to trade over the income from his altars to a relative who contracted to keep him for life, providing " meat and drink as an honest man ought to have . . . an honest chamber . . . with honest bedding, fire and candle in time convenient." His linen clothes were to be kept washed and he was to have, in addition, twenty merks of money per year.[51]

It will be remembered that the affairs of the worldly sort of chaplain were more likely to get into the records. Less is heard of such devoted priests as Sir Robert Rhind, "daily orator and chaplain of Perth", who in 1547 was given the freedom of the city because he kept such "good hour" that " the whole community and neighbours, who rise early to their labours " could easily hear God's service, because he left all other duties for the business of his chaplaincy, and because his " sober annuals " would " not give him sustentation once in the day ".[52]

The approved dress of a chaplain was a gown or cassock of coarse woollen cloth,[53] dark in colour and girded with a belt. In churches and populous places he was to wear a long gown reaching to the ankles, but on a journey a short one was allowed.[54] He was to wear a white shirt. His head-dress was the round bonnet (biretta). These rules were not always observed. Archbishop Forman found cause to forbid gowns ornamented with pleats at the back, with long, wide and spacious sleeves such as might be worn by a wealthy burgess. He also condemned dangling hair, full beards and bonnets laced with small cords after the fashion of the laity.[55] These complaints were taken up again by the provincial council of 1549, which ordered priests to shave off their beards so that they might be distinguished from lay people. They were also to see that the tonsure which they had received, before or with minor orders, was kept becomingly cut.[56] They were not to wear top-boots and doublets

---

45. *Ibid.*, no. 175.
46. *Ibid.*, no. 266.
47. *Protocol Book of Gavin Ros*, no. 273.
48. *Prestwick Burgh Records*, pp. 23, 29.
49. *Protocol Book of Gavin Ros*, no. 324.
50. *Protocol Book of Dominus Thomas Johnsoun*, no. 655.
51. *Ibid.*, no. 815.
52. *The Perth Hammermen Book*, p. xxii.
53. *Statutes of the Scottish Church*, p. 94.
54. *Statutes of the Scottish Church*, p. 176.
55. *Ibid.*, p. 269.
56. *Ibid.*, p. 93.

or oddly-cut coats or coats " of forbidden colours, as yellow, green and such kinds of parti-colour ".[57] This predilection of some clerics for unorthodox hair styles[58] and gay raiment,[59] like other failings of the clergy, was not just a feature of the period. It had been a problem for the bishop from the thirteenth century, not only in Scotland, but also in England and on the continent.[60]

There were no seminaries for the training of priests. In burghs, clerical students were trained for the priesthood in the song school and grammar school, and through service in the church. At the parish church of St. Nicholas, Aberdeen, the town council granted clerkships, a kind of scholarship collected from the parishioners, to choir boys who were expected to go through the schools and so qualify to act as chaplain or parish clerk. A reference to this arrangement is found in the burgh records of Aberdeen where, in 1503, the choir boy, John Marr, having received permission to pass to the schools, appointed Christie Nairn, a choir boy who had been through the song school, to deputise for him in the choir while he studied in the little school and the grammar school.[61] It was through study in the schools and through practical service in the church that young clerics in Aberdeen reached major orders. In 1531, the provost and council engaged Patrick Cumming to sing in the choir till he " be promovit to the order of prestheid "[62] when he reached the canonical age of twenty-four, having received the first tonsure and the four minor orders from the bishop at one ceremony when a boy.

Priests pursuing higher studies attended one of the three universities, St. Andrews, Glasgow and Aberdeen. The number of university graduates among the clergy was naturally not high, but at a university centre this might not be so. For example, out of seventy-eight chaplains who served in the church of the Holy Trinity, St. Andrews, at one time or another, thirty were graduates.[63] Graduate priests were called " Master " and non-graduates (or bachelors proceeding to the degree of master) were given the honorific title " Sir ", which might be compared with the title " Father " accorded to parochial clergy within the last century. Up to mid-nineteenth century it was customary among catholics to address a priest, if secular, as " Mr.", while " Father ", now commonly given to all, was reserved to priests of a religious order. The title " Sir " became the sport of critics of the church, like Sir David Lindsay, but was the official title of, for instance, John Kipper, who was released by the St. Andrews Kirk Session on recanting, describing himself as " sumtym knycht of the Papis Kirk ".[64] So, according to Foxe, Walter Myln was formally addressed in court, " Sir Walter, arise," but he replied; " They call me Walter, not Sir Walter. I have been over long one of the Pope's knights."[65]

Although bishops were ordaining priests unskilled in music " who ought to know Gregorian chant at least ",[66] chaplains in burgh churches

57. *Ibid.*, p. 92.
58. *Ibid.*, p. 12.
59. *Ibid.*, p. 12.
60. *Ibid.*, p. lxviii and footnote.
61. *Cart. S. Nich. Aberd.*, ii, p. 342.
62. *Cart. S. Nich. Aberd.*, ii, p. 327.
63. Rankin, *Parish Church of the Holy Trinity, St. Andrews*, p. 35.
64. *St. Andrews Kirk Session Records*, pp. 81-82.
65. Laing's *Knox*, i, p. 552.
66. John Major, *De Gest. Scot.*, lib. i, p. 20.

were expected to be singers. Town councils were insisting at this period that priests employed in the parish church should not merely be " plain " singers, that is, able to sing a Gregorian melody in unison, but also be able to sing " pricket " song, that is, to sing one of the countermelodies pricked or set down against a Gregorian melody. The chaplains at Crail in 1517 had " understandyng to sing plane sang, priket sang."[67] In 1508, the town council of Aberdeen had reserved all perpetual chaplainries in St. Nicholas's church "tile sangstaris that can sing plane sang ande prik sang at the lest."[68] At Holy Trinity, St. Andrews, likewise, it was agreed between the parish clergy and the town council, in 1527, that no priest was to be granted an altar in the church unless competent in " playn sang prickit sang and descant."[69] In 1553 Edinburgh town council allowed a chaplain of St. Giles leave of absence for a year to go to England and France to " get better eruditioun in musik and playing "[70] on the organs, which by this time were installed in every considerable church and taught by the master of the song school or the parish clerk.

There was much contemporary criticism of the training of the parish clergy. John Major complained that some could not sing Gregorian chant. Archibald Hay, who became principal of St. Mary's College, St. Andrews, warned Cardinal Beaton against the ordination of men who " hardly know the order of the alphabet ". The provincial council of 1549 declared that very many of the parish clergy were deficient in " learning, morals and discretion ".[71] This is only one side of the picture. In the burgh churches, the only kind of parish church of which we have fairly adequate records, the priests were apparently well enough educated for their jobs, some of them being notaries, schoolmasters, or common clerks charged with the duty of keeping the burgh records in Latin. The provincial council of 1552 required the rector or curate to read from Archbishop Hamilton's Catechism " for the space of half an hour before high mass, in a loud and audible voice, distinctly, clearly, articulately, and with attention to the stops ",[72] an impossible task for a man who hardly knew his ABC (litterarum series). The parish clergy were also charged with keeping various written records, registers of deaths, births, marriages, excommunicated persons and lists of parish clergy.[73]

Because of their training, chaplains were able to perform duties for the parishioners which were not directly concerned with the cure of souls. At Arbroath, chaplains often appeared in the burgh court as " for-speikers ", agents, for the people. On 6th April, 1530, Sir John Smith, vicar of Airlie, appeared as " forspeiker " in a case concerning a horse.[74] Very frequently they acted as witnesses to deeds executed in the parish church or elsewhere. The parish chaplain witnessed the wills of his parishioners. He might also act as a scrivener as, for instance, when Sir Thomas Russell, chaplain of Carstairs, wrote to his rector, the parson of Carstairs, in 1525; " Maister, I commend my seruice hertlie to zou.

---

67. *Register of the Collegiate Church of Crail*, p. 41.
68. *Spalding Miscellany*, v, pp. 36-37.
69. *Church of the Holy Trinity St. Andrews*, p. 134; cf. *Stirling Burgh Records*, p. 70.
70. *Memorabilia of the City of Glasgow*, ed. John Smith, p. 15.
71. *Statutes of the Scottish Church*, p. 110.
72. *Ibid.*, p. 146.
73. *Ibid.*, pp. 274-8.
74. G. Hay, *History of Arbroath*, p. 115.

Pleis zou to wit thar is ane barne callit Robe Jonston, rentalit in xl pennevorth of land in the towne of Carstaris quhilk is now liand seik lik to de. Alan Jonston in Ravinstruthir is this barnis fader brother and quhen his brother decessit left the barne to him. The barnis moder was sib to Andro Clerkson and was last possessor of this pece of land . . . and now the barne . . . hes left his kyndnes and gude will to Alan Jonston. Quharfor he hes causyt me wryt to zour M. . . . Jesus keip zou . . . Schir Thomas Russell, chaplane." [75]

Much of the information which we have on parish life at this period is found in the protocol books, or registers of deeds, which notaries public were bound by law to keep. The notary public was an important figure in the life of the parish, conducting much of the chamber practice now the concern of a lawyer, besides performing parochial functions such as chaplain and schoolmaster, like Gavin Ros of St. John's, Ayr: chaplain and parish clerk, like Sir Henry Loch of St. Giles', Edinburgh: or chaplain and town clerk, like Sir John Allan of Peebles. He enjoyed a good social position, sometimes staying with the laird and going to church with him.[76] In Scotland at this time, notaries public enjoyed a much superior status to their brethren in England where Edward II had confined their influence to the church courts. Notaries were enrolled by a protonotary apostolic at a ceremony of admission, at which they received a pen and pen case after examination,[77] enjoying thereafter the privilege of authenticating legal acts by the addition of their docquet and sign manual. Notaries were registered by the bishop and had power to act as his commissary and induct clerks to their benefice.[78] For the public, they made out instruments on leases, indentures, betrothals and marriages, dispensations, admissions and inductions of parish clergy and, often enough, on quite trivial matters, such as protests recorded on a legal instrument for persons mildly calumniated. The town council of Linlithgow, for example, took out a notarial instrument in 1539 to register their annoyance at the fact that James Brown, schoolmaster of Linlithgow, had in public expressed critical concern at the disruption of the work of his pupils caused by the parish priest's habit of taking the children from the school to St. Michael's church on feast days, which would be a considerable number, not only to morning mass, but also to vespers, there to sit " on cauld stanes ".[79] The great majority of the deeds made out by these priest-notaries (the lay notary begins to appear about 1540[80]), for small fees,[81] were evidence of title. Much of the work of some notaries, particularly those who were chaplains, was done in the church or the churchyard.

The parish clerk who assisted the parish priest in the church and parish appears in Scottish records in the early fourteenth century. Our fuller knowledge of him belongs to the period from the middle of the fifteenth century to the date of his disappearance at the time of the reformation. He was appointed directly by the bishop, or, more usually, presented to the bishop by a patron. The parishioners themselves were

75. *Diocesan Registers of Glasgow*, i, p. 55.
76. *Protocol Book of William Corbet*, no. 93.
77. *Protocol Book of Nicholas Thounis*, no. 46.
78. British Museum, Additional Charters, no. 19087.
79. *Protocol Book of Dominus Thomas Johnsoun*, no. 177.
80. *Reg. Epis. Aberd.*, ii, p. 323.
81. D. Murray, *Legal Practice in Ayr and the West of Scotland in the Fifteenth and Sixteenth Centuries*, pp. 71-72.

very frequently patrons, confirming the choice of clerk by a popular election often held in the church on Sunday before high mass, in the tolbooth, or at the homes of the people, or at all of these places. A notary public conducted the election orally with the assistance of the only candidate who asked the parishioners for their votes. The names of the voters were recorded on a notarial instrument to be sent to the bishop as a guarantee that the " greater and sounder " part of the parishioners accepted the choice of clerk. To this instrument the bishop attached a writ ordering the induction of the clerk-elect before returning it to the parish of origin. As the right to vote was based on the possession of land and the ability to pay parish dues, the names of women, always a small minority, and frequently widows possessed of the husbandlands of their dead spouses, appear among the voters. The *principales*, the greater landowners, had a ruling voice in this society conducted according to " degree, priority and place " with the result that the choice of clerk was usually a member of the local gentry, if possible a younger son, a Buchanan at Killearn,[82] a Gordon at Tullynessle,[83] a Kennedy at Colmonell.[84] The member of the landed family was, however, merely the principal parish clerk and acted through a paid deputy in many cases. The practice of appointing a well-born parish clerk brought little honour to the office because these gentle clerks were expected to take part in the quarrels of their class, the burnings, mutilations and killings which disturbed the peace of the countryside and town at this period. Rival families in a parish sometimes came to blows over the possession of the clerkship and the pension that went with it, as, for instance, when the Muirs and the Cunninghams fought at the parish church of Stewarton in 1508. When a parish clerk committed murder, he escaped the rope or axe because he was a tonsured cleric enjoying " benefit of clergy ". He was repledged from the civil court to the bishop's court, which could not deal in blood. These feuding clerks were generally from landward churches and were married men in minor orders. In burgh churches, however, the clerk was often in sacred orders and a chorister, sometimes a notary or schoolmaster and organist and, on occasion, town clerk as well.

The parish clerk was the vicar's clerk making the responses at mass and other services. A chaplain could only have the services of the parish clerk if the parish priest did not need him.[85] The clerk, or his servants, had to care for the high altar at which the vicar celebrated the parish mass, and look after its furnishings and vestments. Chaplains attended their own side altars but had the right to be supplied with a light and sufficient water, freshly drawn, by the clerk, for cruets, fonts and ablutions, under pain of report to the council. The parish clerk also had to see to the cleaning of the kirk and its regular sweeping with heather besoms, especially before greater feast days, and to the periodic renewal of rushes on the floor. His characteristic duty to the parishioners was his weekly tour of the parish with " holy water styk and stop " to asperse them in their homes.[86] As a reward for his services, the parish clerk was given a house and garden in some parishes. In every parish he

---

82. Fraser Charters, no. 97-1.
83. *Collns. Aberd. and Banff*, p. 628.
84. Protocol Book of Henry Preston, p. 3 (transcription, Register House).
85. *Reg. Epis. Glas.*, i, p. 247.
86. Reg. Evid. Civitatis S. Andree, fol. 57.

could claim " clerk meal ", a measure of milled grain, usually of oats or barley, at the rate of one firlot per plough. He also collected " clerk mail ", a money payment, which was, in some cases, a commutation of " clerk meal ". He received small offerings at ceremonies requiring holy water: for example, churching of women after childbirth, and he shared in the " bell money " left for requiem masses and dirges. It is also possible that the clerk collected a fee at the payment of the mortuary fine or corpse-present. In small landward parishes at the lower end of the scale, a clerk-depute might receive a mere pittance, obviously the remuneration of a part-time officer. The clerk was poorly paid in parishes whose clerk-ship had been appropriated, as, for example, at Lenzie, where the fruits of the clerkship went to the support of the choir boys at Biggar, and at Lochwinnoch, where the parish clerkship helped to support a prebendary of the collegiate church. In burgh churches the income and status of the parish clerk were relatively good.

In towns the proportion of priests to people was very high, about one in forty in Aberdeen,[87] one in seventy in Dysart,[88] and perhaps one in eighty in Linlithgow—too many for *Utopia* where " there are only thirteen in every town, one for every temple in it ". Great burgh churches like St. Giles', Edinburgh, St. Nicholas', Aberdeen, St. John's, Perth, and Holy Trinity, St. Andrews, might have as many as thirty priests attached to the church at one time. These priests did not live together in a common presbytery but had each his own dwelling. The manse and glebe of the vicar stood beside his church, as might also the house of the parish clerk. The clerk's house and garden at Logie, Stirling, stood on the north bank of the stream which flowed past the church.[89] The gift of a chaplainry normally brought with it a chamber,[90] possibly, but not frequently, situated within the church like the priest's cell above the south transept in St. Michael's, Linlithgow. The practice of giving parish clergy separate establishments tended by a housekeeper took away the excuse for non-residence, but it no doubt contributed to the scandal of concubinage which marred the life of some of the clergy at this time. The housekeeper was sometimes a concubine, a situation largely accepted by the parishioners who appeared lax and not sufficiently condemnatory in their attitude, although contracts of chaplains and charters founding altarages often specify dismissal for confirmed concubinage. It was not thought unusual, to take one example, that Sir William Clerk should cherish his son and retain his office of chaplain and schoolmaster of Banff.[91]

Parishioners of both sexes[92] were summoned to the church to witness the induction of their priests and clerk, which took place normally in the church and exceptionally in the churchyard.[93] The oral ceremony of presentation before witnesses, the essential element of early feudal conveyancing, was not yet superseded by the written record which a notary made of the proceedings. Notaries were also empowered by the bishop to induct parish clergy, but it was usual for one priest of the church

---

87. J. Robertson, *History of the Reformation in Aberdeen*, pp. 7-8.
88. *Antiquities of Dysart*, p. 14.
89. *Register of the Great Seal*, 1580-1593, no. 1782.
90. *Protocol Book of Dominus Thomas Johnsoun*, no. 257; *Protocol Book of Gavin Ros.* no. 281; *Cart. S. Nich. Aberd.*, ii, p. 366.
91. *Annals of Banff*, ii, pp. 14-15.
92. *Diocesan Registers of Glasgow*, no. 252.
93. Protocol Book of James Colville, f. 8a.

to induct another into office. Thus, on Christmas Eve, 1534, Sir Andrew Skeocht, presbyter, inducted Sir Adam Reid to the vicarage of Monymusk, having asked the assembled parishioners for possible objections, by delivering to him the key of the door of the church which was closed and re-opened, and by causing him to touch the corner of the high altar, the chalice, the missal, vestments and altar cruets, the baptismal font, the bell ropes and hand bells. He next installed the new vicar in the temporalities of his benefice by leading him to the manse, toft and croft pertaining to the office. He then charged the parishioners present to answer to Sir Thomas for the sum of ten pounds per year, the amount of pension allowed him by the rector of Monymusk, a canon of Aberdeen.[94] These acts were registered by Sir John Cristisone, notary public, in his protocol book and a copy was supplied to Reid as evidence of title. A service book, for example, a chrism book giving the order of baptism, might be presented along with the missal.[95] Chaplains were similarly inducted by presentation of the vestments and missal of the altar. Sometimes a chaplain was inducted by the presentation of a single simple symbol of possession, a plack,[96] a glove,[97] a ring,[98] a round bonnet or a surplice.[99]

Chaplains were frequently inducted by a lay patron who, like a trade guild, might preserve the chalice of the altar in his own possession.[100] Induction by lay people was the rule at the installation of the parish clerk, which often took place on Sunday morning before the principal mass of the day, the high mass said by the parish priest sometime between the hours of nine and noon. The principal parishioner in the church at the time gave the new clerk the holy water stoup and sprinkler and presented him to the vicar, who took the sprinkler from him and began the ceremony of the *Asperges*, proceeding through the church and round the baptismal font sprinkling the people as he went and saying or singing the psalm antiphonally with the clerk.[101] At his induction, the parish clerk might also receive the key of the church as *ostiarius*,[102] the bell ropes,[103] the handbell,[104] and whenever he was a priest, a bonnet or ring.

This was a rough age. The absolute authority of statute was not even recognised, far less observed. The concept of obedience to the central authority had less chance of developing in the weak Scotland of the Stewarts than in the England of the Tudors who had ended the grandscale feuding of the Wars of the Roses. Scottish local history of our period is a story of family feuds. In prosecution of a quarrel, a member of the gentry or nobility would organise a punitive expedition, consisting of his relatives and tenants, to march against his enemies. Priests and clerks were often involved in these breaches of the peace. The St. Andrews Statutes (fourteenth century) allowed a cleric going on a journey to carry his " whinger ", a kind of long dagger, to defend himself in case

---

94. *Protocol Book of John Cristisone*, no. 139.
95. *Diocesan Registers of Glasgow*, no. 252.
96. *Protocol Book of Gilbert Grote*, no. 152.
97. *Peebles Burgh Records*, p. 145.
98. *Liber Officialis S. Andree*, p. xlviii.
99. Herkless and Hannay, *Archbishops of St. Andrews*, ii, p. 244.
100. *Protocol Book of Dominus Thomas Johnsoun*, no. 10.
101. *Diocesan Registers of Glasgow*, no. 11.
102. *Protocol Book of Gavin Ros*, no. 777.
103. *Protocol Book of James Young*, no. 486.
104. Protocol Book of James Colville, no. 10.

PLATE VII.   THE SCONE ANTIPHONARY.

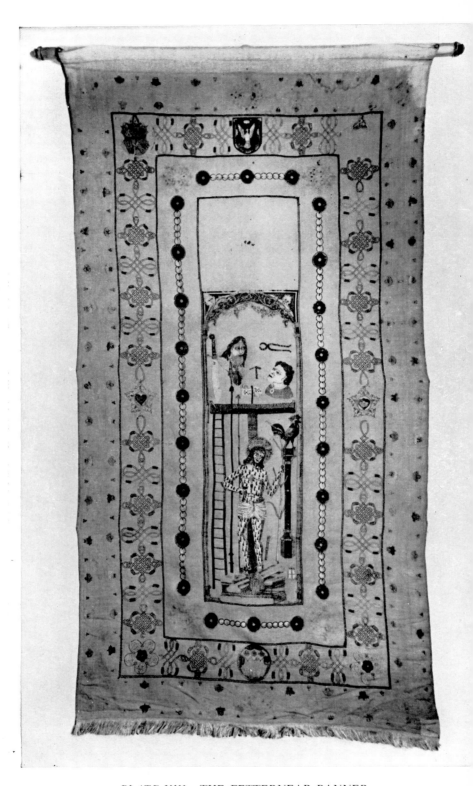

PLATE VIII.   THE FETTERNEAR BANNER.

of attack.[105] No doubt the chaplain in the retinue of the second Earl of Cassilis was so armed when he and his fellow-servants were threatened by some Kennedys in a street of Ayr in June, 1520, and would have used his dagger if necessary.[106] The records also tell of priests murdering and being murdered. A notable affray in which clerics were involved was "The Bloody Vespers", a sacrilegious struggle which took place in Elgin Cathedral on the feast of the Circumcision, 1555, when William Innes of Innes, with a following of thirty-two kinsmen and eighty men-at-arms, attacked the prior of Pluscarden at the altar steps at the time of vespers. Innes was at odds with his stepmother's family, the catholic family of Dunbar, over the progress of the reformation which he supported, and over the succession to his father's position as provost of Elgin. When the Dunbars heard that Innes meant to attack the prior, they gathered in Elgin under cover of night and fought a battle with the Innes faction inside the cathedral.[107]

In burgh churches the parish clergy were controlled by the burgh council elected by the burgesses. The council were able to overcome some of the difficulties inherent in the rectorial system: for instance, the temptation for a distant rector to neglect a church which he never saw. In 1494, the provost and bailies of St. Andrews made an agreement with the prior of St. Andrews, who was rector of Holy Trinity Church, regarding the upkeep of the chancel which the rector had to maintain in good repair. A similar agreement was made, in 1443, by the town council of Dundee and the abbey of Lindores. Besides maintaining the whole fabric of the church through their kirkmaster, the council enjoyed a great deal of power by favour of the bishop in the management of the parish church. It engaged the chaplains under terms of a contract, any breach of which might lead to dismissal, sometimes without report to the bishop.[108] The principal chaplain at Arbroath, as " collector of the choir ", that is, receiver of the monies due to the chaplains and of fines imposed upon them for absence from duty,[109] was given a copy of an agreement drawn up by the burgh council, in 1530, to regulate the services in the Lady Chapel. At St. Michael's, Linlithgow, details of the duties of chaplains at anniversary masses, founded in the church, were furnished by the common clerk, to the priests concerned, at their own expense.[110] These terms of service were registered in the burgh records. At Linlithgow, the council approved the hours of services, the number of lights to be placed on the altar and the regulations for dress in the choir. They fined chaplains who failed in their duties and dismissed them for continued delinquency after warning.[111] " Even the vicar, or parish priest, although the scion of an influential family, and occasionally an important officer of state, and as such enjoying the favour of the king, did not possess an absolute immunity from the supervision of the magistrates: for, if only he were neglectful of his duties, they would summon him before them and, if he proved rebellious to their authority, take steps

---

105. *Statutes of the Scottish Church*, p. 70 and footnote.
106. *Protocol Book of Gavin Ros*, no. 414.
107. Pitcairn, *Ancient Criminal Trials of Scotland*, i, p. 376; *Scottish Notes and Queries*, vii (1929), p. 28, and x (1932), p. 86.
108. *Reg. Cart. S. Egidii*, p. 214.
109. Hay, *History of Arbroath*, pp. 126-127.
110. J. Ferguson, *Ecclesia Antiqua*, p. 50.
111. *Ecclesia Antiqua*, pp. 40-41.

to enforce his band."[112] Priests who did not fulfil their duty might be called " before their Ourman (bishop) with a sharp summons ".[113] In 1530, the town council of Arbroath decided to complain to the bishop because the chaplains of the Lady Chapel had failed to perform the services for Holy Week.[114]

Discipline in the parish church stemmed from the bishop through the official, archdeacon, and rural dean or dean of christianity. On his yearly visitation, the rural dean was to be entertained by the vicar in his manse.[115] He held a court in the parish church to hear causes and complaints. For example, the curate of Insch, in 1535, suspended the parish clerk and placed his complaint before the dean of the Garioch, who had " power of punishing faults within the deanery ".[116] The rural dean also dealt with cases which we should regard as purely civil: for example, an alleged theft of nails at Lanark, in 1514.[117] He inquired whether the parish clergy were performing their duties[118]: whether parish clerks were properly admitted: whether the Blessed Sacrament was suitably reserved in a pyx hanging over the altar or in a sacrament house or aumbry in the wall of the church: whether the Eucharist were suitably escorted with bell and candle on sick calls: whether the fabric of the church were well maintained and the baptismal font kept covered and locked. He also enquired into offences like adultery, incest, rape, usury, scandal, witchcraft, mass-missing, failure to make the Easter communion, clandestine marriages, infidelity of spouses and the defrauding of heirs by executors.[119] He would also hear the complaints of local busibodies, like Bessie Moodie of Kilbarchan, who alleged that a priest breakfasted on honey plums before saying mass.[120] The dean might also undertake special commissions for the bishop: for example, to collect money to help to build Glasgow Cathedral,[121] to protect German miners working at Wanlockhead,[122] admonish non-residents,[123] summon clergy who failed to pay royal taxes,[124] excommunicate offenders, and, in certain cases, relax the sentence of excommunication. Major crimes were reserved for a higher court. The complaint of the parishioners of Liberton, made in 1536, was heard by the official of Lothian and resulted in the suspension of the parish priest for three years.[125]

*   *   *

The parish church might be a splendid cathedral as at Glasgow, a great abbey as at Melrose, a large collegiate church like St. Giles, Edinburgh, or a simple *ecclesia parochialis* not distinguished by any special form of organisation. The simple parish church was sometimes a large

---

112. *Ibid.*, p. 42.
113. *Ibid.*, p. 39 and footnote.
114. *History of Arbroath*, p. 126.
115. *St. Andrews Formulare*, i, p. 142.
116. *Protocol Book of J. Cristisone*, no. 171.
117. *Protocol Book of Gavin Ros*, no. 106.
118. *Statutes of the Scottish Church*, p. 276.
119. Laing MSS., Division iii, no. 322, flyleaf.
120. Protocol Book of Sir John Craufurd, f. 60 *v*.
121 *Statutes of the Scottish Church*, p. 25.
122. *St. Andrews Formulare*, i, p. 179.
123. *Ibid.*, ii, p. 136.
124. *Ibid.*, p. 57.
125. *Liber Officialis S. Andree*, p. 136.

foundation like the royal church of St. Michael at Linlithgow and the churches of St. Mary at Dundee and St. John the Baptist at Perth, but in some landward parishes it might be " bot ane kirk scant coverit with hadder ", a simple, oblong structure with a floor of beaten clay. The parish altar in cathedrals, abbeys and colleges was in the outer kirk or nave, the inner kirk or chancel being reserved for the clerks of the foundation. Liaison with the parish clergy was maintained through a member of the corporation, at Dunfermline and Holyrood, through the monk who was the sacrist. The parish clergy did not join in the liturgy of the greater foundation. At St. Machar's Cathedral, for example, the cure of souls was held by the vicar serving the altar of St. Maurice, assisted by his parish clerk, and acting under rules laid down by the bishop.[126] At the collegiate church at Cullen, the third prebendary, who was parish priest, was expected to join in the common services of the college, except when absent on parochial duties.[127]

The choir, separated from the nave in great churches by the rood screen stretching between the pillars of the chancel step, with a rood loft or gallery above, was reserved for clerics. The clerk, or *bedellus*, at Cullen had the duty of expelling lay people who entered the choir, as well as clerics, not suitably clad in surplice and other vestments proper to their office in the choir.[128] The privilege of being in the chancel during divine service was accorded the king and lay persons of noble birth,[129] and might be reserved to himself by the founder of a church. James IV had a double right to sit in the choir of Glasgow Cathedral, as monarch and as a canon of the chapter. It was the mark of nobility and importance to worship in the choir during life and after death to be buried beneath its flagstones.

In collegiate churches and great burgh churches, with many chaplains serving at the side altars, services went on from five or six in the morning till that time in the evening,[130] The day's liturgy began with " morrow mass," frequently a mass of the Blessed Virgin, celebrated by the Lady priest. In burgh churches, mass might be celebrated hourly or oftener, up to the time of the " high mass ", which was a sung mass with organ, celebrated by the vicar or curate and attended not only by the chaplains of the choir, that is, the chaplains bound to serve in the choir in terms of their agreement, but also the chaplains of the nave, that is, chaplains of side altars, who were independent of the parish priest as far as salary was concerned, but who were supposed to add to the dignity of the vicar's mass by being present in the choir, whether they could sing or not. The " high mass " in some burgh churches would, indeed, be a solemn high mass and an impressive ceremony, attended by some thirty priests. Vespers were said or sung, possibly with organ, some time in the afternoon between the hours of two or five, or earlier,[131] depending on the rules of the particular church and the season of the year, and were followed by compline. Taking part in the singing at the high mass and vespers in some churches and hospitals there might be seen bedesmen or bedeswomen, " bodily weak, poor and old, and dragging out their days ",

---

126. *Reg. Epis. Aberd.*, ii, pp. 99-100.
127. W. Cramond, *Church and Churchyard of Cullen*, p. 43.
128. W. Cramond, *Church and Churchyard of Cullen*, p. 41.
129. *Statutes of the Scottish Church*, p. 44.
130. *Ecclesia Antiqua*, p. 142: D. S. Rutherford, *Biggar St. Mary's*, pp. 34, 35
131. *Church and Churchyard of Cullen*, p. 27.

who had been hired to pray for their patron, receiving in return for their services food and shelter.[132]

Two ceremonies, now not practised in Scottish parish churches, which took place at mass were the kissing of the " paxbrede " or *pax*, and the distribution of the " kirk-lafe " or blessed bread to the people by the priest. The *pax*, a small tablet of silver or other metal, stamped with a sacred sign such as an image of Christ or a crucifix,[133] is commonly mentioned among the furnishings of a parish church. Among the pious gifts made by William Howe to the church of St. Nicholas, Aberdeen, in 1492 were two " paxbredes ".[134] It was the custom to hand round the *pax* to be kissed as a symbol and, instead of the actual kissing and embracing, performed at the *Agnus Dei* at mass, first by the ministers in the choir and thereafter by the faithful in the nave to whom the sacred tablet was carried by a clerk. In 1625, on the island of Eigg, an old lady in her eighties complained to Cornelius Ward, a Franciscan missionary, working in the Western Isles, about the innovation he introduced in his mass when he failed to let her have the " kiss of peace " by omitting to circulate the *pax*. He was able to satisfy her that the *osculum pacis* was not an essential part of the rite, was not universally observed and, even in her time, was omitted at requiem masses.[135] According to the Aberdeen statutes[136] and the St. Andrews statutes,[137] the kiss of peace, like the sprinkling of holy water, was to be refused to any concubine of a priest.

The " kirk-lafe " or holy loaf was an ordinary loaf which was blessed, broken and distributed by the priest to the people at the time of mass. The author of *Ane Schort Catholik Confession* regarded it as a kind of spiritual communion marked by the symbolic reception of the blessed bread. It was received by those who were not disposed to receive the Holy Eucharist because of the guilt of sin or by reason of the eucharistic fast.[138] Like holy water, the blessed bread was held to have power to strengthen the soul against the attacks of evil spirits. According to the *Holyrood Ordinale*, the symbolic communion was distributed after mass to the people who came forward to the choir to receive it. "Venientes autem qui communicare non debent vel possunt . . . eulogias id est oblatas accipiant quas sacerdos benedicat in hec verba."[139] The *Catholik Confession* (c. 1575) which answered an attack on sacramentals made in the *Negative Confession*[140] traces the origin of the " kirk-lafe " to the primitive church and the custom observed by the fathers of sending one another hallowed bread (*eulogias*) as a token of their membership of one communion and in remembrance of the miracle of the loaves and fishes.

According to the statutes, each church was to have proper books for reading and chanting.[141] At St. Michael's, Linlithgow, there was a

---

132. D. S. Rutherford, *Biggar St. Mary's*, pp. 31, 35.

133. R. G. Cant, *College of St. Salvator*, p. 160.

134. *Cart. S. Nich. Aberd.*, ii, p. 244.

135. Report of an Irish Franciscan missionary to Scotland written in St. Anthony's College, Louvain, 17th August, 1626, supplied by Rev. C. Giblin, O.F.M.

136. *Reg. Epis. Aberd.*, ii, p. 35.

137. *Statutes of the Scottish Church*, p. 60.

138. *Catholic Tractates*, ed. T. G. Law, Ane Schort Catholik Confession, p. 253.

139. *The Holyrood Ordinale*, ed. F. C. Eeles, p. 122.

140. The King's Negative Confession was printed as an appendix to John Craig's *Catechism*. It attacked " all his vayne allegories, rites, signes and traditiones brought in the kirk ".

141. *Statutes of the Scottish Church*, p. 37.

yearly stocktaking of the furnishings and books of the high altar, the property of the town, which were duly " tekkatit " in the town register.[142] At St. Mary's, Dundee, there was a library of books bound in oaken boards and housed in the south aisle of the choir. At each altar there would usually be a missal, which the chaplain of the altar was charged to preserve at his induction. One missal might, however, be made to serve two altars, just as one altar might be made to serve two dedications, by erecting the appropriate statue. At St. Mary's, Crail, there were nine altars but only seven missals, three manuscript and four printed.[143] Among practical handbooks, there might be a *manipulus curatorum* (a compendium of canon law),[144] a *crede michi*[145] (a parson's guide), and prayer books, primers,[146] such as those containing prayers before holy communion and recommended by Archbishop Hamilton to those who could read. As the number of worshippers able to use a primer would be few, the archbishop also prescribed the devout recital of the Lord's Prayer in preparation for holy communion.[147] Instead of reading from a book, some would tell their beads which might be of coral[148] or amber[149] with silver ornamentation, or say the psalter of our Lady on a chaplet.[150]

Among the collecting books would be the Pasch Book[151] (*rotulus paschalis*[152]) in which the parish priest kept a list of parishioners, probably to check on the fulfilment of Easter duties and the payment of Easter dues, and the Clerk Book[151] in which the parish clerk listed payments of clerk mail. At the church of St. Nicholas, Aberdeen, there was a " fault book " kept, " according to the pattern of that at the cathedral church ", by the two most diligent chaplains of the choir, or by a chaplain taking his turn as hebdomitar,[153] in which were recorded absences of priests from the hours and services, the rate of fining being twopence on a ferial day, fourpence on a feast day and eightpence on a double feast.[154]

The books kept in the choir at St. Mary's, Crail, a burgh and collegiate church (erected 1517), included two breviaries in two parts, *temporale* and *sanctorum*, and two new ones in four parts, two for summer and two for winter. There were three old antiphoners containing the music of the canonical hours, which were probably used by the priests and clerks of the previous foundation. There were ten psalters or books of psalms and antiphons, written on parchment in a fine " text hand ", that is to say, in " book hand ", a careful script opposed to the cursive " court " hand of the legal records which sometimes degenerates into a scrawl: a new *legenda* or book of readings containing a *temporale* and proper and common of the saints (properte and comone of sanctis): an epistolary and an evangeliary, separate books of epistles and gospels for the use of the subdeacon and deacon at solemn high mass: a great lectern book, con-

---

142. *Ecclesia Antiqua*, p. 46.
143. Rogers, *Register of the Collegiate Church of Crail*, pp. 65-66.
144. *Statutes of the Scottish Church*, p. 266.
145. *Cart. S. Nich. Aberd.*, ii, p. 245.
146. Cf. C. W. Dugmore, *The Mass and the English Reformers*, p. 73, seq.
147. *Archbishop Hamilton's Catechism*, ed. T. G. Law, p. 215.
148. *Protocol Book of James Young*, no. 384.
149. Liber Officialis S. Andree infra Laudoniam, f. 32 *r*.
150. J. Gau, *The Richt Vay to the Kingdome of Hevine*, p. 85 (Scot. Text Socy.).
151. *Acts of the Parliaments of Scotland*, ii, p. 614.
152. *Liber S. Thome de Aberbrothoc*, ii, p. 84.
153. *Cart. S. Nich. Aberd.*, ii, p. 232.
154. *Ibid.*, pp. 360-361.

taining the music of anthems, hymns and rounds, as well as *graduales* and *alleluias*, for use of the choristers at mass. There was also a printed *ordinale* (ordinarium divinorum) giving the proper office for the whole year, which was chained to a desk at the high altar.[155]

At the end of the period, the written records to be kept in the parish church included registers of births, marriages and deaths, and a register of excommunicated persons, all required by the bishop. From the fourteenth century[156] at least it had been the duty of the parish church through its rector, vicar, parish priest, or chaplain, under pain of fining, to keep and bring to consistories a written record of the deceased of the parish " of whatever condition or rank or age . . . testate or intestate . . . " in order to check on the manner in which executors were discharging their duties, especially with regard to bequests made for religious purposes[157] and for the provision of heirs.[158] The register of births and marriages is of later date, having been required by the general provincial council of 1552, probably in imitation of the injunction issued to the clergy in 1538, by Thomas Cromwell, the vicegerent of Henry VIII for ecclesiastical jurisdiction. The earliest extant record of a birth, possibly made in response to this order of the provincial council, deals with Christiane Hay, daughter of Peter Hay and Jonet Fermland in Errol.[159]

How far the parish pulpit was used for religious instruction is not clear. It was expected that each parish church would have its pulpit[160] with its frontal (pulpet clayth[161]). It was from this pulpit that the parish priest was to give readings from Archbishop Hamilton's Catechism.[162] It is possible that the statute asking for these readings indicates a neglect of the sermon as a means of popular instruction. In 1559, there were elderly clergymen who had not been accustomed to preach. Sermons were, however, given " from time to time " on feast days, not only by religious (by Franciscan friars, for example), but also by " ordinary preachers ".[163] Each time that a friar deputised for the parish priest in the pulpit a report was to be made to the bishop.[164] Chaplains of side altars at St. Nicholas, Aberdeen, were forbidden to say mass during the time that a sermon was being preached in the church.[165] The concern of the councils in the matter of preaching was lost on some of the parishioners who appear to have gone out of the church during the sermon,[166] and on those who did not trouble to attend mass at all.[167] Learned audiences had their addresses in Latin, such as the sermons of Adam Elder at Kinloss.[168] In the parish church, the preaching would be of a simple nature, possibly on the popular devotions of the day, to the

155. *Register of the Collegiate Church of Crail*, p. 65.
156. *Statutes of the Scottish Church*, pp. 74-5.
157. *Ibid.*, p. 75.
158. *Ibid.*, p. 266.
159. Errol Parish Register, i, 27th December, 1553. MS., New Register House; cf. J. M. Thomson, *Public Records of Scotland*, p. 128.
160. *Statutes of the Scottish Church*, p. 146; *Protocol Book of James Young*, no. 665.
161. *Reg. Cart. S. Edig.*, p. cviii.
162. *Statutes of the Scottish Church*, p. 146.
163. *Ibid.*, p. 147.
164. *Ibid.*, p. 125.
165. *Cart. S. Nich. Aberd.*, i, p. 262.
166. *Statutes of the Scottish Church*, p. 139.
167. *Ibid.*, p. 138.
168. *Adami Senioris Scoti, Monachi Ordinis Cisterciensis, Monasterii Kynlossensis . . . Conciones Capitulares, Parisiis*, 1558.

Souls in Purgatory, to the Blessed Virgin in her many titles, our Lady of Pity, our Lady of Loretto, etc., the Passion, the Holy Blood, St. Sebastian, etc.[169] There would also be instruction in the common prayers, the *Pater Noster*, the *Ave Maria*, and the *Credo*, containing the chief articles of faith, which all were expected to know. Psalm cxxix, *De Profundis* was also commonly known.

The sacred vestments and ornaments of the altar were stored in locked chests in the vestry or behind the individual altars of the church.[170] The high altar might have several " stands " of vestments—at Crail the number of sets was seven, each providing for a celebrant and the deacon and subdeacon[171]—and side altars had each a set of black vestments, an essential part of the equipment of a chaplain constantly engaged in intercession for the souls specified in his foundation. A side altar might also have more than one set of vestments, allowing a chantry priest to wear a colour other than black on occasion.[172] Thus, in a great church served by twenty or thirty priests, the quantity of sacred vestments would be very great indeed. At St. Mary's, Crail, the sacristan had to look after at least nineteen sets of vestments used by its ten priests and parish clerk.[173] The vestments, which, in towns, were the property of the council, were to be kept in good condition. They were also to be kept clean, a formidable task in view of the clouds of dust which must have risen as the daily processions shuffled round the church whose floor might be partly paved and partly beaten earth.[174] At St. Machar's Cathedral, Aberdeen, the duty of washing the altar linen was given by the sacrist to some worthy matron or virgin.[175] Perhaps the sun and pure air would make up for the primitive detergents she would use.

There was no fixed and common sequence governing the colour of vestments to be used. Dr. Eeles thought it highly doubtful that anything approaching a diocesan scheme of colours was known until the sixteenth century, and then only on the continent.[176] The seven liturgical colours now used in catholic churches in Scotland were all seen, and, in addition, colours no longer used, blue, silver, tawny, brown, grey and dun.[177] Individual churches could have their own rules.[178] At St. Mary's, Crail, blue or red was specified for ferial days, each stand of vestments being in sets of three, celebrant, deacon and subdeacon, to avoid the use of different colours at the same time, which may have been the practice at some churches.[179] It is unlikely that there was uniformity of practice throughout Scotland, except in the use of black for requiem masses[180] and " off-white " for the " Lenten array ".[181] On certain days requiem mass was not, and is not, permitted. On Sundays and feast days the mass

---

169. Cf. Rev. D. McRoberts, *The Fetternear Banner*, pp. 12-16.
170. Maxwell, *History of Old Dundee*, p. 558.
171. *Register of the Collegiate Church of Crail*, p. 64.
172. *Ibid.*, p. 66.
173. *Ibid.*, pp. 64-66.
174. " Pavimentum partim lapidibus partim nuda stratum," Theiner, *Vet. Mon.*, p. dccccxxviii.
175. *Reg. Epis. Aberd.*, ii, p. 105.
176. *Trans. of the Aberdeen Ecclesiological Socy.*, iii, part 3, p. 313.
177. *Edinburgh Burgh Records*, ii, p. 28; *Register of the Collegiate Church of Crail*, p. 64; *College of St. Salvator*, pp. 152-153.
178. F. C. Eeles, *King's College, Aberdeen*, p. 54.
179. *Register of the Collegiate Church of Crail*, p. 64.
180. Though it is to be noted that the Perth Dominicans apparently used blue vestments at requiem masses in 1525 (Fittis, *Ecclesiastical Annals of Perth*, p. 184).
181. *King's College, Aberdeen*, p. 57.

of the day would be said in coloured vestments, chantry priests adding a collect *de mortuis* to satisfy the terms of the altarage. At St. James', Roxburgh, these feast days were given as Christmas, Easter, Whitsunday, the Feast of the Holy Trinity, the five great feasts of the Blessed Virgin, the feast of All Saints, St. Andrew, St. Catherine and St. Mary Magdalene.[182] Unusual symbols sometimes replaced the *nomina sacra* now commonly known: for example, the skull embroidered on the black worsted chasuble at Crail,[183] a decoration no longer allowed, and heraldic signs, still permitted, such as the arms of James IV sewn in gold on the three black copes in the Chapel Royal, Stirling.[184]

The bells of the parish church were an expression of the integration of lay and ecclesiastical interests at this time. The great bells and the small bells in the bellhouse regulated the working day of the burgh craftsman, besides marking the canonical hours for the clergy and those of the faithful disposed to assist at the services in church. A mason contracting with the town council of Stirling, in 1529, entered on his duties at five in the morning at the sound of the matin bell. His midday break was also regulated by the canonical hours because he was required " Ilk day till entyr at the houre of pryme eftyr none."[185] The requirement of strict canon law that the church bell be rung for liturgical purposes only was freely interpreted because the bells were rung for such secular purposes as to welcome a distinguished visitor like the king or the bishop, to warn off threatening dangers, *signis concrepantibus*, to dispel storms, and on occasions of national or local rejoicing. The bells of St. John's, Ayr, were rung, in 1537, when the " Kingis grace come out of France " after seeking a bride.[186] They were rung daily for the public purpose of announcing curfew. However, the ringing of the curfew bell was also a liturgical act, like the modern Angelus Bell, because it was a signal calling the parishioners to prayer. At Lochwinnoch, the bells were rung for " ignitegium et preces ".[187] Specific detail about curfew prayers and the manner of ringing the bells are given in a Lincluden charter of 1547 providing " 10s. yearly to the prebendars or chaplains of the said church, at the two usual terms of Whitsunday and Martinmas, by equal portions, for causing the bell to be rung nightly about the eighth hour for the space of one quarter of an hour or thereby, vulgarly called the " aucht houris bell ", in all time coming, with three strokes at the end so that between each stroke there be said a *Pater Noster*, *Ave Maria* and *Credo in Deum*, for the souls of all and sundry predecessors, founders and all others dead and living, in the name of feu ferme."[188]

There was an increased interest in the bells of the church at this period. Not every church had a belfry with its clock. The only bell in landward churches might be a handbell, but the larger foundations like Holy Trinity, St. Andrews, St. John's, Ayr, and St. Giles', Edinburgh, possessed several bells, " obtained usually at different times and often without regard to their respective sizes or to the relation between their notes ".[189] The bellringer knew his bells, as he knew the doors of his

182. *Origines Parochiales Scotiae*, ii, pp. 457-458.
183. *Register of the Collegiate Church of Crail*, p. 64.
184. *Trans. of Scottish Ecclesiological Socy.*, iii, part 3, p. 318.
185. *Stirling Burgh Records*, pp. 35-36; Cf. *Reg. Epis. Brech.*, ii, p. 318.
186. *Ayr Burgh Accounts*, p. 20.
187. *Reg. Epis. Glas.*, ii, p. 510.
188. McDowall, *Chronicles of Lincluden*, p. 117.
189. *Trans. Aberd. Eccles. Socy.*, 10th year (1), p. 207.

church, by a christian name.[190] The five great bells of King's College, Aberdeen, a university college, were christened Trinity, Maria, Michael, Gabriel and Raphael. Each was rung for the service at the corresponding altar and all were rung for the high mass celebrated by the principal.[191]

The responsibilities of the bellringer were increasing as the desire to ring the bells in a methodical, musical way led to the addition of a carillon to the existing collection of heavy bells, an example of continental influence at variance with the English tendency to make the existing heavy bells make part of a diatonic scale.[192] A carillon was introduced at St. John's, Perth, in 1526. But the progress of the reformation limited interest in this form of ecclesiastical art. On 8th May, 1560, Edinburgh town council instructed James Barroun, dean of guild, to take down the Marie bell at St. Giles, leaving three bells hanging, one for prayers, one for the knok and one for the common bell.[193] The church clock remained a subject of civic pride. Fines levied in the burgh court at Peebles were directed to the upkeep of the clock, which was often under the care of the parish clerk or a chaplain as being a person suitable for the job.[194]

The church was not heated. Illumination was provided more by candles than by oil lamps. Singers in the choir could count on the light shed by the altar candles, two or more, burning smokily in their sockets of silver, brass, bronze, tin or pewter, or on spikes of iron, and serving a practical rather than a liturgical purpose. More light came from the gleam of the oil lamp hanging in the sanctuary, which was raised and lowered by a rope for attention.[195] The sacrament lamp, lit before the Blessed Sacrament, usually burned continuously but it might be extinguished at night, probably on grounds of economy, in some churches, as, for example, St. Michael's, Linlithgow.[196] In addition, there was the light from the candles guttering on the herse, a wooden or iron frame, usually circular in shape, which rested on the floor or more commonly hung from the roof.[197] At St. Giles', Edinburgh, there was a " pann " or candelabrum swung aloft by a rope in the " myds of the kirk ".[198] In St. John's Kirk, Perth, a Cistercian, John de Bute, who died in 1470, provided for the maintenance of lamps before the statues of St. Lawrence and St. Sebastian for two hours nightly during certain periods of the year.[199] On dark days this accumulation of light enabled the priest and assistant ministers to follow the words of the service in the large-hand or large-type books of the day. The congregation standing in the gloomy nave or resting on stone benches at the wall of the church did not require extra lighting because they did not follow the service from books, although some might read devotional works at mass. Light required in other parts of the church was usually supplied by candles. The organ loft of St. John's, Ayr, was lit by candles.[200] Candles were also used by the monk of Kilwinning when he repaired the organ at St. John's.[201]

190. *Cart. S. Nich. Aberd.*, ii, p. 352.
191. *King's College Chapel, Aberdeen*, p. 45.
192. *Trans. Aberd. Eccles. Socy.*, 10th year (1), p. 208.
193. *Reg. Cart. S. Egidii*, p. cviii.
194. *Peebles Burgh Records*, p. 195.
195. J. Smith, *The Hammermen of Edinburgh*, p. 51.
196. *Ecclesia Antiqua*, p. 282.
197. *Burgh Records of Dunfermline*, p. xliv.
198. *City of Edinburgh Accounts*, ii, p. 23.
199. Fittis, *Ecclesiastical Annals of Perth*, p. 37.
200. *Ayr Burgh Accounts*, p. 86.
201. *Ibid.*, p. 112.

In winter, when services in the parish church at Perth were not concluded till after dark, care seems to have been taken to light the worshippers through the kirkyard as they left the church. By a minute of the town council, in 1515, William Ross, baxter and burgess of Perth, was allowed the privilege of building a dyke near the kirkyard on condition of showing a lantern in his foreland, adjacent to the Kirkstyle (evidently at the south end of the Kirkgate) during divine service at even, and until, the kirk be cleared of people by six hours.[202]

Solemn feasts were marked by extra lighting in the church. At Linlithgow, it was the custom to light the candles on all the altars on feast days.[203] The celebration of the Nativity of our Lord saw the church brightly lit with candles. At St. John's, Ayr, an allowance of six shillings was made by the dean of guild for candles to celebrate the Yuletide of 1551-1552.[204] The individual parishioner also donated candles to the church at this time. John Webster, a member of the Websters' Guild of Stirling, took his own candle to church at Yuletide, 1551.[205] A particular section of the town undertook the lighting of the church of St. Nicholas, Aberdeen, at Christmas. In 1553, the council " ordained all the takismen of the watteris of this guid toun to pay and deliver zeirlie at the nativite of our lord callit zowill the lichtis of wax to the honor of god our lady and thar patroun sanct Nicholace conforme to the auld vse and consuetud." Some of the rentallers were to bring three candles, some two and some only one, according to the value of their holding. Each candle was to weigh half a pound.[206]

Some customs observed in administering the sacraments are of interest. As opposed to the many chapels which dotted the countryside (serving the needs of those who lived in areas where parish churches were five to ten miles apart[207]), the parish church was always a baptismal church, having a font of stone or wood furnished with a leaden basin. When not in use, the font was to be kept locked by the parish priest[208] against improper use of the sacramental water, as, for example, for witchcraft. Seven days after a child was immersed in the font the water had to be changed. Lay persons administering baptism in a case of necessity were charged to deliver the vessel and the water used in the ceremony to the parish church, unless the container was destroyed and the water poured into a fire.[209] Confirmation was given by the bishop or his suffragan on visitations,[210] prior notice having been given to the parish priest so that he could admonish the people to bring their children for anointing. Children could be confirmed before they had come to the use of reason and had made their first confession. Adults were enjoined to receive the sacrament of penance before confirmation.[211] Confessions were heard in the chancel behind a veil or the rood screen. Women penitents were heard in some other part of the church, in full sight of the

---

202. Fittis, *Ecclesiastical Annals of Perth*, p. 38
203. *Ecclesia Antiqua*, p. 286.
204. *Ayr Burgh Accounts*, p. 115.
205. *Stirling Burgh Records*, p. 70.
206. *Cart. S. Nich. Aberd.*, ii, p. 363.
207. *De. Gest. Scot.*, John Major, lib. i, p. 20.
208. *Protocol Book of Mark Carruthers*, no. 1.
209. Dowden, *Medieval Church*, p. 140.
210. *St. Andrews Formulare*, ii, p. 123.
211. *Statutes of the Scottish Church*, p. 32.

faithful, but out of earshot.[212] Expectant mothers about to undergo the perils of childbirth were to seek confession at the beginning of the ninth month.[213] The Blessed Sacrament was to be received once a year. Parish priests were urged in "Ane Godlie Exhortatioun" to try to make the people come forward to the altar in an orderly way,[214] not too easy a task in a church which was not marked off by regular rows of seats. An assistant minister or ministers were to accompany the priest with bell and light when he went on a sick call with the Holy Eucharist, unless the sick man lived too far away. Archbishop Forman complained that this rule was not always kept. The Eucharist was being taken on sick calls *inhoneste et occulte* through the streets and parishes. To remedy this abuse and to ensure that greater reverence and due honour for the Blessed Sacrament might be shown by the common people, the priest was in future to bear the Blessed Sacrament through the city and diocese publicly, preceded by at least one lighted candle or lamp and an attendant ringing a bell. Forty shillings were to be the fine for non-observance of this order.[215]

The celebration of the sacrament of matrimony began at the door of the church, "the wedding kirk door". Formal betrothal before the priest was to precede marriage, at which the principals bound themselves *per verba de futuro* to contract marriage at some later date. Thus, David Boswell and Janet Hamilton, daughter of the late James, Earl of Arran, appeared before Dominus Henry Louk, parish priest of Linlithgow, at 8 a.m. on 13th February, 1532, and were duly married in St. Michael's church on the following day at 4 a.m.[216] This marriage, possibly presuming on the noble birth of the bride, was irregular in that the banns of marriage had not been read in the parish church of each contractant "on at least three festival days" beforehand.[217] The legacy of irregularity facing the bishops of Scotland at this time, the intricacies of the law of consanguinity and affinity, the handfasting and clandestine marriages "celebrated in private chapels" by priests "ignorant of the law", can only be mentioned here.[218]

Plays and pageants continued as a practical method of edifying and instructing an illiterate people in the mysteries of their faith. Pageants depicting biblical scenes were a notable contribution by craft guilds to the social and religious life of the community. At Haddington, these dramas were still held regularly during this period (1530, 1537, 1541, 1552) on Midsummer Day.[219] At Aberdeen, however, there is evidence that the Candlemas and Corpus Christi processions at which all the guilds of the town went, two by two, in procession before the Blessed Sacrament, were in decline, probably, as was the case in England at an earlier date, because of the expense involved.[220] In 1531, the town council of Aberdeen, itself made up of guildsmen, had to re-enact the statute of 1510, calling on all the crafts to maintain the processions and

212. *Ibid.*, p. 67.
213. *Ibid.*, p. 48.
214. *Statutes of the Scottish Church*, p. 190.
215. *Statutes of the Scottish Church*, p. 273.
216. *Protocol Book of Dominus Thomas Johnsoun*, nos. 40, 41.
217. *Statutes of the Scottish Church*, p. 268.
218. Cf. Cosmo Innes, *Lib. Off. S. Andree*, Preface, xii-xxvii; Professor Anton, *Scot. Hist. Rev.*, xxxvii, pp. 89-102; Bishop J. D. Scanlan, in *Introduction to Scottish Legal History* (Stair Socy.), p. 72.
219. *P.S.A.S.*, ii, p. 398; A. J. Mill, *Medieval Plays in Scotland*, pp. 247-253.
220. E. Lipson, *Economic History of England*, i, p. 412.

prescribing fines and banishment for failure.[221] The Corpus Christi pageant continued, however, not only at Aberdeen but in other burghs.[222]

Certain parishes and their churches were centres of popular pilgrimage. Shrines, at home and abroad, some hallowed by the life and work of a saint, for example, the internationally-known shrine of St. Ninian at Whithorn[223]: some preserving relics of a saint such as the arm of St. Giles with the diamond ring on the little finger, at Edinburgh,[224] or professing some cult, for example, devotion to the Blessed Virgin, as to our Lady of Paisley, or our Lady of Kyle, attracted many pilgrims. Pilgrimages provided an exercise in piety but were more usually undertaken in expiation of a crime, frequently murder. The feud between the clans of Scott and Kerr was temporarily ended by an agreement between the parties to ally and do penance for the killings by doing pilgrimages (or having them done) to " the four heid pilgrimages of Scotland " (Paisley, Melrose, Scone, Dundee) and by having masses said for the victims.[225] The " chapel called the *scala celi* outside the walls of Rome "[226] was often mentioned as a suitable church for these expiatory masses. Sir James Sandilands was licensed in 1526, to pass to Rome in penance for the crime of murder.[227] John Erskine of Dun, who had killed a priest in the belfry of the church of Montrose, was licensed, in 1537, to pass to France[227] (probably to St. John the Baptist of Amiens, a very popular centre at the time[228]), Italy (probably to Rome and the shrines of the apostles, a great centre for priest-pilgrims towards the end of their days[229]), and other places beyond the sea,[227] for example, Naples, Compostella, Cologne, the Holy Land and Wilsnack, in Brandenburg, a shrine of the Holy Blood.[230]

A departing pilgrim, wearing his pilgrim's badge,[231] cloak and cap,[232] and bearing his pilgrim's staff and wallet,[233] took formal farewell of those assembled to wish him Godspeed.[234] In his wallet he might carry a licence to depart the kingdom granted by the mercantilist prince[235] and a testimonial from the papalist bishop as to his faith and orthodoxy, requesting that he be admitted to the sacraments and given alms on his journey. Henry Wardlaw, bishop of St. Andrews, granted William Brown, a pilgrim to Rome and Compostella, a licence to receive the sacraments and solicit alms. He also granted an indulgence of forty days to all who gave alms to help him on his journey.[236] Pilgrimages, often prescribed as a penance for murder, were richly indulgenced, remitting part or whole of the temporal punishment due to sins of which the guilt had been forgiven in confession, and enabling the penitent, in appropriate cases, to resume

221. *Aberdeen Burgh Records*, pp. 448-451.
222. *Medieval Plays in Scotland*, pp. 115-291.
223. *R.S.S.*, i, no. 2844.
224. *Edinburgh Burgh Records*, p. 27.
225. Wade, J.A., *History of Melrose*, p. 66.
226. *Cal. Papal Letters*, xii, p. 3; *Protocol Book of John Foular*, no. 592.
227. *P.S.A.S.*, iii, p. 168.
228. *R.S.S.*, i, 103, 1251, 1257, etc.
229. *Diocesan Registers of Glasgow*, i, p. 281 and footnote; p. 488.
230. *Book of Carlaverock*, ed. W. Fraser, ii, p. 447; *Rotuli Scotiae*, ii, 347.
231. *P.S.A.S.*, xli, p. 431.
232. *Diocesan Registers of Glasgow*, ii, p. 372.
233. *Ibid.*, i, p. 281.
234. *Ibid.*, p. 488.
235. *R.S.S.*, i, nos, 103, 1251, passim.
236. *Cop. Prior. S. Andree*, ed. J. H. Baxter, pp. 84-85.

divine service or proceed to holy orders.[237] Thus, he was rewarded for the hardship of his journey (especially arduous for an aging priest), the penitential garb, and the begging. Besides the perils of the journey, he had to face moral dangers[238] and was the gullible prey of pedlars in bogus relics. At shrines, it was customary for pilgrims to place offerings in the " offerand stok " or altar box. James IV, on pilgrimage to Tain, placed his offering in the " stok " in St. Duthac's kirk, and on many occasions at the altar of our Lady of Whitekirk.[239] The pious habit of making pilgrimages to holy wells, as at Elgin, Stirling, etc., was so much a part of the life of the people that the kirk sessions and presbyteries had to issue repeated summonses against those accused of making these pilgrimages.

As a consecrated building protected by the sanctions of religious belief, the parish church was used for other purposes than the direct worship of God. An apprentice might hallow his indenture by making it in the church.[240] The criminal in flight could seek sanctuary within its girth,[241] although at this time the church and its cemetery were sometimes the scene of violence, mutilation and murder.[242] Mad persons were tied to the pillars of the college at Borthwick, " where St. Kentigern's merits often cure them ".[243] As it was hoped that the sacredness of the place would deter thieves, the church was also used as a bank. In 1529, the sum of twenty merks was delivered to Friar Arthur Park, warden of the friars minor of Ayr, in sure custody for the children of a deceased parishioner.[244] The church at Minto,[245] and at Forres,[246] was considered a safe place to store gold coins. The fear of the sin of sacrilege did not always hinder a burglar of the character of Robert Rutherford in Todlaw, who broke into the church at Jedburgh, in 1502, to steal altar linen and cushions on which the missal rested at mass[247] for his own profit: neither did it deter the iconoclasts, who began to despoil churches a decade or two later. Business transactions were thought to be made more binding by being executed in church, money being counted out on a specific altar, a practice which, according to Richardinus, led to little edification and many idle words (verbis ociosis).[248] After the reformation, business dealings in church were carried out at the spot " where the altar formerly stood ".[248]

Sunday at the time of the " high " mass, the last and principal mass of the day, was an occasion for the exchange of parish news. Public announcements were also made at the parish mass: " after the Gospel at mass ",[249] being a common time for such announcements. In 1491, a royal nominee for the parish clerkship of Musselburgh appeared at the requiem being celebrated for the late clerk and, at the time of the offertory,

---

237. Cal. Papal Letters, xii, p. 2-3.
238. Wilkins, Concilia, i, p. 91.
239. Trans. Scot. Eccles. Socy., ix, part iii, p. 151.
240. Diocesan Registers of Glasgow, ii, p. 7.
241. Statutes of the Scottish Church, pp. 17-18.
242. Pitcairn, Ancient Criminal Trials, i, pp. 56-57, 328, 376, 382, 400.
243. Commentary on the Rule of St. Augustine by Robertus Richardinus, ed. G. G. Coulton, p. 73.
244. Protocol Book of Gavin Ros, no. 1027.
245. Pitcairn, Ancient Criminal Trials, i, p. 18.
246. Ibid., p. 394.
247. Ibid., p. 37.
248. Protocol Book of Dominus Thomas Johnsoun, no. 431.
249. Statutes of the Scottish Church, p. 25; J. Primrose, Medieval Glasgow, p. 26.

presented his letter of nomination.[250] The subject matter of letters of reversion and redemption might be read aloud in church by a notary public.[251] Parishioners also used the time of mass to announce matters of common interest, as, for example, when Thomas Charteris, one day in the year 1531, at the high altar of St. Monidan of Midmar, openly, before high mass, warned and required certain persons to desist from the grazing and pasture of his lands of Hill of Fayr . . . under a penalty for each beast or animal of 11 shillings, except the animals of Sir David Reche, the vicar, who had his express permission.[252] Another example is provided by the Banff Charters, where all the lairds being present in Alyth kirk to hear the marches read out, " on 14th June, 1534, Sir David Freirtoun, vicar pensionar of the samyn (i.e., Alyth) for the time in presence of the parochinars and uthers in tyme of the hie mess, the said Sir David beand in the pupit presentlie ressavit the said granatour and read the samyn be oppin proclamation and dulie execute his office conforme to the poynts and artikles thairintill."[253] We are reminded by Knox's ridicule that such Sunday announcements might easily, in a small community, degenerate into mere trivialities.[254]

Perhaps the commonest service held in the parish church was a requiem. Votive masses, by far the commonest kind of mass celebrated in the pre-reformation church, were very frequently *misse de requie*. For the one mass proper to the day said at the high altar of a great parish church there might be as many as thirty requiems celebrated at the side altars: that is, a trental of masses said on one day instead of being spread over thirty days as a " Month's Mind ".[255] Obits, or commemorations of an anniversary, founded at Holy Trinity Church, St. Andrews, called for thirty chaplains to say or assist at requiem mass. Sir Mark Jameson's anniversary, founded in Glasgow Cathedral, provided for thirty-six masses to be said annually on 1st June.[256]

A strong belief in the doctrine of purgatory and in the power of prayer, especially at the hour of death, to terminate its pains, was a feature of medieval piety and led to the foundation of monasteries, churches, chantries and obits, with the distribution of money and food to the poor; *sicut aqua extinguit ignem ita elimosina extinguit peccatum*.[257] By his pious act of foundation, the donor hoped not only to obtain present grace but also after death secure for himself and his deceased friends perpetual supplication at the altar. Sir William Myrton endowed the college at Crail in 1517 because " he was inflamed somewhat with devout zeal, and trusting by religious supplication not to let the merciful Redeemer wholly go and also to assuage and terminate the pains of purgatory ".[258] The daily tolling of the great bell of the church was a constant reminder of the reality of purgatory. It is not remarkable that thoughts of death constantly re-awakened by the celebration of the " sawl mess togiddir with the ringenye of the bellis " were never far from

250. *Protocol Book of James Young*, ii, no. 484.
251. *Protocol Book of John Cristisone*, no. 75.
252. *Ibid.*, no. 211; cf. *Protocol Book of John Foular*, iv, no. 560.
253. *Banff Charters*, no. 45.
254. Dickinson's *Knox*, i, p. 16.
255. *St. Andrews Charters*, Hay Fleming Typescript, no. 199.
256. *Glasgow Protocols*, iv, p. 118.
257. *Reg. Cart. S. Egid.*, p. 139.
258. *Register of the Collegiate Church of Crail*, p. 31.

men's minds in an age when sudden and premature death from violence, malnutrition, primitive gynaecology and medicine, the ever-active pest and less dramatic forms of illness, was a commonplace.

The solemn dirge, which in modern catholic practice in Scotland is recited or sung only on the death of priests and prelates, is not a common service, but at this period was constantly celebrated in burgh churches. Solemn ritual was not reserved only for those parishioners rich enough to endow an anniversary by founding a ground annual. At Dundee[259] and at Haddington,[260] the " passing bell " was tolled for all the burgesses and neighbours. Evidence from the Dunblane Testaments[261] suggests that it was the common practice to leave " bell money " in a will, a few shillings being sufficient to provide for the solemn ritual of burial. On the vigil of a requiem mass the common bellman (preco, campanarius, bedellus) went through the town ringing a handbell, calling out the names of the deceased and " exhorting the people to pray for the souls aforesaid ", and requesting them to attend the solemn dirge to be celebrated in the church that afternoon. The memorial service announced through the town by the bellman was referred to in contemporary records as Placebo and Dirige and consisted of vespers and matins for the dead performed in larger churches when the body was brought in procession to the church on the afternoon of the day preceding burial.

The " body " was placed before the altar and covered with a " mort cloth " or pall, with two or more candles burning. The " mort cloth " was a prized possession of a trade guild and could be richly woven and embroidered. The hammermen of Edinburgh, who maintained an altar in St. Giles, had a common " mort cloth " to cover the bodies of dead brethren, elaborate enough to cost thirty pounds, fifteen shillings and elevenpence.[262] At anniversaries, the " mort stool ", a kind of catafalque, was set up and covered with the pall, or alternatively, the " mort cloth " might just be spread on the floor where the body was normally laid, or " abone the lair " if the person were buried in the church. At obsequies of nobles and knights, coats-of-arms might be placed against the " mort table ".[263] During the requiem mass the great bell of the church was tolled thrice in the " menyng ", *tres pulsus singillatim cum mediis intervallis ad excitandum populum.*[264]

Burials were carried out in the church as well as in the churchyard, the most fashionable place of burial being within the choir as near the altar as possible. Well-to-do parishioners and craft guilds donated money and lime and lead for the privilege of having lairs under the pavement of the church floor. The whole choir at Arngask was reserved for the founder's family to the exclusion of the parishioners.[265] George Spalding of Dundee, a great benefactor of St. Mary's, Dundee, was to be buried " in ye quer . . . of ye said kirk under ye farrast gree before ye hye altar " on the epistle side.[266] Priests might be buried within the church with symbolic lead or wax patens and chalices enclosed in the tomb. As burial

259. Maxwell, *Old Dundee*, p. 42.
260. *P.S.A.S.*, ii, p. 397.
261. Commissariot of Dunblane, *Records of Testaments* (Register House).
262. J. Smith, *The Hammermen of Edinburgh*, p. lvii.
263. *Trans. Scot. Eccles. Socy.*, iii, part 3, p. 323.
264. *Reg. Cart. S. Egidii*, p. 117. " Menyng ", warning, probably a corruption of *monicionem*; cf. *Cart. S. Nich. Aberd.*, i, p. 115, " *pulsantes mencionem annuatim* ".
265. *Reg. Mon. de Cambuskenneth*, no.22.
266. *Reg. Epis. Brech.*, ii, p. 317.

space inside the building was used up, fees were raised and lairs let sparingly. In 1531, the sacristan at St. Nicholas', Aberdeen, was ordered to refer all applications for lairs to the burgh council.[267] The desire for burial within the church and the family prestige that went with it had a strong hold on the minds of the people and, although the General Assembly condemned " kirk-burial " in 1582, the practice continued.[268]

The least favoured site for a grave was the northern part of the cemetery. Archbishop Hamilton's Catechism condemned the superstitions of those who broke the First Commandment, " trowand that thair is mair halynes or vertew on the South syde than on the North ".[269] It was at the end of the medieval period that it became necessary to seek new cemeteries away from the church. In 1561, the town council of Edinburgh decided that " ane buriall place be made farer fra the myddis of the toun " because the available space was nearing exhaustion. The council were also against " kirk-burial " and hoped also to avoid " the savour and inconvenientis that may follow thairupoun in the heit of somer ".[270] The atmosphere in a crowded medieval church must often have been offensive, even apart from times of burials. This may be one reason why mass at Ayton was said " whiles in the kirk yaird." Services in the open air would be limited by the northern climate.

Sometimes a chapel was built in the churchyard, such as that founded at St. Giles', Edinburgh, by Walter Chepman, Scotland's first printer, for requiem masses to be said for himself and his relatives and those slain at Flodden, as well as for all persons buried at St. Giles'.[271]

It was the duty of the parish clerk to keep the churchyard clean out of reverence for the sacred precinct, as well as respect for the parishioners buried there. Following the orders of the bishop, the kirkyard was to be kept enclosed by a dyke against the entry of farm animals attracted by the good grass that covered the graves.[272] This wall or fence was maintained partly by the people and partly by the rector who was responsible for that part of the enclosure round the chancel.[273] Entry to the churchyard was by a gate or kirk-stile, an effective enough barrier against animals, if kept in repair: but animals did get into the churchyard, apparently quite frequently, through a gap, or having been set there to graze by their owners.[274] At Old Aberdeen, they might have been seen sheltering beneath the eight great oak trees planted to protect the church from the full force of the wind.[275] The town council of Aberdeen had their own " pundler of thar kirkyard ".[276] At Peebles, in 1468, the parish clerk was empowered to impound any horse, sheep or nolt found wandering in the churchyard.[277] As at Aberdeen, he could collect a fine of fourpence for every animal. Swine were to be slaughtered. As a central and open place, the churchyard was used for irregular purposes, such as

267. *Burgh Records of Aberdeen*, p. 143.
268. Fittis, *Ecclesiastical Annals of Perth*, pp. 129-131.
269. *Catechism of John Hamilton* (1552), ed. T. G. Law, p. 51.
270. *Edinburgh Burgh Records*, iii, p. 106.
271. *Reg. Cart. S. Egid.*, no. 132.
272. *Statutes of the Scottish Church*, p. 57.
273. *Ibid.*, p. 58.
274. *Burgh Records of Aberdeen*, p. 143.
275. *Scot. Antiquary*, iv, p. 129.
276. *Burgh Records of Aberdeen*, p. 149.
277. Renwick, *Peebles in the Reign of Queen Mary*, p. 18.

holding markets and courts. It had been found necessary also to ban the use of the cemetery for wrestling and other sports on holidays.[278] Fairs in kirks and kirkyards had been prohibited by act of parliament in 1503,[279] but, according to the statutes of 1552, trading was apparently permitted in churchyard and porch outside the time of divine service.[280]

The doors of the church were opened by the parish clerk for matins and " morrow mass " at five in summer and six in winter. At St. Mary's, Haddington, it was the custom to " stik the durris " after evensong.[281] The church was thus made safe from night marauders like the thief who broke the church of Jedburgh in 1502.[282] In burgh churches, for example, St. John's, Ayr, the locks of the doors were kept in efficient order on the report of the clerk who locked the church in the evening after compline, having made a search for " maisterful beggars " seeking a night's shelter[283] On special occasions a watch was set in the church steeple at night to guard against fire and sudden attacks by the " auld enemy ", just as watch was sometimes set by day to guard against the entry of undesirables, like beggars or persons smitten with the pest.

Cases of scandal were very common. Cosmo Innes found a multitude of them in the St. Andrews records.[284] Injurious words were not to be used lightly, however. Richard Barclay, parish clerk of Dundee, was dismissed in 1558 after " doing contemption " to the bailies.[285] A person who had been calumniated might hire a notary public to register a deed of protest and bring a charge before the court of the bishop or before the bailies of the town sitting in the burgh court. In 1506, Sir Thomas Forsyth, chaplain, hired Cuthbert Simson, notary public, to protest that he had been called " ane verray erratik and a Jow ".[286] The reek of heresy in the air made the name " heretic " a popular expression of opprobrium. Public penance, a commonplace before and after the reformation, might be ordered by the courts for slander and other offences. Women offenders were particularly liable to a spell in the " cucking stool ", an elevated stool or chair in which persons guilty of minor offences were placed and exposed to public derision. In 1523, Margaret Smith, a parishioner of St. Giles', Edinburgh, who had committed slander, was ordered by the bishop's official to appear in the church before the altar of our Lady of Pity at the time of high mass and on her knees beg forgiveness of the injured party. A man and woman who came before the burgh assise in Aberdeen in December, 1544, for a breach of the peace, were sentenced to a spell in the " gowife ", or pillory, and thereafter to march before the procession of clerks and priests at the beginning of the high mass, clad only in their shirts and each carrying a candle, one pound in weight, for the church, and then to seek forgiveness on bended knee.[287]

The organisation of the church was used to provide many services now of public concern: for example, education, the care of the poor,

278. *Statutes of the Scottish Church*, p. 77.
279. *Acts of Parliaments of Scotland*, ii, p. 245.
280. *Statutes of the Scottish Church*, p. 139.
281. *P.S.A.S.*, ii, p. 397.
282. Pitcairn, *Ancient Criminal Trials*, i, p. 37.
283. *Ayr Burgh Accounts*, pp. 91, 107, 120, 126.
284. *Liber Officialis S. Andree*, p. xxxiii
285. Maxwell, *Old Dundee*, p. 159.
286. *Diocesan Registers of Glasgow*, no. 201.
287. *Aberdeen Burgh Records*, p. 212; cf. pp. 154, 282.

public health. The church was asked to help to control leprosy.[288] The authority of the church was also called upon to help to preserve the peace. One weapon used for this end was excommunication, a sanction not now commonly invoked. At this period, it was used freely not only for major offences, like heresy, but often for matters which appear trivial to us. For instance, Archbishop Gavin Dunbar of Glasgow (1524-1547) excommunicated persons who had removed march stones and encroached upon his land.[289]

Four times a year the parish priest pronounced a general form of excommunication in church before his parishioners assembled for mass, condemning all who had been guilty of such offences as resisting the bishop, contravening the marriage laws, disturbing the king's peace, failure to pay teinds, perjury, usury, infanticide or failure to turn away from evil-doing after three monitions in church.[290] A particular act of excommunication might be pronounced against persons guilty of offences like theft, murder, Lutheran heresy, or reading the English New Testament.[291] Laymen could invoke the aid of the sentence of excommunication against those who wronged them. In April, 1545, for example, Jonet Newton, lady of Dalcoiff, and Adam Ker, her husband, obtained satisfaction in this way against seven men.[292] The king invoked a monition against clerics who failed to pay royal taxes.[293] The penalties of excommunication were formidable when put into effect. They meant social ostracism, the denial of the rites of the church and of christian burial. Excommunicated persons forfeited the ordinary rights of citizens at civil tribunals. They could not bear testimony and might be seized by the sheriff after forty days of defiance. The case of Sir John Borthwick, excommunicated by Cardinal Beaton in 1540, illustrates the serious consequences of excommunication. All his goods were confiscated and he had to remain in the safety of exile till the success of the reformers made it safe for him to return to Scotland. Even then he had to go through the necessary process of public " absolution " pronounced by the " superintendent and ministrie " of St. Andrews in September, 1561.[294] As the free use of excommunication brought its power into disrepute, the general provincial council of 1552 ordered all parish priests to keep a register of excommunicated persons and publish their names on chancel rails and other public places[295]: and although this council complained that excommunication " has in many places become almost of no account ",[296] there is evidence that the ordinary parishioner was anxious to avoid its spiritual consequences. In 1516, William Smith sought absolution in Glasgow.[297] In 1532, William Leslie appeared at the court of the dean of christianity of the Garioch offering to obey the mandate of the church and humbly requiring the dean to give him absolution " that he may dwell among the faithful of Christ ".[298] In 1555, Robert Stark, a parishioner of

288. *Acts of Parliaments of Scotland*, ii, p. 16.
289. *St. Andrews Formulare*, ii, no. 366.
290. *Statutes of the Scottish Church*, p. 6.
291. *St. Andrews Formulare*, i, no. 185.
292. Cf. *Protocol Book of Dominus Thomas Johnsoun*, no. 48.
293. *St. Andrews Formulare*, i, nos. 66, 313.
294. Dowden, *Medieval Church*, p. 307.
295. *Statutes of the Scottish Church*, p. 140.
296. *Ibid.*, p. 140.
297. *Protocol Book of Gavin Ros*, no. 147.
298. *Protocol Book of John Cristisone*, no. 90.

Lenzie, appeared in the court of Malcolm, Lord Fleming, and admitted that he had confessed to one priest and had taken the sacrament at the hands of another without having a certificate of absolution. Pitcairn has many examples of parishioners trying to avoid the prohibition of holy communion.[299]

These notes, gathered together during the course of a study of the parish clerk in the Scottish church, are to a great extent juridical in character. That is because they are based largely on legal sources, protocol books, burgh records, registers, statutes, court books. This class of record is the most trustworthy and is more to be depended upon than literary sources such as the works of Sir David Lindsay: but, like Lindsay, certain legal records tend to emphasise the coarser side of the story, the immorality which co-existed with the devotional life of the period. There are not many examples of medieval piety to be found, for instance, in a work like Pitcairn's *Criminal Trials*. Protocol books, on the other hand, as David Murray has pointed out,[300] show that parish life at this period was regulated by strong family feeling and affection, that parents and children and other relatives were anxious to fulfil their duties to one another, and that there was a greater exercise of charity and less self-seeking than we experience today. Alongside the evils and abuses condemned by the provincial councils there was much in the parish life of the period that was admirable.

299. Pitcairn, *Ancient Criminal Trials of Scotland*, i, pp. 365, 375 and footnote.
300. David Murray, *Legal Practice in Ayr and the West of Scotland in the Fifteenth and Sixteenth Centuries*, pp. 88-89.

CARE OF THE POOR:
PRE-REFORMATION HOSPITALS

by

JOHN DURKAN

The gospels command us to do good by stealth and our forefathers certainly lived up to that command. There is, nevertheless, no doubt that they took their duties to the poor seriously, believing that they would be closely questioned upon them at the last judgment. Examination of conscience included self-scrutiny regarding " spendand ye gud yat god has lent me in helpe and refreschyng of ye pure his creaturis."[1] The poor were " Christ's poor ": their common house was " God's House ", not only because the hand of God had touched them, but because Christ had already equated them with himself. There were, of course, many forms of provision for them: besides the offerings to poor and sick beggars gathering in church porches, there was the surplus given from the " offerand stokis ", or collections made on alms boards and alms dishes. There were the annual doles to those who attended anniversary services; as many as sixty at times.[2] There were the daily doles given at monastic houses; even at the reformation these appear to have been considerable at Paisley.[3] Almoners were attached to kings and even to bishops, and noblemen, as well as royalty, had their personal bedesmen. In this essay, one aspect alone of the subject will be treated in detail; the provision of hospitals. Even so, the result will be to provide an interim report in the absence of more technical investigation.

The late Dr. Easson listed 112 hospitals in medieval Scotland; for the estimated Scots population of the time a rather remarkable total.[4] Not all these hospitals can be shown to have a continuous existence throughout the middle ages, of course. Yet the figure is an under-estimate, though it is hard to say by how much. The existence of the place-name Spittal is often the only clue we have, a clue to be followed with circumspection. Sometimes such sites are not hospital sites at all but areas contributing to the upkeep of the Knights Hospitallers or a hospital elsewhere. Nevertheless, in a country so barren as ours in surviving records, such clues cannot be ignored.[5] The name Maisondieu is much less likely to be misleading, and will usually indicate the site of a hospital, whether constituted in being or extinct. Frequently the only part of the hospital that comes into view is the chapel, so that dedications characteristic of hospitals are possible guides to the searcher. One solitary mention in our scanty records does not impose the conclusion

---

1. *Asloan Manuscript*, i, 75. For comparison, Macpherson's *The Kirk's Care of the Poor* deals with the post-reformation period in one sector of Scotland.
2. *Glasgow Protocols*, ii, no. 618. Most of this charity was on a parish basis. There was a confraternity in Edinburgh in 1544 called " pietas pauperum " (associated with a foundation made by Henry Mow, chaplain, and of which another chaplain was member). Protocol Book of Andrew Brounhill (G.R.H.), ii, 156v. This is hardly likely to correspond to the *montes pietatis* of contemporary Italy.
3. Edinburgh Univ. Lib. Ms, Dc.4.32, f.28r, " pro elisimosino (*sic*) pauperum hepdomatim distributa per elemosinarium huius loci."
4. *Medieval Religious Houses: Scotland*, pp. 135-159. Cf. also *Innes Review*, viii, 132-4.
5. The site " Hospitale " mentioned in 1290 clearly designates the hospital of St. Magnus, Caithness, and so pushes back by two centuries the foundation date. Stevenson, *Documents Illustrative of History of Scotland*, i, 184.

that the hospital was short-lived. We need not, for instance, conclude that because Smailholm and Nenthorn Spittals are only mentioned in the mid-sixteenth century (when the English burnt them) that they were both sixteenth-century foundations.[6] Similarly, certain hospitals like those of Inverkeithing and Musselburgh, which are recorded only in one century, can be traced in others: Inverkeithing in the fifteenth and Musselburgh in the mid-sixteenth.[7] Certain hospitals come into frequent record as chapels merely; St. Anne's chapel where the Perth hammermen met:[8] the Magdalene chapel where the Edinburgh hammermen met:[9] St. Paul's in Perth often mentioned as a chapel:[10] and many others, such as Helmsdale in Sutherland, likewise. The matter is complicated in that the chapel continued to be served, even when, as at Uthrogle, the hospital itself had been abandoned.[11] Other place-names, such as Magdalenes, could be clues to the existence on or near the site of a former hospital.[12]

Of course, the word "hospital" is not to be understood rigidly in its modern sense. Quite apart from the enormous advances in medicine since those days, the word describes institutions for which nowadays we should employ a variety of terms. Even medieval terminology is not uniform; spittal, leperhouse, Maison Dieu, infirmary, almshouse, bede-house, and, for venereal disease, grantgore, are all found. Some were rest houses for travelling beggars or pilgrims, no doubt carrying certificates from bishops or priests, as were St. Martha's, Aberdour, and St. Laurence's, Haddington. Some were isolation hospitals, as were leperhouses. Some housed the blind, dumb and lame, especially if aged, superannuated workers (like the workers on the Dee Bridge at Aberdeen or old abbey servants at Holyrood), wounded war veterans, respectable people who had come down in the world; such types are found at St. Mary's, Aberdeen, and St. Leonard's and St. Mary's (the Spens foundation), Edinburgh. Widows appear to have been catered for at St. Leonard's, Dunfermline, but this hospital does not come to light till after the reformation, although clearly existing before.[13] As to provision for orphans and exposed children we have no information, and the relationship of poor scholars to hospital foundations in Scotland is obscure, as in their association in one document with the hospital of St. Nicholas in St. Andrews.[14] Another type was the rest home for sailors provided by the abbot of Kinloss at Findhorn.[15] The masters and mariners of Leith

---

6. Easson, *op. cit.*, pp. 151; 156.

7. Stephen, *History of Inverkeithing*, p. 25; *Dunfermline*, p. 454.

8. Hunt, *Perth Hammermen Book*, pp. 15, 27, 69. Mentioned already in 1488, *Acta Dominorum Concilii*, 1478-95, p. 96, as a hospital chapel. In addition, later foundations are confused with earlier ones. The hospital in North Berwick, founded by Duncan, earl of Fife, is not to be confused with that in the patronage of Lauder of Bass in 1560. Annual rents from Edinburgh and the town of Lauder maintained the latter hospital, described in 1542 as newly-founded for almsmen (Prot. Bk. Andrew Brounhill, ii, 70v-71r). Cf. also James Young, *Notes on the Scottish Family of Lauder* (1884), p. 51. For hospital architecture, Walter Godfrey's *The English Almshouse* is enlightening.

9. Smith, *Hammermen of Edinburgh*, p.119.

10. E.g. in *Brechin*, i, 134; *Arbroath*, ii, 91.

11. *Soltre*, p. 109.

12. That at Darnley (*R.M.S.*, iv, 111) may designate lands belonging to the Magdalene Hospital in Polmadie. " Bethlehem " in Ayrshire may be a similar clue, as may the " Thomas, canon of Bethlehem ", c.1180 (*Kelso*, ii, 277).

13. As has been pointed out already, *Innes Review*, viii, 134, the St. Leonard's recurring in the Dunfermline register was at Perth.

14. *Highland Papers*, ii, 127.

15. Stuart, *Kinloss*, p. 38; cf. *R.M.S.*, iii, 1172.

seem to have had a similar purpose in mind in their foundation of 1555, of which a stone inscription alone bears witness.[16]

The siting of hospitals is often revealing. Some, of the hostel type, are at ferry terminals; Ardross, North Queensferry, Portincraig, possibly Cree (if identified with the site marked Spittal on Pont's map of Galloway). Others are within chanonry areas; St. Nicholas, Glasgow, facing the bishop's castle: St. Mary's, Aberdeen, just west of St. Machar's. Many stand just outside the gates of towns. Dunfermline had three; at the south gate, St. Leonard's, at the west St. Catherine's and the almshouse at the east.[17] A bridge-end was a favourite site; St. Ninian's, Glasgow, and St. James's, Stirling, are examples. They are also found at lonely spots such as Bertram Shotts, at the entrance to a glen, as at Biggar, or as stations on a pilgrim road. Almonries attached to religious houses are omitted from Dr. Easson's lists. Such were the poors' infirmary at New-battle: and such almonry halls as those at Kelso and Arbroath.[18] Sometimes the almonry hall was so distant from the main building as to disguise its main purpose, the distribution of doles, as, for instance, at St. Catherine's, Dunfermline.[19] Cities where the king was frequently in residence abound in hospitals; Edinburgh and Perth are notable exam-ples. There appear also to have been two additional hospitals in Linlithgow, one an almshouse outside the east port next to the chapel of St. Mary, and another the almshouse in the Kirkgate.[20] At Stirling, there seem to have been five; the original hospital, probably identical with St. James's: the leperhouse: the hospital of Sts. Peter and Paul, probably the Over Hospital: the hospital founded by Mary of Gueldres on the Castlehill: and the Nether Hospital.[21]

Dedications, as we have said, may help significantly in disclosing the existence of hospitals. St. Leonard, St. Mary Magdalene, St. Catherine, St. Laurence, St. Thomas of Canterbury, St. John Baptist, St. Ninian and St. James are characteristic. These are found throughout the period. Others are pointers to a fifteenth-century or sixteenth-century foundation: for instance, our Lady of Pity at Lasswade, St. Anne at Perth and Aberdeen.[22] The choice of St. Leonard and St. John the Baptist is explained by their eremitical nature, of St. Mary Magdalene because she was equated with Mary of Bethany who housed our Lord. But the hospitallers had two famous hospitals in Jerusalem, one dedicated to the Baptist and one to the Magdalene, and these served as prototypes. The association of St. Thomas with Acre also points to crusader models, and there was land of a hospital of St. Thomas of Acre in Symington, Ayr-shire.[23] There was also land of St. Mary of Bethlehem at Hamilton.[24]

16. Irons, *Leith and its Antiquities*, i, 303, 306. Mason, *History of Trinity House, Leith*, p. 4. This hospital was evidently maintained by a confraternity of the Trinity, as at Kingston-upon-Hull. Sometimes private persons gave a booth for the use of one poor man or vagrant, as did a citizen of Canongate in 1495. *Protocol Book of James Young*, no. 779.

17. Beveridge, *Dunfermline Records*, no. 21; *Dunfermline*, pp. 253-4.

18. *Newbattle*, p. 142. Scholars lived in the *domus pauperum* at Kelso (*Kelso*, i, 142).

19. *Dunfermline*, loc. cit.

20. Ferguson, *Ecclesia Antiqua*, p. 347; *Prot. Bk. of Jas. Foulis*, 213; *Prot. Bk. of Nicol Thounis*, 45; *Dominus T. Johnsoun*, 953.

21. The St. James' Hospital is evidently identical with that in *Dunfermline*, p. 132, at Causewayhead. The subject of Stirling hospitals needs fresh investigation, but see *Stirling Nat. Hist. Soc. Trans.*, 1910-11, pp. 106-122.

22. The latter was not the leperhouse but the hospital for poor ladies and the chapel was added by Alexander Galloway in 1519 (*Aberdeen Council Register*, i, 96; cf. the reference to land of *badeis wyffis* at Futty Port in *Aberdeen*, ii, 213).

23. Article of W. J. Dillon, *Ayrshire Post*, 7th September, 1956.

24. *Glasgow*, i, 283. In 1369, therefore, the suggestion in *Medieval Houses: Scotland*, p. 162, is untenable.

The wonder-working powers of the shrine at Compostella influenced dedications to St. James. St. Ninian is found at the leperhouses of Kingcase and Edinburgh and Glasgow.[25] A change of dedication may mean the extension of a foundation, as at Polmadie, first recorded as St. John (Baptist?) and later as St. Mary Magdalene, but it may also indicate a multiple dedication, as with Blacader's hospital in Glasgow, dedicated to Sts. Nicholas, Serf and Machutus.[26] There are some problem dedications. For instance, it is fairly clear that the tenement of the hospital of St. John Baptist in Edinburgh refers not to an Edinburgh hospital but to a property belonging to the hospitallers of St. John of Jerusalem.[27] On the other hand, there seems no good reason for rejecting the existence of the hospital of St. John Baptist in Dundee.[28] In Edinburgh the hospital of St. Catherine and St. Andrew is identical with the hospital of St. Thomas, the two chaplains having, by Bishop Crichton's foundation, to serve the altars of the former saints in Holyrood Abbey. In the foundation, there is no mention of St. Thomas's chapel, which may have been added after the building of the almshouse.[29] The problem of the hospital of our Lady and St. Paul (St. Paul's Work) is more intractable. Here two hospitals may have been combined, one founded by the abbot of Holyrood in honour of St. Paul and one by Bishop Spens of Aberdeen in honour of our Lady, both using a common chapel, the Lady chapel in St. Paul's hospital mentioned in 1495.[30] The problem of " the new place " at Sanquhar (often in medieval documents " Seneware " or a variant) is less soluble. Was it a hospital at all? " Place " is used occasionally for hospital, as with St. Nicholas's place, St. Andrews. A chapel of St. Nicholas, Newark, is mentioned in 1554.[31] It may be that we have here a superannuated foundation. Confusion also arises between the hospitals of St. Leonard and St. Laurence at Ednam, clearly the same institution.

The control of hospitals was sometimes in the hands of religious orders.[32] Bethlehemites ran St. Germains, Augustinians Soutra and Segden, the order of St. Antony of Vienne Leith and the Trinitarians Fail.[33] It was not always practicable for religious to serve such institutions and, at the same time, fulfil their obligations as religious; yet Soutra had a master and nine or ten canons.[34] But some of these institutions acquired semi-independent status under an almoner-religious or a secular chaplain. There does not appear to be any further record of a hospital in Pilrig, founded by Sir William Crichton for six poor in conjunction with the preceptor of St. Antony's, Leith.[35] The pigs of St. Antony's have been

---

25. Kingcase is surely related to " Spetelcrag " mentioned in the thirteenth century (*Paisley*, p. 21). On the meaning of *casa*, see note by John MacQueen in *Innes Review*, vii, 123.
26. *Glasgow Protocols*, ii, 618.
27. *St. Giles*, pp. 27, 63.
28. *Medieval Religious Houses: Scotland*, p. 161.
29. Maitland, *History of Edinburgh*, pp. 154-5. Since writing the above, a reference has been found to the poor almsmen (seven are named) of the hospital under the invocation of Sts. Andrew and Catherine, receiving a tenement (apparently in their almshouse) in Bell's Wynd on 1st April, 1541. Prot. Bk. Vincent Strathauchin, iii, ff. 134v-135v. Cf. *R.M.S.*, v, 1242.
30. *Acta Dominorum Concilii*, 1478-95, p. 405.
31. A chapel does not usually have a warden as this had. There was a hospital in Leicester called Newark. For the Sanquhar Newark, see Wilson, *Folklore and Genealogies of Upper Nithsdale*, p. 174.
32. Religious houses also were associated with the upkeep of chapels at remote sites where their lay tenants had to keep beds for poor travellers. Cf. Lees, *Abbey of Paisley*, Appendix, pp. cxxvi, cxxix.
33. Cf. " four ald men of the convent " and " four auld beidmen of ye convent ", in Edin. Univ. Lib. Ms. Dc4.32, ff. 48r, 52v.
34. *C.P.R.*, x, 164.
35. *St. Giles*, p. 82. Sir Wm. Crichton is in the obit list of St. Antony's.

celebrated by Sir David Lindsay in his satire, and the confraternities that went to support it are on record (no doubt a pardoner circulated these letters of confraternity). The plague decimated the hospital ranks in the sixteenth century.[36] The Knights of St. John had a hospital at Torphichen but the hospitallers are a specialised study outside the scope of this essay.

The most frequent arrangement is that hospitals were administered by a secular chaplain, variously called rector, preceptor, master, warden and even prior: the last title is confusing, as such a " prior " is not necessarily a religious, and " prioress " is also found in charge of hospitals for women. Such a person usually had general administration, while more particular surveillance of the sick was in the hands of some lay person, an attendant, nurse, janitor or lay warden. The tendency of the chaplains to regard themselves as mere holders of benefices to be held in conjunction with other benefices, or to be non-resident, led to abuses, neglect of the fabric, dilapidation of hospital funds and the demand in the Scots parliament for a system of inspection. In 1425, it enacted that crown foundations should be subject to visitation by the chancellor, as in previous reigns, while episcopal foundations and those founded by other spiritual and temporal lords should produce their foundations for episcopal inspection. Some remedial action was taken but evidently not enough (Arbroath, as we shall see, was inspected in 1464 by visitors authorised by James II and Bishop Kennedy). In 1466, the enactment was repeated and the inspectors were to reform the hospitals in accordance with their deeds of foundation: and if these could not be procured, the poor were to have the benefits of existing funds, such as these were. Three years later the royal almoner-general, backed by the civil and ecclesiastical authorities, was empowered to enforce this act.[37] His activities can be traced at Montrose, where he was critical of the secular chaplain who was master, and at Haddington, where his refoundation is a remarkable document, for which the almoner-general, Richard Guthrie, professor of theology and abbot of Arbroath, deserves great credit.[38] Guthrie was associated with St. Salvator's college, whence some other distinguished hospital founders, such as Bishop Brown of Dunkeld, also came.

There can be no doubt that there was mismanagement and neglect by some patrons, especially in appointing wardens who were non-resident or under age. A hospital mastership for some clerics was a mere office of honour carrying revenue but no particular responsibility. The hospitals had acquired valuable stores of vestments and fine furnishings, which such masters were prepared to pawn and alienate; it was against such Judases in charge of the poors' purse that legislation was aimed. At the same time, there is little doubt that many abuses were the consequence of lack of adaptation to changed conditions. With the relative decay of pilgrimages in the later middle ages, some hospitals on pilgrim routes would lose their raison d'etre, and with the decline of leprosy the leper-house had an altered function. Moreover, with the depreciation in land values, some foundations were economically hard pressed. St. Leonard's hospital, St. Andrews, is an example of such constant adaptation. Before

---

36. Rogers, *Historical Notices*, pp. 16, seq. Irons, *Leith*, i, 559.

37. *Acts of the Parliament of Scotland*, ii, 7, 86, 97.

38. *Transactions of East Lothian Antiquarian Soc.*, vi, 9 seq. The visitation of Montrose (now lost) was in existence in 1590, as noted by *Fraser Papers* (Sc. Hist. Soc.), p. 152. In 1548, Sir William Layng was empowered to visit endowed hospitals, with no known results; *R.S.S.*, ii, 2590. The earliest mention of St. Laurence's, Haddington, is in 1312 (Bain, *Cal. of Docs. Scotland*, iii, p. 405).

the introduction of Augustinian canons to St. Andrews, it had been a small Culdee hospital receiving six pilgrims: after it, the house took on a new character and acquired a hospital church of St. Leonard which replaced St. Andrew in the dedication. It clearly became the priory almonry and is called " the almonry of St. Leonard " and its master the " alms master ". The pilgrims to St. Andrews decreased, and it received permanent tenants, aged women and apparently men, too. The women are said to have been disreputable, and the foundation was converted into a college of poor clerics and the hospital buildings (latterly of the almshouse type with separate houses) adapted.[39]

When there was a change of foundation such as this, it did not mean that the hospital was necessarily terminated. For instance, when the church of St. Peter in Rathven was made a prebend of Aberdeen Cathedral, the hospital was diminished and the number of bedesmen reduced to three. In 1536, the prebendary of the time, Master Thomas Hay, restored the three other prebends, and something similar may have happened at Turriff and Kincardine O'Neil.[40] In the same way the hospital of St. Peter, Aberdeen, was apparently terminated, in order to provide for two chaplains in 1427. But there again the sick were still being maintained in the hospital a century later.[41] Similarly, when the hospital of St. Germains in Lothian was united to King's College, Aberdeen, by Bishop Elphinstone, it was not extinguished, for provision was made for a master and three poor brethren to remain.[42] Nevertheless, as already noted, it could not be maintained that all hospitals, recorded as existing at some time in the middle ages, were still extant at the reformation. In some instances the hospital chapel is clearly being served, and that may have been the total extent of survival in a proportion of cases.

Moreover, foundations were occasionally extended. Extra beds were founded and sometimes extra quarters. The Crosshouse, at the corner of the Cowgate and Candlemakers Row, was added to St. Mary Magdalene's hospital in Edinburgh to accommodate four extra cubicles.[43] The back almshouse of the Glasgow hospital of St. Nicholas, founded by Bishop Andrew, made room for four additional bedesmen.[44] Dumbarton had some extra bedesmen founded in the hospital of the collegiate church by Walter Abernethy, provost, who died about 1517.[45] On the other hand, we do not know if anything came of a proposal to found an elaborate new hospital in Edinburgh. The proposal, made in 1552, for execution within seven years from that date, mentioned " dekeyit hospitalis and all wthir your nychtbouris dekeyit be the weris ". It envisaged a staff of

---

39. Herkless and Hannay, *College of St. Leonard*, pp. 9, 137. The " poor clerics " were often part of an almonry foundation, but here they are brought into the foreground at the expense of others on the foundation, in a way that can be paralleled in contemporary France at that period.

40. Cramond, *The Church and Churchyard of Rathven*, pp. 83-6. The new foundation was not extinguished or diminished by the annexation of Rathven to the collegiate church at Cullen in 1543, Cramond, *Church and Churchyard of Cullen*, p. 39. An allowance for hospitality at Turriff is mentioned in 1521, *Aberdeen*, i, 386. And although Kincardine (founded in 1234, *Aberdeen*, ii, 268) was made a prebend of Aberdeen in 1330 (*Ibid.*, ii, 225), yet the hospital was there at a later date (*Ibid.*, i, 83).

41. *Aberdeen*, i. 226, *Powis Papers*, pp. 127-9.

42. *Fasti Aberdonenses*, pp. 9-11. One hospital that did not survive was the rough wattle hospice built for receiving pilgrims to the shrine at Old Kilpatrick (*Paisley*, p. 166).

43. *R.M.S.*, iv, 950. *Book of Old Edinburgh Club*, viii, 51.

44. Beds were founded by Martin Wan, John Hawston (Mark?) Douglas and Michael Fleming: *Glasgow Charters*, i(2), p. 92; *Glasgow Protocols*, iv, 1064, 1204; *Paisley*, pp. 394-5. Incidentally, Bishop Andrew's foundation is mentioned in 1464 (*C.P.R.*, xi, 662). Wan was grand almoner of the realm in 1471 (*R.M.S.*, ii, 1020).

45. Smith, *Parish of Strathblane*, pp. 319, 321, 324 (the last gives preliminary negotiations for collegiate church foundation).

priest, surgeon and mediciner, with forty beds at an upkeep cost of sixpence per day, to be met by a charge of a penny a week from every house with a fire and the surrender of a furnished bed by all who died in possession of 1,000 merks of free goods.[46] It is doubtful, however, if a start was made on this elaborate scheme, and it certainly never came to ultimate fruition. Nevertheless, it shows that even Edinburgh did not consider itself well supplied with hospitals.

To provide for better administration, some hospitals came to be centralised in collegiate churches, where a resident staff was available to provide the sacraments and keep a constant eye on administration. The original foundation at Turriff in 1273 had been practically collegiate with generous provision for chaplains, as well as for the sick. The later idea appears to have been to keep the collegiate and hospital establishments separate to a greater extent, as at Trinity College in Edinburgh, Dunglass, Biggar and at St. Giles.[47] The proposed hospital at the college of our Lady and St. Anne (on the present Tron Kirk site) at Glasgow was to fulfil the will of Roland Blacader and not of the college founder, who was only executor.[48] Evidently the hospital was an afterthought. On the foundation of Biggar collegiate church, the preceptor of the ancient hospital of St. Leonard became schoolmaster, and it is probable that the new almshouse in charge of another of the prebendaries replaced it.[49]

We have no information about medical attention in these hospitals. Doubtless, and especially in towns, doctors and surgeons were from time to time called in, although full-dress doctors of medicine were a rare commodity and surgeons were barber-surgeons. Some chaplains who were interested in hospitals were students of medical literature: for instance, Mark Jameson, vicar-choral in Glasgow.[50] Emergency arrangements were made during plague. In 1530 we hear of the master and governor of the foul folk on the moor near Edinburgh, who appear to have been accommodated in temporary sheds, intromitting with clothes in St. Roch's chapel there.[51] The casual poor in Roland Blacader's hospital at the Stablegreen Port of Glasgow had a resident layman with his wife as keeper, who had charge of bedclothes and a kist of meal to make white gruel when there was no garden produce and a broth when there was. There was a great two-quart-size pot for cooking and a similar cauldron for washing the feet of the travellers.[52] Richard Guthrie's foundation of St. Laurence, Haddington, provided for four wayfarers and one elderly nurse. Each was to have a suitable meal of porridge and a 12-oz. loaf of wheat or oatmeal, with a pint or two of drink. If seriously ill, a wayfarer was to be cared for till he recovered and to be buried decently if he did not recover. The nurse was to receive the poor with kindness, wash their clothes, attend diligently to invalids, prepare and serve the food. The chaplain had to take oath to consider the poors' advantage and not his own, and he was removable by the grand almoner.

46. *Edinburgh Records*, ii, 170.
47. Easson rejects St. Giles, but a hospital is mentioned, o one bed in which the abbot of Kilwinning was patron, and the curates of St. Giles were almoners, Prot. Bk. Andrew Brounhill, ii, ff. 9r-10r (G.R.H.).
48. *Liber Collegii Nostre Domine*, p. lxxii.
49. *Spalding Miscellany*, v, 299, 300, 302, 314 (the new " house of hospitality " or " alemosineress " was still not erected in 1547). Biggar hospital is mentioned in 1446, *Charter Chest of Earldom of Wigtown*, no. 409.
50. *Innes Review*, ix, 119-120. They included surgical and other treatises and a herbal of Leonhard Fuchs.
51. *Edinburgh Records*, ii, 45.
52. *Glasgow Protocols*, ii, 618.

Coal fires were an important item in all such hospitals.[53] The relationship of St. Laurence's to the leperhouse seems to be that it was the original leperhouse and that, owing to the decline in numbers, its funds were now being redistributed by the grand almoner after his inspection.

Blacader's hospital gives a picture of the simplest type of building. It was a two-storey building, the upper storey with the chaplain's chamber reached by a gallery stairway, and the laich house having six beds of oak. There was a coalhouse and pantry, a walled yard with the usual well, an ell above the ground, in the centre. There was no oratory.[54] St. Mary's, Aberdeen, was for resident bedesmen and more elaborate. The whole building was constructed on the infirmary pattern, with six private cubicles (each 14 feet by 12 feet) on opposite sides and a corridor eight feet broad between. At the eastern end of the corridor were two doors, one leading to the common room (36 feet by 16 feet) and another to the oratory of the same size. The dining-room was overhead, but the oratory was a lofty room reaching to the full height of the building and having a timber steeple.[55] There was a little baptistery on the south wall of the oratory, in which were the arms of James V and Gavin Dunbar, as well as the first recorded words of Greek in a Scottish inscription set up by the bishop's executors. The oratory was furnished with a lectern and seats.[56] The altar furnishings consisted of four similar complete vestment sets, three linen cloths, two cruets, two towels, an antependium and frontal with the arms of bishop and king, two settles, a stool for the serving clerk, and a fine illuminated psalter presented by that generous donor to many northern charities, Alexander Galloway, rector of Kinkell, who also gave a new antependium. The cell adjacent to the oratory was adapted as a sick room with a window looking into the oratory for a bedridden patient to follow mass. There were fruit gardens and a yard, where the bedesmen worked.[57] These hospitals were, of course, all small: nevertheless, many of them must have been far from negligible architecturally, and have accumulated quite a treasure of pictures, furnishings and plate over the years. The bigger hospitals, such as St. Mary's, Edinburgh, planned to accommodate forty-eight, and Lincluden, which at the reformation still had twenty-four bedesmen,[58] gradually vanished and of their architectural design we have no record.

The dress of bedesmen was characteristic. Red gowns were to be worn at St. Thomas's hospital, Edinburgh: white at St. Mary's, Aberdeen, St. Nicholas's, Glasgow, and St. Mary's, Biggar: blue at St. Mary Magdalene's, Edinburgh.[59] The term " blew freris " used of poor children in Dunkeld appears to indicate children maintained in St. George's hospital there.[60] Special hoods were another distinguishing feature. Those of the bedesmen of Biggar had to be attached to the gown, while in the refoundation of Rathven the bedesmen had to wear white

---

53. A reference to " rolys " at a Haddington hospital should clearly be to " colys ". *Trans. East Lothian Ant. Soc.*, vi, 10-11.
54. *Glasgow Records*, i, 148.
55. *Aberdeen*, i, 401 seq.
56. Orem, *Chanonry*, pp. 99-100.
57. *Aberdeen*, ii, 199; i, 405.
58. McDowall, *Chronicles of Lincluden*, p. 78.
59. Maitland, *History of Edinburgh*, pp. 154-5; *Aberdeen*, i, 403; *Glasgow Records*, i, 115-6 (a post-reformation record); *Spalding Club Miscellany*, v, 302; *Scottish Ecclesiological Soc. Trans.*, iv, 97, with which cf. *R.M.S.*, iv, 950, which shows that additional bedesmen had to accommodate their dress to the first foundationers.
60. *Rentale Dunkeldense*, p. 342.

gowns with hoods sewn on Carthusian fashion.[61] Badges would also provide distinctive marks, like the cross on the sleeves of the bedesmen of St. Mary Magdalene's, Edinburgh.[62]

The property of hospitals was often fairly scattered. St. Mary Magdalene's, Edinburgh, was largely supported out of Carnwath mill.[63] St. Nicholas in Glasgow drew a portion of the revenues of the churches at Glencairn, Cummertrees and Cambuslang.[64] Even lepers claim their property: for instance, John Fidlare and Eugene Fleming, lepers in Dumbarton, with claims to the Spittal lands of Akinbar in 1518 and 1522.[65] A marsh is not an uncommon property of a leperhouse or hospital as being unattractive to the healthy and productive of the necessary peats for fuel. The " Bedeis Myir " at Cullen suggests the existence of a hospital there in pre-reformation, as in post-reformation times.[66] On the other hand, where there was no danger of contagion, bedehouses were attractive places. In the earliest days, hospitals acquired important milling and fulling rights, as at St. Leonard's, Lauder, and at Ednam, where the abbey of Dryburgh, somewhat reluctantly, conceded the right of fulling four ells of white cloth at its mill in the same way as the laybrothers of Dryburgh.[67] Similarly, exemption from tithes was not uncommon. The early statutes of the church, while naturally anxious that even the sick should contribute to the support of their parish priest, humanely observed; " But if they cannot be persuaded to do this, let no constraint be put upon them: for affliction should not be added to the afflicted, but rather pity should be shown to their miseries."[68]

The patronage could be in the hands of the king, some prelate or lord, the provost and council of a burgh and, latterly, of a trade guild. The earls of Lennox and captains of Dumbarton Castle had the patronage of bedesmen at Dumbarton.[69] The subchanter at Glasgow appears to have been the patron of the fore hospital of St. Nicholas at Glasgow, and is sometimes entitled master.[70] Not all prelates, alas, like Gavin Dunbar, considered themselves " guardians of the patrimony of the Crucified and not its lords ". Yet there appears to be an awakening of conscience in regard to these matters towards the end of the fifteenth century.

The patron had the right of inducting, often quite a ceremony. For instance, when John Stewart was made a " hospitaller " of St. Leonard's, Edinburgh, in 1555, the prior of Holyrood gave him possession by delivery of beads, brought him to the vestibule of the chapel and gave him a place where he could put his bed and provision, pointed out to him his personal garden and plot and made him swear on the gospels to keep the abbey's statutes regarding the " hospitallers ".[71] At Dumbarton, in 1526, a bedeswoman was inducted by touching the bellstrings, which, as also in

61. Cramond, *Church and Churchyard of Rathven*, pp. 83-6.
62. *R.M.S.*, iv, 950.
63. Pennecuik, *Historical Account of the Blue Blanket* (1722), p. 35.
64. *Glasgow Charters*, ii, 626.
65. Prot. Bk. Matthew Forsyth (G.R.H.), ff. 19r, 63r. No site for this leperhouse has been found. The spittal called " Ostellarie de Brigend " at Geilston (1582) was in Cardross parish. *Inquisitiones: Dumbarton Retours*, no. 100.
66. Cramond, *Church and Churchyard of Cullen*, p. 47.
67. *Dryburgh*, pp. 113-4, 267-9. The hospitals sometimes took over hermits' land, as in St. Leonard's, Edinburgh, and Rathven (*Book of Old Edin. Club*, xxiii, 116; *Moray*, p. 32).
68. In this way hospital churches acquired their own kirkyards, even baptisteries and sometimes a separate parochial existence. Patrick, *Statutes of the Sc. Church*, p. 41.
69. Smith, *Strathblane*, p. 319 seq.
70. *Dioc. Reg.*, ii, 190. The " stallars " here are chaplains, not bedesmen (*Glas. Recs.*, i, 115-6).
71. *Book of Old Edinburgh Club*, xxiii, 111 seq.

the case of bedesmen there, points to the duties of bellman taken in weekly rota.[72] Each bedesman in turn was janitor at St. Mary Magdalene's in Edinburgh and had elaborate bellringing duties.

If hospitals were to be reasonably efficient, there had to be a system of inspection. In the foundation of St. Leonard's, Lauder, although the hospital church did not have baptismal rights, it was stated that the priest administrator was not to be subject to any ecclesiastical or secular person, but only to the correction of the visitors appointed by the patron or to the wardens and masters of adjacent hospitals, who, however, were not to take advantage of the situation by removing the hospital's belongings, but were to enjoin penalties in accordance with his priestly status.[73] These regulations were obviously designed against episcopal or lay appropriation, and were unsatisfactory otherwise. Four centuries later the provincial council of 1549 takes episcopal inspection for granted, while in 1552 deans of christianity were ordered to investigate them in their visitations and report on their observance of the statute. Charters and instruments of foundation were to be produced if extant. The hospital's rents and rights, its purpose and nature, to what extent there had been dilapidation of funds or sequestration to other than the original uses, the title of the present possessors, the condition and state of repair of the fabric, all had to be investigated. Abbots, provosts of collegiate churches and similar dignitaries were required to ensure that alms formerly given to poor beggars be paid once again and payments kept up. The distribution of these alms was to be in the hands of trustworthy men whose responsibility the care of the poor was to be.[74]

An inspection was carried out at the almonry of St. Michael in Arbroath in 1464.[75] The two inspectors were Richard Guthrie and John Graham, Dominican prior of St. Andrews, representing James III and Bishop Kennedy. They summoned an assise and held an enquiry, the results of which are all too briefly given;

(1) Was the almshouse of royal or episcopal foundation or founded by a temporal lord or by the abbot and convent? Agreed that it was an almshouse but there was no record of its foundation.

(2) Which king or lord founded it and what was its nature and purpose? Agreed that it was a house such as other monasteries have, in which the daily surplus of the common table is used for maintaining the weak and poor, but unable to say who founded it.

(3) Were the letters of foundation known? No.

(4) Were any poor kept in the house? The answer must have been self-evident as it is not recorded.

(5) Were any annual rents annexed to it and, if so, what? Only a garden and croft known to be so.

(6) What was their opinion of the Spittalfield and the chapel of St. John (i.e., of St. John the Baptist, mentioned at an earlier date as a leperhouse)? The land was not thought to be the property of any, but the abbey, and the almoner received two merks from it annually.

---

72. Mathew Forsyth, f. 161r. *Strathblane*, p. 319.
73. *Dryburgh*, pp. 267-9.
74. Patrick, *Statutes*, pp. 119, 139-40.
75. *Arbroath*, ii, 141-3. It is not correct to say that St. John Baptist was the almonry. The chapel of St Michael was to the south-west of the almonry (*Arbroath*, ii, 154, 188), but adjacent; St. John Baptist's was outside the town.

(7) What is the master, and how is the house governed and furnished inside and outside? The almoner is a monk of the monastery, elected by and removable at the will of abbot and convent, the house competently built, the chapel well adorned.

(8) Why is the said almshouse sited outside the monastery with a chapel, barn, yard, court and great hall of its own? No reason given, except that it pleased the builders.

(9) What is thought of the popular belief that the almshouse of Arbroath had as rich an endowment as the bishopric of Brechin? This opinion was not held by prudent or authentic persons.

It is a pity that we have no record of visitations by the deans, even if of similar brevity.

For the medieval, mind healing was largely spiritual healing. Hence, when, in 1464, Friar William Gibson founded " a houss of almous " at Peebles, it was " for tyl harbry in it pur foulk for saull heile ".[76] Lepers and other incurables could only be distracted from their despair and consequent lawlessness by the confidence that one day their corrupt bodies would be changed into spiritual bodies, as St. Paul reminds us. Henryson has given us a tender and moving picture of the leper's fate in *The Testament of Cresseid* and the words inscribed inside St. Mary's hospital, Aberdeen, summed up the threefold duty of bishop, priest-in-charge and bedesmen; the glory of the first was to provide for the poor, the shame of the second to study his personal enrichment at their expense, and the duty of the third to persevere in patience till death brought an end to their trials.[77] Patience was upheld by prayer. As leprosy declined, very precise regulations for the day's religious observance, often amounting to an approximation to the religious life, were laid down: even more explicitly than the old foundations, the newer ones were first and foremost houses of prayer. The number of bedesmen was often of the apostolic number of twelve or the mystical number of seven. In St. Catherine's, Perth, which was for the casual poor, one poor man was to be maintained to serve the daily mass, a man of ripe years and good " condition and state ".[78] There does not appear to be any trace in Scotland of recitation of the divine office in almshouses, but they were required to say the Lady office or the rosary, which was considered its equivalent. The penitential psalms could be memorised from a primer. Night office is not usual, but at St. Mary's, Aberdeen, they were required to wake at three and pray in their separate cells.[79] A typical foundation in this respect was St. Mary Magdalene's, Edinburgh. The bedesmen there were to receive the sacraments at Easter, Whitsunday and Christmas and at other suitable times, especially when seriously ill. They were to be present at the annual requiem, at requiem masses for their founders on ferial days, at masses on festivals, on warning from the chapel bell rung for a quarter of an hour beforehand. Other important days were St. Mary Magdalene's and the day of indulgences granted to the hospital; on the former, two candles

76. *Peebles Records*, i, 151. The earliest mention of a hospital in Peebles is in 1305 (*Cal. of Docs. relating to Scotland*, ii, 1675).

77. Inscription is cited in Orem, *Chanonry*, p. 99.

78. Fittis, *Ecclesiastical Annals of Perth*, p. 291.

79. *Aberdeen*, i, 404. The illuminated Sarum psalter formerly in this hospital is now Advocates Ms. 18.8.14 and gives the hospital's full dedication. On the calendar under July we read: " Septimo huius altare hospitalis visitationis beate marie infra canoniam Aberdonensem per Willelmum Aberdonensem (dedicatum fuit?) Anno millesimo quadragesimo nono A. galloway." The Psalter includes the Lady office and litany of the saints.

were to burn before the statue of the patron saint. One of the bedesmen took weekly turns as bellman, ringing for a quarter of an hour before the gates opened (at 6.30 in summer, at 7 in winter) and a quarter after closing (at 8 in summer, at 7 in winter), upon which the bedesmen were to recite five paters, fifty aves and a creed, which they also recited communally on their knees before the high altar after dinner at night. Before dinner, they had to recite two Lady psalters and also before the midday meal at 12.[80] Nowadays, when psychological medicine is coming into its own, these requirements will seem less otiose than they might have done fifty years ago.

One of the methods employed to adapt foundations to changed circumstances was to be subjected to strong criticism. Just as Archbishop Stewart and Prior Hepburn felt that it was better that St. Leonard should support poor clerks rather than old women giving little return in devotion or virtue, so others felt that it would be better to support mendicant friars of the observance, men of intelligence leading an austere and studious life, rather than bedesmen, frequently quarrelsome, occasionally decayed burgesses who had bought their bedemanship from a grasping hospital master. To the blind, poor, widows and cripples, who figure in the Beggars' Summons of 1559,[81] however, the friars seemed the very model of the " sturdy beggars " against which much medieval legislation had been aimed.[82] Yet it is hard to see that their criticism had the force sometimes assigned to it. Apart from the similarity of this allegedly spontaneous warning to the Simon Fish incident in England, it is not clear that the friars did utterly extinguish the hospitals with which they were associated. The hospital of Montrose continued to exist in some form, however diminished, after its annexation.[83] So also did the leper-house of St. Nicholas in St. Andrews.[84] And so also, in diminished form, did the Maison Dieu at Elgin.[85] What must have happened was some reduction in the numbers of beneficiaries, and this, of course, could be serious enough and may explain, in part, the unwillingness of certain lay patrons to pay up to the new occupants. The annexation in 1438 by the Carthusians of the hospitals of St. Mary Magdalene and St. Leonard in Perth presents a rather more difficult problem. Here, again, it is not altogether certain that they were immediately extinguished by the new owners. The hospital chapels certainly continued, and the Carthusians received a royal allowance explicitly destined for these hospitals for many years to come.[86]

There is evidence that a new stringency in the regulations of hospitals was designed to avoid the abuses ventilated in the fifteenth century. Chaplains were appointed as masters to reside, not to take another benefice, to swear not to seek derogation from the original foundation and with more precise duties. Bedesmen, too, had their days mapped out

80. Pennecuik, *Blue Blanket*, pp. 40-3. Translation is somewhat garbled, but can be compared with the Latin (again garbled) in Cramond's *Church and Churchyard of Rathven*, for example.
81. Dickinson's *Knox*, ii, 255.
82. The dedication of St. Peter's, Roxburgh, which appears to go back to the time of Alexander III, suggests that it was controlled by the Conventual Franciscans there. *Cal. of Docs. relating to Scotland*, iv, no. 991.
83. Legacies to Montrose Hospital were made in 1523, 1538 and 1543. Low, *Memorials of the Parish Church of Montrose*, pp. 34 seq.
84. *R.M.S.*, v, 883. Here the " sick brethren " are in possession during the Blackfriars' tenure of the mastership. The increase of unemployed and able-bodied poor created a new problem.
85. Easson, *Medieval Religious Houses*, p. 144. Three bedesmen are recorded c.1561.
86. *Dunfermline* p. 368; and, for instance, *Exchequer Rolls*, xvii, 51, 471; xviii, 54. After 1543, the payments for the hospitals are merged with other allowances to the Carthusians.

more fully. They had more control over their funds, and at Aberdeen we find them authorised to appoint one of their own as provisor or steward. The Dunbar foundation was enlightened enough not to insist that all the bedesmen sit down together to one common meal, but hoped that they might agree at least to eat in pairs.[87]

Nothing has been said here about hospitals abroad, such as that founded at Dax by Thomas de Dysart about 1457 for pilgrims to Compostella: nor the hospice for Scots pilgrims in Rome, the predecessor of the present Scots College, whose students wear cassocks similar in colour to the ancient bedesmen's gowns: and there may have been beds in similar hospices in other towns: for instance, in Copenhagen, where the funds that went to the support of St. Ninian's altar in the Vor Frue kirk were later used to maintain two beds for the Scots there.[88]

There can be no question that when the reformation came it gave all hospital foundations a severe temporary jolt. Certain foundations went out of existence altogether and some struggled on for a few decades only. Some certainly survived: notably the Aberdeen group, St. George's, Dunkeld, and the Magdalene hospital in Edinburgh, for instance.[89] The funds of some of these medieval foundations, such as Dunkeld and St. Nicholas in Glasgow, to cite two only, are still being applied to charitable purposes at the present day. The Book of Discipline had plans for the poor, and it was evidently hoped to convert friaries to hospitals, as in Denmark—a process somewhat defeated by the policy of destroying the conventual buildings of friaries. It is not merely catholic observers like Nicol Burne who are severe in their criticisms. James Melville, after noting the damage done by the appropriation of chaplainries and altarages (which had as much to do with the non-survival of hospitals as anything else) wrote; " The rents, lands, and leivings of the Hospitalls, Almeshousses and Maisone Dieus are tean in few be gentilmen and burgesses for richt nocht: in sic sort that thair buildings is alwhare deceyit, and thair fundations lost and abolished. The Pure, partlie for want of thair awin patrimonie, and partlie for yeirly oppresioun, goes throw the countrey in swarmes . . . without mariage, baptesme, or knawlage of dewtie to God or man."[90] If by the seventeenth century the kirk had rallied and showed itself a true inheritor of earlier traditions of service to " Christ's poor ", its achievement need not lead us to neglect or minimise the generosity and idealism of earlier ages.[91]

---

87. *Aberdeen*, i, 404.

88. Dunlop, *Kennedy*, p. 424 n. *Innes Review*, i, 112-7; vii, 5.

89. Naturally, we are better informed about hospitals that survived, and of at least one, St. Leonard's in Dunfermline, we only know because it did survive. Of St. Leonard's, Cambuslang, only a single reference, apart from the place-name, Spittal, informs us that it existed in 1455. *Hist. MSS. Comm. Report, Hamilton*, p. 19. Edin. Univ. Lib. Ms., Dc.4.32, f. 15r.

90. *Autobiography and Diary*, p. 191.

91. The above essay is only a preliminary enquiry into the question. Regarding the canonists' view on care of the poor, Brian Tierney's *Medieval Poor Law* is a useful statement, with judicious observations (in special reference to the earlier Middle Ages in England) on topics such as: the existence or otherwise of widespread monastic charity; the problem of the able-bodied poor; parish relief; the charge of indiscriminate charity; whether medieval charity was " selfish " or otherwise.

PLATE IX.

DUNBAR'S HOSPITAL, ABERDEEN.

From a lithograph by Andrew Gibb, based on an eighteenth-century drawing.

TRINITY HOSPITAL, EDINBURGH.

From a Drawing by William Douglas, 1845.

THE
SACRAMENT
OF EXTREME
UNCTION.

THE PARISH CLERGY
AND THE REFORMATION
by
GORDON DONALDSON

The service of the Scottish parishes in the pre-reformation church was in the hands of priests whose status and emoluments varied widely, because the parish ministry was only one part of a highly complex ecclesiastical structure. In the vast majority of the parishes a very large proportion of the revenues which derived from the parish, in the shape of teinds, offerings and the profits of kirklands, was diverted to the endowment of a cathedral chapter, a bishopric, a religious house, a collegiate church or a university foundation, leaving usually only a small residue to provide a stipend for a vicar in the parish. In only a very small number of parishes—perhaps only 10% to 15% of the whole[1]—did the entire revenues remain in the hands of a parson properly so called[2]. There were indeed the many cathedral canons who held parsonage revenues as their endowment and who were known as 'parsons' of this parish or that, but they must not be mistaken for resident parish priests, because they did not as a rule take any part in the service of the parish from which their title derived, but left parochial duties to the vicar. In general, therefore, it was a vicar who was parish priest. Not infrequently, however, the vicar was himself inactive in the parish: he might be a pluralist, he might be engaged in some secular occupation, he might be unable or unwilling for one reason or another to minister in person; and when this was so, the work of the parish might be in the hands of an assistant priest or curate[3]. There were also, of course, very large numbers of chaplains, serving altars in private chapels, parish churches, collegiate churches and cathedrals, and while they were not, strictly speaking, parish clergy, some of them were in effect attached to the parochial system.

The priests serving the parishes, whatever their status and titles, were in the main secular clergy, but there were exceptions. When a parish was appropriated to a house of canons regular (Augustinians or Premonstratensians) it was a common practice for a canon of the house to be appointed as vicar of the parish, and it would appear that such canon-vicars very often served their parishes in person. Monks of other orders were not as a rule associated with parochial ministrations except to the extent that the nave of an abbey church was itself not infrequently used as a parish church for the district in which the house was situated. Friars, it need hardly be said, performed no parochial work, although they carried on a very active ministry of an extra-parochial kind.

Ideally, the foundation for a study of the attitude of the parish clergy to the reformation would be the compilation of biographies of several

---

1.   This is the estimate of Mr. Ian B. Cowan, who has been making a special study of appropriations, and to whom I am indebted for some information about specific appropriations referred to later in this paper.

2.   The Latin term was *rector* but " rector " was unknown in the Scottish vernacular in this sense, and the idiomatic translation of *rector* is " parson."

3.   The *curatus* was properly the man who had the cure of souls in the parish, whether he was parson, vicar or assistant, but there are undoubted instances of the use of *curatus* and " curate " in sixteenth century Scotland to mean a priest deputising for, or assisting, the parson or vicar.

hundred individuals—the parsons, vicars, curates, canons regular and monks who were concerned in the service of the thousand or so Scottish parishes in 1560. The material is not inadequate, but, while the careers of a proportion of the clergy can be sufficiently traced simply by the use of a limited number of official records[4], there are a good many cases where the requisite evidence can be found only as a result of prolonged and laborious searches in a variety of other sources, printed and manuscript, so that the systematic compilation of a complete survey is possibly beyond the power of any individual scholar. It would be very useful to have a series of regional studies, each of which would be worth while in itself besides yielding its contribution to the general picture (though the regional approach has its snares, if only because it can hardly hope to deal adequately with the numerous pluralists and the many clergy who moved from one part of the country to another). The essay which is now offered is a mere introduction, based only on a general acquaintance with the record evidence and on special investigations, of greater or less thoroughness, of three areas—the dioceses of Orkney[5] and Galloway[6] and the sheriffdom of Perth— and it must be understood that the conclusions tentatively put forward are based on such limited research.

A realistic approach to the subject must involve a readiness to acknowledge that the motives which shaped the attitude of the clergy were diverse. Many would argue, with some reason, that there was probably less altruism and disinterestedness in those days than in our own, and few would be found to contend that there was more, but judgment on such an issue is not possible. If little is said in the following pages about the effects of individual conscience and intellectual conviction, the reason is not that such effects are discounted, but because they are not merely imponderable but incalculable. The historian must confine himself to discussion of those motives which can be calculated from the evidence at his disposal, and among such motives were compliance with the law of the land, financial considerations and leadership or pressure from superiors.

The legal situation was shaped by events extending over several years before and after 1560, for the Scottish reformation was somewhat less precipitate, as well as in some respects less radical, than is popularly believed. Ever since 1543, when the administration of the Governor Arran had made its brief experiment in official support for a reformation, to the extent at least of authorising the scriptures in the vernacular and entering into an alliance with Henry VIII, there had been recurrent phases when ecclesiastical properties, especially the friaries and monastic houses in or near burghs, were threatened with violence. Then, during the late 1550s, not only did separatist reformed congregations develop in a number of towns, but some of the clergy in possession themselves began to use unauthorised forms of service[7]. The events of 1559-60 were therefore no sudden and unforeseen shock. This meant, for one thing, that many ecclesiastics had the opportunity to secure their financial position by feuing their property and thereby raising capital

---

4. For an account of those records, see " Sources for the study of Scottish ecclesiastical organisation and personnel," in *Bulletin of institute of historical research,* xix.
5. *Cf.* "Bishop Adam Bothwell and the reformation in Orkney." in *Scot. Church Hist. Soc. Record,* xiii.
6. *Cf.* " The Galloway clergy at the reformation," in *Dumfriesshire and Galloway Nat. Hist. and Antiq. Soc. Trans.,* 3rd ser., xxx.
7. *Cf.* G. Donaldson, *The making of the Scottish Prayer Book of 1637,* 6-7.

sums in anticipation of the deluge; it meant also that, among the regulars, certainly some of the more zealous reformers, and possibly also some of the more timorous conservatives, had already left their communities before 1560.

When the storm came, it was violent enough. There was a phase, in 1559 and 1560, when many clergy, especially of higher rank, were forcibly dispossessed and when ecclesiastical property generally was regarded as being at the disposal of anyone who cared to resort to force. But the violence did not last, for those proceedings did not receive the sanction of law, and when stability returned to the country in 1561 the situation was one in which neither the hopes of the reformers nor the fears of the conservatives were fully realised. It is true that the parliament of 1560 adopted a new Confession of Faith; but there was no compulsion on anyone, cleric or lay, to subscribe it—unless, of course, he actually held office in the reformed church or taught in a school. It is true, too, that the same parliament passed an act forbidding the use of the Latin rite, and it is true that there were in succeeding years some prosecutions of 'mass-mongers'; but there was no penalty for a negative refusal to join in the work of the reformed church. Not only so, but the parliament did not legislate on ecclesiastical polity, except to the extent of abrogating papal authority, nor did it legislate on endowments; and the consequence was that, while the reformed church received recognition in things spiritual, the entire structure of the old regime remained intact as a financial system, still upheld by the law[8]. It followed that the great majority of the clergy were guaranteed the continued enjoyment of a substantial part of their revenues.

The one group of clergy who appear to have suffered expropriation were the possessors of certain chaplainries and prebends founded on revenues within burghs, for those revenues were assigned by act of council to ' hospitals, schools and other godly uses '[9] (though, at least in some cases, it was not until 1567, when the queen gave the burghs formal gifts of those revenues[10], that this proposal took effect, and it seems likely that the holders kept their life rents). The position of the remaining holders of benefices was governed by the ' assumption of thirds,' likewise in terms of an act of council[11]. The intention was that while the ' old possessors ' retained two-thirds of their income, the thirds should be uplifted by the crown, partly for its own purposes and partly to pay stipends to the clergy of the reformed church. The scheme itself was not unstatesmanlike, designed as it was to avoid needless dislocation and to satisfy the competing claims of the government, the existing clergy and the reformed ministry. Not only was it not revolutionary, it was not wholly novel, because there were several precedents for heavy financial exactions from the church, and at one earlier stage, when the ' three tenths ' and the ' Great Tax ' were being exacted by James V in the 1530s, the prelates had learned what it meant to be mulcted of not much less than a third of their revenues[12]. Further, the assumption of thirds was in many ways even less unfavourable to the existing clergy than it threatened to be. For one thing, while the majority of the holders

---

8.   See *Registrum Secreti Sigilli*, v, Intro.
9.   *Reg. Privy Council*, i, 202.
10. *Reg. Sec. Sig.*, v, p. xiv.
11. See in general *Thirds of Benefices* (Scot. Hist. Soc.), x *et seq.*
12. *Ibid.*, xii, note.

of benefices obeyed the law which required them to produce rentals showing their revenues, and while such figures as can be tested suggest that most of the rentals were probably reasonably accurate, a good many men did not give up rentals at all and others gave up rentals from which some of the fruits had been negligently or fraudulently omitted; and the machinery for the detection of such defaulters seems to have been so inadequate that in the 1570s particulars were still being elicited of revenues which had been concealed in 1561 and which the old possessors had been enjoying all those years[13]. Moreover, thirds were regularly ' remitted ' not only to certain classes of benefice-holders—university teachers, senators of the college of justice and the dignitaries and canons of the chapel royal—but also to individuals, sometimes on grounds of hardship, sometimes apparently for no other reason than that they had influence at court. And finally, although failure to pay the third was followed by the process of ' putting to the horn, ' this had become a mere formality with no serious consequence, so that many ' hornaris ' went for years with their thirds unpaid[14]; only rarely does ' horning ' seem to have been followed by escheat of moveable goods, and not until 1573 did it result in the loss of the liferent of the benefice[15]. The operation of the assumption of thirds was much criticised for its unfairness to the reformed church[16], but it can hardly be regarded as other than tender to the rights of the old possessors. Not only did the old possessors retain their livings, but until 1566 it was not the law that clergy of the reformed church should even succeed them as they died. In the intervening years, the entire machinery for appointments to benefices went on very much as before, and the queen, the bishops and lay patrons disposed of benefices at their will, very often to laymen, whose rights thus formed a new set of vested interests, identical legally and financially with those of the old possessors. It is quite a mistake to believe that the law with regard to benefices and their fruits was on the side of the reformed church before 1566[17].

It should perhaps be added that the last word on the financial position cannot be said until a thorough examination has been made of the scores of volumes of Acts and Decreets of the Court of Session which relate to this period and record the lawsuits relating to ecclesiastical revenues. However, the general impression one forms is that the old possessors had no more difficulty in collecting their revenues after 1560 than they had had before 1560, and no more difficulty than the reformed ministers had in collecting their stipends, for in every period—and certainly not least in the generation before 1560—a vast amount of litigation has arisen from the reluctance of a proportion of the laity to render to the clergy what has been due to them. It is also worthy of note that with the retention of the two-thirds of the revenues there went, of course, the retention of the title, so that everyone who had held office in the church in 1560 continued for the rest of his life to be designated as he had been before 1560—parson of X, vicar of Y, and so forth. It is an elementary, but not uncommon, error to believe that there was any

---

13. There is much evidence in Reg. Sec. Sig. See also " The ' new enterit benefices,' 1573-1586," in *S.H.R.*, xxxii, 93-8.
14. The evidence is in *Thirds of Benefices*.
15. *A.P.S.*, iii, 74 c. 8. The occasional escheats are in Reg. Sec. Sig.
16. *E.g.*, *Thirds of Benefices*, xxi, xxv-xxvi.
17. See *Reg. Sec. Sig.*, v, Intro.

religious significance in the use of such titles: they were nothing more than designations, denoting the enjoyment of certain revenues, to which the individuals bearing them were by law and custom entitled, irrespective of whether those individuals were old priests, new ministers or lay titulars. The retention of old styles was as true of regulars as of seculars: John Henderson was officially designated ' ane of the bruther conventuall of Dunfermeling ' when he was appointed reader at Cleish in 1575[18].

Another source which requires examination from this point of view is the Record of Testaments, which can be relied on to yield conclusive evidence of the financial position of the clergy. Inspection of a number of entries, taken at random, confirms the impression conveyed by other records. Some of the clergy (such as William Ainslie, vicar of Maxton, who kept three servants, and David Barchane, vicar of Suddy and Kilmure, who had 16 oxen, 4 cows and 68 sheep) were very comfortably off in the years after 1560. Many more had a fair competence, and if some of them were poor and the payments due to them in arrears, they were in no worse case than some of the clergy of the reformed church. Thus, William Abercromby, prior of Scone, had ' chamber gear and clothing ' worth only £20 and the debts due to him amounted to £264; but Robert Blinseill, minister of Wigtown, had ' books, chamber gear and clothing ' worth only £13 and the debts due to him (including part of his stipend over a period of ten years) amounted to £286. Examples could be multiplied.

The situation may be summed up as follows. A priest's conscience *might* dictate that he must celebrate mass in the old way, and he *might* be unlucky enough to be caught during one of the very occasional phases of prosecution. Again, he *might* have scruples about paying his third (though if he wanted to quiet his conscience he could remind himself, with perfect truth, that the third was a tax collected by the crown, and partly to supply the financial needs of the goverment); he *might* decline to pay and he *might* incur legal proceedings on that account, but even so the consequences were unlikely to be serious. On the whole, therefore, the old possessor had a good chance of living without interference and with a guaranteed income, whether or not he accepted the reformed faith, though in certain areas and at certain times he would have to be circumspect. It can be said in general that for a dozen years or so after 1560 no legal disabilities and only limited financial disabilities were attached to refusal to take part in the work of the reformed church and even to refusal to accept its doctrines.

The financial considerations with a bearing on the question of active participation in the reformed ministry were complex. In general it may be said that there was only a limited financial inducement to the beneficed clergy to conform to the new regime and serve as ministers, exhorters or readers. The cathedral or diocesan dignitary, the parson or the vicar, did, indeed, usually lose his third; he lost his right to offerings, the levying of which ceased in 1560 or 1561[19]; and, from 1563, in terms of one of Queen Mary's acts, he also lost his right to a parish manse—or at least his exclusive right to the manse, for the act envisaged the possibility that the manse might be shared between the possessor of the benefice and the minister or reader now serving the parish. On the other hand, he was still assured of two-thirds of his stipend for life, in effect by

18. Reg. Sec. Sig., xiii, 135.
19. *Cf. Thirds of Benefices*, xiv.

way of retirement pension, and if he undertook service in the reformed church, his only reward, as a rule, was permission to retain the other third of his stipend and the exclusive possession of his manse. Such a proposition can hardly have had more than limited attractions except to men who were either sincerely interested in the reformation or subjected to some manner of pressure or persuasion. It can at least be said that the prospect of a 50% addition to a man's stipend, and the enjoyment of a free house, were considerations to be weighed in the balance against the contrast between a life of leisure and the strenuous labours of a parish minister. If the balance in material considerations was about even, then conviction or influence would easily turn a man one way or the other.

In practice, a very considerable number of the beneficed clergy of all ranks took part in the work of the reformed church, and the parish clergy who did so generally continued to minister in their own parish churches and to their own parishioners. Such men are for the most part easily identifiable and traced. The clearest cases are those in which a parson or vicar who was in office in 1560 is subsequently recorded[20] as having his third ' allowed ' to him in consideration of his service as a minister or a reader, but even when we find merely that the vicar in office before the reformation and the minister or reader in office after the reformation were men of the same name the identification hardly admits of dispute. When a parish priest served after the reformation in a new parish, it is sometimes less easy to be sure of his identity, and there were instances of quite surprising mobility. One would not, for example, expect the vicar of Terregles and Twynholm, in the south-west, to appear as minister of Perth, and, but for the fact that he happens to be the well-known John Row, the identification might have escaped notice[21]. Even more unexpected is the identification of Matthew Litstar, who became reader in two Shetland parishes, first Delting and later Fetlar; he has no known antecedents in Shetland, and would never have been identified with Matthew Paterson, who appears as curate in Kirkcaldy from 1553 until 1557, but for a solitary reference to him under the style ' Pauterson alias Litstar' in a Kirkcaldy protocol book[22], combined with the knowledge that there were numerous links, through commerce, between Shetland and Kirkcaldy[23]. Such an example shakes one's confidence on any facile assertion that any particular cleric of the reformed church had not been one of the pre-reformation clergy, and there may be many cases where there was a change of parish (not to mention a change of name, in an age when surnames were not yet wholly stabilised) and where conclusive evidence of identity is not forthcoming. ' Curates ' attached to parishes but unbeneficed are much more obscure figures than the parsons and vicars, many of them probably not on record at all, and in the few instances where the post-reformation reader can be identified with the pre-reformation curate, even of the same parish, the evidence is quite fortuitous: e.g., but for an unusual entry in the Books of the Assumption of Thirds, referring to ' Thomas Manderstoun, quha wes curat and now reidar ' we should not know that the curate in the parish of Tynninghame

---

20.   In the Accounts of the Collectors of Thirds of Benefices or in the Registers of Stipends.

21.   *Dumfries and Galloway Soc. Trans.*, loc. cit., 44, 58.

22.   David Bowsie's Protocol Book (in Register House), 1065, 1071, 1077, 1091, 1099, 2000. For these references and other particulars of Litstar I am indebted to Rev. L. Nowosilski, who has devoted to the clergy of that part of Fife an industry probably unparalleled in this field.'

23.   *Cf.* G. Donaldson, *Shetland life under Earl Patrick*, 70 ; *Court Book of Shetland* (Scot. Record Soc.), 105.

became reader there after 1560[24]; and only an incidental reference in a criminal trial discloses that John Allan was curate and minister at Mennar[25]. Other known examples of curates who became readers are John Thomson, at Kinkell in Aberdeenshire, and John White, at Tullycheddill[26].

While there is, therefore, ample evidence about so many of the parish clergy, until much more work is done statistics will remain so incomplete that it is dangerous even to suggest figures at all, but it seems likely that over the whole country the proportion of those who conformed and continued to minister in their old spheres under the new regime was at least a quarter[27]. At the top there were four bishops (two of them, indeed, unconsecrated)[28], who committed themselves without qualification to the reformed cause, and three of them continued to act in the oversight of their dioceses after 1560[29]. Of the dignitaries, the treasurers of Dunkeld, Brechin and Ross and the archdeacon of Shetland were already in 1561 numbered among the ministers of the reformed church[30], and others followed their example later. The " parsons " who took the same course—whether genuine parsons or cathedral canons— are too numerous to specify, and it is somewhat remarkable that the earliest official list of beneficed men who were recognised as ministers— a list certainly incomplete but giving a rough and ready indication of the proportions of the ranks of conforming clergy—names ten parsons and includes only twenty-two vicars, while in a second official list— again incomplete—there are seventeen parsons and thirty-seven vicars[31]. These figures might suggest that parsons, who were in the main of higher educational attainments than the vicars as well as of better ecclesiastical standing, showed more independence and initiative in making a decision; and certainly as the years passed and the number of conforming clergy in general increased, the proportion of vicars among them rose considerably.

But if some such picture, however sketchy, represents the situation for the whole body of clergy, it also emerges very plainly that the situation was by no means uniform over the entire country, In Galloway, out of about thirty-six vicars who can be traced, twelve continued to serve in their own parishes under the new regime, four more probably did likewise, and a further three seem to have served in other parishes. In Orkney, out of thirty-four clergy who are certainly known, or who may be strongly presumed, to have been in office in 1560, fourteen continued to serve the parishes attached to their benefices, four or five others may have done so and four more served in the reformed church in other spheres.

---

24. Books of Assumption, i, 75. Another entry on the same page refers to the unnamed curate of another parish " quha is now reidar."
25. Pitcairn, *Criminal trials*, I, i, 422.
26. *Reg. Mag. Sig.*, iv, 948, 2062 ; *Thirds of Benefices*, 224, 254.
27. This is the figure suggested by a rough check made in the *Thirds of Benefices*, xxiii. There are two qualifications, which may cancel each other out : (a) some of the holders of benefices so counted were men appointed after 1560 ; and (b) there were, as work on individuals demonstrates, many conformers who are not shown in the *Thirds of Benefices*.
28. Unconsecrated bishops were not rare in the two generations before 1560, but the doubts which have occasionally been thrown on the consecration of Alexander Gordon and Adam Bothwell are quite unfounded. Gordon was consecrated for the archbishopric of Glasgow in 1550 (and, having been consecrated, was made titular archbishop of Athens); Bothwell's charters regularly give the year of his consecration.
29. See in general *Eng. Hist. Rev.*, lx, 355-7.
30. *Thirds of Benefices*, 91-3.
31. *Thirds of Benefices*, 91-3, 149-51.

In Perthshire, by contrast, out of about a hundred clergy who held parochial benefices at the reformation, only seven can be shown unquestionably to have continued to serve their parishes; in another ten instances the evidence is inconclusive, while two served as ministers but not in their old parishes[32]. Thus the percentage of those who may be called active conformers can be put at about fifteen for Perthshire, at nearly fifty for Galloway and at over sixty for Orkney. One possible explanation of these quite remarkable figures may be this: Galloway and Orkney had bishops who supported the reformation and presumably influenced their clergy to come over with them, whereas the bishops among whose dioceses the Perthshire parishes were distributed were Robert Crichton of Dunkeld, William Chisholm of Dunblane and John Hamilton of St. Andrews, all of whom took a conservative line. Other examples, however, make it clear that leadership from the bishop was not the only influential factor. It would probably emerge on examination that a higher proportion of clergy conformed in Fife, the heart of the diocese of St. Andrews, than in Perthshire, but if so this could reflect the strength of reforming opinions among the burgesses and lairds there as well as the probability that Archbishop Hamilton made less strenuous efforts against the reformation than did Crichton of Dunkeld; on the other hand, in the twenty-five parishes of East Lothian (also in St. Andrews diocese), only four parsons and vicars and one or two curates joined the reformed ministry, although in that area also there were lairds zealous for reform[33]. A series of detailed investigations would certainly be necessary to determine the influence, varying from district to district, of the local lairds who were sometimes the patrons of the parish priests and were often partly responsible for paying stipends. One demonstrable example of what may have happened quite often is the case of Colin Campbell of Glenorchy, who established William Ramsay, formerly his chaplain at Finlarig Castle and curate of Killin, as minister of Kenmore, in the heart of Perthshire, and contracted to pay him a stipend[34]. Between priest and patron there might, however, be influence either way, for the opinions of a convinced reformer in a parish church might affect the attitude of the local people of all classes. Yet another possibility to be kept in mind is that the bishops and superintendents who were organising the reformed ministry may not have pursued a uniform policy towards the old clergy. The official attitude of the reformers in 1560 was, if not to discourage the acceptance of priests as ministers or readers, at any rate to do nothing to facilitate it[35], and some superintendents may have tried to follow this policy; bishops like Bothwell and Gordon, however, were almost bound to take a different view, and this might partly explain the high proportion of conformers in their dioceses. Whatever the precise nature of the pattern, the explanation of it is not a simple or a single one.

Monks and canons regular were in a different financial position from the secular clergy. Their portions, or pensions in lieu thereof, continued

---

32. The survey of Perthshire has been less thorough than those of Orkney and Galloway, but it is unlikely that further study would alter these figures very substantially.

33. Dr. John Durkan has suggested to me that the influence of St. Andrews Priory (see p. 139 *infra*) may partly explain the situation in Fife, and Mr. Cowan has suggested that the number of conformers may have been higher in districts where vicarages were mostly very poor and lower in districts where two-thirds of a vicarage often provides a competence.

34. William A. Gillies, *In famed Breadalbane*, 261-3.

35. Dickinson's *Knox*, i, 337, ii, 269 ; *Acts and proceedings of the General Assemblies*, i, 5.

to be payable to them, without deduction of a third, after the reformation as before it, and those emoluments were valuable: the monks of Glenluce had quantities of meal, bear, butter, cheese and peats, in addition to cash, and the whole " portion " was worth about £60 in the Scots money of the time[36]; the monks of Dunfermline received, in satisfaction of their portions, £50 each with £1 for coals[37]; and the figures for other houses are comparable[38]. In addition, the monks were still entitled to their " chambers " and " yards " in the abbey precincts[39]. Altogether, therefore, a monk enjoyed a fair competence, far greater than the average stipend of a vicar, and was not likely to feel any financial compulsion to supplement his income by working for the reformed church; on the other hand, however, should he become a minister, he retained his monastic income and received a full stipend in addition. Such at least was the position where the law was observed and the machinery of monastic finance worked smoothly. But neither the observance of the law nor the smooth working of financial machinery was characteristic of sixteenth-century Scotland, and monks did not, any more than seculars, always receive what was due to them. There were many instances where a monk had to resort to litigation to extract his portion from the commendator[40], and, while it would be hard to determine whether this kind of thing was a novelty for regulars any more than it was for seculars[41], or whether monks were in fact any more irregularly paid after 1560 than they had been before 1560, that does not alter the fact that the monk was in some sense at the mercy of the head of the house, who could clearly put pressure on men who were not of the same mind as himself: an example of sorts had been set by Mary of Guise in 1559, when she " stopped the portions " of the canons of Cambuskenneth who had " foresaken papistry "[42]; and where the abbot or commendator went over to the reforming side, then it might of course be the turn of the conservatives to suffer. At the same time, hasty generalisation may be curbed by consideration of the action raised by John Philp, a monk of Kinloss, against his abbot, for his portion for no less than ten years[43], because the abbot was on the reforming side and Philp, who had become a minister, had actually received financial help from the abbot when his ministerial stipend failed in 1565. Again, of three canons of Scone who had to sue for their portions, one was a minister and one a reader, the third not a member of the reformed ministry[44]. It is plain that disagreement on principles between abbot and monk did not lie behind every instance of litigation over portions.

The identification of the monks who passed into the ranks of the reformed clergy tends to be more difficult than the identification of the seculars who did so. There is no record evidence comparable to that of

---

36. Acts and decreets, xxxiv, 141, 352.
37. *Ibid.*, xxxvii, 30 ; *Reg. Sec. Sig.*, v, 3037.
38. E.g., Acts and decreets, xxxiv, 114 ; R.S.S., xlv, 78-9 ; *Charters of Inchaffray* (Scot. Hist. Soc.) xcix-c ; *Acts of the lords of council in public affairs.* lvi.
39. Acts and decreets, xxxiv, 141 ; Reg. Sec. Sig., xlvi, 11 ; *cf.* Hay Fleming, *Reformation in Scotland*, 613.
40. E.g., Acts and decreets, xxxiv, 114, 141, 352 ; Reg. of deeds, vii, 175; *Reg. Sec. Sig*, vi (volume in the press), 134, 171 ; R.S.S. (MS.), xiv, 78-9.
41. In *Acts of the lords of council in public affairs*, 505, we find a nun suing her prioress for a payment due to her, and (611) the commendator of Kelso granting a pension in lieu of a portion which, owing to English depredations, could not be enjoyed.
42. Dickinson's *Knox*, i, 213.
43. *Reg. Privy Council*, i, 680-81.
44. Reg. Sec. Sig., xliii, 27. For a similar case at Whithorn, see *Reg. Privy Council*, ii, 331-2.

the " allowance " of thirds to parsons and vicars, and we do not even have the assistance of continued location in a parish as evidence, except in a few cases where a monk is of the same name as the post-reformation minister of the parish in which the monk's house was situated. It can hardly be doubted, for instance, that Thomas Haliwell, monk of Melrose, was identical with the Thomas Haliwell who appears as reader at Melrose; other examples are Patrick Cowill, monk of New Abbey and reader there; Walter Miller, monk of Culross and reader at Clackmannan, Tulliallan and Culross; William Kirkpatrick, monk and minister at Kilwinning; and John Sanderson, monk of Glenluce and reader there. Again, when a minister or reader in a parish lying near a monastery, or in a parish appropriated to that monastery, has the same name as one of the monks, we can be reasonably confident that they are one and the same: for example, John Hutchison, monk of Culross, was minister at Crombie, a parish formerly appropriated to his abbey; John Mason, monk of Lindores, was reader at Auchtermuchty, a parish formerly appropriated to his abbey; and William Hood, monk of Coldingham, was reader at Stitchill, a parish formerly appropriated to his priory. But when the only evidence is identity of name, without any association in place, it is better to reserve judgment, though much depends on how common the name is, and a fair degree of certainty is sometimes attained when it emerges that, years later, a minister and a monk of the same name died about the same time[45].

The positive evidence is thus far from complete, though there is a good deal of negative evidence, for there are very many monks with names which are not to be found among those of the reformed clergy. The general picture which emerges is that the monks were not a conspicuous element in the ranks of the new ministry. It is possible to say with some confidence that among the Cistercians only one monk from Melrose and one from Glenluce became readers, although each of those communities had about fifteen members in 1560; there may have been no more than one from Dundrennan; there were perhaps two from Coupar and two or three from New Abbey, there were at least three from Culross and three from Kinloss. Among other orders, there seems to be little or no evidence that there were any recruits to the reformed church from Paisley or Crossraguel; there was one from Coldingham, perhaps two from Kilwinning, two or three from Dunfermline, and a few from Arbroath[46]. The conservative line taken by abbots like John Hamilton at Paisley and Quentin Kennedy at Crossraguel may explain the negative response of their monks; at Kinloss, by contrast, Abbot Walter Reid embraced the reformation, and the intellectual activity which had been fostered there by his predecessors may have brought about a readiness to accept new ideas and new ways but it is hard to detect comparable influences at work in other houses. Possibly the determining factor was often simply this: accustomed to a fairly secluded life in the shelter of the community, a monk generally preferred to enjoy his portion, which was adequate to support him, without undertaking ministerial labours, and to continue a life of comparative ease and

---

45. The approximate date of the death of a monk may often be found from the Register of Presentations to Benefices and the Register of the Privy Seal, which record the gifts of monks' portions made as the monks died off.

46. Dr. John Durkan has given me some information on the recruitment of monks to the reformed ministry, which suplements my own very supperficial investigations.

comfort which did not differ materially from the life he had lived before 1560. It would require a certain effort to uproot himself and enter on a life which involved constant dealing with the public, and it is significant that at Glenluce, for example, the solitary monk who entered the reformed ministry was the member of the house who had already been responsible for its parochial work before 1560; to him the exertions of a parish minister represented a less radical change in his way of life. Nor is it hard to understand the preference of a monk, if he was going to serve in the reformed church at all, for service in a parish close to his monastery, for only thus could he make much use of the " chamber " and " yard " to which he was entitled.

When we turn to the canons regular, who so often held vicarages, the task of identification becomes much easier, because the same evidence is available for them as for secular vicars. Their record is demonstrably different from that of the monks, and it is not surprising that men already accustomed to parochial ministration took quite readily to work in the reformed church. In the Premonstratensian houses of Whithorn and Tongland the canons were peculiarly subject to the influence of their reforming bishop, Alexander Gordon, because the canons of Whithorn were the chapter of the bishopric of Galloway and the bishop was commendator of Tongland. In Whithorn there was, indeed, the contrary influence of the prior, Malcolm Fleming, who was a rigid conservative, but his views evidently did not command much following among the monks. At any rate, out of eleven canons of Whithorn who survived the reformation, two clearly did not take part in the work of the reformed church, but seven certainly became readers and one or two more may have done so. At Tongland, eight canons survived the reformation, and of them five appear as readers. With hardly an exception the churches in which the canons of Whithorn and Tongland served as readers were churches which had been annexed to their houses before the reformation. The Perthshire Augustinian houses of Scone and Inchaffray likewise made an important contribution to the ministry: it is unlikely that in 1560 the two communities together numbered as many as thirty canons, of whom some would be beyond the age for active service; yet nine canons from those two houses appear as ministers, exhorters or readers. The commendator of Inchaffray was Alexander Gordon, the reforming bishop of Galloway, and the commendator of Scone was Patrick Hepburn, bishop of Moray, who, while he may have done little to aid the reformed church, did nothing to hinder it[47]. At the Augustinian priory of St. Andrews, where the office of commendator was held first by the Lord James Stewart, one of the leaders of the reforming party, and then by Robert Stewart, the reforming bishop of Caithness, and where the subprior was John Winram, who became a superintendent, there was every encouragement to the canons to enter the reformed ministry, and no less than twelve canons who had taken service in the reformed church were still alive in 1572[48]. Augustinian Holyrood and Cambuskenneth, too, made their contributions, with at least four ministers and four readers respectively, and the small Premonstratensian houses of Holywood and Soulseat each produced at least two readers. On the

---

47. *Cf.* p. 142 *infra.*
48. *Acts and proceedings of the general assemblies*, i. 222.

other hand, from Augustinian Jedburgh and Premonstratensian Dryburgh there may have been no more than one recruit to the new ministry[49].

Although the friars did not form part of the pre-reformation parish ministry, something should be said of their work in the reformed church. They were entitled to pensions, or " wages, " but only at the modest figure of £16 per annum, and, unlike the monks, they no longer had free quarters, so that the financial attraction of a minister's or reader's stipend may well have been considerable. Yet it is certainly clear, negatively, that a good many friars, although recorded as receiving their " wages " in Scotland after 1560, did not serve in the reformed church, for no men bearing their names appear on the roll of its ministry. On the other hand, to determine positively how many friars did become ministers or readers would be a task of peculiar difficulty, because identification is nearly always hazardous. Friars are on the whole more poorly documented than secular priests, monks and canons regular, and they were not associated with benefices or parishes, so that evidence of location is of little help. Occasionally, indeed, the evidence from proximity may be convincing: *e.g.*, it can hardly be doubted that Alexander Young, prior of the Carmelites of Tullilum, near Perth, became minister of Methven; William Smith, prior of the Carmelites of Banff, may well be identical with the man of that name who appears as vicar and reader at Banff in the 1560s; Charles Hume, friar of Dumfries, is probably to be identified with the reader at Kirkbean and Troqueer, especially as Charles was at that time a very uncommon christian name; John Auchinleck, warden of the Greyfriars of Haddington, may be presumed to have become reader at Athelstaneford and John Black, a Perth friar, may have become reader at Dunning. But promixity is not enough: even although Smith was a much less common name in Scotland then than it is now, who can say whether John Smith, friar in Dundee, is to be identified with the John Smith who became reader at Inchture, eight miles from Dundee? Sometimes there are complications: James Ramsay was a friar at Inverness or Elgin; but James Ramsay was the name of a monk of Melrose; there was a reader called James Ramsay at Alloway in Ayrshire and another of the same name at Fearn in Angus—have we here two, three or four individuals? Friars were in any event probably more mobile than most other priests, and too often, without any evidence from location or proximity to help us, there is nothing except identity of name, which is far from sufficient. An excellent illustration of the kind of work which is necessary to investigate the biographies of friars but which in the end may lead only to possibilities and probabilities is a note by Rev. Ian A. Muirhead which demonstrates the likelihood that out of ten friars of Inverness and Elgin who are known to have survived the reformation, five became ministers or readers[50]. Elizeus MacCulloch and Henry Smith, Dominicans of Ayr, may be identical with the readers at Balmaclellan and Glasserton, and James Dodds, prior of the Dominicans of Wigtown, may have become minister at Dalry in Galloway[51]. Others who deserve investigation are Robert Fisher, reader at Dalyell, James Fothringham, reader at Covington, James Carruthers, reader at Eastwood and Parton, and John Paton, reader at Dunnottar, all of whom bear the names of friars.

---

49. The prior of the small Augustinian house of Blantyre, William Chirnside, became a minister, but he seems to have been a secular, holding the priory *in commendam*.

50. *Scot. Hist. Rev.*, xxviii, 89-90.

51. I am indebted to Dr. John Durkan for these suggestions.

Contemporaries were well aware of the number of clergy who conformed and carried on their work in their parishes. It was to them that Ninian Winyet was alluding when he wrote: " At Pasche and certane Soundays efter, thai techeit with grete appering zele, and ministrate the sacramentis till us on the Catholic manere; and be Witsonday thai change thair standart in our plane contrare "[52]. But he also points to the numbers of monks (including, of course, canons regular) who entered the reformed church: " Quhy admit ye to be your prechouris . . . [men] of na experience, nor yit haifand praeeminence by utheris of godly leving, except ye call that godly to covet a fair wyfe and ane fatt pensioun, by the lawis of the monastik lyfe, quhilk sindry of thame hes professit ? "[53] Another observer, the Jesuit de Gouda, also speaks of the monks who had turned ministers, but remarks as well on the acceptance of men with no previous clerical experience: " The ministers, as they call them, are either apostate monks, or laymen of low rank, and are quite unlearned, being tailors, shoemakers, tanners or the like "[54]. The historian who surveys the ministry of the reformed church and, after listing those who had previously been secular priests, monks, canons regular and friars, notes how many of them are apparently without antecedents among the pre-reformation clergy, is at first inclined to agree with de Gouda. But a little reflection suggests that such a view may be ill-considered. For one thing, the reformed church drew not only on parsons, vicars, and regulars, but also on chaplains and on unbeneficed clergy: e.g. Walter Pyle, exhorter at Southdean, had been a chaplain in Jedburgh; Thomas Skirling, reader at Crail, had been chaplain of St. Nicholas in the collegiate church of Crail; Alexander Ramsay, reader at Aberdour (diocese of Aberdeen), had been " chaiplane of Oure Lady Pietie in the yle of the parroche kirk of Abirdoure "; and John Sinclair, reader at Dumfries, was presumably the sir John Sinclair who had been the possessor of an altarage in Dumfries church. Further investigation would probably reveal many similar cases, and there were in addition men who had not held benefices but to whose former priestly status the appellation " sir " is a safe guide: for instance, Michael Boncle, minister at Innerwick in 1567, must be identical with sir Michael Boncle, the natural son of a burgess of Dunbar, legitimated in 1558[55]. It would in any event be worthy of note that, while a very high proportion of the ex-priests and ex-monks were fit only to be readers, a good number of the men found capable of the full ministry of word and sacraments in the reformed church were men previously unknown to record, and if they had indeed been tailors, shoemakers or tanners they must have been reasonably well educated, albeit possibly self-educated, men. Further, on looking through the lists of priests who were prosecuted for saying mass in 1563 one observes that a good many of them, too, have no known career in the pre-reformation church, and this makes one cautious about stressing the non-priestly element in the post-reformation ministry[56].

---

52. Winyet, *Works* (Scot. Text. Soc.), i, 53.

53. *Ibid.*, 101.

54. Pollen, *Papal negotiations with Queen Mary*, 135.

55. *R.M.S.* iv, 1304.

56. The dangers arising from incomplete records, or incomplete examination of records, hardly need stressing : *e.g.*, Gilbert Foulsie, who became Archdeacon of Orkney in 1561, had evidently been a member of a religious order (*Reg. Sec. Sig.*, v, 3308), and Francis Bothwell, who became treasurer of Orkney about the same time, had been a friar, but I have not found either of them recorded as a member of a Scottish community.

The record of service in the reformed church, while it is the easiest evidence to come by, is not the only evidence which shows the attitude of the clergy to the reformation. There must have been many who accepted the reformed faith but did not undertake work as ministers, and proof of this may occasionally be found. There are, for example, some lists of priests who formally renounced their former doctrines, but by no means all of the men named appear among the reformed clergy[57]. There is, again, the case of the dignitaries and prebendaries of the chapel royal. They were in a specially privileged position, because, as thirds were not exacted from them, they were therefore in possession of their full pre-reformation revenues. It is perhaps hardly surprising that few of them served in the reformed church, though one conspicuous exception was John Carswell, the chancellor of the chapel royal, who became superintendent of Argyll[58]. Yet it must not be concluded that the other prebendaries were out of sympathy with the reformed cause, because the testament of George Clapperton, the subdean, shows that he died in the reformed faith[59]. No doubt examination of the testaments of other clergy would yield similar information, for in his will a man often made a kind of profession of faith. Again, some light is thrown on the opinions of the bishop and canons of Moray by their agreeing, in 1569, to contribute to the repair of their cathedral so that it could be used for reformed worship[60], and on the attitude of Henry Sinclair, bishop of Ross, by the fact that he did not scruple to furnish bread and wine for the communion service of the reformed church[61]. There is a dearth of memoirs and private letters for that period, but the *Correspondence of Sir Patrick Waus*[62] shows how easily a parson accepted the change in 1560. Andrew Blythman, one of the Charterhouse monks, seems to have become an elder in the parish church of Perth.

Another kind of evidence which may be used to throw light on the attitude of individual clergy to the reformed church is proof of their entering into matrimony. It is easy to find examples of men whose names do not appear among the reformed clergy but who married in or after 1560: Robert Douglas, provost of Lincluden, scandalised his prebendaries early in 1560 by intimating his intention to marry[63]; Magnus Halcro, chantor of Orkney, married in 1563[64]; after Malcolm Reid, vicar of Reay, died in 1567, we hear of his widow[65]; Alexander Dunbar, dean of Moray, was another dignitary who married[66]. The Dunfermline parish register discloses that Andrew Law, " sometime a popish priest " but otherwise unknown, married in 1562[67]. Marriage need not, however,

---

57. *St Andrews kirk session register*, 11-18.

58. John Stoddart, who had been presented to a prebend in the chapel royal in 1559, became parson and minister of Campsie, and Henry Yair, another prebendary, is said to have become an exhorter.

59. Edinburgh Testaments, 21 Sept. 1574.

60. *Reg. Privy Council*, i, 677.

61. *Ibid.*, 492.

62. Ed. Robert Vans Agnew.

63. *Protocol Book of Mark Carruthers* (Scot. Rec. Soc.). 190.

64. *Protocol Book of Gilbert Grote* (Scot. Rec. Soc.), 229.

65. *Thirds of Benefices*, 211.

66. R.S.S., xlv, 115*v*.

67. *Dunfermline Parish Register* (Scot. Rec. Soc.), p. 9.

in every case prove that there had been a change of conviction. There were only too many priests who before 1560 had been married in all but name, and they did not all react in the same way to the change of custom —for there was no change in law, in the sense of a specific enactment— which came at the reformation. Some of them had no doubt already adopted the reformers' opinion that compulsory celibacy was wrong, and those who had done so would presumably hasten in 1560 to make their mistresses " honest women " by marrying them. But others, in spite of their manner of life, may yet have upheld clerical celibacy in theory, and may still have adhered to that view after 1560—only to find, however, that it was no longer permissible for them to live in sin and that the courts of the reformed church did not acknowledge that their priestly character was any excuse for abstaining from matrimony. Sometimes, therefore, the marriage of former clergy took place under constraint and does not indicate any change of opinion[68]; but John Anderson, vicar of Cleish, after being compelled by the kirk session of St. Andrews to marry Eufame Pattoun in 1564, subsequently carried his acceptance of the new ways a stage further and became reader in his parish[69].

It must not be thought, even when it is recorded of a priest that he accepted office in the reformed church, that he had necessarily undergone a profound change in his convictions. There were vicars of Bray at the Scottish reformation as at other ecclesiastical revolutions, those who conformed to what seemed for the time to be the fashion, the prevailing opinion, but who were equally ready to change again. For instance, William Telfer, canon of Whithorn and vicar of Cruggleton in Galloway, appears as reader there in 1562 and so continues for twenty years; yet in 1563 " sir William Telfer " was convicted for saying mass at " Crugiltoun, " so it appears that this vicar-reader was quite prepared to do a little " mass-mongering " when he thought that the mass was coming into fashion again[70]. John Colville, vicar of Cathcart, was reader there in 1563 and 1568, but he also was prosecuted for saying mass in 1563[71]. And John Morison, who after his " recantatioun " had been " admittit reader in Mithyll (Methil)," was subsequently summoned for administering baptism and marriage " efter the papistical fasson "[72].

The periodical changes in the government's policy, and not least the vacillations of Queen Mary herself, were such as to tax the agility of even the most determined vicar of Bray. Anyone who hoped that the queen's return in 1561 would lead to the nullifying of the reformers' achievements of the previous year would be disappointed by Mary's proclamation forbidding any alteration in the state of religion which she found on her arrival in her kingdom[73]; those who looked to the influence of the conservative north-east to bring about a reaction against the reformation found their hopes blighted by the queen's campaign against Huntly in 1562; again, if the " mass-mongers " of 1563 expected official countenance, they found instead that the law would take its course in terms of the queen's own proclamation, and indeed the year 1563, with its act about the manses and its prosecutions of " mass

68. *St. Andrews kirk session register* (Scot. Hist. Soc.), xiv.
69. *Ibid.*
70. Pitcairn, *Criminal trials*, I, ii, 428 (" Congiltoun " is a mis-reading).
71. *Ibid.*
72. *St. Andrews kirk session register*, i, 226-7.
73. *Reg. Privy Council*, i, 266-7.

mongers, " represented a high-water mark for the time being of crown favour towards the reformed church. From 1564 to 1566, official policy was much less favourable to the reformers, and the expansion of their ministry was seriously hampered by lack of funds, for very little of the income from the thirds was allotted to stipends[74]. Towards the end of 1566, however, Queen Mary's attitude changed radically. She ordained that benefices worth less than 300 merks should, as they fell vacant, go to ministers; she gave a very substantial assignation for stipends from the thirds—£10,000 in money, and victual worth perhaps nearly as much; she made several gifts to burghs of the ecclesiastical revenues within their bounds[75]. On top of all this, in April 1567 she formally took the reformed church under her protection and undertook to defend it against any interference from overseas[76]. After Mary was deposed, the government of the new reign did not at first go any further than she had gone, for proposals made at the parliament of December 1567 to dispossess the " old possessors " of benefices were not accepted, and instead their titles were confirmed[77]. Meantime, however, the attitude of the reformed church towards the beneficed clergy had changed. In 1560, so far from being given any specific encouragement to serve in the reforming ministry, they had not received any recognition in virtue of their existing status; but in 1566 an invitation was issued to all beneficed men to support the reformed church[78], and from that time onwards the whole drift of the reformers' policy was towards imitation of the policy pursued in England, whereby the reformed church would take over the existing benefices and their holders. It was a logical development of this policy that in 1573 a statute was passed[79] whereby every beneficed clerk was to take an oath to the king, to acknowledge a bishop or superintendent of the reformed church as his ordinary and formally to give his assent to the Confession of Faith, on pain of deprivation. This measure represented a challenge to men who had hitherto been under no compulsion to admit their refusal to comply with the new regime[80]. The number of deprivations does not appear to have been very large, for the records of crown presentations contained in the Register of the Privy Seal reveal only some twenty between the date of the statute and the end of 1574 and only another four between that date and the middle of 1577. It must, of course, be borne in mind that these records are only of benefices to which the crown had the right to appoint, and, while the number of such benefices was certainly very large in that period, what proportion of the whole it represented has not been worked out; and it must also be taken into account that by this time probably about a third of the men who had been in office in 1560 were dead. Yet, with all qualifications, the figures are not very impressive, and suggest that the amount of determined and persistent recusancy was limited. Certainly, if particulars are to be sought of priests who carried their resolution to adhere to their old beliefs to the extent of incurring financial loss, they are to be found in those records of deprivations.

---

74. *Thirds of Benefices*, xxvi-xxvii.
75. *Reg. Privy Council*, i, 487 seq., 404 ; *Reg. Sec. Sig.*, v, Intro., xiv.
76. *A.P.S.*, ii, 548.
77. *Ibid.*, iii, 37cc. 2, 5 ; 31c. 26 ; 33c. 36.
78. *Acts and proceedings of the general assemblies*, i, 92.
79. *A.P.S.*, iii, 72 c. 3.
80. There are indications that the threat of deprivation may have stimulated some priests to a belated decision to become active conformers and to undertake work as readers, but there was no obligation on them to do so.

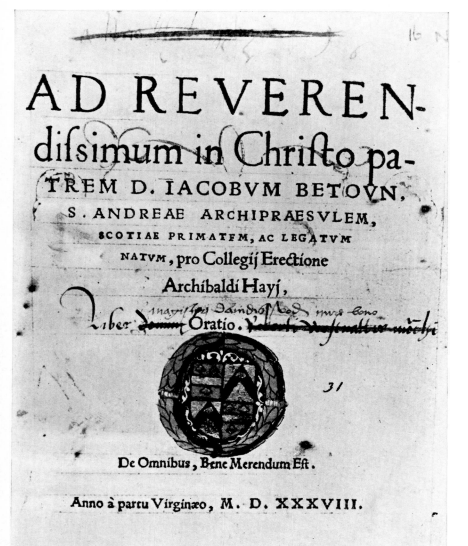

AD REVEREN-
dissimum in Christo pa-
TREM D. IACOBVM BETOVN,
S . ANDREAE ARCHIPRAESVLEM,
SCOTIAE PRIMATFM, AC LEGATVM
NATVM , pro Collegij Erectione

Archibaldi Hayj,

Liber ~~domini~~ Oratio.

31

De Omnibus , Bene Merendum Est .

Anno à partu Virgineo, M . D . XXXVIII.

PLATE XI. TITLE-PAGE OF ARCHIBALD HAY'S ADDRESS, PROPOSING
THE FOUNDATION OF ST. MARY'S COLLEGE, ST. ANDREWS.

PLATE XII.

ST. MARY'S
COLLEGE,
ST. ANDREWS.

EDUCATION IN THE CENTURY OF THE REFORMATION

by

JOHN DURKAN

" I grant that our Fatheris of immoderat zeill (besyde the teindis
and necessarie rentis of the Kirk) gaue thairunto superfluously, and
mair than aneuch," claimed David Fergusson, minister of Dunfermline
a decade after the reformation.   But he had just been accusing his
hearers of impiety and sacrilege, " quhairby ze spuilze the pure, the
schuilis, the Tempilis, and Ministeris of Goddis word, zea Christ him
self."[1] Writers of an earlier day were inclined to exaggerate the extent
of the church's contribution to education in medieval Scotland; some
nowadays would rather suggest that there were few schools or scholars
to despoil.   David Fergusson's text can, of course, be interpreted to
mean that what has been jeopardized by the greed of vested interests are
merely the paper schemes of the Book of Discipline, and no doubt he
does in part mean that.   Nevertheless some schools were despoiled at
the reformation, the reason being that their revenues were attached
to collegiate churches or chaplainries, revenues that the kirk was only
partially successful in recovering and in some cases re-applying to
scholastic purposes. Moreover the existence of medieval schools is often
masked by the fact that they were usually part of a larger foundation
dedicated in the first place to the worship of God; and that the schoolmaster generally preferred to be described as a chaplain or prebendary,
for that was what he primarily was (and no doubt the same is true of
some ministers and readers later).   So that when we hear of schools
being founded in later days, or merely emerging into record, we cannot
be altogether certain that they are not re-foundations and can only wish
that we had the parish records in medieval times that we have in post-
medieval.

The following essay attempts a reassessment in the context of the age.
Leaving aside university education for the moment, it deals with
elementary and grammar school education and other forms of higher
education, with schoolmasters and schoolboys, and with comtemporary
attempts to reform the educational framework, in such a way as to
illustrate the thesis set out above.

LITTLE SCHOOLS: SONG AND READING

Little school is a more comprehensive name than song school, apt
as that name is.   It is the term found in France and elsewhere, and is
implied by the name " great school," or " high school " given to the
grammar school by contrast.   In smaller places the reading school and
the song school were naturally identical.   In the burghs they were often
separate; in Edinburgh, for instance, in 1524, schools outside the grammar school were to be devoted to the " teching and lering of lectouris

---

1. Fergusson, *Tracts*, p. 76. The work of A. F. Leach is here accepted as the standard source for the
structure of medieval education. But Joan Simon's articles in *Past and Present* and the *British Journal
of Educ. Studies* provide modifications especially regarding the activity of religious in education, which
Leach somewhat underrated.

alanerly.²" Why was it that generally the grammar schoolmaster had no authority over little schools?

The authority over every song school in a diocese was originally the precentor, but we have no record of his exercising his authority in Scotland outside the cathedral. In Elgin, for instance, the precentor, or the chanter as he is usually called in the vernacular, was responsible for singing lessons and choirboy discipline, for holding song schools " in the college of the church ", and for deputing a fit man to rule and teach youths and other comers in song and reading.³ The purpose of the song school was to staff the choir, and therefore the learning of the alphabet and memorising by rote of the psalter, etc. were incidental. But all clerks had to have a minimum of reading; the alternative name for a tonsured cleric was " psalmist ".⁴ In Edinburgh there were little schools which taught the primer, the grace book and " plane Donat ", that is, the *Ars Minor* of Donatus, which contains the rudiments of Latin grammar.⁵ Four grace books were bought in Edinburgh and sent on to Dunkeld in the time of Bishop Brown.⁶ And the " Grate Buik " put into James Melville's hands at the age of five was clearly a grace book and not a bible.⁷ Acquiring the rudiments (*puerilia*) was a more considerable achievement than mastering the ABC and some song schools obviously aimed higher than others. James Melville spent two years at home with his grace book and there are indications that that was the average time spent at such little schools.

Theoretically, as laid down by the early church councils, there should have been a song school in every parish. Moreover all such schools should be " public " (or " general "), that is open to all comers. It has been remarked that we can only point to one such school in a rural parish in Scotland. In an unidentified parish in the diocese of St. Andrews we hear of parishioners wishing to found a chaplainry of the Holy Rood, of which the chaplain is bound to hold a public song school at the church for the teaching of scholars in Gregorian chant, the organ and descant⁸. But when we find scholars from the Isles enrolling themselves as university students⁹, we can be less confident that there were few rural schools, even if we must suppose them as coming straight from a parish school to study in the university. Moreover it is really quite inaccurate to speak of burgh schools, as some do, as early as the twelfth century; the wording of the charters shows that they are church schools sited in a burgh. Of a number of notaries educated in the first half of the sixteenth century, who must have had as a minimum both song and grammar school education, a surprising porportion came from remote country areas: Cruach in Strathearn, Orchard in Glasgow diocese, the Mains of Dollar, Newburgh in Buchan, Ochiltree, Kirkchrist near Insch, Trinity Gask, Bold (near Innerleithen), Dornoca,

---

2. *R.M.S.*, iii, 918.
3. *Moray*, p. 263, or 270. Episcopal and monastic registers are cited here in this form, rather than the cumbrous *Registrum Episcopatus Moraviensis*.
4. John Major, *In Quartum Sententiarum* (1521), fol. cliii explains.
5. *Edinburgh Burgh Records*, i. 193-4.
6. *Rentale Dunkeldense*, p. 252.
7. *Autobiography* (Wodrow Society), p. 16.
8. *Formulare*, edited Donaldson (Stair Society), ii, 185-7, and comments of the late D. E. Easson in *Records Scottish Church Hist. Soc.*, vi.
9. *Munimenta Universitatis Glasguensis*, ii. 61.

Douglas, Dalry in Galloway, Abington[10]. Many may have attended the nearest song school and been maintained by an interested cleric as landward scholars at the grammar school of the nearest town.

Sometimes a youth came from the country to the cathedral song school. Master John Panter left his home near Hamilton to become one of the six endowed choirboys at Glasgow cathedral[11]. He shone, and in 1508 received an extra salary of ten merks, besides his daily upkeep such as the other choirboys had[12]. Later he went off to an expert teacher to learn more advanced singing and organ-playing, promising solemnly to return. The earl of Arran, however, persuaded him to accept the parish clerkship in the collegiate church of Hamilton for a fee of £40, perhaps as prebendary in charge of the song school. However, remembering his pact, he returned to Glasgow. The archbishop was grateful, and, in addition to the preceptory of the song school whose profits he already enjoyed, gave him a stipend of £20. Panter also composed: we hear of an *Ave Gloriosa Virginum Regina* written by him in three parts of " prickat singing " for which first and second trebles were necessary[13].

Among Panter's duties was daily service at the Lady mass and on certain other days at matins, high mass and vespers, taking the organ in the organist's absence. As will appear from this a great deal of medieval learning was learning by apprenticeship. At Aberdeen St. Nicholas in 1496 we find Robert Hutchinson, sangster, taking the song school, for burgesses's sons especially, and they were to pay him scholage. Besides teaching them to sing and play, he had to be at the lecterns at mass, matins, evensong, compline, psalms, responses, hymns and all other services: it is a wonder he had any time for a school[14]. There were, however, at least two masters. In 1483 Richard Boyle was principal master. Boyle was a choir clerk: that is a choirboy or singing man receiving a fee[15]. The parish clerkship income was evidently divided up to provide for several clerks. It is not surprising therefore, that elsewhere the income of a parish clerkship was thought suitable for annexation to collegiate churches. Another way of providing for the income of a young scholar was as server to a chaplain: as with the chaplain of St. Gabriel in St, Giles in Edinburgh, who by his foundation had to pay a scholar 21 shillings yearly. Occasional smaller windfalls for poor scholars came in the same way: for instance for the six who served six chaplains in the nether kirk of Glasgow cathedral or the one who served the altar of St. Eloi in Edinburgh[16].

What happened to a boy when his voice broke? There appears to be a rough distinction between *puer* and *iuvenis*, the latter an adolescent, the former one whose voice has not broken. James Melville speaks of a boy of 14 as " now almost past from the age of bernheid ",[17] no longer a boy. The *puerilia*, rudiments, were the studies of boys. At the collegiate church of our Lady in Glasgow, the three endowed choristers had to

---

10. Register of Admission of Notaries, MS in General Register House, i, passim.
11. *Formulare*, ii, 263-4.
12. *Diocesan Registers of Glasgow*, ii, 252.
13. Renwick, *Glasgow Protocols*, i, 118.
14. *St. Nicholas*, ii, 339.
15. *Ibid.*, ii, 334, 335.
16. *St. Giles*, p. 202; *Glasgow Protocols*, i, 119; Smith, *Hammermen of Edinburgh*, p. 44.
17. *Autobiography*, p. 20.

leave when they lost their voices, but they could continue in the city grammar school for a further two years, after which the endowment passed to another boy.[18] A similar arrangement is evident at Semple where the sixth prebendary had to teach the boy foundationers grammar, after they left the song school where the fifth prebendary taught and maintained them.[19] At Aberdeen St. Nicholas one of the choir clerks was licensed to pass to the grammar school, appointing a substitute, who likewise left for the grammar school, and had in his turn to be replaced.[20] The burgh was not always anxious to let a singer go even to improve his organ playing: Gilbert Robertson was released for two years with fee, only on promising to give a year's service on return and to give Aberdeen his preferences. In fact he later became a prebendary of St. Giles.[21]

All collegiate churches had their own song schools, whether explicitly mentioned as such or not. In some cases, as as Biggar, they may have taken over a parish school. But at others they were separate. Restalrig had its own song and grammar school, and the grammar school at Dumbarton was in the parish church, where St. Peter's altar was held by the master[22]. While the number of endowed boy choristers was small, others attended the school who were not endowed, as for instance at Brechin[23]. Scottish collegiate foundations are small compared with certain English ones, but the comparison should rather be with similar small countries abroad. An advantage of the collegiate church was the discipline of the common life, but that was characteristic of some burgh churches too, where the choir members were known as the " brethren, " and which were collegiate in all but name. As a cleric was required to be of " good conversation," the common life as well as precept taught him manners, and the youth acquired that stock or moral and proverbial wisdom for which the middle ages are famous. There were of course textbooks such as the Distichs of Cato or the books of Solomon such as they evidently used at Crail.[24]

The song school is at times associated with the Lady mass, which was often either rehearsed or held in some private place, where the master could direct his scholars without distracting worshippers. In 1540 Sir Robert Aikenhead, chaplain, was hired to deputise for the aged Lady chaplain at Linlithgow and eventually to replace him. He had also to " uptake ane sang schull ", evidently a public one, as he had to " leir all bairnis that will cum thereto " and take customary payments. However he broke the engagement by becoming a chaplain to the Lady altar in Torphichen. Nevertheless he was re-engaged in 1543 as permanent chaplain to teach and present himself as the rest of the brethren of the church did and reside in the burgh.[25] Similarly at the parish church of St. Andrews the *rector chori* has to keep the bairns of the song school as well as any other choirmaster in any parish church in Scotland, and cause the Lady mass to be sung as well as or better than any of his predecessors.[26]

18. *Liber Collegii Nostre Domine*, pp. 43-4.
19. *Glasgow*, ii, 509-510.
20. *St. Nicholas*, ii. 342.
21. *Ibid.*, ii, 359; *St. Giles*, p. 254; he was also in 1532 parish clerk of Kenmay, *Protocol Bk. Sir J. Cristisone*, no. 188.
22. *Collegiate Churches of Midlothian*, p. 283; Fergus Roberts, *The Grammar School of Dumbarton*, p. 2.
23. *Brechin*, ii, 26-7. This is a collegiate foundation attached to a cathedral.
24. Cf. *Innes Review*, ix, 79, under Bowman.
25. Ferguson, *Ecclesia Antiqua*, p. 286; Linlithgow Burgh Court Book, MS (G.R.H.), ff. 267r, 307r.
26. Rankin, *The Parish Church of Holy Trinity*, p. 134.

In St. Salvator's college, the song schoolmaster had to sing the Lady mass daily in Gregorian chant at the Lady altar in the cloister: at Paisley the *Ave Gloriosa* was to be sung by the sangsters in the chapter-house before the Lady altar there[27].

The parish clerk acted sometimes as master. In 1551 at Ayr, for instance, George Cochrane was licensed by the burgh to hold a song school for the neighbours' bairns and others whomsoever for payment.[28] In 1539 the clerk who is also burgh clerk was presented by the burgh of Inverness to the bishop; he is " to rule the school, to instruct and teach the chaplains and scholars coming thereto in the art of music, not only in chant but in organ playing[29]." A similar arrangement existed at Dundee.

The attempt to teach everything through Latin had been partially abandoned by the sixteenth century, and many little schools had become in reality vernacular schools: Sir David Lindsay himself in his *Monarch* uses the phrase "Latin school" for a grammar school. As Grant illustrated in his work on the burgh schools, the grammar of John Vaus of Aberdeen was taught through the vernacular. English was being taught in Dundee by one of the doctors deputed by the grammar schoolmaster appointed there by the abbot of Lindores[30]. In this school, which had not managed because of burgh opposition to obtain possession of the official premises, song and grammar school were probably together and one of the doctors perhaps taught English while the other (Andrew Kemp, the composer) taught singing.

More advanced music was also taught in some centres. Sir Thomas Binning, chaplain and sangster at Aberdeen, had both bairns and students under him in 1505[31]. John Malison, master of the song school in Old Aberdeen, would appear from Boece's account to have done likewise[32]. In 1464, John Hutchinson, a graduate of Glasgow, received a dispensation from the authorities to go and learn music in Edinburgh after his mastership[33]. In 1553 James Lauder, a prebendary of St, Giles, received licence to go to England and France to study music and the organ[34]: many years later he composed Lord March's Pavane. Alexander Scott appears as a student of the fife in Paris, in 1540, besides being singer and organist (with canon's portion) at the priory of Inchmahome[35].

Some of the teachers were musicians of considerable ability. Thomas Wood, vicar of St. Andrews in post-reformation times, did his best to get some of them to use their talents in the making of the Scottish Psalter. He appears to have been a monk himself, probably of Lindores[36]. Other composers had a similar history. John Angus had been a monk of Dunfermline; Andrew Blackhall, a canon regular of Holyrood; David

---

27. Cant, *St. Salvator*, pp. 25, 28; note. MS Rental, National Library of Scotland, Adv. MS 15.1.17, p. 148.
28. Grant, *Burgh Schools*, p. 68.
29. Hutton Collections (Shires) in N.L.S., xi, 71.
30. Maxwell, *Old Dundee Before the Reformation*, p. 153.
31. *St. Nicholas*, ii, 344-5.
32. Boece, *Bishops of Aberdeen*, p. 79; *Aberdeen*, ii, 98.
33. *Munimenta*, ii, 202.
34. *Edinburgh Records*, ii, 176.
35. *Fraser Papers*, p. 223; *Bibliotheque d'Humanisme et Renaissance*, xii, 113.; he appears to be the poet of that name, who wrote the lament for the Master of Erskine.
36. Thomas Wood, monk, was at St. Andrews University in 1576.

Peebles, although he married, preferred to style himself in his will as a member of the convent of St. Andrews. Others can be traced as teachers in various towns: John Fethy, for instance, who about 1532 returned to Scotland, and " wes the first Organeist that euer brought in Scotland the curius new fingering[37]." Andrew Kemp taught the song school at Dundee and was later one of the chaplains in St. Salvator's college St. Andrews[38]. John Buchan we shall meet later as a grammar schoolmaster. Alexander Smith, who taught James Melville his music after the reformation, was brought up among the novices in the priory of St. Andrews, where was David Peebles, " ane of the principal musicians in all this land." Some of the novices had already considerable skill, Francis Heagy, for instance[39]. It is a remarkable fact that the Englishman, Andrew Borde, who disliked most things Scottish, and maintained that the Scots reciprocated as far as he was concerned, could still say that " the people of the countery be hardy men, and well favored, and good musycyons[40]."

There can be no doubt about the national passion for music. The immediate post-reformation reaction in favour of plain psalm tunes can best be understood against a background where music still mattered very much; and Thomas Wood's prophecy that if nothing were done music would perish utterly from the land was in fact fulfilled[41]. The Regent Moray was not the first person to refer to the elaborate music of his time as " the curiosity of music ", when he advised David Peebles to abandon it for plain sweet tunes. The provost of the collegiate church of Semple was expected to be expert not only in Gregorian chant but in *cantus precatus* " which others call curious[42]." Alexander Paterson of the Chapel Royal, Stirling, is one of those described as believing in the theory of one note to a syllable.[43] And there are many other indications that there were centres which valued plain song and *patrum more cantus* in preference to elaboration, an indication as the latter is, however, of high musical culture[44]. The great advantage of the new psalm tunes was less their greater musical simplicity than the fact that, being in the vernacular, they were within the understanding of all.

What can we say about the spread of such schools outside the urban areas ? Were there, as in England, chantry schools in rural districts ? In the nature of things education is an urban thing, and Latin was a less useful instrument of communication away from the centres of tiade and ecclesiastical organisation. But that is not to say there was no rural education at all. The word chantry (*cantaria*) is seldom used in Scotland: " chaplainry " and " altarage " are commoner. We have few foundation deeds. Even in England, however, " the foundation deeds . . . even when it is known from the statutes, where extant, that a school was intended . . .

---

37. *P.S.A.S.*, vii, p. 455.
38. *Old Dundee*, p. 153; *Laing Charters*, no. 846.
39. *Musica Britannica*, xv.
40. *Works* (Early English Text Soc., extra series no. x), p. 137. Borde denounced all Scottish ale except Leith ale (p. 136) and even took exception to those Scots he met at Orleans on their way to Compostella (p. 205).
41. In spite of later efforts by James VI.
42. *P.S.A.S.*, vii, p. 448; *Glasgow*, ii, 514.
43. *Robertus Richardinus* (Scot. Hist. Soc.), p. 81. Robert Paterson, master of the song school, Ayr, and organist there, was trained by the parson of Crieff, evidently another Paterson who held that prebend in the Chapel Royal. Alloway Barony Court Book (G.R.H.), unfoliated, under 13th May, 1535.
44. Boece, *Lives*, p. 79.

rarely mention a school[45]." We are not so fortunate as to possess statutes for such foundations, nor have we evidence like the chantry certificates granted in England at the reformation and which are often the only evidence of pre-existing medieval schools. Even the foundation of the chaplainry at Carmyllie in Angus mentions schools quite incidentally[46]. We have it is true references, immediately after the reformation, to the eradication of idolatry in colleges and schools in Cunningham, Kyle and Carrick; between Spey and Dee; and in Caithness and Sutherland[47]. A recent tendency is to read these general commissions as having no particular application to the region in question, a tendency that is as unfounded as the easy assumption of others that all chantry foundations had a scholastic end in view. It may, I think, be taken for granted that there were other rural chantry schools apart from Carmyllie.

GRAMMAR SCHOOLS OR HIGH SCHOOLS

Grammar schools were schools in which "grammar subjects" (*grammaticalia*) were taught. The elements of rudiments were expected to be mastered in some degree before entry; the other subjects of the *trivium* (rhetoric with versification, and dialectic) were often added. At King's College, Aberdeen, the university grammar school segregated grammarians and logicians (who were in the first year of their arts course anyway) and held a class "elementarians" who could not speak Latin at all or at any rate not sufficiently: these were allowed to speak the vernacular, but not to the grammar students proper[48]. The term "principal grammar school" is sometimes used, as at Perth, to differentiate it from the little school where some grammar was taught[49]. The term "high school[50]" or "great school" is also found (cf. *magna missa*, rendered in the vernacular as high mass). Grammar schools can be identified in various burghs, in cathedral towns and in collegiate churches. Unlike the little schools they came under the chancellor of the diocese (even where the patron was an abbot, it appears).

The length of the course varied, but it was longer than the two years or so of the little school. In sixteenth-century England utilitarian minds described it as " long and tedius ".[51] Mathurin Cordier, the well-known French grammarian of reformed opinions, found burgesses all too eager to shorten the course for their offspring. While there were many advantages in the transfer of much of the power over the grammar school from the church to the burgh authorities, there were some disadvantages too. Adam Mure, the "maister of the Hie Scule" of Edinburgh, was only appointed on condition that he promised to make the bairns perfect grammarians in three years: Mure was a Paris graduaate[52]. Yet this does not mean that this was the fullest possible course available: " perfect grammar " means perfect mastery of spoken Latin. Similarly Andrew Melville was trained up " in letters " till the age of twelve under Mr. Thomas Anderson in Montrose grammar school. But

---

45. Leach, *English Schools at the Reformation*, p. 52.
46. *Registrum de Panmure*, ii, 266.
47. *Acts of the General Assemblies*, i, 63, 73, 311.
48. Simpson, *Bon Record*, p. 99.
49. *Dunfermline*, p. 394.
50. *Protocol Bk. of John Foular*, i, nos. 271, 565.
51. Tawney and Power, *Tudor Economic Documents*, iii, 436.
52. *Edinburgh Records*, ii, 48; Paris, BN Ms Lat. 9952, f. 125v.

there we are left to infer that he might have continued if his mother had not been widowed[53].

It would be pleasant to be able to illuminate the grammar school course in the early sixteenth century. At King's College there is mention of the table of confession and of a modicum of counting[54]. But this evidently refers to " elementarians " and new boys. Roman figures (although Arabic are also common) must have made sums a bugbear. Reckoning by tallies as well as in paper notebooks and " bills " (*cedulae*) is found[55]. At Aberdeen the Scots tongue is confined to elementarians, whose Latin is not adequate to permit converse with the grammar students, who, however, have a choice of Greek, Hebrew, French and Gaelic as well[56]. It is well-known that, according to Bishop Lesley, Aberdeen students were able to greet James V with Greek prose on his visit there in 1540. The school statutes of 1553 quote from Terence, Virgil, Cicero and Quintilian, and use a Latinised Greek— the headmaster is *archididascalus*, the under-teachers *hypodidascali* and the enforcers of the statutes are *nomophylaces*. At Musselburgh grammar school in 1547 (otherwise unrecorded at this date), Patrick Waus was reading Ovid, Caesar's Commentaries, Sallust and the *Silva* (perhaps of Statius), in addition to the New Testament and the psalter[57]. As to the learning of French, Edinburgh had a separate French School[58].

The grammar of Alexandre de Villedieu, as edited by John Vaus, was probably in use. At Semple collegiate church, for instance, the first and second parts of Alexander were taught in the grammar school[59]. At the monastery of Deer the grammar of Despautere was evidently used.[60] Despautere was also favoured by William Nudrie, who taught at Ayr in 1551 and at Peebles in 1555[61].

James Melville informs us that the languages, Greek and Hebrew, " war nocht to be gottine in the land[62]." He shows how Andrew Melville astonished his regents with his grasp of Greek, having learnt it from Pierre de Marsilliers at Montrose. A certain amount of evidence has, however, been accumulating which makes it clear that this statement cannot be accepted without qualification. Some additional considerations suggest themselves. Nudrie, already mentioned, had some knowledge of French, Greek and Hebrew, all of which he proposed printing in his textbook: it can hardly be believed that he had not already begun teaching these subjects at Ayr and Peebles. William Seton, a pupil at St. Leonard's in 1563, had by the age of nineteen learned some Greek in both Scotland and Paris[63]. William Crichton had certainly studied abroad, as had so many of his compatriots, Wishart included[64].

---

53. James Melville, *Autobiography*, p. 38.
54. *Bon Record*, p. 99.
55. *Rentale Dunkeldense*, p. xxvii.
56. *Bon Record*, loc. cit. " Perfect " Latin appears to mean Latin without the frills, as used in *Acts Parl. Scotland*, ii, 238, c.3, and in *Records of Elgin*, ii, 395. (The latter includes rhetoric, but Greek, Hebrew, logic ,etc., are extras.)
57. Waus, *Correspondence*, pp. 2-3. A Mr. George Nisbet was schoolmaster in 1580 (*Yester Writs*, no. 823).
58. *Edinburgh Records*, ii, 241.
59. *Glasgow*, ii, 515.
60. *Innes Review*, ix, 165.
61. *Ayr Burgh Accounts*, p. 110; *Peebles Records*, i, 209; *R.S.S.*, v, 658.
62. *Autobiography*, p. 30.
63. Pollen, *Papal Negotiations*, p. 511. He had been at school since five and had done logic and rhetoric.
64. Father Chadwick, S.J., tells me that a *catalogus* of 1593 describes Crichton as having studied before entering the Society in the following cities: St. Andrews, Paris, Rome, Leipzig, Louvain.

But when he arrived at the Jesuit novitiate in Rome in December, 1562, he carried a Latin Scottish history (Boece or Major), a Roman breviary, a diurnal, a small New Testament in Latin and French, a compendium of theology, trilingual prayers from scripture, a book by Hessels of Louvain, a Hebrew psalter, Marcus Aurelius in Scots and a Machiavelli in Italian[65].

Curiosity about the Greek alphabet, as James Melville suggests, may have been the whole of Greek learning in some centres. Already in 1531 we find a Linlithgow burgess wanting " Jhesus amor meus " transliterated *more litere Grecorum*[66]. We are told about George Wishart's familiarity with Greek, and this is not surprising as he studied at Louvain[67]. We do not know the date of appointment of Duncan Nevay (or Nevin) as school-master in Dunblane. He is first mentioned as such in 1567[68]. But he was certainly there earlier, having come from Aberdeen. After the reforma-tion, being then 32, he was readmitted as a notary by the Lords of the Council, and was at least sufficiently familiar with Greek to use it in his notarial sign[69]. It appears probable that in some of the more notable towns some degree of familiarity with Greek, and to a lesser extent Hebrew, was already a fact by the time of the first Book of Discipline. Nor can St. Andrews have been quite so backward as James Melville suggests, for a student there in 1564 was offering to teach Greek and Hebrew in Elgin two years later[70].

The main grammar school aim was the acquisition of Latin. Versifi-cation was taught and there are some samples in the printed books of the period. Translation into Latin was important. When Winzet was at Linlithgow, his boys almost daily got some theme, argument or saying on the basis of which they wrote a prose or letter in Latin. For instance when the Edinburgh burgh council ordered the doors of catholics to be chalked (a sign of eviction ?) on Easter Monday, Winzet drew up a declamation to be addressed to them " for caus of excercise and priuat studie, as usis to be in sculis." There is only a modicum of rhetoric in this sample, as Winzet himself noted: but it illustrated the use of every-day material in such exercises[71].

Less is known about the other end of the educational scale. What weight must be given, for instance, to the accusation that many clerics did not know their alphabet ? Was Sir John Latinless so completely Latinless as the Latin scholars of the time make out ? What precisely did the provincial councils mean by their " crass ignorance ? " There do not appear to be any clerics without a modicum of Latin or unable to write their names, although the use of *manu propria* after the signature shows it is not a universal skill. Many could no doubt read, who (at any rate after their schooldays were long past) could not construe: but country parishioners would hardly feel strongly about that. Yet even the poor bedesmen of the hospital in Haddington prayed their Lady psalter in Latin and their common prayers at curfew-time likewise: and

65. *Archivum Historicum Societatis Jesu*, v. 272.
66. Protocol Bk. of Thomas Johnsoun, f. 10v.
67. " Georgius filius georgii Wijer de dono dei " (Aug. 31, 1529.) Brussels, Royal Archives, Liber Intitu-latorum, iv, f. 21v. See also *S.H.R.*, xxxii, 98.
68. *R.M.S.*, iv, 2378.
69. Reg. of Admissions (G.R.H.), i, f. 66r.
70. Patrick Balfour. *Early Records*, p. 271; *Elgin Records*, ii, 395.
71. *Tractates* (Scottish Text Soc.), i, 25.

the Franciscan warden had to test their ability beforehand. If they knew their letters, they could add the *De Profundis*[72]. Similar requirements are found at our Lady's hospital, Aberdeen. There the poor bedesmen carry their beads in processions, no doubt answering the litanies in Latin[73]. Four categories of literacy are observable in one Aberdeen obit: the lepers who can pray to our Lady; the blind and other poor who can do likewise; the poor grammar schoolboys who are to read the *De Profundis* and the seven penitential psalms; the choirboys of King's and the cathedral who are to read the latter, with the litanies, prayers, suffrages, and collects (along with the *De Profundis*) to be found in their Books of Hours[74].

SCHOOLMASTERS

As already stated, grammar schoolmasters were subject to the diocesan chancellor, and in dioceses where none existed, such as St. Andrews and Whithorn, to the archdeacon. By the sixteenth century it is quite evident that most of the control had been won over by the burghs, but there was always the possibility of conflict and even of appeal to Rome.

The dominie was usually *Dominus*. He was quite frequently a master of arts in burghs: Patrick Blair at Dundee in 1490; James Makneiss at Ayr in 1516; Hugh Congilton at Leith in 1557[75]. A cleric styled Dominus was generally a person in sacred orders and who had not fully graduated in any subject. Theoretically nobody but a cleric could have authority (*regimen*) over other clerics. Married men are occasionally found as schoolmasters: Hugh Munro in Aberdeen and Andrew Simpson in Perth[76]. The commonest class of schoolmaster were chaplains. The burghs appear to have been disinclined to appoint a permanent chaplain to the school or to appoint for life, perhaps from the fear that permanency of tenure would lead to his neglecting his work and taking his ease in Sion. More often they appointed a stipendiary chaplain with an annual fee or pension. We have Winzet's word for it that in almost no burgh was the income sufficient[77]. It is not always clear what the schoolmaster actually collected. In Ayr he received £13 6s. 8d. from the burgh treasurer, but this would be augmented by collections (generally his service there was the Trinity service) and such casualties as entry silver, book silver, bent silver and candle silver. While the earliest records of these are post-reformation there can be no doubt that they were traditional payments. Entry silver was paid by new boys; book silver was paid when the master started a new book; bent silver was paid when rushes were being collected to strew the floor; candle silver (sometimes called the Blaise candle after the feastday immediately following Candlemas) was paid at Candlemas and no doubt at other times[78]. Scholage, a fee that may have originated as a charge towards the upkeep of the

---

72. Bryce, *Scottish Grey Friars*, ii, 14. Here the Lady psalter means some form of rosary (150 Aves, 15 Paters, 3 Creeds), the curfew prayers being 5 Paters, 5 Aves, the Creed.

73. *Aberdeen*, i, 405.

74. *Ibid.*, i, 426. Scholars at Glasgow who could not say the 7 psalms and had the rosary (*Rosarium*) as alternative are cited in *Liber Collegii N. Domine*, p. 50.

75. *R.M.S.*, ii, 1935; Alloway Court Bk. (G.R.H.), p. 96; Haddington Burgh Ct. Bk. 1555-60 (G.R.H.), f. 168r. For an early use of Dominie (c. 1580), *cf.* Row, *Historie*, p. 456.

76. *Bon Record*, p. 14; *Laing Charters*, no. 673.

77. *Tractates*, i, 24.

78. *Bon Record*, p. 38. Other explanations given of these terms are unsatisfactory.

school building, appears to have become a perquisite of the school-master. Some schoolmasters may have treated the post as a benefice: for instance, in November 1529, at Linlithgow, " ye sis deliueris yat maister finlaw forest get ane suffiiciand gramariar to tech ye skole or ellis ye balzeis to discharge ye said maister finlaw of ye skole and to discharge all ye nychtburis yat yai put na barnis to hime for he hes donne gret hurt to ye townne[79]." Possibly in the same connection, James Fyntoun, chaplain, appealed against the decision of the prin-cipal official of St. Andrews calling on him to demit office as school-master there; if so, Forest prevailed, and the chaplain had to demit[80].

Vicars are occasionally found teaching, usually as stopgaps. For instance, there is Andrew McCormyll, mentioned as " scul maister aire " on the 29th March, 1501, but shortly afterwards as vicar of Straiton and master of Ayr grammar school (*studium*)[81]. Again, Sir William Tunno, vicar pensioner of Manor in 1555, was next year appointed to the school at Peebles on a temporary basis, but was gravely ill shortly afterwards and had to be replaced[82]. The legend that monks were in charge of all medieval education dies hard. The nuns who taught girls at Aberdour probably taught embroidery and perhaps some reading (certainly not writing) and the Cistercian nuns who kept school at Elcho may be presumed to have done likewise[83]. Pedagogues, usually chaplains, were to be found in noblemen's houses, as we might expect; but Scots noble-men somewhat neglected their children in this respect. A page in a bishop's household would attend school in the bishop's absence[84]. Similarly some clerics would make themselves responsible for the tuition of their relatives[85]. Training of chaplains in those pre-seminary days in most cases ended with the grammar school and perhaps with an abbrevi-ated course, though refresher courses were not unknown: to which was added apprenticeship among his fellow-chaplains in choir. A typical instance is that of Thomas Palmer of Dumbarton, who made an agree-ment with a relative in 1518, whereby in return for certain lands his relative guaranteed to maintain him in food and clothing at "the grammar schools or school" (there may have been two in Dumbarton), " always and until he is made a chaplain," promising also a letter that " the said Thomas might well and freely celebrate and sing his mass or masses at the usual time, that is in the 24th year of his age "[86].

Under-teachers were known as doctors; monitors, however, occur also. Their appointment was in the hands of the principal master. They were far from wealthy. Dr. Small, for instance, at Edinburgh, kept the kirk watered and swept on eight days in summer and fifteen in winter, for which he received £3: no doubt his pupils did the work[87]. They were often helped out of burgh funds. Dr. Smith, alias John Nicolson, ended his days as one of the bedesmen of St. Mary's hospital, leaving in 1555 a wife and six children in extreme poverty[88]. Another

---

79. Linlithgow Burgh Court Bk., 1528-65 (G.R.H.), f. 45r.
80. *Protocol Bk. of Thomas Johnsoun*, nos. 36, 39.
81. Acta Dominorum Concilli (G.R.H.), x, f. 68v; *Ayr Burgh Charters*, p. 96.
82. Renwick, *Peebles in the Reign of Queen Mary*, p. 110; *Peebles Records*, i, 233.
83. Theiner, *Vetera Monumenta*, no. 884; *Calendar of Scottish Papers*, i, 56.
84. *Rentale Dunkeldense*, p. 107; this scholar became parish clerk of Forgandenny, *Ibid.*, p. 241.
85. *Ibid.*, p. 329.
86. Protocol Bk. of Matthew Forsyth (G.R.H.), f. 12v.
87. *City of Edinburgh Burgh Accounts*, i, 89.
88. *Edinburgh Records*, ii, 211.

Edinburgh doctor, Robert Drummond (or Dormont), was appointed in 1554 to the Canongate grammar school. However, the principal master in the Edinburgh grammar school objected and Drummond appeared shortly afterwards as a doctor in his school.[89]

Unofficial " adventure " schools are also found. At Peebles in 1558, the council appointed Walter Haldane on approval, paying him forty shillings and his " adventuris " (i.e. fees and casualties) for a few months till they found a qualified man, in which event he was either to relinquish or work with him as doctor[90]. At Elgin, Sir Thomas Rag, chaplain (and parish clerk) was commanded to desist from teaching, whether the children were few or many, but later he was still teaching in his room and was ordered by the council to join the principal grammar master in the common school[91]. David Ellis, who hailed from Aberdeen and was created notary at Innerpeffray, acted as adventure schoolmaster in Stirling, but was commanded to desist, under an agreement made with the grammar schoolmaster, Mr. William Gullane, from teaching anybody over the age of six without Gullane's licence, except those learning to read, write and count[92]. In other words, boys of seven who were ready to start grammar proper were the exclusive concern of the grammar schoolmaster. The schools in the charge of women, mentioned in Edinburgh in 1499, were undoubtedly of the little school type[93].

One surprising fact that emerges is the mobility of many of these teachers, no doubt in quest of better rewards or a post nearer home, motives not unknown nowadays. Mr. John Lowis was at Elgin and meditated removal to Peebles; Mr. Alexander Hepburn at Elgin, and after the reformation, Dundee and Dunkeld; Mr. William Nudrie at Ayr and Peebles; Sir John Fethy at Aberdeen, Dundee and Edinburgh; Mr. John Buchan (a graduate of St. Leonard's college) at Ayr and Dundee; Andrew Kemp at Dundee and then as prebendary in St. Salvator's college; Sir Thomas Burrell was at Haddington as an under-teacher before going to Perth; Mr. Robert Maxwell, preceptor of the Glasgow grammar school before the reformation, had previously been at Paisley[94]. With this mobility there was little danger of arterio-sclerosis in the educational body.

Ninian Winzet indicates one reason for such mobility, in that in many towns there was no common schoolhouse. In country districts a church or chapel was used, as in the case of the schoolmaster chaplain of Carmyllie[95]. Even in burghs the schoolhouse was often rented and the schoolmaster's house also; it is probable that in some places he stayed with different neighbours in turn. A good illustration is provided in Dundee at the reformation, where grammar pupils proper and readers under the doctors paid graduated fees towards the rent, but even at that the schoolmaster got into arrears with the rent and had to be rescued by

89. *Edinburgh Burgh Accounts*, i, 59; Grant, *Burgh Schools*, p. 40; *Register of Privy Council*, iii, 305.
90. *Peebles Records*, i, 244.
91. *Elgin Records*, i, 89, 118.
92. *Stirling Records*, i, 71.
93. *Edinburgh Records*, i, 76.
94. Lowis: *Elgin Records*, i, 105; *Peebles Records*, i, 243. Hepburn: *Innes Review*, ix, 116; *Old Dundee*, p. 156; *Protocol Bk. of Thomas Johnsoun*, no. 957. Nudrie: *Peebles Records*, i, 209; *Ayr Burgh Accounts*, p. 110, 114. Fethy: *St. Nicholas*, ii, 367; *Old Dundee*, p. 152; *St. Giles*, p. lxxxix. Buchan: *Ayr Accounts*, p. 119, 123; *Old Dundee*, pp. 152, 155. Kemp: *Old Dundee*, p. 154; *Laing Charters*, no. 846. Burrell: Grant, *Burgh Schools*, p. 42; *Dunfermline*, 394. This list is not exhastive. There are also persons like Mr. Adam Mure, master in Edinburgh and later pedagogue to Alexander Beaton at Crail grammar school (*Edinburgh Records*, ii, 48; *Rentale Sancti Andree*, pp. 95, 199.)
95. *Brechin*, i, 226.

the council[96]. There were towns with permanent buildings: Glasgow, Elgin, Dumfries are only a few examples[97]. Old traditional buildings had for one reason or another been abandoned: the old school (*schola antiqua*) is mentioned in 1480, for instance, in Stirling.[98]

Some of the schoolmasters rose above the common run of chaplains and some were notable men. At Ayr in 1515, " Maister John Law " was feed "to mak service at ye trinite altare and in ye queir *sicut solebat* and to haif xii merkis of fee of ye commone purss and to haif ye scuyll for fiwe zeris with ye profettis yairof." Actually a new schoolmaster was appointed next year, the probability being that Law had entered religion and is identical with the Augustinian canon regular who was principal of St. Leonard's in the university of St. Andrews and is the author of a manuscript chronicle[99]. John Doby, a grammar schoolmaster in Peebles later emerges as principal of Glasgow university[100]. Simon Young, successively dean of Christianity and official of Dunkeld, was schoolmaster in Perth[101]. Sometimes he was called upon to write the clerk play, as was Mr. Patrick Anderson, schoolmaster in Ayr[102]. The most notable of all was of course the schoolmaster of Dunfermline, Robert Henryson, all too often described as a court poet although it is extremely unlikely that he was ever near the court. When incorporated at Glasgow university in 1462 he was already a licentiate in arts and bachelor of decreets. By 1468 we hear that the abbot of Dunfermline has provided a house for the town schoolmaster and lands and rents worth eleven merks yearly maintaining poor scholars to be taught there gratuitously[103]. The gift of the schoolhouse may have encouraged Henryson to stay[104]. All school-masters of the time loved to moralise and Henryson is a superb moralist as his *Testament of Cresseid* shows. His successor, Sir John Moffat, perhaps the poet of that name, is not entitled schoolmaster till 1519, but he may have been doctor in the school as early as 1493 when he took the morrow mass in the parish church[105]. Henryson appears in the Dunfermline register as a notary in the year 1478, but his life-span is unknown[106].

SCHOOLBOYS

Who went to school in sixteenth-century Scotland ? We have many complaints about the unreadiness of the nobility to take advantage of its educational opportunities, and the act of parliament shows that there were some noble households that did not provide for more than a little reading and writing even for the eldest son: on the other hand some noble youths as well as sons of lesser lords went to school at six or nine.[107] Winzet complains that so few children were held at the study of gram-

---

96. *Old Dundee*, p. 155.
97. *Glasgow Charters*, i (2), 436, 557; *Elgin Records*, i, 51; *Transactions of Dumfries and Galloway Nat. Hist. and Archaeol. Soc.*, series 3, xxi, 107.
98. *Cambuskenneth*, pp. 302-3.
99. Alloway Barony Court Bk. (G.R.H.), p. 94; Herkless and Hannay, *College of St. Leonard*, p. 29. The chronicle is in Edinburgh University.
100. *Peebles Records*, i, 155; *Munimenta Univ. Glasguensis*, ii, 108.
101. *Dunfermline*, p. 394.
102. Mill, *Medieval Plays*, p. 165.
103. *Munimenta*, ii, 69; *Calendar Papal Registers*, xii, 297.
104. For site see *Dunfermline Burgh Records*, nos. 280, 287, 324, 336.
105. *Dunfermline Records*, nos. 47, 298.
106. The printed register omits witnesses; but David Laing quotes from the manuscript in *Poems of Henryson* (1865), p. xiii.
107. *Acts Parliament Scotland*, ii, 238, c.3.

mar, but we do not know his standards and we have no reliable figures. Many will be inclined to doubt that as many as 300 scholars could have attended the grammar school at Perth on the eve of the reformation[108]. Shrewsbury, however, claimed 400 in the same century[109]. But we really have no check on numbers. We do know that there must be a minimum of 24 poor scholars in Glasgow in 1494 and of 15 at Old Aberdeen in 1544[110]. We also find that, in spite of the burgh's anathemas and fines, 32 townspeople were attending opposition schools in Dundee in 1556, held by Master Henry Livingstone, a Paris graduate and colleague there of the humanist, Archibald Hay[111]. Details of scholars may be found occasionally in protocol books when the notary is himself a schoolmaster. Matthew Forsyth of Dumbarton is one. Every now and then we hear of an unspecified number of "scholars of the whole town" being witnesses, evidently when the protocol was drawn up in the schoolroom: as at Dunfermline in 1433 and at Newburgh in 1526[112]. Cuthbert Simson, who taught grammar in Glasgow university, occasionally has scholar witnesses, both at Glasgow and at Irvine where he practised originally[113]. The latter fact incidentally points to the conclusion that James VI's foundation of the grammar school of Irvine, like his foundation at Paisley, and like that by a bishop of the Church of Scotland at Banff, was a refoundation[114].

In theory education was free, and fees charged were not for education as such, at least where the school was endowed. Private schools were known as " particular " schools in opposition to free schools or " general " schools, such as that at Elgin[115]. Schools described as " public " are also free schools and otherwise the terminology often indicates that teaching was free as when the master is required to teach all comers (*omnes confluentes*, or similar phrase). In practice poor scholars probably did not pay scholage, just as they were released from university fees. In burgh schools the practice may have grown of charging landward pupils higher scholage, and unless they stayed with friends they would have to pay for board in town. In 1538-9 Andrew Kynneir's board in St. Andrews cost £12 and his clothes cost over £2 more; yet in 1540 his board was a little over £1 a term when he was lodged with the canons of the priory[116].

Poor scholars were sometimes provided for in a schoolhouse and sometimes in a hospital. The schoolmaster was often chaplain of the hospital. As the schoolmaster of Glasgow is rather a good illustration of what we must envisage, his position is worth describing at some length, especially as some details have not hitherto appeared in print.

In Glasgow the grammar schoolmaster was also chaplain of the leper hospital of St. Ninian beyond Glasgow bridge. Each week he had to celebrate four masses in the chapel with commemoration of the dead,

---

108. Row, *History* (Wodrow Society), p. 7.
109. Tawney and Power, *Tudor Economic Documents*, i, 199.
110. *Glasgow*, ii, 490; *Aberdeen*, i, 426.
111. *Old Dundee*, p. 153; Paris, BN Ms. Lat. 9953, f. 58r.
112. Hutton's Collections, Shires (in N.L.S.), vi, 113; A Laing, *Lindores and Newburgh*, p. 518.
113. *Munimenta*, i, 39; *Diocesan Registers*, ii, 6, 228.
114. *Annals of Banff*, ii, 165, mentions the *preceptor schole grammatices de Banff* in 1544. Also *ibid.*, i, 19, 28, ii, 165-6, 381 and *R.M.S.*, iii, 3062.
115. *Edinburgh Records*, i, 193-4; *Moray*, p. 270.
116. Figures given for scholars' board in the *Treasurers' Accounts*, are hardly likely to be average; *noblesse oblige* was a principle very often at work in such payments. For Kynneir, see *Rentale Sancti Andree*, pp. 83, 95.

that is on Sundays, Mondays, Wednesdays and Fridays, but if he had to celebrate for a double feast on the spare days he was excused the Wednesday or Friday mass. If absent for over a fortnight per term, his chaplainry would be declared vacant. If not impeded through sickness he yet failed to carry out these duties and did not supply a chaplain in default, then he paid sixpence to the lepers for their prayers instead; but if he let his duties lapse on ten occasions and refused to pay five shillings, the chaplainry was declared vacant. He had to find security to the patron of the chaplainry (the diocesan chancellor) for the safety of the missal, worth 12 merks, and the chalice, containing 14 ounces of silverwork. He had to use the chapel offerings to glaze, roof and ornament the chapel, and had to buy 8 dozen coals (price, 3s 6d a dozen) for the lepers during the summer season. Obviously the chaplain lived at the hospital, which was some distance from the school, and the 24 poor scholars who were to be paid for attending the obit lived there too[117]. One of these deputies of the schoolmaster appears to have been Sir Alexander Roberton who collected the Rogation day offerings at the chapel in the year 1510[117]. A similar arrangement may have prevailed for a time at Stirling, where schoolmasters act sometimes as hospital chaplains.[118]

Discipline was no doubt in those rough days somewhat harsh. John Mair (or Major), the famous theologian, complained that the harshness of his master in Haddington (George Litstar, a St. Andrews graduate) was such that he thought of giving up a clerical career altogether, had not his devout mother insisted[119]. Even a Hebrew scholar, William Nudrie, also a St. Andrews graduate, was prosecuted by a boy's relatives for binding his hands by way of correction[120]. One chaplain, doubtless a schoolmaster somewhere, was summoned to Glasgow for killing a schoolboy[121]. And the principal master at Glasgow, Mr. John Reid, fell foul of the relatives of another boy for cruelly wounding him, the boy's own master (a chaplain of the chapel of St. Roch) having apparently delegated the duty.[122] The rights and wrongs of some of these cases are past recovery nowadays, and it has to be remembered that equally typical may have been Ninian Winzet, whose relations with his Linlithgow pupils appear to have been of the friendliest[123].

SOME CONTEMPORARY LEGISLATION

The provincial councils of the sixteenth century legislated to some extent regarding education, in this respect copying the legislation of the Council of Trent. There was little time to enforce such legislation before the reformation happened.

Churches whose annual revenues were slight or which had few clergy and laity so that no theological lectureship was possible had to have a grammar master chosen by the bishop. The master was to be paid by means of a benefice or other arrangement but only so long as he continued

117. Advocates Ms. (in N.L.S.), 9A.1.2, f. 1451 seq. A note adds that the chaplainry was dedicated in honour of St. Ninian on the 11th September, feast of SS. Prothus and Iacinthus, in 1494, by Archbishop Blacader in the presence of the chapter and other religious men.
118. Cf. Sir Robert Cristison, chaplain of St. James' chapel beyond Stirling Bridge, *Stirling Records*, i, 17. It is probable, but not certain, that St. Ninian's chapel belonged to the lepers there, and of that another schoolmaster was chaplain; *R.S.S.*, iv, 1229.
119. " New Light on John Major " in *Innes Review*, v. 84.
120. *Peebles Records*, i, 209.
121. *Diocesan Register*, ii, 398.
122. *Ibid.*, ii, 501.
123. *Tractates*, i, 24.

teaching, and was to teach clerics and other poor scholars freely so that afterwards they might take up theology. Princes and governments were encouraged to found theological lectures in grammar schools, especially where they previously existed (as they would in some cathedral schools in the earlier middle ages) but we are unaware of any such initiative on the part of Scottish kings and queens[124]. It does, however, appear that most sizeable burghs, if not most burghs, in Scotland, already had grammar schools. What appears probable is that the church authorities regretted in some ways the hold the burghs had acquired over their schools. The archdeacon of St. Andrews seems to have lost his hold over the burgh school there; the council directed him to ensure that the schoolmaster was well versed in grammatical subjects and amply competent in other ways to teach boys and those who do not know the rudiments (*puerilia*)[125]. The meaning appears to be that the grammar schoolmaster of St. Andrews had no authority to teach beyond the rudiments, presumably because the university colleges took care of the higher flights, a situation that can be parallelled in Paris. The university rector for his part was to ensure that nobody who had failed to master spoken Latin could be admitted to study logic, a proviso the more necessary where students came to the university direct from their parishes. The burgh schoolmaster was the chaplain of St. Peter in the parish church and as such can be recognised; before the reformation the chaplainry was held by Andrew Oliphant, an excellent Latinist, and later by Mr. James Douey, who had studied at Paris[126].

Also in accordance with Trent was the requirement that in cathedral churches or elsewhere in cathedral cities a theologian should lecture to the canons and a canonist to the canons and other clergy; the theologian to get a benefice worth £100 and the canonist one worth 100 merks. Moreover, every monastery was to have a theologian, whether regular or secular[127]. The nearest attempt to carry out this requirement, apart from those cathedral towns which were also university towns, was made in Kirkwall by Bishop Reid. There the chancellor of the diocese was to be at least a bachelor in canon law and lecture publicly once weekly[128]. In 1547 in Aberdeen John Watson, licentiate in theology, was appointed to lecture publicly in the cathedral twice weekly[129]. We find a Dominican professor of theology, Andrew Abercromby, holding a canonry of Dunkeld, but it is uncertain when he was first appointed[130]. A hitherto unpublished letter is worth citing in this connection. In 1547 the clergy of the provincial council wrote to Paul III saying that Cardinal Beaton before he died had laid down that all bishops should assign benefices for theological professors and preachers of the orthodox word, but that many had not done so, with the result that after his death the council of 1547 repeated the statute; which council, under the presidency of John Hamilton, bishop of Dunkeld, added the rider that such professors and preachers as failed to accomplish their duties should suffer withdrawal of their daily commons. Moreover it added that prelates who

---

124. Patrick, *Statutes of the Scottish Church*, pp. 99-100.
125. *Ibid.*, p. 109.
126. Douey or Dowye had also been a student of St. Salvator's. See Rankin, *Parish Church of Holy Trinity*, p. 98. Paris, BN Ms. Lat. 9953, f. 87 shows Douey at Paris in 1538.
127. Patrick, *Statutes*, p. 105.
128. Clouston, *Records of the Earldom of Orkney*, pp. 264-5.
129. *Aberdeen*, ii, 318.
130. *Protocol Bk. of Gilbert Grote*, no. 276.

had no benefices or insufficient funds at their disposal should assign what they could to an adolescent candidate in other subjects or a student in theology. The letter reminds the pope that these requirements were based on Trent, adding that if the pope added his backing to the provincial council's recommendation, and gave mandate of execution to the two archbishops and the abbot of Newbattle, there would be greater likelihood of the statute being observed[131].

Some evidence is also available of theological preaching. The provincial council required a preaching benefice in each diocese and in every monastery[132]. John Watson, the supernumerary canon of Aberdeen, was required to preach to the people once yearly in the cathedral and in all the churches united to the cathedral chapter; a tall order, which was soon modified to include the mother churches only and not annexed and subordinate churches, and power was given to depute a fit subordinate[133]. A few more theological preachers can be descried; besides the provost of Kirkwall appointed by Bishop Reid[134], the rest are in association with Archbishop Hamilton who was at once abbot of Paisley and archbishop of St. Andrews. They are Andrew Davidson, bachelor in theology, appointed to preach in his diocese[135]. Others are Master John McQuhyn, *concionator Pasletensis*, and Friar James Johnstone, who was also maintained out of the revenues of Paisley, and was evidently the Dominican prior of St. Andrews. We are told that even after the reformation Patrick Adamson, minister of Paisley, turned a blind eye to their activities:

> "Freir Jhonstoun and Maquhane about him,
> Tua pallartis that the Pope professes,
> Rysing at mydnycht to there messis . . ."[136]

The great defect of a clerical education then was the lack of specific theological training, even though in the teaching of all subjects there was a definite religious climate: not for nothing was the grammar schoolmaster of Aberdeen admitted to office by the presentation of a pair of beads[137]. This is a theme that could be developed, but would take us beyond the bounds of the present essay. But even for theological reading, grammar was the universal key. Hence the grammar schools in the Dominican houses of Glasgow and Ayr[138]. Hence also the necessity to import a secular master to teach novices, as at Arbroath where a master of arts taught the novices and the children of those laypeople who had letters of fraternity[139]. In the 1537 mitigation of the statutes of the abbey of Deer, it was enjoined that there should be a daily lesson in grammar or the arts to junior brethren and even to seniors capable of following it or having need of it[140].

Of those embracing the reformation before 1559-60, there do not

---

131. Royal Letters (1524-1548), Blairs Archives (*penes* Rev. W. J. Anderson), p. 120.
132. Patrick, *Statues*, pp. 121-2.
133. *Aberdeen*, ii, 319-320.
134. Clouston, *Records of Orkney*, p. 365.
135. Advocates Ms. 17.1.3 (3rd foliation), f. 19r.
136. *Early Records*, p. 255; their pension as *predicatoribus* is mentioned in the E.U.L. Ms. DC. 4.32, f. 29r; Cranstoun, *Satirical Poems of the Reformation* (Scot. Text Soc.), i, 356. Another attached to Dunfermline is mentioned in the essay on the cultural background of the reformation, *q.v.*
137. *Bon Record*, p. 7.
138. Durkan, *Turnbull*, p. 60; Dunlop, *James Kennedy*, p. 5, note.
139. *Arbroath*, ii, 245. He signs along with the monks a decade or so later, but that only proves he had a monk's portion. *Ibid.*, 316.
140 *Antiquities of Aberdeen and Banff*, iv, 15.

appear to be many schoolmasters. One was Mr. Henry Henryson, preceptor of the Edinburgh high school, convicted of heresy about 1540[141]. There were of course those, like Mr. Andrew Simson of Perth, who were zealous " papists " on the eve of the reformation and who very soon conformed[142]. Some, like John Black, master of the song school of Aberdeen, left the country[143]. Others were openly critical. Apart fromWinzet himself, there was Mr. Robert Cumming, schoolmaster of Arbroath, accused of corrupting the youth with papistry and, as such, to be deposed[144]. Some years later, Ninian Dalzeill, schoolmaster of Dumfries, was the victim of similar allegations[145]. Mr. Robert Maxwell, schoolmaster in Glasgow, disputed publicly with Willock, superintendent of the west[146]. Great corruption of the youth by Mr. William Roberton, master of the grammar school of Edinburgh, " an obstinat papeist, " was alleged by the Edinburgh town council in 1562. Roberton, who had graduated in 1537 at St. Salvator's college as a poor scholar,[147] had been appointed by Lord Robert Stewart, then abbot of Holyrood, at that time in his minority. At the reformation, Roberton had taken the precaution of moving his books and goods out of town, and could only produce the letters of appointment of his predecessor, which the council refused to accept[148]. The case dragged on, while the council, through the earl of Moray, tried to influence Lord Robert to cancel the gift. In the interim Roberton produced his letters of appointment. He also offered to procure the testimony of Edward Henryson, the Greek scholar, among others, that he was qualified in Greek and Latin grammar, but the procurator of the council alleged that he " had nane or litill eruditioun in grammer greik or latene, bot empty thairof." More pointedly, he was accused of neglecting to frequent sermons and to communicate, being an enemy to God's word. He rejected the council's crafty offer to subject him to the examination of a commission of learned men, headed by John Craig, the minister. Eventually the queen intervened with two letters, one written on the 21st February, 1564, and the other in the following December, ordering the council to pay his stipend and school mail, The council tried to trick him into handing over the royal letters, without success[149]. He won his point, continuing in office for many years to come, and even sitting on a committee for the revision of grammar teaching along with George Buchanan and others.

It is too often forgotten how sparse are the medieval records on which we have to base our conclusions. On the facts in front of us we can no more say that every parish had its school, however rudimentary, and whether ruled by chaplain or parish clerk, than we can say it had not. The first occurrence of a parish school in a kirk session or presbytery record, especially before the act of 1616, can hardly be accepted as evidence of its date of foundation; and this is not to deny the contribu-

141. *R.M.S.*, ii, 2179.

142. Row, *History*, p. 8.

143. *Aberdeen Records*, i, 325, 370. There is, however, a person of that name in later records.

144. *Acts of General Assemblies*, i, 25.

145. *Ibid.*, ii, 432.

146. Leslie, *Historie* (ed. Cody), ii, 464-5. In 1563, " sometime preceptor of the grammar school," *Glas. Protocols*, v, 1480.

147. *Early Records*, p. 138.

148. *Edinburgh Records*, iii, 131-3; Perhaps he was one of the sayers of Mass who were exiled out of Edinburgh, *Acts of General Assemblies*, i, 6.

49. *Ibid.*, iii, 142, 145, 149-150, 190, 193, 196. Roberton was appointed master about 1546.

tion of the seventeenth century to Scottish education.[150] Pre-reformation parish records, however imperfectly kept they may have been, have not survived. Burgh records seldom survive before 1560; where they do, they are not always informative. The first surviving Wigtown register does record a school in 1513;[151] but Lanark records tell us nothing about Lanark school, although the monastic register of Dryburgh shows it in existence as early as the twelfth century.[152] The monastic and episcopal chartularies for the west of Scotland (apart from Glasgow and Paisley) have vanished: registers for Whithorn and Kilwinning certainly once existed.[153] Such registers would have provided additional information regarding schools in the west, especially burgh schools, although other evidence makes it plain that the east was much better provided. As to the highlands proper we know nothing at all.

On the other hand it is clear that contemporary observers were dissatisfied with what had been done. Winzet remarked that rich endowments had been given to religion and learning, but not to grammar schools. The bishops of the period were accused of failing to provide for poor scholars and men of talent. The grammar schools, he contended, were the gateways to knowledge; now that everybody was a would-be theologian, it was prophetic of the catastrophe of 1560 that so many were still unlettered. The bishops had failed to cope with a rapidly changing situation, and no doubt many schoolmasters in their degree were also culpable; for instance, in continuing to charge book fees for the copying of their master copies of textbooks like Donatus, when printed books were becoming widely available (although not as yet available in Scots). The country priest, too, who knew little more than his rudiments, and had forgotten much even of them, laid himself open to ridicule as he mumbled and stumbled over the frequent Latin interpolations, and perhaps over some of the vernacular (although that is less readily credible), in the catechism of Archbishop Hamilton;[154] a ridicule that would have been rare in an earlier age, but not in an age when the literate layman was an increasing phenomenon.

The evidence does suggest, however, that there is more in formularies, such as the commissions of visitation in remote areas to eradicate " idolatry " in schools and colleges, than many are prepared to grant; whatever they mean, they cannot mean that there were no schools. When one considers that scholastic duties were almost invariably associated with chantry duties (" idolatry "), the eradication of idolatry must often have meant the eradication of schools as it did usually of colleges. One must scrutinise carefully the terms " foundation " and " erection " in the reformation era (as indeed throughout the middle ages); the Book of Discipline even talks of the " erection " of the three traditional universities. Similarly, it is true that survivals of Celtic schools, as at Turriff and Ellon, are not on record after the early middle ages; but it

---

150. For this contribution, see article by J. M. Beale in *The Scottish Genealogist*, ii, 7 seq.
151. Wigtown Burgh Court Bk., 1512-35 (G.R.H.), ff. 11r, 12v.
152. *Dryburgh*, p. 194.
153. *Hist. Mss. Commission Report xi, pt. 7*, 150 (Whithorn, 1504); *Memorials of the Montgomeries*, ii, 130 (Kilwinning, 1544).
154. *Catechism*, ed. T. G. Law, pp. xlvi-xlvii; citations are mostly from the Bible, but there are others in Latin from Chrysostom, John Damascene and Theodoretus. In the towns the position was better. The prebendaries of Cullen had to have a good grasp of grammar (*sufficenter eruditus in grammatica*) but the grammar master a thorough grasp (*bene eruditus in grammatica*). Cramond, *Church and Church-yard of Cullen*, pp. 42, 46.

would be quite hazardous to deny that they survived in however altered a form.

It is sometimes implied that not all cathedral schools had a continuous history, even when we have record of the establishment there of a chancellor. Were there schools always at Whithorn (where, however there was no chancellor), Lismore, Dornoch, Rothesay (seat for a time of the Sodor diocese), Fortrose ? As to continuous existence, it is often said that the cathedral school at Dunkeld was founded about 1506 by Bishop Brown. The appearance in 1475 at Glasgow university of " a scholar of Glasgow school and Dunkeld diocese " would appear to confirm that no grammar school existed there at that date.[155] It is, of course, impossible to dogmatise; but it ought to be observed that in essence the foundation of a perpetual chaplainry for the grammar schoolmaster (Mr. John Thompson, later dean of Angus) in St. George's hospital, Dunkeld,[156] is no more likely to be a completely new beginning than the similar foundation described above of a perpetual chaplainry in Glasgow at St. Ninians hospital; the motive being rather to attract a more qualified schoolmaster and to provide for more grammar scholars among the relatively poor.

Collegiate churches were often in rural areas or small towns. Where there were boys on the foundation, a song school was a *sine qua non*. Sometimes a pre-existing school was taken over; for instance, there was a grammar school in Cullen before the college foundation of 1543.[157] Even where no school is specifically mentioned, as at Seton, two boys and a clerk had to have free instruction " in the rite of the said church," and there would be other local boys to join them.[158] At Dalkeith college the prebendary had to teach the boys sufficiently and well, but probably in the rudiments only, as they were removable when their voices broke.[159] " Idolatry " in Tain seems to have been effectively eradicated, for in 1588 we hear of the ruinous structure " foundat besyde the said colledge kirk and chaptor, ane hous of auld dedicat for a scuilhous callit the boith."[160] At Crichton college there was both a song school and a grammar school, not specifically provided for in the foundation.[161] Moreover, sometimes the schools are attached rather to parish churches than to collegiate, where these are separate institutions, as at Dumbarton. There the chaplain of St. Peter altar took the grammar school and the chaplain of the Rood altar the song school and the organs; the latter had to maintain two choirboys, but also to teach all burgesses' sons who were learning the psalter and singing, *psallere et canere addiscentes*. After the reformation the revenues of both altars went to the upkeep of the grammar master.[162]

---

155. *Munimenta*, ii, 85.
156. *Rentale Dunkeldense*, pp. 323, 148; *R.M.S.*, ii, 3482; a song school also existed, *Rentale*, p. 342.
157. In 1541; the master was William Malison; Barclay, *Schools and Schoolmasters of Banffshire*, p. 95. It is interesting that the parish clerkship (often closely associated with song schools) was split up to provide maintenance in food and blue tunics for the choirboys, Cramond, *Church and Churchyard of Cullen*, p. 40.
158. *C.P.R.*, xii, 346.
159. *Registrum Honoris de Morton*, ii, 230.
160. MacGill, *Tain and Balnagown Documents*, i, 26.
161. *R.M.S.*, iv, 2169.
162. Fergus Roberts, *The Grammar School of Dumbarton*, pp. 2-3; cf. Protocol Bk. of Matthew Forsyth, f. 177r.

From Ayr and Paisley in the west to Montrose and Musselburgh in the east, and from Kirkwall in the north to Wigtown in the south, there were grammar schools in the burghs of Scotland. Of their products well over a hundred were fitted for universities in 1539, which in view of the country's population is no discreditable number, especially as it must be a small proportion of those actually finishing at grammar schools.[163] When we consider other imponderables, lawyers trained in the ecclesiastical courts, apprentices to writers in Edinburgh, servants of notaries, friars such as Dominicans, Franciscans and Carmelites with theological degrees acquired in their respective houses of study, it is fair to conclude, that, in spite of reservations adduced above, provision for education, and especially for musical education, was remarkable for the time, and to be assured that, besides so much that makes for sombre reading in the history of Scotland at that date, its educational record is something of an achievement and a boast.

APPENDICES

Paisley Grammar School.

An earlier generation of Scottish historians took it for granted that with the establishment of a Benedictine abbey the establishment of a school automatically followed, but this belief is not so universal as it used to be. As regards Paisley, owing to the absence of references to a school in the abbey's published chartulary or the town's published charters for the period before 1560, it is now being generally assumed that no school existed prior to the foundation by King James VI.

The undermentioned document is therefore of interest. It is a foolscap paper folio folded in two, written in a good italic hand, with what appears to be a Scots watermark (hand with a star), and is to be found in Blairs Archives, Letters, 1/C.9. It is a piece of Latin verse addressed to Archbishop Beaton of Glasgow for whose patronage the writer is looking. He describes himself as " moderator (i.e. rector) of the Paisley youth." The theme is fairly humdrum even if skilfully expressed: the object appears to be to get some benefice in Glasgow (probably the grammar school), for which the chancellor or the chapter are unwilling to give their names, and therefore Maxwell suggests the device of using the common seal. At Paisley, he points out, the abbot has one seal, the convent another, and both are surrendered to him without difficulty.

The writer, Robert Maxwell, did, as Lesley tells us, become master of the grammar school of Glasgow, and was there at the reformation, when he disputed with the reformers. On the 5th November, 1563, he is described as sometime preceptor of the grammar school of Glasgow (Renwick, *Glasgow Protocols*, v, 1480). He was then involved in a reversion of certain property from which we are able to identify him as the person described as vicar of Killallan in October, 1561, by which time he was presumably no longer at the grammar school (*Ibid.*,v,1417). In 1551 Alexander Crawford is said to be " master " and in 1555 Archibald Crawford " preceptor " of Glasgow grammar school (*Munimenta Universitatis*, ii,279,299): these may of course be the same person, but in any event Maxwell's appointment to Glasgow must have been after 1555.

---

163.   20 Matriculations at Glasgow, 80 at St. Andrews, no numbers known for Aberdeen (*Munimenta*, ii, 165; *Early Records*, p. 241).   In addition, there was a constant trickle abroad, especially to Louvain, Cologne and Paris.   At the last in 1542 there were 50 matriculands from Scotland, Paris, B.N. Ms. Lat. 9953, ff. 183r-186v. Numbers, of course, varied.

He was already described as vicar of Killallan and son of the laird of Stanelee in 1550 (*Ibid.*, ii,170): he was then a student at Glasgow, but probably went on to St. Andrews, where other Glasgow students of the period also went. If so, he can be indentified with the student of that name who graduated from St. Leonard's College in 1553 (*Early Records of St. Andrews*, p.151). The versified letter given below can therefore be narrowed down to the dates 1554-1559, and at some time in that period Maxwell was rector of Paisley grammar school.

Reuerendissimo in christo patri et domino: domino Jacobo Beton Archipraesuli glasguano longe omnium vigilantissimo, Robertus maxuel pasletanae iuuentutis moderator: s.d.p.

> Pastorum sublime decus, doctissime praesul:
>   Dura morae longae damna tulisse queror.
> Quis malus, ah, genius nostris sua numina votis
>   Opponit? vel quod crimen obesse potest?
> Crimen id aut vitium si sit subscribere praue:
>   Censorem, non me, iure notare potes.
> Hic tuus est censor seu scriptor, doctus ut aiunt,
>   Qui castigate scribere multa solet.
> Qui mihi persuasit quod nil subscribere iuuit:
>   Et sic nominibus littera nostra vacat.
> Credenti facile est imponere, plusque peritus
>   Qui fertur fallit famaque saepe nocet.
> Sed mihi praeualida sese ratione videtur
>   Tutari censor, si bene cuncta notes.
> Mos siquidem fuerat, qui longum creuit in aeuum,
>   Ut sine nominibus charta notata detur,
> Communi (ut dicunt) tantum insignita sigillo:
>   Idque bipartitum tumque biforme manet.
> Alterutram seruat partem conuentus, et abbas
>   Alterutram: mihi pars utraque sponte datur.
> Hinc liquet abbatem cum coetu relligioso (*sic*)
>   Litterulas missas rite probare satis.
> Ergo moecenas, O spes et anchora sacra.
>   Huc ades, et elegos concipe mente meos.
> Tu potis es nostros in gaudia vertere luctus
>   Te penes es nostri nunc medicina mali.
> Faxis ne vacuus discedam, ne ve repulsam
>   Pro nihilo patiar, sic tibi vinctus ero.
> Tv mihi quod Daunus Diomedi: quodque Maroni
>   Augustus: doctis quod Philadelphus erat:
> Quod fuit Aeneae pius Euander: quod Ulyssi
>   Alcinous: mestis quod vel Jesus erat:
> Si me praesenti iam sollicitudine tollas
>   Atque oculos flectas in mea vota tuos.

Another Paisley schoolmaster who precedes the foundation of the grammar school by James VI is Sir Thomas Robeson, a priest called to give evidence at the trial of Archbishop Hamilton, " sumtyme maister of the scule of Paslay " (*Diurnal of Occurents*, p.204; *The Historie of King James the Sext*, p.71). Whether he preceded or succeeded Maxwell is unknown.

LINLITHGOW SONG SCHOOL

The following is typical of appointments made by the burghs to a song school. It is taken from the Linlithgow Burgh Court Book 1528-65 (G.R.H.), f.307r, and dated 30th April, 1543

"Ultima die mensis aprilis anno domini xliii.

The quhilk day the prowest, baillies and communitie and consale of the hale town as (*sic*) gewen and grantit haim wace for the wele and honor of god and halykirk and for gude seruice to be maid be ane discret man Sir robert akynhed chaplan the altarage of our ladies altar situat and fundit within the kirk of linlithqw to be permanent and byddand to him for all the dais of his lyff with all proffetis, commodoteis, annuell rentis, housis, landis with all richwyss pertinentis pertenand to the samyn, with oblatiounis and uthir dewteis in haly kirk as his predecessouris had of befor, he doand sufficient and thankfull seruice in kirk and queyr, efter the alud wse and consuetude of his predecessouris, and sall ken and leir the barnis yat will cum to him to syng, as wthir sang schullis usis, and sall causs the ladie mess to be swng be yame on sondais and halydais and uyer dais quhen he is disposit, and sall present him self in queyr and kirk to mess, matynnis, ewynsang and uther deuyn seruice, as the laif of the breyer of the kirk dois daylie, and sall mak daylie residence within the said burgh, quhilk to do the said sir robert akynhed as (*sic*) tane on him and falzeand he do it nocht the said alter sall waik and be at the disponyng and prouiset off the prowest, balleis, consale and communitie of the said burgh as it was at his entress . . .

(signed) dominus robartus akynhed."

SCHOOLMASTER AT AYR.

The word " scule master " used by itself invariably means grammar master. Those who are familiar with *The Protocol Book of Gavin Ros* (Scottish Record Society) will be aware of Gavin Ross as a notary and chaplain, but may not suspect that he was also a schoolmaster, as many other chaplain notaries must have been. He was first appointed to the Trinity service with 12 merks from the common purse in May, 1519, and reappointed in 1520 (Alloway Barony Court Book, pp.112, 118). The following extract is from the same manuscript, now in the General Register House, p.149: its date is the 14th May, 1526.

" Conductio capellanorum.

Maister Gawyne Ross feit to be scule master for all ye daes of his lyve and to mak serwice at ye trinite altar and in ye queyr as he wes wont to do. And to haue yairfor zeirlye ten li(bre) of ye commound purs at twa usuale termes in ye zeir, Witsunday and mertymes. And ye said Maister gavyne is bund to remane yairupone, and to mak gud thankfull service yairfore. And siclyk ye gud toune to pay him thankfullie yairfore. In witnes of ye quhilk thing, we haiff causit stene prestoun our commond clerk to subscrive yis present act togyddyr with ye subscripcione of ye said maister gawyne public notar."

SCOTTISH PRE-REFORMATION SCHOOLS.

Schools of cathedral and collegiate churches not specifically recorded as such are excluded from these lists, which can therefore be regarded as incomplete. Abbreviations used are:

G(Grammar) ; S(Song) ; W(in charge of women).

Aberdeen,
    Old, Cathedral (G.S.)
    King's College (G.S., of
    which the grammar school
    perhaps replaced the cathe-
    dral one)
    New, (G.S.)
Aberdour (W.)
Abernethy
Arbroath (G.)
Arbuthnott
Ayr (G.S.)
Banff (G.)
Biggar (G.S.)
Brechin (G.S.)
Berwick on Tweed (G.)
Carmyllie
Crail (G.S.)
Crichton (G.S.)
Cullen (G.S.)
Culross (G.)
Cupar
Dalkeith (S.)
Dumbarton (G.S.)
Dumfries (G.)
Dunbar (G.S.)
Dunblane (G.)
Dundee (G.S.)
Dunfermline (G.S.)
Dunkeld (G.S.)
Edinburgh, Canongate (G.)
    Town (G.S.W.)
Elcho (W.)
Elgin (G.S.)
Ellon

Glasgow, Cathedral and Town
    (G.S.)
    Lady College (S.)
    University (G.)
Haddington (G.)
Inverness (G.S.)
Irvine (G.)
Kelso
Kirkcudbright
Kirkwall (G.S.)
Lanark (G.)
Leith (G.S.)
Linlithgow (G.S.)
Lochwinnoch, Semple (G.S.)
Montrose (G.S.)
Musselburgh (G.)
Muthill
Newburgh, nr. Lindores
Paisley (G.S?)
Peebles (G.S.)
Perth (G.)
Restalrig (S.)
Roxburgh
St. Andrews,
    Cathedral, etc. (G.S.)
    St. Leonard's (G.)
    St. Mary's (G.)
    St. Salvator's (S.)
Seton (S.)
Stirling (G.)
    Chapel Royal (S.)
Tain
Turriff
Wigtown

THE POPULAR LITERATURE OF
THE SCOTTISH REFORMATION

by

BROTHER KENNETH

In Row's account of the early stages of the reformation in Scotland, mention is made of the various " means " which contributed to the spread of the knowledge of God's truth in a time of great darkness, but " the more particular means," it is stated, " were such as Sir David Lindsay's poesies . . . Wedderburn's psalms and the godly ballads of goodly purpose, a complaint given in to England against the bishops, priests . . . There were also some notable histories acted in publick . . . "[1]

The works listed by Row might well be considered as typical of the popular literature of the period and to them could be added the various unlicensed publications—pamphlets, tracts, placards, bills, most of which have disappeared—the imported literature, the several *Complayntes* and, in the second half of the century, the ballads and broadsheets of the Sempill variety. To include in the description of popular literature all works having a popular appeal would mean bringing in almost the whole body of Scottish reformation literature, since, apart from some lighter verse of a courtly type, almost everything that was written was heavy with the theme of reform and was aimed at convincing the nation of the justice of one cause or another in this crucial period of its history.

The term popular literature might easily convey the impression that it is representative of the nation at large, or of a substantial section of the people. The views expressed in such literature tend also to be accepted as primary historical evidence. If we wish to form a more precise estimate of the evidential value of popular literature, we do well to look at its origins and character and to view it in its political setting.

We do well also to remember that the movement for reform originated within the church, that it was widespread in western Europe and was of long duration, coinciding with the gradual development of the spirit of nationalism, before it erupted in the religious revolt of the sixteenth century in Germany and central Europe. The spirit of revolt spread to adjoining countries and, wherever it found suitable social and political conditions, it accelerated the progress of reform and gave it a more radical character.

In Scotland, the movement for reform was largely directed by the political relations with France and England, and it was through intercourse with England and the continent that the spread of heretical beliefs received impetus in the first phase of that movement. The importation of heretical literature and unlicensed publications was a constant preoccupation with the authorities. In 1525, parliament passed an act against heresy, proclaiming that, as the christian faith had always been preserved clean of such filth and vice within the realm, any stranger arriving by ship and bringing the works of Luther and his disciples would forfeit ship and goods and suffer imprisonment. The act was renewed in 1535.[2]

---

1. *Historie of the Kirk of Scotland* (Maitland edition), i, p. 3.
2. *A.P.S.*, ii, 295, c.4.

In 1527, the English ambassador at Antwerp informed Cardinal Wolsey that " there were divers merchants of Scotland that brought many of such like books (Tyndale's New Testament) and took them to Scotland, a part to Edinburgh, and most part to the town of St. Andrews."[3] It was from a press in Antwerp that the first protestant document, *Patrick's Places*, came to Scotland, and Antwerp served Ninian Winzet for the publication of his *Fourscore Questions* after his difficulties with the Edinburgh magistrates. John Gau's *Richt Vay to the Kingdom of Heuine*, another early protestant work, came from a Danish press at Malmö, and it was a London press that printed Wishart's *Confession of Faith of the Churches of Switzerland* about 1548 and which probably gave us also the first edition of the *Good and Godly Ballads*. Paris, of course, was the regular asylum for the Scottish exile who had something to say about home affairs. The foreign press was, of course, the only answer to the licensing laws. The answer to the foreign press was the customs officer and, in 1541, we find Thomas Davidson and James Bannatyne, burgesses in Edinburgh, appointed searchers generally in every part of Scotland of all Englishmen, their ships, merchandise and goods coming within the realm without sufficient conduct.[4]

England served in a special way as the source of the prohibited editions of the bible. In Lindsay's *Satire*, Dame Veritie appears bearing a copy of the New Testament in her hand and is questioned by Flattrie,

> " Quhat buik is that harlot, into thy hand,
> Out walloway, this is the New Test'ment,
> In Englisch toung, and printit in England,
> Herisie, herisie, fire, fire incontinent."

The prohibition was directed, of course, not against the bible as such; but against editions carrying " pestilential " glosses, prefaces of unorthodox character and tendentious translations. Such an edition was Tyndale's, which Henry VIII used almost as a secret weapon in his joint campaign against the crown and faith of Scotland. To be sure, every translation is tendentious, but Tyndale's particular slant was such that in the estimate of the contemporary Sir Thomas More, " the folk unlearned cannot discern falsehood from it."[5]

But the greatest menace was the use of the bible as an argument against authority and tradition by demanding scriptural warrant in chapter and verse for every development in christian doctrine and practice in the past fifteen hundred years;

> " The water of lyfe we gaue them neuer to drink,
> Bot stinkand pulis of euerie rottin synk:
> For haly Scripture allutterlie we haue mockit,
> And with traditionis of men we haue them zockit (yoked):
>
> And euer this was the blating of our queir (choir),
> Fatheris of haly kirk this Xv. hunder zeir."

So speak the *Good and Godly Ballads* and their readers, " the folk unlearned ", soon became expert in this easy exegesis;

---

3. Anderson, C., *Annals of the English Bible*, ii, 409. The ambassador, John Hackett, was busy burning up copies of prohibited English works in Antwerp and the neighbourhood. He just missed intercepting a consignment of such books by the early departure of a ship bound for Scotland. For the " Influence of the English printers on the Scottish Reformation," see the essay with this title in *S.C.H.S.*, i, 75.

4. R. Dickson and J. P. Edmond, *Annals of Scottish Printing*, p. 105.

5. Schwarz, W., *Principles and Problems of Biblical Translation*, p. 14. W. E. Campbell, *The English Works of Sir Thomas More*.

" For limmar lads and litle lassis, lo,
  Will argue baith with bischop, priest, and freir,"
as Alexander Scott complained.

With such a bible complex, it is not surprising that the literature, both serious and popular, is saturated with scripture. You meet it everywhere; in sermons, of course, and theological " reasonings ", but also in political pamphlets, history, drama, scribblings at the market cross, battle song, love song and satire. Understood as exploited in this sense, the bible was easily the most popular literature of the period.

We are not to suppose, however, that the nation whose faith and devotion had been nourished for centuries on the bible narrative spontaneously demanded the text. The stimulus was obviously external and the correspondence of Sir Ralph Sadler, the English envoy to Scotland, suggests the origin of the demand and the supply. After the death of James V in 1542, Sadler reported that the new regent, the Earl of Arran, was asking for heretical books as he was coming to the conclusion that if there were no purgatory, then they had good grounds for getting rid of the monks and friars.[6] In another report, Sadler could write that the bible, the New Testament and other books in English, such as the primer and the psalter, were " marvellously desired now of the people in Scotland ", and that if a cartload were sent, they would be all bought up.[7] Parliament, under Arran, sanctioned the reading of the scriptures in the vernacular in 1543 and, in the invasions of 1544-45 that followed the renunciation of the marriage treaty, Somerset considered that a supply of preachers and bibles was indispensable.

In view of the ready supply of English bibles, it is not surprising that no real attempt was made to print the bible in the Scots vernacular until 1579. Even when it comes to composing the *Scottish Psalter* of 1564, it is the English version of the psalms by Sternhold and Hopkins that will form its basis and not the translation appearing in the *Good and Godly Ballads*. Here we probably see the influence of Knox, whose preference, as far as doctrine was concerned, would be for something more radical than that offered by the ballads, and, as regards language, for a less strongly flavoured Scots. His own English accent had laid him open to the charge of " knapping Suddron".[8] One regrettable result of the extensive use of the English bible and of English influence generally at this period was to hasten the assimilation of Scots to English which is observable in the course of the century.

Arran's espousal of the English cause and reform would no doubt have had the approval of Sir David Lindsay, Lord Lyon at the Court of James V. Although he never uprooted himself from the ancient faith nor identified himself completely with the cause of the reformers, there is no doubt of Lindsay's strong reforming tendencies as shown in his various works.[9] The *Dreme*, the *Complaynts*, the *Testament* and the *Dialog*, or *Monarche*, all have reforming themes: but when Row speaks of the influence of Lindsay's poesies in spreading the knowledge of God's truth, he has most likely in mind the *Satyre of the Thrie Estaits*.

At the time of the first performance of his play, 1540, Lindsay was

---

6. *Letters and Negotiations of Sir Ralph Sadler*, p. 148.
7. *Hamilton Papers*, i, 445.
8. Millar Patrick, *Four Centuries of Scottish Psalmody* (Oxford, 1949).
9. *Works of Sir David Lindsay*. S.T.S. Ed. D. Hamer.

influential at court and well acquainted with the mind of his master, James V, who had constantly resisted the pressure of his uncle, Henry VIII, to establish a royal protestantism in Scotland. But Lindsay's own mind had long pondered the problems of his country which had not known continuous central government for over a century and had been, in consequence, a prey to civil strife and all its attendant social disorders. From his earliest works, the *Dreme* and the *Complaynts*, he had urged the need to " mak reformatioun " in the broadest sense of setting the national house in order at all levels and these " complaints " were to become frequent in the literature of the times, giving full time occupation to the social satirist and reformer.

In the *Satire of the Three Estates*, written some twelve years after his first work, Lindsay is merely continuing his crusade for all-round reform, but it has been the fate of this morality play to have become the text-book for anti-clericalism. The business had begun with Row setting up Lindsay and Wedderburn as lights shining in the darkness, but even after four centuries, if the play is resurrected, all the efforts of the producer will be directed to spotlighting the First Estate, the Spirituality. This is a strange misreading of the text, and of Lindsay's main purpose, which was to rouse the whole nation, king, nobles, clergy and commons to a sense of duty and realisation that all reform must begin from within. And they were an unreformed lot as Lindsay sees them. To forget that the play was performed in the first instance before the assembled court and council of lords spiritual and temporal at the close of the Christmas festivities is to miss the whole psychology of it.

The spiritual leaders of the nation are naturally the most severely censured—two thirds of the acts passed by the people's parliament at the close of the play concern church reform—but, in truth, all three Estates " gang backwarts ". The office of the king should be " to caus his leigis live in equitie ", but the king, alas, is " overset with sensualitie ". Greed leads in the reverend fathers of spirituality and Publick Oppression the temporality. Good Counsel is banished from the land and Dishonesty dwells among the merchant men. The circuit courts fail to function and the consistorial courts specialise in delays. Idlers of all types swarm in the land; fiddlers, pipers, pardoners and fat friars. Thieves have the run of the border lands and the commonfolk sink daily into extreme poverty. Bishops' palaces are like paradise, the parson cannot preach but is an expert at handball, cards, dice and football. And so on.

The general indictment is pressed home with a wealth of detail and variety of wit, coarse humour, buffoonery, comic interludes, solemn orations, pageantry, piety and clever characterisations—all for " pastyme and for play." The play was popular because of this skilful blending of pantomime and earnest pleading, and not because it was considered the final word on church or state. But it had good propaganda value.

It was no doubt owing to its pulpit value, apart from its intrinsic merits, that Lindsay's play is the sole survivor from the period of a long dramatic tradition in medieval Scotland which died hard but surely as the century wore on.[10] The municipal authorities subsidised and controlled the popular expression of the art in its varied forms and the burgh records tell us of this tradition of minstrelsy, folk plays of the Robin Hood

---

10. A. J. Mill, *Medieval Plays in Scotland.*

type, morality and clerk plays of a sacred character performed at Christmas, Passiontide and on the feast of Corpus Christi, secular plays or farces on royal occasions with tableaux, tapestries, orations at the scaffolds erected and potations at the market cross. We have a good idea of the kind of miracle or mystery play performed from the surviving English Cycles, such as the York Cycle of forty-eight plays covering the whole of biblical history and performed by the various guilds of craftsmen. Lindsay's *Dialog* or *Monarche*, which is a continuous verse narrative of universal history from the creation to the last judgment, can easily be imagined split up into sections and cast similarly in dialogue form.

Besides the facilities afforded by the erection of platforms in the public places of the town, the principal burghs had playfields adjoining for open-air performances. On the 12th August, 1554, a performance of the *Three Estates* was given at the Greenside on the lower slopes of the Calton Hill, Edinburgh, in the presence of the regent, Mary of Lorraine, a great part of the nobility and a concourse of people, lasting from nine o'clock in the morning to six o'clock at night with a break at the end of part one, when the higher ranks retired and the people made a meal.[11] We can sense the atmosphere of " pastyme and play " at such performances and it is difficult to imagine the audience taking the satire of themselves too seriously, on the odd occasions when satire was the theme and not the usual one of edification or diversion.

Row speaks of some notable histories acted in public which made the people sensible of the darkness they were in, and Knox is our source for the account of a Good Friday performance of a passion play by a certain Friar Kyllour at Stirling in 1535, the king being present. "All things in the play," says Knox, " were so lively expressed that even the simple people understood and confessed that as the Priests and obstinate Pharisees persuaded the people to refuse Jesus Christ, and caused Pilate to condemn him, so did the Bishops and men called Religious blind the people and persuade the Princes and Judges to persecute such as profess Jesus Christ's blessed Evangel." Dramatic criticism was hardly Knox's line and he possibly enlarges also on the reception of the play, but he records that three years later Kyllour, along with others, was burned for heresy and he attributes the friar's fate to the effect that the plain speaking of his play had on those " who bore the mark of the beast ".[12]

The historian, Calderwood, writing in 1636 and speaking of the Wedderburn brothers, relates, with some of the enthusiasm of Knox, that the eldest brother, James, " had a good gift of poesie and made divers comedies and tragedies in the Scottish tongue wherein he nipped the abuses and superstitions of the time. He composed in form of tragedy the beheading of John the Baptist, which was acted at the West Port of Dundee, wherein he carped roughly the abuses and corruptions of the Papists. He compiled the History of Dionisius the Tyrant, in form of a comedy, which was acted in the playfield of the same burgh, wherein he likewise nipped the Papists."[13] Not all the compilers would have the skill, still less the humour of Lindsay, and it is not difficult to imagine the effect of the Wedderburn zeal at work on a subject like John the

---

11. *Ane Satyre of the Thrie Estaits.* Ed. James Kinsley. Introd. Agnes Mure MacKenzie. Foreword Ivor Brown (1954).
12. Laing's *Knox*, i, 62.
13. For an account of the Wedderburns, see Calderwood, i, 141-143.

Baptist in a time of great darkness. Much depended on the locality for the reception given to such productions, but it is safe to assume that any form of nipping the papists would be popular at that time in Dundee.

John Wedderburn, the second eldest of the three brothers, was, according to Calderwood, a priest in Dundee who had to flee to Germany because of his beliefs and there, " he heard Luther and Melancthon, and became very fervent and zealous. He translated many of Luther's dytements into Scottish metre, and the Psalms of David. He turned many bawdy songs and rhymes into godly rhymes. He returned after the death of the king in December, 1542, but was again pursued by the Cardinal, and fled to England." The full title of Wedderburn's work as it appears in the earliest extant edition, that of 1567, reads; *A Compendious book of godly Psalms and spiritual Songs collected forth of sundry parts of the Scriptures, with divers other Ballads changed out of profane Songs into godly songs, for avoiding of sin and harlotry. With augmentation of sundry good and godly Ballads not contained in the first edition.*[14] This is the collection variously known as the *Wedderburn Psalms*, the *Psalms of Dundee*, the *Good and Godly Ballads*, whose influence in the spreading of the reformed doctrines is commonly reckoned as second only to that of the bible.

As the descriptive title indicates, the book falls naturally into two parts, one of which is doctrinal and devotional, the other profane but spiritualised. To replace the liturgical books in use in the church—missal, breviary, antiphoners—and the layfolk's primer of prayers and devotions, the reforming churches introduced various service manuals. In England, the *Bishops' Book* and the *King's Book* had prepared the way for the *Book of Common Prayer* of Edward VI. Henry's book had not found favour with James V, but the *Book of Common Prayer* was circulating in Scotland about 1560. The reformed kirk adopted the *Book of Common Order* in use at Geneva.

Wedderburn's book, which never received the sanction of the assembly, was of German origin and inspiration, at least as regards its first part, which would appear to have been lifted almost bodily out of the Magdeburg and Strasbourg hymnbooks. It has borrowings also from Coverdale's earlier work of *Ghostly Psalms and Spiritual Songs*, and Sadler, we remember, spoke of a demand in Scotland for English primers. The new service manuals retained certain features of the medieval primer which usually contained the Hours of the Blessed Virgin, the seven Penitential and the fifteen Gradual Psalms, the Litany of the Saints, the Office of the Dead, various Graces and Devotions and a Calendar.[15]

Our *Compendious Book* opens with an almanack which gives the important feasts and holidays; the Circumcision on January 1st, St. Mungo and the Glasgow holiday on January 13th, the Purification on 2nd February, St. Patrick and the Dumbarton holiday on March 17th: with important dates in history; the crowning of James VI at Stirling on 29th July, 1567: the birth of Alexander the Great on 6th of June: of Martin Luther on 10th November: and Noah's exit from the Ark on 27th May.

A short prologue quotes the advice of St. Paul to the Colossians and explains how profitable it is for the young and the unlearned to sing the

14. *Gude and Godlie Ballatis*, 1567. Ed. A. F. Mitchell. S.T.S. This is the standard edition. A convenient edition, without Mitchell's bias, is that of the 1578 text by D. Laing.
15. *The Prymer, or Prayer-book of the Lay People in the Middle Ages*. Ed. Henry Littlehales (London, 1892).

word of God in the mother tongue and eschew the unseemly songs of the world. Passages specially selected from scripture and presented in hymns or psalms to be sung by the faithful with " sweet melody ", such is the formula and there can be no doubt of its efficacy in promoting the spread of new beliefs. Hymns, spiritual songs, psalms and ballads not only fed devotion but served also as sermons inculcating the reformed doctrines and rousing to battle.

The prologue is followed by the text of the catechism or instruction for christian men which gives the Ten Commandments from Exodus, the " twelve Articles of our Faith, as they were written by the Apostles to the Three Persons in Trinity ", the Lord's prayer from St. Matthew, Baptism from a mixture of St. Matthew and St. Paul, the Lord's Supper from St. Paul's account of its institution and St. Matthew on the power of binding and loosing, " granted to the true preachers of God's word ". The catechism is then repeated, this time, " put in metre, to be sung to the tune."

Corresponding to the passages from scripture on baptism and the Lord's Supper, which constituted the whole sacramental system for the continental reformers, we have, in the metrical catechism, two hymns by Luther, that on the Lord's Supper being a translation of the Latin hymn by John Huss which, in turn, has frequent echoes from the *Lauda Sion* of St. Thomas. Belief in the real presence is explicit in the verse;

> " And he, that we suld not forget,
> Gave us his body for to eit,
> In forme of bread, and gave us syne
> His blude to drink in forme of wyne."

In startling contrast to this traditional note, we find the crudest of jibes at this same belief in a ballad at the end of the collection whose theme in an all-out attack on the idolatry of the mass;

> " Give (if) God was maid of bittis of bread,
> Eit ye not ouklie (weekly) sax or sevin? "

Likewise, the quotation from St. Matthew, " Quhais sinnis ze forgive, ar forgeuin vnto them, and quhais sinnis ze retene, ar retenit vnto them," appears to offer embarrassment, although the early reformers approved of some kind of confession. It is not versified in the metrical catechism. These and similar contrasts point to the composite character of the authorship of the book and indicate the span of years between its covers.

The catechism is followed by spiritual songs and ballads of scripture, all selected or composed on the theme of sin and salvation, with special emphasis on the all-sufficing merits of the Saviour. So we have many pleasing Nativity hymns, old and new, celebrating the birth of the Saviour; *In Dulci Jubilo, Ane Sang of the Birth of Christ to be sung with the tune of Balulalow* (Luther's Christmas Carol), *Onlie to God on heich be gloir* (Gloria), and Simeon's *Nunc Dimittis*. But even these glad tidings are not announced without a sombre note on sin and the tedious repetition of justification by faith which is dragged into nearly every item in the collection, be it song, psalm or ballad. *To us is borne a barne of Blis* opens pleasingly, but is soon singing of our poisoned nature, and Simeon looks forward to his " rest and peace " through faith in Christ his only trust, in spite of St. Luke. One wonders how this new note echoed in the minds of those who had been accustomed to a tradition of sacred song, drama and processional hymns which were not all sung, surely, in mystifying

Latin or to sophisticated music.[16] The spiritual songs and ballads which echo at times in moving accents the deep medieval devotion to the passion[17] tend also to be marred by a depressing note on our corrupt nature and the strife between the flesh and the spirit.

The twenty-two psalms of David that follow seem to correspond in number to the seven penitential psalms and the fifteen gradual psalms of the primer, but they are not so representative of the psalter in scope and incline to illustrate the one theme of the righteous struggling against their own and God's enemies; *Quare fremuerunt Gentes, Salvum me fac Deus, Usquequo Domine, In Exitu Israel, Super flumina Babylonis*; nearly all strike this note.

They are " translatit ", but there could be no question of an exact rendering where verse was the medium of translation: and while they remain faithful enough to the original, their general drift is to drive home the new teaching with an occasional outburst, as in psalm 32, where David's unsuspecting Edomites and Moabites find themselves transformed into pope, cardinals, monks and all the Roman tyranny. Fuller's observation on the work of the English translators that they had drunk more of the Jordan than the Helicon applies equally to their Scottish contemporaries, but we must not expect to find gems of literature where the translator has to fit his meaning into a verse form which is already set to the mould of the psalm tune. There is piety, however, and occasional skill, as in the paraphrase of the *Miserere*, but the business of keeping in step with the tune and the bother of the rhyme keeps the average performance low and sometimes, as in the song of the exiles, leads to desperate shifts;

> " They bad us sing sum psalme or hymne
> That we sum tyme sang Sion in."

But it was not so much the psalms and hymns that gave the collection its special character and did most, one suspects, to keep it alive as the " divers other Ballads changed out of profane Songs into godly songs." Some half-dozen of the songs metamorphosed in this way are mentioned in the *Complaynt of Scotland*, but most have disappeared with their tunes and it is difficult at times to gauge their effect, which depended on the mood of the moment. Where the opening lines of the old air are retained, the sudden shift to top spiritual gear is disconcerting;

> " In till ane mirthful May morning
> Quhen Phebus did up spring,
> Walkand (awake) I lay, in ane garding gay,
> Thinkand on Christ sa fre."

For others, we must take the religious appeal they made largely on trust; *Johne, cum kis me now*. Others again linger in the mind; *Grevous is my sorrow, Go hart, vnto the Lamp of Licht*, and the lovely *All my lufe, leif me not. Our Brother let us put in graue* is a noble rendering of a German burial service hymn which served, no doubt, to replace the primer's Office of the Dead. The joyful *All my hart, ay this is my sang* is probably traditional, as indicated by the stanza;

16. Frank Ll. Harrison, *Music in Medieval Britain* (Oxford, 1958).
17. *Devotional Pieces in Verse and Prose*. Ed. J. A. W. Bennet. S.T.S. (1955).

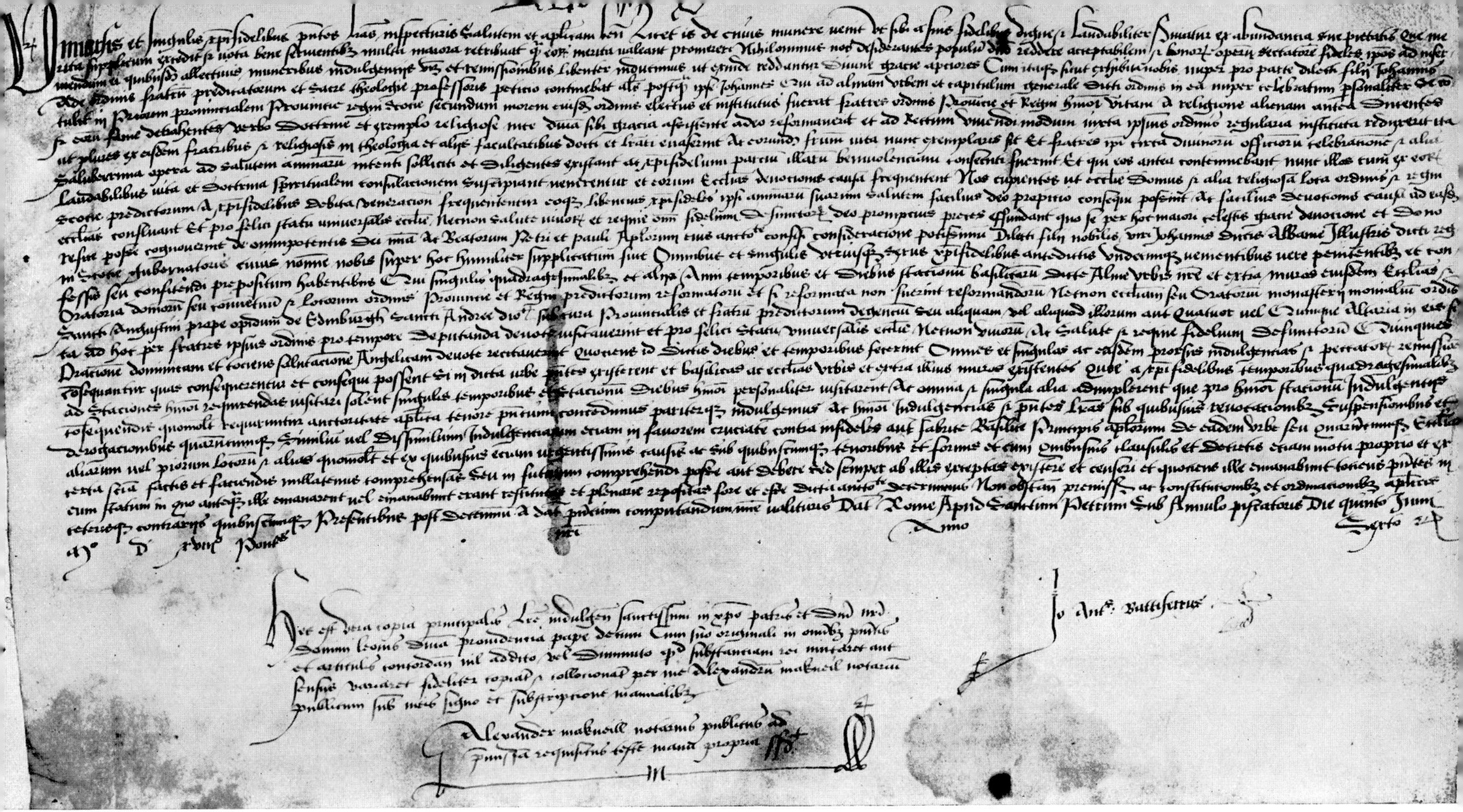

PLATE XIII. NOTARIAL COPY OF PAPAL BULL, COMMENDING THE REFORM OF THE SCOTTISH BLACKFRIARS.

Io. Francisci Pici

MIRANDVLAE DOMINI, ET

Concordiæ Comitis, &c. De Animæ
immortalitate docta & arguta
Digreßio, nunquam prius
in Gallijs excusa.

A diecimus huic digreßioni Io. Ferrerij Pedemon-
tani Entelechiam, cum nonnullis aliis.

PARISIIS,

Apud Ioannem Roygni, via ad D. Iacobum,
sub Basilisco, & quatuor Elementis.

1541.

PLATE XIV. HENRY SINCLAIR'S COPY OF THE
DE ANIMAE IMMORTALITATE.

" Nixt him, to lufe his Mother fair,
With steidfast hart, for euer mair:
Scho (she) bure the byrth, fred vs from cair;
Christ hes my hart ay."

An occasional reference in the collection to contemporary events, such as the presence of French troops, the policy of the queen mother, the steeples no longer standing, and the general sermonising tone of the book, indicate a period of the militant preaching of the " Word " which would correspond with one extending from the death of James V to the reign of his daughter, Mary Stewart. The closing ballads reflect the aggressive attitude of the young Congregation and its campaign to stamp out idolatry.

The ballads probably had a greater influence in the second half of the century. It is hardly likely that an edition was printed in Scotland before 1560, but copies of Scottish editions have come to us with the dates 1567, 1578, 1600 and 1621. In the earlier period, they would have served much the same purpose as the bible and the *Book of Common Prayer* for the reformers. Later, they would have satisfied the needs of those who preferred a milder doctrine and a more traditional piety than was being offered officially. The tunes and the satire alone do not explain their sustained popularity. If their appeal was to a more restricted circle, this would seem to imply a less wider distribution than is commonly claimed for them, and there has always seemed to be more of assertion and conjecture concerning their wide circulation than real evidence.

The years immediately following the first performance of Lindsay's *Satire*, in 1540, were filled with events momentous for the fate of Scotland. The disgrace of Solway Moss and the death of James V: the brief ascendancy of the anglophile party under Arran and the equally brief triumph of Cardinal Beaton ending in his murder: the defence of the castle of St. Andrews by the reformers: the campaigns of Somerset, the defeat of the Scots at Pinkie and the arrival of French reinforcements—such was the sequence of events leading to a situation that demanded more than ever a decision on the part of those who were wavering in their allegiance to tradition. Where did the duty of a true patriot lie in these circumstances? The unknown author of the *Complaynt of Scotland*[18] gave an answer in his stirring appeal to the three Estates to heal their mutual discord and unite in the defence of the public weal against the old enemy, England, and all it stood for at that time—about 1549.

It is a remarkable work, written in " domestic Scots language for the vulgar people ", but elevated in tone and eloquent in the style fashionable of the day which combed the scriptures and the classics for imagery and example. It was a reply also to the war of nerves that Henry and Somerset had waged with the help of preachers, bibles and political tracts, such as; *Henry VIII's Declaration of the just causes of the war with the Scots and his Majesty's title to the sovereignty of Scotland*, published in 1542: or *James Henryson, a Scottishman's Exhortation to Unity and Peace sent to the inhabitants of Scotland*, which appeared in 1548: or *Nicholas Bodrugan alias Adam's Epitome of King Edward VI's Title to the sovereignty of Scotland*, belonging to that same year. [19]

---

18. *Complaynt of Scotland.* Ed. J. A. H. Murray. E.E.T.S.
19. All four tracts are printed in the appendix to the *Complaynt.* E.E.T.S.

Amidst all this noisy propaganda, the *Complaynt* strikes a note of scorn and protest at the prospect of a satellite Scotland, and exposes the root causes of national decay. In the allegorical form that the work takes, Dame Scotia reproaches her three sons, the Estates, for their disunity and pusillanimity in repulsing the extravagant claims of England, which are based on fairy tales and false prophecies. It is battles not books that decide the fate of nations. The English king might patronise renegade Scots, but he would be better pleased if every Scotsman had another Scot in his belly. Familiarity breeds treason. Twenty hours suffice for a determination of the Scottish council to be known in Berwick, and three days for the Berwick post to have it in London.

Only the youngest son, the Labourer, is allowed to reply, but he is silenced with a reproof of the vices of the fickle, thriftless, intemperate lower classes, who only lack the opportunity to commit the very crimes of which they accuse their superiors. As for the nobility, there is not one spark of honour among the majority of them, for whom the nights are too short to indulge their vices and the days not long enough for their crimes of oppression of the poor. Horses and dogs are the ruin of Scotland. Some excuse may be found for the nobles and the commons on the grounds of ignorance, but the clergy sin against the light and fail to give the example demanded of their state. Let them take warning from the fate of their brethren in England and have recourse to arms without scruple in this holy war against the southern infidel.

Many suggestions have been made regarding the authorship of the *Complaynt*,[20] The youngest of the three Wedderburns, Robert, has been mentioned, but, as C. S. Lewis observes,[21] no claim should be made for anybody who had a hand in the *Good and Godly Ballads*. It is natural to compare the *Complaynt* with the *Satire of the Three Estates* and a common authorship has been assumed on the grounds of certain similarities between the works. But neither will this claim bear scrutiny. The note of patriotism in the *Complaynt* is not Lindsay's, nor does he ever show the same restraint and calm assessment of affairs as appears in the *Complaynt* and which offers a more balanced view of contemporary Scotland. (We will forget that Lindsay's play is a satire !) Perhaps his earliest and finest work, the *Dreme*, comes nearest to anything in the *Complaynt* by the resemblance between it and the delightful interlude, *A Monolog Recreative*, which affords us a brief glimpse of another Scotland full of song, dance and story, and of that " blythness " whose loss Sir Richard Maitland was to lament later on in the century. It sends a shaft of light through the prevailing gloom and fully explains, itself alone, the nostalgic note that fills the *Complaynt* with a plaintive patriotism.

In the decade or so following the appearance of this work, the Scottish church held at least four provincial councils, the first in 1549. The canons of those councils provide sufficient evidence of the need of disciplinary reform in the Scottish church. Moreover, they had behind them the weight of responsible authority and received a publicity that no satire, tract or ballad could hope to have. They implied a state of affairs that was remediable, but the very reforms that they proposed alienated those

---

20. The latest suggestion in *Notes and Queries*, July-August, 1959, makes an interesting claim for Patrick Cockburn of the Merse. It is difficult, however, to reconcile Cockburn's subsequent career—he was recommended to Cecil by the English ambassador, Randolph, in September, 1560, and came to terms with the reformers—with the mentality of the *Complaynt*.

21. C. S. Lewis, *English Literature in the Sixteenth Century* (Oxford History of English Literature Series), is indispensable for a study of the literature of the period.

whose interests were affected and prevented the reforms from taking effect. It was not a church reformed along the lines of Trent that was the aim of the anti-catholic party, or was called for in the party literature, but rather the renouncement of all " idolatry ", the false fire of purgatory, the whispering of sins and the mumbling of the mass, as the ballads have it. Arran's argument had been; no purgatory, no need for monks or monasteries that had been founded to pray for the " souls being in the pains of purgatory ".

The extirpation of idolatry meant, then, in practical terms, the expulsion of the friars and on the 1st January, 1559, the *Beggars' Summons*, claiming to come from every city, town and village of Scotland, was posted up on the doors of the friaries. It was addressed to the " Flocks of Friars within this realm " and demanded the patrimony of the poor in the name of the " Blynd, Cruked, Beddrelles (bed-ridden), Wedowis, Orphelings, and all uther pure, sa viseit be the hand of God, as may not worke."[22] The inspiration of the *Beggars' Summons* no doubt came from the *Supplication of the Beggars* of Simon Fish which had been widely distributed in England, and Row mentions such a tract as coming in from England. The idea appears to have been maturing for some time in Scotland as there is notice of a work, called *Querela Pauperum*, being in the country about 1540.[23]

An early start had also been made on discrediting the friars, since, whatever their failings, it was necessary to build up a case against them. The Earl of Glencairn's *Epistle from the Holy Hermit of Loreto* was directed against the Grey Friars, Buchanan satirised them in the *Franciscanus*, Lindsay pokes fun at the friars and few orthodox ballads could afford to forget them. Calderwood repeats a story from Knox of one who was ridiculed as Friar Pater Noster for having advocated the saying of the Lord's Prayer to the saints and he reprints two pasquils that were set up on the abbey church of St. Andrews, one in Latin and the other in English;

> " Doctors of Theologie of forescore of yeeres
> And old jollie Lupoys, the bald Gray Friars,
> The would be called Rabbi, and Magister Noster,
> And wot not to whom to say their Pater Noster."[24]

The fun of it all seems to fade away with time.

The writing, printing and posting up of such defamatory literature was the subject of legislation in 1543, 1549 and 1552. The act of 1552, which forbade the printing of books, ballads, songs, " blasphemations ", " rhymes or tragedies in Latin or in English ", seems to presume the presence of several printers in the country. Two of them, John Scot and Robert Lekpreuik, are well known for their enterprise and co-operation with both sides in the controversies of the times.[25] Scot enjoyed the patronage of Archbishop Hamilton and printed his *Catechism* in 1552, and in 1559 his *Godlie Exhortation*, a leaflet on the Eucharist, which modern historians have perhaps too readily identified with the pamphlet which Knox dubs the *Twapenny Faith*.[26] He was imprisoned in 1562 for

---

22. The full text of the *Summons* is given in *A Source Book of Scottish History*, ii, 168.
23. *St. Andrews Formulare*, ii, 72.
24. *History of the Kirk of Scotland*, i, 273.
25. Dickson and Edmond, *Annals of Scottish Printing*.
26. The price of the leaflet was probably two pence.

printing Ninian Winzet's *Last Blast of the Trumpet*, but was busy again in 1568 on an edition of Lindsay's works. Lekpreuik, who did more business with the reformers, likewise suffered imprisonment in 1573 for printing Davidson's *Dialog* without a license. His press in Edinburgh was seldom idle and there issued from it a constant stream of ballads and broadsheets during the troubled times of Mary's short reign and the subsequent regencies of Moray, Lennox and Mar.

In 1567, parliament found it necessary to renew the earlier legislation against unlicensed publications. The preamble of the act complains of the licentious abuse of the setting up in the silence of the night in public places of bills and " tickets " slandering the queen and members of the nobility. In spite of the penalties imposed by the act, not only on the bill posters but upon those who failed to destroy these notices at first sight, they continued to pour from the press so long as the queen was alive and constituted a threat to the new regime. The period was a stormy one with the tide of battle fluctuating now in favour of the queen's party, now in that of her enemies, with support for both sides supplied by the enthusiasm of known and unknown authors of satirical effusions. [27]

Of the author of the greater part of the ballads that have survived, nothing definite is known, but writing under the real or assumed name of Robert Sempill, he speaks with no uncertain voice and in much the same political language as we are accustomed to hear today from self-styled representatives of the people working for a party. His style and themes are uncomplicated; Mary and the mass are an abomination: Moray and Elizabeth are the salvation of Scotland. It is, no doubt, Sempill who under the signature of Maddie of the Fish Mercat, or Maddie of the Coil Mercat, claims to be retailing the gossip of the day, but the fund of inside information on which he draws and his rooted prejudices mark him obviously as the party spokesman. And he was well equipped for the role of mouthpiece with his uncompromising views, journalistic flair for the sensational and talent for vituperative scorn.

There was no lack of " hot " news. The murder of Darnley provoked, among other protests, the *Testament of umquhile King Henrie Stewart of gude memorie, Verses underneath an Answer to a Challenge made by the Earl of Bothwell, offering to prove by law of Armes that he was the chief and author of the foul and horrible murder of the King*, with Bloody Bothwell, Mary Dowbill Dalyday and Rizzio, " a manifest enemy to the Evangell ", all cast in sinister roles. Various " Exhortations " are also made to the lords in their just quarrel, calling upon them to " mak reformatioun, with Goddis buik for guide ", to " depose all wickit papists proud and Christis fois ", and to keep a watchful eye on "Aberdene, of Sophistis the well-spring ". [28]

One of the rare replies from the other side came in a ballad by Tom Truth entitled *A Rhime in defence of the Queen of Scots against the Earl of Murray*—this murderer Moray, Caco's offspring and Satan's seed, the perfect pattern of deceit, who, with confederate lords, killed the king and laid the blame on the queen, and was now plotting to reign in her stead as regent of the land. He were better employed looking after his monastery;

---

27. *Satirical Poems of the Times of the Reformation*. Ed. James Cranstoun. S.T.S. 2 vols. Cranstoun prints forty-eight of these poems with an introduction and biographical notices in volume one. The second volume is devoted to copious literary, linguistic and historical notes.
28. Aberdeen symbolised papistry and St. Andrews protestantism.

> " A cowle, a cowle for such a Greek
> Were fitter far to wear,
> Than this apostate Deacon should
> Such princely rule to bear."

For Sempill and his co-balladists, Moray was very much the " good Lord James ", and his assassination in 1559 let loose a stream of protests against the crime and in praise of the virtues of " that Innocent ", the child of Honour and Good Fame, endowed with the faith of Abraham, the wisdom of Solomon, the strength of Sampson, the justice of Jethro, the chastity of Scipio, the benignity of David, the liberality of Titus— " Quhat wald thou moir? " The shot that laid the regent low is " The Poysonit Schot " that has split the realm in twain and allowed idolatry to shoot up again.[29] Possibly the truth about Moray lies somewhere between the views expressed in these two ballads.[30]

In the spring of the following year, 1570, Sir William Kirkcaldy of Grange declared for the queen and held the castle of Edinburgh on her behalf till the end of May, 1573. In his fine *Ballat of the Captan of the Castell*, he expresses his sentiments regarding the party he had hitherto supported; " These wicked vaine venerianis " who had abused the queen and accused her " with serpent wordis fell." Sempill replied in a ballad proclaiming the virtues of Elizabeth whose forces had come to avenge the death of Moray and support the besiegers of the castle. He recalls Elizabeth's manifold good deeds, particularly the reforming of idolatry, and concludes that as regards Scottish interests a better sovereign never ruled in England. After this exchange of shots, the batteries open up. In *The Cruikit liedes the Blinde*, the influence of the able Lethington and his subtle loyalties—he was now working for the queen—come under fire;

> " Thay say he can baith quhissell and cloik
> And his mouth full of meil."

He is the " Bird in the Cage " (castle of Edinburgh) according to Maddie the Prioress of the Cail Mercat who predicts his end on the gallows where Death the Traveller with dusty feet shall call him forth to his last dance. *The Lamentation of the Commons of Scotland* describes the misery and hardship resulting from the siege for the common folk—whose cause it was always good policy to espouse—the colliers, carriers, tinkers, chapmen and craftsmen, and calls down the wrath of heaven on the author of their woes (Kirkcaldy);

> " O thow ! O Lord and God in persoun thre
> Consume this Wratche with Brinstane, fyre and thunder."

A noose was to prove equally effective. Kirkcaldy was hanged at the mercat cross of Edinburgh on the 3rd August, 1573.

The raising of the siege of Edinburgh in May, 1573, gave a breathing space to the contending parties and allowed attention to be focussed again

---

29. The regent was assassinated in the High Street of Linlithgow by James Hamilton of Bothwellhaugh, a kinsman of the archbishop, on 23rd January, 1570. The Hamiltons were naturally on Sempill's black list and he ridicules the prelate in a scurrilous ballad, *The Bischoppis Lyfe and Testament*. According to the *Diurnal*, the archbishop admitted complicity in the plot and expressed repentance on the scaffold at Stirling, where he was hanged in April, 1571. Two Latin verses were affixed to the scaffold:
> Cresce diu, felix arbor, semperque vireto
> Frondibus, ut nobis talia poma feras.
(Grow on, blessed tree, and flourish evergreen bearing us fruits so rich.) *Satirical Poems*, ii, 140.

30. In *The Reign of Queen Elizabeth*, 1558-1603 (Oxford, 1959), Professor J. B. Black feels " that the time has come boldly to eliminate the ' Buchanan myth ' and the ' legend of the good lord James ' which between them have bedevilled our text-books and distorted the truth beyond recognition." *The Tablet*, Sept. 19th, 1959.

on the general conditions of the country. The same causes that had operated for so long—divided allegiance and civil strife—had produced the same effects—much social and moral misery and a new crop of *Complayntes*. Reflecting on the *Miseries of the Tyme*, Sir Richard Maitland, who remains aloof from party strife and is critical of both old and new regimes, observes that eating meat on Fridays is no claim to righteousness and that calling the pope Antichrist and the mass idolatry does not cure human nature of its follies. The charge is backed up with less restraint by the author of *A Lewd Ballat*, who accuses the reformers of the same frailties of the flesh as were imputed to their predecessors. Nicol Burne adds his testimony in a poem, entitled *Ane Admonition to the Antichristian Ministers in the Deformit Kirk of Scotland*. The *Admonition* is attributed to Burne because it is found attached to copies of *The Disputation concerning Headdes of Religion*, which Burne wrote in Paris in 1580 and in which he describes himself as a former professor of philosophy in St. Leonard's College, in the city of St. Andrews, brought up from his tender age in the perverse sect of the Calvinists and now by a special grace of God a member of the holy and catholic church.

In the *Admonition*, Burne pours scorn on the apostate clergy, religious and others, naming some fifty of them,[31] who transferred their allegiance so easily from Rome to Geneva in 1560. Many of their names are to be found in the early annals of the reformers—Willock, the " loun " who pulled the plough steered by Knox, Row who returned from Rome to oppose the movement and joined it, Craig, Winram, Davidson, the " poet ", Melville, the " elect Arbuthnot ", the ambitious Simpson of Dunbar, little David Howe, Glas and Tom Makghe. These are the men, says Burne, who have to answer for the state of Scotland since 1561—the sacrifice of the altar abolished, the sick and dying deprived of the last rites—and he calls down upon them the
> " Curse of the people quha on the Lord do call
> For Pastors and Sacramentis, the saulis remeid."
" On your way," he cries contemptuously,
> " Kilt up your Conneis and hie the to Geneve."

Burne's shafts would have pierced few skins in those days and would have made little impression, one feels, on John Davidson, the sincere admirer of Knox who is eulogised by him in *Ane Breif Commendatioun of Vprichtnes*. Davidson had modelled himself on the master, was fearless in denouncing whatever he disapproved of and seems to have inherited, along with the reformer's mantle, his habit of dropping bricks within royal earshot. For James VI, Davidson had only a nuisance value and for Lennox he was just *un petit diable*.

The question of patrimony was one of plain survival for the kirk and the Regent Morton's project of uniting four parishes under one minister spurred Davidson to protest in his *Dialog or Mutuall Talking betuix a Clerk and ane Courteour*. In a way, Lennox's proposal was a renewal of the old practice of pluralities, with this difference; that the surplus revenues would be pocketed by the crown. Courteour's argument is that there are not enough ministers—barely two hundred all told—and that many parishes have been neglected for seven years.

We have a picture of these neglected parishes in the anonymous *Lamentatioun of Lady Scotland*—parish kirks like sheepcots, crows and

---

31. Cranstoun identifies most of them with biographical details in *Satirical Poems*, ii, 218.

" dows " drowning the minister's voice, feathers and filth everywhere, the people cold in devotion, the Sabbath ignored—one remembers Archbishop Hamilton's report on the state of the churches in the Merse in 1556—scripture, to be sure, has now ousted superstition, but somehow all is not well and Lady Scotland blames the lords, lairds and commons, who will not pay for the upkeep of the kirk, the dishonesty of the merchant-men and the failure of the leaders to give example.

Few want to preach, continues Courteour in the *Dialog*, and fewer still are worthy of it. Give them a living wage, says the Clerk, and you will have able preachers enough. Always talking money, cries the scandalised Courteour, can they not imitate the itinerant apostles ? And, as for wages,

> " The teindis will not cum in thair neuis (fists)
> Sa lang as one of us leuis."

For a time the controversy grows even more bitter and humourless; a popular ballad of the period, *The Bonnie Earl o' Moray*, with its wild, haunting air, seems to echo the grim mood of the still undecided battle-field. Old Lethington, who had witnessed the whole course of the revolution (and profited by it) and who castigated popery and Calvinism alike with poetic indifference, sensed a profound transformation in the national mentality; he looks back wistfully beyond the economic, social and religious changes to that earlier Scotland of his youth where devotion, compassion, mirth, equity and honour were (he seems to remember) cherished and esteemed. And to his disillusioned mind, that bygone " time of superstition and popery " took on the aspect of " the good old days ". The poem, in which he voices his misgivings, strikes a curiously authentic note amid the somewhat repellant theology and morality of the pamphleteers;

> " Quhair is the blyithnes that hes beine
> Baith in Burgh and landwart sene
> Amang lordis and ladyis schene
> daunsing, singing, game and play
> Bot now I wait not quhat thay meine
> all merines is worne away.
>
> For now I heir na worde of yuile
> In kirk on calsay nor in scuile
> Lordis lattis thair kitchingis cuill
> and drawis thame to the abbay
> and scant hes ane to keip thair muile
> All houshaulderis is worne away.
>
> I saw na gysaris all this yeir
> Bot kirkmen cled lyik men of weir
> That neuer cummis in the queir
> Lyik ruffiaris is thair array
> To preiche and teiche that will not leir
> The kirkis gudis thay waist away.
>
> Kirkmen afoir wer gud of lyfe
> Preichit, teichit and stainchit stryfe
> They feirit nather sworde nor knyfe
> For love of god the suith to say
> All honourit thame bayth barne and wyff
> Deuotioun wes not away.

Our fatheris wyse wes and discreit
Thay had bayth honour men and meit
With luiff thay did thair tennentis treit
and had aneuche In poise to lay
Thay wantit nather malt nor quheit
And mirrines wes not away.

And we had nather yuill nor pace
Bot seikis our meit from place to place
and we haue nather luck nor grace
We gar our landis doubill pay
Our tennentis cryis alace alace
That reuthe and pitie is away.

Now we haue mair It is weill kend
nor our foirbearis had to spend
bot far less at the yeiris end
and neuer hes ane mirrie day
God will na ritches to us send
So lang as honour is away.

We waist far mair now lyik vaine fuillis
We and our page to turse our muillis
Nor thay did than that had greit yuillis
Of meit and drink sayid neuer nay
They had lang formis quhair we haue stuillis
And mirrines wes not away.

.   .   .

The kirkmen keipis na professioun
the temporall men committis oppressioun
puttand the puire from thair possessioun
Na kynd of feir of god haue thay
Thay cummer bayth the kirk and sessioun
And chasis Cheritie away."

.   .   .

But Sir Richard Maitland of Lethington had something of the sensitivity and insight of the genuine poet and was perhaps exceptional. Nevertheless, as the century moves on and the controversies cool a little, the picture of contemporary Scotland, as reflected in the writings of men like Nicol Burne, John Davidson or the anonymous versifiers, is still one of Scotland's " lang dolour ". The picture is not a complete one, nor wholly representative, any more than that offered in the rest of the literature that has been under review. Without doubt, there is a more encouraging aspect, as there always was, and the influence of England is moving to a climax in the union of the crowns. But as he turns the pages of the latest *Lamentation of Lady Scotland* and hears once again the complaint against the Three Estates in the same language, and often in the very phraseology of Lindsay, the reader may be excused who lays it down with the reflection—this is where we came in.

SOME NOTES ON THE RELIGIOUS ORDERS IN PRE-REFORMATION SCOTLAND

by

ANTHONY ROSS

I

It must be evident to anyone who has done even a little research on the subject that an attempt to produce a synthetic account of the religious orders in sixteenth-century Scotland is still premature. There are so few monographs to draw upon, there is so much unedited material to be examined at home and abroad. The documents already in print require re-interpretation in the light of material with which their editors were unfamiliar. They are also, unhappily, almost entirely limited to matters of legal or economic interest to the later owners of monastic property; they throw comparatively little light on the internal life of the communities concerned. One longs for the intimate pictures of monastic life which have come down from Bury, Rievaulx, or St. Albans, but which are paralleled in Scotland only by Adamnan's life of Columba against the background of Iona. The lack of such documents has been some excuse for slight interest in monastic history; nevertheless, it needs to be emphasised that although we do not have the rich documentation of religious life available to English church historians there is more material for the study of religious orders in Scotland than most writers on the subject have appreciated. It is scattered, but it exists. When I began to investigate the history of the Scottish Black Friars a very distinguished historian, who has done more to promote the serious study of Scottish history than any man now living, suggested that there was not enough matter to engage attention for very long. Soon he was agreeing that it would take half a lifetime and two considerable volumes to cover the subject thoroughly. It has been too readily assumed that unless we find great chartularies or monastic chronicles not much can be discovered. That might be true, if it could be assumed that the religious orders in Scotland made no impact on the life of the nation. In fact, however, monks and friars played a part up to the end of the middle ages which has left significant traces in local and national records at home, and in academic and ecclesiastical records abroad. It can be discovered by reading, in addition to the printed records of parliament or the exchequer or the register of the great seal, the unpublished records of burghs and law courts, and the protocol books of notaries; the records of foreign universities, of general chapters of monks or friars, letter-books of masters-general or procurators-general, Vatican records, dedicatory epistles in contemporary literature, and of course diplomatic correspondence.[1]

The list may sound formidable, but it is not impossible, given a revolution in the idea of what constitutes research. In Scotland, only too

1. The following pages owe much to Dr. John Durkan and the Rev. Joseph O'Dea, O.C.R., who placed results of their own research at my disposal, and gave me the benefit of their critical judgment on many points. Father O'Dea was to have written this essay originally, but was unfortunately prevented from doing so by ill health. He very generously sent me all the material which he had collected, some of which proved so new and valuable that I have felt obliged to put it aside until he can publish it himself. Perhaps it is scarcely necessary to add that neither he nor Dr. Durkan is responsible for the use made of their notes; nor are they committed to agreement with what follows, in any way.

often, reputations are built on the kind of work which in some other countries would qualify for the simplest research degree, namely the transcribing and editing of a text for the printer. But historical research should not have to wait for the printer, especially in these days of photostat and microfilm. The work of examination, interpretation and synthesis of evidence characteristic of the great medievalists or the great students of the sixteenth century, ranges over printed or unprinted sources with ease. In Scotland we are too content to wait upon print. This has the effect not only of ensuring merely partial examination of the evidence for sixteenth-century church history, but of lending sometimes an exaggerated distinction to the few writers whose references include manuscript sources.

So it comes about that Hay Fleming or Dr. Coulton rank as quarries for raw material, and are employed without close examination of the documents they used, still less those they did not use. Yet each touched only a small part of the relevant material, and each was blinded, as we are all liable to be, by too great devotion to a particular hypothesis. Hay Fleming could misinterpret so simple a phrase as " schola canonum," being unsure apparently of the elementary facts of medieval curricula.[2] More seriously perhaps, he could make play with a scandal about an abbot of Kilwinning abducting a lady, not mentioning—what he must have known—that the abbot was no monk but a commendator pushed in by the king, nor—what perhaps he did not know, if he did not probe sufficiently into the evidence—that the so-called abbot was bitterly opposed by the monks and by the long established abbot whom royal chicanery was busily removing.[3] The uncovering of the whole story which he so lightly touched requires collation of a range of material from different sources, and a less reverent attitude, incidentally, to royal letters than is customarily shown when they seem to support an anti-monastic brief. Dr. Coulton, in his account of the feuing of Drygrange by the monks of Melrose, is another example of how hasty and prejudiced reading can result in complete missing of the significance of a document, so that an amicable adjustment of rent becomes an example of monastic exploitation.[4] It is not surprising that he failed to notice that the " rack-rented " tenants sympathised with the monks at the reformation!

It is, in fact, all too easy to practise that kind of writing which selects random detail, even accurately recorded, to build up a picture which, in spite of documentation, is essentially distorted, because insufficient effort has been made to gather the available evidence or to understand what was happening. It is possible to produce two utterly opposed character sketches with the same basis of facts, but judged in the light of different principles, or simply in and out of their proper context. The distortion or misinterpretation need not be calculated; it almost certainly never is, in the works of Scottish history under comment. Nevertheless, up to date, it is hardly an exaggeration to say that the most valuable contributions to a knowledge or understanding of the pattern of monastic life in Scotland before the reformation are to be found by the average intelligent reader

2. See St. Andrews Charters Transcripts, by David Hay Fleming, in the Scottish Record Office, no. 18, (on p. 29), where " scholae canonum " has been translated as " the schools of the canons " and " facultatem canonum " as " the faculty of canons "; or no. 213 (on p. 206) where William Ghume and John Annand are described as " professors of canon law " (which they were not) instead of " canons professed."

3. Cf. *The Reformation in Scotland*, Appendix D, pp. 570-77.

4. *Scottish Abbeys and Social Life*, p. 123 and Appendix 5, p. 263. A more just assessment of the Drygrange case was given by the late Dr. Marguerite Wood in *Melrose Abbey*, (H.M.S.O. 1932), pp. 34-5.

in the guides to ruined abbeys or priories issued by H.M. Stationery Office. Their authors have been primarily archaeologists concerned to reconstruct a range of buildings and to discover their function, to know in fact why they were built and what they were normally used for, and not to demonstrate whether monks were a good or a bad thing. Limitations of space have perhaps helped also to discourage them from wandering far into moral or romantic speculations. A better idea of what went on in the medieval religious houses of Scotland will be gathered from Mr. Stewart Cruden's small book on their ruins,[5] in spite of its occasional errors, than from Dr. Easson's much larger and more comprehensive survey of their history.[6] The latter set out " to indicate the significant features of their history, so far as these are ascertainable." But if the religious listed could read Dr. Easson they would find little reference to what was significant in terms of their own constitutions, or their own particular and local effort. The friars, for example, might wonder what had happened to obscure their relationship to the universities, or the very important part they played, on both sides, in the course of the Scottish reformation.[7]

What Dr. Easson's pages note are almost exclusively details of benefactions or wartime disasters, dates of foundation or dissolution. The dates of dissolution are themselves unreal since they so often record simply the termination of legal formalities by which titles were preserved when the reality which they once covered no longer existed. To refer to the year 1606, or 1609, as the end of an abbey's religious history, is to perpetuate a legal fiction which both before and after 1560 covered the depredations of the crown and the nobility among monastic property. Religious life in the sense understood by St. Benedict or St. Bernard existed in the abbeys of Arbroath and Melrose as long as they held communities living, even imperfectly, under a rule of monastic obedience, and concerned primarily with maintaining the *opus Dei*, the recitation of the Divine Office and the celebration of mass. Such communities came to an end, for a time, with the reformation. Vows were no longer recognised; religious were compelled to cast off their traditional dress; the choral office and the mass were no longer allowed, even if they may have been found occasionally after 1560, in exceptional circumstances. Nor is Dr. Easson's attempt to suggest some sort of continuity after 1560 strengthened by talking, as Dr. Donaldson does, about the suppression of " the Latin rite " in that year.[8] What the reformers repressed was the mass in any form. They would have had no more to do with Greek or Armenian or Celtic rites than with Sarum or Roman, and indeed they would have been busily engaged in " casting down " Scoto-Catholic or Anglo-Catholic rites and altars if such had existed in their day. No " Iona Community " appears before the twentieth century; no Scottish Mirfield or Nashdom was set up in 1560. There were Scottish members of religious orders after that date, but if they followed traditional forms of community life it was abroad, in houses of their orders in France or the Low Countries, or in the Scottish Benedictine Abbey of Saint James at Ratisbon. The ideals of religious communities could not be pursued in Scotland, but they did survive, though tenuously, among her people. Before 1560 there were

---

5.   *Scottish Abbeys: An Introduction to the mediaeval abbeys and priories of Scotland*, (H.M.S.O., 1960).
6.   *Medieval Religious Houses: Scotland.* (London, 1957).
7.   Professor J. H. Burleigh, *A Church History of Scotland*, (Oxford 1960), is even more vague about the friars, who are dismissed in eight pages, of which only four concern their activity in Scotland.
8.   *The Scottish Reformation*, p. 55: cf. *Scotland, Church and Nation through Sixteen Centuries* (London, 1960), p. 54.

Scots in the newly established Society of Jesus and there were many more after that date. That the older forms of religious life also continued to exercise an attraction, even after the reformation, is illustrated by the slender but unbroken line of Scottish Benedictines stretching from before 1560 to the present day.[9] Such facts are perhaps a little more relevant to the history of the religious orders in relation to Scotland, than the recording of empty titles of abbot or prior.

They are mentioned here chiefly because they point to something not sufficiently noticed, and which is true also in its way of the secular clergy. Despite the scandals that there were in the fifty years before the alteration of religion, and in spite of what happened after 1560, the appeal of the priesthood and of the religious life continued to attract recruits from Scotland who undertook to lead lives of chastity and obedience, to recite the traditional prayers of the catholic church, and to celebrate mass and administer the seven sacraments. Such establishments as the abbey of St. James and the Scots colleges in Paris and Rome were real links between the medieval and the later periods of Scottish catholic life.[10] There was still some vitality in sixteenth-century Scottish catholicism, but it is usually overlooked in the preoccupation with the material aspect of life which is uppermost in the Scottish chartularies and in such a work as Dr. Easson's. It is indeed true that there was a great crisis in the sixteenth century, but it is not just a story of the collapse of the religious orders but rather of a struggle between forces of decadence and the defenders of an ideal within, and without, each of the older orders. By " decadence " is meant not simply the obvious scandals implied in such lines as Lindsay's

> Speir at the monks of Balmerinoch
> Gif lechery be sin,

but any notable decline from the ideals expressed in the constitutions of a religious order. So we may speak of the elaborate decoration of Melrose as a sign of Cistercian decadence because it is so plainly a departure from the pattern of simplicity professed by the order. If monks generally in sixteenth-century Scotland lived like members of a country club that too may be described as decadence, especially if it can be shown that leisurely comfort was secured at the expense of parish needs, or by rack-renting their tenants. If there were Scottish Dominicans like that Benedict de Scotia who was pilloried in the *Epistolae Obscurorum Virorum*, with minds closed to new ideas and blind to the spiritual needs of the age, then that also was decadence. The attempt attributed to Friar Walter Laing, to restore spiritual authority by bogus " miracles " was a sign of grave decadence, if the word is not too mild to describe a blasphemous deceit.[11] By one word many things are covered, from mediocrity to open sin, which were recognised not only by those in the church who became protestants but also by some at least, and more than is usually supposed, who worked to change them within the obedience of the Holy See. The rest of this essay will be chiefly concerned to suggest some of the difficulties which stood in the way of an orthodox reform, from the point of view of the

---

9. On the Benedictine connection, see Appendix II to this article, by Mark Dilworth, O.S.B. See also Aubrey Gwynn, S. J. " Some Notes on the History of the Irish and Scottish Benedictine Monasteries in Germany," *Innes Rev.*, v, pp. 5-27, and Fr. Dilworth's " Two Necrologies of Scottish Benedictine Abbeys in Germany," *Innes Rev.*, ix, pp. 173-203.

10. On the Scots abroad see, for example, David McRoberts, " Scottish National Churches in Rome," *Innes Rev.*, i, pp. 110-130. William McGoldrick, " The Scots College, Madrid," *Innes Rev.*, iv, pp. 92-109. M. V. Hay, *The Blairs Papers*.

11. Cf. Dickinson's *Knox*, ii, p. 334, n. 11. For Benedict see Letter xlvii in F. G. Stokes ed. of *Epistolae Obscur. Vir.* (London, 1925), pp. 230-3.

friars and of the monastic orders, and to give a glimpse of the struggle which went on for the preservation of a religious ideal.

II

To begin with, it must be conceded that Scotland was overstocked with religious houses. A religious foundation can outlive its usefulness; so can an order for that matter. The very success of a foundation brings dangers; urgency fades, and with it zeal slackens and routine takes hold. Effort and risk that seemed natural to pioneers are shunned by their descendants in the name of prudence, or even of humility. Vested interests grow, sometimes almost without their growth being noticed; the preservation of corporate rights, privileges, and possessions, originally granted for the assistance of some particular work, becomes more important than that work itself. So medieval abbots might tend to appear less and less as spiritual fathers and rather more as feudal barons, or perhaps as kindly squires. Admission of novices tended to be made easier, to facilitate the staffing of foundations established in the first enthusiasm of great religious movements, like those of the eleventh or thirteenth centuries; although, as enthusiasm waned, contraction of foundations in the interest of quality would have been wiser policy at times. It was very likely so in friaries as well as in monasteries. And if monasteries tended to be assimilated to the feudal pattern, the friaries which were settled in small burghs in the thirteenth century tended to become pleasant social centres for the business or gossip of burgesses, for members of the trade guilds, people to whom members of the community were often closely related.

Such a situation is not scandalous, and when it exists it is defended not only by the clergy involved but also by the laity. The religious communities so knit into secular life are not simply organs of prayer, insurance companies for the hereafter; they are usefully engaged in the social and economic structure of the lay society around them. This can be seen at every level of society in medieval Scotland. The Blackfriars at Perth, or the Greyfriars at Stirling, becomes the centre of the court life while a king stays there;[12] another house is a convenient meeting-place for the officials of the exchequer,[13] or for the hammermen of a burgh;[14] one gives hospitality to ambassadors,[15] another regularly provides lodging for a nobleman;[16] legal documents are witnessed for burgess connections.[17] We find one friar actually functioning as a customs officer;[18] another is called in to mend the town's clock;[19] one is in demand as a carpenter;[20] another apparently possessed outstanding skill in making lawns;[21] yet

---

12. James I was staying in the Perth Blackfriars when he was murdered. James V's residence with the Stirling Greyfriars prompted one of Dunbar's liveliest efforts. Cf. Mackay Mackenzie, *Poems of William Dunbar*, pp. 56-9.
13. See, for example, *Exchequer Rolls*, viii, p. 295.
14. John Smith, *The Hammermen of Edinburgh*, (Edinburgh, 1906), pp. 12, 47.
15. *Exch. Rolls*, viii, pp. 292, 294.
16. *Liber Collegii Nostre Domine*, (Maitland Club, 1846) p. 166.
17. An interesting example in C. Fraser-Mackintosh, *Invernessiana*, (Inverness, 1875), p. 109.
18. *Exch. Rolls*, iii, p. 14.
19. Aberdeen Burgh Court Books, xv, 567. (Town House, Aberdeen). " Georg bissat pait tol yndsa blakfreir in part of paiment for the mending of the knok of the tolbuith . . ."; there is no ceremony in this entry!
20. *Exch. Rolls*, vi, Fr. Andrew Lisouris appears seventeen times in five years, a wright who dealt with royal artillery as a regular thing.
21. *Exch. Rolls*, x, pp. 511, 554.

another, a Dominican, received royal appreciation for his skill in making whisky.[22] These are all admirable skills, no doubt, but rather off-beat in relation to the friars' vocation to a life of prayer and penance which would overflow into preaching and teaching the Word of God. The situation which they help to illustrate was one of compromise between sanctity and laxity, with a respectable and comfortable mediocrity which avoided both extremes. Such a condition is unsound partly because it is so static; there is no longer that sense of the needs of one's own time which inspired the founders of the various religious orders. And so the orders become out of touch with the times to a greater or less degree, conservative, self-centred, maybe quite plainly reactionary, but certainly not alert to signs of strain in the social structure and the need for change. When crisis comes at last, they must waken up or perish.

The twelfth and thirteenth centuries had been a time of new growth, during which most of the religious houses of Scotland were founded. The fourteenth century had been a period of crisis, making regular observance difficult in the context of war and plague. The fifteenth century on the whole had been quiet, with English energy so largely engaged in France, and there had been a certain amount of good government at home. That century had seen a slow increase of wealth in the burghs, the establishment of three universities, and important changes in some sections of church life; partly for the worse, such as the introduction of the commendatory system into Scotland, and partly for the better, for example the introduction of the Observant Franciscans to several important burghs. Among churchmen elsewhere there were ideas current which demanded serious attention, and received it from at least a fair minority among the Scottish clergy. Those who had studied on the continent could not fail to be cognisant of questions touching the nature of papal authority, especially the relationship of pope and general council; at least a few in the reigns of James III and James IV were aware of the new classical interest among scholars abroad; others were caught up in the disagreements which were disturbing contemporary scholasticism, for example in Cologne; others must have been aware of the movement for reform which was slowly making way among both regular and secular clergy. People like Archbishop Scheves, with his Louvain background, would have known something about the Brethren of the Common Life and the spiritual revival which was under way in the Low Countries. Others knew of the reforming spirit at work in Italy itself and associated with such oustanding figures as Raymond of Capua, Catherine of Siena, and Antoninus of Florence. Scholars like John Mair and John Annand at the beginning of the sixteenth century formed an even closer link with some of these movements, being familiar with no less a figure than Standonck. The reformed Franciscans already mentioned were a significant link with Italy. Scotland in fact was not a stagnant backwater cut off from ideas or new forces, though it may be true that these were not contemplated, except by a few, with much sense of urgency, and probably not contemplated at all by the lawn-mowing or whisky-making experts. But then there were few who would realise that the Lutheran disturbance was urgent, until it was too late, and there would be many in Scotland in 1560 who thought they were being buffeted by a rough but only passing storm.

---

22. *Exch. Rolls*, x, p. 487. Friar John Cor can be identified as an Edinburgh Dominican from references in the Protocol Book of Peter Marche (S.R.O.), ff. 38v., 39r.

III

A hundred years of the history of the Scottish Black Friars offers amplification of some of these points and will serve to illustrate certain enduring problems. The first mention of reform among them is as early as 1468, associated with a Friar Andrew of Cruden and stemming from the reform of Raymond of Capua.[23] What reform took place then appears to have been very gradual, rather mild, and linked with the desire to establish a distinct Scottish province. This aim was achieved in 1481, under Friar John Mure.[24] The new province appears to have been respectable, but perhaps not highly idealistic. This at any rate might be one interpretation of the favour enjoyed by its provincials at the courts of James III and IV and their willingness to act as commendatory superiors of the wealthy Trinitarian house at Failford, whose numbers had shrunk almost to extinction.[25] Such appointments were not unknown on the continent at the time and were sometimes intended to promote reform in the house concerned.[26] At other times, and this would seem to apply to the Failford appointment, they were a way of financing a promising movement. The new Scottish province needed financial support if it was to grow, or even if it was to maintain a sufficient income for necessary expenses; the commendatorship of Failford was legally and economically an easy means of providing such support. Nevertheless it was far from ideal, and certainly not in keeping with strict Dominican observance, although in harmony with the picture of the friars indicated above.

There may, of course, have been one or more houses of stricter observance in the new province. Such an arrangement was recognised at the time as a way of retaining unity between the reforming and the more relaxed schools of thought among the brethren. Certainly there was some difference of opinion on the subject of observance in the Scottish province and it came to a head in the early years of the sixteenth century. There was a sharp struggle between two parties, one advocating a return to primitive observance and the other trying to retain a mitigated practice. The latter had the sympathy of the king, but not enough to prevent its defeat by the advocates of strict reform who were associated with the famous Congregation of Holland, then making headway in northern France and recently successful in taking over St. Jacques, the great Dominican study-house in Paris.[27] The support given by the French king to the reform of St. Jacques may have carried weight at the Scottish court. At any rate official visitors from the Congregation of Holland were admitted to Scotland, notable members of the Congregation, whose personal standing was high in Paris, and backed by the authority of the Master-General Thomas de Vio, better known later as Cardinal Cajetan.[28]

23. Reichert, *Acta Capitulorum Generalium Ordinis Praedicatorum*, iii. (Rome, 1900), p. 312.
24. *Op. cit.*, p. 369.
25. See James IV's letters in support of Dominican tenure of Failford. *Letters* (S.H.S., 1953), nos. 114, 119.
26. There are numerous examples of such appointments in *Bullarium Ordinis Fratrum Praedicatorum*, iii and iv. (Rome, 1731-2).
27. For a useful short account of the conflict centred on St. Jacques, see M-D. Chenu, *Le Couvent Saint-Jacques et les Deux Renaissances du XIIIe et du XVIe Siècles*, (Cahiers Saint-Jacques, 26: Paris, n.d.). A. Renaudet, *Préréforme et Humanisme á Paris*, 1494-1517, (2nd ed. Paris, 1953) is an indispensable work for any student of the intellectual and religious conflicts of the sixteenth century.
28. Albertus de Meyer, *Registrum Litterarum Fr. Thomae de Vio Caietani O.P. Magistri Ordinis 1508-1513*, M.O.P.H. XVIII. (Rome, 1935), p. 37: Fr. Jean Frelin, prior of Lille, appointed visitator of Scotland, June 28th, 1508. On January 23rd, 1510, the Vicar-General of the Congregation of Holland, Fr. Nicholas Gonor, was appointed visitator and commissary over the Scots province with the fullest power for himself or his nominees, whom all the members of the Scots province were bound to obey under pain of excommunication. (Meyer, p. 51). On December 4th, 1510, Livinus Baudouin, Jean de Tourcoing and Jean Frelin, priors of Ghent, Valenciennes and Lille, were given the most emphatic mandate to carry out reform in Scotland. (Meyer, pp. 56-7). Letters of Feb. 20th, Oct. 10th and 14th, 1511, illustrate their work and the replacement of David Anderson as provincial of Scotland by John Adamson. (Meyer, pp. 317-8).

The provincial David Anderson was removed from office, and John Adamson appointed in his place in 1511. The change was not made quietly. As in Paris, when St. Jacques was reformed, the power of the state had to be invoked to secure the transfer of authority and to protect members of the reformed observance. Not for the first time since the setting up of the Scottish province several brethren fled to the milder regime which still prevailed across the border in England.[29] During the ensuing decade however, a thoroughgoing programme of reform was carried out by John Adamson, with the approval eventually of the papacy, the king and the Scottish parliament, and the highest authority in the order itself. It was a remarkable programme, being in every respect a plain attempt to restore the primitive ideals of the Black Friars. It is remarkable also in this, that all the available evidence suggests that John Adamson was educated wholly in Scotland. The only university to which he can be assigned, before appearing among the professors at Aberdeen, is St. Andrews.

Perhaps the most striking glimpse of him comes from outside Scotland, from a Spanish Dominican who recorded his impact on the general chapter held in Rome in 1518, which had to find a successor to carry on Cajetan's work as Master-General when he was promoted to the cardinalate. There were five outstanding candidates according to Sebastian de Olmeda, and one of these was Adamson, " a man famous for his prudence and religious observance." The primitive zeal of the Scottish provincial had been shown in the fact that he and his companion had made the journey across Europe on foot, as St. Dominic himself would have made it, and had kept the customary rules of the order as to fasting and abstinence all the way. It was no secret that Cajetan personally favoured two candidates: the Spaniard Garsias de Loaysa, who was actually elected, and John Adamson. Cajetan had received much information about both, and it had always been to their credit.[30] It is almost certainly safe to suggest that no other Scottish or English Dominican has made so profound an impression on a general chapter, with possibly one exception in more recent times. None certainly has ever been considered for such high office at so critical a time in his order's history.

The chapter of 1518 approved Adamson's work in Scotland and his plans for development of what had been started.[31] He stressed, with similar minds elsewhere, three essentials in the lives of preaching friars: prayer, penance, and study. Something of his own penitential spirit has already been noticed. In his journey across the continent he illustrated the ancient ideal of apostolic poverty and self-discipline preached by St. Dominic and also by St. Thomas Aquinas. It was bound up with an emphasis on prayer, on contemplative prayer as a real force in the background of any public ministry. St. Dominic had founded a priory of enclosed nuns as a power-house behind the work of preaching, even before he established the first regular house of friars. Similarly Adamson associated with the reform in Scotland the enclosed community of St. Catherine of the Sciennes, that convent of nuns on the outskirts of

---

29. *Letters of James IV*, no. 30.

30. " Frater Johannes Adae, similiter Magister et Provincialis Scotus, vir prudentia et religionis observantia celebris, quem a Scotia in Urbem et pedetim venisse et cibaria Ordinis non mutasse multi commendabant. Hunc et Garsiam se diligere affirmabat Thomas Cardinalis et Magister, eo quod multa referrentur de illis beneque semper audiret de eis." Canal Gomez, *Fr. Sebastiani De Olmeda, O.P., Chronica Ord. Praed.*, (Rome, 1936) p. 196.

31. *Acta Cap. Gen. O.P.*, iv, p. 173. See also Calendar of St. Andrews Charters (S.R.O.), no. 215.

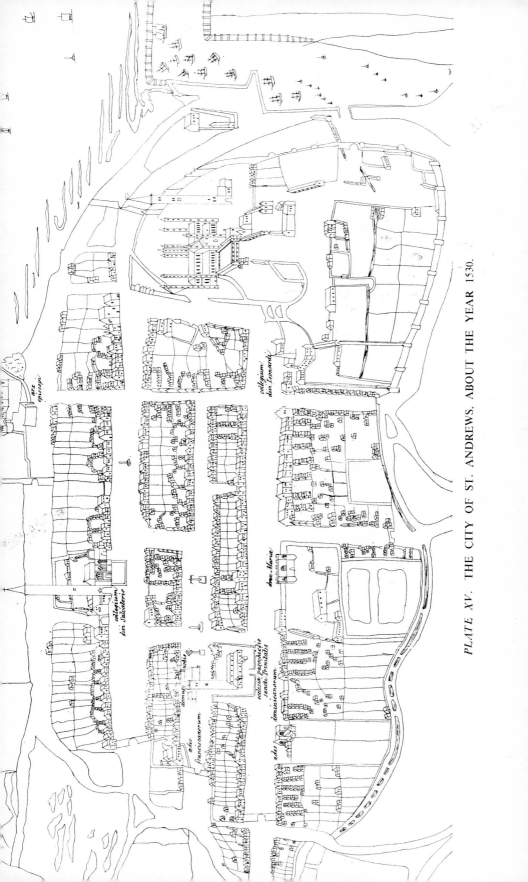

PLATE XV. THE CITY OF ST. ANDREWS, ABOUT THE YEAR 1530.

DAVID BETONIVS S·R·E· CARD· ARCHIEP· S·ANDI
'N· SCOTIA AB HOSTIBVS FIDEI BARBARE TRVCIDA

PLATE XVI. CARDINAL DAVID BEATON.

Edinburgh to whose chastity and poverty no less a critic than David Lindsay is witness, and whose foundation was made possible by the appreciation of Adamson's work by members of the clergy and laity.[32]

For the kind of study which engaged the reformed Dominicans both penance and prayer were indispensable. They were concerned with theology, and were taught in the *Summa Theologica* the need for balance and harmony in body and spirit as a pre-requisite of theological study and the life of contemplation which would overflow in preaching. They were taught also that theological study is dead without prayer. It is prayer which brings us into direct relation with God, the subject of true theology, to whom we must address ourselves and to whom we must listen if our talk about divine truth is not to be unreal, or, worse still, distorted by intellectual pride. The movement of which Adamson was so distinguished a representative was well aware that contemporary theology had too often become arid and sterile. Cajetan's approval of him as a potential Master-General suggests that the Scottish provincial was in agreement fundamentally with the effort being made by Cajetan and others to replace the decadent scholasticism, so often satirised then and later, by a more vital theological activity which would draw directly on scripture and the early fathers of the church. In fact the connection between the Scottish reform and the Congregation of Holland is itself evidence of Adamson's intellectual ideals and their probable derivation immediately from that movement for high scholarship and severe living which was already so much alive in the Low Countries among representatives of secular as well as regular clergy. Jean Standonck, more medieval perhaps than Cajetan, but still to be counted among those who inspired great developments, was a friend of several leading members of the Congregation of Holland, including those responsible for the reform of St. Jacques. He was ardent for the creation of " a new model clergy " to serve the needs of the church, and worked not only to establish a new kind of diocesan clergy but also to promote the reform of the older religious orders.

Standonck had his admirers in Scotland and we find Adamson associated with several among them. Bishop Elphinstone, John Mair, Hector Boece, John Hepburn of St. Andrews, and Alexander Mylne of Cambuskenneth witness to a common ideal, and appear as supporters or admirers of what John Adamson was attempting. At Aberdeen the bishop was the inspiration of a remarkable group of priests, regular and secular, associated with his new university. Adamson was one of them as professor of theology, and Boece, who left a post under Standonck at Elphinstone's request to become principal of the bishop's new college, wrote an unusually long eulogy of the Dominican in his *Aberdonensium Episcoporum Vitae*: " John Adamson, professor of sacred theology, a man notable for piety and learning, the first in Aberdeen to achieve the crowning honour of master in that faculty. He now holds the supreme office among the friars preachers (what they call the provincialate) in the kingdom of Scotland; by his devout and religious character he deserves to be set as an example among the foremost members of his order. For, indignant that the holy way of life of the order of preachers was so neglected among our people as to be almost a subject of contempt, dreading neither perils by sea, nor the

---

32. See Moir Bryce, " The Convent of St. Catherine of Siena," in *Book of the Old Edinburgh Club*, x, pp. 96-153. *Liber Conventus S. Katherine Senensis prope Edinburgum* (Abbotsford Club, Edinburgh, 1841). Lindsay, *The Complaynt of the Papingo*, (Works, ed. Chalmers, i, pp. 339-341) Roland Blacader, subdean of Glasgow, bequeathed 300 pounds for a similar foundation in Glasgow: cf. *Liber Collegii Nostre Domine*, p. lxxii.

ferocity, the threats and outrages of opponents, sparing no exertion nor his bodily strength, taking upon himself his really difficult province, with great and incredible labours he effected the restoration of the ruinous structure; so that now there are many learned, pious and religious men of that order to be found among us, who expound, practise and preach the scriptures. It is indisputable that all this is to be attributed to the pious exertions of John. The authority of Bishop William, who had considerable power both at home and abroad, contributed not a little to this state of things."[33]

The bishop's will offers confirmatory evidence of his support for the reformed Dominicans. Enough has been said above to indicate the factual basis of Boece's renaissance superlatives about Adamson's journeys and character. The reference to threats and violence recalls the popular opposition which the reform met with in Scotland where the arrival of the visitators from abroad was accompanied by rioting which did not subside even in the church, and which led to an application by the observant party in Aberdeen for letters of royal protection.[34] The affair seems to have been rather similar to the riots in Paris which were touched off by the reform of St. Jacques and which John Mair explained as having been worked up by angry tradesmen who faced a serious decline in profits when the friars returned to their ancient customs of fasting and abstinence.[35]

There is sufficient evidence of Adamson's efforts to establish erudition among his brethren, and again it should be pointed out that he was not alone among the Scottish clergy in attempting to revitalise study. The evidence of their libraries' surviving items would be enough to indicate that Boece's praise of the Aberdeen circle was not without reason;[36] the old and the new learning came together in the company of Elphinstone, Adamson, Boece, Vaus, Alexander Galloway, James Ogilvie and William Hay. Thomas Chrystall, abbot of Kinloss, had started his work of restoration among the Cistercian monks while Adamson was still prior of the Aberdeen Black Friars. Giovanni Ferreri, the Italian humanist whom Abbot Chrystall later engaged to teach the humanities at Kinloss, records the fact that two young Cistercians were sent by the abbot to study theology under " a devout man . . . a notable doctor of scholastic theology." John Adamson.[37] The Italian came to Scotland after Adamson's death, but the connection between Aberdeen and Kinloss remained close, carried on by a younger generation in which the mingling of humanist and scholastic interest was even more marked. Not only at Kinloss but in Elgin, Inverness and Beauly, and at Deer, the influence of

33. *Aber. Episc. Vitae*, ed. and translated by James Moir (Aberdeen, New Spalding Club, 1894), pp. 92-3. Moir's translation is unsatisfactory and I have given my own version. The Latin is as follows: Joannes Adamus, sacrae theologiae professor, pietate insigni atque eruditione; primus qui Aberdoniae magisterii fastigium ea in facultate est adeptus; nunc praedicatorum fratrum intra Scotorum regnum summum (quem provincialatum dicunt) agit magistratum: is pio et religioso animo exempli locum meretur inter primos sui instituti. Indigne siquidem ferens sacram praedicatorum religionem neglectam inter nostros adeo ut pene contemptui daretur, non maris pericula horrens, non aemulorum saevitiam minas, injurias, non laboribus, non corpori parcens, duram admodum subiens provinciam ut labefactata repararetur, magnis et incredibilibus obtinuit laboribus; effectumque ut nunc eruditi, pii, et religiosi, qui sacras literas enarrant, profitentur, concionantur, illius instituti viri frequentes inter nos reperiantur: quae omnia Joannis piis sudoribus ulla sine controversia accepta sunt ferenda. Ad haec Wilhelmi auctoritas, qui et domi et foris plurimum potuit, haud parum conduxit.

34. *Letters of James IV*, no. 348. *Reg. Sec. Sigilli*, i, p. 342.

35. Mair's support for reform among the friars is well illustrated in his commentary *In Quartum Sententiarum* (Paris, 1521), ff. ccxxiiii B, ccxxviii C, ccxxix A, and elsewhere in the same work.

36. See John Durkan and Anthony Ross, *Early Scottish Libraries, Innes Rev.*, ix, pp. 5-167. Reprinted, with addenda and corrigenda, Glasgow, 1961.

37. Stuart, *Records of the Monastery of Kinloss*, (Edinburgh, 1872), p. 39.

the Aberdeen circle would be felt. Among the Black Friars who were influenced by it directly we may mention John Grierson, John Black, Andrew Macneill, Andrew Abercromby, Alexander Lawson, John Spens and Robert Lile, who can be found engaged in Aberdeen, Glasgow, St. Andrews, Edinburgh, Inverness, Elgin, Stirling, Perth, and Wigtown in the half century before 1560. There will be something to be said about most of them later in this essay; they are mentioned now simply to draw attention to the mobility of the friars, a quality of significance when we are considering the extent of the influence which a man like John Adamson might have.

He appears also in connection with St. Andrews university, where similar ideas to those already described were finding support. Like Aberdeen, St. Andrews had admirers and former pupils of Standonck. John Hepburn, prior of the Augustinian Canons, founded St. Leonard's College as a " college of poor clerks " whose austerity was patterned on the Collège de Montaigu and which was directed by John Annand, a disciple of Standonck, as principal. It was John Hepburn who gave authority for the disposal of Bishop Elphinstone's estate, a great part of which went to build a Dominican priory in St. Andrews as a centre of higher study associated with the university. Hepburn's younger brother George, dean of Dunkeld, also actively assisted Adamson's scheme for St. Andrews, and the general chapter at Rome in 1518 approved an agreement between the dean and the provincial for a foundation for five or six students *in conventu universitatis sancti Andree*. It approved also the provincial's proposal to close the house at Cupar and transfer its resources to the new centre of studies. There were only two friars at Cupar and the town itself was described as reduced from affluence to poverty, the dwelling house of the friars in ruins and only the church standing, while the St. Andrews house on the other hand had a skilfully constructed dormitory and well-endowed church with no lack of benefactors to assist in completing and maintaining the buildings. The house at St. Monance was also to serve the needs of St. Andrews, but two priests were to remain as custodians of the shrine of St. Monan. Both St. Monance and Cupar were, in Adamson's judgment, unsuitable places for religious whereas St. Andrews, as a university town, was a place where a sufficient number of friars might live according to rule, serving God night and day, and continuously applying themselves to the study of theology. The picture which he put before Leo X and the general chapter in Rome, and before a Scottish provincial chapter in 1519, reveals the idealist.[38] In 1519 it looked as though idealism was triumphant and that the Black Friars in Scotland had truly embraced reformation. So it seemed to many, including Alexander Mylne, Abbot of Cambuskenneth, (and himself associated with a movement of reform among the Augustinian Canons), who recorded the help given by the dean of Dunkeld " when John Adamson . . . that great and inspired man, the provincial of the Preachers in Scotland, brought about a thorough reformation of the order."[39]

It would be possible to give a longer list of those who gave their assistance to John Adamson, or who showed their high regard for him in

---

38. *Reg. Episcopatus Aberdonensis*, ii, (Edinburgh, Maitland Club, 1845). pp. 310-2. *Acta Cap. Gen. O.P.*, ix, p. 173. Cal. St. Andrews Charters, nos. 207, 215, 282.

39. " Et postquam ordo praedicatorum in Scotia per magnum et illuminatum virum Johannem Ade, sacrarum literarum professorem, ordinis provincialem, reformationi deditus esset, magno auxilio affuit . . ." Myln: *Vitae Episcoporum Dunkeldensium*, (Bannatyne Club, 1823), p. 55. cf. also Hannay, *Rentale Dunkeldense*, (S.H.S., 1915), p. 320.

one way or another. The list would include Gavin Douglas bishop of Dunkeld, and other members of that family; greater and lesser figures among the laity; Archbishop Forman of St. Andrews, James Hepburn, bishop of Moray (a nephew of John and George Hepburn) Patrick Panter, who made possible the restoration of the house at Montrose.[40] It has been suggested that James IV had Adamson in mind when proposing an auxiliary bishop to administer the diocese of St. Andrews during the minority of his own son Alexander, and that Archbishop Forman later sought to have him as a coadjutor.[41] It is interesting to see, as we go through the names of his admirers, a phenomenon especially marked in the renaissance period, namely admiring and practical recognition of idealism and reforming zeal on the part of some who, although they could share enthusiasm for study, had indifferent control over their own moral behaviour. It is indicative of Adamson's real greatness that it won recognition from such varied witnesses at home and abroad. It is to be remembered also that he was not conducting a counter-reformation. His effort sprang from his appreciation of the ideals of the religious life and he died, burnt out we may surmise by the intensity of his effort, somewhere about the year 1523, having to all appearance achieved what he set out to do. The protestant reformation was not yet appreciated as the cataclysmic movement it would prove to be, and in Scotland those clergy whose outlook Adamson shared, could still hope for success in their spiritual and intellectual task.

The time was one of transition. John Adamson had presided at the inaugural lecture in theology given by another Dominican, Robert Lile, in Glasgow in March 1521-2.[42] The class text was still the *Sentences* of Peter Lombard compiled in the twelfth century. His own interest may have been conservative, although he was influenced by the Cajetan reform; the volumes of Augustine, Gregory and Bernard which we know he used are no proof one way or another, although they fit well enough the picture of a man who found inspiration, like Standonck, outside the later forms of scholasticism in the writers of an earlier and more zealous age, but especially in the fathers of the church. He sent his students not only to Aberdeen and St. Andrews but also abroad, some to Paris, an important group to Cologne, possibly some to Italy. But wherever they went they would find on the continent that the time was one of serious intellectual disagreement, with few of those clear distinctions with which later writers have been able to separate so neatly different ways of thought.

Facile contrasts of humanists and scholastics are here utterly misleading, as are the old-fashioned equations of catholic and scholastic, humanist and protestant, scientist and humanist, which still appear from time to time. A man might be a scholastic and a humanist at once, like Guillaume Petit of St. Jacques, a supporter of Lefèvre and Erasmus and Cajetan against the obscurantists of the Sorbonne, but also a student of Thomas Aquinas (Lefèvre himself was an admirer of Aquinas, and Pico della Mirandola defended the use of the *lingua parisiensis* by theologians). Men like Petit and Cajetan were revolutionary in their attempt to get back to the great

---

40.　See, for example; Fraser, *Douglas Book*, iii, pp. 218-221; Cal. St. Andrews Charters, nos. 214, 282 (involving Douglas, Errol and Sandilands families); *Reg. Magni Sigilli* 1513-1546, no. 113 (Panter's Montrose benefaction); N.L.S. Adv. MS. 34.7.2. (James Hepburn's benefaction to Elgin Blackfriars). The published chartularies of the Scottish Blackfriars contain numerous other examples.

41.　*Letters of James IV*, no. 24; *St. Andrews Formulare* (Stair Society), i, 54. Query: In the *Formulare* is Forman merely repeating a formulary of Alexander Stewart, his predecessor?

42.　*Liber Collegii Nostre Domine*, p. lxi, n. 7.

thirteenth-century scholastics and away from the dusty commentaries upon commentaries which put books instead of reality before their students. They were keen to study the authentic text of Aristotle, to establish a deeper knowledge of the bible with the aid of Greek and Hebrew texts, drawing upon Jewish scholarship in their zeal to establish the latter. Opposition came not only from cautious doctors of the Sorbonne but also from members of their own order. A recent church history of Scotland has an inconsequential remark about the Dominicans of Cologne in the sixteenth century being the laughing stock of Europe. But those Cologne friars were also in strong disagreement with other Dominicans in France and Italy, who supported the very things which they were attacking, and that fact is also relevant to events in Scotland. There can be no adequate discussion of the friars at the time of the Scottish reformation until more attention is paid by Scottish writers to the European intellectual scene to which they belonged, whose tensions they shared. They were at the very centre of what happened in Scotland, on both sides of the main conflict, because they were already at grips with moral and intellectual issues which were not simply national but which were deeply engaging many of the best minds in Europe.

The point may be illustrated by noting briefly a few other figures among the Scottish friars, both black and grey. Adamson's successor as provincial was John Grierson (or Greson) who had been one of his pupils at Aberdeen, then procurator and later prior of the house in that city. He was professor of theology in St. Andrews and dean of the faculty of theology in 1553. For nearly fifty years of his life he held some senior office in the province, over thirty-five years as provincial, until the crash came which he foresaw but found himself and his brethren powerless to prevent. There is nothing to show whether he shared the asceticism of his predecessor, but we do know enough about his intellectual interests to support the suggestion that he was a christian humanist of the type which combined study of the early scholastics with an interest in Greek thought. He appears to have maintained the priorities emphasised by Adamson. It is significant that his headquarters were in the ecclesiastical capital, not in the court capital—which was where the pre-reform provincials had resided. Educated apparently, like Adamson, wholly in Scotland, he moved widely about the country in the course of his work which brought him into contact with such varied characters as Boece, Ferreri, Cardinal Beaton and other members of the hierarchy, John Mair, John Winram, and in fact probably most of the clerical leaders and many of the lay leaders in contemporary Scotland. On the very eve of the revolution he was still sending his province's financial contribution to the headquarters of the order, but expressing frustration and weariness owing to the state of his country and the "impossible tasks" which he and his brethren were being asked to undertake.[43] In his extraordinarily long provincialate he had been presented with problems, internal and external, enough to strain any man. More than one of the books he used points to an awareness of what went on elsewhere; the discussions of Henry VIII's divorce proceedings, for example, and the resolutions of the Council of Trent and the German council at Mainz. He also read Orosius, Geoffrey of Monmouth, the

---

43. See the letter printed in Michele Pio, *Della Vite degli Huomini illustri di S. Domenico*, (Bologna, 1607), of which an English translation by Dr. Durkan appeared in *Innes Rev.*, ix, pp. 216-7. Another letter was printed in *Analecta Sacri Ordinis Fratrum Praedicatorum*, (Rome, 1895), p. 484, as a footnote to a generally unreliable article about the houses of the Scottish province. The letter contains a rapid survey of the province just before its fall.

letters of Cicero, John Mair's *History of Greater Britain*, and works of Erasmus. " What an elegant style! " he remarked on a passage of Augustine. The evidence is fragmentary but one may perhaps wonder if it does not give a real glimpse of an intelligent, cultivated and perhaps moderate character, enjoying the confidence of the province because he embodied the ideals of reform in a less awe-inspiring, less extreme figure than Adamson. As Hay Fleming pointed out, he must have been an old man when he made his supposed recantation of faith at St. Andrews in 1559.[44] I have queried the value of such recantations at St. Andrews elsewhere in this volume,[45] and Grierson's has some curious features about its form. For the present it must suffice to point out that at least its sincerity is brought in doubt by the fact that he appears at Seton in 1561 transferring Dominican property to lay ownership but " providing that if in the mercy of God it shall happen any of those men who were some time religious in the foresaid place (St. Andrews) or any other place of the said order in Scotland to be recalled to the service of God in the said place in regular habit conform to the statutes and rules of the order of preachers " the new owner shall renounce his title.[46]

Among those who were subject to Grierson as provincial we find a considerable group who studied abroad, mainly as young friars of the Adamson period. Among them, probably older than the rest, is James Crichton whose mastership in theology was approved by the general chapter of 1525 together with the lesser degrees of eight other Scots.[47] The fact that at one stage he was in receipt of a pension from George Crichton, bishop of Dunkeld, may indicate an influential family connection.[48] He certainly moved in very high circles, travelling abroad with letters from his own sovereign, in touch with the courts of Francis I (whose confessor was Petit), Margaret of Navarre, and Pope Clement VII, who found him a learned and entertaining conversationalist.[49] He seems to have been an actual pupil of Cajetan who refers to him in one of his books.[50] It is interesting to find this foreign-trained, far-travelled, influentially connected friar holding the office of subprior at Montrose in 1531, but not so surprising when one remembers the Montrose priory's long struggle with the Earl of Crawford or its connection with Patrick Panter, himself an associate of James Crichton's patron, the bishop of Dunkeld.[51] The books which Crichton used carry an echo of classical humanist fashion, in a copy of Erasmus's *Adages* inscribed in his very beautiful hand, but they also show an interest in the thirteenth century theologians and in Cajetan. He is one of a number of Scottish Dominicans who can be shown to have possessed copies of Cajetan's writings and who were contemporary with the

44. *Register of the Kirk Session of St. Andrews*, pp. 16-18. Grierson was prior of Aberdeen, earlier than Hay Fleming thought, in 1512. Anderson, *Aberdeen Friars*, p. 70. Confirmed as provincial, March, 1523. Meersseman—Planzer *Magistrorum ac Procuratorum generalium O.P. Registra Litterarum Minora* (1469-1523), (Rome, 1947), p. 149. For Grierson's books, as for those of others mentioned in these pages, see *Early Scottish Libraries*.

45. See below, " Reformation and Repression."

46. Cal. of St. Andrews Charters, no. 343.

47. *Acta Cap. Gen.*, iv, p. 206. He is probably the Fr. Iacobus " Rupton " from the Edinburgh priory who received permission to study in Italy, in 1522: cf. Meersseman-Planzer, p. 106.

48. Cf. Theiner, p. 542.

49. Theiner, pp. 552, 553. Arch. Vat. xl, f. 12, no. 331. A. Fraikin, *Nonciatures de Clement VII*, p. 417, Letter of Clement VII to Francis I regarding Crichton.

50. *Quaestiones atque omnia quodlibeta.* Lyons 1554. " Ad fratrem Jacobum Crecton Scotum lectorem Theologie. Petitionibus tuis fili charissime deesse nolens, ad proposita duo dubia respondere curavi."

51. A note of the Rev. Ian Muirhead gives the names of the community at this date; Alexander Barclay was prior. There are transcripts of the main documents belonging to the Blackfriars-Crawford controversy in the Hutton Collections (N.L.S.), Vol. ix.

disputes about the orthodoxy of his teaching which raged in Paris. Grierson was one; others were John Spens, closely associated with Adamson, and touching in his affection for his order;[52] Andrew Macneill, the prior of Stirling, forcibly expelled by the reformers;[53] John Hunter, prior of Glasgow, who was to end his days as a highly respected member of a Dominican priory in France;[54] John Black and Andrew Abercromby, both among the preachers supported by Mary, Queen of Scots, and the former to be murdered with Rizzio.[55] They were not the only ones concerned with new ideas, and with them should be noticed a number of Observant Franciscans, such as John Scott, John Roger, John Hay and Alexander Arbuckle, all of whom were on the side of orthodox reform and one of whom was to die a martyr's death in the Low Countries.[56]

All these friars represent the new theological revival, opposed to heresy and schism, but itself under attack from many vested interests, which was to reach success in the third session of the Council of Trent. Fathers Arbuckle and Scott (who is not the same as the champion faster), may have been out of their depth in the surge of demagogic argument which swept round them when Knox, Willock, Goodman and Methven got under way. They were scholars, not demagogues, belonging to a different mental climate from three at least of the opponents just mentioned. Knox's account of his disputation with Arbuckle is intended to show the latter as a fool, but even in the pages of Knox one can see the contrast between the academic mind on the one side, entering slowly and formally into discussion, and on the other side the passionate, impulsive mind of Knox, not ignorant of the syllogistic method, but impatient of it in the heat of battle.[57] One may be allowed to doubt if Arbuckle was so much a fool. Like Lefèvre of Etaples he read Bonaventure; like Andrew Melville at a later date, he possessed the *Isagogae ad sacras literas* of the famous Dominican Hebrew scholar, Santes Pagnini; he read and heavily annotated Cajetan's opusculum *De potestate papae*, which he had in a volume of Aquinas and Cajetan presented, or possibly bequeathed to the Grey Friars by John Mair (whose own writings testify to his warm admiration for the Observants and the type of reform with which they were identified). At least in his reading, Father Arbuckle represents that union of biblical, patristic and early scholastic study which lies behind the achievement, not only of Trent, but also of such figures as Vitoria, John of the Cross, Teresa of Avila and Suarez.

There were other Franciscans and Dominicans of whom we can say less but who remained in the same tradition as those just listed. There was John Paterson, for example, the provincial of the Grey Friars, who

52. He accompanied Adamson, as diffinitor, to the general chapter in Rome in 1518: *Acta Cap. Gen.*, iv, p. 157. He was prior of Edinburgh in June, 1512: Moir Bryce, *The Blackfriars of Edinburgh*, (Edinburgh, 1911), p. 85; prior of Glasgow in May, 1517, when he is described as Bachelor in Sacred Theology: *Lib.Coll. Nostre Domine*, p. 213; he was still alive, prior of Elgin, in 1546: Adv. MS. 34.7.2. f. 64v. Inscriptions on two of his books suggest that he died at Elgin. Another inscription reads: *Ad usum Reuerendi patris fratris Johannis spens almi ordinis predicatorum.*

53. *Reg. Mag. Sig.*, iv, 1373.

54. Quétif & Echard, *Scriptores Ordinis Praedicatorum*, ii, p. 211. Mortier, *Histoire des Maîtres Généraux de l'Ordre des Frères Prêcheurs*, (Paris, 1903-20), v, p. 514 n. Forbes-Leith, *Narratives of Scottish Catholics*, p. 196 n.1. has the name of a Father Hunter who is probably the same. A treatise on whether it is lawful to deny the faith verbally, with a mental reservation, when living among heretics, is attributed to him; he held it unlawful. Cf. Paris, Bibliothèque Nationale MS. Lat. 3478, pp. 568-597.

55. Dickinson's *Knox*, ii, p. 175, which refers to Andrew Abercromby and John Black, (Dominicans), and John Roger, (a Franciscan). The editor's insertion of the word (Friars) is mistaken. On Fr. Black's death see below, " Reformation and Repression."

56. See plate xxxvi in this volume.

57. Dickinson's *Knox*, i, pp. 90-2.

went abroad at the reformation and died in Louvain in 1573.[58] There was James Johnstone, whose preaching had been supported before 1560 from the revenues of Paisley Abbey and who worked on after that, appearing in 1563 among those arrested for saying mass and hearing confessions in Paisley. He had been sometime Dominican prior in St. Andrews.[59] Thomas Aitken, one of seven men delated in July, 1572, for " contravening of the Actis and Ministratioune of the Sacramentis in the Papisticall maner," was a Franciscan; the same probably who appears with Robert Veitch, of the same order, under the protection of Robert Crichton, bishop of Dunkeld, in his island stronghold.[60] The Franciscan James Peebles, at one time vicar of the St. Andrews friary, and apparently interested in the new Latin style since he used Angelo Poliziano's *Virorum Illustrium Epistolae*, was among those noted by the Privy Council in 1574 as " rebels abroad."[61]

There were those, however, with a similar background to the friars already mentioned, who took a different road eventually; in some cases as much as twenty-five years before 1560. The important posts held by certain of them underline the seriousness of intellectual disagreement. It must have been a severe shock to the Scottish Dominican province when, in the middle of the thirties, three such men as John Macalpine, John Macdowell and Alexander Seton left the country because of their unorthodox views. All three were prominent members of the province, priors at the time of their flight, or shortly before it, of Perth, Wigtown and St. Andrews respectively. Macalpine and Macdowell had studied at Cologne and were among the graduates in theology whose degrees had been approved in 1525.[62] Seton may have studied in Paris.[63] Despite their similarity in that they became protestants, these three reflect even among themselves the intellectual divisions referred to above. Macalpine and Seton were humanist in tendency, the former associated later with Coverdale and Melanchthon, and becoming Lutheran professor of

---

58. He was superior of the Greyfriars at Ayr in 1520: *Protocol Book of Gavin Ros*, no. 417; superior in Glasgow in 1531: *Glasgow Protocols*, iv, 101; at St. Andrews when Sir John Borthwick was accused, in 1540: *Reg. Kirk Sess. St. And.*, i, p. 94; cleared David Guild of heresy in 1541, when he is described as *predicator et theologus*: Herkless & Hannay, *College of St. Leonard*, p. 222; as superior of the Scottish Greyfriars at the provincial council of 1549: Patrick, *Statutes*, p. 87; according to Hay's *Chronicle* he was twice provincial, and went abroad with eighty friars, (a very questionable figure) in 1559: Moir Bryce, *Scottish Grey Friars*, ii, pp. 182, 193—on the latter page, and in the index, read *Paterson* for *Patrick*; having been incorporated in the province of Lower Germany, he died on Feb. 20th 1573: Molanus, *L'Histoire de la Ville de Louvain*, ed. F.X. de Ram, i, p. 259.

59. *Reg. Mag. Sig.* 1546-80, no. 693 shows him prior in 1552. See also Pitcairn, *Criminal Trials*, i, p. 429; and his Paisley connection is discussed elsewhere in this volume.

60. Pitcairn, i, pt. 2, p. 35. *Proceedings of the Soc. of Antiquaries of Scotland*, ii, 106.

61. *R.P.C.*, iv, 334.

62. The graduates were: James Crichton, already mentioned; Alexander Campbell, prior of St. Andrews when Patrick Hamilton died, (cf. Dickinson's *Knox*, i, pp. 12, 14); Alexander Barclay, who was successively prior of Wigtown (*Exch. Rolls*, xv, pp. 189, 279) Glasgow (*Exch. Rolls*, xv, p. 425), Montrose (see above, n. 51), Aberdeen (*Exch. Rolls*, xvii, p. 69), and Lector, i.e., lecturer in theology, at Elgin in 1549 (Adv. MS. 34.7.2. f. 64r.); Alexander Lawson, who had become a Dominican after a distinguished career as a secular priest, (see *Early Records of the University of St. Andrews*, pp. 91, 198; *Fasti Aberd.* p. 75; Boece *Episc. Vitae*, pp. 92, 109, *Reg. Sec. Sig.* i, 2793; *Reg. Episc. Aberd.*, ii, 355, 382), and was prior of Edinburgh at the date of the conferring of the degrees, (cf. *Prot. Bk. of John Foular*, iii, 343, 466, 702, 713); James Hewat who later taught James Wedderburn in Dundee, and, says Calderwood, " confirmed the doctrine which the other had receaved in his youth, in St. Leonard's College under Mr. Gawin Logie." *History*, i, 142. He was also at Perth. Francis Wright, who was to appear later as an Exhorter in the new Kirk (cf. *Thirds of Benefices*, pp. 97, 153, 209, 212, which probably refer to the same person); John Macalpine, famous among Lutherans after his flight from Scotland, and discussed at length elsewhere in this volume; John Macdowell, who was also to fly from Scotland; and James " Pryson," so far unidentified. The list, read in relation to the history of the persons named, illustrates vividly the quality of the friars at the time, and the depth of their divergence ten years later. Macalpine's Cologne connection is witnessed to in Foerstemann, *Liber Decanorum Facultatis Theologiae Academiae Vitebergensis*, p. 29; Macdowell's is not so certain. John Hunter is said to have been at Cologne, (Camerarius, *De Scotorum Fortitudine*, p. 180).

63. Was he perhaps that Alexander de Scotia whose study at Paris was approved by the chapter of 1525? *Acta Cap. Gen.*, iv, p. 208.

theology in Copenhagen, chaplain to the king of Denmark and one of the translators of the bible into Danish. Yet he was also in many ways a scholastic, as his writings show, not to mention the formal scholastic disputation in which he engaged at Wittenberg in 1541 under the presidency of Luther himself. He displays something of that wide range of scholastic and patristic learning already noted among some of the representatives of orthodoxy; Clement of Alexandria, Cyprian, Irenaeus, Chrysostom, Ambrose, Jerome, Pierre de Palu, Scotus, Albert, Aquinas, Bonaventure, Innocent IV, councils and canonists, are drawn upon in support of his arguments.[64] It would be interesting to discover how wide were his contacts with Scotland after he settled in Denmark; he certainly had some.[65]

While Macalpine may be counted a moderate reformer and a humanist in temper, like his friend Melanchthon, Macdowell was apparently more old-fashioned intellectually and strongly opposed to any toleration of humanism.[66] In his student days, presumably spent at Cologne, the anti-Reuchlin campaign was still raging and we may suppose that he was in sympathy with the conservative Dominicans of that city and displeased, like them, with the popes who refused to condemn Reuchlin. Seton, who had Erasmus's edition of the works of Origen, was perhaps more inclined to the new learning than Macdowell, but his later history seems to show him as less assured of his position than either of the others. All three are united in their reaction against the moral decadence of contemporary Scotland, and we can see how Macalpine, especially, was exercised over the seeming futility of expecting popes or bishops to take positive steps to mend the situation. In the law of clerical celibacy he saw a major cause of current scandals. Soon he would attack all ecclesiastical law as the vain tradition of men and come to the conclusion that something was so radically wrong with the existing hierarchy as to throw doubt upon its title to existence and its right to obedience. He had been a young friar in the days of Adamson's reform, when the future must have looked very hopeful. He was a contemporary of that prior of St. Andrews, Alexander Campbell, who is said to have been so distressed by Patrick Hamilton's death, and it may well be that he shared that distress. In one way or another events were too strong for him. John Black and others had a similar anxiety about scandal in high places but would distinguish between the man and the office, and struggle on with a firmer faith and hope than Macalpine. Yet even in the case of Black and Grierson we can see the weariness they felt in what seemed an unending and increasingly frustrated effort, an effort in which Grierson had been engaged for half a century. Black protests in a marginal note, (in a book which he used), perhaps with his wandering brethren in mind, that we must not hold the sins of man against God. The times were indeed dark, but he believed that he should struggle on, trusting in the mercy of God and his providential supervision of all things.

---

64. Something of Macalpine's mind is revealed not only in the theses he defended at Wittenberg, and in his posthumously published commentary on Deuteronomy, but also in a treatise " De coniugio sacerdotum " which illustrates the extent of his learning and his attitude to celibacy. N.L.S. MS. 485, (a photostat copy of the original, which is in Corpus Christi College, Cambridge).

65. The Earl of Rothes and Sir David Lindsay were in Copenhagen in 1548 and 1550 as Scottish ambassadors. The former visited Macalpine. Did Lindsay? What lay behind the fictitious title-pages of his poem *Ane Dialog betuix Experience and ane Courteour*, better known as *The Monarche*, supposed to have been printed in Copenhagen at the expense of Macalpine? Cf. *Treasurer's Accounts*, ix, pp. 259, 347, 387, 395, 428. Dickson and Edmond, *Annals of Scottish Printing*, pp. 182, 186.

66. On intellectual differences see Dr. Durkan's chapter, " The Cultural Background " below and see also his account of Macdowell in " Some Local Heretics," *Trans. Dumfries and Galloway Natural History and Antiquarian Soc.*, xxxvi, pp. 69-77.

IV

Given such qualities among the Black and Grey Friars as have been sketched in the last few pages, the question rises why they, and those who thought like them, failed to avert the collapse of the medieval church. Up to this point attention has been directed mainly to their intellectual activity and the divisions in thought which partly provide an answer. They were active in many other ways in the sixteenth century, and this must be taken into account before we can hope to meet the question adequately. There is evidence of their preaching, and even in Gaelic. The bishop of Dunkeld who arranged that " Friars Minor and Friars Preachers well acquainted with the Irish tongue should preach at least once a year in the upper parts of the diocese and hear confessions " may have been more or less exceptional than we can say.[67] Nevertheless, there are traces of both orders of friars preaching by mandate of the bishops, not only in Dunkeld but in Moray, Aberdeen, St. Andrews and Glasgow. Both Archbishop Beaton of Glasgow and Archbishop Hamilton of St. Andrews appointed friars to preach, and when the provincial councils referred to preaching by " religious " they would almost certainly have had friars in mind. According to David Lindsay, who repeats the charge more than once, the bishops were satisfied that they had discharged their duty with respect to preaching if they employed friars,[68] and indeed but for the work of the friars

> Tint war the faith amang the seculeris.[69]

Lindsay frequently indicates such preaching, without particularly distinguishing members of the four bodies of Carmelites, Dominicans, Observant and Conventual Franciscans. The favourable recognition of their work, in the line just quoted, is typical of the earlier Lindsay, the same who said in *The Dreme*:

> Devotioun is fled unto the freiris,[70]

and who in *The Complaynt of the Papingo* devoted nearly fifty lines to explaining those principles which inspired the community of Dominican Sisters in the Sciennes.[71] It is illuminating to see how his attitude changed over the years, to note the difference between his hope for kirk and state in the early years of James V and the bitterness which came into his work after the king's premature death. The bitterness is there perhaps in the latter years of James's reign, but in view of the uncertain dating of much of Lindsay's work it is hard to be sure. At any rate the friars seem to have disappointed him, and it is not so hard to see why if we look at a passage like that in *The Three Estaitis* which gives Flattery's reply to the objection that he cannot disguise himself as a friar because he is unable to preach.

> Quhat rak, man, I can richt weill fleich.
> Perchance I'll cum to that honour
> To be the kingis confessour.
> Pure freiris ar free at ony feist,
> And marshellit ay amang the best.
> As God hes lent to them sic graces,
> That bishopis puts them in thair places,

---

67. *Rentale Dunkeldense (Vitae Episc. Dunkeld)*, p. 304.
68. On friars preaching see Lindsay, *Works* (ed. Chalmers), i, p. 401; ii, pp. 62-65, 71, 78, 85, 88-97, 101, 110, 117, 146-54, passages which illustrate his hostile criticism.
69. Lindsay, i, p. 345.
70. Lindsay, i, p. 241.
71. Lindsay, i, pp. 339-341.

> Out-throw thair dioceis to preich,
> Bot, ferlie nocht, howbeit thay fleich:
> For, schaw thay all the verite,
> They'll want the bischopis charite.
> And thocht the corne war never sa skant,
> The gudewyfis will not let Freiris want:
> For quhy, thay ar thair confessours,
> Thair hevinlye prudent counsallours.
> Tharefor the wyfis plainlye taks thair parts,
> And shawis the secrets of thair harts
> To Freiris, with better will I trow,
> Nor thay do to thair bed-fellow.[72]

The passage implies influence in important places, of a kind which has been almost universally resented, since it has been taken as excluding others with a better right to position in the places concerned. Have courtiers—and Lindsay after all was a court official by profession—ever accepted clerical privilege at court, whether well or ill used, without spleen? Resentment would be greater at the Scottish court if the friars involved were usually of lowly or indifferent origin in the eyes of the nobles, which they almost certainly were in view of what we know about their recruitment at the time. James Crichton has been mentioned, and he was apparently engaged in carrying royal letters to foreign courts, the sort of work that Lindsay himself might have done. More elusive, and tantalising, is the figure of another Dominican, Friar Gill. There are scraps of evidence to suggest that he had a long career of privilege at home and abroad, (little touched even by Adamson's reform), but enough to secure the rare distinction of a personal reference in Lindsay's lines, when Falset says to Flattery:

> Now gang thy way quharever thow will,
> Thow may be fallow to freir Gill.[73]

How much of Lindsay's satire, one may wonder, was directed under the stock costumes of a morality against real figures who would be fairly easily recognised by the courtly audience for which his play was chiefly written and staged. Friar Gill must have been rather old when Lindsay wrote *The Three Estaitis*. Was he, one wonders, also rather stout?

There is, however, deeper criticism in the lines which touch the friars' relationship to the bishops. It is very likely that as a rule the mendicants would avoid statements in their sermons which might be construed as direct or even veiled attacks upon somebody like Cardinal Beaton. As Lindsay points out, there were financial reasons for this; it simply does not pay to offend one's employers. Preaching brought fees to financially

---

72. *Op. cit.* p. 401.
73. *Op. cit.* p. 402. In 1491 a Fr. Johannes Aegidii represented the Scottish province at a general chapter: *Munimenta FF. Praed. de Are*, (Ayr and Wigton Archaeological Assoc., Edinburgh, 1881), p. xxxiii; in 1508, " Fratri Johanni Gyl conceditur, quod possit usque ad capitulum generale proxime futurum manere extra ordinis nostri conventus et praedicare suis conterraneis et ipsorum confessiones audire." That was on Feb. 6th; on June 26th we find, " Fratri Johanni Aegidii conceditur illa, ubi benevolos." Meyer, *Reg. Litt. Caietani*, p. 317. On Dec. 2nd, 1511: " Fratri Johanni Aegidii conceditur licentia morandi in conventibus ordinis, donec habeat opportunum tempus eundi in provinciam suam Scotiae." Meyer, *op. cit.*, p. 318. Entries in the royal accounts show grants to " freir Gill " in 1526, 1527, 1538. *Treas. Accts.* v, 311, 318: vii. 21. An entry in the *Exchequer Rolls* in 1527 reads " Et Fratri Egidio ad supportationem sui habitus de mandato dicti domini regis de hoc anno tantum, iiij li." *Exch. Rolls*, xv. p. 390. There seems no doubt that Fr. Johannes Aegidii and Friar Gill are the same, that he was a royal favourite who had been prominent in the Scottish province in the pre-Adamson period, and that he must have been nearly eighty when Lindsay first wrote *The Thrie Estaitis*. Was he in Rome in 1508 and 1511 on behalf of David Anderson, the provincial who was removed by the Master General's authority? Dr. Wittig's view that Lindsay does not identify symbolic figures with particular historical personalities or events may need to be modified. Cf. Kurt Wittig, *The Scottish Tradition in Literature* (Edinburgh, 1958), p. 99.

straitened priories. It no doubt made possible the buying of some of those scholarly volumes whose users inscribed them as being " *Ad usum et ex industria.*" But it has also to be pointed out that the itinerant preaching of the friars required episcopal license to take place at all, with or without fees. The bishops, and especially a primate with the fullest legatine authority, could silence the friars by withholding faculties to preach or hear confessions in their dioceses. A friar with orthodox principles, who recognised episcopal authority accurately, even when it was set about with scandal, might groan under the burden which was being imposed upon him and his like, but he would not rebel, least of all by public demonstration. He might remonstrate in private to an approachable prelate, but his preaching would be directed to preserving some spiritual life among his hearers, to the strengthening of faith and morals in spite of the misery and discouragement of the times and not to personal attacks upon his ecclesiastical superiors. Someone like Friar Henry Adamson, graduate of St. Andrews, penitentiary of Lothian under Cardinal Beaton, might have understandably considered he had enough to do in the simple performance of his office.[74] Nevertheless, to many minds, such men as Henry Adamson would be compromised by their very obedience, and would come to be regarded as accessories to scandal. Lindsay for one seems to have thought that there was not enough blunt speaking. Was he unaware of the pressure brought to bear upon the provincial in 1534?[75] What did he think of Friars Kyllour, Beveridge, and Russell, who were burnt? What were his connections with Friars Arth, Seton, Macalpine, Macdowell, Willock, Gilyem and Rough, all of whom fled eventually to England? Some of these he certainly knew, for example Rough and Seton, and some of the views he expressed on such things as celibacy and confession would have had support from them. Was he so opposed to the Grey Friars because they had proclaimed the heresy of those other friars, as Knox says they did?[76] Even to ask these questions suggests the enormous tension in which Lindsay eventually was involved, and with him those equally whom he satirised or defended.

Tension must have been greatest among the friars themselves. The maximum number of men in the two main orders was probably never more than 200, at any time in the sixteenth century.[77] During the period 1540-1560 their combined strength was perhaps about 150, distributed in some twenty or so friaries from Inverness to Wigtown, each holding on average between 5 to 8 friars. Enough has perhaps been said already to suggest the intellectual divergences which divided them. There was very probably also a deep cleavage between Black and Grey Friars on more issues than the Pater Noster controversy. Both were in the thick of matters of life or death. We have mentioned two Black Friars and one Grey Friar who were burnt as heretics; another Black Friar died on the rocks under

---

74. *Rentale Sancti Andree*, pp. 94, 121, 137.

75. In 1534 Grierson and the Franciscan John Bothwell, each with a friar of his order, were summoned to sit with the Privy Council, which was concerned with the spread of heresy through books, strangers lodged in the burghs, and the activity of certain friars. It was resolved " to put remeid to the freris at ar tholit to pas furth of the realme in apostasy and of the haly preching making to the peple without ony rehers of opinionable materis bot in the sculis, and to gar warne all the governouris of religioun sic as priouris and wardanis that thai tak diligent tent and cuir apoun thair brether for eschewing of inconvenientis." The two friar superiors promised to see that new opinions were not put forward in the sermons of their brethren. Hannay, *Acts of the Lords of the Council in Public Affairs*, p. 422.

76. Dickinson's *Knox*, i, p. 21, specifically in connection with the attack on Seton: and p. 42, with regard to Gilyem and Rough.

77. See Appendix I, below.

his prison in St. Andrews.[78] We have named seven other friars, of whom six were Black Friars, who fled the country within a short time. So high a number of casualties, among the Dominicans especially, must have had an emotional impact which would be difficult to over-estimate and which was increased by the fact that some zealous heresy-hunters were to be found in the friars' own ranks. There was, in fact, no united front, no high-powered drive in spite of much deep concern with events. The divisions among friars were publicly and dramatically illustrated during Arran's regency. Several of the preachers appointed by him were Black Friars, including John Roger and Walter Thomson. The Aberdeen burgh records preserve the town council's acceptance of " our lord the governours request to gif to the religiouss men frer Johnne roger and to frer Waltir thomsoun his marrow to thair honest sustentatioun daylie induring thair will thre s. with ane honest chalmir . . . and that for the leill and trew lawtefull service to be done in preching and teching of the trew word of God and thair daylie Prearis for the estait of the lord governouris grace the commont weill of this realme and of this guid towne."[79] What discussion there must have been in Aberdeen, and not least in the Dominican priory itself, when this dissident establishment of two set up in the town. In other towns also at this time there were friars who were irregular, whose activity must have served to weaken the credit of their orthodox brethren with higher ecclesiastical authority, and must have troubled some at least among their own former colleagues.

Further internal difficulties are suggested by the history of John Rough, if it is true, as he is reported to have said, that he became a friar at the age of seventeen to spite his relations. After eighteen presumably difficult years in the order, he received due permission to live as one of the secular clergy. That did not bring him peace, nor does he appear to have found it as a protestant until he met his death at the stake at Smithfield in 1557. " Death," he wrote, two days before his burning, " is to my great advantage; for thereby the body ceaseth from sin, and, after, turneth into the first original; but after shall be changed, and made brighter than the sun or moon. What shall I write of this corporal death, seeing it is decreed of God that all men shall once die? Happy are they that die in the Lord, which is to die in the faith of Christ, professing and confessing the same before many witnesses. I praise my God I have passed the same journey by many temptations. The devil is very busy to persuade, the world to entice, with promises and fair words; which I omit to write, lest some might think I did hunt after vain glory, which is furthest from my heart."[80] He was no doubt writing for posterity, with more than an echo of St. Paul, and a suggestion of apostolic resemblance which has brought the accusation of vain glory against him since. (A similar verdict has been passed on Mary Stuart's death, although christians might leave such final judgment to God—in both cases.) What is surely clear about John Rough is that his soul was in anguish, whatever the reason; and he accepted hardship and death rather than deny his convictions. Knox calls him "simple," and one wonders what the word means. There are elements in the story which could be paralleled in any age, a reminder of the difficulty which religious communities have found in rejecting recruits when short of men.

---

78. Dickinson's *Knox*, i, p. 56.
79. Aberdeen Burgh Court Books, xvii, 489. P. J. Anderson is mistaken in saying that the provost and council were acceding to the *bishop's* request. Cf. *Aberdeen Friars*, p. 85.
80. See Foxe, (ed. Townsend), *Acts and Monuments*, viii, pp. 443-9, for the main account of Rough's life, and the letter quoted here.

John Rough should never have been a novice, and his stay in a religious order could only mean trouble for himself and others the longer it lasted; he was giving himself to an exacting life without a sound understanding of what it entailed; the religious life must be attempted for the love of God, and is an impossible burden if undertaken for any other reason. So Rough discovered, and he claims our sympathy.

It was a weakness of Adamson's reform that although he suppressed Cupar and demoted St. Monance, twelve other houses remained in existence. It was essential for the type of observance which he envisaged to have larger communities than was to prove possible; three priories would have been enough for a total of between 80 and 100 friars, if itinerant preaching was to be combined with study and regular choral observance. At first it may have looked as though the reformed province was to recruit successfully. It attracted not only young Rough but such a person as Alexander Lawson, a distinguished lawyer in Aberdeen who gave up a notable career to become a Black Friar, and others such as John Hunter, Andrew Macneill and John Black. But we may reasonably suspect that there were some insufficiently tried vocations, and in any case the general decline in the quality of the nation's life which gathered momentum in the forties, was not favourable to mendicant vocations. In the small communities of friars low numbers meant increasing burdens at the best of times, even without the strain involved in carrying misfits. There must have been some unenthusiastic survivors, for a time at least, from the group of friars who had opposed Adamson. It has been remarked that he achieved something unique in bringing the whole province under the stricter observance, instead of dividing it into reformed and un-reformed congregations after the device used on the continent.[81] The fact was, of course, that the Scottish province was too small for such treatment to be workable, and although some recalcitrant elements fled to England, the province after 1511 consisted, it may reasonably be assumed, of some strong supporters of strict observance, some reluctant conformers who regretted the old regime, and some sort of group between two extremes; such a mixture, given the " democratic " method of the Dominican order, would entail frequent compromise on sharper issues. If, and when, there was no compromise, but a clear decision by some one party, an increase of tension might well result among those who were in the minority.

Internal strain caused by small numbers, and misfits among them, would lead to developments inviting satirical attention of the sort illustrated in the last few lines of the passage of Lindsay already quoted, and in many other places; various forms of escape which gave no ground for scandal of a lurid kind but which could cause misunderstanding, gossip, and sometimes considerable irritation. Here it is significant that there was a close relationship between the friars and the burgh communities among whom they lived. The greater number of friars whose antecedents can be traced seem to have come from the burgess class or the families of the smaller lairds. A friary was no high road to wealth or promotion in church or state, and so usually had little attraction for members of great families. In spite of the movement of personnel from friary to friary, of which there is ample evidence, it may well have been true that there was often too great intimacy between the friars and the inhabitants of the

---

81.   Mortier, *Maîtres-Generaux*, v, p. 111.

burghs. The neurotic would find an escape from the community in a citizen's house, accepting hospitality eagerly, giving entertainment perhaps, or advice, receiving alms, and excusing much comfortable inactivity by a little space given to advice or alms-gathering. There are always women ready to encourage that kind of apostolate, without any shadow of grave temptation in their minds. The religious situation in Scotland at that time, and the general decline in morals, would lead to many women seeking and finding friars who would listen to their worries and escape from their own in doing so. Fashionable friars in burgesses' houses would be quite enough to account for the accusations of idleness and flattery flung against the orders from time to time. (And for the gibe which said that the Dominicans were no longer *mendicantes* but *manducantes*). The very circles in the burghs which originally encouraged social intimacy would produce the critics. The phenomenon has been so familiar in other times and places that it is reasonable to suppose its existence in medieval Scotland though perhaps not among the Observant Grey Friars—and there is enough in contemporary literature to confirm the supposition.

Economic problems pressed heavily on most of the mendicant communities, and are reflected in a mass of litigation which can hardly have improved relations between them and sections of the town populations. The Observants with their stricter poverty, and refusal of money payments, were exempt from a vicious circle which held the other bodies of friars, and especially the Dominicans.[82] The economy of the country went from crisis to crisis, owing to bad government, civil strife, foreign invasion, bad seasons, and general dishonesty. An important part of the friars' revenues came from small annual rents in the burghs, from ancient grants levied on customs or burgh fermes, from their own crofts and occasionally from fishing rights. All of these brought trouble, settled only at the expense of legal proceedings. Years after the expulsion of the friars, Edinburgh town council found the collection of their former annuals so great a nuisance that it disposed of the lot.[83] But more than fifty years before the reformation we find the friars involved in a struggle, to secure their legal income, which had decreasing success as the century advanced, and which must have constantly militated against their popularity as well as forming a major distraction from their essential work. Yet the work demanded resources; money for repair or extension of buildings, for books, travelling expenses, the maintenance of students both at home and abroad; and even those benefactors who helped with such projects as the building of the Blackfriars in St. Andrews would expect annuals to be collected. Their assistance in fact often meant there were more annuals to be collected. The Elgin Blackfriars were exceptional in possessing landed property of some extent, which they feued in 1545, thus securing a revenue and freeing themselves from the worries of administration and collection of rents. They presented a target to certain critics, however, since the bulk of their property had been transferred to them from the Maison Dieu. So also did the Blackfriars of Montrose whose restored foundation had been similarly assisted by transfer of a hospital foundation, a transfer

---

82. Between 1480-1560 I have found only two cases involving the Grey Friars in the Aberdeen Burgh Court Records, and neither had to do with money, In the period 1489-1560 there were over 50 cases involving the Blackfriars, and about 60 involving Carmelites or Trinitarians. Some of the processes dragged on for years, so that there was rarely a time in which the friars were not engaged in some litigation and it was not always to their credit. It is perhaps significant that there was a marked reduction in litigation between 1511-41, and an equally marked increase after 1543.

83. *Edinburgh Burgh Extracts*, iv, p. 462.

which offended the Erskines of Dun, who had enjoyed the hospital's goods for some decades. We might be more impressed by the indignation of John Erskine of Dun, and others like him, on behalf of the " poor oratours " of the hospitals if there was no evidence to suggest that they were perhaps also roused by loss of a vested family interest.[84]

The attack on the friars in the name of the poor by those like Moray, Erskine and Knox, who benefited richly by the reformation, is a good example of an artificially contrived movement covering a quite different issue. The friars were in no way responsible for the economic distress which existed in the country at the time of the revolution, and they had no power to effect a change in the situation. Almost every writer in sixteenth-century Scotland points to the true cause of poverty and beggary; the wars, the callousness of landlords, the dishonesty of merchants, the almost universal indifference to anything but private interest which characterised the monarchy and the nobles, the merchants and the craftsmen. The attack on the friars provided a scapegoat for " the rascal multitude " and simultaneously suppressed the most serious obstacle to the progress of the reformation. It is easy to mount a riot when there is serious distress and a large population of beggars, and to direct it where one will; the distribution of placards against the friars throughout the kingdom on January 1st, 1559, the blatant exaggeration of the charges put forth, and the presence of large bands of reformers and their retainers at the critical points, all indicate a contrived and centrally directed campaign.[85] It was some years later that Knox attributed the attack on the friaries to " the rascal multitude "; at the time he seems to have been in no doubt, at least in his private correspondence, that it was the work of " the brethren " of the Congregation.

The attack was in fact a testimony to the importance of the friars and their continued vitality. Even the phrases of the *Beggars Summons* about the success of " cloiket and hudit simplicitie " and " feynseit halynes, quhilk now is declared superstitioun and idolatrie," indicate an influence among the people generally, which had to be destroyed by the reformers. It is indicated also by such things as the alarm of the burgh council in Edinburgh about friars creeping busily about the town shortly after the overthrow of their houses, but perhaps most of all by the hard-worked references to the " miracles " of Friar Walter Laing, the " gude kail " of the friars at Failford, and the bad character of the friars of Tullilum. Whether fool or knave Walter Laing provided a much appreciated stick with which to beat the friars. The Trinitarians at Failford were the only ones who could possibly be called wealthy:

> The Friars o' Fail
> They made gude kail
> On Friday when they fasted,
> And never wanted geir enough
> As lang as their neighbours lasted.

So the rhyme about then. In another context the same ideas turn up;

---

84. Erskine was confirmed in possession of Montrose Blackfriars lands, etc. in 1567-8. Cf. Reg. of Presentation to Benefices (S.R.O.), f. 3v.

85. See also Dr. Donaldson's illuminating note, " ' Flitting Friday,' The Beggars' Summons and Knox's Sermon at Perth," in *Scot. Hist. Rev.*, xxxix, pp. 175-6 For a text of the *Summons* see Dickinson's *Knox*, ii, pp. 255-6.

The Monkis of Melros maid gude kaill
On Frydayis quhen thay fastit.[86]

In the disturbances of 1543 the Perth Blackfriars had been broken into and the broth pot stolen from the kitchen and paraded through the town. Much ado about plain enough food. On a par with Knox's remarks about the store and plenishing of the Greyfriars and the Blackfriars of Perth when their houses were destroyed, which ignores the fact that the Greyfriars bedding came to them by gift, not purchase, and begs several other questions. The theme was a good one with which to appeal to the beggars in the street, but if there was any valid criticism of the friars in Perth on the score of poverty it would have had to come from someone who shared John Adamson's ideals, and not from one who enjoyed servants and a wine cellar and wore fur about his neck.

It is significant too, that the suggestions of grave scandal are so often directed against the weaker orders of friars. The Trinitarians, or Red Friars, were in no very healthy state, perhaps, being an example of an order which had served its day. There is an odd incident in connection with a visitation of the Trinitarians in Aberdeen in 1554 when the bailies ordered that one Agnes Lowsoune should restore a chalice which had been delivered to her by John Quhitcors, one of the Red Friars, in consideration of six pounds which he owed her. The visitor " oblist him of his awin guidnes to deliver to the said Agnes fourty s. mair nor the said sowme of sax li. at the restitioun of the said chalice in maner aboune writtin sua the same be deliverit to him with plesour and thankfulnes but ony forthir of cumyr or coist."[87] There is here obvious anxiety to settle some unpleasant business; it certainly points to an odd state of affairs when a religious pawns a chalice to a woman. At the same visitation the administration of Trinitarian property in Aberdeen was made over to Robert Lumsden who was to supply the Red Friars with what they might need and undertake the repair of the Trinity Kirk and place.[88] It appears that, although much may have been wrong, an effort was being made at correction.

V

The Carmelites deserve closer attention than they have yet received. Their houses were evidently small, usually half-timbered, with chapels rather than churches attached to them, the communities, in the sixteenth century in Scotland, averaging three or four friars and totalling probably less than forty in the country. Few though they were, and whatever may lie behind the references to the community at Tullilum, they had a share in the movement to raise the standard of religious life which has been described above. In 1512 we find Friars Musch and Pareis of Tullilum going to Aberdeen to study, subsidised by the same bishop of Dunkeld, George Brown, who employed Franciscans and Dominicans to preach in Gaelic, and who gave considerable help to the Carmelites by building the nave of their church at Tullilum and improving their conventual accommodation.[89] The Scottish Carmelite province was not without some

---

86. The rhyme about Failford is one of a number. Hutton has it, with another: " The Friars o' Fail/Gat neir owr hard eggs or owr thin kail/For they made their Eggs soft with butter, and their kail thick with bread." Collections, xiii, 60, p. 17. The Melrose rhyme: Mitchell, *Gude and Godlie Ballatis* (S.T.S.), p. 206.

87. Aberdeen Burgh Court Books, xxii, p. 149.

88. *Op. cit.* p. 150.

89. *Rentale Dunkeldense*, pp. 226, 238-9.

learning. David Balbirny, " the little doctor " (or " teacher ") of Dunkeld, was patronised by Bishop Brown and later became prior of Greenside (Edinburgh), and of Tullilum.[90] He is mentioned as early as 1506, which is about the time Fr. Thomas Lyell, Bachelor in Theology, was appointed to make a visitation of the province as vicar-general, with a view to reform.[91] In Aberdeen, where financial help was given to the friars by Bishop Elphinstone,[92] the Carmelite William Shewan acted as scribe to William Hay, subprincipal of King's College, and also transcribed some of the Aberdeen cathedral registers for Alexander Galloway of Kinkell. Galloway, who was generous with gifts of books, presented the Aberdeen Carmelites with the works of Gratian published in Paris in 1507. Also at Aberdeen, prior and later provincial, was Friar Andrew Storour who bought a volume of Duns Scotus for the community library with the fruits of some work which he did in 1507. As the volume was printed in Venice in 1505 the acquisition was fairly up-to-date. Compared to the Dominicans and Franciscans the Carmelite claim to learning is modest, but enough to show that they must not be written off too easily.

Abroad, two Carmelites of Scottish origin took part in the reforming activity of the Master-General Audet and one of them, William Gregory, became vicar-general of the Congregation of Albi.[93] A review of the state of the Carmelite order, compiled while he was at Albi, says that little is known of the Scottish province, owing to distance, but that its provincial is " good enough."[94] That was in 1531; ten years later the Scots were certainly better known to headquarters when disagreement about internal reform came to a head. There were rival provincials, John Malcolmson —the same who had been described as quite good—and William Stob, the former with backing at court which for a time proved formidable to his opponents. The battle opened at the end of August, 1539, when William Stob summoned Malcolmson and the other Carmelite superiors to attend a provincial chapter to be held at Aberdeen on September 14th immediately following. This citation was by virtue of authority from the general and the general chapter of the order. Malcolmson, who at this date must have been at least sixty years of age, replied warmly that he would see Stob hanged before obeying him or his summons and declared several times his determination to take the matter further. What he meant by this last statement is clear from his counter-citation to Stob and his companion John Cristeson to appear at Greenside or Linlithgow, " wherever our sovereign lord the king should happen for the time to reside," on September 26th, to answer to him as their provincial regarding their religious life and other things to be investigated. He also attempted to frustrate the reform by sending a false report of the situation to Rome and appealing beyond the authority of his superiors in the order. For a time it looked as though he might succeed. William Stob and the prior of Tullilum, with several other Carmelites, were put to the horn. In the end Stob appears to have been vindicated, Cardinal Beaton, acting under

90. *Ibid.* pp. 79, 88, 108, 218, 221, 283. Prior of Tullilum, 1540: *Exch. Rolls*, xvii, p. 311. Prior of Greenside, 1539, Prot. Bk. of Robert Lawson (N.L.S., Riddell Collection), f. 73v., and 1544: *Notes and Queries*, (1870), 4th series, vi, 521.

91. See Zimmerman, *Acta Petri Terrasse, Magistri Generalis Ordinis Carmelitarum*, 1503-11, (Rome, 1931), pp. 28, 53.

92. Boece, *Vitae*, p. 100.

93. See Ian Johnson, " Scots Carmelites and the French Reform," *Innes Rev.*, v. pp. 141-3.

94. Staring, *Der Karmelitengeneral Nikolaus Audet* (Rome, 1959), p. 429.

a papal commission, having pronounced him to be lawful provincial in February 1540-41. Malcolmson afterwards protested that his own submission to this judgment had been made under threat by the cardinal of perpetual prison and was null and void; nevertheless Stob and his supporters were freed from the horning and recognised by the Lords of the Council, and it was his colleague Cristeson who later succeeded Stob as provincial.[95]

The whole case is illuminating as an illustration of the difficulty experienced by those who were associated with orthodox reform. Opposed at first by influence at court, the supporters of strict observance were involved in legal proceedings at home and in the Roman curia which ended naturally, but in a way ironically, with a decision in their favour promulgated by the highest ecclesiastical authority in Scotland, the cardinal. This is part of the background to *The Three Estaitis*; Lindsay was at court, and presumably directing preparations for the production of his great play which was to take place on the feast of the Epiphany immediately following William Stob's summons to John Malcolmson. He must have known, he may even have heard, Malcolmson's appeal to the king. What are we to make then of lines like these, spoken by Deceit to Flattery in the play? Were they in the text of 1540? It is impossible to say. They occur in both the later texts.

> Heir is thy gaining, all and sum,
> This is ane coull of Tullilum.[96]

Tullilum was in fact on the side of strict observance, to judge by the association of its prior with William Stob. Lindsay's gibe was on the side of the party which was resisting strict observance, with the help of the king and members of the court, and is no evidence against the community of friars which it names. The success of the observant party—a success here linked in Lindsay's eye with David Beaton—would not have helped to endear the friars of Tullilum to Lindsay and his friends. In fact, apart from more local and personal considerations, the success of any reform among the friars, of whatever order, must have worried a number of people. Flattery, about to be disguised as a friar, advised Deceit:

> And let us keip grave countenance
> As we war new cum out of France.[97]

To the pro-English party in Scotland the reformed observance among the friars meant a very likely increase of ties with France, through which, as we have seen in the case of the Black Friars, so much of the impetus to reform actually came. It certainly would mean a strengthening of opposition to English influence as the nature of Henry VIII's religious changes became clear. One wonders also how burgh traders, to whom connections in Lutheran areas of Scandinavia and Germany mattered so much, must have viewed the observant movement among the friars. There were more things than protestant zeal to win applause for Lindsay's verse, and his thrusts cannot be taken simply at their face value.

These notes on what was happening among the friars may be enough to encourage a new approach to the history of the religious orders, and a re-assessment of some familiar material. There is of course much more to be said, and not all of it in their favour, but at least it should be clear

---

95. The stages in the conflict can be followed in the Protocol Book of Robert Lawson, ff. 73v., 74r., 82r., 82v.; and *Acts of the Lords of Council in Public Affairs*, pp. 486, 497, 500.
96. *Works*, i, p. 402.
97. *Ibid*, p. 399.

that there was a real vitality among the orders. This is true not only of the friars, but also of some at least of the monastic communities. That these were by no means entirely cut off from contemporary thought will have been gathered from some previous references in this essay to the appreciation of John Adamson's ideals and character by abbots of Kinloss and Cambuskenneth. There is more work to be done on the connection between monks and friars in the movement for reformed observance. How much preaching to monastic communities was undertaken, for example, by the friars? When the Dominican Richard Marshall was appointed preacher to Dunfermline in May 1558 his duties included not only preaching in kirks appropriated to the monastery; it was also stipulated, " he sall teache as god gyffis him grace ane lessone of the scripturis or sum uther convenient doctrine to the bretherin of the said abbay thryce in the owlke and ofter gyf thay requyre hym thairwyth."[98] Was his colleague Mark Hamilton thinking of addresses to Benedictines when he filled one and a half flyleaves of a book with notes on the greatness of monastic tradition and the qualities desirable in a religious? Very possibly, since about a quarter of the notes concern the black monks.[99] However, the monastic communities were not dependent on the friars for ideas of reform or strict observance. Their own traditions were by no means dead, and something must be said briefly about them before finishing this essay.

VI

One caution must be made, in any approach to Scottish religious history of the sixteenth century, which has been reserved until now because it is of even greater importance in studying the monks than in studying the friars. We must be careful about comparing what happened in Scotland with the dissolution of the monasteries in England. The comparison can be useful, but conditions for Scottish medieval establishments were so different from those obtaining in England that ideas gathered in discussing English history can be seriously misleading when carried over to Scottish affairs. We have to remember, for example, that the fifty years before the dissolution of the English monasteries were years of peace and good government, while in Scotland not one decade had been free from trouble since 1286 and there had been seven foreign invasions between 1513-1560, during which some of the great abbeys and priories had suffered severely. Internal anarchy imposed extra strain on communities so closely knit into the general economic and social life of the country as were most monastic establishments. We have mentioned how the Blackfriars of Montrose were defrauded and bullied by the Crawfords for nearly thirty years after Flodden. Other communities were often worse treated. Iona was occupied, for example, in 1551 by the Macleans of Duart, who retained it at the reformation.[100] Lindores was sacked in the premature revolution of 1543. Glenluce suffered repeated invasion by local lairds, especially the earl of Cassillis and Gordon of Lochinvar between 1544-60. During the invasions of 1543-48 by English forces the following were burnt: Coldingham, Kelso, Balmerino, Melrose, Newbattle,

---

98. See the appendix to " The Cultural Background " below, on Marshall.

99. The volume is Aquinas, *Comm. in beati Pauli apostoli epistolas.* See *Early Scottish Libraries*, p. 111. The notes contain an interesting summary of traditional monastic ideals: " Tria in religioso laudabilia pondus maturitatis/amor communitatis/et fuga proprietatis. Tria in religioso reprobanda/indevocio dissolucio/et evagacio. Tria decent omnem religiosum/ pauca loqui/paucos familiares habere/multum orare."

100. Easson, *Medieval Religious Houses: Scotland*, p. 52. The details which follow are based on Easson, or on articles appearing in this volume; it seems unnecessary to repeat references.

Holyrood, Jedburgh, Dryburgh, the Trinitarian house at Peebles, the Cistercian convents at Eccles, Elcho, St. Bothan's and Haddington, and several houses of friars, notably in Dundee, Haddington and Edinburgh. During the same period the party which occupied the castle of St. Andrews, after the assassination of Cardinal Beaton, burnt the houses of the Black and Grey friars in the city. Some of the monasteries listed were repaired after a first attack, only to be destroyed a second or a third time. It is impossible to say how many members of the communities may have been killed or taken prisoner, although occasionally some information is available; in 1548, for example, we learn that six monks from Newbattle were taken to England as prisoners. The monastic islands in the Forth had to be abandoned years before the storm of 1559-60; May was waste by 1550; Inchcolm had been occupied first by English, then by French troops in 1547, so that monastic life must have become virtually impossible. It was the set intention of some of these military actions to help on the conversion of Scotland to protestantism by the destruction of religious communities. When we add to the work of English protestants the attacks launched by their Scottish friends and allies in the next decade very few religious houses are excluded from the catalogue of destruction. The Scottish reformers were to wreck or destroy most of what had escaped English attention: Dunfermline, Crossraguel, Paisley, Kilwinning, Lindores, the Charterhouse at Perth, Scone, Cambuskenneth, and friaries in Stirling, Perth, Edinburgh and elsewhere.

More serious than this record of violence, in the century which led up to 1560, was the establishment of the commendatory system, something which English monasticism escaped but which in Scotland had a deplorable effect on monastic life. The subject is immense, and would have produced an extensive literature by now if the study of medieval church history had been developed in Scotland as it has been elsewhere. For the present, the main point which I want to stress is that there was real resistance to the commendatory system by Scottish religious communities right up to 1560. In the early stages of the struggle they opposed the appointment of secular clergy who were backed by the king or the Roman curia, or both; this struggle had some success up to 1496. After this early stage, the battle was against the appointment of royal state officials, members of the royal family (usually illegitimate), and members of the great noble families supported by royal letters. By 1535 most appointments were effectively in the royal power and a head-on conflict was useless; abbatial office would go either to young nobles or the king's illegitimate offspring. In spite of this an attempt was still being made to save the situation from the type of disaster which we shall see presently, with reference to Melrose, by securing young commendators who might be trained as monastic prelates. This attempt to solve the problem of how to preserve monastic observance under commendatory abbots can be seen at Kinloss, Deer, Coupar-Angus, Culross and Glenluce. It is remarkable that four of these prospective abbots were sent to study at universities, three at Paris, one at St. Andrews. (Two died in 1552)[101]. It is significant

101. At Kinloss, Reid attempted to train his nephew Walter, who was sent to study at Paris in the care of Adam Elder. (His course included Greek). Stuart's *Kinloss*, p. 66. Robert Keith, commendator of Deer, also had a successor-nephew at Paris, Robert Keith II, who died there on 25th April, 1552. Pollen, *Papal Negotiations*, p. 415. John Colville, the young commendator of Culross, also a student in Paris, died there in 1552. *Scots Peerage*, ii, p. 546. At Glenluce, Walter Malin sent young James Gordon to study at St. Andrews, in the care of Andrew Langlands. *Early Records of St. Andrews*, p. 256. These were to have been monastic prelates, even if commendators, and Gordon and Colville seem to have promised well. The letter of Adam Elder, and the two from Ferreri summarised by Pollen, show three of these youths to have been in the humanist circle associated with Kinloss.

that all five appointments were Cistercian, as the most stubborn resistance to royal interference came from that order; and also that they can be attributed to the influence of two prelates, who were themselves originally appointed *in commendam*, but who proved supporters of religious life and of the movement for sound observance and a revival of study—Robert Reid, abbot of Kinloss and bishop of Orkney, and Walter Malin (or Malynne), abbot of Glenluce.

Kinloss has already been mentioned, in connection with John Adamson and the promising movement fostered by Bishop Elphinstone at Aberdeen. The work of Abbot Chrystall was continued by his successor, in spite of his onerous duties in church and state, and Kinloss affords a picture of healthy life. The abbot of Kinloss was Father Immediate of Deer and Culross, i.e., responsible for maintaining standards in these houses by regular visitation. Both Chrystall and Reid were conscientious about this responsibility, and appear to have followed the directions given by the visitor from Citeaux who came to Scotland in 1531, Simon Postel, abbot of Chaalis, who was charged with securing strict observance. Although Chaalis does not seem to have gone farther north than Coupar-Angus, the monks of Kinloss had the latest edition of the Cistercian usages, printed at Paris in 1531, in a volume whose scored and well-thumbed condition testifies to its use. This was simply continuing what had begun earlier in the century at Kinloss. Thomas Chrystall had been personally associated with the work of Thomas Fassington who had been sent to Scotland from Citeaux in 1506, with a commission to visit all the Cistercian houses there, accompanied by an abbot of the country. The intention was that the reform of Abbot Jean de Cirey should be extended to Scotland. Fassington's labours in Scotland stretched over ten years, hindered by James IV, (who tried to have Robert Beaton, whom he had foisted on Melrose as abbot, appointed visitor of the Scottish houses instead of him), and by others who were profiting by the commendatory system. *Mercenarii ymmo peiores sunt*, remarked the Abbot of Fountains in a letter to the Abbot of Citeaux on Fassington's hardships.[102] But something had been achieved and not only in Kinloss and its dependencies, for at Glenluce also the abbot, Walter Malin, had considerable success against greater difficulties.

The type of life established by these reformers was well-balanced and suited to the needs of Scotland at the time. It included the traditional Cistercian pattern of prayer, with rising for the Night Office included; the observance of laws of fasting and abstinence; an enlightened appreciation of the value of study which is illustrated not only by the provision made for the education of young monks but also by the libraries of the abbots of Kinloss, which testify to a thoroughly contemporary appreciation of the necessity of going back to the sources of Catholic theology. Thomas Chrystall's devotion to St. Jerome is significant; the great example of early biblical scholarship was the patron saint of Erasmus and the christian humanists. There was a huge bible in six volumes in the library of Kinloss; many works of Jerome, Ambrose, Augustine, Chrysostom, Gregory, and Bernard were there; the *Summa* of Aquinas, and his commentaries on St. Paul; all that was needed in fact to develop that *docta*

---

102.   The change in James's attitude to Fassington can be seen in his *Letters*, pp. 29, 61, 66. The Abbot of Chaalis's visit, and a number of other events in Scottish Cistercian history, are illustrated in Canivez, *Statuta Capitulorum Generalium Ordinis Cisterciensis*. I have had the benefit of reading some of Fr. O'Dea's transcripts of material in archives at Rome and Dijon, including the Abbot of Fountains' letter.

pietas which is part of the Cistercian ideal.[103] The results of the educational programme at Kinloss can be glimpsed in the writing of Adam Elder, in the books used by various members of the community, the continued connection with King's College illustrated by the book-borrowing of John Cameron, and in the note book of John Smyth[104] which contains arguments for and against strict observance in the matter of " portions."[105] Smyth was in favour of a rigorous interpretation of the law, a significant attitude when we remember that he was *confessor monachorum* at Kinloss. He would not have approved of Adam Elder's selling cabbages from his garden without permission!

Giovanni Ferreri has made historians familiar with many aspects of life at Kinloss; the work in the gardens, and the importing of a gardener from Normandy to improve the cultivation of fruit trees at Kinloss and Beauly; the regard for pastoral responsibilites shown in the repair of the appropriated churches at Ellon and Avoch and the supply of vestments for mass; Thomas Chrystall celebrating mass daily himself; his social services, such as the hostel for seamen, the dowries for poor girls, his alms to the poor. But it is not only at Kinloss that we can see a complex of useful activities. The little abbey at Culross deserves more appreciation than it received from Dr. Coulton, who concluded one of the stranger passages in his *Scottish Abbeys* as follows: " Even the reforming abbot Reid, at Kinloss, had to buy for his library many of the most important volumes in the 16th century, and paid for the writing of two of his service-books at Culross. From this it has been unsafely inferred that the monks of Culross were noted scribes; it is more probable that they had a competent hired copyist."[106] (It was not Reid, but Chrystall, who ordered the service-books; de luxe volumes, a gradual and a missal).[107]

The probability of a hired copyist is established only in the writer's own prejudice, and is questioned by record evidence. Setting aside the Culross psalter as an argument for the existence of a scriptorium at Culross in the second half of the fifteenth century, we find a number of entries in royal accounts which point to the existence of a scriptorium in the sixteenth and permit identification of one individual associated in its work.[108] Between July 1502 and January 1503-4 the king ordered, and paid for, more than £60 worth of books written at Culross for the Greyfriars of Stirling. (Did the poet William Dunbar regard this as extravagance?) The accounts specify *ane monk* of Culross and *the monkis* of Culross. In April, 1517, appears: Gevin to ane monk of Culros for bynding and alummyng of twa bukis to the Kingis Chapell of Striveling . . . 56s. In February, 1531-2, we find: Be the Kingis preceptis to ane monk of Culros for foure anti-phonallis to the Kingis Chappell . . . £32. In January 1538-9: Item, deliverit to Dene Mycheall Donaldsone, monk of Culross for ane grete antiphonal deliverit to the Chapell. Surely this suggests that Culross may have had a scriptorium noted for work above the average. The Stirling Greyfriars may be presumed to have had among themselves someone as

---

103. For Chrystall's devotion to St. Jerome, see the *Life* by Ferreri, Stuart's *Kinloss*, pp. 30, 32-34. The list of books is given on p. 36 of the same work.
104. Harleian MS. 2363. Smyth's *Chronicle*, contained in the same manuscript, is printed in Stuart's *Kinloss*, pp. 3-13, which also contains selections from Adam Elder's chapter sermons, pp. 69-91.
105. Harleian MS. 2363, ff. 8-17.
106. *Scottish Abbeys and Social Life*, p. 160.
107. Stuart's *Kinloss*, p. 36.
108. *Treas. Accts.*, ii, pp. 68, 69, 73, 250, 252, 254, 255, 257; iv, pp. 409, 513; vi, p. 22; vii, p. 132.

competent as the Carmelite friar William Shewan for ordinary work; they got 48 Flanders skins in 1503.[109] The books ordered for them and for the Chapel Royal would have been above ordinary as the prices themselves suggest. Quite apart from these entries, the likelihood of a scriptorium at Culross is by no means startling when we remember the references in Ferreri to fifteenth-century monks of Kinloss who were copyists, and to Abbot William Culross of Kinloss who transcribed books of ritual *decenter*;[110] or if we recollect the Cistercian of Newbattle, Alexander Scot, who transcribed the Cistercian *Institutiones* in 1528;[111] or the beautiful floral designs in the Cambuskenneth Chartulary; the Scone antiphonaries; Thomas Guld's manuscripts;[112] or some of the material reproduced elsewhere in this volume; or even the quantities of fragments of graduals, written indifferently on coarse Scottish parchment, which still survive.

The king was at Culross himself several times between 1500-13, and drew on the monks for more than books. Dene Matthew Takket, monk of Culross, appears to have been in charge of glazing and laying out of gardens. He was being paid in 1497 for work on windows, on the " yard bigging," and for buying peas and beans for the yard. In February 1502-3 appears an entry: " To Dene Matho Taket, monk of Culros, for " xv^c plowme tries to the garding of Strivelin . . . 25s." One wonders if the plum trees came from Culross, especially as a little later the gardener at Stirling was given three shillings " to pas to Culros for floures to set."[113] Bedding plants and young trees, glazing and building, writing and illuminating of books; why didn't the king hire his own secular craftsmen, unless the monks were in fact skilled themselves? Robert Wedale, monk and later abbot of Culross, was actually Master of the Works in the palace of Linlithgow.[114] The small community at Culross cannot have done everything itself, but among its score or so of monks there were certainly men of skill. The abbey's own burgh was a flourishing concern, with a harbour kept in good repair from which ashlars cut in the Culross quarries were ferried across the Forth for the building of Holyrood.[115] There must have been considerable activity in the quarries at the beginning of the century when Abbot Andrew Mason was engaged in extensive reconstruction of the church and the building of its fine tower. Workers were engaged also in the salt-pans and the coalheughs, and it has been suggested that salt was exported to the continent.[116] The burgh's girdle-makers were famous; a planted industry, or a spontaneous development?[117] There was a grammar school. Abbot Chrystall studied at it when a boy.[118] In 1589 the inhabitants of the burgh were asserting that the school which had been " in all tyme bygane within the abbey of Culros " was in danger of being neglected. In it " the youth of the burgh and land of Culross wer instructit in grammar, and trainit up to vertew and lettres, to the commounweill of

---

109. *Ibid*, ii, p. 250.
110. Ferrerius, *Historia Abbatum de Kynlos* (Bannatyne Club, 1839), p. 35. "Consueverat manibus propriis multa facere: plurimum scribebat et decenter rituum libros hujus loci . . . vir satis pius, nisi carnis voluptatibus et veneri succubuisset." See also p. 35—Dom David Eliot, another copyist.
111. N.L.S., Adv. MS. 18.4.1.
112. In the library at Abbotsford.
113. *Treas. Accts*, i, pp. 364, 370, 378, 388, 497; ii, pp. 358, 433.
114. *Exch. Rolls*, iv, pp. cxxxix, 554, 555, 610, 652.
115. See *Accts. of the Masters of the Works*, i, pp. 3-36, passim.
116. See I. F. Grant, *Social and Economic Development of Scotland before* 1603, p. 316. Coal from Culross to the king: *Treas. Accts.*, iv, p. 511.
117. Cf. Beveridge, *Culross and Tulliallan*, ii, 143 seq.
118. Stuart's *Kinloss*, p. 20.

216

the haill cuntrey."[119] The monks of Culross were not idle, even if we limit their share in the activity of the burgh to planning and general direction. With its industries growing, the beginnings of an export trade, the formation of groups of skilled labourers, an established grammar school, Culross was a fine plum for those who took it over from the monks.

Kinloss and Culross were favoured in many respects compared to abbeys in Galloway and the borders. It is tempting to enlarge on their struggles and especially on the story of Glenluce and that great fighter for Cistercian observance, Abbot Walter Malin, but space will not allow more than some brief remarks. It is to be hoped that Father O'Dea, the Cistercian historian who has done so much research on Abbot Malin, will soon give us the fuller account of him which he is so well qualified to write. For the moment it may be noted that before going to Glenluce Walter Malin had been the Duke of Albany's secretary and confidential agent,[120] well acquainted therefore with the reform among the friars which Albany strongly supported. He was also one of Ferreri's Scottish patrons, for the latter writes: " Nor can I pass over in silence an Abbot of Glenluss, Dom Walter Malynne, to whose courtesy, learning and plenitude of virtues I owe so much."[121] Malin was a university man, and the general chapter of Citeaux also refers to his learning with respect.[122] As abbot he provided for the education of the young monks, without lowering the strength of his originally small community, by introducing a graduate of theology, Andrew Langlands, from the sister abbey of Newbattle. What rouses admiration more than anything he did, however, is the long, stubborn fight which he waged, with the backing of Citeaux, to restore strict observance at Glenluce. Roman curia, Scottish king, archbishops, bishops, commendatory abbots, the sheriff of Galloway, the earl of Cassillis and the predatory Galloway lairds were resisted step by step from his appointment by papal provision in 1519 to his death in 1556, when his clauseless will gave a final illustration of the true Cistercian ideal.[123]

His story is extraordinary, for he began it would seem unpromisingly, granted an abbey as a reward for services to the regent. The provision stipulated that he should rule as a regular abbot, taking the habit within one year. He insisted on postponing that step until Glenluce was freed from payment of a crippling annual pension to Cardinal Grimani, and then, from 1523, ruled as a regular superior who followed the programme of reform laid down by Citeaux, and attempted to have it adopted elsewhere. Only one aspect of his work will be described further now, as an example of the shifts and ambiguities of royal policy and a caution for readers of royal correspondence. In 1530 he was appointed visitor-general for Scotland, by Citeaux, in place of the worldly Andrew Durie of Melrose whose indolence and absorption in secular affairs made his tenure of the office worthless. Malin, whose work with Albany must have taught him a lot, knew what he would have to face, and fortified his authority from the general chapter by securing an apostolic brief from the pope to

---

119.   Quoted by Hay Fleming, *The Reformation in Scotland*, pp. 515-6.
120.   *Exch. Rolls*, xiv, pp. cxxxv. cxliii. cf. *Treas. Accts*, i, p. 237.
121.   Stuart's *Kinloss*, p. xx.
122.   *R.S.S.*, i, 2610. *Early Recs. St. Andrews*, pp. 107, 207, 252.
123.   I have drawn on Fr. O'Dea's transcripts for the following account of Malin, but much of his struggle can be traced in the following: Acta Dominorum Concilii, xxxii, f. 191; xxx, f. 75; xlii, ff. 2, 24v; xliii, f. 17v. Acta Dom. Conc. et Sessionis, vi, f. 180; xiii, f. 209; Donaldson, *St. Andrews Formulare*, i, p. 56; ii, pp. 345-9: (He spells his name *Malynne* usually); *Letters of James V*, pp. 187, 202, 210-11, 238, 286, 339; Canivez, *Statuta*, vi, pp. 713, 739. Reid, *Wigtownshire Charters* (S.H.S.), pp. 46-51, etc.

the king, and papal confirmation of all his Cistercian commissions, directed to the various abbots and communities. So armed, he acted with such vigour that the abbot of Melrose and the archbishop of St. Andrews had to invoke the Lords of Council to protect them. James also evidently became alarmed by such zeal and appealed to Citeaux for a French abbot to reform the Scottish houses. There must have been something like glee at Citeaux when this letter arrived. The abbot of Chaalis was dispatched to Scotland, but he also was too much for some of the monks and abbots —like Malin he had strong views on property, and would not tolerate private gardens. Gardens and portions were means of keeping monks quiet while commendators milked the revenues of the abbeys, so it is not entirely surprising to find James trying to wriggle out of the dilemma which he had brought upon himself and others by asking for a French abbot. He wrote to the general chapter suggesting, of all things, that the abbots of Melrose and Newbattle should smoothe things out after the " strange and unusual orders " of the visitor. The attempt to block Malin had failed. The latter, with the co-operation, at least nominally, of the abbot of Coupar, insisted on strict poverty at Melrose, Balmerino and Newbattle, and would only tolerate mitigated observance on condition that the position should be investigated by the general chapter, before which he cited the abbot of Melrose to appear in 1535. The resistance to reform again invoked the king's help, and we find James trying to excuse the abbot of Melrose. The issue was serious for all who profited by the commendatory system. The rigorous adoption of common property advocated by Malin and the Citeaux reformers would have forced abbots —commendatory or regular—to depend on the control of the monastic officers and to allow heavy sums to go to the upkeep of buildings, and works of charity.[124]

The subject of the financial relations of commendators and monks constitutes another chapter of Scottish monastic history still to be properly written. Unlike England, Scotland does not seem to have known a clear separation of conventual and abbatial incomes. When a commendator put in an *economus*, therefore, to manage the affairs of an abbey for him, the members of the community were dependent on him not only for their personal livelihood, but also for whatever sums were necessary for maintaining the church and the monastic buildings, the requisites for divine service, study, and the social obligations of the community. What this meant can be seen in the case of Melrose. When the extravagant Durie retired in 1541 an *economus* of royal nomination took over, and in 1542 an act of parliament sequestered all the revenues of the abbeys belonging to the king's sons until they should come of age.[125] (His illegitimate offspring then held Kelso, Melrose, St. Andrews, Dryburgh and Coldingham *in commendam*). James Stewart, commendator of Kelso and Melrose, was only 14 in 1541, and the *economus* acted until at least 1549. The disastrous years of that decade saw Melrose with practically all its lands leased out, and its rental in the hands of laymen using royal authority and interested in

---

124. For an illustration of Malin's personal economy see Acts and Decreets, x, f. 262. Expenses of 6 men, 2 boys, and 7 horses, and himself, 24s. a day. For the ideas which were being urged by the representatives of Citeaux see the Abbot of Chaalis's " Charta Visitationis," printed in *Anitiquities of the Shires of Aberdeen and Banff* (Spalding Club, 1862), iv, pp. 5-14 and the subsequent modification, pp. 14-16. For the connection between Malin's appointment as visitor and that of Chaalis, sec Canivez, *Statuta*, vi, pp. 674, 689, 695, and James V, *Letters*, p. 187, and the appeal of Melrose to the Lords of the Council, Jan. 21st, 1530-1: *Acts*, p. 347.

125. The economus was William Hamilton of Sanquhar. See *Acts of the Parliaments of Scotland*, ii, 424. *Acts of the Lords of Council*, p. 582.

securing as wide a margin of profit as possible for themselves. After the sack of 1545 the *economus* himself was in debt,[126] and hardly likely to be much concerned about the monks, who must have experienced real hardship in those days. They were reduced in numbers to 16 at the most in 1549, when the commendator assumed personal control of the abbey's property.

It is surprising perhaps that there was still a community of monks at Melrose. To continue they needed three things urgently: large sums of money for the restoration of the abbey buildings; some clearly defined rights in the direction of the monastic estates, which would secure sufficient revenue to maintain the fabric and regular worship; and their own daily bread. The remainder of their history is largely the story of the struggle, led by the old sub-prior Thomas Mersar and by Ralph Hudson to meet these needs. It must be emphasised that they fought for much more than was required for their own personal needs, for the future of the abbey, which they could scarcely ensure simply with the produce of their small private gardens and their portions. In Scottish abbeys the fight for portions might be an attempt to retain old slack customs; it might also be a desperate effort to save a little more from the rapacity of a commendatory superior. In James Stewart the monks of Melrose had a non-resident commendator who was a heavy spendthrift in constant search of more money. He died, at the end of 1558, bankrupt, leaving a deed in which he had pledged all his goods, even his table spoons and his clothes, to his half-brother the future Regent Moray[127]—who was also named James Stewart, also a natural son of the king, and also a commendator, able to help his brother of Melrose from the greater revenues of the priory of St. Andrews. James Stewart bled Melrose through a lay chamberlain and deputy bailies, who defied the monks to their faces.[128] We find the latter protesting that lead had been sold which was meant for the church, that unless immediate repairs were carried out God's service would cease in the coming winter (1556), that they would refuse to assent to feus unless the abbot kept his promise of money for repair of the church.[129] Protest after protest was drawn up by Ralph Hudson.[130] With the help of Walter Malin one concession was wrung from the commendator, an allowance of rents from lands near Melrose to the total of £227-3-4 with 20¾ chalders of victuals, which means about £30 a head, with no allowance for overheads or the running costs of the abbey. Even this concession gave the commendator a new lever against the community, the threat to withdraw it altogether if they refused to sign the documents which were drawn up in their name.[131]

The story is long and complicated, and full of incident; the rages of the commendator when opposed by the monks—" his body grew crawbit," and he tore up documents which they presented and " cast thame doun at his feet ";[132] the impeding of divine service and the administration of the sacraments by two of the commendator's bailies who occupied the

---

126. *Acts of Lords of Council*, p. 638.
127. Morton Papers (S.R.O.), box 54.
128. *Melrose Regality Records*, (S.H.S.) iii, pp. 158-161.
129. *Ibid.*, pp. 217-219.
130. See, for example, *op. cit.*, pp. 155-7.
131. *Ibid.* pp. 191-195: cf. p. 156.
132. *Ibid.* pp. 156, 217.

church;[133] the protest of Ralph Hudson, who took over as conventual superior after Thomas Mersar's death, against the action of the earl of Arran's agents sent to despoil the abbey;[134] he remained indomitable, although so weak in body that he could not return home after his protest. James Stewart's death did not help the monks. The Cardinal of Lorraine was named commendator by Rome, with a burden of pensions on the abbey amounting to £1070.[135] The community was down to eleven monks, still trying to keep some form of monastic life after twenty years of anarchy. It is ironic that it should have had to bear the obloquy of so much that was done in its name, in spite of its protest. The commendator took the money from the tenants, but through agents who claimed to act in the name of the abbot and the community; it was the latter which was stuck with the ill-fame of it all. It seems, again ironically, to have often escaped notice that Ralph Hudson's protest against Arran's depredations was made from the house of Drygrange, where the very family which the monks are supposed to have rack-rented was sheltering and nursing him, moved by a more just appreciation of his life than those more distant from it would know.

Enough has been said perhaps to suggest that the story of Scottish monasticism is not one of simple decay from within, but that on the contrary there was a real striving to attain ideals which were made extremely difficult of achievement in an age of curial corruption, royal exploitation, an avaricious nobility, and disastrously frequent wars. The Cistercians in some ways were better equipped to fight against the system of exploitation since they had a more centralised organisation than most monastic groups, and received strong backing from Cîteaux, which was spending vast sums of money to defend the rights of its daughter houses, in Scotland and elsewhere, in the Roman curia. But others fought also for an ideal, and like the Cistercians of Glenluce and Kinloss were sometimes fortunate to find commendators who came to appreciate what they represented, and supported reform. The Augustinians at Cambuskenneth had Alexander Mylne; the Benedictines at Crossraguel were to finish with Quintin Kennedy at their head; Paisley was well cared for by Archbishop Hamilton, in spite of his many serious faults; even Donald Campbell at Coupar was persuaded to give his community a chance; from 1546, Adam Forman, sent over from La Grande Chartreuse, was doggedly battling against threats to Carthusian life, from the usual sources. There were educated, even learned men among the religious, especially among the Canons Regular; some of the evidence for this has already been published elsewhere. The quality of their contribution to agricultural life has been assessed in a useful essay by Dr. Bedford Franklin;[136] after their expulsion there would be nothing like it for two hundred years.

This is not to say that all was perfect. Men like Ninian Winzet, Archibald Hay and Quintin Kennedy, appreciated what we can see more clearly than many of their contemporaries, that there were too many monasteries, and too many small ones. Everywhere small houses tended to decadence and deserved to be closed. Places like Monymusk and Pittenweem should have been suppressed, just as Adamson suppressed

133. *Ibid.*, p. 161.
134. July 19th, 1560. Morton Papers, box, 54.
135. Pollen, *Papal Negotiations*, p. 28 note.
136. T. Bedford Franklin, *A History of Scottish Farming*, chaps. vi–xii.

Cupar and St. Monance. Yet that was not so easily done, in an age which placed so much importance on chantry obligations and family associations. Adamson had not managed to suppress St. Monance entirely; it was a recent royal benefaction, and a centre of devotion, and his treatment of it must have caused uneasiness, if not positive opposition within and without his order. We have to remember also that the nobles who exploited so many religious foundations in one way or another held on to them with that odd mixture of avarice, immorality, superstition, and piety, which appears in the highest circles of church and state at the time. They wanted prayers and cash. The progress of the catholic reformation would have given them more of the first, and less of the latter, thus testing the proportions of superstition and piety in their characters. The protestant reformation presented a means of acquiring more wealth, with a more secure title, while retaining a lien upon heaven too. By 1560 only four Scottish monasteries had regular abbots; restoration of the regular monastic system would have involved reversing the trend of three generations and would have been impossible without strong backing of reform by an efficient and orthodox ruler.

The commendators as a whole helped to blacken the reputation of regular religious life in Scotland. As was pointed out earlier in this essay, historians have not been particular about distinguishing between regular and irregular superiors. Patrick Hepburn brought notoriety to Scone, as another commendator did to Kilwinning, another to Arbroath, another to Balmerino. Passages from Lindsay about abbots and their mistresses have been very familiar in volumes of Scottish church history, regardless of the fact that so few of the abbots involved were ever monks. Not only their immorality but also their financial exactions brought their subject monks into disrepute. After the death of James V, Lisle wrote to Henry VIII: " Douglas told that the late King of Scots had gotten his hands on 4 of the best churches of Scotland for 4 of his bastard sons—Kelso, Melrose, Holyrood, St. Andrews, all of which he hath greatly exhaunced the rents and kept the profit to his own use and had put out all the fermers of them with which they were sore discontent."[137] What was done in this way was done in the name of the whole community by the officers employed in collecting the revenues; it would have been better for the actual maintenance of religious observance, and for the reputation of the monks who were trying to preserve it, if the king had confiscated outright part of the abbey's excessive accumulation of property, leaving enough near a monastery for the community's needs. As we have noted above, this would have required more radical thinking in Scotland and in the Roman curia than the times produced; it might also have led to awkward comparisons, somewhat to the royal disadvantage, because as landlords the monks were usually so much more desirable than nobles or kings.

Something of what happened at Melrose under one of James V's sons has already been noted. There is a queer twist in later history which may be remembered. When James Stewart, later regent, took over his half-brother's assets, he employed as agent Sir John Bellenden of Auchnoull, so well-known as justice-clerk. Bellenden's ruthless efficiency did not help Melrose, nor in the end did it help the regent. As a result of his callousness elsewhere, Hamilton of Bothwellhaugh's wife was to go mad and die.[138] Her husband laid the blame at Moray's door, much as Moray

137. *Hamilton Papers*, i, 358.
138. *The Historie of King James the Sext*, (Edinburgh, 1804), pp. 74-7.

and his confederates threw blame for other happenings upon the religious orders. There was no monastic life at Melrose or St. Andrews any longer, but James Stewart, prior of St. Andrews, earl of Moray and regent of Scotland, was still using commendatory titles when he was killed at Linlithgow, shot by a man whose hatred expressed not simply ideological opposition but reaction to a great complex of injustice towards individuals and communities.

VII

There are numerous glimpses of personalities and personal relationships in sixteenth-century Scottish history, religious or secular, which are suggestive and demand to be followed up; there are glimpses also of practices familiar to later periods which suddenly kindle the reader's imagination and give a sense of contact with the earlier age; illuminating examples of contemporary problems appear unexpectedly in such sources as protocol books. A few examples may help to underline some of the points already made in the course of these notes, and to remind readers of the great field of Scottish monastic history not even touched in these pages.

A little before the century opened, in February 1496-7, Dene George Hume, Canon of Holyrood and vicar of Balmaghie, demitted the vicarage in the hands of the abbot and community, desiring them for love of Jesus Christ to receive the vicarage because he could not live therein as a good catholic and religious (*tanquam bonus catholicus et religiosus vir*). Renewing his oath of obedience to the abbot, he was received by him as a canon regular of the monastery, as he had been before. This was the climax of a personal history whose beginning is obscure, although we know that in 1488 George Hume had disappeared from his monastery.[139] What would have happened to him had he lived a little later? As noted elsewhere in this volume a successor as vicar of Balmaghie, Dene William Forman, fell into heresy. How many regular clergy in the years before the reformation found it hard to be good catholics and religious while in charge of appropriated parishes? How many were farmed out by their superiors because they were awkward members of their communities, as John Saunders (or Sanderson) appears to have been by Abbot Malin of Glenluce?[140]

In 1518 the duke of Albany wrote to Rome about the state of the Trinitarians in Scotland. He mentioned that three or four professed members of that order usually resided at Houston, which had recently been given *in commendam* to a secular cleric, who would be less likely to secure a distribution of goods for the redeeming of prisoners than a member of the order itself would be. He requested that an inquiry should be set up, so that the indemnities of captives and the good state of the religious should be maintained. How sincere was Albany?[141] Were the Scottish Trinitarians still employed in redeeming captives? What was the result of the inquiry which the pope did in fact commision? Houston, occupied by only one friar, was annexed later to Peebles.[142] The Trinitarians were undoubtedly short of men and there is evidence to show that

---

139. See *Protocol Book of James Young*, nos. 103, 120, 564, 859.
140. See Acta Dom. Con. et Sess, xxii, 115; xxiii, 20. Acts and Decreets, xxxvi, 213. After the reformation he appears as an Exhorter at Glenluce. *Thirds of Benefices*, p. 292.
141. Arch. Vat., Armarium, xxxix, vol, 32, ff. 113-4.
142. Hutton Collections, iv, 30.

they adopted a policy of staffing their wealthier houses and abandoning the less wealthy to the care of a single friar or a secular chaplain. So we find Robert Arnot, Minister of Scotlandwell, setting all the teinds of their church of Moonzie, parsonage and vicarage, to his half-brother, so that more brethren could be placed in the house of Scotlandwell. (The reddendo to Scotlandwell was in oats, barley, and other readily marketable goods). The prior of Dirleton, Friar William Madder, resigned the priory of Dirleton in January 1539-40 " for the augmentation of divine service at Scotlandwell." reserving a life-rent and arranging for a secular chaplain to be maintained at Dirleton to pray for its founder. Dirleton in fact was annexed to Scotlandwell as Houston had been to Peebles, but even after that reinforcement there was anxiety about conserving the order's rights at Scotlandwell. The picture suggested by a number of documents associated with Scotlandwell and Dirleton[143] is one of a failing organisation whose members were desperately trying to avoid total eclipse, holding on to a number of appropriated churches, among their other assets. Whatever personal scandals there may, or may not, have been among the Trinitarians, their general condition gave ample material for severe criticism by those interested in pastoral reform and those interested in a new distribution of property.

The affair at Kilwinning referred to early in this essay should be noted at greater length. In 1512 James IV was writing to the pope, and to the Cardinal Protector of Scotland, to the effect that William, abbot of Kilwinning, had promised to resign and that Master John Forman, precentor of Glasgow cathedral, was the royal nominee to the vacant abbatial throne. (The vacant precentorship would go to a royal servant).[144] Certain apostolic bulls were eventually produced in favour of John Forman, and it may be presumed that the documents were genuine. This is more than can be said about the resignation of Abbot William, as the method of inducting Master John Forman was to show. Shortly after Palm Sunday, 1512, the Earls of Angus and Glencairn with a force of about sixty armed men broke into the abbey, the representatives of John Forman having been refused entry by the monks. The abbot refused to have any discussion with Glencairn, " whereupon the earl seized the abbot (who resisted, and often called out, and earnestly entreated to be set at liberty) with force and violence by the arms, throwing off his sword and shield and giving them to one of his followers; and while the armed men surrounded him, sometimes threatening, sometimes fawning upon him, to make him submit himself to the pleasure of Mr. John Forman, the pretended Abbot of Kilwinning, and open the gates of the abbey to the king's herald and others of the same opinion standing without the gates, held him long in his embrace, until induced by the persuasion of Alexander Scott, Prior of Kilwynning, and of some of the armed men, he let him go, panting for breath, and calling out, Suffer me to sit here, and cut off my head, because, while I live, I never shall agree to what you propose. Nevertheless, after he had sat and rested a while, and was desirous to rest longer, the earl seized him a second time, while he struggled and called out, and dragged him against his will to the gates of the place. When there, trusting, as he alleged, to his appeal, and besides being under the protection of the Roman pontiff, he refused to open the

---

143. See Protocol Bk. of John Feyrn, ff. 38v., 73r., 77v., 129v., for Dirleton and Scotlandwell transactions.
144. *Letters*, p. 280.

gates to the king's herald, and Archibald Earl of Angus, and others, who were standing without, although earnestly requested by the earl to do so." The anxiety to have the gates opened by the abbot in person, so that he could be said to have admitted the supplanter in the person of his pro-curator, is typical of medieval legalism. Eventually Abbot William, exhausted by rough treatment and unable to expel the men, who had invaded the abbey church itself, "their armour clanging." took refuge elsewhere. still protesting. His appeal against what had taken place was read publicly at the doors of Glasgow cathedral on April 7th, 1513, and then fixed to the cathedral door.[145] It is a curious reflection on some historiography that John Forman's abduction of a woman should be recorded as an event in church history, rather than his eviction of Abbot William. "A critical evaluation of royal letters on Scottish ecclesiastical affairs " might be an interesting subject for a research thesis.

In 1536 Thomas Brown, monk of Kilwinning, made the town's organs for Ayr. There was some dispute about payment: the town treasurer asserting he had given £5 to Dene Thomas, who denied having received it. Was the same Dene Thomas the monk of Kilwinning who was paid £13-6-8 in 1550-51 for mending the organ? He had a servant to help him then, whoever he was, and the servant received 13s. 4d., and they had a quart of wine between them into the bargain.[146] Presumably the monk of the same abbey who was paid in 1535 for binding a mass-book for the town kirk was another colleague of Dene Thomas, unless the latter was something of a jack-of-all-trades.[147] Was he more mechanic than musician? And where had he learned the craft of organ building? There were, as is now well known, many religious who were noted musicians; several were canons regular of St. Augustine, such as Robert Carver at Scone, James Baldowy at St. Andrews, Andrew Blackhall at Holyrood, David Peebles at St. Andrews. Not that their musical activity was appreciated by all their brethren, to judge by the strong objections voiced by Robert Richardson of Cambuskenneth, a devotee of plain chant in good Gregorian tradition.[148] What is the good of singing in unison, he asks, if there is no unison of charity and love? And how have Augustinians, of all people, come to accept musical novelties so easily, since the rule of St. Augustine plainly condemns those who are now introducing peculiar masses con-cocted according to their own fantasy? Did not Petrarch point out that Athanasius actually forbade singing in church? And what a waste of time the modern music is, so ridiculously prolonging a single mass. It leaves too little time for study, and in any case violates the ideal principle of ecclesiastical music, which is to give equal value to words and notes. Richardson's strongly worded criticism of the composers among his brethren (he exempts the abbot of Inchcolm from his criticisms—" that striking example to our whole order in Scotland ") is a reminder of the intellectual quality of the Augustinian canons in other fields than music, witnessed to so impressively by their activity in the university of St. Andrews where they produced such men as John Annand, John Law,

---

145. *Archaeological and Historical Collections of Ayr and Wigton*, i, pp. 180-3. The relevant documents were printed from the Protocol Book of Cuthbert Simson by Bain and Rogers, *Diocesan Registers of Glasgow*, vol. ii, pp. 477 seq. There is much more to be said about the case than I have attempted here; it illustrates the fundamental problems in the contemporary relationship of papacy—crown—and monastic community.

146. *Ayr Burgh Accts.* (S.H.S.), pp. 28-9, 73, 74, 112.

147. *Ibid.*, p. 73.

148. *Commentary on the Rule of St. Augustine* (ed. G. G. Coulton, S.H.S., 1935), pp. 77-81.

RODERICI MACLENII HECTO=
ROGENIS SCOTI GATHAELICI
IONITAE DE INTVITV PRO=
PHETICO D. COLVMBAE
IONIDOS LIBER
PRIMVS.

ΙΑΚΩΒΟΥ ΤΟΥ ΘΟΎΡΧΘΟΝΟΣ
ΤΟΥ ΤΗΣ ΕΚΚΛΗΣΙΑΣ ΡΟΣ
ΣΕΩΣ ΥΠΟΔΕΚΑΔΟΡΟΣ
ΕΙΣ ΦΙΛΕΧΘΡΟΝ ΑΝΔΡΑ
ΣΤΙΧΙΔΙΟΝ.

Πᾶτα φιλεχθρος ἀνὴρ, συλλαίνει σεμνο πεοσωπῶν,
ὡς ἀγαθόν τε κακοῦ, μήποτε μᾶλλον ἔχει.

Et dixi, Quis dabit mihi pennas ficut columbæ?
& uolabo, & requiefcam?
Pfal. LIIII.

Excufum Typis Antonij Bladi Romæ apud
Campum Floræ Menfe Maio
M. D. XLIX.

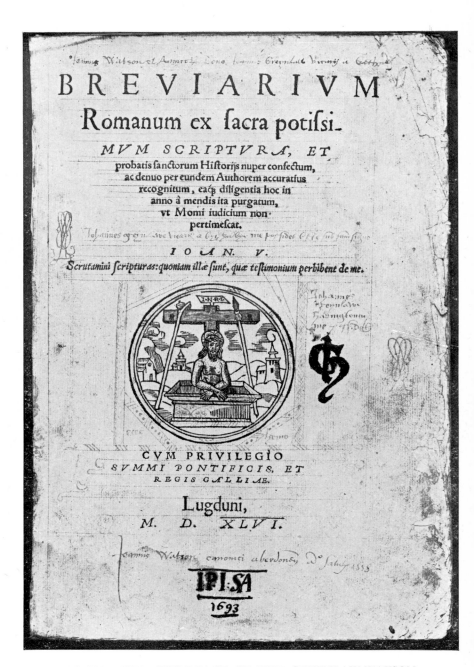

PLATE XVIII. TITLE-PAGE OF THE GREENLAW-WATSON
BREVIARY.

John Duncanson, and other pillars of St. Leonard's. Did Richardson speak as strongly as he wrote? Were there many others like him in Scottish Augustinian houses? If so there must have been sharp, even acrid, discussion at times.

An example of decadence in an Augustinian house is provided by the visitation of Pittenweem carried out by John Winram, subprior of St. Andrews, in 1554.[149] It illustrates the type of problem which might well arise in a small community, yet there is nothing in it that might not be found in earlier medieval visitations elsewhere; nor is there anything novel in Winram's provisions for reform in his charter of recession in the same year. He had received witnesses, including the rector of Muckart and some laymen, in the prior's cell; the prior, who had to receive canonical correction, was presumably absent. Patrick Forman, who was subprior and six other canons, are named. The chamberlain produced the book of accounts, which seems to have excited no comment. The divine office appears to have needed stricter attention. Winram ruled that in summer matins should be recited chorally at 6, in winter at 7, and the need for audibility was stressed. To stir up popular devotion, lauds were to be sung on solemn feasts; then the bell would ring for the Lady mass, after which the brethren would celebrate masses in turn until the time of the community high mass. Failure to observe these arrangements would be penalised by loss of the pittances and other commons.

There were regulations for the dormitory, where boys or youths were not to be allowed to spend the night. Women were to be excluded from it, and also from the canons' little houses in the priory gardens. No member of the community was to leave the priory's bounds without permission from the subprior, nor (an enforcement of the ordinary *socius* rule) without a companion. No one was to be out late after the *Salve*, or pass the night in town or make a habit of getting special permission to do so. Such allowances as habit money were to be put to their proper purpose, and not used by the canons to provide gifts for parents or friends, without the subprior's permission, and even then only if their habits and room furnishings were respectable; nor were they to be used by the canons to oblige themselves in the official of St. Andrew's books, on behalf of a debtor. The subprior was to see that members of the community were kept occupied as scribes, or in other religious exercises, when not actually at divine service; and there was to be spiritual reading daily at both meals.

Some particular offenders against the rule were named; one for absence from the common table and gossiping about his fellow canons; another for entering a lady's house; another for paying social visits; another for sharp words about a female neighbour. This last offence may have had more to it than the record suggests; the offender was to be confined to the cloister and to receive the discipline for a month. Who was the lady so firmly vindicated? Some of Winram's provisions may touch on abuses more or less serious, according to our interpretation of the text and what we read into it. Taking it straightforwardly it presents a picture of the kind of relaxation of religious life to be expected in a small community pulled between its traditional obligations in church and cloister and its pastoral obligations and social connections outside.

---

149. See Hutton Coll., vi, 23.

Signatures to documents sometimes draw attention to the probability of discussions which must have played a part in shaping the future. John Rough was resident in the Edinburgh Blackfriars for some time, with Richard Marshall as one of his colleagues.[150] Did they discuss the actions of Henry VIII? Marshall was a fugitive from Henry's rule; Rough was one of his agents.[151] What effect on religious communities in Scotland did the English exiles have? Marshall was not the only one among the Dominicans; he and Henry Mason were to spend many years in St. Andrews, in close association with the life of the university. We know the names of eighteen Franciscans who fled from England to Scotland.[152] Bearing in mind the numerical strength of the Franciscan friars, this is a large increase north of the border. How did it affect the Scottish houses economically? Did it intensify their begging for alms? Did the English refugees appear to " fleich " more than the natives? How far were they really absorbed into Scottish life? Some, Marshall for example, became closely identified with Scottish affairs. When Friar Andrew Cottis preached his foolish sermon, advocating that the Our Father should be addressed to the saints as well as to God, was he already hostile to the English friar who had reached such eminence in St. Andrews and who opposed his views? And what did the more learned among the Greyfriars have to say about the absurd position into which Friar Cottis had blundered, perhaps in his too rash and simple zeal to defend the cult of the saints, already under attack from heretics? It is surely unreasonable to imagine that all the other Greyfriars in Scotland were his staunch supporters.

There are so many other questions which come to mind. What was the real trouble at Monymusk in 1534-5 that prompted the prior, David Fairlie, to command Alan Galt, one of the canons, " to keip his chalmer in the dormitour and pass nocht furth of it bot *ad necessaria* and that he be in continuale seilence with all maner of man except hyme that mackis hyme ministratioun and that he be all this tyme in breid and aill and twa dais in the ouik *videlicet* Vednisday and friday at his discipline."[153] The canons supported Alan Galt and were suspended from all divine service by the prior, whereupon they appealed to the bishop of Aberdeen and the pope.[154] Was David Fairlie acting unjustly, as the canons said? Or was he trying to reform a small and decayed community? As he was at St. Andrews university in 1515 he may have been actuated by ideals of reform. He seems to have been a man of some culture, since he possessed the *Poetae Latini* published by Aldus at Venice in 1502, and the *Arithmetica Boethii* which was edited by Lefèvre and published at Paris in 1514.

There was trouble at Monymusk, but whatever it was has been generally forgotten, and it is Balmerino which bears the most scandalous of reputations, set in Lindsay's much quoted couplet. The effect of the commendatory system on other Cistercian houses has been discussed slightly already, and credit given to such men as Malin and Reid who took their responsibilities seriously. Balmerino illustrates the worst effects of the system, and much of its unsavoury reputation was due to that old

150.   Cal. of St. Andrews Charters, nos. 287, 290.
151.   See A. G. Dickens, *Lollards and Protestants in the Diocese of York*, 1509-1558 (Oxford, 1959), p. 197.
152.   *Letters and Papers of Hen. VIII*, vii, no. 1607.
153.   *Antiquities of the Shires of Aberdeen and Banff*, iii, p. 492.
154.   *Protocol Bk. of Sir John Cristisone*, (Scottish Record Soc.), nos. 144-7.

reprobate abbot, Robert Forester, whose illegitimate children would have continued the exploitation of the monastic property if he had succeeded in his plans. Life under the Forester regime must have been attractive to a number of rascals. It does not appear to have attracted the royal interest in reform professed by James V, who wrote in 1530 that it would be " for the great advantage of the church " if Forester were allowed to feu the lands of Balmerino. The activity of the abbots of Chaalis and Glenluce would have given serious cause for anxiety at Balmerino if the king had been behind them. As it was, they failed; and Balmerino remains notoriously associated with such characters as Forester and his chamberlain Alexander Car, and John Yestir, homicide and fornicator, who features in the St. Andrews Kirk Session Records.[155] It would seem from the extant records of Balmerino that he was attracted to the monastic life, when it was almost extinct, by the usefulness of a monk's portion. How many others were there, like him, but a little more respectable outwardly? Inchaffray was another centre of opportunity, and Newbattle under Mark Ker, for those in search of an unearned income. Were there also monks in these houses who kept quietly to a life of private devotion, receiving their portions, cultivating their gardens, and hoping for better things?

There may have been, when we remember the midnight funeral of an abbot and the election of his successor, at Newbattle in 1529; quashed in favour of a royal nominee.[156] Or the battle of the monks of Coupar-Angus to have Alexander Spens as abbot, who " was put to the horne for perseuing his just title anent the said place of Cowper."[157] Or the Premonstratensians of Dryburgh who dared to elect one of themselves as abbot, in contempt of royal authority and contrary to the privilege of the realm, and went to prison for it in 1518.[158] From Fearn to Glenluce there was a story of resistance which has still to be written. The Roman curia had a hand in what happened, but only gave Scotland what Scotland, in the person of its rulers, plainly wanted. As so many of the dates mentioned in these pages will have indicated, the monastic ideal was fighting for survival before there were any protestants to attack it.

VIII

It is surely astonishing that the struggle was still going on, even after the fight against the system of commendators had been lost. There was real vitality among the friars, monks, and canons regular as late as 1560, in spite of all the frustration they experienced, their internal weaknesses, and the external pressure. Benedictines of Paisley and Crossraguel, the Cistercians of Kinloss and Glenluce, the Augustinian canons of St. Andrews and Cambuskenneth, the Blackfriars and the Greyfriars, these religious were not merely spectators of the revolution which took place in Scotland. They produced men who were in the thick of the conflict, on one side or another. The list of those who died for their beliefs shows it. So does the life of Knox himself, who was first drawn to the new teaching by Friar Gilyem and called upon to preach by Friar Rough. John Winram was an Augustinian canon, Willock and Craig were at one time Dominicans. The Earl of Argyll had an ex-Carmelite chaplain, John

---

155. *Reg. Kirk Sess. St. Andrews*, i, p. 146, for Car, pp. 180-1, for Yestir, see also *Letters of James V*, p. 286.
156. *St. Andrews Formulare*, i, 280-1.
157. Easson, *Charters of the Abbey of Coupar Angus* (S.H.S.), ii, 275-6. *Acts of Lords of Council*, p. 197.
158. *Acts of the Lords of Council*, pp. 130-1.

Douglas, one of the leading preachers. (Not to be confused with that other John Douglas who was Rector of the university at St. Andrews and also joined the reformers). The part played by men like Alesius, Macalpine and Seton is well known.

On the other side were men like Robert Reid, Quintin Kennedy, and others already named elsewhere in this essay, especially that later generation of friars which came to the fore when John Hamilton became archbishop of St. Andrews. Knox names some of them who got permission from Queen Mary to preach; Black, Abercromby, Roger. Leslie in his *History* has a story of Father Andrew Leich, a Dominican employed by the archbishop of Glasgow, who was saying mass in Leith when it was besieged by the English forces and carried on at the altar unmoved by bombardment, even when a shot crashed through the church.[159] There was something of the spirit of John Adamson in him, as there must have been in Father Black. The latter's experience of being waylaid and wounded was not unique, for the case of two Franciscans has come to light, of whom one was that Father Thomas Motto who helped Father Hay to compile his chronicle of the Scottish Greyfriars, and was still alive in the friary at Rouen in 1586. The attack on Thomas Motto and his companion, Friar Thomas Cristeson, appears to have been late in 1558, or early in 1559, and a servant of the laird of Fordel was involved, which suggests the activity of the Congregation and its supporters in Fife.[160] One wonders how much beating up there really was. It would become unsafe to say much about such happenings if one wanted to avoid kneeling at the mercat cross, or sitting in the stocks, with a label round one's neck saying " Behald the contempnar " or " False toung he leyd." Would the Regent Moray's men have handled gently the friars whom they hunted out of shelter at Dalhousie? And to where did those friars escape?[161]

In addition to the friars who have been mentioned, Johnstone, Black, Leich, Roger, Abercromby, Macneill, Aitken, Arbuckle, Veitch and Hunter, there were others who refused to join the reformers and either entered communities abroad or kept up some sort of fugitive ministry at home. We cannot be sure at present what happened to many of them; about half are still unaccounted for.[162] Even if their names are found among those of pensioners, in the *Thirds of Benefices*, nothing is proved thereby as to their real allegiance, as we see, for example, in the case of David Craig, Carmelite of Aberdeen, of James Hopper, Carmelite prior of Linlithgow, and of William Henderson, sometime prior of the Dominicans in Stirling. David Craig eventually entered the Scottish Benedictine community at Ratisbon.[163] Friar Hopper's life pension of £16 from the fruits of the Linlithgow house was cut off by royal authority in June,

159. *De Rebus Gestis Scotorum* (Rome 1578, reprint 1675), p. 524.

160. Justiciary Records, (S.R.O.), xi, f. 3v. For an example from the other side, a foray from Castle Semple in 1559 with which two Dominicans (Friars Allan Peter and Thomas King) were associated, see f. 37v.

161. Thomas Archibald to Archbishop Beaton, 18th Dec., 1560: " The laird of Dalhousy is in ward in the Castell of Sanctandrois, becaus he gaif three or four puir Friars meal in his place. My Lord of Arran and my Lord James seirchit all his place, and gatt thame not; but brunt all the bukis and mess—claiths that was in the place." Keith, *Affairs of Church and State*, iii, p.8.

162. There are various problems requiring elucidation in connection with such material as we have in, for example, the *Thirds of Benefices*. Aliases are a problem, and variant forms of a name: one man can appear as Henderson, Henryson, Litstar, or—in a Latin document—Tinctor. A man might be known by a patronymic or a geographical designation, e.g. John Gibson or John Elgin. Thomas Chrystall is also called Wawan. In most cases to do with religious we have no means of knowing their standing in the communities to which they belonged; were they students or seniors, invalids or in sound health? Such questions are relevant to any attempt to draw conclusions from the existing evidence.

163. See Appendix II, n. 18.

1576, because " the said freir James has not gevin the confessioun of his faith nor his assent and subscriptioun to the articles of religioun;" he had not promised in the presence of James' bishops or superintendents to accept his authority, nor brought testimonial of this in writing, but had departed from Scotland to live overseas " in the cumpany of freiris and papists," and so lost his pension *ipso facto*.[164] Henderson was one of those who went abroad, by February 1573-4 at least, when he was denounced, with the Franciscan James Peebles, as a rebel.[165] A reference to him in the protocol book of Gilbert Grote, (no. 306), suggests that he went to Flanders.

The Scottish exiles settled abroad in a way that itself suggests how much they were part of a European and not simply a national tradition. Sometimes an epitaph witnesses to the regard in which they were held. The provincial of the Observant Greyfriars, John Paterson, who died at Louvain on February 20th, 1573, is the subject of the one which follows:

> Impiger in sanctis, lustris bis quinque tribusque,
> Ordine Francisci serviit ille Deo.
> Ordinis et sacri summa cum laude minister,
> Quum late patuit, Scotia tota fuit:
> Coniuge cum cara Scotorum rex Iacobus
> Quintus ab hoc solitus sumere sacra fuit.
> Lovanii ter quinque annos fuit exul in isto
> Conventu eximii signa dedit viri.[166]

He was not the only Scottish Franciscan in the Low Countries, (one, as we have already noted, was martyred there), nor were the Franciscans the only refugee religious to be found in Flanders. Two monks of the Charterhouse at Perth died at Bruges in 1568, according to a Dutch source which gives their names as Walter Towris and Alexander Calant.[167] Both appear as signatories in Scottish Carthusian documents, along with Dom William Clapen, the last professed monk of Perth, who died in the Charterhouse of Vallis Profunda, in the diocese of Sens, in 1590.[168] Three years later William Chisholm, formerly coadjutor bishop of Dunblane, died, a Carthusian also, having resigned his French see of Vaison. Adam Forman, the prior of the Perth Charterhouse, remained in Scotland until 1567, attempting to secure the order's property in the hope of a religious restoration, and to obtain in the meantime adequate pensions for some of the " poor brethren " of the place. After holding office in Swiss, French and Bavarian houses he died in 1574. *De Ordine optime meritus*, wrote a Carthusian historian, giving him the highest form of praise current in their order.[169]

A rapid note of some of the names which appear, in connection with the effort to maintain traditional sacramental practice in Scotland itself, may encourage further inquiry into the history of catholic resistance. Malcolm Fleming, prior of the Premonstratensians of Whithorn, was among those accused of saying mass and hearing confessions in 1563.

164. Reg. of Presentation of Benefices, (S.R.O.), f. 129v.
165. *R.P.C.*, ii, 334, 575-6.
166. Molanus, *Hist. de la Ville de Louvain*, i, p. 259.
167. A Dutch correspondent of Fr. O'Dea forwarded the names as *Tolbridge* and *Calant*, from a misreading of *Towris* hardly surprising in someone quite unfamiliar with sixteenth-century Scots names. Towris had been sacristan of the Charterhouse; cf. Hutton Coll., vii, 39.
168. Cf. James VI Hospital Writs, sect. 2, nos. 70, 71.
169. See *R.P.C.*, i, p. 250; *R.S.S.*, v, 3435; Leon Le Vasseur, *Ephemerides Ordinis Cartusiensis* (Montreuil, 1891), i, p. 579; Molin, *Historia Cartusiana*, (Tournai, 1904), ii, p. 428.

Dene Mungo Wilson and Dene James Jamesoun, along with Dene John Lun of Coldingham, were in trouble for saying mass at Dryburgh.[170] A monk of Melrose, Dene John Watson, was another offender. John Logan, sometime monk of New Abbey, was accused of profaning the sacraments, as late as 1590.[171] He had been a reader in the new kirk, but his name now appeared with those of several notorious catholics, including Gilbert Brown, abbot of New Abbey, that " famous excommunicat, foirfaultit and perverting papist, who evir since the reformatioun of religioune had conteinit in ignorance and idolatrie allmost the haill south-west partis of Scotland, and had been continowallie occupyit in practiseing of heresy." Was Gilbert Brown responsible for John Logan's recovered orthodoxy? The names of both are a reminder of the revolution in personal belief and morals which could and did take place, even if rarely, in the post-reformation period. The change in Gilbert Brown's life after his ordination in 1586 is truly remarkable. Who, incidentally, was Freir George Levingstoun, also called to account for his actions in 1590?

The Franciscan Thomas Aitken was summoned for celebrating mass in 1572.[172] Another Franciscan, John Affleck, perhaps a Conventual friar of Haddington, was accused in 1569 of " abusing " the sacraments at Greenlaw.[173] As late as 1580 the Jesuit Father Abercrombie could write of the Franciscan Fathers Veitch and Leitch: " I know only two of those religious who constantly go about the kingdom, saying mass, now in one place, now in another; they are often in my father's house, sometimes together, sometimes separately, but at Easter he has one of them. One is called Robert Veitch, the other N. Leitch, both good scholars, skilled in the Bible, Fathers and Councils, good preachers; they are Franciscans, dressed in lay clothes they do good work. When I came to the town where they were they came to me and said: ' Would that you had brought a hundred of your order with you ' "[174] By then, of course, the Society of Jesus contained a number of excellent Scots recruits, some with considerable seniority. Among these Scots was John Durie, son of the commendator of Dunfermline at the time of the reformation. What was happening at Dunfermline itself in 1580, if Father Abercrombie's account of a residue of monks who still recited the Divine Office in private is reliable?[175]

Resistance among the Augustinian canons is represented by Denes James Abircrummy, John Ged, and William Heslop, who were summoned in 1571, and failed to appear.[176] But it is among the Benedictines of Paisley and Crossraguel that the strongest monastic opposition to protestantism is found. The names of a number of monks appear in summonses on charges of " mass-mongering,"[177] but of even more interest perhaps than these charges is the will of Dene John Mure,[178] subprior of Crossraguel, who died on November 15th, 1585, a few months after it was

170. *R.P.C.*, ii, p. 40.
171. *Ibid.*, iv, p. 522.
172. Pitcairn, i, pt. 2, p. 35. With Thomas Aitken was a monk, Dene John Shaw—order unidentified.
173. *R.P.C.*, ii, p. 40.
174. *Innes Review*, vii, p. 32.
175. In 1584 certain monks of Dunfermline refused to sign the commendator's tack. *R.P.C.*, iii, p. 643.
176. *R.P.C.*, ii, p. 91.
177. Some appear in the list of 1563. In 1568, Dene John Maxwell in Crossraguel, and others in Maybole and Girvan, were to be arrested for " their accustomat ydolatrie of mess saying." (Ailsa Papers, Inventory (S.R.O.), v, 112).
178. Edinburgh Testaments, (S.R.O.), vol. 14, ff. 278-81.

drawn up. " In ye first I leif my saule to almyte god, the glorious virgin marie and ye haill company in heavin, my body to be bureit in ye chaptre kirk in ye abbay of corssragwell." There are legacies to Dene Michael Dewar, Dene John Maxwell, Dene John Mure, Dene John Bryce. His executor is Dene Gilbert Kennedy, brother in Crossraguel. The will refers also to a monk of Paisley and a catholic layman in that town : " to dene thomas locheid in paslay to pray for me twa crounis of ye sone Item henry houstoun in paslay ane angill nobill in rememberance. The rest of all my guidis dettis and geir I leif to ye pure seik and indigent personis," and he curses any who prevent them from getting the legacy. The John Mure who appears among the legatees made his own will in 1595, a few days before he died, and Gilbert Kennedy was one of the witnesses, along with Mr. Michael Hamilton, reader in Maybole.[179] Gilbert Kennedy lived on, last of them all, it would seem. On December 7th, 1614, " Mr. William Birnie moderator of the presbyterie of Air requested be my L. of Glasgow to tak ordour with Sir Gilbert Kennedy priest reported that Sir George Hamilton brother to my L. abercorne quhen he came out of Ireland came in to him be ye waye and comforted him and gave him ane hundreth merk."[180] The kirk was much exercised in those parts at that time on account of another priest, the Jesuit John Ogilvie, and also by two painters " who came in secreitlie to the town (Glasgow) and painted in divers houses the crucifix, qlk gave slaunder to many."[181] It would seem that the work of Quintin Kennedy had not been entirely vain, nor that of the Blackfriars appointed to preach in his diocese by the archbishop of Glasgow. John Hamilton, archbishop of St. Andrews and commendator of Paisley, who for all his sins dealt well with the abbey and town of Paisley, should also have some credit for the survival of a catholic community there. In many ways he was so representative of sixteenth-century catholicism in Scotland, and of many of the higher clergy who were closely associated with the religious orders; bastard son of a great earl, closely related to the royal house, pushed into an ecclesiastical career before he was old enough to make a sound or independent choice, hopelessly mixed up with his family's politics, a self-proclaimed scandal in his attachment to a mistress, grasping at his doctor's certificate to excuse his immorality, but an educated man and appreciative of goodness in others. The man who questioned him about his religion, just before he was hanged, " culd find nathing bot that he wes ane papyst, and exhortit sik as wer neir hand upoun the scaffold to abyd at the catholick faith, sua he termit the papistrie." He asked for a priest to hear his confession, and " sua he continowit to the death in his papistrie as he levit."[182]

The system which John Hamilton represented was not dead, although its problems were so heavy and so many of its members were, like himself, a paradox of belief and practice, something not unusual in christians of any age. Religious orders were suppressed in Scotland and the vast property of the great abbeys alienated from its former use. Those who had hoped to see it used to endow a national system of education, and of care for the poor and the sick, were to be bitterly disappointed. It went, as Knox said, to the devil for the most part; only not to the old kirk, but to

---

179. *Ibid.*, 28, ff. 257-8.
180. Gilbert Kennedy was a cousin of the subprior, John Mure: cf. Edinburgh Testaments, 14 f., 280.
181. *Miscellaneous Papers Principally Illustrative of Events in the Reigns of Queen Mary and King James VI* (Maitland Club, 1834), p. 170.
182. *Diurnal of Occurrents*, p. 205.

the same rapacious nobility which already had most of it under an insecure ecclesiastical title. The call to a monastic life would have a different ring henceforth for Scots. Before Dene Gilbert Kennedy was dead, the Scottish Benedictine house at Ratisbon was well established. The Minims, the Augustinian Friars and the Capuchins had their Scottish members. The new kinds of community would also find Scottish novices. The Society of Jesus received them in its early days. St. Vincent de Paul, in the middle of the seventeenth century, had a Scot among his priests, whom he sent with two Irish Fathers to work in Scotland. There was still work for religious orders, old and new, taught by bitter experience in the past what to avoid.

Nor was appreciation of conventual life confined to catholics. That great protestant, Robert Boyd of Trochrague, who died in 1627, left a commentary on the epistle to the Ephesians, which was published posthumously in 1652, and which contains a remarkable plea for the restoration of some form of monastic life, deploring the " sacrilegious wickedness" of his own times which had done away with those " religious places once well and abundantly established through the whole kindom." He would have had them purified and restored so that those drawn to embrace a more strict form of christian life than ordinary might there take up the cross and give themselves wholly to the divine service. He saw in the restoration of such establishments a means of providing a training ground for the young, places of prayer and quiet for the aged, comfort for the bereaved, refuge for the poor; they would shelter virginity and widowhood, and ensure a continual round of prayer.

With Boyd's statement of the ideal of religious life this attempt to stimulate a re-assessment of its forms in sixteenth-century Scotland will have to close. Those readers who have themselves studied the subject will not, I hope, discover many serious errors in what has been written, even though they may differ over points of emphasis or interpretation. They will certainly regret omissions. There is so little about the nuns; although their houses were very few they also had their struggles, and there is more to their story than Cardinal Sermoneta's well known letter might suggest. If some orders of men have been passed over almost in silence it is sometimes because readers can be referred to studies already published. We have, for example, Moir Bryce's two monumental volumes *The Scottish Grey Friars*, on Franciscan history, and the valuable work of Father Backmund and Dr. Gordon Donaldson on the Scottish Premonstratensians.[183] Similarly certain important topics have been left aside which are relevant to the life of several orders; in other sections of this volume Dr. Durkan has much to say, in connection with schools, hospitals, and universities, which illuminates aspects of religious life. Almost nothing has been said about monastic farming, not because the topic has been exhausted but because a considerable introductory survey is available in Dr. T. Bedford Franklin's *History of Scottish Farming*. On many points nothing has been said because it is assumed that anyone at all interested in Scottish religious life will be familiar with the late Dr. Easson's indispensable reference book, *Medieval Religious Houses: Scotland*.

It would have been pleasant to dwell more on details of personality and the everyday life of communities, especially those things, like the reference

---

183. Norbert Backmund, " The Premonstratensian Order in Scotland, " *Innes Rev.*, iv, 25-41. Gordon Donaldson, " The Bishops and Priors of Whithorn," *Trans. Dumfries and Galloway Nat. Hist. and Antiq. Soc.*, xxvii, 128-154.

to the crimson coat for " the baby Jesus of the Senis " which reveal forms of devotion;[184] or the community librarian's inscription, on a book belonging to the Edinburgh Blackfriars, revealing the brethren's affection for a deceased member of the house;[185] or John Knox's vivid story of the conversation of Father Arth and some citizens from whom he had begged a drink[186] " Yes, Father, (said one of the gossips), ye shall have drink; but ye must first resolve a doubt which is risen amongst us, to wit, What servant will serve a man best on least expenses?" Did the friar laugh at the answer which his questioner gave? And did any bystander pass the word around that he had laughed at a cynical joke about the bishops? The passage is a reminder of work still to be done on sixteenth-century preaching. There is much also waiting to be investigated which will throw light on popular devotion and the kind of prayers used. The rosary was used, in various forms, and was presumably preached by the friars. There was a devotion to the name of Jesus, and of course to the Passion. One wonders who used a work such as Friar William Touris' *Contemplacioun of Synnaris*, or read Walter Kennedy's verses on *The Passioun of Crist*, or those other devotional pieces edited by Dr. J. A. W. Bennett for the Scottish Text Society. This essay will have served its purpose if it prompts further investigation of these and similar questions, and if it has shown a little, however slightly, of the human interest of Scottish monastic history in the sixteenth century.

---

184. " ane el crammesy satyn to be the bawby Jesus of the Senyis ane coit, price iiii li." *Treas. Accts.*, v, 301.
185. A copy of Cajetan's *De peccatis summula*, " Codex communis librarie fratrum predicatorum de Edinburgh ex industria olim dilecti patris fratris Johannis Touris." See *Early Scottish Libraries*, p. 154. Were Fr. John Towers and the Franciscan, Fr. William Towers, related to each other or to the Carthusian, Walter Towers? There are many interesting family connections of this kind which can be established (e.g. the Baldowy family).
186. Dickinson's *Knox*, i, 16.

APPENDIX I

I. STATISTICS OF RELIGIOUS ORDERS

| | NUMBER OF CONVENTUAL HOUSES | | | NUMBER OF RELIGIOUS | | | |
| | Major | Minor | | 1520-1540 | | 1559 | |
			Total	Max.	Min.	Max.	Min.
MONASTIC							
Benedictine	8	3	11	220	190	160	150
Cistercian	10	1	11	200	190	160	152
Carthusian	1	—	1	15	10	12	8
Valliscaulian	—	1	1	3	3	3	3
			—24—	438—	393—	335—	313
CANONS REGULAR							
Premonstratensian	6	—	6	85	77	65	56
Augustinian	7	4	11	160	147	130	105
Trinitarian	—	5(?)	5	26	20	15	10
			—22—	271—	244—	210—	171
FRIARS							
Dominican			12	120	100	80	70
Franciscan Conventual			7	45	35	40	30
Franciscan Observant			9	95	80	80	70
Carmelite			10	45	40	40	30
			—38—	305—	255—	240—	200
HOSPITALLERS			1	?	?	?	?
NUNS							
Cistercian			7	90	80	70	65
Dominican			1	18	12	12	10
Franciscan			2	6	4	6	4
Augustinian			1	10?	5?	8?	6?
			—11—	124—	101—	96—	85
Sum Totals			96	1138	993	881	769

(NOTE—Trinitarian Friars are placed among canons regular for statistical purposes, to draw attention to the fact that they often serve their appropriated churches in the way of canons regular.

In addition there are at least 7 non-conventual houses not recorded in the above totals.

Between 1500 and 1560, these new foundations were made: Dundee, Dominicans and Franciscan nuns; Sciennes, Dominican nuns; Greenside, Carmelites.

In the same period some ceased to function as conventual: Cistercian, Saddell; Augustinian, Canonbie (suppressed by Henry VIII); Benedictine, Fyvie (united to Arbroath); Trinitarian, Dunbar and Houston (? remain hospitals); Dominican, Cupar and St. Monance.

Between 1400 and 1500 there were 18 new foundations: Carthusians, Perth; Franciscan Observant, nine; Franciscan Conventual, Kirkcudbright; Dominican, Haddington and St. Monance; Carmelite, Inverbervie, Kingussie, Linlithgow, Queensferry; Franciscan nuns, Aberdour).

II. NUMERICAL ANALYSIS OF HOUSES

The figures are the actual number of signatories and can only be taken as an indication. Figures followed by (?) indicate that there certainly were others; otherwise they are the net figures in the house as stated.

Monks	1520-1540	1559	*Remarks*
BENEDICTINE			
Arbroath	24	20	Theiner in 1517 gives 42
Coldingham	6	8	2 in 1461
Crossraguel	10	12	
Dunfermline	26	25	
Fyvie	—	—	United to Arbroath (1508)
Iona	?	?	
Kelso	21	12–15	Theiner gives 36-40
Kilwinning	15	12	
Lesmahagow	?	5	
Lindores	25	17	
Paisley	15	16	
Pluscarden	12	10	
Urquhart	—	—	United to Pluscarden (1454)
CARTHUSIAN			
Perth	13	8	
CISTERCIAN			
Balmerino	20	12	
Beauly	8	8	
Coupar Angus	29	19	
Culross	17	11	
Deer	12	12	
Dundrennan	14	10	16 portions
Glenluce	17	16	
Kinloss	20	18	
Melrose	31	13	
Newbattle	25	14	
Saddell	—	—	United to Isles bishopric
Sweetheart	10	10	
VALLISCAULIAN			
Ardchattan	3	3?	3 in 1510
Canons Reg.			
AUGUSTINIAN			
Blantyre	—	—	Non-conventual (Jedburgh)
Cambuskenneth	14	14	
Canonbie	?	—	Suppressed
Holyrood	17	14?	In 1488, prior and 23, *Jas. Young Protocols*, no. 103
Inchaffray	15	10	
Inchcolm	15	?	3 names only recognised

Inchmahome	8	6	
Jedburgh	?	?	Plus or minus 8 (1545)
Lochleven	?	?	
Monymusk	6	—	

AUGUSTINIAN

Oronsay	?	?	Still in existence in 16th century
Pittenweem	9	6	Nine, 1542 (*Yester Writs,* 591)
St. Andrews	34?	28?	
St. Mary's Isle	—	—	Non-conventual
Scone	15	15	
Strathfillan	—	—	Cell?

AUGUSTINIANS (Vienne)

Leith	—	—	Preceptor only?

PREMONSTRATENSIAN

Dryburgh	17	10	
Fearn	9	5	
Holywood	12	10	
Soulseat	?	?	No lists
Tongland	12	11	
Whithorn	25	13	

TRINITARIAN
See additional remarks below

FRIARS
See additional remarks below

Orders of Nuns

AUGUSTINIAN

Iona	?	?

CISTERCIAN

Coldstream	12	8	
Eccles	?	?	No lists
Elcho	12	7	
Haddington	24	19	
Manuel	5	5	
North Berwick	22	17	
St. Bothans	7?	4	

DOMINICAN

Sciennes	?	12	Foundation bull says 30 (1517)

FRANCISCAN

Aberdour	5	4
Dundee	3–4?	2–3

236

III. ADDITIONAL REMARKS

Abbots and prioresses have been included only when it is certain that these were religious—at least in the sense of having made a profession and normally forming part of the effectives of the house.

Benedictines

ARBROATH: Abbot and 29 (1486) in *Arbroath*, ii, 245.
> Prior, Subprior, 40 in 1517, Theiner, *Vetera Monumenta*, no. 926.
> Commendator and 21 (*Glasgow*, 561-2) in 1546.
> In lists for 1527 and 1558 only 3 names identical (*Laing Charters*, 360, 684).
> 1560, Comm., Sp., 18 (*Ibid.*, 712).

COLDINGHAM: 2 in 1461 (C.P.R., xi, 425-6).

CROSSRAGUEL: Statutory quota of 10 (1405) Coulton, *Scottish Abbeys*, p. 48.

KELSO: Prior, Sp. and 36 or 40 in peacetime, 1517 (Theiner, no. 927).
> 1462, 17 or 18 (Suppliche, 550, f. 256r).

PAISLEY: Statutory number, 25 (Coulton, *Scottish Abbeys*, p. 48).
> Comm. and 15 (1539), Lees, *Abbey of Paisley*, app. LV.
> Comm. and 16 (1559, July 18), Paisley Library Ms. PC 1766, f. 73.

PLUSCARDEN: Only 5 in Rental (no comment in Anson), yet in 1558 a Sp. and 9 sign (Macphail, p. 125).

Carthusians

PERTH: 1478, Prior John Davidson, 14 monks, 1 novice, 2 conversi (in visitation quoted in C.Le Couteulx, *Annales Ordinis Carthus.*, vii, 589-90).
> 1529, Prior and 13 (N.L.S., Hutton, Shires, vii, 36).
> 1558, Nov. 13, Prior and 7 (S.R.O., James VI Hospital, Perth, Writs, Section 2, no. 73.)

Cistercians

COUPAR: 1521, Abbot and 28 (*Cupar*, i, 97).
> 11 of 1521 still in abbey in 1539 (13 new recruits in 18 years), cf. *Coupar Angus*, ii, 154-162.
> 12 portions are vacant in 1588, *Coupar Angus*, ii, 246.
> 1607, " the convent . . . all now deceist," *Ibid.*, ii, 251.

DUNDRENNAN: 1545, Comm. and 10, *Laing Charters*, no. 497.
> 10 in 1559 (S.R.O., Calendar of Chs., 1786, 1820).

MELROSE: 1517 to 1527, ten new names in ten years (*Scotts of Buccleuch*, ii, 134; S.R.O., Morton Papers, Box 54).
> 1536, Abbot and 28 (*Melrose Regality Records*, iii, 386).
> 1556, Comm. and 12, and 4 novices to be added by order of Visitor, S.R.O., Miscellaneous Ecclesiastical Papers, Rental.

NEWBATTLE: 1559, 28 Feb. Comm., Sp. and 7, J. McArthur, *Old Monkland*, p. 20.
> 1559, 23 June, Comm. and 14 (*Laing Charters*, no. 699).

Augustinians

ST. ANDREWS: 1555, 34 according to Martine, *Reliquiae Divi Andreae*, p. 169. But this may have been a joint deed with Pittenweem, like that in S.R.O., St. Andrews Chs., no. 323, of which 10 signatories are apparently Pittenweem. Similarly some of the " cannons of St. Andrews " at that university in 1525 are only temporarily there, one being a canon of Cambuskenneth, and two " fratres " being perhaps Irish (Burke, Macbrayne), Anderson, *Early Records*, p. 220.

Premonstratensians

SOULSEAT (Saulset): A few names of canons, but no lists, are found in R. C. Reid, *Wigtownshire Charters* (Scottish Hist. Soc.), pp. 107-110 In 1532, there is " dane Johne mcblayne " vicar of Kirkchrist in " ye ile of man " and " dene bartylmew," vicar of Cruggleton (N.L.S., Hutton, Shires, i, 99). In 1537, the former was subprior of Tongland and in 1546 the latter is said to be a canon of Whithorn (*Wigtownshire Chs.*, pp. 31, 111).

Trinitarians

ABERDEEN: Only 2 names recognisable in *Thirds of Benefices*.

HOUSTON: Held by Thos. Nudre against Christopher Howson in 1516, usually had 3 or 4 " expresse professi " (Arch. Vat., Armarium xxxix, vol. 32, ff. 113-4).

FAILFORD: Minister and 6, 1528, *Gavin Ros Protocol Bk.*, no. 912. Minister and 7, 1545-6, Feb. 9, S.R.O., Fraser Inventory, no. 137.

PEEBLES: Minister and 4, 1556, Yester Writs, no. 672.

GENERAL: Service of external churches, cf. Torthorwald (*Diocesan Reg. of Glasgow*, Grampian Club, ii, 310).

Carmelites

GENERAL: 12 names in *Thirds of Benefices*, some houses being omitted.

ABERDEEN: 6 names in *Thirds*.

BANFF: 1544, 3 sign, *Notes and Queries*, 1870, p. 472.

IRVINE: None in *Thirds*, but the prior, Robert Burn, is reader at nearby Dundonald, p. 265.

LINLITHGOW: 1545, John Scot, prior, Thos. Young, Andrew Haw, John Blyth, Hutton, Shires, Linlithgow, f. 3.
1559, James Hoppar, prior, John Blyth, *Ibid.*, f. 5.

LUFFNESS: 1560, John Rankine, prior, S.R.O., Robt. Lawder Prot. Bk., f. 205v.

QUEENSFERRY: Thomas Young, prior, 1565, but not in *Thirds*. David Balbirny being prior in 1557, S.R.O. Cal. of Charters, 1717.

Dominicans

GENERAL: Some known survivors are not in *Thirds*, e.g. Friars John Black, John Hunter, Andrew Leich and Andrew MacNeill. 38 names in *Thirds*, possibly half of total numbers.

AYR: 8 in 1557 (*Charters of Friars Preachers Ayr*, pp. 98-9).

EDINBURGH: 13 in 1479 (*Laing Chs.*, no. 177). 8 in *Thirds*, but 2 of these are Carmelites, Hoppar and his " marrow " (socius), Blyth.

GLASGOW: 10 on 6 Nov., 1557, 8 on 20 Dec., 1554, 8 on 6 Dec., 1558, in Glasgow University Archives, Miscellaneous Tacks.

INVERNESS: Andrew Philp, mentioned as prior on 28 Feb., 1570 (Feus of Kirklands, i, 198v.) is not among the signatories of 1559, *Rose of Kilravock*, p. 227.

MONTROSE: 8 sign on 28 Nov., 1531 (communication of the Rev. Ian Muirhead). 1564, 18 May: Prior (John Dodds), subprior (Wm. Gibson), Robert Jackson, John Adamson, friars, S.R.O., Abbreviation of Charters of Feus of Kirklands, i, 169v.

ST. ANDREWS: Refounded in 16th century for 6 and 6 sign on 27 Aug., 1517, N.L.S., Hutton Collections, Shires (Fife), f. 20.
10 in 1545, *Laing Charters.* 5 on 22 Apr., 1560, of whom 2 (Alexander Balcanquall and John Akynross) are not in *Thirds*: S.R.O. Morton Inventory Box 44. 4 sign in the previous June, when they are said to be " violently expelled from their destroyed place." (S.R.O., Calendar of Charters, no. 1788).

WIGTOWN: Prior, four named friars and one unnamed, of whom only the prior is in *Thirds*, in S.R.O., Abbrev. Feu Chs. Kirklands, ii, 145. Also in *Wigtownshire Charters*, p. 132, where the date is 1560.

Franciscans, Conventual

GENERAL: For period 1556-60, Moir Bryce gives 15 names in all, of whom only 9 are in *Thirds*.

Franciscans, Observant

GENERAL: 5 only recognisable in *Thirds*, survivors such as John Roger and Simon Maltman being unrecorded.

ABERDEEN: 24-30 (Hay's Chronicle), but only three get pensions in *Thirds*, p. 219. 15 deaths in period 1500-60. Some are lay-brothers, who, with novices, never signed.

PERTH: 8 in 1559, Moir Bryce, i, 159 note.

ST. ANDREWS: 24 plus novices (Hay's Chronicle), but only 2 names given in 1559 (Moir Bryce, *The Scottish Grey Friars*, ii, 202). Dr. Durkan gives me these names of St. Andrews friars: 1527, Robert Hay and Wm. Martyn, 1551, James Winchester, warden, James Peblis, vicar; 1530, Andrew Carnis, warden, Finlay Ramsay; 1558, Herbert Carneill, John Geddy, John Burrell, John Knycht. Some of these names are absent from Moir Bryce.

GENERAL OBSERVATIONS

Understaffing is evident, but there were reasons:

    (i) economic;

    (ii) the action of Commendators (notably at Melrose, Holyrood, Dryburgh, Kelso, and probably Jedburgh, Whithorn, Soulseat);

    (iii) the effects of war.

In 1573, Jedburgh had a Comm., 1 canon (Wm. Todryk), and the prior of Canonbie (James Oliver). S.R.O., Cal. of Chs., 2286.

12 monks of Kelso are said to be killed in siege in Sept., 1545, *Letters and Papers Henry VIII*, xx, pt. ii, 456.

Newbattle monks were taken prisoner by the English, but 6 returned and recommenced monastic life; *Calendar of Scottish Papers*, i, 237 and Canivez, *Statuta O. Cist.*, vii, 37.

Coldingham monks were evicted time and again, 1532, 1542, 1544-5, *Letters and Papers*, v, 1460; xvii, 1086, 1197; xx, 129.

Moreover, not all religious are by any means recorded in *Thirds of Benefices*, which limits its indisputable value as a guide to numbers. Of three Trinitarians at Failford in 1558 (S.R.O., Calendar of Chs., 1741) none are in *Thirds*.

In conclusion, it ought to be said that more precise statistics regarding the state of the religious must await the publication of individual studies on the various orders.

JOSEPH O'DEA, O.C.R.

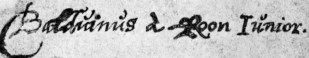

Baldianus à Loon Iunior.

CONCLV
SIONES DE SA,
CROSANCTO MISSAE
sacrificio, & com,
munione
laica, ·

R. Vauchop Schoti Theologi
Parisiensis, nunc In,
golstadij.

1.Timoth.3.   Matth.16.
ECCLESIA Dei viui columna est &
firmamentum ueritatis: Et portæ
inferi non præualebunt
aduersus eam.

ANNO M. D. XLIIII.

J F Vandevelde

PLATE XIX.   ROBERT WAUCHOPE'S CONCLUSIONES DE
SACROSANCTO MISSAE SACRIFICIO.

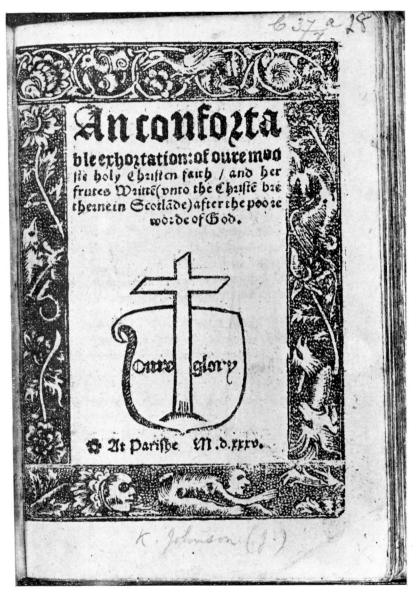

PLATE XX. JOHN JOHNSONE'S *AN CONFORTABLE*
EXHORTATION.

APPENDIX II

THE SCHOTTENKLÖSTER AT THE REFORMATION

The study of Scottish monasticism in the sixteenth century is incomplete unless the Benedictine abbeys in Germany are taken into account. Although they were all Irish in origin, those which survived in Irish hands until the sixteenth century became Scottish after 1515. In view of their omission from Easson's *Medieval Religious Houses; Scotland*, it will be best to clear the ground by establishing which monasteries concern us here. Foundation by *Scoti* has been claimed for a fantastic number of houses, but only those which belonged to the Ratisbon congregation need be considered.

The original foundation was the priory of Weih St. Peter, founded by Marianus Scotus in Ratisbon about 1075. Subjects flocked to it, and soon, perhaps as early as 1090, the abbey of St. James was founded in the same town to house the increased numbers. A period of expansion followed, no fewer than seven foundations being made between 1130 and 1170: St. James in Erfurt, Our Lady in Vienna, St. James in Constance, St. James in Würzburg, Holy Cross in Eichstätt, St. Giles in Nuremberg, St. Nicholas in Memmingen. In 1215 the nine monasteries were grouped into a congregation whose head was the abbot of St. James' in Ratisbon.[1]

Studies by Irish scholars[2] and the documents calendared by Renz[3] reveal how this flourishing Irish congregation went to pieces in the fifteenth century. The exact status of some of these houses is not easy to determine. Renz quotes documents—not at first hand, however—according to which all but Weih St. Peter would be abbeys (*Renz*, 32, 60). A tenth house, the priory of Kelheim on the Danube, was founded in 1232.[4] Dr. Binchy on the other hand says that Memmingen and Eichstätt were never more than priories, and that at the beginning of the fifteenth century Kelheim, Eichstätt and Memmingen had long been held *in commendam* by German secular priests.[5]

Certainly the status of several of these houses declined. Memmingen sank until it was a mere property or chaplaincy, the ownership of which was constantly disputed; it was eventually demolished in the first years of the sixteenth century. A similar fate overtook Eichstätt: it became a mere property, administered however for the monks in Ratisbon and surviving as such until 1566.[6] Kelheim likewise ceased to be a religious house, although it remained in the possession of the monks of Ratisbon until the

---

1. There is general agreement on certain central facts concerning the early history of these houses, but no satisfactory study of the congregation as a whole exists and the uncertainties are very great.

2. P. J. Barry: *Zustände im Wiener Schottenklöster vor der Reform des Jahres 1418*; idem: *Irish Benedictines in Nuremberg* (in *Studies*, xxi, p. 579 ff. and xxii, p. 435 ff.). D. A. Binchy: *The Irish Benedictine Congregation in Medieval Germany* (in *Studies*, xviii, p. 194 ff.); idem: *Die irischen Benediktinerkloster in Regensburg* (unpublished thesis in Munich University Library, U1924-8130). Cf. also A. Gwynn: *Some notes on the history of the Irish and Scottish Benedictine Monasteries in Germany* (in *Innes Review*, v, p. 5 ff.).

3. G. A. Renz: *Beiträge zur Geschichte der Schottenabtei St. Jacob und des Priorates Weih St. Peter in Regensburg* (in *Studien und Mittheilungen aus dem Benediktiner- und dem Cistercienser- Orden* xvi-xviii, 1895-7). This is a series of 396 documents, numbered and arranged chronologically from 1075 to 1499, and will be quoted as *Renz*.

4. *Renz*, 44, 54. It is significantly omitted from J. Hemmerle: *Die Benediktinerklöster in Bayern*. The author no doubt considered that it was never a properly constituted religious house.

5. *Studies*, xviii, pp. 195, 210. It would certainly seem that Eichstätt at least had not abbatial status.

6. There is a brief account of the end of Memmingen and Eichstatt in J. Hemmerle, *op. cit.*, pp. 41, 68-9. For evidence of the interest of the sixteenth-century Scots of Ratisbon in Eichstätt and the final compensation given to Ninian Winzet, see Blairs Ratisbon MSS., C 7, 5b; Eichstätt Ordinariatsarchiv, Salbücher B175, B177, B44x.

final dissolution of the congregation in 1862. Würzburg was given to German monks in 1497 and not restored to the Scots till 1595, so that it concerns Scottish reformation history only indirectly. Vienna and Nuremberg had been given to German monks in 1418.

These six houses can therefore be excluded from consideration.[7] The situation, however, was not quite as simple as would appear from this bald outline. Kelheim is called a priory in 1464 (*Renz*, 324), but this is merely a legal title. Eichstätt actually had an Irish prior from 1461 to 1465 (*Renz* 319,326), while Memmingen is called an abbey in the acts of the general chapter of 1479 and an Irishman was elected to succeed his fellow countryman as abbot there in 1485 (*Renz*, 340, 356). Superiors were no doubt given to Memmingen and Eichstätt to strengthen the legal position of the Irish claimants to the property.

Much the same, in fact, is true of all the houses except St. James' in Ratisbon, which alone possessed a community. Superiors were elected to Erfurt, Constance, Würzburg (until its loss) and Weih St. Peter, but each was elected at Ratisbon by the other prelates and the monks of St. James', Ratisbon (*Renz*, 340 and *passim*). A true picture of the Scoto-Benedictine congregation at the dawn of the sixteenth century would be that of a handful of Irish monks, never exceeding ten in number,[8] of whom four were superiors of houses independent of each other; and of these four, three were without subjects.

This situation is important for understanding what the first Scots abbot succeeded to in the years 1515-20. John Thomson became abbot of St. James' in Ratisbon and thereby was head of the Scoto-Benedictine congregation. His ally, John Denys, was appointed prior of Weih St. Peter by him. For generations the abbots of Constance and Erfurt had been elected at Ratisbon from among the monks of St. James'; accordingly, when the Irish abbots of these two houses died, the local authorities notified Ratisbon, and a Scot was quietly provided from the community that Thomson was in process of gathering.[9] Scottish Benedictines thus had in Germany one community, besides three prelacies which were little more than benefices. Thomson's work prospered, and when he died in 1525 eleven monks (including these prelates) met in chapter.[10] We do not know the surnames of all, nor do the ones we do know correspond very well with the entries in the monastic necrology,[11] although it is worth noting how many were said to have been professed in Scotland.

John Thomson was previously a secular priest (*Necrology*, n. 11), John Denys a Cistercian of Newbattle.[12] David Cumming (*Necrology*, n. 27), a monk, was made abbot of Erfurt in early 1518; Thomson was not yet installed as abbot and could hardly have professed him, so presumably he was a monk already. Presumably too the first Scots abbot of Constance, provided that same year, was already a monk. The necrology mentions

7.   The priory of Ross (mentioned, for instance, in *Renz*, 289, 311, 340) was in Ireland and need not be considered either. The same is true of Altenfurt (given in Brockie's *Monasticon*), Oels in Silesia (given by Wattenbach and repeated by other writers), and other names which occasionally crop up.

8.   *Renz*, 306, 317, 319, 332, 340, 394. Before Würzburg was lost there were occasional subjects there (e.g. *Renz*, 393).

9.   K. T. Gemeiner: *Regensburger Chronik*, IV, pp. 323, 349.

10. Blairs Ratisbon MSS., C 6, 3.

11. Edited in *Innes Review*, ix, p. 173 ff. This will be quoted often (as *Necrology*) to save lengthy reference to archives.

12. *Necrology*, n. 14. Denys was already a monk of Newbattle and in Scotland in November, 1501, as we know from the *Protocol Book of James Young*, 1485-1515 (Scottish Record Society, 1952), n. 1169, 1176-8.

Andrew Ruthven of Arbroath, John Gordon of Inchcolm, Servanus Thomson of Dunfermline, William Fleming of Paisley and Thomas Maxwell of Dunfermline. Of these five, we have contemporary evidence of the existence of Ruthven alone; there is no evidence either for or against Gordon; Servanus Thomson looks suspiciously like an invention, while Fleming and Maxwell are almost certainly inventions.[13] Apart from John Thomson and Denys, no contemporary indication is available of the religious background of these early monks of Ratisbon.

The period of prosperity did not last long. Two abbots disputed for the prelacy of St. James' in 1531-2, while in 1538 the town authorities undertook the financial administration of the house (*Necrology*, n. 27). On the credit side must be recorded the co-operation with Robert Wauchope's efforts for reform in 1542.[14] A disastrous fire destroyed much of the monastery in 1546; whatever community was left must have dispersed, for now begin the documents mentioning the lack of any community.[15] Abbot Bogg seems to have squandered monastic property, thereby involving himself in litigation with Prior Dawson of Weih St. Peter in 1550-1 (*Necrology*, n. 33). The latter succeeded to St. James' by default in 1555 and was the sole Scots monk in Ratisbon in 1560 (*Necrology*, n. 41).

The three prelacies had fared even worse. Constance was demolished in 1530 (*Necrology*, n. 26) and Weih St. Peter in 1552, in both cases because they stood too close to the city walls at a time when sieges were feared. Erfurt was in territory which became Lutheran; the Scots abbots had a difficult time, and the last one, Andrew Hunter, is said to have fled in 1561.[16]

In the years following 1560, therefore, the Scoto-Benedictine congregation apparently boasted one monk living in his monastery. The picture of the German houses providing asylum for faithful monks exiled from Scotland is quite fanciful. And yet it has a grain of truth. Thomas Anderson, a secular priest of Brechin, assisted Abbot Dawson, became a monk and succeeded him as abbot. When he in turn died in 1576 the town authorities administered the abbey, but two young Scots had joined him and were there when Winzet arrived the following year (*Necrology*, n. 44). Erfurt was meanwhile given by the Holy See as a benefice to an exiled secular priest of Aberdeen, William Chalmer.[17]

With Winzet, a new era of endeavour and achievement began, and a community of Scots gathered together. We know very few names of monks who were at Ratisbon between 1560 and 1590. The two abbots, Anderson and Winzet, had both been secular priests in Scotland; John Hamilton had been a monk of Paisley (*Necrology*, n. 53) and David Craig a Carmelite.[18] Few if any of the others we know of could have been old

---

13. *Necrology*, n. 12, 13, 17, 23, 37, respectively. For the last two see also p. 178 and n. 16.

14. *Innes Review*, i, pp. 53-6.

15. For instance, a deed of Abbot Alex. Bogg: " Wir Alexander Abt . . . such an statt eines ganzen Convents dieweil wir diser Zeit aus mannge der Personen keinen Conventual haben . . ." (Kloster-Urkunden St. Jakob, Regensburg, Fasz. 7, Nr. 61, dated 23rd Nov. 1553).

16. *Necrology*, n. 28; J. Scholle: *Das Erfurter Schottenkloster*, pp. 34-6.

17. Dr. J. H. Burns, in his study of Ninian Winzet (*Catholic Truth Society of Scotland*, 1959), pp. 37-9, accords equal monastic status to Winzet and Chalmer. According to Brockie (*Monasticon*, ad. loc.) the Ratisbon chapter and the ordinary, the archbishop of Mainz, protested, and the latter refused to confirm Chalmer as abbot. Chalmer went to Prague, received the monastic habit from the nuncio and succeeded in obtaining confirmation, but found the benefice a poor one and resigned it, in exchange for a better one, into the hands of the pope in 1581.

18. *Necrology*, n. 49. The date 1587 given in *Hewison* for his reception at Ratisbon is no doubt a misprint for 1578. David Craig, a white friar of Aberdeen, is mentioned as receiving a wage in 1563 in *Thirds of Benefices*, p. 219 (Scottish Hist. Soc., 1949).

enough to take vows or orders before 1560. Winzet and John Leslie, Bishop of Ross, made strenuous efforts to obtain possession of the former Scots monasteries which still survived, hoping to fill them with Scotsmen,[19] but their only success was in Erfurt, where John Hamilton became abbot in 1581. An important success fell to Winzet's successor, Abbot Whyte, who gained possession of Würzburg in 1595 (*Necrology*, n. 138, 139).

These three abbeys had a not undistinguished history until the nineteenth century. Würzburg was in a healthy state when it was suppressed in 1803.[20] Erfurt remained without subjects and became eventually a dependency of Ratisbon, achieving a quite remarkable place in the realm of scholarship until its suppression in 1819.[21] Ratisbon itself, crippled by the anti-religious laws, struggled on till 1862. Plans had already been adumbrated for a foundation in the mother country, and Lord Lovat already had a site for it.[22] The last surviving Scots monk, Dom Anselm Robertson, and Lord Lovat played an important part in the foundation of Fort Augustus, which was constituted the successor and continuation of the old Scots abbey of Ratisbon (*Necrology*, no. 135). Even though one must abandon the picture of the Schottenklöster enabling the monks of the suppressed Scottish monasteries to persevere in their vocation, the fact remains that they were important counter-reformation centres and provided the means for pre-reformation Scottish monasticism to survive into the twentieth century.

MARK DILWORTH, O.S.B.

19. Some of the documents are printed in the Introduction of Hewison's edition of Winzet's works (*Scottish Text Soc.*, 1888-90).

20. M. Wieland: *Das Schottenkloster zu St. Jakob in Würzburg* (in *Archiv des historischen Vereins für Unterfranken und Aschaffenburg*, Band 16, 1864, p. 19).

21. *Necrology*, n. 124 and *passim*; Scholle, *op. cit.*, pp. 55-9. The studies by Dr. Ludwig Hammermayer which have appeared recently stress this aspect and deserve to be known in this country: —*Gründungs und Frühgeschichte der bayerischen Akademie der Wissenschaften* (Münchener Historische Studien, 1959); *Die Benediktiner und die Akademiebewegung im katholischen Deutschland* 1720-1770 (Studien und Mitteilungen des Benediktinerordens, 1960); *Zur Geschichte der Schottenabtei St Jakob in Regensburg* (Zeitschrift für bayerische Landesgeschichte, 1959); *Neue Beiträge zur Geschichte des Schottenklosters St. Jakob in Erfurt* (Jahrbuch für das Bistum Mainz, 1958-1960).

22. Letter of Fr. Anselm Robertson, 17th March, 1857; letter of Bishop Kyle, 15th March, 1861. (Both are in Oban Cathedral collection of letters of Vicars-Apostolic of Western District).

THE CONFLICTING DOCTRINES OF THE SCOTTISH REFORMATION

by

Maurice Taylor

1525-1546

The Scottish reformation, if considered as a conflict in religious beliefs, may be dated from 1525. Luther had made public his theses at Wittenberg in 1517 and had been formally excommunicated as a heretic in 1520. In the years following, Lutheran literature and opinions reached Scotland, brought here by those whose callings made them travellers between this country and the continent—seamen, merchants and students. The first public mention of heresy in Scotland occurred in an act of parliament of 1525, which forbad the bringing into the country of Lutheran books and the spreading of such doctrines. Shortly afterwards, James V thought it necessary to write to Pope Clement VII: "As to the Lutherans, others must judge of the king's detestation and the strength of his opposition; James will strive to follow his predecessors in defending the Catholic Faith and ecclesiastical liberty; neither Lutheranism nor any other heresy will be suffered to invade Scotland."[1] Reassuring words at the time, perhaps, but seen now as the small cloud on the horizon, heralding the storm.

It is correct to regard the twenty-five years after 1525 as only the preliminary stage in the theological conflict in Scotland. There are two reasons for this. In the first place, heresy in Scotland during the period was mainly Lutheran in outlook, yet the crucial struggle of the late 1550s and early 1560s was waged and won by Calvinists. Secondly, one may speak of doctrinal *controversy* in Scotland at this time in only a limited sense. There was heresy, certainly, and catholic opposition to it, but the church, with the aid of the state, was still in a position of sufficient strength to confront the heretics with coercion as its principal weapon, rather than with argument alone.

The Scottish protestants of these years[2] faithfully reflected the teaching of the German reformer, the same small group of theological topics, differing sharply from catholic orthodoxy, being found again and again among their recorded opinions. Probably most reasoned was the question of man's justification. This theological problem, concerned with the means whereby a man passes from a state of damnation due to sin to a state of grace, is admittedly most difficult and complicated. It is also true that, when the Lutheran views with regard to it were first advanced, there was no definite catholic pronouncement with which to oppose them. Not until 1547 did the Council of Trent (in its sixth session) give the church's solemn and codified declaration on the matter.

---

1. R. K. Hannay, *The Letters of James V*, p. 134.
2. Accounts of their lives and trials are found in   Knox's *History* and in Foxe's *Actes and Monuments*, relevant parts of the latter being reprinted in Laing's *Knox*, i, Appendix.

But in brief, the position was this. Luther and his followers taught that, of ourselves, we are completely corrupt because of sin, that we have no truly free will and that, without grace, we can do nothing which is not sinful; when a change takes place in our relationship with God, i.e., when we are "justified," we are totally passive and contribute nothing to the change; Christ made satisfaction to God the Father for our sins, redeemed us and intercedes for us, and we become partakers in his redemption by that faith which is a special kind of trust and which is itself passive rather than active, a receiving rather than a doing; "faith is the firm and certain thought or confidence in God, that through Christ he will be propitious, that through Christ he will think thoughts of peace towards us;"[3] those who have been justified, those who have Christ's grace, still retain their sins, but they no longer consent to them and so the sins are no longer imputed to them; good works have no merit in God's sight but, on the other hand, the state of justification can be lost only by the sin of unfaithfulness.

The catholic position agrees with the Lutheran that man's justification is brought about by divine grace which Christ, our Redeemer, merited on Calvary, but differs profoundly from it in the further explanation of this basic point. We have free will and are not constrained, without grace, only to sin; indeed, if adults, we must freely prepare ourselves for justification, which we receive by Christ's grace, conferred in baptism. However, the beginning of this preparation for justification is due to the grace of God alone (to which we freely consent and with which we then co-operate); nor do we, by our self-preparation, merit justification, which, when it is received, is the free gift of God. We may lapse from our justified state by any mortal sin but can regain our position by a similar method to that by which justification was acquired in the first place (except that the sacrament now is penance, not baptism); we can also increase our state of justification (i.e., our state of grace) by the performance of good works. Faith is the essential beginning of salvation, the necessary foundation of justification, but by it the church implies not trust or confidence in divine goodness and mercy (though such is related to faith as both a stimulus and a consequence), but the intellectual acknowledgment of divine truths revealed by God.

So much for the standpoint of the two sides on this matter. The Lutheran exposition of their views, so well known in the German disputes and controversies, is also found among the early Scottish protestants. In fact, Murdoch Nisbet's *The New Testament in Scots* has, as prologue, a translation made about 1525 of Luther's own preface to the New Testament, in which the necessity of a trusting faith is much stressed, for the gospel "does not require our works for any such intent that we should be made righteous or saved by them," but "specially sets forth the faith in Christ and provokes men to believe in him, namely that he . . . saved us not by our works but through his own works, even by his death and passion."[4]

---

3. Luther, *Opera Omnia*, 42, 563.

4. *The New Testament in Scots*, (The Scottish Text Society), i, p. 4. Tyndale's Prologue to St. Paul's Epistle to the Romans, a later addition to Nisbet's translation (iii, pp. 315-347), also expounds the Lutheran explanation of justification by faith. (Quotations throughout the present article will be made in modernised spelling.)

Patrick's Places, the work of Patrick Hamilton, the first Scottish Lutheran to be tried and executed (1528),[5] is entirely concerned with explaining how man is justified. Parts of the book could be accepted or interpreted in an orthodox sense, but it is Lutheran in emphasis; the absolute necessity of faith is reiterated many times, as is also the relative unimportance of our actions, for " none of our works neither save us nor condemn us."[6] Frequently, too, the Lutheranism is explicit: " The faith of Christ, is to believe in him; that is, to believe his word and to believe that he will keep thee in all thy need, and deliver thee from evil;"[7] " He that keepeth one commandment, keepeth them all."[8] At his trial, likewise, the judgment allegedly pronounced on Hamilton was as follows: " We have found also that he hath affirmed, published and taught divers opinions of Luther and wicked heresies, after that he was summoned to appear before us and our council: that man hath no free will; that man is in sin as long as he liveth; . . . no man is justified by works, but by faith only; good works make not a good man, but a good man doth make good works; that faith, hope and charity are so knit that he that hath the one, hath the rest, and he that wanteth the one of them, wanteth the rest. . . . "[9]

The means of justification continued to be prominent in heretics' teaching. About 1535, the Dominican, Alexander Seton, is reported as preaching that " to satisfy for sin lies not in man's power, but the mission thereof comes by unfeigned repentance and by faith apprehending God the Father, merciful in Christ Jesus, his Son "[10]—a view which, as in other cases, is more dangerous because of its vagueness and omissions than for any express error. John Gau, a Scot exiled in Malmö, in his work of 1533, *The Richt Vay to the Kingdom of Heuine* (practically a translation from a Danish treatise of Christiern Pedersen), clearly approves the Lutheran outlook: " Faith is a living trust in God which makes us sure without any doubt that we are in his favours and he will be gracious and merciful to us and will gladly, for his son's sake, forgive us all our sins."[11]

The Scottish Lutherans also attacked several Catholic doctrines affecting the day-to-day lives and conduct of the faithful. The sacrament of penance, then more commonly called by the heretics auricular confession, was probably rejected by Patrick Hamilton[12] and certainly by George Wishart;[13] prayer to our Lady and the saints was very frequently repudiated[14] as also was the custom of praying, and offering mass, for the souls in purgatory.[15] Such denials were, at least in theory, founded upon the basic principle that the only source of revelation, and therefore

---

5. Dickinson's *Knox*, ii, pp. 219-229.
6. *Op. cit.*, ii, p. 228.
7. *Op. cit.*, ii, p. 224.
8. *Op. cit.*, ii, p. 221.
9. Laing's *Knox*, i, p. 511.
10. Dickinson's *Knox*, i, pp. 19-20.
11. *Op. cit.*, p. 74.
12. Laing's *Knox*, i, p. 509.
13. Dickinson's *Knox*, ii, p. 237.
14. For example, by the " woman of Leith ", Robert Lambe and George Wishart (respectively, Laing's *Knox*, i, pp. 519 and 523, and Dickinson's *Knox*, ii, pp. 240-241). It is interesting that, in Gau's book, the Hail Mary (i.e., the first part of the present-day form) is recommended since " there is no prayer here " but only a remembrance of the great grace that God gave to the Blessed Virgin. (Gau, *The Richt Vay to the Kingdom of Heuine*, pp. 102-103.)
15. Cf. Patrick Hamilton (J. Herkness and R. K. Hannay, *The Archbishops of St. Andrews*, iii, p. 180), Norman Gourlay, David Straton (Laing's *Knox*, i, p. 519) and Wishart (Dickinson's *Knox*, ii, p. 241).

of christian belief and practice, was scripture. Wishart, in particular, made this plain: " I say that auricular confession, seeing that it hath no promise of the Evangel, therefore it can not be a sacrament . . .; it is found plainly and certain in scriptures that we should worship and honour one God . . . but as for praying to, and honouring of saints, there is great doubt among many, whether or not they hear invocation made unto them; therefore I exhorted all men equally in my doctrine that they should leave the unsure way . . . except it stand by the Word of God, I dare not be so bold to affirm anything "; and he denied purgatory because, " without express witness and testimony of scripture, I dare affirm nothing."[16] The same principle that relegated tradition from partnership with scripture to a subservient, merely confirmatory, position was also sometimes used to limit acceptance of ecclesiastical authority. John Borthwick, for instance, asserted that some decrees of the fathers of the church were contrary to the law of God[17] and Wishart's attitude was " if that they (i.e. the laws of general councils) agree with the Word of God, I will not disagree."[18]

The mass does not seem to have been a primary target of these early protestants, though Wishart was accused of having denied its usefulness, his reply being that he had merely taught the need for all worship to be interior as well as exterior.[19] But bitter animosity towards the papacy and denial of its authority and power were found in the opinions of very many of the Scottish Lutherans[20]—an outlook attributable not only to theological considerations, but also to the disedification given by several popes in their lives and activities.

During this period, there were some Scottish catholic writings which upheld the church's doctrines and exposed the Lutheran heresies.[21] Doubtless, too, the same task was undertaken in oral teaching in the centres of learning[22] and by many priests in their instruction of the people. But despite this and the frequent discussions and arguments which would take place on the theological issues, particularly in the universities and colleges, the rôle assumed by the church in Scotland towards heresy in these early years was mainly that of the inquisitor rather than the arguer. Though less interesting historically, such a state of affairs is understandable—an established church, outraged at heresy and not deigning to descend to the level of controversy with its attackers. The result was, too, that the theologians did not have to commit themselves positively concerning those doctrines (including justification, the sacrifice of the mass, and confession) on which the church had by then given no authoritative lead. After the definitions of the Council of Trent (which began in 1545), the task of catholic controversialists in knowing exactly what the church taught was greatly simplified.

---

16. Dickinson's *Knox*, ii, pp. 237, 240, 241.
17. R. Keith, *History of the Affairs of Church and State in Scotland*, i, p. 338.
18. Dickinson's *Knox*, ii, p. 242.
19. *Op. cit.*, ii, p. 236.
20. For example, Patrick Hamilton, Norman Gourlay, John Borthwick and George Wishart (respectively, Laing's *Knox*, i, pp. 509 and 519, Keith, *op. cit.*, i, p. 337, and Dickinson's *Knox*, ii, p. 239).
21. For example, John Major's Commentary on the Gospels (published in 1529) has a preface praising James Beaton, Archbishop of St. Andrews, for his measures against Lutherans and stating that he himself hoped by the commentary to " root out from the good seed in the Lord's field the pestilential tares " of (among others) the Lutherans; in the preface to a new edition of his commentary on the First Book of Lombard's Sentences (1530), Lutheranism is declared "a detestable calamity . . . an execrable heresy." (Scottish History Society, X, pp. 447 and 450.)
22. The theological lectures delivered at King's College, Aberdeen, by William Hay, its vice-principal, and published in manuscript in 1535, show a reasoned yet uncompromising opposition to Lutheran teaching. Cf. *The Innes Review*, ii, p. 91.

1547-1553

It was in 1547 that John Knox first came to prominence. With his advent, accounts of Scottish protestant opinions at once become more detailed than previously, due partly to Knox's obvious facility in advancing and arguing his views, his love of the opportunity for expounding his beliefs; but it is also a result of the fact that Knox's sayings and writings have been preserved to a much greater extent than those of his predecessors. During the first few years after Wishart's execution and until Knox went to Geneva in 1554, he must be regarded as continuing in the general Lutheran, rather than Calvinist, tradition of previous Scottish protestants. Most of the period was spent as a minister in England and, in spite of the fact that there is no record of his having engaged in controversies with catholics, it is possible to discover, from several sources, what were his principal beliefs at the time and how well he had developed his thought regarding them.

His view on justification was made public right from the start of his ministry for, in the *History*, he gives the following summary of how he expounded the matter in his very first sermon: " This he proved by conferring the doctrine of justification expressed in the scriptures, which teach that man is ' justified by faith only, that the blood of Jesus Christ purges us from all our sins '; and the doctrine of the papists, which attributeth justification to the works of the law, yea, to the works of man's invention as pilgrimage, pardons and other baggage."[23] The second half of this statement is, of course, quite wrong and unfair. The first half may be rather vague, but one finds an excellent account of Knox's view on justification in his warm approbation of Henry Balnaves' treatise on *Justification by Faith.* This work reached Knox in exile in 1548, and he sent it on to Scotland with his commendation and with a summary, written by himself, of each of its chapters. The treatise of Balnaves, a Scot, is a very competent exposition of Lutheran teaching on justification, each assertion being referred to the places in scripture on which the author claims that it is based. In his summary, Knox also makes the same points as in the main work: "And albeit in diverse men there be diverse opinions of justification, yet they alone in whom the Holy Spirit worketh true faith (which never wanteth good works) are just before God. The substance of justification is to cleave fast to God by Jesus Christ, and not by our self nor yet by our works . . . He (i.e., Christ) plainly taught that by faith, without all works, man is reckoned just. . . . The just live by faith, ever trusting to obtain that which is promised, which is eternal life, promised to us by Jesus Christ. . . . Works are an outward testimony to faith, by which only man is first made just, and thereafter his works please God because the person is acceptable. . . . All works preceding faith is sin."[24]

Perhaps the other most prominent feature of Knox's theology in these pre-Calvinist days was his hatred of the mass and of the catholic claim that it was a sacrifice offered for the living and the dead. In his first sermon, he referred disparagingly to the " merits of the mass " having " power to relax the pains of them that were in purgatory,"[25] and,

23. Dickinson's *Knox*, i, p. 85.
24. Laing's *Knox*, iii, pp. 15, 17, 20 and 22.
25. Dickinson's *Knox*, i, p. 86.

by the commission of catholic theologians before which he had to appear because of his sermon, he was accused of having preached, among other things, that " the mass is abominable idolatry, blasphemous to the death of Christ and a profanation of the Lord's Supper."[26] No record is preserved of Knox's defence against that accusation, but circumstances repeated themselves in Newcastle three years later, when Knox was called upon publicly to defend his teaching that the mass was idolatrous. In this latter instance, there has been preserved the very lengthy reasoning which Knox employed. The kernel of his defence lies in two syllogisms, a type of reasoning which he used fairly often and with which he was familiar because of his youthful studies in scholasticism: "All worshipping, honouring or service invented by the brain of man in the religion of God, without his express commandment, is idolatry; the mass is invented by the brain of man without any commandment of God; therefore it is idolatry;"[27] and secondly, " All honouring or service of God, whereunto is added a wicked opinion, is abomination; unto the mass is added a wicked opinion (that the mass is a sacrifice and oblation for the sins of the living and the dead); therefore it is abomination."[28] The premises of both syllogisms are defended by a great many reasons and examples, the whole effort being a painstaking and fairly complete exposition of all the usual reasons for protestant hostility towards the mass.

In Knox's speeches and writings of this time, there is the expected antagonism towards the pope, bishops and priests. His report of his first sermon tells that " then began he to decipher the lives of divers popes and the lives of all the shavelings for the most part; . . . in handling the notes of that beast, given in the text (i.e. the Man of Sin, Anti-Christ, the Whore of Babylon), he willed men to consider if these notes . . . could be applied to any other but to the pope and his kingdom."[29] On other occasions, however, a more reasoned, but still hostile, attitude is adopted, for at the examination which followed his sermon, he was accused of holding that " no mortal man can be the head of the church "[30] (as perhaps he assumed the pope claimed to be) and that " there are no bishops, except they preach even by themselves "[31] (an attitude not yet rejecting episcopacy as such, but regarding the principal duty of bishops to be the instruction of the people in the scriptures).

Other opinions held by Knox at this time were common enough among protestants—rejection of purgatory and, therefore, of prayers for the dead, rejection of praying to the saints[32] and of prayers and ceremonies added to the method, instituted by our Lord, for administration of the sacraments. All of these can be seen as applications of the doctrine that non-scriptural belief or practice is inadmissable.

It will have been noticed that one of the greatest points of contention between catholic and protestant—the real presence of our Lord in the Blessed Sacrament—has not yet been mentioned. In fact, there is little evidence that the Scottish protestants until Wishart were other than

---

26. *Op. cit.*, i, p. 87.
27. Laing's *Knox*, iii, p. 34.
28. *Op. cit.*, pp. 52 and 54.
29. Dickinson's *Knox*, i, p. 85.
30. *Op. cit.*, i, p. 87.
31. *Op. cit.*, i, p. 87.
32. Cf. especially Laing's *Knox*, iii, p. 95.

Lutheran in their opinion on this matter. Lutherans admitted the real presence (though they denied transubstantiation and maintained that the bread and wine also remained), but the Blessed Sacrament is not prominent in accounts of the early Scottish heretics' views.[33]

With the coming of John Knox, however, the subject receives attention at once. He claimed that, even in 1547, at the start of his protestant ministry, he rejected Luther's "halfway" opinion and certainly by 1550 he was denying the real, in the sense of physical, presence—though by then he was in England. In that year, he wrote a short statement of opinion on "the Lord's Supper, called the Sacrament of the Body and Blood of Our Saviour, Jesus Christ," in which the following passages occur: "In setting forth bread and wine to eat and drink . . . (Christ) giveth unto us Himself, to be received with faith and not with mouth, nor yet by transfusion of substance ";[34] and again, "We believe God's word and confess that it is true, but not so to be understood as the papists grossly affirm; for, in the Sacrament, we receive Jesus Christ spiritually as did the fathers of the Old Testament."[35] In this affirmation of a merely spiritual presence and reception of Christ[36] he is repeating the views of the sacramentarians in general and of Oeculampadius, Zwingli's lieutenant, in particular. Such Zwinglianism amidst the otherwise still Lutheran outlook of Knox may well be traced to his friendship with Wishart and to the contact which the latter had had with the Swiss reformation.[37]

Apart from Knox, there is little of note in Scottish protestant theological activity between 1547 and 1553.[38] In detailing its plans for the discovery and extirpation of heresy, the provincial council of 1549 gives an indication of the chief errors of the time: attacks on the sacraments, sacramental ceremonies, ecclesiastical councils and their decrees, statues, fasting and feast days; denials of rewards for good works, of prayers to the saints, of purgatory, the soul's immortality and the body's resurrection.[39] This suggests the prevalence of errors in doctrines of the more popular kind, rather than in technicalities such as the sources of revelation, the correct interpretation of scripture, and justification. An explicit reference of the council to "Sacramentarians and chiefly those who inveigh against the Sacrament of the Eucharist "[40] indicates that Knox

---

33. At a later date George Buchanan stated that, about the time that he fled from Scotland in 1539, he had had doubts concerning the real presence but that these doubts disappeared when he realised that "in the Sacrament of the Eucharist there is both the body and the symbol," so that texts of St. Augustine suggesting a symbolic presence did not exclude the real presence of our Lord. (Cf. J. M. Aitken, *The Trial of George Buchanan before the Lisbon Inquisition*, pp. 18-19, 81-82.)

34. Laing's *Knox*, iii, p. 73.

35. *Op. cit.*, iii, p. 75.

36. The name of Knox is associated with the last-minute addition to the Second Book of Common Prayer (1552), stating that kneeling at communion is not to be taken as adoration, "for that were idolatry." It was this English Prayer Book that was frequently used in Scottish protestant celebrations of the Lord's Supper in the later 1550s and even, in some cases, after 1560, until replaced by the Calvinist Book of Common Order.

37. The Swiss Confession of Faith, drawn up at Basle in 1536 and translated by Wishart, denies our Lord's "carnal" presence in the Eucharist; instead, "the Body and Blood of Our Lord are received verily of a faithful soul," the bread and wine being "tokens by which the very communion or participation of the Lord's Body and Blood are exhibited of the Lord Himself" to be the spiritual nourishment of the soul.

38. The enigmatic figure of Sir David Lindsay should receive some mention. Of great influence at the time, yet apparently not a Lutheran in the full sense of the word, he is most critical of papal abuses while accepting the pope's primacy, probably orthodox on justification and the mass, but perilously close to heresy with regard, inter alia, to confession and prayer to the saints. (Cf. *The Innes Review*, i, pp. 79-91.)

39. *Statutes of the Scottish Church* (Scottish History Society), pp. 126-127.

40. *Op. cit.*, pp. 123-124.

in England was not out of touch with protestants at home in his rejection of the real presence.

In the only heresy trial of consequence during the period, that of Adam Wallace in 1550, he was accused of the usual Lutheran outlook on the scriptures and their interpretation, on the mass, purgatory, praying to the saints and for the dead; in addition he admitted, after showing considerable ability in the intricacies of theological argument (which belies Knox's description of him as "a simple man without great learning "[41]) that he denied the physical presence of Christ in the Blessed Sacrament.[42]

One can say, therefore, that the Scottish protestants followed faithfully in the steps of the European reformers, most of all Luther. After the simple and uncomplicated Lutheranism until 1545 or so, they moved even further away from catholicism by the acceptance of additional heresies whose origins were in Zurich.

. . . . . .

It is time now to consider how the catholic church in Scotland was replying theologically to those attacking its doctrines. Despite widespread neglect of preaching by the clergy, many priests must, in their sermons, have been continuing to warn their hearers against protestant errors and explaining catholic doctrine in the points at issue. Indeed, Knox bears this out by his spirited attacks on catholic preachers and in particular on the friars. But no balanced or reliable account of such efforts to combat protestantism has been preserved.

However, as a result of a decree of the provincial council of 1552, there came the first publicised theological rejoinder to the spread of protestantism. This was the catechism of Archbishop Hamilton,[43] so called because it was under the presidency of John Hamilton, archbishop of St. Andrews, that the council had met and ordered the work to be prepared. The catechism is a document of great importance in the doctrinal history of the reformation, being an avowed attempt by the Scottish church, at a crucial moment in its life, to give a complete, yet brief, account of what catholics believe. The writing of the catechism was ordered because preaching, and therefore the religious instruction of the people, had been much neglected for years, with the result that protestant errors had made serious inroads into the faith of many. Although a long-term improvement in preaching was attempted, the catechism was to supply the immediate need, a section of it having to be read by the priest to the congregation at the principal mass each Sunday, if no preacher was available. The catechism is not in question and answer form, but is a continuous narrative or exposition, divided into chapters and logically working through the various heads of catholic teaching— the twelve articles of the creed, the ten commandments, the sacraments and prayer. The style is generally reckoned a fine example of Scottish prose of the period and even as far as its matter is concerned—in spite of the short time devoted to its preparation—it is clear, orderly, not diffuse, yet unhurried.

---

41. Dickinson's *Knox*, i, p. 114.
42. Laing's *Knox*, i, pp. 544-548.
43. Reprinted at Oxford, 1884, edited by Thomas Graves Law.

If that were all to be said of it, the catechism would have to be accounted an admirable publication, a credit to its author and to the Scottish hierarchy, even if too late to change the course of reformation history. But one must confess that, in addition to having good qualities, the catechism is a most perplexing work. Indeed, the question has to be faced: is it always orthodox in its treatment of catholic doctrine? There are several reasons that make one regard the catechism with suspicion, reasons both extrinsic to its actual matter and intrinsic to it. With reference to the former, recent research has shown that the main author was probably Richard Marshall, a Dominican and an Englishman in exile who remained loyal to the church, and not (as previously supposed) John Winram, sub-prior of St. Andrews, who publicly apostatised in 1560. However, it seems possible that Marshall used, among his sources, several heretical works and it is almost certain that he made much use of the *Enchiridion* of John Gropper, a Cologne theologian and faithful catholic but who, in the *Enchiridion*, attempted to achieve a compromise between catholic and Lutheran doctrinal differences, particularly in regard to justification, was adjudged to have gone too far, and incurred the condemnation of Rome. Moreover, there are some grounds for believing that the author of the catechism was influenced by the compromising spirit of the Interim of Augsburg (already rejected by Trent) and evidence that he intended his book to have an appeal for the moderate, Henrician protestants in England.[44]

But, in the final analysis, the orthodoxy of the catechism must be judged on intrinsic evidence. Certainly there is a great deal in the catechism which is unexceptionable—and this is so, not only concerning doctrines on which both catholics and protestants agreed, but also on several matters bitterly attacked by the latter. For example, the attitude to tradition, the church's authority in interpreting scripture, the sacraments (and the Blessed Eucharist in particular), prayer to our Lady and the saints, and prayers for the dead is unequivocal and correct.

On the other hand, there are several parts of the catechism that are strange, to say the least. Perhaps most noticeably because so often repeated, the catechism's instruction on justification has a protestant tone to it. We are told that Christ suffered his passion " to make satisfaction and amends for the sins of us all who have a true and loving faith in him."[45] There is frequent insistence on this " true and living faith," which the catechism distinguishes from " general faith " or acceptance of revealed truths; the former " is the special faith of a true christian man which stands in the general faith before rehearsed and in sure confidence and hope of God's mercy."[46] The " I believe " of the creed is equated with " I trust,"[47] and with this special faith we are enabled " to believe with certainty that he died for our salvation "[48] and " to commit ourselves wholly to God, to put our whole trust and confidence in his help . . . in all our necessities."[49] In addition, the catechism stresses that, to be fruitful, the sacraments must be received with the special, trusting faith,

---

44. Dr. John Durkan deals with these last two points in the following article, "The Cultural Background"; an appendix of that same article gives an account of his research and findings on the question of the catechism's authorship.
45. fol. civ,a, p. 154.
46. fol. xciii,b, p. 126.
47. fol. xcv,a, p. 129.
48. fol. ciii,b, p. 153.
49. fol. xcii,b, p. 126.

while the words of baptism, " I baptise thee," are interpreted as meaning, " I *declare* to thee plainly that all thy sins are forgiven thee,"[50] and, by the sacrament, we are said to " clothe ourselves with his (i.e., Christ's) righteousness and repute it as our own."[51]

The mass, too, is treated in a most unsatisfactory manner in the catechism. In the chapters on the Blessed Eucharist, the chapters in which the mass would normally be explained, there is no set teaching on it at all, but only four unconnected sentences which can be said to have some bearing on this topic so much attacked by protestants. The two most important of these references consist only in the following: " It (i.e., the Sacrament of the Altar) is called the Sacrifice of the Altar because it is a living and special remembrance of the passion of Christ, as it is said in the Gospel of St. Luke, ' Do this in My remembrance ' ";[52] and " This blessed Sacrifice of the Altar is a living memorial ordained to recall to our mind the passion of Our Saviour, Christ."[53] The actual word " mass " remains unused in these chapters, to add to the peculiar lack of prominence and the enervated treatment that the subject receives. To be sure, there is some satisfaction to be gained from an appendix to the final section of the catechism, (on praying for the souls departed), because there the word " mass " is used several times and the propitiatory value of the mass for the souls in purgatory is clearly stated. But one's perplexity remains. Why is the sacrifice of the mass dismissed so inadequately at its proper place in the catechism ? In particular, does not the change in style that is obvious in the last few pages suggest that a different author wrote them and managed to supply some of the main author's omissions regarding the mass ?

There are other criticisms of the catechism, most notably the treatment accorded to the papacy. Because of the confusion resulting from conciliarist theories in the church, it would perhaps be expecting too much of the catechism to deal with the pope's position in matters of authority and jurisdiction. However, the fact is that, throughout its whole length, the catechism never as much as mentions even the mere existence of the pope.

These are the reasons based on intrinsic evidence which must make one question the orthodoxy of Hamilton's catechism. Taken along with the suspicions concerning some of its aims and sources, they undoubtedly make a strong case against the book. But sentence cannot be passed easily. It is hard to accept the suggestion that omissions concerning, for example, the mass or the pope were due to oversight or hasty compilation, or even to the fact that no good catholic ever thought of rejecting such matters. But an attempt to produce a doctrinal compromise was certainly not the intention of the catechism's sponsors, the bishops, whose decision to publish it was occasioned by the admission that " many frightful heresies have, within the last few years, run riot in many diverse parts of this realm " and whose purpose was to secure that the " true, Catholic and Apostolic Faith may, by the exclusion of all kinds of error, be kept intact and uninjured."[54]

---

50. fol. cxxvi,a, p. 184; italics mine.
51. fol. cxxviii,b, p. 188.
52. fol. cxl,b, p. 203, quoting Luke 22, 19.
53. fol. cxli,b, p. 205.
54. *Statutes of the Scottish Church* (Scottish History Society), pp. 143-144.

The difficulty in reaching a decision on the catechism's peculiarities is not lessened by the fact that it presents many catholic doctrines, even those then in dispute, in an irreproachable way. This aspect has not been given its correct proportion in the quotations made above, which have tended to isolate the strange passages. Furthermore, one must beware of judging the words and phrases of the catechism with a twentieth-century, or even post-Tridentine, yardstick. The catechism was written in 1552, long before many of the later decrees of Trent, especially those on the mass, were enacted and this may go a long way towards explaining away the meagre quantity and quality of some of the catechism's teaching. Even though the Tridentine definitions on justification, the sacraments in general and baptism had been made in 1547 and these decrees were known in Scotland by 1552, the impact of the doctrinal clarification that they made was probably hardly felt by then, so that the catechism's phraseology may be adjudged not so much heterodox as old-fashioned and unenlightened by Tridentine standards. It is possible to see traces of Gropper's compromise theory of " double justification "[55] which the Council of Trent rejected in 1547 and which Gropper then abandoned. But one may claim that the peculiarities regarding justification are all susceptible of a catholic interpretation; nor is the " special faith " exactly the same as the Lutherans' faith, for the catechism states that " special faith . . . stands in the general faith before rehearsed " or, in other words, can be had only if there is also intellectual assent to revealed truths. There is no one statement of which it can undoubtedly be said, " this is heretical." Finally, if it be argued that doubts about the catechism's orthodoxy arise only on doctrines on which protestants disagreed with catholics, and that this increases the liklihood of the catechism having protestant tendencies, the retort may well be made that the peculiarities are due to the fact, not that the protestants denied these doctrines, but that they also happened at the time to be the most difficult to explain precisely and authoritatively.

The enigma remains, despite the 1552 council's statement that the catechism was, " after the most elaborate revision," to be " approved by the opinions and votes of the most prudent prelates in the whole realm and of the most learned theologians and other churchmen."[56] But this much can surely be said. No matter whether well-intentioned conciliatory motives in its author or carelessness and ignorance in those appointed to inspect and approve his work are important reasons for the catechism's deficiencies, the value it had for its projected task was seriously impaired. Explanations of the reasons for the book's inadequacies do not remove them. Perhaps the catechism came too late anyway, and perhaps the method appointed for its use was of little value, but the undoubted failings that have been noted in the work, together with the absence of any rejection of the Calvinist errors soon to be so prominent, must have meant that appreciation by the faithful of the church's teaching in controverted matters would be little improved by the catechism.

1554-1559

With the death of Edward VI and the accession of Mary Tudor, Knox left England early in 1554, went to Geneva and thenceforward came

---

55. Cf. *D.T.C.*, vi, 2, 1880-85 and viii, 2, 2160-62; Gropper's *Enchiridion* (Venice, 1543), fol. 194-220. In passing, one should mention that the *Enchiridion* deals very fully with the sacrifice of the mass (fol. 77-109) and explains the basis and extent of the primacy of the pope (fol. 253-254).
56. *Statutes of the Scottish Church* (Scottish History Society), p. 144.

under the influence of Calvin. During the next five years, he travelled much, but Geneva may be regarded as his headquarters, in the spiritual as much as in the material sense. A prolonged visit that he made to Scotland from September, 1555, until July, 1556, is said to have greatly strengthened and increased the Scottish protestants. During these months, he preached in several parts and " ministered the Lord's Table." The record of his teaching in Scotland during these months is very scanty, and one cannot say that there is as yet positive evidence of Calvinism in his sermons; but that he was now the established and acknowledged doctrinal leader of the Scottish protestants, there is no doubt. This was so, not only during his stay in the country, but even after his return to Geneva. In a farewell letter, Knox gave to protestants his directions as to how in future they should hold and conduct regular meetings for prayers and scripture reading and explanation in their own homes; but he went further, indicating that, if they should find difficulty or disagreement in the correct interpretation of any passage of the scriptures, he would be ready to act as arbiter: " Of myself, I will speak as I think; I will more gladly spend fifteen hours in communicating my judgments with you, in explaining as God pleases to open to me any place of scripture, than half an hour in any other matter."[57]

Very soon, we find Knox answering the difficulties of his followers in Scotland regarding various matters. In these replies, one sees, perhaps explicitly for the first time, the influence of Calvin in his religious thought. His teaching on the sacraments is exactly that of Geneva: baptism must be received because our Lord commanded it, not as a means to re-generation (for regeneration is acquired by trusting faith in the merits of Christ), but as an external sign or seal by which we are reassured of our regeneration; the only other sacrament, that of the Lord's Table, is a sign or declaration to " assure our consciences that the league between God and us is permanent and sure."[58] The two sacraments are also " a declaration of our profession before the world " that we belong to the household of God.[59]

Of course, much more characteristically and obviously Calvinist is the doctrine of predestination, which, while accepting the usual protestant teaching on justification, lays down that, without reference to their manner of life or works, God has irrevocably predestined some men for heaven and the rest for eternal damnation. It is possible to detect this most famous of Calvin's doctrines in the answer of Knox just quoted, though not yet fully and blatantly stated. Such statements as " the league of God (i.e., between himself and the regenerate) is of that firmity and assurance that rather shall the covenant made with the sun and the moon, with the day and the night, perish and be changed than that the promise of his mercy made to his elect shall be frustrated and vain "; " He has chosen us in Christ Jesus, his only well-beloved, before the foundation of all worlds were laid "; " His gifts and vocation are such, as of the which he cannot repent himself towards His elect "[60]—these at least suggest the course that Knox's thought was taking.

---

57. Laing's *Knox*, iv, p. 138.
58. *Op. cit.*, iv, p. 123.
59. *Op. cit.*, iv, p. 120.
60. *Op. cit.*, iv, pp. 123-124.

Indeed, there is other evidence that Knox was already an out-and-out Calvinist, for he was one of the five compilers of *The Form of Prayers and Ministration of the Sacraments, etc., used in the English Congregation at Geneva,* 1556[61] to which there is prefixed a short confession of faith, succinctly yet unashamedly Calvinist. Knox at the very least approved this document in which it is written that " Jesus Christ, Our Lord . . . made us (through faith) the children of God "; that he will come again " to separate the lambs from the goats, the elect from the reprobate "; that there is a church " not seen to man's eye, but only known to God, Who, of the lost sons of Adam, hath ordained some, as vessels of wrath, to damnation, and hath chosen others, as vessels of his mercy, to be saved "; that the sacraments " Christ has left unto us as holy signs and seals of God's promises," baptism signifying " that although this root of sin lie hid in us, yet to the elect it shall not be imputed."[62] The same document enjoins the Calvinist practice of ministers and elders being appointed by election of the congregation[63] and the Calvinist belief that, at the sacrament of the Lord's Supper, " we spiritually eat the flesh of Christ and drink his blood,"[64] refusing " to seek Christ bodily present in them (i.e. the elements) as if he were enclosed in the bread or wine, or as if these elements were turned and changed into the substance of his flesh and blood."[65]

In a letter that Knox wrote in 1557 " to his brethren in Scotland," predestination is stated explicitly: "And further they (i.e., who think as he does) acknowledge that this salvation doth not proceed of our works nor yet that it was appointed to us in time, but that before the foundation of the world was laid, did God elect us in Christ Jesus that we should be holy and blameless before him by love, by which he loved us even when we were dead in sin and did predestinate us and freely choose us to be his inheritors with Christ, according to the good pleasure of his will."[66] Moreover, on the eve of his return to Scotland to assume direct leadership of the reformation movement, the whole Calvinist doctrine of the eternal predestination of the elect and the reprobate had become so much a leading feature of Knox's convictions and had assumed such vital importance for him that he made it the subject of his longest, most exhaustive and greatest theological composition. In this work, *An Answer to the Cavillations of an Adversary respecting the Doctrine of Predestination,*[67] he uses the various statements hostile to predestination, made in an Anabaptist treatise, as the occasions for a systematic and extremely lengthy exposition of the Calvinist teaching on the matter.

Many of the continental protestants, taking the view that the unity of Christ's church had been broken and that the Council of Trent represented only a fraction of christendom, had been calling for a general council to settle the religious differences then prevalent. Knox himself, in his *Appellation to the Nobility and Estates of Scotland* (a rejoinder to his condemnation *in absentia* by an ecclesiastical court), allies himself to this

61. It is this " Order of Geneva " which, in an augmented form and called the Book of Common Order or Knox's Liturgy, was made the official prayer-book in Scotland by the General Asembly in 1564.
62. Laing's *Knox*, iv, pp. 169 seq.
63. *Op. cit.*, iv, pp. 175 seq.
64. *Op. cit.*, iv, p. 192.
65. *Op. cit.*, iv, p. 194.
66. *Op. cit.*, iv, p. 273.
7. *Op. cit.*, iv, pp. 21-468.

attitude and suggests the assembly of " a lawful and general council, wherein may all controversies in religion be decided by the authority of God's most sacred word."[68] But it is clear that, for Knox, the decisions of such a council, as with the teaching of all previous councils and the fathers, could be granted only conditional authority and acceptance, the condition being that they conformed to his interpretation of the scriptures; for he later adds: "And if they think to have advantage by their councils and doctors, this I further offer, to admit the one and the other as witnesses in all matters debatable . . . (provided) that no determination of councils nor man be admitted against the plain verity of God's word. . . . "[69]

. . . .

During his Genevan days, Knox retained his theological influence at home as the regulator of his followers' beliefs. The evidence[70] is that these last were very much as one would expect: attacks on the mass, the real presence, the other sacraments except baptism, prayers for the deceased and to the saints.

Antagonism towards the catholic clergy is expressed with an increased frequency, sometimes on theoretical, as well as practical, grounds. As the Letter of the Congregation, written in 1559 to the catholic nobility, puts it, the sign of true ministers of the church, who " have the same power which our Master, Christ Jesus, granted to His Apostles," is that " they preach and we believe the same doctrine which is contained in his most blessed word."[71]

In another of the several manifestoes which they issued late in 1558 and early in 1559, the protestants in Scotland echo Knox's request by suggesting a " general council lawfully assembled " to decide the religious controversies of the time; but the same prejudicial proviso is added: " We require that our brethren be not damned for heretics unless, by the manifest word of God, they be convicted to have erred from that faith which the Holy Spirit witnesseth to be necessary to salvation."[72]

. . . .

During the period leading up to Knox's return in May, 1559, catholics of influence were showing increasing realisation and anxiety about the danger to the church. A petition of some nobles, probably catholic, besides suggesting reforms of a disciplinary nature, stressed the importance of doctrinal matters, especially that the mass be properly revered and the sacraments correctly administered and received.[73] In the provincial council of 1559, catholic doctrines admittedly have a minor role, but it is noticeable that Calvinism as well as Lutheranism is named among the " nefarious heresies being propagated everywhere in this realm "[74] and

---

68. *Op. cit.*, iv, p. 489.
69. *Op. cit.*, iv, p. 518.
70. Cf. the dying words of Elizabeth Adamson, Knox's spiritual pupil; the anti-protestant sermon of the well-informed Dean John Sinclair of Restalrig; the condemnation of Walter Myln; and the reported catholic reaction to the protestant nobles' petition of November, 1558; (respectively, Dickinson's *Knox*, i, pp. 119-120 and 131; Laing's *Knox*, i, pp. 552-553; and Dickinson's *Knox*, i, p. 152).
71. Dickinson's *Knox*, i, p. 170.
72. *Op. cit.*, i, pp. 155-156.
73. *Statutes of the Scottish Church* (Scottish History Society), pp. 157-160.
74. *Op. cit.*, p. 150.

that, in concurring with the petition's recommendations, the council provides a list of subjects to which preachers were to give special attention and which includes most of the usual disputed matters noted above—the authority of the church, the mass, the real presence, the priesthood, prayers to the saints and for the souls in purgatory.[75] The mention made of the mass is short but especially valuable, as it may be regarded as an official, if unintended, rebuke to the inadequacy of the catechism: " The Sacrifice of the Mass, being instituted in commemoration of Christ's passion, benefits both the living and the dead by the efficacy of his passion."[76]

1558-1563

In 1560, the roles of the two sides in the Scottish reformation were reversed. But, from the point of view of the history of doctrinal opinions, 1560 hardly starts a new chapter. On the other hand, a novel element in events, not previously mentioned, was introduced in the year 1558. For it was then that, for the first time, a catholic apologist appeared, who defended catholicism and attacked the protestant heresies by the writing of polemical works. He was later joined by another protagonist and for a few years the two men, Quintin Kennedy and Ninian Winzet, were excellent advocates for catholic doctrine during the period of the church's downfall. So it is that, from the catholic point of view at least, the period from 1558 until 1563 may be regarded as a separate chapter in the doctrinal history of the reformation.

These years saw not only the overthrow of catholicism and the triumph of the protestants, but also the production of two very important protestant theological documents. These were the Confession of Faith and the Book of Discipline, both published in 1560, very shortly after the fateful proceedings in parliament. By them, Calvinism in Scotland was made official, explicit and complete, since they contain the first full Scottish statement of the doctrines of John Knox. It is, therefore, against a background of strife, destruction of the catholic edifice and consolidation of a thorough-going Calvinism that we have to view the controversial writings and debates of Kennedy and Winzet. As far as is known, they were the only two catholic protagonists of consequence during the critical period under consideration; and this, in spite of the fact that many priests and ecclesiastical institutions of the time took an evident interest in the works of catholic controversialists on the continent.[77]

Both men were about forty years old in 1558. Kennedy, son of the earl of Cassilis, had studied at the universities of St. Andrews and Paris and, shortly after ordination to the priesthood, had been appointed commendator-abbot of the Cluniac abbey of Crossraguel. He continued to hold that position during the period 1558-1563. Winzet was not of noble birth but was priest-schoolmaster at Linlithgow until 1561, when he was dismissed for his refusal to abjure catholicism.

---

75. *Op. cit.*, pp. 173-175. One continues, not unexpectedly, to have the impression that doctrinal errors bearing on matters of common religious practice were more prominent, at least with ordinary people, than those of a more technical nature.
76. *Op. cit.*, p. 175.
77. Cf. *The Innes Review*, ix, p. 15.

The literary output of neither was very large. Four tracts or treatises by Kennedy are known and in these he deals with only three topics of theological dissension: the method of settling religious controversy (this is the main subject of his first treatise, *Ane Compendius Tractive*[78] of 1558), the real presence of Christ in the Eucharist, and the sacrifice of the mass (which is the subject of the other of his two major works, *Ane Compendious Ressonyng*[79] of 1561).

Winzet, though not more prolific at this period, ranges much more widely in his choice of subjects, at least in the most important of his three works, *The Buke of Four Scoir Thre Questions*. These eighty-three questions are addressed to " the Calvinian preachers " and demand to know the reasons for their opinions on a great variety of religious topics. His other two works, as far as disputed theology is concerned, deal with the claim of Knox and others to be true ministers of Christ.[80] Winzet also translated several Latin works of the fathers and, of these, the only one still preserved in his translation of the Commonitorium of St. Vincent Lirinensis, a most popular work with catholic apologists of the sixteenth century.[81] Besides their writings, both men were engaged in direct arguments with prominent protestants and the more important of these will be noticed in their place.

In order to appreciate the methods used by Kennedy, Winzet and their opponents, it will be sufficient to consider three important topics of controversy—the way to interpret scripture correctly, the sacrifice of the mass, and the validity of Knox's protestant ministry. This consideration will also give an insight into some of the special difficulties facing catholic apologists of the period.

. . . .

In a sense, the first of these topics, even as it is fundamental in theological argument, is also the hardest in which to reach a satisfactory conclusion. Catholics hold that divine revelation is to be found in tradition as well as in sacred scripture—a position that protestants reject. But the problem now is not that, but this: all christians admit that the bible contains the revealed word of God, but they likewise realise that, unfortunately, the contents of the bible frequently require interpretation; in other words, the meaning of many of the statements in scripture is not immediately clear, either because the statements themselves are capable of being understood in different ways, or because an apparently obvious statement may be confronted by a seemingly contradictory passage from elsewhere in scripture. Indeed, a great many of the theological controversies of the reformation can be traced to different meanings being attached to the words of scripture. So the question is: what is the correct method of arriving at a true interpretation of scripture ?

The Calvinist answer has already been indicated[82] and was given its definitive Scottish statement in the Confession of Faith: " The interpretation whereof (i.e., of scripture) . . . apperteineth to the Spirit of God, by the which also the scripture was written. When controversy

---

78. Reprinted in *The Miscellany of the Wodrow Society*, i, pp. 95-174.

79. In manuscript and never printed; the preface is printed in Laing's *Knox*, vi, pp. 166-168.

80. All three works, and the translation of the *Commonitorium*, were reprinted by the Scottish Text Society (1888-90) under the general title, *Certain Tractates by Ninian Winzet*.

81. Thirty-five editions, twenty-two translations (Cf. *D.T.C.*, xv, 2, col. 3046).

82. Cf. *supra*.

then happeneth for the right understanding of any place or sentence of scripture . . . we ought not so much to look what men before us have said or done, as unto that which the Holy Ghost uniformly speaks within the body of the scriptures and unto that which Christ Jesus himself did, and commanded to be done. . . . If then the interpretation, determination or sentence of any doctor, kirk or council repugn to the plain word of God written in any other place of the scripture, it is a thing most certain that theirs is not the true understanding and meaning of the Holy Ghost, supposing that councils, realms and nations have approved and received the same; for we dare not receive and admit any interpretation which directly repugneth to any principal point of our faith or to any other plain text of scripture or yet unto the rule of charity."[83] That these words mean, in effect, " our interpretation is always correct " is confirmed by the assertion in the same chapter that " the doctrine taught in our kirks is contained in the written word of God, to wit, in the books of the Old and New Testaments."[84]

Thus the difficulty confronting Kennedy and Winzet. To suggest that the right of interpreting scripture lay with councils, fathers of the church or doctors met with a denial; their agreement with the Calvinist interpretation provided a valuable confirmation that they, too, possessed the Spirit of God, but disagreement simply meant they were mistaken. To lay down that at least the church of God had the power to interpret simply brought the rejoinder that the true church was not any visible organisation, least of all catholicism, but was the company, known in its entirety only to God, of the elect through the ages; it was this company, of whom the antagonists of Kennedy and Winzet claimed to be part, which could know infallibly the meaning of the scriptures. Both Kennedy and Winzet made attempts to tackle the problem of forcing the Calvinists from their entrenched and (in the literal sense) prejudiced position concerning scriptural interpretation.

Kennedy's effort was made in the work which, as far as is known, is his first: *Ane Compendius Tractive, conforme to the Scripturis of Almychtie God, Ressoun and Authoritie, declaring the nerrest and onlie way to establische the conscience of ane Christiane man in all materis (quhilks are in debate) concernying Faith and Religioun.* In this, his thesis is straightforward and direct enough, but perhaps, for that very reason, of little trouble to his opponents: in doctrinal matters which are the subject of dispute, and especially in controversies concerning scriptural texts, the church is the only true judge; but it is evident that all of the members of that body cannot meet to settle these matters and hence it is that, even from the time of the apostles, general councils, in this connection representing all the members of the church, have decided controverted matters with the same authority and strength as the church as a whole. That this is true of general councils, Kennedy proves scripturally, historically and by reasoning. Therefore, " let every private man, what vocation that ever God has called him to, flee curiosity in seeking the secrets and mysteries of the scripture, in special, such as the sacraments, predestination, free will and justification."[85]

---

83. Chapter 18, (Dickinson's *Knox*, ii, pp. 266-267).
84. *Op. cit.*, ii, p. 266.
85. *The Miscellany of the Wodrow Society*, i, p. 133.

Ane Compendius Tractive made sufficient impact among the protestants to elicit an answer, published in 1563 by John Davidson, then principal of the college of Glasgow.[86] This takes the form of short extracts from Kennedy's work, followed by a lengthy reply from Davidson. His answer to Kennedy is, as one would expect, a restatement of the Calvinist position: the word of God is not only the witness in controversies of religion (as Kennedy had said) but also the judge; general councils have been merely the assemblies of godly and learned men in order that the interpretation of each of them (given to them in the ordinary way and, as to all the elect, by the Holy Spirit) may be heard and noted.

Winzet's approach to the problem is less studied, more animated than Kennedy's. Without yet deciding what or where it is, the holy catholic church, he says, undoubtedly has the true understanding of the word of God in scripture, because of Christ's promise to the church: " When he, the Spirit of Truth, is come, he will teach you all truth."[87] The question is to decide where the church is and, therefore, where the true interpretation of scripture is to be found; here, there are two alternatives: the church's judgment is to be found either in the ancient fathers and councils (whose interpretations have always, until recently, been accepted and observed by all christians) or in the opinions of Calvin and his followers. To justify this claim, Winzet gives many examples to show that (a) the doctrines of contemporary catholics were taught by the fathers and early councils (so that the term " papistry," insinuating that these doctrines were of recent invention, was misleading) and (b) Calvinist teaching had no ancient confirmation. Hence, if Calvinism is correct, the scriptures have never previously in the history of Christianity been correctly understood—a conclusion that Winzet seeks to ridicule as in conflict with common sense. He suggests also that his opponents are illogical in accepting the judgment of tradition in determining which books are truly part of scripture and which are apocryphal[88] but in refusing to use the same criterion in anything else.

The force of Winzet's argument is not necessarily dependent on accepting the catholic view of the church as a visible organisation. It is true that, against the protestant concept of an invisible church of the elect, he argues that scripture and tradition, when speaking of the church, make no mention of such, but always imply a visible church with good and evil persons among its members; and that many suspect that the protestant view is " to the end that you and your private opinion be not judged by men of superior powers."[89] But even though his opponents would not accept his outlook on this matter, his alternative—the true church must either be Calvin and his followers alone, or else all previous christians—would still have its point. Certainly, Calvinists were able to adduce other ancient testimonies apparently in their favour (or at least themselves in need of interpretation) and, as for the rest of antiquity, its witness was to be rejected. But even so, because they valued the confirmation which they maintained the early church's views held for them, the more instances Winzet gave of their doctrinal isolation, the more disconcerting would their position become.

---

86. *Op. cit.,* i, pp. 181-258.
87. John, xvi, 13.
88. Confession of Faith, chapter 18, (Dickinson's *Knox,* ii, p. 266).
89. Question 72, p. 120.

Notice of this problem provides the opportunity of dealing with the attitude of the catholic church in this country towards the vexed issue of papal authority, especially in its relation to general councils. The question was the subject of a great deal of dispute in Europe among catholic theologians of pre-Tridentine and Tridentine times, nor was the matter settled at Trent; for some, the decrees (nowadays recognised not to have been solemn definitions) of the council of Contance[90] that a general council represents the whole church militant and has authority from God in such manner that even the pope is subject to its decrees concerning faith, heresy and reform, were the basis of their opinion; for others, papal primacy, not only in conjunction with general councils but independently of them, seemed to be the truth; and naturally there were some more theologians striving to achieve a compromise solution acceptable to both extremes.

When the relevant Scottish documents[91] are dealing with the question of the supreme authority in matters of faith, etc., it is true that, on the face of things, they may seem conciliarist. However, it is to be noted that none of these documents attacks the papal claims vis-à-vis general councils (as the true conciliarists did), but simply keeps silent about the whole problem. Moreover, in other places, there is no antagonism shown to the pope, but rather deference.[92]

The clergy were by no means ignorant of the disputes about papal authority among European theologians, many of the main works, both from the two extreme points of view and from the attempted middle ways, forming a significant part of their libraries.[93] It is quite probable that, because many of the Scots clergy had been educated in France, where the conciliarist opinion was strongly maintained (nowhere more than in the university of Paris), there may well have been a tendency towards this viewpoint in Scotland. But, leaving aside the complete omission of the pope from Hamilton's catechism (for in a work claiming to be a summary of all matters a christian should know, some mention of the pope would seem almost unavoidable), one can conclude as follows: of documents where only the restricted question of supreme ecclesiastical authority is being discussed, it would be unjustified to say more than that their silence regarding papal power is a judicious acknowledgment of the confused state of the question in those days.

. . . .

The hostility that Knox bore to the mass even in his early days of prominence has already been mentioned.[94] His attitude, and that of

---

90. Session 5, 5th April, 1415.

91. Hamilton's catechism, the statement of the 1559 provincial council, Kennedy's *Ane Compendius Tractive*.

92. The Throne more than once sent to Rome reassurances concerning its fidelity to the catholic church; parliament enacted against those who denied the authority of the pope; at the trials of heretics, attacks on the pope were regarded as matters for punishment; the protestants' hatred of the pope is evidence of the position he held in the minds of catholics; William Hay taught, in his lectures previously mentioned, that " above all these " (i.e., patriarchs, primates and all bishops) " is the pope, successor of St. Peter and vicar of Christ, with the plenitude of power . . . and thus is assured the unity of the church, because all the members are under one head; hence those who deny this power are schismatics and dividers of the unity of the Church," (*The Innes Review*, ii, p. 98); and, not least, Winzet writes of his special love and obedience for " the successor of Peter now commonly called pope," (*Book of Questions*, Preface, p. 59), and adduces the testimony both of scripture, to prove that Christ gave authority over the other apostles to St. Peter, and of tradition, to show that superiority was attributed to the bishops of Rome as the successors of St. Peter. (Question 39, pp. 102-103.)

93. *The Innes Review*, ix, p. 15.

94. Cf. *supra*.

his followers, in no way weakened in later years, the celebration of mass being proscribed as a " wicked idolatry " immediately after the Calvinist victory of August, 1560. In brief, the view was that adoration and reception of the consecrated elements, in the belief that they were truly Christ, were a travesty of what he instituted, that the priest-celebrant was attempting to set himself up as a mediator between God and man, and that the claim that the mass was a sacrifice and could be offered in propitiation of sin was a blasphemous insult to the one and all-sufficient sacrifice of Calvary.[95]

Winzet's reactions to these opinions are of mixed value. The real presence is adequately vindicated with several of the usual arguments, and the point is made that the priest, far from seeking to intrude between God and man, is acting as Christ's minister and as merely a participant in the priesthood of Christ, the only high priest.[96] But the relationship of the mass to Calvary is not explained and the propitiatory nature of the mass only indirectly stated.[97] Moreover, among some proofs, very sketchily presented, that the mass is a sacrifice is a claim that " no christian of the former age and few of the protestants at this present in Germany and other countries deny the right use and practice of the Lord's Supper to be called a sacrifice or oblation."[98] Lutherans, who allowed the Eucharist to be called a sacrifice, but only of praise and thanksgiving, would probably have been surprised at this rather ingenuous enlistment of their support by a catholic.[99] Winzet's orthodoxy is not in question, of course, for the whole tone of his work is illustrative of his wish to be in complete doctrinal conformity with the church; also, at the time of writing, Winzet, who was not a trained theologian, had to a great extent to rely on his memory of previous reading and was working prior to the Tridentine definitions on the mass;[100] nor was he under any obligation—as, for instance, the catechism's author was—to deal with his subject fully.

However, it is evident that the church's teaching on the mass is the branch of theology in which Quintin Kennedy excels. In addition to his disputes with Willock and Knox, two of his written works deal with the subject. In *Ane Oratioune*,[101] Kennedy seeks to show that protestant condemnation of the mass as idolatrous was mistaken, and, for this purpose, he recalls the first of Knox's famous syllogisms of 1550.[102] Before passing to the minor premise, Kennedy delays to reject the major also, showing that the incidents adduced by Knox did not prove what he claimed, namely, that all worship not commanded by God is wrongful; indeed, he gives several examples of such worship being pleasing to God. For his refutation of the minor premise, Kennedy refers his readers to the fuller and more important treatise, *Ane Compendious Ressonying*.

---

95. Cf. Confession of Faith, chapter 22, (Dickinson's *Knox*, ii, p. 270).

96. Questions 20, 21, 25, 26, pp. 86-88, 90-93.

97. Question 22, p. 89.

98. Question 11, p. 80.

99. Indeed, Calvin himself speaks of the Lord's Supper as a sacrifice of praise (*Institution de la Religion Chrétienne*, bk. 4, ch. 18, no. 16-17; Corpus Reformatorum, 32, 1074-1076)—though whether Winzet overlooked this or considered it further condemnation of the Scots Calvinists, it is impossible to say.

100. Session 22, 17th September, 1562.

101. Reprinted in Laing's *Knox*, vi, pp. 157-165.

102. "All worshipping, honouring or service invented by the brain of man in the religion of God, without His express commandment, is idolatry; the Mass is invented by the brain of man without any commandment of God; therefore it is idolatry."

This latter work is in the form of a dialogue or conversation between an enquirer, who plies the other with questions and objections about the mass, and a catholic, thereby enabled to make a refutation of protestant errors and an explanation of catholic teaching. Kennedy's is not the scornful, pointed, hard-hitting style of the born controversialist that Winzet often achieved; but as a painstaking and detailed exposition of the church's teaching on the mass, borne out by many apt references to authority, *Ane Compendious Ressonyng* is an admirable work. In it, Kennedy is not content merely to establish that the mass is not a human invention. He proceeds to show that it is " the sacrifice and oblation of the Lord's body and blood given and offered by him at the Last Supper," and this he does with no fewer than nine proofs. These range from Old Testament figures of this sacrifice, through New Testament texts, to authoritative statements and opinions in the early church. His proofs are usually much more than simple assertions (as Winzet's tended to be) and are also supported by frequent references and illustrations.[103]

Good though Kennedy's explanation is that the mass is a sacrifice, there is an even better feature of *Ane Compendious Ressonyng*—the explanation of the *nature* of this sacrifice. Consideration of this matter is essential if one is to be able to answer protestant objections previously mentioned and based on St. Paul's teaching that " Our Saviour was offered up once a sacrifice on the cross for man's redemption and is never to be offered up again."[104] In fact, it was to meet such objections that the Council of Trent produced its definitions to show that St. Paul's words and the fact that the mass is a propitiatory sacrifice are in no way irreconcilable and that the solution of difficulties is only a matter of understanding properly the special type of sacrifice that the mass is. The Tridentine teaching thus provided all catholic writers with the answer to protestant objections, but the intriguing feature in Kennedy's case is that *Ane Compendious Ressonyng* preceded by a year the council's definitions. Although in the years immediately before the latter, and because of the need adequately to reply to the protestants, catholic theologians had been attempting detailed explanations of the sacrificial nature of the mass, the church's official teaching was greatly lacking in exactness. It was clear that the mass was a sacrifice with the same victim and principal offerer (Christ) as the sacrifice of Calvary and that it was in some way representative and commemorative of that sacrifice, but writers of the time had to work out their answers, without authoritative guidance, as to how the mass was a sacrifice in a stricter sense than as a mere representation or depiction of the cross and how, as a true sacrifice, it did not in any way detract from the one sacrifice of Calvary and its infinite merits.

Just how good were Kennedy's answers will be seen from the following comparison. In its decrees of 1562, the Council of Trent defined that " in this divine sacrifice performed in the mass, that same Christ is contained and bloodlessly offered who on the altar of the cross once offered himself in a bloody manner . . . the victim is one and the same, now offering by the ministry of priests who once offered himself on the cross, only the manner of offering being different; indeed, the fruit of his bloody oblation is most plentifully obtained by means of

---

103. It is perhaps noteworthy that he, like Winzet, appeals to the unanimity of history for his point but, unlike his colleague, he names Luther as one of the few exceptions to the general rule.
104. Hebrews, x, 10 seq., etc.

this bloodless one."[105] In 1561, Kennedy had anticipated this decree by stating that, whereas the sacrifice of the cross was performed in a bloody manner, " the Lord's body is offered up after another manner in the sacrifice of the mass . . . as an unbloody sacrifice. . . . It is the selfsame body that is offered up . . . not as a new satisfaction or re-demption but as a new sacrifice in commemoration and remembrance of Christ's death and passion, by the use of which we are made partakers of the fruits of the death and passion of Jesus Christ, our Saviour."[106]

This explanation, so close to the future definition, enables Kennedy to show that St. Paul's words refer to a repetition of a sacrifice in the same visible bloody manner as the cross and for the same purpose of securing salvation for mankind; the mass may be called a " new sacri-fice " because our Lord is offered in a different manner and its purpose is not to duplicate, or to be a substitute for, the work of the cross, but to apply the merits gained there; therefore, far from being a derogation of Calvary, the mass in fact enhances that sacrifice since (along with the sacraments) it is the means whereby our Lord has decreed that the merits he gained for us on the cross should be distributed. (Needless to say, Kennedy can hardly be blamed for not mentioning a modern tendency among theologians which provides a further safeguard for the words of St. Paul—a tendency to go even further than the Council of Trent did in relating the mass to the sacrifice of the cross.) However, what he has said allows him to explain accurately but easily the propitiatory value of the mass. He shows that, by its function in applying our Lord's merits gained on the cross, the souls in purgatory are helped in their sufferings and the living also benefit, not in the sense that the mass remits their mortal sins but because, by it, they may receive graces to bring them to repentance, the remission of punishment due for past sins, and graces to fight future temptations to sin. These details once again closely an-ticipate the Tridentine teaching and set the seal on a portion of *Ane Compendious Ressonyng* that is a tribute to its author's theological skill.

One must not omit to mention that on the two occasions on which Abbot Kennedy directly disputed with the protestants, the mass was again the subject at issue. In 1559, John Willock had returned from exile and was preaching at Ayr, his theme being that the mass is idolatrous. Kennedy tried to counteract Willock's influence by his own preaching and thus a public debate was arranged between the two. In the prelim-inary correspondence, Kennedy undertook to show in the debate that the mass is not idolatrous. Willock replied, accepting the challenge, and laid down that the debate was to begin with the scriptural evidence. Kennedy was agreeable but, foreseeing differences about interpretation, stressed the need for authoritative judges and stipulated that these be the fathers of the church. At this, Willock invoked the usual Calvinist attitude: " I will allow all the doctors, so far as their sayings and judg-ments agree with the said word of God expressly contained in the holy scriptures."[107] That ended the dispute since the projected debate did not take place. Willock alleged that Kennedy was late in arriving, but the latter's explanation of the cancellation is that Willock arrived with

---

105. Session 22, chapter 2.
106. fol. 5.
107. The correspondence between the two is printed in Keith, *History of the Affairs of Church and State in Scotland*, iii, pp. 393-404.

several hundred followers instead of the twelve, which, to prevent violence, had been mutually agreed; because of the danger of a riot, therefore, the debate was called off.

In 1562, Kennedy spent three days in public debate at Maybole with John Knox himself. The only account extant is Knox's own,[108] according to which Kennedy was confounded several times so that the laurels of the debate rested with Knox. However, the catholic side maintained that Knox's friends were so annoyed by his performance that they said it would have been better for him not to have appeared.[109]

The debate opened with Kennedy's explanation of catholic teaching on Melchisedech, the figure of Christ. Melchisedech made an oblation or sacrifice of bread and wine to God; Christ is a priest for ever according to the order of Melchisedech;[110] there is " no place in the gospel where Our Saviour . . . declares himself to be a priest after the order of Melchisedech but in the Last Supper, where he made oblation of his precious body and blood under the form of bread and wine, prefigured by the oblation of Melchisedech . . . then are we compelled to affirm that Our Saviour made oblation of his body and blood in the Last Supper, or else he was not a priest according to the order of Melchisedech."[111] This is very customary catholic theological reasoning (though since St. Paul did not exclude the sacrifice of the cross when explaining Christ's priesthood according to the order of Melchisedech, it is more accurate to show merely that our Lord exercised his priesthood according to Melchisedech at the Last Supper without asserting that this was the only occasion on which he did so). On the first day of the debate, therefore, reasonable progress was made on one of the traditional proofs that the mass is a sacrifice. However, the second and third days were completely occupied by a long-drawn-out wrangle on whether Melchisedech offered bread and wine in sacrifice to God or only as refreshment to Abraham, Kennedy, of course, defending the former view customary with catholics.

The debate was adjourned at this impasse and after these two unprofitable days without progress. The intention to resume at a later date was never carried into effect, so that the affair remains no more than a partial, and therefore unsatisfactory, attempt to argue the merits of catholic claims concerning the mass. One may, perhaps, regard it as a monumental example of the basic difficulty in the interpretation of scripture, as well as of the futility of hoping to reach a decision in theological argument.

· · · · · ·

If the mass is Kennedy's principal interest, it is clear that Winzet's favourite matter on which to taunt his opponents was the claim they made to be true ministers of Christ. He raises the subject time and time again in his writings, choosing as his test case and particular target, Knox himself, " as to him who was held . . . principal patriarch of the Calvinist court."[112]

---

108. Laing's *Knox*, vi, pp. 169-220.
109. Lesley, *De Origine, Moribus et Rebus Gestis Scotorum*, p. 540.
110. Psalm 109, 4; Hebrews v and vii.
111. Laing's *Knox*, vi, p. 186.
112. *Book of Questions*, Preface, p. 56.

Towards the end of February, 1561-2, Winzet sent to Knox a copy of his *Book of Questions*, still unpublished. Among these, the question that most attracted Knox's attention, and which therefore had certain consequences, was the thirty-third, entitled " If John Knox be lawful minister ? " In it, Winzet explains that this is not a matter of Knox's lawful ministry as a catholic priest since, even though he will remain a priest for ever, he claims to " renounce and esteem that ordination null, or rather wicked, by which formerly he was called Sir John."[113] Therefore, Winzet's point is this: the scriptures[114] lay down that no man may undertake the ministry of God's word and the sacraments without a lawful vocation, either immediately from God or else mediately, from men with the requisite power; moreover, an immediate divine vocation is always accompanied by some proof (namely, the explicit testimony of Holy Scripture or the ability to work signs and wonders)[115] and, for the other type of vocation, only the apostles and their successors, catholic bishops, possess the requisite power;[116] " therefore if you, John Knox we say, be called immediately by God, where are your marvels wrought by the Holy Spirit ? . . . but if you be called by men, you must show them to have lawful power thereto."

Knox received the *Book of Questions*, brought from Winzet by " an honourable person of your own (i.e. Knox's) religion who of his charity (as he thought) had often exhorted some of us to a union with you."[117] But instead of a private answer in writing, as Winzet asked, Knox's rejoinder was given in a public sermon. This sermon is not preserved but Winzet, as well as complaining that Knox had distorted what he had written,[118] recounts that, of the eighty-three questions, " one article specially " (i.e., regarding his lawful vocation) " he chose out of so many to confute and confound in the pulpit, to augment his glory."[119]

It is worth remembering that, in 1560, the Book of Discipline had laid down that ordinary vocation to the ministry consisted of three stages: election, or choice of a candidate by the congregation he was to rule, examination in life and in doctrine by ministers and elders of sound judgment, and admission, or the public approbation of the congregation.[120] Here, the vocation is not immediately from God, but from men; the requisite power is regarded as belonging to the congregation. The same outlook is seen in Knox's account, written almost twenty years after the event, of the method by which he himself was called to the protestant ministry in 1547. A sermon was preached, pointing out " what power the congregation . . . had above any man in whom they supposed and espied the gifts of God to be "; the congregation gave the call to Knox, he was charged " that ye refuse not this holy vocation but

---

113. Question 33, p. 99.
114. Romans, x, 15; Hebrews, v, 4.
115. Kennedy had made the same point several years previously in a remark in *Ane Compendius Tractive:* " Read the Scripture all through, I dare boldly say, thou shalt never find any man sent by God only, and not by man, but he confirmed his doctrine by miracles or else the Scripture makes plain mention that he was sent by God." (*The Miscellany of the Wodrow Society*, i, p. 123.)
116. This last detail, implicit in Question 33 as well as Question 34 (pp.98-99), is explicit in *The Last Blast*, pp. 41-42.
117. Winzet's Letter of 3rd March, 1561-2, (pp. 16-17).
118. *Ibid.*, p. 17.
119. *Book of Questions*, Preface, pp. 57-58.
120. Chapter 4, (Dickinson's *Knox*, ii, pp. 283-287).

. . . that ye take upon you the public office and charge of preaching "
and, in these circumstances, he accepted the office of preacher of God's
word.[121]

However, in spite of these facts, the burden of Knox's preached
rejoinder to Winzet's question does not seem to have been a rejection of
the catholic belief that ordination to the priesthood (or, to avoid using
these terms, mediate vocation to the ministry) can be received only from
bishops. Rather does Knox appear by now to have been thinking of
himself as directly called by God to his ministry for, in letters which
Winzet wrote to him some days later,[122] he rejects Knox's attempt to
prove his immediate vocation by the examples of St. John the Baptist
and the Prophet Amos; contrary to Knox's claim, both of these, as well
as the apostles and the seventy-two disciples, showed their immediate
vocations by proofs, " of which, none (as we understand yet) convenes
to you." In the second of these letters, and still more in a third one
two days later, Winzet urges Knox to give up his work as a minister of
Christ if he cannot justify his lawful vocation, at the same time citing
examples of the punishments meted out by divine Providence to those
who had usurped a sacred office.[123]

After receiving the third letter, Knox again preached on this question
of his dispute with Winzet and in his sermon, Winzet says, promised
what the latter had always sought—an answer in writing.[124] But by
July, the promise was still unfulfilled and, in exasperation, Winzet wrote
and had printed *The Last Blast of the Trompet of Godis Worde aganis the
usurpit auctoritie of Iohne Knox and his Calviniane Brether intrudit Precheouris.*
In it, he repeats the complaints he had already made against Knox—no
written reply, no satisfactory proof of vocation, no sign of his demitting
office. He makes the further point that scandalous life and conduct
by some catholics is no reason or excuse for others becoming heretics.

The printing of *The Last Blast* was never completed for, during the
process, the press was seized and Winzet had to flee to the continent.[125]
But there were later echoes to the dispute. Before his debate with
Quintin Kennedy, Knox composed a written reply to the abbot's *Ane
Oratioune* and the illuminating remark is found there: " But my lord
(i.e., Kennedy) perchance requireth miracles to prove our lawful vocation,
for so doth Winzet, the procurator for the papists; to both I answer that
a truth by itself without miracles hath sufficient strength to prove the
lawful vocation of the teachers thereof."[126] Clearly, Knox is here
claiming an immediate vocation from God; but the mere repetition of
the Calvinist assumption that their interpretation of God's word was
true can hardly have been acceptable to his opponents. He adds that the
matter " by the grace of God shall be more fully treated in the answer
to Winzet's questions thereupon,"[127] but again the answer was not made.

---

121. *Op. cit.*, i, p. 83.
122. On 3rd and 10th March, 1561-2.
123. The three letters, together with the original questions on Knox's ministry, were printed on 21st May,
1562, as part of *Certane Tractatis for Reformatioun of Doctryne and Maneris.*
124. *The Last Blast*, p. 39. Knox's behaviour towards Winzet illustrates well the fact that he was happier
as an orator than as a theological thinker. The pulpit was always more congenial to him than the
intellectual discipline and exactitude demanded by written composition.
125. Apart from a brief visit in September, 1571, Winzet never returned to Scotland.
126. Laing's *Knox*, vi, pp. 192-193.
127. *Op. cit.*, vi, p. 193.

By the time that Winzet, now in the Low Countries, had in hand the printing and publication of his *Book of Questions*[128] and was writing a preface to it, he knew of Knox's references and of his intention to produce a reply. Winzet rejoices at this last but, because more than a year had passed since Knox's promise and he had not yet learned of any reply, he suspects that he may again be disappointed; at least, the delay will have given Knox time for thought and perhaps opportunity to see the truth; moreover, " by his long silence after so many promises, he shows himself convicted in conscience, having no apparent reason for the defence of his vocation."[129]

The printed edition of the *Book of Questions* also carries a bitter postscript, directed personally to John Knox: " It appears to me, brother, that you have some great impediment whereby you are stopped from keeping promise touching your answering to this our tractate, after so long advisement."[130] Scornfully, Winzet suggests that perhaps his handwriting was illegible—if so, the present printed copy of the questions will remove that obstacle; or it may be that Knox's absence from Scotland and his years among English speakers have led to his forgetting the Scottish tongue—if so, Winzet would be willing to use Latin. But even these taunts were unavailing and the matter ended there. Whether or not one judges that the absence of a written reply from Knox represents a moral victory for Winzet and however one views Knox's apparent identification of his vocation with that of the prophets of the scriptures— as ludicrous, revealing or tragic—the impression remains, not so much of a dispute between two willing contestants, as of a relentless harrying of the reformer by the schoolmaster.

· · · · · · ·

The years between 1558 and 1563, then, witnessed an activity in controversy, at least from the catholic side, previously unknown and subsequently repeated only from abroad. Without a doubt, Kennedy, the erudite theologian, and Winzet, the astute yet mild-mannered controversialist, were the outstanding catholic representatives, but there were also other priests at this time to defend the doctrines of the church in debate. Little is known in detail of such controversialists. Lesley says that many public disputations between catholics and protestants took place at this time and enumerates the contestants in about six of them, adding that there were others which he has not expressly mentioned.[131] Perhaps the best remembered of them was a disputation before some of the nobility, in which there were about four participants on each side, the mass being the subject under debate.[132]

However, these were special occasions. As far as day-to-day defence of the church's doctrines was concerned, the judgment of the papal legate of 1562, Nicholas of Gouda, is much less impressive: " There are some catholic preachers of note, but they are few in number and

128. Antwerp, October, 1563.
129. *Book of Questions*, Preface, p. 58.
130. *Op. cit.*, p. 138.
131. Lesley, *De Origine, Moribus et Rebus Gestis Scotorum*, pp. 530, 533, 538, 540, 551.
132. *Op. cit.*, p. 530; Dickinson's *Knox*, i, pp. 352-354. In addition, the queen's French confessor, René Benoist, issued a few anti-Calvinist tracts during 1561 and 1562, these being in Latin and in French and later translated.

seldom venture to attack controverted points, being indeed unequal to the task of handling them with effect."[133]

By 1564, the lively polemics of the previous years had died down. Of the two outstanding catholic apologists, Winzet was pursuing a successful academic career at Paris and Douai. He was finally (in 1576) appointed abbot of the Scots Benedictine abbey at Ratisbon and there he spent his last years, until his death in 1592. Unlike Winzet, Kennedy was not forced into exile, in spite of his twice having been threatened with punishment because he continued to celebrate mass. But, unfortunately for the church's cause, he died in 1564 when by no means in old age.

AFTER 1563

With the departure of Kennedy and Winzet from the scene, one reaches the end of a chapter in the history of theological dispute in Scotland. However, it was not long until the church found exponents of its teaching among Scotsmen abroad, with the result that soon religious controversial writings were appearing again from both sides, those from the Calvinists being as a rule in answer to catholic expositions.

Perhaps the most celebrated of these disputes was that which James Tyrie conducted with Knox and others. Tyrie, who had gone abroad in 1563 and had joined the Society of Jesus, had written several letters to try to convert his protestant brother. These were said to have been of great value in converting other Calvinists also, so that when one of the letters, written in 1567, reached John Knox, he quickly wrote a long reply to it. Tyrie's theme is that our Lord founded a visible church and that this is the catholic church, since it alone has universality and doctrinal apostolicity, both necessary characteristics of the true church. Knox, in his answer, holds that the church of Christ is invisible and made up of the godly, denies that many of the contemporary doctrines of catholicism (and especially those of the mass and the pope) are of apostolic origin and, therefore, rejects Tyrie's assertions. This reply was not printed until 1572, but it reached Tyrie in Paris soon after that. He published *The Refutation of Ane Ansuer made be Schir Iohne Knox* in 1573 and, with Knox now dead, the Calvinist response was undertaken by John Duncanson and also by George Hay, though probably neither of their works was published.

A written controversy on similar topics occurred between Archibald Hamilton and Thomas Smeton. Hamilton had written a treatise in Latin, *On the Confusion of the Calvinist Sect in Scotland*, in which he deals with the catholicity and apostolic succession of the true church as well as with the primacy of the pope, to which Smeton replied from Edinburgh, also in Latin, with *The Orthodox Response to the Virulent Dialogue of Archibald Hamilton impiously written, concerning the confusion of the Calvinist Sect among the Scots*. Hamilton's rejoinder was a tract, *Against the Scurrilous Response of the Ministers of Scotland*.

In 1580, John Hay, S.J., published from Paris *Certaine Demandes concerning the Christian Religion and Discipline*, a work of great influence, especially on the continent, being translated into both French and German and adducing several protestant replies. It consists of 166

---

133.   Letter of 30th October, 1562, to Father Laynez, General of the Society of Jesus, (W. Forbes Leith, *Narratives of Scottish Catholics*, p. 75.)

challenging questions to the protestants on a wide range of disputed doctrines and is very reminiscent of the method and style of Winzet.

Ninian Winzet himself, now abbot at Ratisbon, made his reappearance in the field of controversy with two long Latin works, written in 1581 and published at Ingolstadt in the following year. Both have, as their subjects, the rights of rulers and the relationship that should prevail between rulers and people, particularly in matters of religion; but in one of the works, *Flagellum Sectariorum*, he introduces many purely theological topics. These range over practically the whole field of disputed matters: justification, the mass, the real presence, the sacraments, prayer to the saints, religious vows and, not least, the question of the vocation required by God's ministers. Winzet devotes a full quarter of the work to this last, in which he repeats his thesis of 1561-2 and in which there is even a reference to the claims made by " the minister of Calvin in Britain, John Knox, once of great fame."[134]

Other Scotsmen in Europe active in writing in defence of the church's doctrines were William Chisholm, who, in 1584, succeeded his uncle as bishop of Vaison in France, Francis Hamilton, prior of the Scots Monastery at Würzburg at the turn of the century, and John Colville. The last was a convert from Calvinism, whose work, *Paroenesis*, in 1602, reiterated the traditional catholic views on Christ's church: that it is a visible body and that it, and in particular its rulers, has authority in all matters of faith and scriptural interpretation.

Although the most important polemical works of the Scots Calvinists are to be found as replies to catholic statements, there is one other field that is worth brief notice. This is the education of the laity in religious doctrine. Archbishop Hamilton's catechism had been superseded in 1560 by a translation of the catechism of Calvin. This remained in use until 1581, when John Craig, then one of the king's chaplains, compiled his *Shorte Summe of the Whole Catechisme*, a work in the form of question and answer, conceived in a very simple and straightforward manner, but thoroughly Calvinist in teaching. A few examples will illustrate its style and tone: " Question: What is the Church which we confess here ? Answer: The whole congregation of God's elect, called and sanctified. Q: What thing is true faith ? A: An assured knowledge of God's mercy towards us for Christ's sake, according to his promise. Q: Out of what fountain does this our stability flow ? A: Out of God's eternal and constant election in Christ."[135]

Catholics at home during these early years of protestant domination had not the opportunity of either the protestants in Scotland or the catholics abroad to publicise their religious opinions. Nonetheless, the priests who remained faithful to their office and those who managed to re-enter the country after ordination on the continent must, in addition to their ordinary work of celebrating mass and administering the sacraments, also have tried to uphold the church's doctrines and refute those of their opponents. Their efforts are, naturally, not well recorded by history, principally perhaps because they were so seldom able to be written down, let alone printed. But there is at least some evidence of their zeal and that of some laymen, too.

---

134. p. 125.
135. In the Barberini Collection of the Vatican Library, there is a manuscript containing *Ane schort Catholik Confession*, written about 1588 in answer to Craig's catechism.

Prospectus Civitatis TAODUNI ab Oriente. The Prospect of y Town of DUNDEE from y* East.*

PLATE XXI. THE TOWN OF DUNDEE, FROM SLEZER'S *THEATRUM SCOTIAE.*

PLATE XXII. JAMES STEWART, EARL OF MORAY.

Nicol Burne, professor of philosophy at St. Leonard's College in St. Andrews, became a catholic in 1580 and was soon engaged in public disputation on behalf of the church's teaching. Exiled to Paris very shortly afterwards, he published there an account of his apologetic work in Scotland.[136] James Gordon, S.J., of Huntly, disputed more than once, and even (in 1585) with the king himself, on the questions of justification and the mass. Gilbert Brown, abbot of Sweetheart, is said to have been of great influence, not only by example but by instruction also, in the preservation and spread of catholicism in south-west Scotland. He was banished about 1606 but before that, in 1602, he had engaged in a written controversy on matters of religion with John Welsh, a minister of Ayr. The convert, John Hamilton, a theological scholar of some fame in France, rector for a time of the university of Paris and the author of at least three polemical works,[137] returned to Scotland and continued his struggle here in defence of the church's teaching until his committal to the Tower of London, where he died in 1610. This was the time, too, of Blessed John Ogilvie, S.J., who, at the trial in 1614 which preceded his martyrdom, firmly upheld the primacy of the pope in matters of faith. One may also mention Patrick Anderson, S.J., if for nothing else than his use, during questioning at his trial, of a novel *argumentum ad hominem* to meet a difficulty only too familiar to catholic apologists and fundamental in all theological controversy. Speaking of the Calvinists' certainty of true interpretation of scripture, he reasoned as follows: You admit that the Roman church was the true church for the first four centuries and afterwards erred; therefore you have to admit that the true church can err; so even if your church is the true one, you cannot be sure that what it approves is in fact the truth.[138]

. . . .

Such were the doctrines that exercised the minds, the lips and the pens of Scotsmen four hundred years ago.

---

136. *The Disputation concerning the Controversit Headdis of Religion . . . betuix the praetendit ministeris of the deformed Kirk in Scotland and Nicol Burne*, dealing with the nature of the papacy, the universality of the catholic church and its duty to give judgment in religious controversy, the sacraments of the eucharist and penance, the validity of protestants' ministry, and some matters of catholic practice; this published account allows the protestant side to make short objections, to which Burne gives the catholic reply at some length.

137. *Ane Catholik and Facile Traictise* (Paris, 1581) on our Lord's real presence in the Blessed Eucharist *Certane Orthodox and Catholik Conclusions with their Probations* (Paris, 1581), comprising an explanation of the true church followed by thirteen questions to the protestants after the manner of Winzet's *Book of Questions*; and *A Facile Traictise* (Louvain, 1600) on the sure way of distinguishing the true church from the false and on the nature of the seven sacraments.

138. W. Forbes Leith, *Narratives of Scottish Catholics*, p. 322. An account of the disputes, mainly about the catholic church in the first few centuries, which Anderson had with protestants during his imprisonment and trial in 1560 and 1561 was later published as *The Ground of the Catholike and Roman Religion in the Word of God*.

THE CULTURAL BACKGROUND
IN SIXTEENTH-CENTURY SCOTLAND

by

JOHN DURKAN

The literary and religious aspects of the revolution in thought in sixteenth-century Scotland cannot really be kept apart; realising this, many have been tempted to regard the reformation and the renaissance as, for all practical purposes, the same thing. This is not so at all, and indeed it is probable that if the religious revolt had not taken place the new learning would have been digested and assimilated with much less agony and tension. In the main, it would be generally agreed that the sixteenth-century renaissance was a more radical return to the sources, in the Latin and Greek classics, in the Latin and Greek fathers and in the bible that demanded Hebrew as well: sometimes in mere archaising imitation, but also in the intellectual excitement of a rediscovery of the bases of European and Christian culture and in the recreation for modern times of a new Rome, a new Athens and even a new Jerusalem. To this some would add the reawakening of the vernacular. As to the Scottish reformation three main mental pictures are current. There are those who maintain that it was purely a movement of ideas or a great wind of the Holy Spirit, and for whom political and economic aspects are incidental. Others minimise its ideological character and stress the creation by a political revolution or great democratic upsurge of a new kirk of Scotland, one making a clean break with a moribund and irremediably corrupt traditional kirk. There are those too who hardly see the change in ideological or political terms at all, but as the mere temporary purging of a kirk that was not living up to its vocation any longer, with the minimum of sedition and the maximum of continuity in doctrine, polity and personnel, a purification achieved in the main by legislation, both in answer to popular clamour and by the joint efforts, only initially revolutionary, of the major and saner sector of the ruling elite, largely abetted by parliament and nation. None of these explanations fits all the facts as we see them. The limits of this essay allow for only a summary investigation into the matter, for, as regards the reformation it ignores entirely the issue of legality, central as it may be, and, as regards the renaissance, leaves the investigation of art and music to other, more competent, hands. All one can give are indications to authorise some revision of these attitudes in the light of whatever evidence there is, hoping thereby to stimulate closer expert enquiry by professional theologians into theological issues and by other technicians into the other technical issues. For even quite mundane, and, at first sight, irrelevant matters can illuminate the great issues in unexpected ways.

WAYS AND MEANS

The first question is: Did the necessary tools of learning books and schools exist? The Scotland of the period, it will be agreed, did not take the transition from manuscript to printed book in its stride. In the late fifteenth century some monastic scriptoria were busy as far as we can judge: especially that of the Perth Carthusians (whose superiors sometimes were foreign), of the Dunfermline scribe who executed the orders of Archbishop Scheves, or the Culross monks who supplied the Stirling Franciscans.[1] Parchment-makers, or at least parchment-sellers, for parchments were imported from Flanders and elsewhere, certainly existed in universities (at Glasgow in 1468, one, Robert Barbour, is named) :[2] and no doubt bookbinders too (as later, the bedellus may have combined binding with his other duties), yet only one or two Scots binders' names are known, of whom Patrick Lowis is the sole name surviving on an actual book-cover. Moreover the Scheves books were apparently bound in Louvain to Scheves' order after they had lain in his hands for some time unbound; the fine armorial bindings of sixteenth-century Scots bishops are stated by Dr. Mitchell to be definitely French (though since parchments were imported, the existence as end-pieces in them of French parchments would not of itself be conclusive).[3] As to the rise of a paper trade we are again in the dark. The watermarks on the paper used are similar to some in use in northern France, but the matter calls for rigorous investigation. Scots printers borrowed engravings as well as type founts from French and Flemish printers, but John Scot, printer in Edinburgh, describes himself as "engraver" (is this merely type-cutter?) as well as printer.[4] This borrowing of "cuts" was, however, far from being exclusive to Scottish printers.

Some qualifications need to be made before writing off Scotland as a complete backwater in regard to early printing, even if its late start must be acknowledged. In the first place much more investigation is needed. Samples of our early printing too often survive in single copies or even in odd leaves. Up till 1713 the common belief was that the earliest specimen was Thomas Davidson's printed acts of parliament, and it was not till the discovery made in 1785 in Glasgow by Father Alexander Geddes, of the Chepman and Myllar prints, that the date was pushed back to 1508, while the facts regarding the printing for Andrew Myllar at Rouen by Pierre Violete before that date were an even more recent discovery.[5] Moreover there are unsolved problems connected with the printing press of John Story (perhaps a modest affair that could well have coped with the odd broadsheet or ballad) and with the printing of Sir David Lindsay, whether by Davidson, Scot or another. It is at least odd that no Scots printer, not even Myllar, seems to have attempted an ABC, a Primer or a Book of Hours *pro pueris*. Myllar's *Expositio Sequentiarum*, printed at Rouen, is a sort of textbook for cathedral song-schools explaining the proses or sequences very frequent in the Sarum rite.[6] The fragment of a Scots Donatus could have been printed either there or elsewhere in France. It is curious that there was no press in Aberdeen, although Scot may have printed in Dundee.[7] Printing in a university centre was advised by Archibald Hay in his address to

---

1. One of the archbishop's scribes, Magnus Mackulloch, was a Louvain student. Could not his binder likewise have learnt his trade in Louvain ? See however, G. H. Bushnell in *The Book Collector*, 1960, 19-29
2. *Munimenta Univ. Glas.*, ii, 73. Cf. " Henderson " in Pitcairn, *Criminal Trials*, i, 388* (In 1556). The first Scot connected with the book trade appears to be the Parisian bookseller, Nicolaus de Scotia, mentioned Sep., 1323. Denifle. *Chart Univ. Paris*, ii, 273, note.
3. *Treas. Accts.*, ii, 250-7; 93; 411; 419.
4. In 1539. Protocol Bk. of Andrew Brounhill, i, f.105r. (" calcographus ").
5. Beattie, *Chepman and Myllar Prints*, xvi, xix-xxi.
6. *The Library*, xxvi, 256, 258. Thomas Davidson may have learnt his trade in the Low Countries, if he is identical with the person of that name at Louvain in 1522. Brussels, Archives du Royaume, Liber Intitulatorum, iii, 286r. Cf. *Trans. Edin. Bibl. Soc.*, iii, 31, re " cuts " borrowed from Antwerp.
7. Hamer's *Lindsay*, iv, 16, mentions a possible Aberdeen edition, but with a caveat. For Scot in Dundee, see Dickson and Edmond, p. 152.

Cardinal Beaton, but printing in St. Andrews may have had to wait a few years more. Hay, moreover, wanted expensive printing of Latin and Greek classics, similar to the Latin translations of Epictetus and Arrianus by Edward Henryson that Henry Sinclair, dean of Glasgow is believed to have sponsored in 1552, but which were postponed because of the relative poverty of our printers.[8] Moreover, apart from the monopoly of trade acquired by the big European centres as a result of their early start, the cost of printing Latin works on a large scale for continental distribution was such that printing for Scots scholars could be done more expeditiously by a great printer entrepreneur like Josse Bade in Paris. As early as 1470, if not before, Scotland imported printed books, sometimes from Antwerp,[9] though at least one book went first to a bindery in Bruges.[10] Scholars like James Cumming (later mediciner at King's College) and James Watson, a Louvain student, acted as middlemen, usually for other scholars like Scheves himself, the university rector (like Walter Drummond or Robert Keith) or a distinguished lawyer like Richard Lawson.[11] But they also bought for booksellers, of whom John Foular was clearly one, for he did business also with Jean Richard, the Rouen merchant printer, trader in missals and breviaries.[12] Books were imported in larger numbers than is often thought: 500 crowns were spent in one instance for the library of Scheves alone.[13] Several traders in books, who may not have been booksellers specifically, are mentioned as infringing the privilege granted to Chepman and Myllar.[14]

This grant of copyright and partial monopoly was made to Chepman and Myllar under the secret seal.[15] It has features which invite inquiry especially when taken in conjunction with their implementation a year or more later by an act of the Lords of the Council, which lead to the suggestion, developed in the appendix, that another printing centre also existed in Scotland.[16] But, in addition, many Scots authors preferred to print abroad, leaving out of account the edition, certainly adapted, possibly pirated, by Wynkyn de Worde, of *The Contemplacyon of Synners* of Friar Touris.[17] The first of these was James Liddell of Aberdeen, printed in Paris about 1495 by Higman and Hopyl.[18] An Edinburgh proof-corrector, David Lowis, also worked for this firm, and was later friendly with Josse Bade, another Paris printer, but he never appears to have returned home.[19] The works of John Mair (or Major) began to appear in Paris in 1499.[20] But Myllar alone can be shown to have returned home at this time. If he had returned to Rouen, we should expect to find his name on books published there after 1508, or on works

---

8. Hay, *Panegyricus*, f.lx verso. McCrie was sceptical of the Henryson story, unjustly so. Cf. his *Andrew Melville*, i, 444.
9. Where a bookseller seems to be named " Master Garad wan Arnssurd." Haliburton's *Ledger*, pp. 101, 103.
10. *Ibid.*, p. 99. No doubt his account book, which has a " Louvain " binding.
11. *Ibid.*, pp. 100, 204. It is interesting also to note the early connection of Patrick Panter and Hepburn, dean of Dunkeld (*Ibid.*, p. 254).
12. *Ibid.*, p. 102. *Protocol Bk. of John Foular*, i, no. 67.
13. *Ledger*, p. 6.
14. Dickson and Edmond, *Scottish Printing*, p. 84.
15. On the 15th Sept., 1507 (*R.S.S.*, i, no. 1546).
16. In January 1510, Dickson and Edmond, *Scottish Printing*, p. 84.
17. Friar William Touris remained in Scotland, and was a witness in St. Andrews in September, 1504; Acta Dominorum Concilii (G.R.H.), xv, f.226r. His original is printed in Bennett, *Devotional Pieces* (S.T.S.).
18. *Edinburgh Bibliographical Soc. Trans.*, iii, 75.
19. *Ibid.*, iii, 78.
20. *Innes Review*, i, 140.

written by Scots and printed in the neighbourhood.[21] Other Scottish printers, Davidson and Scot, may have learnt the art abroad, but at a later date.[22]

These rather workaday considerations will show a promising development, which, if maintained, would have gained enough impetus by 1530, not to say 1560, to provide the means in Scotland for meeting the flood of Tyndale and other bibles, and external reformation propaganda, such as Patrick Hamilton's *Places* or John Johnsone's *Confortable Exhortation* or John Gau's *Richt Vay*, whether printed by Hoochstraten at Antwerp or (after his press moved) at Malmo; or the Lollard treatise he planned for sale in the Scottish market and northern England; not to speak of the Latin and other treatises printed for Alesius or the later propaganda emerging from English presses.[23]

But Flodden and almost continuous war intervened. John Scot may even have been driven from Edinburgh in 1544. The alarums and excursions in St. Andrews, especially in 1546-7, may have led to some clandestine ballads and placards, but hardly to ambitious big editions. The rest of the history of our early printing is an enigma, due to the lack of surviving specimens, which in part no doubt was the result of small impressions. Apart from the destruction of Scot's stock in 1562, the post-reformation regime was highly unfavourable to its survival. Sufficient survivals of fragments are there to assure us, as we might have expected, that no Scots press could compare with Aldo in Venice or Froben in Basle or even with certain handsome London productions; that, although occasional royal prohibitions[24] suggest not only the disappearance of secretly printed heretical literature but even of the complete output of unknown printers, yet apart from the Catechism we know of no real counter-literature, supported or subsidised by the bishops, till the 1558 edition of Quintin Kennedy. Even so, there is enough not to obscure the fact that some of our finest Scots prose and poetry was able for the first time to see the light of print. Yet of Gavin Douglas (the author of *five* works according to David Lindsay) we have no pre-reformation Scots edition except a fragment of the Palice of Honour printed by Davidson.[25]

There were difficulties in printing for an international market without funds, especially as so much of the trade had been cornered by continental centres to which distribution presented fewer difficulties; printers like Bade in Paris could afford to handle an immense volume of international business. If we may judge from *Early Scottish Libraries* the import trade did not present the same difficulties. Thus we find works printed for Scots authors in Paris and elsewhere being bought in all sorts of places after publication: Liddell and Crab in Louvain or London: David Cranston in Medina del Campo or Cologne; Robert Galbraith

---

21. For instance Mair, published at Caen by the university binder there, printed by the Rouen printer Hostingue; Liddell printed by Forestier at Rouen, and a hitherto unknown edition of Gilbert Crab printed at Rouen by Richard Goupil (for which see the printed facsimile of the Seville Colombina catalogue, no. 1411; Huntington, *The Catalo ue of Ferdinand Columbus*, New York, 1905).
22. At Louvain, Davidson is described as " de marouia abordinensis." Is Scot the John Scot at Dieppe in 1524 (*Prot. Bk. John Foular*, iii, 484) ?
23. The Lollard treatise was to be the examination of Thorp and Oldcastle to serve " both for the northern men and the faithful brethren of Scotland." Johnsone's work (written by " a humble professor of divinity " and eyewitness of Hamilton's martyrdom) was supposed to be printed at Paris by Peter Congeth.
24. E.g., the " divers prentaris " of 1552 (Dickson and Edmond, p. 154).
25. The five works present difficulties, as *King Hart* is no longer accepted as Douglas's.

and George Lockhart in Louvain; and John Mair in Louvain, Seville and Nuremberg.[26]

This international clientele for works in Latin points to its utility as the international language of culture (and even of trade). How much the world of learning has contracted since can be gauged from the fact that Scots were buyers in all the great book-markets of Europe. But the level of Latinity even of educated men varied extraordinarily. Some of the lower clergy may have had very little: although here again, for much of the middle ages, it was primarily a matter of spoken, not written, Latin. As to-day with English, some men, even educated men, wrote it ungrammatically and spelt and punctuated it somewhat eccentrically. On the other hand, numerous humble chaplain-notaries, admittedly often trained on formularies, never seem at a loss for even the most recondite Latin word. Another useful index to learning may be handwriting. There are some fine examples in this century of Gothic hands: there are also a few who use an italic hand and some who use both. The subject has yet to be investigated.

Schools and universities were the main agents for the spread of learning. The numbers attending universities were relatively few: it is doubtful if St. Andrews, Glasgow and Aberdeen between them had as many as 100 new members each year. But modern preconceptions ought not to lead us astray. For while Oxford had an average of 191 matriculations in the years 1571-1580, and in 1564 Cambridge had an aggregate total of 1,267 members,[27] these figures must be related not only to a population five times as dense, but to the greater number of Scots students abroad (apart from those recognisable in surviving matriculation lists of foreign universities, there are many graduates, named in our national records, who are neither in foreign nor in native university lists), and also to the greater antiquity of Oxford and Cambridge as university towns. Moreover, the Cambridge figure obviously includes all *members*, and not merely matriculated members of that year, and so accounts not only for permanent staff but also for those following the relatively longer arts course in England. All in all, the Scots figures are creditable for the time.[28]

INFLUENCES FROM ABROAD

As already noted, owing to the late foundation of the Scottish universities, Scots students were more frequent at universities abroad (except perhaps in Italy or in certain centres at certain times) than were English. Few Scots are found at Oxford or Cambridge, after the fourteenth century anyway; but, of course, it was not always necessary to attend English universities in order to be subjected to English intellectual influences.

To those familiar with the period, there is no need to labour the

---

26. Huntington *Catalogue*, nos. 136, 142, 178, 413, 821, 1411, 1417, 1557, 1673, 1701, 2020. No. 821 may be an unrecorded edition of Liddell.

27. Mullinger, *University of Cambridge*, ii, 192, 214. The average matriculations in St. Andrews in the 1530 decade were 47, compared with 53 in the 1570 decade. On the other hand during 1578-1584 (during part of which time Andrew Melville was active) graduates averaged ten per year. (*Mun.*, iii, 3). For Scots abroad in the previous century, see Dunlop, *Scots abroad in the Fifteenth Century* (Historical Assoc.).

28. Unfortunately we have no Aberdeen matriculations for this period, but local protocol books, etc., list many graduates not to be traced at either St. Andrews or Glasgow. There was a catastrophic drop in numbers in all the traditional universities of Europe as a result of the impact of the reformation: in the mid-16th century, reformed centres, like Wittenberg and Leipzig, and counter-reform centres, like Ingoldstadt, took a new lease of life, but Cologne and Heidelberg declined. Oxford *graduates* around 1555 totalled 67 only per annum, although it had 1,000 *members* in 1552 (*New Cambridge Modern History*, ii, 432).

importance of Paris. Paris was not only the main filter for European culture; it was also, in the phrase of Gabriel le Bras, the second capital of Christianity. But at Paris Scots students were not only under French influence, although this was increasingly so by the time of Mary of Lorraine, as it contracted into a much more national institution, with a much decreased inflow of foreign, and especially of German, students; for it tends to be forgotten that the Scots there were members of the German (formerly English) nation in the university, and so most closely associated with Dutch, Flemish and German students by the very nature of the university organisation. When our Hector Boece left Paris his most vivid memories were of Jean Standonck of Malines and Erasmus of Rotterdam. Moreover, men like John Mair were admirers of the Spaniards, treating themes of interest to their expanding empire, and acquiring Iberian followers such as the young Vives, the Coronels, the Enzinas, Juan Gelida, who became the patron of many Scots teachers at Bordeaux. At Paris also Buchanan made the contacts that brought him later to teach at Coimbra. Orleans, which was, as regards foreign students, merely the civil law faculty of Paris (where in theory no civil law was taught), Bourges, Toulouse, Bordeaux, Poitiers, Angers and Montpellier were overshadowed and provincialised by the Parisian monopoly, although all sheltered the odd Scots student during their occasional spells of temporary brilliance.

Of Italy we know little. Some indecipherable Scots appear in the Padua lists, as given by Andrich. At Bologna from 1512-1526 was a John de Scotia, bedellus at the time of his death, who left his goods to the German nation.[29] Thomas Erskine, secretary of James V, was at Pavia.[30] The Dominican, James Crichton, studied at some Italian university, apparently also under Cajetan.[31] Several Scots also followed the court of Rome, but until the papal supplications of the period are published we cannot be more specific. Certain reformers are better documented: James Melville, a runaway Observant, was known to Cardinal Cesi; John Row, one of the authors of the Book of Discipline, was patronised by Cardinal Sforza and took degrees at Padua and Rome (doctorate at the former and licence in laws at the latter); while John Craig is said to have been patronised by Cardinal Pole. Robert Richardson, a runaway canon regular, was on friendly terms with Cardinal Ghinucci and appears to have canvassed Padua on behalf of an annulment for Henry VIII (he sometimes employs a fine elongated italic hand and affects the Italian name, Roberto Ricardino).[32] Florence Wilson (Volusenus) was friendly with the Italian colony in Lyons and employed by the Italian bishop of Carpentras, Cardinal Sadoleto.[33]

But Scots students, and even Scots teachers, were important elements at both Louvain and Cologne in the previous century; there were times

---

29. Malagola, *La Nazione Germanica*, pp. 275, 405ff.

30. William Fowler, *Works*, iii, p. xcii.

31. A note on Crichton will appear in a later *Innes Review*.

32. See *Wodrow Society Miscellany*, i, where Melville's tract is reprinted; also Row's *History*, Wodrow Society, for Row and Craig. I hope to write of Richardson at greater length later; meantime, see my note in *Edin. Bibl. Soc. Trans.*, iii, 83.

33. As schoolmaster, the other choices made for the school being highly unfortunate: Cassandro, Bording and Baduel, all of whom were heretics. Baduel was later at Geneva university; Bording later physician to Christian III of Denmark. Richard M. Douglas, *Jacopo Sadoleto, Humanist and Reformer*, pp. 183, 287. Italian contacts are glimpsed in unexpected places, as with Thomas Dalgleish of Scotland, scribe on the 19th July, 1467, to M. Jacobus de Gottifredis, physician to Paul II. See Mazzatinti's *Inventari*, i, 1, Volterra, p. 182, no. 17: "Comment. in tract. de anima." Dalgleish had been a Glasgow student (*Mun.*, ii, 64, 193).

when they were even more important than Paris, and were its only serious rivals till the religious revolution made men wary of sending their sons to the Low Countries and Germany. The resulting decay was assigned by catholics to protestants and vice versa, an example of the latter being the oration of Alexander Alane (Alesius) at the university of Frankfurt on Oder in 1540.[34] Some Scots who later joined the reformers are found at Louvain: notably George Wishart and Patrick Hamilton. Others were at Cologne: notably Henry Balnavis, John Macalpine (the Machabaeus of Melanchthon's correspondence), Thomas Forret and John Lyne.[35] Vienna had a few Scots in the Saxon nation.[36] As the reformation got under way we find Scots at Wittenberg, Greifswald, Frankfurt and Leipzig.

Some probably went as far as Denmark, where from 1542 Macalpine was in the theological faculty at Copenhagen. One of these may have been William Christeson, future minister at Dundee, who certainly spoke Danish, and who lived for a time in Bergen under the protection of the bishop Geble Pedersson, one of the leaders in the reformation there.[37] The Thomas Alane found at Copenhagen was no doubt related to the fugitive Alesius who arrived at Malmo before proceeding to Wittenberg.[38]

Many of these wandering Scots returned as teachers, more particularly to St. Andrews, which was seldom without former students of European universities among its teaching body. It will be seen that a movement of ideas, that had in earlier ages been beneficial to the church in Scotland and was now to prove inimical to its very existence, was facilitated by this study abroad, and nourished a strong current of early Lutheranism which is reflected even in the 1560's among ordinary observers and in royal charters which speak of the reformation as happening in "illis periculosis Lutheranis diebus" even when the reformers now looked to Zurich and Geneva as well as to Germany and Denmark.[39]

¦ It is difficult to trace the movement abroad from university to university. John Lesley, later bishop of Ross, for instance, graduated in arts at Aberdeen, studied some theology at Paris, then went to Poitiers where he studied for four years in canon and civil law, thence to Toulouse where he spent nearly a year in "repetition" and conference with the doctors of law before taking his licence in civil law, thence finally back to Paris, where he was created a doctor in decreets and was public reader *ordinarius* in the schools of decreets for almost another year before returning to King's College.[40] Another student styled Sinapius (actually Alexander Snape or Snype) can be traced successively at Paris, Cologne and Greifswald.[41]

---

34. *Corpus Reformatorum*, xi, 487-495.
35. See Appendix. MacBrair is said to have lived in Belgium, possibly therefore as a student; *Musa Latina Aberdonensis*, iii, 121.
36. Given in Appendix.
37. The official language in Norway at the time was Danish, and Pedersson was bishop from 1536-1557. *Musa Latina Aberdonensis*, iii, 129; *St. Andrews Kirk Session Records*, i, 48-9. For Nicol Burne's allegations about his behaviour in Bergen, see *Disputation*, f.184r.
38. Matzen, *Kjobenhavns Universitets Historie*, i, 192-3. For Alexander Kinghorn, professor of medicine at Copenhagen, see *Dansk Biografisk Lexicon*, s.v.
39. A good example is the country chaplain who in his chronicle still sees reformers as Lutherans. Of James Campbell of Lawers who died in 1562 he says, " Vixit tunc temporis in lege Lutereana." See others in *Black Book of Taymouth*, p. 130, etc.
40. Jas. Anderson, *Collections relating to Mary, Q. of Scots*, i, 2.
41. See appendix. Called " synape " in Paris, c. Oct.-Dec. 1537, Paris B.N., Ms Lat. 9953, f.67r; also " snipi," Bibl. de l'Univ., Reg. 15, f.410r.

Much remains to be discovered about the place of study of members of the religious orders. John Hunter Dominican prior of Glasgow, was in Cologne and presumably studied theology there.[42] John Macalpine was definitely a bachelor in theology of Cologne, and it is by no means improbable that many of his fellow graduates whose degrees were recognised by the general chapter of 1525 were also at Cologne: Friars James Crichton, S.T.M., Alexander Campbell, Alexander Barclay, Alexander Lawson, James Hewat, Francis Wright, John MacDowell and James "Prysen," all S.T.B. John Willock, stated by Lesley to have been an Ayr Dominican, was also a bachelor in theology, most probably of Cologne; he knew some Greek, but we are not told where he acquired it.[43] However, in 1525 also, a certain Friar Alexander of Scotland was assigned by the general chapter to Paris.[44]

The possession of French-owned books by the Franciscans John Scott and Alexander Arbuckle suggests studies in a French house, possibly Paris.[45] Two friars of uncertain order and uncertain name matriculated at Paris in 1542.[46] Indeed many uncertainties remain, about which speculation is tempting, but enough has been said to indicate that Scotland was far from being an intellectual enclave and nothing to support the conviction that the reformation as a movement of ideas was any less foreign-influenced than any previous Scottish intellectual crisis.

THE OLD LEARNING

Towards the beginning of the sixteenth century, there had been a revival of scholastic thinking at Paris headed by John Mair (or Major) of Haddington. If we think of scholasticism as the old learning, then Mair is its last distinguished representative. There is no scholastic thinker in the England of the time with which to compare him and none in Paris itself. His great published output in logic and theology, physics and ethics, illustrates his European reputation. Yet Mair cannot be written off merely as a representative of the old learning, because circumstances forced him gradually to come to terms with the new situation in the world of learning: it is true that his pupil, Buchanan, considered himself "badly instructed," but he was not alone in that age of incredible doctrinal advance in finding himself out of the running. In theologically more tranquil times, Mair admitted, it was all very well to discuss "intension of forms" and similar questions of natural philosophy in a theological treatise. But Luther had done one good thing: he had recalled theologians to the scriptures.[47] And he showed himself appreciative of the times by temporarily deserting the Sentences of Peter Lombard, the traditional textbook along with the bible, to comment on the "sacred page" itself. Yet he saw things through the eyes of the fourteenth-century thinkers of the English school, and it is not till after his death

---

42. Camerarius, *De Scotorum Fortitudine*, p. 180, citing Hunter.

43. Appendix: Reichert, *Acta Cap. Gen. O.P.*, iv, 206; Hennessy, *Novum Repertorium*, p. 25; *Original Letters* (Parker Soc.) ii, 392.

44. Reichert, iv, 208.

45. *Innes Review.*, ix, 71 (no. 3), 142 (no. 7). Arbuckle was an arts graduate of St. Andrews, as was also Crichton the Dominican; while Alexander Lawson studied arts at St. Andrews and law at Aberdeen.

46. Paris, B.N. Ms Lat. 9953, 184r has " fr. Iacobus Malynne, Glasquensis; fr. Jacobus Heppardio, Sancti Andree." Perhaps the latter name is Hoppar and, if so, he was Carmelite prior of Linlithgow in 1559. (N.L.S., Hutton Collections, Shires, vi, f.6.). In addition, Alexander Cockburn was at Basle in 1555. Peter Young was at Geneva in 1559. For the latter, Stelling-Michaud, *Le Livre du Recteur*, i, 49. Other university connections will be discussed in passing.

47. Major, *History*, p. 441.

that the universities were redirected to the thirteenth-century masters Aquinas and Bonaventure.[48]

John Mair has been much studied in the pages of the *Innes Review*. He is clearly a figure of the greatest importance. There is scarcely a theme on which he did not touch. Although profoundly influenced by Ockham and the nominalists and a vigorous exponent of the conciliar theory he opposed Luther and Lutherans in no uncertain terms. Yet he influenced and was respected by many of them: it is significant that Gilbert Winram, who accompanied Patrick Hamilton to Marburg, should have left behind in Scotland his personal copies of both Mair and Erasmus.[49] As a theologian he has not as yet been the object of detailed investigation. But he was more than a theologian. He was a shrewd observer as well as a logical analyst of ability, and this not only in his *History*, but, as Dr. J. H. Burns has shown, throughout his works.

CONTEMPORARY PORTRAIT OF JOHN MAIR

From title-page of John Mair's *In Petri Hyspani Summulas Commentaria* (Lyons, 1505).

By courtesy of the Librarian, Glasgow University Library.

His anticipation of "infinitist" views in mathematics is discussed by Elie, who also notes the important initiative in editing and further extending the discoveries of medieval precursors of later scientific theory (such as Buridan, precursor of Galileo in the theory of impetus), work developed still further by disciples of Mair, like George Lockhart of Ayr;[50] his contribution to the theory of international law has been discussed by Grabar, Villoslada, Leturia and Carro; and his political theory has been studied at close quarters by Dr. Burns. Among the Scottish members of his "school" at Paris may be cited William Manderston, Robert Galbraith, Gilbert Crab and David Cranston.

48. Patrick, *Statutes of the Scottish Church*, p. 109.
49. *Innes Rev.*, ix, 161. Also Lefèvre's edition of Aristotle.
50. *Innes Rev.*, i, 131 seq. Elie, *Le Traite de l'infini de Jean Mair*; and his important article (with occasional trivial errors of fact) in *Archives d'Histoire Doctrinale et Litteraire du Moyen Age*, 1951, 193-243. The significance of this great enterprise of editing the impetus theorists and the Merton authors is appreciated by Clagett, *Science of Mechanics in the Middle Ages*, pp. 653, 658. For a short but sober evaluation of Buridan's contribution see Weisheipl, *Development of Physical Theory in the Middle Ages*, p. 62 seq.

But the renaissance of the fifteenth century had been embraced with bouyant confidence in the highest ecclesiastical quarters; its firmest patrons were the renaissance popes. Mair held to the theory, advanced by certain Italians like Battista Mantuano, though characteristic of French humanism, that the new Athens was no longer Rome, but Paris. In their view, shared by Guillaume Bude, there had been a *translatio studii* and Paris had become the real heir of Athens and this view was held enthusiastically, not only by Mair's contemporaries like John Annand but even by others of a later date and different stamp, like Andrew Melville, not to speak of Mair's warmly Francophil if highly disrespectful pupil, George Buchanan, who not only rejoiced openly at the recapture of Calais, but became a naturalised French citizen.[51] The French had not yet taken up the cult of the noble savage, for, unlike their Italian brethren they were convinced that the barbarians had something to teach as well as the Romans; it seemed barbarous to the Italians that French humanists thought nothing of transliterating Greek, as Mair did in his epistles, although here and there he inserts the odd Greek characters in his text (written in by the printers).[52] He could also turn a respectable line of Latin verse.

The open attitude of Mair is probably the key to the nature of the conflict between old and new learning in Scotland. There is no doubt that there was a type of curial humanist of whom Mair was impatient, a type incarnated in Lorenzo Valla; for him no rhetorician could be a thinker, and Valla's open paganism (in his early writings) obviously repelled him. For him the proper preparatory studies were the seven arts that grew out of the ancient schools of grammar rather than out of the schools of rhetoric; hence his animus against the rhetoricians and their successors in the church, the canon lawyers. Sometimes he expressed himself more mildly: Augustine wrote in homilies, but we express ourselves in the style more appropriate to our times. He little envisaged Melanchthon's rhetorical approach, so successful because student-centred rather than subject-centred. It is curious that Mair never attacks Erasmus by name, Erasmus who was also suspicious of lawyers for their barbarous glosses and who thought little of Valla as a theologian, while otherwise his admirer.[53] To a newer generation Mair seemed a "cold commentator"; compare the fervent phrases on justification in Patrick Hamilton with Mair's distinctions and counter-distinctions. But Mair had the advantage of Erasmus and the rather aristocratic if unspeculative humanists in one respect: sharing the Erasmian delight in adages and paradoxes, he also savours homely sayings, and while equally critical of superstition and abuse, he is less willing to sit in judgment on the piety of simple men. Erasmus approached the bible as a philologist and scholar; for Mair as for the Scottish reformers it was the easier part of theology. How often they cite the plain text of scripture, where subsequent events were to show it was not quite so plain. The "sophisms" of these thinkers have been much misrepresented.[54] They are actually a

---

51. *Innes Rev.*, i, 140-157. William Cranston is really a disciple of Rudolph Agricola. Paris BN, Dupuy Ms. 755, f.109 verso, shows that Buchanan's letters of naturalisation were dated in August, 1557, at Paris.

52. In his commentary on the 4th Book, " eucharistia " (f.xxvii A, where a sixteenth century Scots owner has duly noted " Littera greca "), f.clxiii B, " episkopos." The owner in question was John Duncanson, canon regular of St. Andrews.

53. Major, *History*, p. 444 says, " Ego pro virili Christianam modestiam tenui, neminem qui in gremio ecclesiae se continet nominatim taxo . . . "

54. Duncanson frequently writes " sophisma " in the margin of his copy of Mair, but he is often more appreciative, " Doctor pie loquitur " or " bona opinio doctoris."

kind of intellectual game, like crosswords or Latin versification; tricks to exercise the immature minds of youths, not yet ready for the deep water of metaphysics.[55] But the time was unpropitious: tortured Latin epistles and neat hexameters were in, and sophisms were out.

As for many readers nowadays, scholastics like John Ireland and John Mair are associated with arid works written in difficult hands or printed in indecipherable black letter, it may be useful to draw attention to their real grasp of the object they studied as theologians: God and man's last end in him. To be compared with the fine "testament of John of Ireland, servant of Christ Jesus,"[56] is the following prayer of Mair's which I take the liberty of citing *in extenso* :

"I am alpha and omega, the first and the last, the beginning and the end. Since, thy grace forestalling and co-operating to this end, thou hast deigned to lead me from the start to the finish of this little work, and because, through writing and study, we come, following your lead and by our merit as pilgrims, to the glory of the blessed which we glimpse from afar, which from the waters of this sea we already salute, for which from this valley in which we live we sigh, and try in the midst of our tears to see if somehow we may reach it, we therefore beg thee, O hope of the human race, Jesus Christ, God born of God, our refuge and our strength, our sole consolation, whom in the distance, like the star of morning and the sun of justice, standing on the shore of our heavenly home, we long to see and yet can barely discern for the tears in our eyes, govern our ship with thy right hand, marked as it is with the nails of thy cross, lest we perish in the waves; grant us, we beg, Lord Jesus, to hold a mid-course between Scylla and Charybdis, so that, avoiding vice and error and all dangers, we may, our ship and our gear safe, securely come to port at last. Through thee, Jesus Christ, our Saviour and Captain, who with the Father and Holy Spirit lives and reigns . . ."

The man who wrote that prayer, whatever Buchanan may say, was no little man, or, at least, no little Christian.

THE NEW LEARNING

In investigating the effects of the renaissance it is important to distinguish two moments: the moment when a movement first shows itself and the moment of the greatest doctrinal impact. Failure so to distinguish has led many historians to be impatient with any suggestion that places a revival before George Buchanan or even Andrew Melville. Moreover, it is mistaken to think that any reorientation must come from one source: from Italy; from Wittenberg or Geneva; from the universities of France. The origins and growth of this reorientation in Scotland require excavation rather than investigation; but there is enough to indicate more complexity than some have been prepared to allow.

For instance, can we really believe that Germany and the Low Countries had no influence on the Scottish students who went there, or who met their inhabitants as fellow-members of the German nation at Paris ? Besides the well-known (but not fully appreciated) influence of the more medieval figure of Jean Standonck, there was the lively admiration of men like Hector Boece, Alexander Stewart, Florence

---

55. Mair does say they go in for this sort of thing much more at Oxford than we do at Paris.
56. *Meroure of Wyssdome*, i, xxxii.

Wilson and Archibald Hay for Erasmus, but he after all was in the tradition of the *clerici vagantes* of earlier days, significant less of Rotterdam than as an international symbol of christian humanism. Yet contiguity served to strengthen his influence. But cities like Augsburg and Strasbourg were like the monasteries of earlier days (or the Kinloss of the sixteenth century) symbols of something more than themselves: through its great presses the latter influenced Scots book purchasers as much in its earlier days as when it had become the city of Calvin and Bucer. Augsburg was the native place of Johann Gaisser, whose juristic learning Hector Boece celebrates; both had a common interest in Marsilio Ficino.[57] The confession of Augsburg was accepted by Alexander Alane[58] and the Interim of Augsburg may have influenced Scots religious policies; there, as we shall later note, Henry Scrimgeour supervised the famous library of Ulrich Fugger. In addition, orthodox German influences were mediated through Robert Wauchope, in active contact with the German and Italian counter-reform.

Nullus doctus in Gallia: such was the battle-cry of the Italians, inflated somewhat with the new wine of antiquity, and some ultra-Ciceronians in France were not disinclined to agree, at least as regards the cultivation of poetry and oratory. Even so, a Frenchman, John Carpenter, was giving public lessons in St. Andrews in the time of Archbishops Forman and Alexander Stewart, and under their patronage.[59] At the same time in France, David Lowis of Edinburgh was active, first as a proof-reader in connection with an edition of Lefèvre and later as a schoolmaster in Arras to whom the printer Josse Bade dedicated his editions of Sulpizio and the *Epistolae* of Filelfo (Bade's edition of Virgil was that used by Gavin Douglas). It must have been through the school at Arras that Lowis became acquainted with Robertus Brittannus, a native of Arras of the French "Ciceronian" school, later to be principal of the College of Guyenne at Bordeaux.[60] The later cluster of Scottish humanists at Bordeaux and Poitiers is better known through the biographies of Buchanan and Melville, but the connection of Lowis with Brittannus has not been adverted to, while few are aware of the jurist, Robert Ireland, who left St. Andrews university for Poitiers and had Rabelais among his hearers.[61] Friendly also with Bade, the printer, was John Vaus of King's College, Aberdeen, who collaborated with him in editions of Alexandre de Villedieu made for the Scottish market: the excuse for neglecting the newer Italian grammarians being that schoolboys are very conservative![62] Somewhat later these Aberdeen schoolboys are borrowing their prayers from the Colloquies of Erasmus.[63]

One French humanist to win some favour in Italy was Jacques Lefèvre of Etaples. The French-domiciled Piedmontese, Giovanni Ferreri, was a propagandist for him among the monks of Kinloss, among

---

57. Both owned works of his; Boece had the *De Triplici Vita*, Gaisser Ficino's commentary on Plato. See: *Innes Rev.*, ix, 79; Boece, *Vitae Episcoporum*, p. 88; *Humanisme et Renaissance*, vi, 290.

58. Alane says so in his inaugural address at Frankfurt, *De Restituendis Scholis*. (1540).

59. I hope to study this figure in fuller detail later. Meantime I suggest identifying him with the Johannes Carpenter alias Boquillon, who published *Litigium liberalium artium* at Rouen (Le Forestier) before 1522, Huntington, *Ferdinand Columbus Catalogue*, no. 1135.

60. See note in Appendix.

61. Anderson, *Early Records*, p. 198; *Rentale Dunkeldense*, p. 327. He was *lector ordinarius* when Mylne wrote, He also taught the celebrated Eguinaire Baron, the legal theorist. Boissonade, *Universite de Poitiers*. pp. 167-8.

62. Delisle, *L'Imprimeur Parisien, Josse Bade, et le Professeur Ecossais, Jean Vaus*, p. 3 seq.

63. See Appendix.

whom, before he settled down to marry in Paris, Ferreri had hoped to end his days. For Buchanan the dead Lefèvre was the first reviver of learning,

> " Qui studiis primus lucem intulit omnibus, artes
> Edoctum cunctas haec tegit urna Fabrum."

A French apostle in Lefèvre's cause was Symphorien Champier, friend of Robert Cockburn, bishop of Ross, whose *Duellum Epistolare*, in which Cockburn features, defended French culture against Italian accusations of barbarism in an epistolary duel with Girolamo da Pavia. The Italian view echoed that of Valla: we Romans have lost our temporal dominion over the civilised world, but have acquired a newer and more splendid spiritual dominion wherever the Roman Language is spoken. But Champier objected to accepting the posture of servile adulation that the Italians hoped to force on the French: the French, he reiterated, were the real heirs of Athens, just as Erasmus was to claim that the present-day Romans were more likely to be offspring of the Goths and Vandals than of the Romans of antiquity. Budé particularly attacked the French Ciceronians who were willing to accept that France take a back seat in humane studies. He made a point of indicating errors in the scholarship of Poliziano and other Italians. But while refusing to concede that the Italians might not be rivalled and even surpassed in their chosen field, he softened the arrogant claim of an outright transference of culture that bypassed Italy. Buchanan's graceful exaggeration that it was due to Budé that the Greeks were no longer regarded as barbarians and that France had become Greek itself summarised his aim:

> " Gallia quod Graeca est, quod Graecia barbara non est,
> Utraque Budaeo debet utrumque suo."

Ferreri, who went so far as to claim Cicero not only as a prosewriter, but as a poet of stature, echoed Buchanan in his *Cicero Poeta*. The views of Champier were familiar to James Liddell and his other Scottish friends: Cockburn had met Champier's circle of humanist acquaintances at Lyons, had corresponded with him as a fervent admirer, and had discussed with him the defence of Lefèvre published by Champier in his *Evangelistarum Symphonia*. Later French influences are better known: for instance the Spaniard domiciled at Besançon, Guillaume Cassanate, physician to Archbishop Hamilton, or Pierre de la Ramée or Ramus, the vigorous anti-Aristotelian. It is true that he was somewhat frowned on, by official catholicism and official protestantism: but some like John Fraser made a distinction between "Ramus' dreames in religion" and his philosophical outlook. Official Geneva thought him too extreme, so much so that Andrew Melville was compelled to follow his course at Lausanne.[64] But already some decades earlier a certain John Stewart had defended him.[65]

Direct Italian influence on Scottish letters was, it would seem, much less; but it was not non-existent. It is well known that Boccaccio influenced both Gavin Douglas and Sir David Lindsay; but the former was also familiar with several works of Valla and with Poggio.[66] A French

---

64. *American Historical Review*, v, 298.
65. Briefly in his *De Adventu Henrici Valesii* (1549) and at more length in his " Dialogus in librum primum institutionum dialecticarum Petri Rami " (Paris, B.N., Ms Lat. 8479). Another early Scots writer on Ramus was Roland Makilmenaeus (London 1574), a student previously of St. Andrews and Paris (of Galloway diocese), *Early Records*, p. 273; Paris, B.N. Ms Lat. 9955, f.57r.
66. Major, *History*, p. 428.

edition of Macchiavelli was appropriately dedicated to the earl of Arran.[67] The Italian poet, Gianfrancesco Conti, called Quinziano Stoa, wrote epigrams on James IV and a monody for his widow, but whether Quinziano had any closer connections with Scotland is less evident.[68]   Mair and David Cranston were among Scots who attended the Greek courses of Aleandro, given in Paris.   The occasional Scots reader of Italian can be detected: one who owned a manuscript of Leonardo Giustiniani and an archdeacon of Lothian interested in Ariosto.[69]   Many curial Scots, however, must have been familiar with Italian literature, or at least had a smattering of the language: for instance, John Hay, brother of Archibald. Doubtless also some of the nobility were interested.[70]

The influence of Marsilio Ficino on Boece through Johann Gaisser has already been suggested;[71] his influence on Cockburn and others of his circle through Symphorien Champier can also be postulated. Champier has been described as "the only true disciple Ficino had in France."   The appeal of Ficino to a man like Boece, scholastically formed but with humanist aspirations, is understandable in the context of the disturbance caused by the sceptical attitude to things christian found in Poggio's *Facetiae* or in Valla's *De Voluptate* or by the ferment of Aristotle still at work in the schools, oscillating dangerously between the outright materialism of Alexander of Aphrodisias and the Averroistic world-soul of which all men were mere parcels, both mirrored in contemporary nominalism and realism.   Even those who would not concur with Ficino that if men must philosophise let them Platonise, since Plato was a short-cut to the faith, welcomed his statement, *Adversus Averroem graeca Aristotelis verba reclamant*.   The important issue as to whether clerics ought to be concerned with philosophy, so strange to us who habitually think of philosophers in terms of laymen like Kant or Hume, was already being aired.   There was no question where John Mair stood on this question: he was a convinced Aristotelian.   But if one comes straight from the reading of the preface to Ficino's *De Religione Christiana* and his edition of Iamblichus to Mair's dedicatory letter to James Beaton, archbishop of Glasgow, with its very Platonic colouring and its defence of the status of priests in the pursuit of philosophic wisdom, the resemblance is too overwhelming to be accidental:

"Aegiptiorum olim famigerabilis propago (quem solem autumabat) vano delusa idololatritio venerabatur, illique mirandae venustatis sceptrum insculpebat in quo oculi effigies depingebantur.   Quo significaret eos qui sunt et prothomiste et antecellani sacros codices celestiave charismata linceis Argi luminibus et altissima cogitatione circumspicere oportere utpote qui sunt aliorum ideae et imagines.   Qua propter, non abs re instituit prudens mundi archetypus divina mysteria dumtaxat ab iis pertractari qui sapientiae deosculatores essent.   Proinde Hebraeorum vates et Essei sapientiae non minus quam sacerdotio vacabant . . ."[72]

---

67. *Le Prince de Nicolas Macchiavelli*, Poitiers, 1553, dedicated to Arran, by Gaspard Dauvergne, advocat au duche du Chastelleraut. A *Robert* Darvegny is a bearer of Arran's letters in 1554. (*Balcarres Papers*, Scot. Hist. Soc., ii, 213).

68. *Epistolae Poetarum Italicorum*, ii, 525-6.

69. Paris, B.N., Ms Ital. 1032, owned by William Crichton, 1522; it had other Scots connections, E. Pellegrin, *Les Bibliotheques des Visconti et des Sforza*, p. 390. *Innes Rev.*, ix, 75.

70. Archibald Hay, *Panegyricus Cardinalis*, v, verso. A French-Italian grammar (1548) was in Darnley's hands, *Heber Library Sale*, i, pt. 2, no. 2342.

71. In France Ficino was known to the de Ganay family, of whom Jean was associated with Elphinstone, Boece's patron. Cf. *Vitae Episcoporum*, p. 64. For Jean and Germain, see references in Ficino, *Opera* (Basle), pp. 957, 960, 963, 1871.

72. Major, *History*, p. 435, cited from *In Matthaeum* (1518). In his prohemium Mair defends Jerome as a Ciceronian and renews his attack on Valla, whose translation is held in contempt, he says.

This notion of the conjunction of theology and arts as the ideal studies of clerics in the pursuit of wisdom is the key to many matters of university policy in medieval Scotland.

The French-domiciled Cardinal Sadoleto, bishop of Carpentras, was patron of Florence Wilson, another northerner who had other Italian associations, both in England and in Lyons where he was still active in 1551.[73] While it was mainly with northerners that he was associated, it is clear from the correspondence of Giovanni Ferreri with certain of the nobles and the bishops that his influence must not be confined to a few Cistercians at Kinloss.[74] His letter (written from Kinloss in 1534) to William Stewart, bishop of Aberdeen, is significant. From it we learn that Stewart and some of the nobility went out of their way to visit him at Kinloss, and Stewart, as far as time allowed, handled some of his classical books and observed the educational apparatus in use there.[75] He can also be found associated with James Balfour (the dean of Glasgow, not Pittendreich), acting through the Italian banker, Cagnioli; and with Gilbert Skene, also of Aberdeen, to whose catholicity he testified when Skene was appointed to a college at Rennes in 1563.[76]

Doubtless it can be objected that much of this Italian influence is either superficial or indirect and has to be set beside the contemporary picture of a Scotland on the edge of the world, a land of unrelieved barbarism. Yet one who started off with a like prejudice against Scots, Girolamo Cardano, found himself forced to admit that this original prejudice stemmed from ignorance and was dispelled by acquaintance; on his visit (he wrote from Milan to Archbishop Hamilton in 1553), he found them a highly refined and incredibly civilised people. Undoubtedly there is a touch of flattery here; yet the terms might not be inapplicable to the circle of learned men then to be found in St. Andrews.[77]

GREEK

In order to test the thesis advanced here regarding the renaissance in Scotland several key inquiries are desirable: for instance, regarding translation (Douglas's *Aeneid* and Bellenden's *Livy*); regarding imitation of the ancients in verse and prose; the more general use of classical constructions; the rebirth of Greek and Greek ideas. There is room to pursue only a few of these enquiries here, and many studies of individuals will be necessary before anything definitive can be said.

For many years it has been accepted that Scotland was Greekless before Row and Melville: *Graecum est, non legitur.*[78] In addition it is alleged that Hebrew was totally unknown till Row brought it back from the Roman curia.[79] As regards individuals, these allegations are highly questionable. As regards institutions, it seems likely that, in spite of Archibald Hay's plea to him not to erect a " languageless college," Cardinal Beaton did not implement his nephew's plan for a trilingual

---

73. Pericaud, *Florent Wilson, Guillaume Postel et Louis Castelvetro*, p. 4.
74. Pollen, *Papal Negotiations*, pp. 413-9.
75. *Cicero Poeta*, sig. A iii.
76. Protocol Bk. of James Harlaw (G.R.H.), f.79v. Skene was to be regent in the College of St. Thomas, *Bibl. d'Humanisme et Renaissance*, xii, 100.
77. Cardano's commentary on Ptolemy, a 3r. (He goes on to celebrate Hamilton's virtues, his liberality to the poor, etc. (Cited from Basle reprint of 1578.)
78. Row, *Historie*, p. 422.
79. *Ibid.*, p. 455.

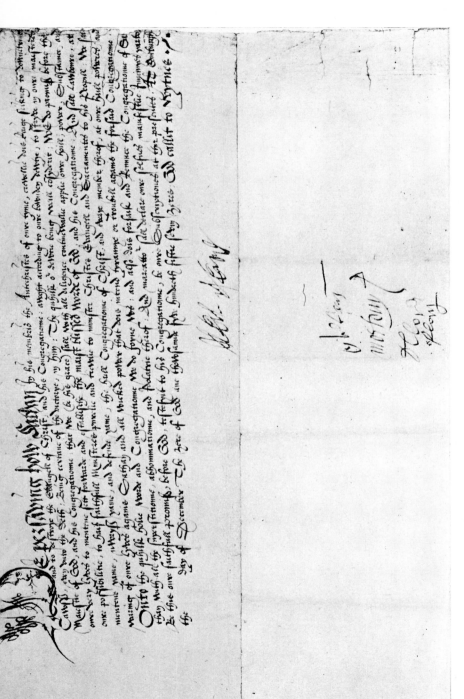

PLATE XXIII. THE BAND OF THE LORDS OF THE CONGREGATION. 1557.

PLATE XXIV. WILLIAM CECIL, LORD BURGHLEY, RIDING IN HIS GARDEN.

course at St. Andrews. Before the fifties Greek in the universities is unlikely except at Aberdeen, where Hebrew was also taught; but it is likely that some Greek (there are degrees of Greek !) was available in grammar schools. Knowledge of Greek even in the fifteenth century is probable in certain scholars: at least in Archibald Whitelaw and John Ireland.[80] Many must have learnt it abroad. Moreover, the fact that they knew it is no proof that as teachers they taught it. Here, however, is a provisional list:

George Dundas; John Mair; David Cranston; William Manderston; Alexander Stewart, archbishop of St. Andrews; John Vaus; George Buchanan; Florence Wilson; Robert Richardson; George Wishart; Alexander Alane (? learnt Wittenberg); Alexander Arbuckle, Franciscan; Archibald Hay; James Bachelor; Robert Stephenson, Cistercian, prior of Deer; William Learmonth, curate of Whitekirk (probably a canon of Holyrood);[81] James Thornton, subdean Ross (Greek verses, 1549); Alexander Beaton; Theophilus Stewart; John Davidson, principal, Glasgow; John Willock; John Knox (? learnt Geneva); John Lesley; George Hay; Adam Blackwood; Adam Elder, Cistercian (possibly from Ferreri[82] at Kinloss); Walter Reid, Kinloss; Henry Sinclair; David Panter; John Sinclair; Ninian Winzet (by 1563 at least).[83]

There are other indications pointing to an interest in Greek; for instance the armorial bookstamps of Bishops Gordon and Henry Sinclair.

IMITATIO VETERUM

Useful comments on this aspect of the renaissance theme already exist in essays by two modern classical scholars interested in renaissance Latin verse.[84] A study of the prose of the renaissance period is still a desideratum however.

The beginnings of the revival of verse in classical metres in Scotland are lost in the shadows as yet. But what may the religious verse of Dunbar for instance have owed to such Latin lines as these of Ireland's ?

> Deficient vatum mentes et tota poesis,
>   Si temptent laudes velle referre tuas.
> O utinam tandem possim te cernere coram,
>   Et quam contemplor, post mea fata fruar.
> Interea nostros, virgo sanctissima, gressus
>   Dirige, nam durus obsidet hostis iter.
> Non sine te tuti per tot discrimina mundi
>   Tendimus. O nostras suscipe, virgo, preces.
> Nos rege, dum vallis silvas erramus opacas,
>   Et rege cum tristis exitus eius erit.[85]

This is moving away from the medieval jingle, and is alive in spite of the odd roughness and the conventional images of nature. But while it is not true to say that Ireland's verse is unmusical, the work of James Foulis is a

---

80. Whitelaw explains the Greek " amnestia " to the English king. *Bannatyne Miscellany*, ii, 47. *Meroure of Wyssdome*, i, p. xix, inconclusive; but see title of poem, p. 177.
81. He was dead by early 1540, his executor dative being Robert Cairncross, bishop of Ross, former abbot of Holyrood, to which Whitekirk was appropriated; Liber Sententiarum Officialis infra Laudoniam (G.R.H.), f.219r.
82. Ferreri cites Greek (e.g., in *Cicero Poeta*, sig. E2 v,). But, of course, Elder was also at Paris.
83. This list is roughly chronological.
84. W. L. Adams in *Scottish Poetry: A Critical Survey*, ed. Kinsley pp. 68-98; D. F. S. Thomson in *The Phoenix*, xi, 63-78.
85. *Meroure*, i, 174.

great advance in metrical handling and in classical conciseness. Here he is asking James Henryson to favour his legal studies at Orleans:

> Dum licet, et caelo miti spes ulla colonis,
> Omnia continuo rura labore sonant.
> Sic mihi si faveas studii pars maxima nostri
> Dulcis erit sudor; tempore grana leges.

Writing to Alexander Stewart, archbishop of St. Andrews, he says his object in publishing was to entice students at home to take up the study of polite letters.[86] A few Latin lines addressed by John Mair to the same archbishop are also very polished.[87]

The greatest of our neo-Latin poets was, of course, George Buchanan. Buchanan was a pupil of Robert Wauchope at Paris.[88] Buchanan has to be linked with Hector Boece, whom he seems to have met in Paris, and whose " companionable " qualities he remembers; with Florence Wilson whom he certainly knew, and who was a skilled metrist; and probably with David Lowis or his pupil Britannus.[89] He outclasses his contemporaries but he is not to be presented as a literary phenomenon without father or mother or any sort of poetical genealogy. Recognition for him in his own country was postponed because of his association with the Scots heretics of 1539 during a brief sojourn in Scotland then and his later appearance before the Lisbon inquisition. The scandal caused made his return impossible, although he obtained an absolution apparently through Archbishop Hamilton's efforts, and was able with a good conscience to take up a canonry at Coutances in France in 1558.[90] His brother Patrick, was employed by the archbishop as pedagogue to one of the Hamiltons at Ave Maria College, Paris, and also at Poitiers.[91]

In addition to the poets there were innumerable versifiers; almost all the logicians of the school of John Mair could turn an epigram, some more convincingly than others.[92] Probably the earliest Latin verses by a Scot to appear in print were those prefixed to an edition of a legal work and composed in 1494 by Robert Abernethy, vicar of Kirriemuir.[93] One lost Latin poet of ability was a certain Master Paul who was preceptor of the young Pierre Ronsard during his Scottish visit, at least in Virgilian and Horatian metres.[94] But a new *Delitiae* would be necessary to illustrate the development satisfactorily.

The history of prose-writers following classical models would soon outrun the limits of an essay. Archibald Whitelaw already writes classically in the reign of James III. A typical theme in the declamatory style is Alexander Stewart's *Declamatio de Morte*, the only survivor of his Sienese compositions under Erasmus's tutorship, edited and dedicated by Erasmus to Henricus Glareanus. Archibald Hay's two works, the first addressed to Archbishop, the second to Cardinal Beaton, are in this genre of the

---

86. Jacobus Follisius, *Calamitosae pestis deploratio.*
87. Major, *History*, p. 420.
88. Paris, B.N. Ms Lat. 9952, f.41.
89. *Rerum Scoticarum Historia*, lib. ii, cap. 47, " Hectorem Boethium, non solum artium liberalium cognitione supra quam illa ferebant tempora insignem, sed humanitate et comitate singulari praeditum."
90. *Exposition France-Ecosse, Paris, Archives Nationales*, no. 329.
91. Edinburgh Univ. Library, Laing Ms, Div. iii, ff. 43r-v., 123v.
92. Also some logicians not of his school like John Gray of Haddington, whose verses are prefixed to Picard's *Thesaurus Theologorum*, Milan, 1506, (the British Museum copy was Cranmer's).
93. Magister Adam: *Summula Pauperum*. Paris. 1494. See *Gesamtkatalog der Wiegendrucke*, i, no. 217.
94. Pierre Champion, *Ronsard*, p. 25. Another Ronsard, Jean, citizen of Nantes, is found in Scotland on a more prosaic mission as procurator for certain French merchants pursuing some Scots pirates in law; Protocol Bk. of Jas. Harlaw, f.61v.

academic set-piece. The former attacks Cornelius Agrippa, whose own virulence, directed at the university curriculum of the time, is also in the genre of *declamatio*. It is hard to say how seriously we are to take the ideal picture of the two Beatons against the sombre backcloth of the clerical corruption of Scotland of the time; no doubt both pictures are overdrawn.[95] Erasmian influence on Hay is quite notable; his attitude to the philosophers is thoroughly Erasmian.

The attempt to write theology in classical Latin was not conspicuously successful. Reading Patrick Cockburn, with his chains of scriptural citations, or Florence Wilson, modelling himself on Erasmus, but unlike Erasmus in not being soaked in early christian Latin, we sense an ambiguity due to the use of a vocabulary reminiscent of pre-christian Rome instead of the " barbaric " terminology sanctioned by tradition. One sympathises with the remark of Gavin Douglas, who personally animadverted against barbarity, but whose own verse has a sharpness and raciness lacking in those brought up on a more exclusively classical diet:

> I compt nocht of thir paygane Goddis a fuddir
> Quhais power may nocht help a haltand hen.[96]

SCHOLARSHIP

George Buchanan was not a pure scholar, although the sixteenth century often seems to choose to think he was; and Andrew Melville is therefore often considered the first of our pure scholars. This is part of the Melville legend, due it would seem to the impact of Melville in fields quite unrelated to pure scholarship and partly of course to Melville's genuinely serious concern with the reform of studies.

But scholarship existed in Scotland before Melville. When he went from Paris to Poitiers to study law he presumably was attracted by the reputation of " that other Aelius Donatus ", Duncan Macruder, a manuscript of whose observations on Pomponius Mela has been overlooked in this country. I hope to write of Macruder and his relative, Andrew, at more length later.[97] Henry Scrimgeour, an uncle of Melville, is even more deserving of attention. He studied at St. Salvator's college in St. Andrews in 1532 before proceeding to Paris and Bourges.[98] While at Bourges, he studied under Jacques Amyot, the famous translator of Plutarch, and succeeded him as tutor to the Bochetel family, whose father held several posts in the French Royal household. He is thought to have supplied a manuscript of Plutarch used by Amyot. At Bourges he also met Ulrich Fugger, originally a chamberlain of pope Paul III, later to become the sole protestant member of this famous family of capitalists. He bought Greek manuscripts for Fugger's library in Augsburg, editing there the Greek text of the Emperor Justinian for Estienne's press at Geneva in 1558. Augsburg was the spiritual capital of the Melanchthonian and Calvinising wing of Lutheranism, as well as the nerve-centre of imperial religious politics, on the elaborate chessboard of which the edition of Justinian was doubtlessly a significant propagandist move: the example of the religious initiatives taken by Justinian being a model set before the modern emperor to follow. Scrimgeour later settled down at Geneva to

---

95. It is true he darkly hints he has more up his sleeve, which kind friends advised him not to put in print.

96. *Aeneid*, prologue to the 10th Book.

97. Paris B.N., Ms Lat. 4854. Annotationes in Librum I Pomponii Melae de situ orbis D. Duncani Macrudaeri Scoti . . . f.106r. Finis Annotationum in Pomponium Melam de situ orbis D. Donati Macrudaeri Scoti. Macruder was at St. Leonard's in 1545, *Early Recs.*, p. 251.

98. *Ibid.*, p. 231. I shall deal at greater length with Scrimgeour soon.

which he attracted Melville, but unlike Calvin, who on his conversion resigned all his benefices at Noyon, Scrimgeour retained his Scottish ones as far as we can see.[99] He was in Italy at Padua buying Greek manuscripts in 1562.[100] Some of his manuscript notes were transmitted to Scotland from abroad. But it is probable that most of the actual manuscripts themselves remained at Augsburg till transferred to the Palatine collection at Heidelberg and so after a few decades into the present Palatine collection in the Vatican.[101]

Another Scot, Edward Henryson, incepted at Paris in early 1543.[102] From there on he went on to Bourges, and his name is also associated with Ulrich Fugger and with translating and editing Plutarch; both the *Septem Sapientium Convivium* and the *Commentarius Stoicorum Contrariorum* are dedicated to Fugger whose hospitality he too enjoyed. He professed civil law at Bourges, was patronised by its chancellor, Michel de l'Hospital, addressed verses to another great jurist, Francois Duaren, and took up the defence of Robert Ireland's former pupil at Poitiers, Eguinaire Baron, against Antonio de Gouveia, was invited back to St. Andrews by Archbishop Hamilton in 1553, but chose instead to have himself commended to Bishop Reid through Ferreri, and so came instead to Edinburgh to lecture on Greek and the laws.[103]

These brief indications are perhaps sufficient to suggest that there is no real evidence for post-dating the Scottish revival of learning till after Andrew Melville, significant as Andrew Melville doubtless was.

It would be a useful exercise to try and compile a history of Scottish anti-humanism in this period; it unquestionably must have existed. The members of the religious orders were so much under humanist fire that they must have had a strong anti-humanist core, not only in reaction to the Epicurean extravagances of some of the pets of the curia like Valla, but because of the mordant ridicule of which they were the continuous butt. Partly this was the old secular-regular conflict resuscitated, although certain secular priests went out of their way to defend them; particularly Mair himself, as regards Carthusians and Franciscans and other Observants (to whose ranks there is evidence of men of learning once more flocking). The clergy were accustomed to teasing, and took it mostly in good part; but the irony of Erasmus could be very wounding, while Margaret of Navarre's *Heptameron* is quite vicious: our own Buchanan followed suit. Doubtless some friars encouraged superstition and often crossed the line from vulgarisation to vulgarity, and deserved censure. That monks should learn to laugh at their follies is desirable, but, in the event, the satire was ill-timed, and some of their more sensitive members were stung into leaving not only the cloister but the church as well.

THE CLIMATE OF THOUGHT

In any age there is nothing more difficult to pin down than a climate of thought, and nothing more necessary to reckon with than this

99. He probably came home after finishing his studies at Bourges as he was commended by Bochetel to Mary of Lorraine; *Balcarres Papers*, Scottish Hist. Soc., i, 209. On 22 June, 1552, he was chaplain of the St. Sebastian chaplainry at Dundee, a benefice he still held in 1564; he was also before his death parson and vicar of Glassary, *Dudhope Peerage Case, House of Lords: Print of Documents*, pp. 100, 118, 137.

100. *Inventario dell' Epistolario Manuziano*, p. 331.

101. Cioranescu suggests that these notes were taken from Amyot's public course at Bourges, but this can not be wholly true. Some of his notes are now at Cambridge; Trinity College Ms 1304. See also Scrimgeour - Buchanan Correspondence. There is quite a literature on the role of Scrimgeour as collector.

102. Paris BN, Ms Lat. 9953, f.217r.

103. A fuller study of Henryson must wait till later.

particular intangible; historians who prefer tidiness to grappling with realities have an understandable impatience with what they feel is a flight from footnotes and factuality. The risks are great; it may be necessary to take them.

A recognised factor in the making of this age is the gradual secularisation of the idea of " wisdom", and consequently of the ideal of the good life, in some ways a necessary secularisation, a necessary recognition of the relative autonomy of merely human values and of the status of secondary causes, due not wholly to the renaissance or the reformation, but also to the Aristotelian ferment at work within the christian framework of thought which the middle ages inherited from the christian fathers principally through Augustine. Thus one can understand the monastic life (or collegiate life for that matter—the Scottish reformation destroyed secular college life) being held in high regard in a society for which wisdom was the contemplation of divine things through the three divine virtues principally of faith, hope and charity, cultivated alone or by some intellectual or spiritual elite set apart from men but abiding in common. The christian Aristotelians had put Augustine into a new context: for them wisdom flowed upwards from man's God-given reason as well as downwards from the revelation handed down from above. Men did not cease to be Aristotelians or Augustinians in spite of a few Ramists and a few Pelagians; but they were either so blinded by God Transcendent that they saw nothing but faith and faith alone, man's God-given reason as utterly vitiated by his original revolt and the Image within shattered in fragments, or they stressed first of all that this human reason had been restored once and for all in God Incarnate, who thus accepted human sanctity, in that he was fully and unequivocally human as well as fully and unequivocally God.

A typical medieval statement of this view of Incarnate Wisdom is found in the prologue to the Glasgow university arts statutes, where all the virtues, moral and theological, and all science, divine and human, refer back to their source in the Saviour;[104] in the St. Salvator of the contemporary St. Andrews college dedication. Bishop Elphinstone's tomb takes up the same theme; with the figures of Contemplation and the divine virtues with it, Action being illustrated by the four moral virtues on which all other human virtues hinge.[105] The " Lady " in the faculty seal at St. Andrews is this Lady Wisdom and not our Lady as Hannay read her. Similarly Perdrizet mistakenly reads a continental example of the same symbol.[106] Understandably, because the middle ages is not consistent in its use of symbolism. Hence Elphinstone used the dedication of the nativity of our Lady for his college in Aberdeen, because in her sinlessness and infused wisdom she was the symbol of a new race; and Beaton used the dedication of the Assumption to symbolise the assumption and transfiguration of human wisdom and human virtue in a divine context.[107] Significantly Elphinstone's profane studies were outside in external manses; the sacred studies (arts were the handmaid of sacred studies) inside. The seminary idea was not altogether new; what was new was its extension to the whole priesthood and not merely to the university-trained.

---

104. *Munimenta Univ. Glasguensis*, ii, 20.

105. Eeles, *King's College Chapel*, p. 10.

106. Hannay, *Statutes of the Univ. of St. Andrews*, p. 23; Perdrizet, *La Vierge de Misericorde*, p. 210.

107. It is surely not just coincidence either that Archbishop Dunbar chose the same feast for his proposed refoundation of the Glasgow college. Cf. *Munimenta*, i, 493.

This unity of doctrine and discipline is based on the traditional view of wisdom, a view alien to hard-headed men of the world then as now, who doubtless found repellent the Sabbath calm of contemplation in which masters and students were to be enveloped; although Elphinstone hoped to attract laymen and particularly the nobility to his " noble college." The university ideal, the studies, the academic acts and exercises are, he says, praiseworthy in themselves.[108] So far from being criticised or crushed they ought to be added to and improved; indeed to be changed into something infinitely better and this requires God's initiative. Clerics were his ministers; the catholic faith was their career, and as its devotees (i.e., as students of the Word and its ministers) they ought to apply themselves to letters. It is my province as their bishop, he says, in accordance with the grace I have received from on high, to see that they are fit and able to do so. But they must do this with the minimum of disturbance, have a higher standard of behaviour, have security and leisure; and must not be exposed during this formative period to lay influence and so get into trouble, or have an excuse for involvement in court cases, etc., or for wandering off and merging with the world outside. Lay contact was maintained, especially in chapel; but in a real sense the artists and theologians were sealed off. A similar ideal exists at the new college of St. Leonard in St. Andrews, where the lay element that was soon to invade it is hardly perceptible in the original statutes (which I hope to publish) and where arts and theology alone are provided for; but there the founder stresses discipline more than doctrine, order rather than wisdom.[109]

This idea of a new model clergy is set before Archbishop Blacader of Glasgow in 1506, in phrases with a somewhat Platonic ring in spite of their Aristotelian context and composed by a convert to the theory of Paris as the new Athens, David Cranston, regent at Montaigu:

" Nihil etenim viro id conditionis dignius quam, sopore funditus euulso, sese coalescere bonis (ut soles) artibus. Idipsum profecto diis superis simillimum fore censeas, quod gymnosophie parens Stageritauus Aristoteles asseuerat summum bonum in supernarum et diuinarum rerum contemplatione consistere: Socrates identidem, Ionici author studii . . . Namque ingenio quodam ad sciendi cognitionem incendimur omnes. Id longe potius enituisse debet qui semidei probatisque simulachra in terris habentur."[110]

The ideal of a civilisation of the sanctuary was being adapted to a new age; with the renaissance, philosophy was no longer cultivated merely as an aid to theology, there was " a republic of letters ", the possibility of a purely human culture, something already envisaged in the thirteenth century with the irruption of Arab Aristotelianism but not fully followed up in subsequent ages. This laicisation of culture was not something utterly unheard of; nor was it really completed till the days of the Enlightenment. The Paris dialecticians accepted the concept of a republic

---

108. Largely paraphrased from Eeles, p. 198.
109. Herkless and Hannay, *College of St. Leonard*, pp. 145, where the Prologue on Order follows the original text closely. The main charge of many fifteenth-century critics, that such " contemplation of divine things " was sterile, is met at King's with the programme of vernacular sermons as well as sermons *ad clerum*. Doctrine and discipline also go together at Glasgow, cf. " Cum philosophie et omnis contemplationis pulchritudo tam anime quam corporis in morum condecencia exigat honestatem . . . "*Munimenta*, ii, 22. Contemporaries were aware of the contrast between other-wordly theory and this-worldly practice, even if to later eyes they seem impotent to overcome it.
110. *Questiones super posteriorum lectura* (Paris), 1506.

of letters without fuss; the tensions were rather between lawyers and theologians, between rhetoricians and logicians, between the uncompromising advocates of contemplation and the patrons of civic virtue. It is a dialectician turned lawyer, Robert Galbraith, who writes thus to James IV's Justice Clerk:

" Quandoquidem praeclara Stoicorum sententia ab Romani eloquii facile principe M. Tullio Cicerone in iis quos de officio scripsit libris citata, ' Homines hominum causa nati sunt, ut interesse alii aliis prodesse possint,' in hoc, natura duce, institi, in hoc animum appuli, ut et studiosis et reipublicae literariae consultum irem . . . "[111]

The argument about wisdom went on throughout the century. For Luther human wisdom was a *sapientia carnis*, " the traditions of men "; Erasmus valued a *sancta eruditio*, such as the times with its superstitious observances and multiplication of printed texts seemed to demand. The rising mercantilist classes were increasingly literate and increasingly inclined to regard their own virtues as pre-eminently worthwhile and the cloistered virtues of monks and university men as the fantasties of idlers.

The whole trend is extremely complex: men like Sadoleto and Cardano often use the old phraseology alongside the new. Language is changing and in itself is betraying men into new ways of thinking. " The college of the godly Leonard " or even " the Leonardine college " displaces " the college of saint Leonard." The " church " becomes " the temple " and soon begins to look like one. The new vocabulary did not always win permanent victories: *ecclesia* eventually won the battle with *templum* and the university rector-elect soon ceased to be *moderator designatus*. This was not the only element contributing to the effect of paganism in late sixteenth-century Scotland (one was the lack of recruits for the ministry), for the effect itself was not entirely novel; but even a man born in 1537, like Alexander Arbuthnot, testified to the decline in his lifetime:

" Religioun now is reknit as ane fabill.
All houpe of hevin is hauldin vanitie
And hellis paine is comptit poetrie."[112]

THE REFORMERS

Before dealing with the reformation proper it would have been enlightening to examine the catholic pre-reform movement too: because, besides secular priests like Mair and Wauchope, there were religious reformers whose careers have unfortunately not been the subject of the detailed enquiry necessary. The association of Cambuskenneth through St. Victor in Paris with Windesheim; of the Dominican reform under John Adamson with Cardinal Cajetan; of the reform at Kinloss under abbots Chrystall and Reid and at Glenluce under Walter Malynne with Giovanni Ferreri and the wider Cistercian reform in Europe; all these are themes whose treatment would carry us beyond the bounds of an essay. Moreover the influence of the ideals of Jean Standonck in the project for creating a more priestly priesthood from the ranks of poor men where wealthy clerics were failing was felt not only by John Hepburn prior of St. Andrews and vicar general and rival to its archbishop magnates, and exemplified in his creation of the college of poor clerks at St. Leonard's,

---

111. Printed in an edition of George Lockhart's *Termini*.
112. *Maitland Quarto Manuscript*, p. 125.

but was also exemplified at least in part by both Bishop Elphinstone and Archbishop Beaton in their college foundations.

It was precisely out of these groups in touch with foreign influence, whether beneficed secular clergy able to study in universities abroad or friars accustomed to be assigned to foreign houses of their orders, that both the antidote to the revolutionary religious theories and the theories themselves came. Of the three greatest religious leaders of the new movement, Knox was a secular priest, influenced by Wishart above all, but also partly by Thomas Gilyem, friar and a native of Athelstaneford;[113] Wishart was surely at least a tonsured cleric and probably in major orders, a brilliant student at Louvain;[114] and Patrick Hamilton, pensioner of Fearn, was certainly in orders, and, if Frith be relied on, a priest, who had studied abroad also. The influence was not always immediate. The following Cologne students for instance entered or remained in religion after the Lutheran revolt: John Lyne, Franciscan; Thomas Forret, Augustian canon; and John Macalpine, Dominican. Some, though not themselves abroad, were first stirred by the burning of Patrick Hamilton. The nature of this influence for many years to come can be broadly described as Lutheran, though Scots Anabaptists are not unknown.[115] Moreover, Zwinglian and Swiss influences are not impossible through Francois Lambert (with whom Patrick Hamilton had been at Marburg), though Lambert did not become decisively Zwinglian till after Hamilton's return home; however, Bullinger, the contemporary at Cologne of some Scots students (1519-22), succeeded Zwingli as pastor at Zurich, and came to be friendly with the ex-Dominican, Willock.[116] Even so, it would not be difficult to multiply references (as late as the trial of Walter Mill) to specifically German influence on our reformation personalities, even where at a later turn of events influences from Geneva and Zurich took over.

The nominalist influence in the German universities is often canvassed by historians of diverse views as decisive in creating the reformed mentality; and there is no doubt that Luther's vocabulary is charged with nominalist overtones. *Imputed* justice in man was taken to mean that man was not in any *state* of justice, was not really justified, but merely that effectually the individual was accepted as just through Christ's righteousness:

---

113. Gilyem was prior of Inverness in 1525 (*Exchequer Rolls*, xv, 192). The name is found in Athelstaneford in 1557 (Prot. Bk. Thos. Stevin, f.178v.)

114. There appears to be some confusion regarding pre-reformation forms of address for the clergy, secular and regular. It is not true to say that " Father " is non-existent or rare, apart from the well-known " venerable father in Christ " of prelates. It was almost certainly used addressing priests in confession (cf. Lindsay's *Monarche*): and is found in the general confession at the beginning of mass in Sarum and Roman rites. It was employed to distinguish lay-brethren from choir-monks and priests; hence a friar was both " brother " and " father " (cf. signature of Friar Towers, *Innes Rev.*, ix, 154). " Father Willock " is used by Quintin Kennedy; " the good Scottish frere Father Donald " by More (*Innes Rev.*, v, 78); and those familiar with Knox will recognise Winram's form of address for Friar Arbuckle (Knox, *History*, i, 90, 92). " Dominus," translated " sir," or among regular canons and some monks as " dean," is applied not only to priests, but to all clergy, secular and regular, in major orders: for examples of deacons and subdeacons, cf. *Diocesan Registers of Glasgow*, ii, 127, 141, etc. (The traditional expression was " diaconus regens populum," hence entitled to dominium over Christ's patrimony, hence all clerks in major orders required to have a title). " Master " is confined to graduates, who may or may not be in major orders or even in orders at all; if in orders they may describe themselves occasionally as " Dominus " (" Magister Dominus " is not unknown and even " Frater Dominus "). For a Master addressed as " sir " see *Dioc. Reg.*, ii, 361. Wishart seems to be similarly addressed (the title could be a title of honour to a distinguished layman, but the moment hardly seems appropriate) by Friar Scott (Knox, ii, 244). For a clerk in the highest minor orders, but still lacking the prefix " Dominus," cf. Baxter, *Copiale Prioratus Sanctiandree*, p. 33. Knox is curiously uninformative about the orders of reformers; Foxe is more forthcoming. Foxe tells us that Henry Forrest was degraded from his " small orders " of Bennet and Collet (i.e., tonsure, *benedictio coronae*—and acolyte), Foxe-Townsend, iv, 579.

115. In 1532 the names of London Anabaptists include " Andrew Pierson, a Scottish organmaker, dwelling in Redcrosse Street." *Letters and Papers Henry VIII*, Addenda, i, pt. 1, no. 809.

116. The dedication of the Fifth Book of Bullinger's *Decades* (of homilies, not of prayers) to Henry, Marquis of Dorset, mentions " Andrew (*sic*) Wullock."

doubtless this phrasing of the doctrine will not be acceptable to all, but, whatever phrasing is used, God's grace seems to strike man at a tangent rather than transform him through and through. Yet if the *via moderna* in this way did influence events, the mentality of the *via antiqua* also lent itself readily to the cause: it tended to a predilection for what was primitive and ancient in the church, a distrust of modern traditions and of later speculation and would favour in principle the return to the sources that resulted mainly from the enormous industry of Erasmus, a return which exerted as much influence over the breakaway movement as over the theological revival in the church. An example of one of those attached initially to both Augustine and Aquinas is Robert Richardson, canon of Cambuskenneth, later a London Puritan divine.[117] Yet something also is due to the fact that the themes of predestination and justification were favourite themes of the fourteenth century when nominalism took its rise.

The defection of clerics, secular and regular, was a European phenomenon, but it can be exaggerated, at least in the decades before 1560. It would not be difficult to show that something similar happened in a contrary sense after 1560. Moreover the mobility of some of the clerics concerned and their relationships must have been potent factors in the spread of their influence. For instance, William Forman was both canon of Holyrood and vicar of Balmaghie, Kirkcudbright.[118] I have suggested elsewhere that Robert Richardson was related indirectly to that other runaway, John MacBrair. It now seems to me likely that Richardson had some relationship to Alexander Alane, who, through his mother, Christina Bigholm, was heir to John Bigholm, a canon of Jedburgh.[119] Now Alane was an important figure in the European reformation, known personally to Melanchthon and to Bucer as well as to Thomas Cromwell and Cranmer in England.[120] Unfortunately his Scottish correspondence is missing.

But Melanchthon is clearly of central importance in the trend followed by Scottish Lutheranism. This point will have to be reverted to; meantime it suffices to note that, besides Alane, Macalpine was in touch with him. In 1542 another Scot, a certain James, was recommended by Macalpine to Alane and Melanchthon, most probably James Balfour, soon to be Knox's galley companion.[121] Melanchthon sent Walter Spalding, a friend of the Spanish reformer, Enzinas, to Cranmer, and he, after a period at Oxford, was active in Ireland, where he died in 1551.[122] He wrote to John Fidelis, Scot, at Frankfurt, recommending John Lyne to him.[123]

During the latter part of the reign of Mary of Lorraine a new phase can be encountered; the phase of the " privy kirks ", secret meeting

---

117. *Robertus Richardinus* (Scottish Hist. Soc.) ed Coulton, whose index gives no idea of the spread of references to Aquinas.
118. Pitcairn, *Criminal Trials*, i, 330*; Liber Sententiarum Officialis infra Laudoniam, f.301v. The mobility of the friars is not generally realised; for instance, Friar William Kelour, whose activity in Stirling is cited, was convoyed south from Aberdeen where he had gone in the interim. Pitcairn, i, *221.
119. *Transactions Dumfriesshire and Galloway N. H. and Antiquarian Society*, xxxvi, 74. Protocol Bk. Thomas Strathauchin (G.R.H.), f.45r Marion Bigholm, relict of James Richardson, burgess of Edinburgh, married Nicholas MacBrair, burgess of Dumfries, A.D.C., xiv, 56. She was Alexander Alane's aunt, *Prot. Bk. John Foular*, i, 895, 899. The Edinburgh family of Baron was also related to Alane.
120. On the 7th Nov., 1540, he wrote from Worms to the elector of Brandenburg. He had been discussing the rumour of new dissensions in protestant Eucharistic theory with Bucer, who informed him there was great concord, *Archiv fur Reformations Geschichte*, viii, 404. He is also mentioned in Luther's *Tischreden* as having strong views on the punishment of public sins. Cf. also his reasons for leaving Frankfurt for Leipzig, *Corpus Reformatorum*, iv, col. 89.
121. *Corpus Reformatorum*, iv, 793.
122. *Ibid.*, iv, 780-1; vii, 189. *Original Letters* (Parker Soc.), ii, 428.
123. *Corpus Ref.*, viii, 815-6.

places for worship in burgess's houses or noble mansions, probably, as in France, behind closed curtains, at night, with stringent regulation of entry. If these privy kirks were organised centrally, presumably they were at that date organised from Geneva. Yet Geneva never acquired anything like the control over the Scottish privy kirk that it did over those in France between 1555 and 1562; for one thing the lines of communication were rather longer and the Scots trainees for the ministry at Geneva appear to be a very small proportion. If the Company of Pastors found control an arduous business in France, the French network was at least supplied with a constant flow of Genevan-trained missionaries; how much more arduous must have been any control over the quality and quantity of missionaries so far away from headquarters. Yet the war with England favoured the cause, and Knox says that they held their conventions and councils with such gravity and closeness that their enemies trembled. Many must have been taken on at this time who were not Calvinists *pur sang*; some were soon dropped.[124] It is curious how little the leaders of the privy kirks contributed to the personnel which drew up the Book of Discipline. Yet these privy kirks were important; the work of indoctrination did not suddenly begin in 1560 nor did protestant armies then spring from nowhere.

English Influence

Before the Henrician schism started in England there were defections from the church in Scotland explicable as originating from influences other than English. By 1534, besides Patrick Hamilton, there were Gilbert Winram, who died at Marburg in 1530, Alexander Alane, who fled to Malmo and so to Wittenberg and Melanchthon, John Gau (in Malmo by 1533), James Melville, ex-Franciscan, who cites Lambert as a pillar of Lutheran doctrine, in spite of his deviations in some things, and whose return to the fold in 1530 was apparently of a temporary nature. Those Scots who did flee to England after Henry's break with the pope were well received by Thomas Cromwell, whose patronage often proved necessary, as they were often too doctrinaire for the stomach of the English divines; doubtless through him the ex-friars, Macdowell and Macalpine, became chaplains to the protestantising bishop of Salisbury, Shaxton; Robert Richardson was provided with a benefice; and George Wishart, fleeing from the mayor of Bristol, but supported by some scurrilous citizens, had to report to Cromwell who appears to have helped him leave for a while. The movement south was given a great impulse by the English schism; but there is no reason to doubt Knox that much of the outflow stemmed from Patrick Hamilton.

It is notable that some found shelter in noble households; John Craig with Lord Dacre;[125] John Willock with the Marquis of Dorset; Alexander Seton with the Duke of Suffolk. But the Englishmen's opinions probably

---

124. Is the ex-Trinitarian, John Wallace of Peebles one of these ? Renwick, *Peebles in the Reign of Mary*, p. 113; *Peebles Records*, i, 258. The situation in Peebles was confused for some time, and even after admission by Willock, Knox, as " superintendent of Edinburgh," had final say, *Ibid.*, i, 275. Knox lists certain names and the additional name of Patrick or Paterson is given by the Provincial Council (*Statutes*, p. 186) and Friar John Christeson by Pitcairn, i, *407, One has the impression that as far as urban centres went the organisation was good, but that the rural areas were less well served. Even in the towns one man did duty in several places; for instance Knox cites William Harlaw as active in Edinburgh, but we find him in the south at the house of Stewart of Garlies and in Dumfries in a burgess's house and defying the authority of Archibald Menzies, official of Nith, in October 1558. (Keith, *Affairs of the Church and State*, i, 495).

125. Is he the John Cragge alias Turner naturalised in 1544 ? *Aliens in England*, p. 57.

affected our nobility more than the clergy, although married clergy like Thomas Cocklaw or Gibson or their sympathisers, like Robert Logie, a fellow canon of Cambuskenneth, might find it easier in England to keep their clerical status.[126] Nevertheless a study of the alien element in England gives no ground for the belief that large numbers from Scotland were sheltering there, and in London among the merchants the Scots were an infinitesimal proportion among the Dutch and other refugees.

Yet it would be flying in the face of commonsense to belittle overmuch the process of Anglicisation in Scotland, and not merely the forcible Anglicisation of English armies, even when this was associated with evangelisation, as when John Willock preached to the Scottish borderers after they had been cowed by the arms of his patron, the Marquis of Dorset.[127] It is true that in the early part of the century a Scots reader still found Chaucer " hard on the ears."[128] However, that did not deter a hardheaded French publisher like Verard from employing a Scots student in Paris, Thomas Lewyngton, to translate *L'art de bien vivre et bien mourir* (Paris, 1503) into a Frenchified Scots in order to cultivate the English market. [129] Verard already cultivated Henry VII with service books and special vellum copies of French works. We can be fairly certain then that English service books would circulate steadily in both countries, even when from 1534 they very gradually took on more a Lutheran hue, with Bucer writing under the name of Felinus and excerpts from Gau's Lutheran catechism and Patrick Hamilton's Places.[130] The effect of this subtle psychological conditioning, whereby traditional orthodox matter was slowly watered down and the new teaching imperceptibly infiltrated, is hard to evaluate, especially as, for decades before the reformation, there was some vernacular matter in these primers. Of course the full effect of Anglicisation was not to be felt till after 1560.[131]

It is in this context that Robert Burrant's account of Wishart's martyrdom must be read. Whether based or not on matter sent south by Knox, Burrant has made of it a subtle work of art, calculated to appeal to secret sympathisers like John Winram (whom it handles gently), but also to the peace-loving layman or the learned priest with an Erasmian outlook, a student for instance of the *Ratio Verae Theologiae*. Like the latter work, it suggests that the peace of the christian world is being shattered for the sake of a few ceremonies, presents Wishart as the Servant of Christ, gentle to the beggars and the plague-stricken and severe only to pharisaical men, a

126. Both of these were associated with Thomas Forret, vicar of Dollar, a Cologne student. Both had been in France, at Paris perhaps with Richardson, who mentions Logie (*Robertus Richardinus*, p. 127). Cf. *Aliens in England*, pp. 105, 155. Richardson and Logie were both at Cambuskenneth on 14th August, 1531, when they were released by Abbot Mylne from an excommunication for disobedience, so that divine office could proceed on " tam sublimi nocte assumptionis." Old Stirling Protocols, Fragments, (G.R.H.), f.18v.

127. *Original Letters*, ii, 428, 431.

128. *Innes Rev.*, ix, 129. Actually the work was by Lydgate.

129. This information came from M. A. Manzaloui, of Magdalen College, Oxford, who also showed that *The Kalendar of Shepherds* (S.T.C. 22407) was a similar work and so not to be ascribed to Alexander Barclay. Livingstone, who translated S.T.C. 791, was, as Manzaloui surmised, a student in Paris. Unfortunately I am not aware that Manzaloui published his findings, nor have I been able to contact him since.

130. Butterworth, *The English Primers*, pp. 19, 127, 282-3; White, *Tudor Books of Private Devotion*, p. 87. The Places follow on the 15 O's in Gough's Primer of 1536 !

131. James Rollock of Dundee, who, in 1539, was a fugitive from the law for heresy, in 1544 was porter at Campvere and buying and probably importing into Dundee service and other books printed by John Mayler in London. (*R.S.S.*, ii, 2962; Maxwell, *Old Dundee prior to Reformation*, pp. 78-9). Martin Balcasky, Edinburgh merchant, was arrested for refusing to deliver his (English ?) matin book to the official of Lothian. (*R.S.S.*, ii, 2936; *Criminal Trials*, i, 218. He was imprisoned in England in 1541. Nicholas, *Acts Privy Council*, vii, 144, 172; *Letters and Papers*, xvi, 1163.) The so-called Matthews bible (actually sponsored by John Rogers, colleague of Macalpine at Wittenberg) had made its way to Dundee also where it was in the hands of David Wedderburn, burgess. (*Innes Rev.*, ix, 158).

true prophet confronted by a Caiaphas and a Pilate.[132] Burrant knew his job: he translated the Cato of Erasmus and the Seven Sages for English readers.[133]

But Wishart may only have been slightly affected by his English contacts, although some of his positions are not unreminiscent of Latimer (and the pointmakers of Bristol appealed on his behalf to Cromwell and Latimer).[134] Still, it is at least noteworthy that Bristol, a Lollard centre, later received Thomas Gilyem, an ex-Dominican who introduced Knox to reformed views and possibly to Wishart. There was also an unidentified Scottish friar, perhaps from Montrose, associated with Latimer in an accusation of heresy in 1546.[135]

The truth is that contemporary English theology was so much under foreign influence itself and Scottish students apparently such rare birds at English universities that it is safe to say that to the clerical element in Scotland it only appealed as a refuge for those already influenced from other sources; although of course this does not apply so much to noblemen amateurs, interested in theological ideas certainly, and no doubt in some *via media*,[136] like Buchanan who affirmed that he saw no difference between Lutheran and catholic views of justification.[137] We can take it that Hector Bain, a former Louvain student, naturalised in 1535, was already influenced abroad. David Peddie, a former student of Greifswald, no doubt turned Lutheran there.[138] A Scot called Dodd burnt at Calais (then English) in 1544 learnt his ideas in Germany.[139] Nicholas Borthwick, a former student of Wittenberg, received an English reward in 1542.[140] Sir John Borthwick, on the other hand was influenced by English ideas,

---

132. Cf. the *Ratio* in Erasmus, *Opera*, v, 75 seq.

133. There clearly was a very attractive side to Wishart's character, but shot with moods of violence. No doubt he regarded the Grey Friars at Inveresk as interfering Pharisees, hence his sudden rounding on them, Dickinson's *Knox*, i, 67. But his Cambridge panegyrist confesses that some thought him severe and " would have slain him." Foxe-Townsend, v, 626. His early preaching was probably extreme; the St. Andrews accusation regarding baptism appears to refer to earlier Anabaptist views (Dickinson's *Knox*, ii, 237-8). The hubbub created by him in Bristol in 1539 led to his departure from England. He appears to have received a reader's licence from Henry Holbeach, suffragan of Latimer, a former Cambridge Benedictine. His artisan-defenders refer to him as " the faithful young man " and " the honest reader " who put the King of Heaven before Henry VIII, but are brutally scurrilous about his critics. He was before Thomas Cromwell for his first offence in January, but in May, according to two Bristol calendars, " he sett furth his lecture . . . the moost blasphemous heresy that euer was herd," which he recanted in July. *Ricart's Calendar* (Camden Soc.); *Letters and Papers Hen. VIII*, xiv, pt. 1, nos. 184, 1095. Seyer's *Memoirs of Bristol* is fuller, ii, 222-3.

134. Latimer resigned Worcester on July 1st, Wishart recanted a fortnight later.

135. " The Scot is more meet for Dunbar than London, having neither wit nor learning for a preacher, but is a very ignorant, and hath framed his sayings after his audience, as to be rid will say now what you will bid him." (*Letters and Papers Hen. VIII*, xxi, pt. 1, no. 803). This has been identified with Robert Richardson, friend of Crome, one of the accused, and who was released two months later (*Ibid.*, no. 1290) but if so the estimate of his ability seems prejudiced. Nor does the cap quite fit Alexander Seton, said to have died in 1542; although a married Scot named Seton fled out of constable's custody in Surrey at this very time (Dasent, *Acts Privy Council*, i, 405). Another possibility is ex-Dominican Thomas Gilyem, said to have fled south about April, 1543, but still in Scotland late in that month, and not made denizen in England till 1549. (Calderwood, i, 160; *Treas. Accts.*, viii, 183; *Pat Rolls Edw. VI*, ii, 243). Moreover the description hardly seems to fit a bachelor of divinity, even if his birthplace is not so very distant from Dunbar. Foxe cites a Learmonth alias Williamson among the Marian exiles (Foxe-Townsend, viii, 739). Moreover a " William Lermounth," Scot, was in trouble for attacking the service-book in 1550 (Dasent, ii, 379-381). This man was also chaplain to Anne of Cleves. The Rev. Ian Muirhead suggests identifying him with William Learmonth, friar of Montrose in 1531, a native perhaps of Dunbar.

136. An exponent of the middle way won no sympathy from the General Assembly of 1563, *Acts General Assemblies*, i, 44.

137. Aitken, *Trial of George Buchanan*, p. 19.

138. *Aliens in England*, pp. 18, 185. Peddie was not naturalised till 1567. But William Bourne, a student at Cambridge was in England for 16 years before becoming a denizen in 1544, p. 27. Peddie held a prebend of St. Paul's in 1559 (Hennessy, *Repertorium*, p. 49.)

139. Foxe-Townsend, v, 523-4.

140. *Letters and Papers*, xvii, no. 880. There are problems. Is the John Penven, vicar of Staines, 1576, identical with the earlier one ? (*Ibid.*, xi, no. 916). Is the curate of Lothbury (1560), whose vices were " unmentionable," the Patrick Freebairn, Scot, in London in 1549 ? (Hennessy, *Repertorium*, pp. cxxiii, 279; *Aliens in London*, i, 354).

and after condemnation for heresy in Scotland, went on to live in England: it is disconcerting to think of him on missions to Sweden and Denmark in 1549 and 1552 to win support for reformed England,[141] while his fellow Scots, Sir David Lindsay and the Earl of Rothes (father of the cardinal's murderer), visited Denmark in 1549 and 1550 on behalf of unreformed Scotland.[142] Did Rothes alone call on their Lutheran compatriot there, John Macalpine?

But there is another facet to English influence, for Scotland was invaded by priests, friars and monks seeking temporary refuge. We know of many Franciscan Observants for instance.[143] There is also a William Fordham, monk of Worcester, with no very happy history behind him, at Dunfermline in 1546.[144] We also know of four distinguished academic Englishmen who took refuge in St. Andrews university: Richard Hilliard, Henry Bretton, Richard Smith, secular priests; and Richard Marshall, Dominican.[145]

When therefore we find Archbishop Hamilton's brother, the Governor Arran, buying some English books, the Paraphrases, the New Testament and Hooper on the Commandments, early in 1552, we need not imagine that he is reverting to his earliest uncertain orthodoxy when he sponsored the preaching of Rough and Gilyem in 1513.[146] The books were presumably bought for the information of the provincial council then gathering in Edinburgh. Hooper, an ex-Cistercian, a somewhat repellent advanced protestant and an old adversary of Richard Smith (who was present at the council), typified the new turn taken by the English schism after the death of Henry and the influx of continental extremists.[147] The elevation of Hooper to the bishopric of Worcester, and in general Northumberland's policy of advancing theological extremists, the positioning of John Knox at Newcastle, Willock's Zwinglian preaching to the Scottish borderers, the arrest of the orthodox-minded northern bishop, Tunstall, all these factors made it imperative to encourage the Henrician survivors and discourage the Edwardine innovators.[148] It may even have been hoped to influence Cranmer himself and nullify the attraction of the Zurich *consensus* of 1549, which patched up the sacramental quarrel between Zurich and Geneva.

This goes some way to explain the inclusion of some passages from Henry VIII's *Necessary Doctrine* and the *Book of Homilies* in the catechism authorised by the provincial council of 1552, an attempt to recall the English to their own earlier orthodoxy. Richard Smith had written to Cranmer stating that Hamilton had urged on him the compilation of a book of commonplaces (i.e., the catechism) but that he was unwilling to

---

141. *Foreign Calendar, Edw. VI*, p. 36; Haynes, *State Papers*, p. 129.

142. *Treas. Accounts*, ix, 259, 347, 387, 395, 428. Moreover, did the paths of this trio ever cross? Borthwick incidentally became a Marian exile in Geneva. (Martin, *Les Protestants Anglais*, p. 337).

143. *Letters and Papers*, vii, no. 1607. We have also to reckon with Scots in England whose sympathies were pro-papal. The Scots friar at Newark in 1534 defending papal supremacy is one such, *Ibid*,. vii, no. 26 and possibly also the Scots surgeon at Mountgrace three years later, *Ibid*., xiii, pt. 2, no. 328.

144. *R.S.S.*, iii, no. 1599.

145. About the stay of the first three in St. Andrews I hope to say something later. For Hilliard see J. H. Baxter in the *St. Andrews Alumnus Chronicle*, no. 44, pp. 2-10.

146. *Treasurers Accounts*, x, 50. The archbishop was treasurer.

147. Smith had also crossed swords with Alexander Seton (over merit) and with Peter Martyr.

148. As early as 1536 several Scottish priests are said to have been in Tunstall's household (*Letters and Papers*, x, no. 364), although the only certain name to be found in his register is that of Alexander Skene (*Registers of Tunstall and Pilkington*, Surtees Soc., p. 66, first tonsure 1535). Knox was active (1549-53) in Tunstall's diocese. One of the refugees, Richard Hilliard, was Tunstall's chaplain (Sturge, *Tunstall*, p. 191). Another orthodox-minded English bishop, Nicholas Heath of Worcester, had an Edinburgh man, Francis Scott, in his household in 1544 (*Aliens in England*, p. 217).

attack *all* the English teachings.[149] The English refugees in Scotland may still have hoped to influence the course of events; the former prior of Newcastle in St. Andrews cannot have been too happy about the new minister of Newcastle, Knox.[150] As Smith was unwilling to undertake the catechism, there was the alternative of another Englishman.

The traditional view which asserts that the catechism was the work of John Winram must be rejected. The reasons for rejecting it and assigning it to friar Richard Marshall, former Dominican of Newcastle, are given elsewhere.[151] Richard Smith, who was in St. Andrews and still hopeful to return to England, wrote to the borders in November forwarding copies.[152] Nevertheless it has to be remembered that such a catechism would undergo the scrutiny of many revisors, some perhaps suspicious of English influence in the provincial council.[153] Indeed, even on the late Professor Mitchell's showing, the influence of Gropper's *Enchiridion* outweighs greatly any other. Its structure, however, is post-Interim, as has been suggested by Mr. Mahoney, and this explains its reserve on papal supremacy, for instance; a reserve shared by the Council of Trent (which otherwise exerted such a powerful influence in re-establishing papal authority).[154] Governor Arran's correspondence with a prominent Melanchthonian like Macalpine in Denmark may also be explained in this context. In any event, the catechism was not going to prove an answer to Calvin; it dealt with a situation still, as far as Scotland was concerned, broadly Lutheran.[155] Augsburg and Strasbourg are more important as yet than Geneva or even Zurich; although the English (including Smith) had now good reason to be increasingly aware of the latter. Indeed the more extreme among them were not only afraid of Trent but of the pacifying effect of the Augsburg Interim, which had somewhat upset the tactic of playing off the pope against the emperor.[156] But the Interim's political consequences were disastrous in many ways: the protestant princes who rejected it lined up with France against the emperor; Mary of Lorraine's own brother the duc d'Aumale was captured near Metz by Albert of Brandenburg;[157] Norman Lesley, the cardinal's murderer, was killed fighting against the emperor at Renty;[158] and Mary Tudor

149. See preface to Gau, *Richt Vay*, p. xlviii and Strype, *Memorials of Cranmer*, iii, App., pp. 735-6.

150. Who echoed the Swiss doctrine, attacking Tunstall as a " murderer " for slaying Christ afresh in every mass, as he asserted, and a " thief," for stealing an authority to remit sin to which, in Knox's view, he was not entitled.

151. In an appendix.

152. " Sir, I have sent you the Doctrine set out here by the Cleargye (only for the Cleargye), as they decreed yn their Assemble at Candlemas last, wheryn I was my selfe . . ." His correspondent forwarded several copies, apparently, to Wharton, warden of the Marches, " I have sent you certen Bookes of Doctryne, set out by the Clergye of Scotlande, sent unto me by the said Doctor Smythe." Haynes, *State Papers*, pp. 129-131.

153. Smith, who remained a loyal Englishman, was suspected of treasonable communications by some in the party of Mary of Lorraine, and was naturally unsympathetic to French projects for taking Ireland under protective custody. A fellow-refugee in St. Andrews, Robert Daly, a priest, was surely Irish. *Ibid.*

154. Notice, however, the cut showing Peter with the keys, badly reproduced in Mitchell's edition, the first occurrence of this cut in Scottish printing. Also, Marshall originally left England because he could not accept Henry's supremacy.

155. The fact that it did not accept the giving of the communion cup to the laity as suggested in some German quarters is due, I believe, to the influence of Robert Wauchope's *Conclusiones de Sacrosanctae Missae sacrificio*.

156. Kennedy's book (1558) is a further stage in the development. The Interim climate has now disappeared, and we have an answer to books like Bullinger's *Decades* (which attacked the Council of Trent, a work aimed at the English Public and in which John Willock has honourable mention). That Tunstall appreciated these products of Scottish presses is shown by Randolph's observation, " the abbot of Corsrogell, the lypperie abbot that made the book the old bishop of Durham so greatly delighted in." (Bain, *Calendar of Scottish Papers*, i, 609).

157. A pupil of Henry Scrimgeour, Bochetel, Sieur de la Forest, was sent to secure his release.

158. This for Ferreri, writing to the cardinal's nephew, was one providential feature of the war, Pollen, *Papal Negotiations*, p. 146.

strengthened the party of the Interim by her alliance with Spain (and incidentally evoked *The Monstrous Regiment* from John Knox.) The advent of Mary Tudor led to a breathing spell as far as religion was concerned, but only for a brief moment in the political tangle of the times.[159]

THE WARFARE OF THEOLOGIES

A cultural history of the times that kept silence on the warfare of theologies would be a maimed history, for while the clash did not reach its culmination till the doctrinal duels of 1559-60, it had been preparing for some decades before. However, even to confine oneself to purely historical considerations relative to the technical theological issues would take us far afield; and Fr. Maurice Taylor has already examined certain specific issues as a theologian. To the modern observer, appreciating that certain central doctrines were never in question, the issue may appear the purely practical one of the reform of morals. Knox indeed wrote off the bulk of the accusations against Patrick Hamilton as " trifles." Yet if they really were *adiaphora*, why all the fuss ? All parties to the quarrel were certainly anxious to dissociate themselves from the attack on the Trinity by the Spaniard, Servetus. A person suspected of Trinitarian heresy was cited before Mair in St. Andrews in 1541.[160] Servetus actually quotes from Mair as putting the orthodox view.[161] Moreover, one of the participants in a Wittenberg discussion of 1545, along with Luther and others, was William Ramsay, who, as a matriculand of St. Andrews in 1540, no doubt followed the St. Andrews disputation.[162] And, of course, with the full approval of Melanchthon and Beza, Calvin burnt Servetus. While then certain doctrines are more fundamental and must not be dislodged by others less cardinal to christianity, yet the whole fabric of christianity is a unity, to undermine any part of which is to risk the overthrow of basic beliefs. It is one thing to criticise accretions, over-emphases and over-formalism from within;[163] it is another thing to reform, not merely the church, but the very concept of the church. The portmanteau word "idolatry" did not mean the mass only or superstition only; for Macalpine it meant that there was no real invocation of God by the Church and therefore no Church there at all: " there is no Church where there is no invocation of God."[164] Of course, the obvious strategy when your opponents hurl excommunications at you is to hurl them back at them,

---

159. There is a letter from Guillaume Cassanate, Archbishop Hamilton's half-French, half-Spanish physician, describing to Mary of Lorraine how at Berwick, York and Cambridge, the tables were being replaced by altars, new images were going up or old ones replaced. " Quant a la messe, Madame, elle est desia fort en usaige." (London, Oct., 1553). *Analecta Scotica*, i, 99.

160. Herkless and Hannay, *College of St. Leonard*, p. 220, printed with some misreadings; Guild, the accused, seems to have been understood by his hearers to maintain three essences. The president of this disputation was Martin Balfour, uncle of Sir James Balfour of Pittendreich, also apparently present at the St. Andrews and Wittenberg disputations. Incidentally, while his stay in Wittenberg shows him as a Lutheran in 1544 it does not prove him a Lutheran when Knox wrote his history. To follow Martin's opinion of the sacrament then means Martin Balfour's not Martin Luther's. Cf. Dickinson's *Knox*, i, 93; actually Knox says he was brought up in Martin's opinion, not surprisingly since he was his nephew. Bell Brander Writs (G.R.H.), no. 37.

161. Bainton, *Michel Servet*, p. 25 shows that he cites his commentary on the first book of the Sentences, both in the *De Trinitatis Erroribus* (1531) and in his *Christianismi Restitutio* (1553). Servetus also found time to edit Santes Pagnini and take up the defence of Symphorien Champier against Leonhard Fuchs !

162. *Early Recs.*, p. 245 (with Balfour). Ramsay, the " fighting cock " in the Wittenberg disputation is described as a Scotist. Luther, *Werke*, xxxix (2), pp. 294, 302. Georg Meier and Luther both oppose Ramsay, who gave the disputation a turn reminiscent of the St. Andrews one. Luther attacks Ramsay, Lombard and the pope, but caution wins the day.

163. " Ecclesiae ceremoniis vehementer faueo . . . sed collocatam in his pietatem." Archibald Hay, *Panegyricus*, f.xlviii r.

164. Luther, *Werke*, xxxix (2), Theses of Johannes Macchabaeus Scotus.

and when they call you an agent of the devil the best defence is to denounce them as the synagogue of Satan.[165]

JUSTIFICATION AND MERIT

The fountainhead of reformed doctrine and the source of its attack on " idolatry " is the doctrine of justification by faith alone; Knox admitted that this was the one serious charge against Patrick Hamilton. In the traditional view justification created in sinful man a real inner order or discipline, whereby man, under God's guidance and through the utterly gratuitous gift of God, grace, was able to fulfil personally the destiny to which God had called him. It is interesting to see how the principles of this solution are already found in two theologians, John Ireland and William Manderston. The latter is particularly relevant, as although commenting on Aristotle's *Ethics* for arts students at Paris, he had Luther in mind, and, a fact hitherto overlooked, was the teacher there of Patrick Hamilton, the first name associated with the reformation in Scotland.[166]

There is no space to do more than refer to Ireland's work here; it is important as it circulated in the vernacular. " It is in our power to wyrk our saluacioun and to wyn ye realme of hevinly paradice," he says, adding immediately, but " nocht be our awne wertu and natur," but through God's assistance, Christ's merits and in virtue of " ye sacramentis of ye kirk ".[167] Human nature, even once elevated by baptism cannot win " the glory and joy eternal without special help of God."[168] Free will is a great natural perfection, disposing us to receive God's initial graces, yet without grace we cannot merit salvation.[169] The idea of man's meriting salvation was of course repugnant to the reformers and hence their ecclesiastical courts tended to regard the sinner as a monster under the sign of divine rejection.[170] Some of their theologians were clearly embarrassed by the human Christ and by his merits; witness the doctrine of the younger Wishart. If not a Socinian precursor, he belongs at least to an Antinomian climate of thought, with his denial in Bristol in 1539 that Christ could merit either for himself (Wishart) or for them (his hearers).[171] The " stiffnecked Scott " fortunately abandoned this view.

Manderston discusses these questions in his *Bipartitum in morali philosophia* (1523). The will is habitually free. To the objection that baptism is a meritorious act and yet not free while morally good, he answers that it is a meritorious act in man's free power, but not in man's free power that it is meritorious.[172] Baptism infuses the theological virtues and gives us the habit of grace, but our acts still remain human acts, made *with* grace, not *from* grace; that is, grace, although transcendent in its source, is not a foreign body within us, but really recreates and regenerates. [173] He agreed that christian infidelity is the worst of all, but

---

165. This last expression, beloved of Knox, goes back to Luther as applied to Rome. Incidentally, the " Bleiter chaplain," who saw the devil in Wishart, is quite evidently Peter Chaplain, doctor in theology, later provost of St. Salvator's, which demolishes the established, though indubitably ingenious, interpretation. ((Dickinson's *Knox*, ii, p. 238.)

166. Paris, B.N., Ms Lat. 9951, f.19v, cited in Appendix to this essay.

167. Meroure of Wyssdome Ms (in N.L.S., Adv. Ms 18.2.8), f.212r.

168. *Ibid.*, f.209v. Cf. f.125v.

169. *Ibid.*, f.126r.

170. The medieval courts had much more the atmosphere of Roman Law. While there may be a touch of hypocrisy sometimes in sentencing a " discreta et provida mulier " for failing to meet her financial obligations or defaming her neighbour, yet the tradition respected the essential dignity of man; here merely was an interim judgment.

171. " . . . openly declaryng that Christ nother hath nor coulde merite for hym ne yett for us . . . " *The Maire of Bristowe is Kalendar.*

172. *Bipartitum*, f.xlvi verso.

173. *Ibid.*, f.xlix verso. Cf. also the discussions as to whether the act of faith is meritorious, ff. lviir-lviiir.

when confronted with Augustine's *Omnis vita infidelium est peccatum* desired to qualify it. This is the teaching Patrick Hamilton imbibed; it is perhaps not fanciful to hear his voice in some of the objections.[174]

There is little continuity between this doctrine and his pupil's. Hamilton's *Places* contrast utterly gospel and law.[175] Man is stripped utterly of his human merit and free will; God was the cause of sin in withdrawing his grace; and, Beaton's citation quotes him as saying that man was in sin as long as he lived, and that there was no reward for good works or bad.[176] For Luther God's grace covered man like a mantle from the Father's ire; for the middle ages the symbolism of the mantle was also precious as in the devotion to the Mother of Mercy through whose Son a new humanity was prepared and Satan definitively conquered:

> Moder of God, ay virgyne doith remane
> Restoring wss the goldin world agane.[177]

But in the one case the mantle signified Christ's power and the fruits of the Victor effectively communicated to man and a fight won once for all. In Dunbar's famous

> " Done is a battell on the dragon blak,"

the stress was on the " done," a word full of vocal thunder.

If some hardened sinners were already under a cloud of rejection (here Hamilton evidently followed Francois Lambert and not Melanchthon) others were under the mantle of acceptance.[178] All christians worthy of the name, he affirmed, knew that they were in a state of grace.[179]

Manderston discusses this question in the context of Ockham's theory of God's twofold power, his absolute power (*potentia absoluta*) and his ordinary (and orderly) workings with men (*potestas ordinata*). God could reveal all truth to anybody, but only exceptionally and by his absolute power; but even by that he could not constrain the will to desire damnation. Some maintained that he could by his absolute power deceive men regarding their merits; but this opinion would make all faith suspect, and the more probable and pious opinion is that the Godfearing man cannot even be deceived by his absolute power. [180] Servile fear of the Lord in other words becomes filial, or as Hamilton's catechism was to put it beautifully, " The first feir bringis in the secund, evin as the nedil bringis in the threid throw ane clayth . . . "[181] As to how a man can be saved now and not then, through not persevering, Manderston says we can be written in the book of life in two ways; one according to our present righteousness, the other according to God's eternal foreknowledge.[182]

---

174. Manderston discusses those seduced by false preaching under two heads: ignorance of doctrine called " crass " through neglect; ignorance called " invincible," accepting it in good faith *propter Deum* from the preacher. (ff. lxiir, lxiiiir, lxvir, lxxxiiir).

175. With the Antinomian experience behind him Melanchthon is more nuanced and this is reflected in his pupil Macalpine: " Nam non solas promissiones intelligimus vocabulo Evangelii, sed etiam doctrinam legis, quia quando de penitentia dicimus, tum etiam de lege loquimur. " Luther, *Werke*, xxxix (2), 166.

176. Mitchell, *Scottish Reformation*, p. 290; Foxe-Townsend, v, 559-560. The later Calvinist gloss on this is that man has no free will " as the papists mean." *Acts General Assemblies*, i, 36.

177. Prologue to 6th Book of Gavin Douglas, *Aeneid*.

178. The Scot, James Melville, in 1530 contrasts Lambert's view, which he found unacceptable, with Melanchthon's (*Woodrow Misc.*, i, 35).

179. This must be a paraphrase of what Hamilton preached. Foxe-Townsend, iv, 560.

180. *Bipartitum*, f.lxviiir.

181. Archbishop Hamilton, *Catechism*, ed. Law, p. 210.

182. *Bipartitum*, f.lxxiv verso.

It will be seen that once *potentia ordinata* and a genuine inner law and order are rejected, every act of faith becomes a blinding revelation of salvation, in which you are secure in your hope of eternal life. This is Patrick Hamilton's position in his *Places* (which Frith's commentary somewhat tones down): the Gospel set in harsh contrast to the Law and Faith to Incredulity, a doctrine which was destined to pass through Europe like a forest fire.

THE LAW AND VARIOUS PROPHETS

The severity of that contrast has been burnt into many a sixteenth-century face. The age loved a paradox just as it loved an adage, and of course even when wild men took possession of the paradox and embarrassed its originators, it could not be abandoned by either catholics or Lutherans, because in their different contexts both recognised it as gospel truth. That is what the Louvain doctors wrote to Scotland about Patrick Hamilton: some of this could be understood in a catholic sense.[183]

The undesirable consequences drawn from Luther's theory by the Antinomians made a shift of emphasis desirable. This Melanchthon achieved, knitting law and gospel together again. For him philosophy (that is, the traditional arts course readjusted in accordance with new scholarship) was associated with the law written on tables, not quite the handmaiden of the Word perhaps, but law and philosophy, like law and gospel, were co-ordinated once more. Against the Stoics and Epicureans he set Aristotle: " Hanc igitur doctrinam, quae quasi vox est naturae, sequamur." The uneasy partnership of a Double Truth was avoided: " Vetus philosophia, hoc est veritas . . . "[184]

Hence Alexander Seton's Lenten course in St. Andrews (c. 1536) wove both strands together again. For many years the law of God had not been truly taught; its purity obscured by men's traditions; Christ not recognised as its end and perfection; men did not realise that where the divine law is not violated there was no sin; and that to satisfy for sin comes from unfeigned repentance and faith discerning the mercy of God the Father in Christ his Son. This is Melanchthon, not Luther. The " faith alone " of Patrick Hamilton is no longer quite alone: it now has conversion as a *sine qua non*. Read in conjunction with the Wittenberg disputation of his former colleague, Macalpine, this brief sermon-course yields up its secrets. Yet the first Lutheran euphoria is not exhausted; a few years later, at St. Martin in the Vintry, London, Seton would reiterate in the very phraseology of Luther that faith alone justified and works were unprofitable save to testify and declare our faith. Evidently both Macalpine and Seton want to cling tenaciously to Faith alone.[185] As curate of St. Antholin's, London, presented apparently, but without episcopal admission or licence to preach, he confronted the orthodox morning sermon at Paul's Cross of Richard Smith on man's reconciliation with God with an afternoon homily of a strong Melanchthonian colouring: man's will was utterly in the power of man's Lord and so not free, but his

---

183. Foxe-Townsend, iv, 562.

184. Hildebrandt, *Melanchthon, Alien or Ally* ?, p. 5. The new scholasticism of a man like Jacob Schegk of the Augsburg circle is reflected in post-reformation Scotland more in Rutherford than in Melville, who in some respects is even untypical of Geneva.

185. Luther, *Werke*, xxxix (2), 146-8; *Letters and Papers Henry VIII, Addenda*, i, (pt. 2), no. 1463.

act and his consent were free.[186] The law and the works of the law as well as the works of faith are gradually regaining admittance, but only on condition that they can be turned as a weapon against the church of tradition.[187]

Knox says that the " dumb doctors " of St. Andrews suspected Seton's course of sermons, and this because he had nothing to say of purgatory, pardons, pilgrimages, prayers to the saints " and such trifles."[188] Knox is right that they would be most suspicious of what he had left unsaid; but listeners like John Mair would have a more crucial reason for being uneasy, for by highlighting the divine law and nothing else, Seton was trying to undermine the whole fabric of the church's traditional discipline. The influence of such views on a diaphanous intellect (in matters theological) like George Buchanan emerges clearly. The " ex-prior of a convent and exceptionally famous preacher " who advised him to eat meat in Lent is surely Seton, who encouraged him in this cavalier attitude to the precepts of the church.[189] No doubt Buchanan heard similar sermons after his flight to England in the role of religious refugee, but his questions there regarding the church, what it was and what was its nature (*quid esset aut quae*) got no answer from Englishmen; yet logically they were the right questions to follow.[190]

The Church and Its Ministry

Before leaving Seton's Lenten course on law, we must interpret them in the light of Macalpine on justice: The justice of christians is not a quality, but a relation, a " reputation of justice."[191] This effects an absolute disjunction between divine law and human. What had been a principle of elevation and supernaturalisation, now became an agent of deflation. Now more than ever the divine law was only what was written in the divine statute book, the scriptures, but above all in Deuteronomy, and not what was written in man's heart by his Creator; and human law would soon be what was written in the human statute-book and act of parliament would be sacrosanct. For the Buchanan of this period (often echoing Seton curiously), who after all had written his *Baptistes* in honour of a Sir Thomas More who had defied an unjust act of parliament, the

---

186. Foxe-Townsend, v, 449. A little over a month later at Paul's Cross on December 18th, 1540, both Seton and his parson (who incidentally owned copies of Frith, Melanchthon and Zwingli) were forced to recant. Millar Maclure, *The Paul's Cross Sermons*, p. 140.

187. Hence Seton says that he does not disapprove of works, fasting and prayers, but only of popish works, fasting and prayer. Foxe-Townsend, v, 450. We are still some way from a theology of works collaborating with faith, as in Georg Meier (whose objections at Wittenberg Macalpine skilfully turns) and in Alexander Alane who eventually adopted Meier's " synergism."

188. Dickinson's *Knox*, i, 19; in London he also preached that private masses and dirges " were not available nor helping to the souls that were departed." *Letters and Papers, Addenda*, i, (2), no. 1463 (18).

189. Nobody had been more critical of the excessive place given to canon law in the late medieval set-up to the detriment of theology than John Mair and John Annand, both of whom would be among Seton's hearers, and no doubt this would be the position Seton started from. Buchanan also would be trained in Mair's views, while Seton probably knew him as a student, for Seton may be identical with the matriculand of Lothian " nation," at St. Andrews in 1522 (*Early Records*, p. 218). In his books he describes himself as Seton of Seton, hence in Lothian. Moreover his books show him in Scotland in 1536, still it would appear a fervent Dominican, and there is no proof that he went to England till his denization of 30th June, 1539 (*Aliens in England*, p. 217, Alexander " Selome "). Cf. Seton's signatures in *Innes Rev.*, ix, 142-3 with the " Dominicus " of 1536. Aitken, *George Buchanan*, pp. xlix, 7, 25, 55. The latter identifies the Dominican as John Rough, not very convincingly, especially as we have no evidence that Rough was ever a prior; moreover he has Buchanan attending " meetings " in England rather than sermons (*conciones*). Cf. " concionibus " at Bordeaux. *Ibid.*, pp. 8-9; 40-1.

190. *Ibid.*, pp. 24-5. Buchanan's comparative orthodoxy at this period (although he was attacked as a sacramentarian by a Scottish Dominican) on the subject of the Real Presence probably reflects Seton's attitude at the same date. There does not appear to be a genuine Zwinglian on the Scottish scene till Wishart's return in 1543. Aitken, *Buchanan*, pp. 19, 81, where " per modum signitatem " must surely read " per modum signi tantum."

191. Luther, *Werke*, xxxix (2), 151.

church could only make laws binding in the same way as the state's laws, under pain at the most of venial sin.[192]

These questions were largely raised after John Mair had published his last book. But the immediate background of them seems to have been his teaching: just, indeed, as his conciliar outlook is the background of the inveterate conference-mindedness of Alexander Alesius. Recently a text of Mair's has been printed in translation which asks, as a result of the agonising experience of christendom in the Great Schism, whether lest he should destroy the church, a pope may be deposed for wrongdoing or heresy. The answer is yes, and the reasons given interesting.[193] It could be said that it is only one more step to go on to say with Macalpine that the whole hierarchy may be deprived so that there may be reformation in head and members. Yet it is surely a very long step. In his disputation Melanchthon asked Macalpine a very relevant question: How can we judge whether the bishops please God or not? The answer was that the Spirit of God gave him certitude. The answer of Mair had been that a legitimately convoked general council could authorise the pope's deposition. There is a world of difference between that and Macalpine's: Desert the bishops, they are anathema, they teach black error.[194]

Moreover Mair's doctrine is not to be seized in a few pages taken out of context. His ecclesiology needs technical study, but meantime a few things can be usefully said. In the first place, it is clear from the text cited by Spinka that the supreme pontiff had supreme jurisdiction and that by divine institution. He is cautious in his handling of the relationship between church and scripture, even a little awkward. But he does safeguard its divine institution, and repels the Lutheran opposition set up between the church of his day and the primitive church.[195] Nor will he accept an artificial contrasting juxtaposition of church and bible.[196] The two go together and confirm each other mutually: Dans superioritatem uni, alteri quasi derogare videtur.[197]

The church's triple ministry of sanctification, teaching (with preaching) and jurisdiction was under fire. The old quarrel of the spiritual estate (*sacerdotium*) and the temporal estate (*imperium*) was rekindled. It was the status of the church that Alexander Seton attacked when he asserted that the bishops were not true bishops because non-preaching bishops, recommending that James V should dispense with ecclesiastical advice and take that of his nobles.[198] There was however no danger of a theocracy; and the bishops were well aware that, in the interests of civil concord, James could withhold the secular arm as Alexander Alane advised in his *Cohortatio ad Concordiam Pietatis*. But what Seton and Alane also demanded was that James, like a Lutheran godly prince, should take specifically *religious* action independently not only of them, but of the

192. Aitken, *George Buchanan*, p. 25.

193. Spinka, *Advocates of Reform*, pp. 175 seq.

194. Luther, *Werke*, xxxix (2), 148.

195. Maiestas huius ecclesiae non est minor quam authoritas ecclesiae erat tempore apostolorum . . . Illa est ultimata omnibus ambiguorum resolutio: a qua fluctuare nefas est . . . Daedalea aenigmata diuini eloquii elucidat: cui elucidationi standum est. *In Quatuor Evangelia*, 1529, f.cccxlviir.

196. Si dicas scripturam esse ecclesiae rectificatricem: tunc cuilibet haeretico fas erit pro voto paradoxa peregrina sustinere: ut hoc tempore videmus. *Ibid.*

197. In his 1529 preface, he boasts of following the "catholicas iuxta Romanae ecclesiae doctrinam per Doctores receptos traditiones." (In Major, *History*, p. 447). Manderston enumerates the degrees of the Church according to their jurisdictional authority from pope, through legate *a latere*, primate, bishop, etc., down to deans of Christianity or " archpriests," judges of parish priests. *Bipartitum* (1523), f.clxviiir.

198. Dickinson's *Knox*, ii, 230-1.

universal kirk of God, and this in point of fact Arran tried to do in 1543 by steering through parliament the act in favour of a vernacular bible in the teeth of the united opposition of the whole episcopal bench. The object was to reduce the status of the Scottish kirk to that merely of a civil society gone over to the gospel; hence William Hay's observation on the *De Abroganda Missa* of Luther that it made of the church " a disordered congeries which did not allow of any polity."[199]

A modern observer may be tempted to comment that a congeries was exactly what the medieval church had become: with its lush diversity and endemic untidiness, its multiple acts of delegation, dispensation and exemption, the arrogance and avarice of many of the monarchs in Christ's kingdom, the venality and laxity of ecclesiastical judges and the bleeding white of local kirks appropriated to cathedral and monastery. But many observers then would have thought that a worm's eye view. For them it was more important that there was an ordered society, with a God-given hierarchical structure, legislating on behalf of a divine Lawgiver, transcending its human membership and so more than the sum of its numbers, a single thing in the unity of the Holy Spirit whose regimen, as Cajetan said, " gives to churches as far apart as those of Scotland and Spain more than agreement in faith, hope, charity, the sacraments and obedience to the same head; there is the bond that unites one part to another in a single community . . . "

To its defenders it was this invisible bond that the new men of Wittenberg were determined to break by a new exegesis of Christ's indefectible promises, by fragmenting the church catholic into parishes, by " demythologising " the eucharistic mysteries, the visible sign of their invisible community in the things of God, which were every bit as real and as much things as any other things.[200] The parish is not to be found in scripture; as it existed in the sixteenth century it was very largely a medieval creation. The nation too is not part of the gospel; but it was part of the human reality the middle ages had largely made. To return to the parish and the nation was to return to something that was already there. But, whatever the evils of appropriation and whatever its benefits, the local mother church, heather-thatched or slated, ill-furnished or physically opulent, shared with its neighbours the real presence of its Redeemer; and it was aware (often to its financial cost) that it was part of a whole majestic christian commonwealth within which it was integrated, that Christ reached out beyond the parish and even beyond the ecclesiastical province to the universe at large. At least it was saved in some measure from the curse of parochialism.

BISHOPS AND PREACHING

" No, no, set your heart at rest," Bishop Gardiner of Winchester counselled Alexander Seton, " and look never to have it said that ye have overcome the bishops, for it shall not be so." Once again Seton has to be related to Macalpine, for whom only the godly bishop need be obeyed, one tied not to Rome, but to the gospel as he understood it.[201] On the other hand, the orthodox view, represented in William Hay,[202] was that the

199. Hay Ms, f. 8 verso, A-B, transcript kindly supplied by the Rev. John Barry.
200. Hence John Ireland understood the *communio sanctorum* of the creed as a communion " in holy things."
201. Bale, *Select Works* (Parker Soc.), p. 433.
202. " Cum oblatio est sancta decet ministros esse sanctos." Hay Ms., f. 19 verso A. Cf. Manderston, *Bipartitum*, f.clxv recto.

ministry was of divine institution, but purely as an instrument of Christ and hence godliness was not requisite but desirable.[203]   Yet, humanly speaking, the church had acquired an institutional momentum which made it simpler to eliminate " the whole rabble of the clergy " (in Knox's phrase) than to rectify the quality of the royal choice of bishops.   Rome had to compromise with secular rulers a great deal, but, while James's appointments were not ideal, he was not yet a Lutheran *summus episcopus*; at least Rome could and did insist on certain minimum requirements.[204] Indeed Seton himself is evidence that the bishops were far from passive instruments in the royal hands.

William Hay's lectures, given in the great schools of King's College in 1535, will illustrate the conception of their authority that the bishops had. Are the terms bishop and priest synonymous, he asks.   He cites two opinions, proposing the second for acceptance.

The first opinion was that of those who followed St. Jerome in denying the sacramental nature of the episcopate as such and maintaining its origins in a purely ecclesiastical institution.   Hence both bishops and priests had the same power over Christ in the eucharist (*corpus verum*) and in his church (*corpus misticum*).   The bishop was a title of an administrative function (*operis*) and not of a more honourable status (*honoris*) and was interpreted " superintendent ", as having charge over those above whom he was placed.   The lower clergy reserved certain things to him by custom and consent.

The second opinion, the common opinion, was that the bishop was of divine institution.   His power was wider than the priest's both as regards jurisdiction and as regards order (examples include consecrating other bishops, clothing religious, ordinations unless in virtue of a special papal commission).

Christ, says Hay, chose for his church a monarchical polity; a single ruler in charge.   Thus there is one supreme person having full power, which he can, within clear limits, delegate to others as well.   From Peter as from a fountainhead this power descends to simple priests in the lowest degree.   Above all priests is the pope, successor of Peter, vicar of Christ; and so the church is one church, all its members united under one head.[205] Hay refers to the contemporary habit of referring affectionately to certain worthy priests as " bishop " and concludes: In the consecration of a bishop there is no distinct character imparted, but it is the crowning and completion of the priesthood,[206] which it amplifies and intensifies.

The medieval mind, for all its love of clear ideas, gloried in symbols and had meditated much on the text *per speculum in aenigmate*.   All that came from above to us was mediated through Christ the Son of God, in whose wisdom as in a burning glass the brilliance of the Father was eternally imaged; to the eye of faith the gospel was the glass in which that

203. Luther, *Werke*, xxxix (2) 179.

204. Gavin Dunbar, a fact overlooked by his biographer, was a graduate in arts of Paris and of canon and civil law of Angers (Major, *History*, p. 445).   William Gordon was also a graduate in both laws (Hay, *Letters of James V*, p. 335).   Andrew Durie had been in several universities, including Montpellier. Montpellier students are perhaps worth citing from the *Matricule de l'Université de Montpellier*: Thomas Hycotor (1509); Archibald Richardson of Ormiston (1515); Andrew Durie (1515); John Gray (1528); John Cunningham, Galloway diocese (1538); Patrick Tod (1548; doctor of medicine, 1558).   Pages 17, 26, 36, 54, 80, 113.

205. In 1540 Sir John Borthwick was accused of maintaining that the pope had no greater authority to exercise over christians than any other bishop or priest.   *St. Andrews Kirk Session Register*, i, 96.

206. Hay Ms., ff. 23vA-25vB.

image was represented and reflected, " l'école particulière de l'évangile," as Calvin would say, the treasure " hid in a croft," as John Ireland wrote, the croft of the devout soul, but mainly mediated through that public school of faith and virtue, the parish kirk, visually or otherwise; and finally the created cosmos mirrored him again in the human microcosm. A school implies leisure but the *otium* was in view of a higher *negotium*. The parish priest, the *persona*, represented and reflected Christ to his parishioners, who through the paschal eucharist were members of him whom they reflected each to each; through him they were in relation to the wider world of the diocese through the bishop, who delegated his own preaching responsibilities to him; and through their bishop related to the *pontifex maximus* who represented Christ's headship to christendom entire. " The kyrk is meroure and exampil to all pepil,"[207] a *congregatio fidelium*, as Hostiensis calls it, called out of darkness into the light. The moving lines of Buchanan in the *Calendae Maiae* may, it has been suggested, originally have commemorated his Easter communion after his temporary return to the faith;[208] if so they give a summary of salvation, a *speculum humanae salvationis*, of the pilgrimage of *homo viator* from paradise lost to paradise regained:

> Salve fugacis gloria saeculi,
> Salve secunda digna dies nota,
> Salve vetustae vitae imago,
> Et specimen venientis aevi.

The age was a rhetorical one: men wrote and spoke to move rather than convince. In his *De Utilitate Verbi Dei* (1551), Patrick Cockburn goes on reiterating, faith comes from hearing—" fides ex auditu." Giovanni Ferreri attacked the established Aristotelian view that sight was the most perfect of the senses in his *Auditum visu praestare*. No service in church without preaching, said Cockburn: " Quid prosint sacrificia sine verbo oblata ? "[209] The reformers attacked private masses not only because the sacrament was not received, but because nobody preached. While there is some reason to think that sacramental exhortations were not so novel as has been made out,[210] the spread of books (and books were still thought of as read aloud) made it desirable that the masses be educated out of their mental immaturity into more adult attitudes. The reformers took advantage of this situation, using it to discredit episcopal authority, preaching without episcopal admission or in ambiguous terms or secretly calling the parishioners by a beadle, as did John Willock.[211] The earl of Arran seems to have tried to enforce a homilies plan in 1543 here and there.[212] Indeed it appears probable that homilies read in church were already a feature in parish churches before the reformation: some provincial council statutes may imply this. Preachers, like John Annand, who wanted a good night's sleep, had already the use of their *Sermones*

---

207. Ireland, *The Meroure of Wyssdome*, i, 13. Ireland sees the bishop's power as delegated, " the bischop has grauntit to him be the pap the power of iurisdictioune and collacioune of ordouris." (Meroure Ms., f.298v).

208. Aitken, *George Buchanan*, p. 101, thinks his reconciliation took place about the 1st May, 1541. His accusation before the Lisbon inquisition, of course, was within the next decade.

209. *De Utilitate*, sig. Dviii.

210. " Monitions sacramentelles au 16e siecle " by J. B. Molin in *Maison Dieu*, lxi, 48 seq. These were not merely bidding prayers.

211. As curate of St. Catherine Coleman, London. Foxe-Townsend, v, 443, 448. Bishop Bonner's monitorial letters of 22 October, 1540, are mainly directed at Willock, presented (by some noble ?) but not admitted by him. Wilkins. *Concilia Magnae Britanniae*, iii, 855.

212. For an example of this in Aberdeen cf. *Council Reg. Aberdeen*, i, 189. *Letters and Papers*, xviii (2), no. 392.

Dormi Secure Dominicales and Eck's *Homiliae* were a controversial sample of the same thing.[213] The enthusiasm for the pulpit outran fervour on behalf of the sacraments and the word, and it seems likely that few Scots post-reformation pulpits were as sober as that of Parton: at Ayr the medieval pulpit was repaired at the same time as a more elaborate one replaced it, and this pattern was probably repeated in places able to afford it.[214] But the kingdom of God is not in speech, but in intenser love of God and neighbour, and it seems that in some respects catholics had the advantage.[215] Moreover, while it is likely that the early post-reformation repressive discipline was gradually replaced by something more like real moral education, it is clear that our ancestors, as they figure in such kirk session records as have been printed, brought with them to the new regime all their moral delinquencies as well as their ancient pieties. As often, for a few who were genuinely virtuous, there were many who were going through the motions. Meantime not a few pulpits were occupied by Scots like Robert Blackwood in Kirton, Nottinghamshire, whose preaching is described as " the roaring of an Oxe in the top of an ashe tree."[216]

AUTHORITY ECCLESIASTICAL AND SECULAR

How far Luther had been thrown into the arms of the secular power, whose patronage he hoped for, is shown by his attitude to the Peasants' Revolt and the bigamy of Philip of Hesse.[217] This resultant exaltation of the secular power is reflected in the letter to James V of Alexander Seton, attacking kirkmen " who put the temporal lords and lieges of thy council out of favour . . . For when thy barons are put down, what art thou but the King of Bean ?"; in the preaching of Robert Richardson in the north after the Lincolnshire rising against Henry VIII that people ought " to obey God's word and the Prince's laws "; and in that of Alexander Alane at the same time repeating that " those Lutheran books . . . would have taught them to die honourably in silence rather than raise a rebellion on account of an unjust exaction, or even on account of religion."[218]

The first sign of a shift in this attitude is after the Augsburg Interim of 1548, Brandenburg and Saxony refusing to accept it, and campaigning against it with a torrent of Magdeburg pamphlets. But there was tension between the party of the Interim and that of the Consensus of Zurich, although officially Calvin, Bucer and Bullinger made no change in Luther's attitude. This served very well under the protection of a godly prince, but among foreign exiles in London, during Edward's reign, other ideas were probably germinating. Friendly with John ab Ulmis and corresponding with Bullinger was the Scot, John Willock.[219] Now while

---

213. *Innes Rev.*, ix, 70, no. 2.

214. Pryde, ed. *Ayr Burgh Accounts*, p. 33.

215. William Lauder compares them favourably with their neighbours in 1568, adding:
> The Mes, that Idoll,—praysit be God !—is past;
> But Covatyce, the quhilk is cum in last,
> Is the worse Idoll of the twa, be fere.
Minor Poems (Early Eng. Text Soc.), p. 21. Cf. pp. 27-8.

216. A. Tindal Hart, *The Country Clergy*, 1558-1660, p. 29. The quarterly communions characteristic of Geneva do not appear to be such an innovation in Scotland, where quarterly communions are not unheard of in pre-reformation days. Cf. Herkless and Hannay, *St. Leonard*, p. 147. But perhaps St. Leonard's was untypical.

217. His attitude shows the traditional outlook but its exaggerations make it new. Cf. Archbishop Dunbar to Peder Swave, the Danish ambassador, congratulating him on what he had written about democracy, the worst form of government: " the peasants wished to tread on the necks of kings, which could turn out ill for them." *Letters and Papers*, viii, no. 1178.

218. Dickinson's *Knox*, ii, 230-1; *Letters and Papers*, xiii (1), no. 305 and xi, no. 987.

219. *Original Letters* (Parker Soc.), ii, 393; i, 314.

it is true that Knox still advocated passive obedience, and did not move till 1557 or thereabouts to an anti-authoritarian position, yet Willock had probably arrived there sooner.[220] Not only is there his statement that princes may be deposed, Mary of Lorraine was an open idolatress, utterly despised by the council, the power of magistrates being in any event limited by the word of God. Willock had been in Emden, which was not only a centre from which inflammatory pamphlets published in Strasbourg or Geneva by such as Ponet or Goodman could be circulated, but was also a centre for the printing of some of it (inclusive of Knox) as Colonel Isaac has shown.[221] We are assured by Knox himself that under cover of his embassies on behalf of Anne of Friesland Willock did much to promote the godly cause.[222] Even more to the point is the fact, hitherto overlooked, that before his exile in Emden, Willock was already involved in active resistance in the rising against Mary Tudor for which Henry, Duke of Suffolk, his patron, was executed in 1554.[223] It is hardly suprising that in the eyes of Quintin Kennedy, who knew Willock, such men were " seditious." Later Willock, whose sympathies were more with Zurich than Geneva, settled down comfortably in England under that godly princess, Elizabeth, whom so many rated as a semi-idolatress, in the rectory of Loughborough with from 1570 the additional living of Ealdland, a prebend in St. Paul's.[224]

Calvin became the leader of the religious revolution after Luther died in 1546 and the opposition between them came to a head in their disciples. Denmark and northern Germany gave a frosty reception to the exiles including Willock who eventually settled in Emden, on account of their eucharistic views. A David Simpson, Scot, was one who opposed Westphal the Lutheran.[225] Thomas Methven seems to have been reading Calvin in 1551, although he clearly was not convinced, for he told the kirk session that he was neither " ane papist nor ane Calwynist, nor of Paul, nor of Apollo, but Jesus Christis man ", which paraphrase of St. Paul did not meet with their approval.[226] The whole genesis of Calvinism in Scotland needs to be examined minutely; until that is done, 1560 will remain an enigma.[227]

But the geography of the reformation has also some consequence for the spread of ideas. Is it not likely that Orkney and the north would turn towards Denmark ? Even the imposed English reformation in Ireland must have heartened Glencairn and Argyll in the west, while the French situation became increasingly relevant for reasons of policy as Calvinism was allowed to spread from 1555.[228] The zeal in Ireland of Alexander Craik, Scots bishop of Kildare and dean of St. Patrick's, Dublin, is notable

220. Compare with the *Monstrous Regiment* the Court complaint during the regency of Loisie de Savoie, regarding pointless Parisian disputations on papal and princely powers, treaties of peace, the conferring of benefices at Rome and if a woman could be allowed to govern a monarchy: " telles et sembiables propositions pourront estre de plus grande consequence qu'en autre temps." Du Boulay, *Historia Univ. Parisiensis*, vi, 186. Cf. also " Political Ideas of the Scottish Reformation " by Dr. J. H. Burns in *Aberdeen University Review*, xxxvi, 252 seq.
221. *The Library*, 4th ser., xii, 336.
222. Dickinson's *Knox*, i, 118.
223. *Patent Rolls, Philip and Mary*, i, 381; iii, 44, Bartholomew Willock, late of Bradgate, gentleman, was pardoned (i, 499).
224. Hennessy, *Novum Repertorium*, p. 25.
225. *English Hist. Rev.*, x, 435.
226. *Innes Rev.*, ix, 130-1, no. 4. *St. Andrews K. S. Reg.*, i, 135, 317; ii, 609.
227. Calvin's gift for slogans helped the movement among those whose theological gifts were rudimentary.
228. Cf. the request of the young Mary *at the instance of the French king* for protection from all spiritual as well as civil courts on behalf of Balnavis and Kirkcaldy of Grange in 1557, Fraser, *Melvilles, earls of Melville*, iii, 94.

from 1560. Unfortunately the imposition of the vernacular there was like its imposition in the highlands a forcible attempt at anglicisation.[229]

THE LAST DECADE

There are many themes in the history of ideas that would require fuller discussion in the last decade before 1560. Calvin had advised Melanchthon (who had supported the Interim of Leipzig, as did also Alane, the Scot) that moderation could be overdone: " moderationis laus non est appetenda."[230] Knox clearly had little time for " sermons penned to offend no man."[231] There must have been a party willing to go to great lengths to compromise; if we are to accept Sir David Lindsay as still orthodox, such a party has to be postulated. There was also a party which has a somewhat defeatist attitude, for which no good could come of discussion in print or in speech: David Panter, bishop of Ross, was one such[232] But there also were many who hoped for national concord: Archbishop Hamilton's preface to the catechism typifies this group and perhaps Patrick Cockburn and William Lauder. The trial of Walter Mill is an interruption of this policy, perhaps because of the spread of secret preaching, athough it was a continuation of the trial begun under Cardinal Beaton.[233] Many attitudes are highly ambiguous. The suddenness of the conversion of John Winram and John Douglas, who in 1558 were judges of Mill, is only paralleled by the sudden reversal of attitude of John Davidson, the Glasgow college principal, in 1559.[234] The humanists generally are hesitant. Henry Scrimgeour was probably one of those who collaborated with Calvin to write about Francesco Spiera of Padua, who died in despair after recanting in 1548; and Cockburn, writing from Orleans in 1552 to the prior of St. Andrews said this should not have been allowed to happen.[235] Buchanan in France had an impressive list of high ecclesiastical acquaintances: Panter, bishop of Ross and abbot of l'Absie, the abbot of Ivry, the cardinals of Guise and Lorraine, Cardinal du Bellay, and the bishops of Tarbes and Condom. This might be explained as reflecting the drop in the controversial temperature after the Peace of Augsburg, did he not also become a canon of Coutances in 1558.[236] As for John Row, he was still active in the curia as late as May of 1559,[237] when Knox had already arrived: but it must have been rather discouraging for him there trying to arrange a titular commendatorship when the curia was being reformed.

229. He graduated at St. Andrews in 1523; later a bachelor of laws; naturalised as an Englishman in 1551 and appointed to a prebend in Lincoln; demitted probably in Mary Tudor's reign; patronised the former Strasbourg exile, the Scot, William Leach, friendly with Edward Cusack, an Irishman, minister in Cardross and Dumbarton. (*Early Recs.*, p. 112; Le Neve-Hardy, *Fasti Ecclesiae Anglicanae*, ii, 127-8 and *Patent Rolls Edawrd VI*, iv, 51, 166; *State Papers Ireland* 1509-73, p. 180 and Grindal, *Remains*, p. 275; *Innes Rev.*, ix, 83; Donaldson, *Thirds*, p. 262; *Fasti Eccl. Scot.*, iii, 341). As to the process of anglicisation in Scotland after 1560, see *S.H.R.*, xxiii, 107 seq. Ferguson in *The Library*, viii (1928) identifies many English books circulating in Scotland, although here and there a little too definitely, e.g., " tua Enchiridion ecce " are more likely to be Eck's *Enchiridion* than that of Erasmus.
230. Hildebrandt, *Melanchthon*, p. 83.
231. Dickinson's *Knox*, i, 93. The preachers were Winram and John Spittal, official of St. Andrews.
232. *Ibid.*, i, 131.
233. *Pitscottie*, ii, 130. The other preacher (a Sir John Petrie or Panter ?) was servant to the laird of Innermeath, whose wife was a Beaton.
234. See appendix; also Mill's trial in *Pitscottie*. Mill's arrest was in Dysart in *Fife* not Angus, as the name of the vicar proves.
235. Cited from 1558 edition of Cockburn's *De vulgari Sacrae Scripturae phrasi*, at which date he was still orthodox.
236. Aitken, *Buchanan*, pp. 96-9.
237. *Analecta Scotica*, ii, 381. On the other hand, the Adiaphorist, Alane, and others who had borne the heat and burden of the day either did not come home or were not invited home. Moreover, apart from Willock and Spottiswood, the privy kirks were excluded in the making of the Book of Discipline. Laurence Duguid, minister at Emden in 1557, is not in our Fasti lists. *Prot. Bk. Gilbert Grote*, n, 135. Willock's knowledge of Zurich may account for the repetition of the 1523 invitation of the 200 of Zurich that those who did not agree with the new Reformation were to point out the errors, with the proviso that they must not abuse this courtesy to resist their authority !

Unfortunately for our purpose, John Lesley was not interested in the history of ideas, and every fact taken from Dempster has to be sifted.[238] However, Knox is informative, even if incidentally. He lets it slip that contemporaries considered the Franciscan Alexander Arbuckle a learned man, although he personally thought him foolish.[239] He treats another Franciscan, John Scott, as a serious opponent, as indeed he was.[240] He mentions that Archbishop Hamilton delegated the Dominican Friar John Black, of St. Mary's college, to preach, and it was probably as a delegate of his that he met Willock (" chosin Primat of thair religioun " and unwilling to match himself against anything short of an archbishop) for a lengthy debate on the eucharist in Edinburgh.[241] This was the new generation of Dominican against the old, as Bishop Lesley did not fail to note.

Ignatius of Loyola was at Montaigu college in Paris from early 1528 till late the following year after which he went to Ste. Barbe, from which he graduated in 1534, founding the Company of Jesus later that year.[242] Calvin was in Paris studying law and reading the humanists at various times in this period. William Cranston, future provost of St. Salvator's, incepted in Paris in 1533-4, and Knox had heard a rumour that Cranston had forced a recantation on some point out of Calvin. Whether the rumour was true or not, and Calvin was asked to comment but failed to do so, Cranston may have known both men.[243] However that may be, at least three St. Salvator's students joined the new Society: Edmund Hay, William Crichton and James Tyrie. Robert Abercromby appears at St. Mary's also.[244] William Murdoch, who also joined appears to have been in the household of Bishop Crichton of Dunkeld.[245] With the Jesuits are also associated the names of Robert Wauchope, archbishop of Armagh, who worked unrestingly in southern Germany and was the link between Scotland and Trent,[246] and also the secular priest, John Greenlaw, who appears to have been in touch with a wide group of junior priests including John Watson, Tridentine preacher at Aberdeen, Ninian Winzet, the catholic pamphleteer, priest-schoolmaster of Linlithgow, and Friar Scott.[247] An instance of one who remained a crypto-catholic till his death in 1583 is the scholarly lawyer, familiar, it would seem, with both Greek and Hebrew, Archibald Crawford, parson of Eaglesham.[248]

---

238. Dempster's wish to exalt his fellow countrymen may be an atonement for his temporary lapse, revealed in this work: " Declaration et Confession de foy de Thomas Dempster, par laquelle il renonce au Papisme." (La Rochelle, 1604.) Taken from p. 182 of *Catalogus Librorum V. CI. D. Phil. de la Coste* (1722)

239. Dickinson's *Knox*, i, 90, 92.

240. *Ibid.*, ii, 242. *Innes Rev.*, ix, 18.

241. Dickinson's *Knox*, ii, 175; Leslie (ed. Cody), ii, 455. Other friars mentioned are Andrew Abercromby, O.P., and John Roger, O.F.M.

242. *Bibl. d'Humanisme et Renaissance*, xvi, 363.

243. Laing's *Knox*, vi, 134; Paris B.N., Ms Lat. 9952, f.188v.

244. *Early Recs.*, p. 255, 257, 264; also 255, 156.

245. Murdoch was with them at Louvain. *Rentale Dunkeldense*, pp. 358 seq.

246. On Wauchope as a new model pastor see " The Pastoral Zeal of Archbishop Wauchope " in *Seanchas Ardmhacha*, ii (1956), 32-60.

247. On all of these see *Innes Rev.*, ix, s.v. Greenlaw is mentioned as heir to the late Elizabeth Scott, his mother. Haddington Burgh Ct. Book (G.R.H.), i, f.77v; note also *Innes Rev.*, ix, 106, no. 8. His curate at Cranston was Robert Acheson (mentioned in his will, Edinburgh Testaments, G.R.H., i, f.95r), accused of saying mass there in 1563 (*Acts General Assemblies*, i, 40.)

248. *Innes Rev.*, ix, 84-5, nos. 2, 5, 6. Excerpt from his will (dated 15 Aug., 1583, three days before his death): " In ye name of ye fader, sone and halie spirit, amen. Jesus . . . Item in ye first and befoir all I commend my saule in ye hand of ye halie and indiuisible trinite, fader, sone and halie gaist, quha creat ye samyn to his image and similitude of nathing, and quha redemit ye samyn with ye deth and passioun of ye sone fra ye power of sathan, with maist humble prayeris prayand yat ye samyn may be brocht to his glorie and honoure into ye cumpanie of heavin." His body he leaves to be buried in the choir of the parish kirk of Eaglesham, if his soul is dissolved from his body there or within 6, 8 or 9 miles, otherwise in the " nixt halie place quhair it sall happin me to depart out of yis warld." (Edinburgh Testaments, G.R.H., xxv, f. 336v).

The reaction of the universities in the crisis years 1559-60 was mixed. The university Rector and the St. Leonard's college staff of St. Andrews joined the reformers. The two Dominicans on the foundation of St. Mary's (Richard Marshall and John Black) were more resilient. John Mair's old college also stood firm, and Buchanan has hard words to say about the provost of St. Salvator's, "haly Doctor Cranstoun", who refused to surrender office, preached in defence of the orthodox eucharistic doctrine in the parish kirk, and had to be threatened with excommunication from the kirk session.[249] Simon Simson, his colleague, like Cranston a doctor in theology and fellow of the Sorbonne, fled to Paris and ended his days as a canon of St. Quentin.[250] Even so at St. Andrews the overall picture is one of conformity, and at Glasgow, where the principal, John Davidson, led the way, although here also there were resisters. Aberdeen, which under Hector Boece had acquired a more than local name,[251] held out successfully till 1569 when a special session of the Privy Council was necessary to depose non-subscribers to the Confession of Faith, the college principal, Alexander Anderson, with four more of its rulers.[252]

It is a pity that these men should have left no formal monuments of their learning, apart from two slim volumes of a logic based on Rudolph Agricola, the work of William Cranston.[253] It was left to men of a more controversial temper, like the abbot of Crossraguel, to take up a written defence of orthodox positions.[254] In January, 1561, under a promise of free speech, Alexander Anderson and others from Aberdeen, inclusive of John Lesley, the canonist, were engaged in a sacramental debate with their opponents in Edinburgh, and after a period in ward were allowed to return to Aberdeen.[255] But the principal was still unrepentant at the date of his death.[256]

The older theory that 1560 came in not with a whimper but a bang has been authoritatively challenged of late. But in so far as it is true that the men of 1560 had risen at the head of a slowly maturing national revolution it is equally true that christian unity and even christian solidarity was being gradually sacrificed and the final hammer blows were delivered in that year. The Congregation came to divide as well as unify and its nascent internal divisions were to tear the nation apart.[257] The vision men may have had of declaring to every man in his own tongue the wonderful works of God (and some catholic reformers in Germany had the same vision) was put into cold storage while they argued about the letter without, as Ireland had put it, "ye hie, divine and hevinlie mynd yat it

---

249. Buchanan, *Vernacular Writings* (Scot, Text Soc.) p. 44; *St. Andrews Kirk Session Reg.*, i, 169-71.

250. He was examining theological candidates at the Sorbonne, 15th April, 1561. Paris, Archives Nationales MM 249, f.124v. Some Latin verses of his when principal of the College Duplessis are in John Hamilton's *Ad Amplissimum Senatum* (Paris, 1586).

251. See the eulogy by Jean Latomus in *Delitiae Poetarum Belgicarum* iii, 107.

252. *Acts General Assemblies*, i, 141.

253. But two known copies out of three editions ! Only one copy has been traced of this work of Wauchope: *Tractatus de compositione propositionis mentalis . . . a magistro Roberto Wanscop (sic) Scoto nouiter recognitus atque in suam integritatem restitutus.* Lyons (A. du Ry). 31 May, 1528. (Oxford: Bodleian). The following work is not as yet traced: *Dialecticae methodus Patritio Todaeo Scoto authore.* Parisiis apud Simonem Colinaeum. 1544. (Renouard, *Bibl. de S. de Colines*, p. 400).

254. Whose work shows that the Faber *Malleus Lutheri* and the *Detectio Nugarum* of the Dominican Jan van den Bundere were circulating in Scotland.

255. Dickinson's *Knox*, i, 353-4; Anderson, *Collections relating to Mary Q. of Scots*, i, 3.

256. *Spalding Miscellany*, ii, 44.

257. In 1583 Thomas Smeaton complained that youths trained in the three tongues were going to France and making shipwreck of conscience and religion, that is reverting to the Catholicism men thought they had exorcised. *Calendar of Scottish Papers*, vi, no. 671.

contenis."[258] In the century when Scots were already to be found in Mexico and the Cape Verde Islands,[259] contemporaries may have had too exclusively European a notion of catholicity, especially when vast tracts of utterly pagan territory were opening up before their very eyes. A *trahison des clercs* was matched by a lay rebellion: the magic name of Geneva was invoked through its English minister. Yet before long many came to abhor " a perfect reformation "; brought up on Luther they wanted a laicised church and were offered instead a clericalised state. And idolatry was popular; different men were of different judgments; a tragic breach was engineered in the peace and consensus of the church.[260] Quintin Kennedy says that if he had all the eloquence of Cicero and Demosthenes he could not summon up " the incredible and wounderfull mistemperance of the air, quhilk continuallie hes bene in this realme sene this deuillis dangeruss dance first begwn."[261] If only the advice of the Latin poet, Roderick Maclean, himself a former alumnus of Wittenberg, had been taken:

> haec vero Indigeti lege qualiacumque Columbae
> pangimus; ut poteris, tu meliora canas;
> dira neotericae ne forte venena Minervae
> amoveant Veteri te Pietate, cave.

* * * *

APPENDICES

EARLY PRINTING

Myllar was printing for Chepman in mid-1508. Yet the 1510 act is in favour of Chepman alone, and relates in effect solely to the importation of printed books into the Edinburgh area. Moreover the 1510 Aberdeen Breviary lacks Myllar's but has Chepman's name. Had Myllar died or become financially a sleeping partner ? Yet there are books which he may have printed elsewhere in Scotland: Dunbar's *Tua Mariit Wemen* which is in a type used by him (1505-6) at Rouen. (He was in Edinburgh, it would seem, in early 1506, which makes it uncertain that he actually did the work of printing at Rouen: *Foular*, i, no. 214). Moreover, it has been pointed out that the so-called Chepman and Myllar Prints were originally owned in Fife (*Innes Rev.*, ix, 129). Obviously, in spite of the accidental absence on some of them of Chepman's device and the presence of Myllar's they were mostly printed in Edinburgh. But the question suggests itself: might not the best centre for the kind of publication Myllar had specialised in at Rouen, the schoolbook, be St. Andrews rather than Edinburgh ? In any event, an Andrew Myllar was incorporated there in 1509, which is an odd coincidence (Anderson, *Early Records*, p.204. Cf. p. 190, where in 1492 the only other Andrew Myllar, perhaps a Fifer, is incorporated; being born in Fife is not of course inconsistent with being a burgess of Edinburgh). If this identification is correct, it means that the king's son,

---

258. *Asloan Manuscript*, i, 4. Even then, men foresaw that " Scriptura sola" might well prove a principle of division.

259. Conway, *An Englishman and the Mexican Inquisition*, p. xxi. *Europeans in West Africa*, Hakluyt Soc., p. 427. The Scot in Mexico was a Thomas Black. The other Scot is unnamed.

260. As Archibald Hay wrote in his preface to *Hecuba Euripidis*: " Quis enim est Europae angulus hoc tempore alienus a tumultibus plusquam tragicis ? "

261. *Ane Oratioune*, p. 13.

Archbishop Alexander Stewart, could have been his patron as Bishop Elphinstone was Chepman's. There is also a leaf of a Donatus which Myllar may have printed, either admittedly in Edinburgh with Chepman, or at Rouen. But there is no reason to see him accepting without protest such an inferior position in Chepman's press that his device was excluded from its productions: and we must conclude that by 1510 he was either dead or had left Chepman.

SAMUEL JASCUY

The problem of the publication abroad of Sir David Lindsay's satires on the Scottish clergy has run up against the insurmountable obstacle of the identification of Mr. Samuel Jascuy of Paris who financed its appearance in the 1558 quarto and octavo, printed, according to John Scot, a contemporary rival, in Rouen. Jascuy has been thought to be some contemporary Scot studying at Paris; but no Scot of that name or an anagram thereof can be found in existing Paris records. The name might be read, it was suggested, as an anagram of " Cujas ", the great jurist of Bourges: and of course the christian name Samuel, comes straight from the book of Judges ! But the Cujas seemed pointless: Calvin, after all, did write the works he published as Alcuin or Lucian, and William Tindal was in fact identical with the William Daltin, matriculand of Wittenberg, whereas Cujas was orthodox and unpolemical, although friendly with a colleague at Bourges, Henry Scrimgeour, whose namesakes had protected the unauthorised press of John Scot at Dundee. Who more likely to have a copy of Scot's earlier edition than Scrimgeour, unless one of the Dundee Wedderburns who settled at Dieppe ? But this is a flimsy foundation on which to build the theory that he had a hand in the printing of it abroad.

No, the only solid basis is Scot's statement that the Lindsay was printed at Rouen; any hypothesis must take account of this, while making room for a bookseller financing it from Paris. Yet Scot could have been mistaken; it may only have been *distributed* from Rouen. It certainly contains the mutilated device of Jean Petit of Rouen; but the edition is dated 1558 and Petit is not known to have printed, at least with this device, after 1557. Even where Rouen is on the title-page bibliographers are often cautious; as with the English and Dutch editions of Abel Clémence. In fact one bibliographer (*The Library*, 4th series, xx, 136 seq.) only accepts Clémence as a Rouen printer with some reservations and hesitations; rejecting his relationship with the Clémence printing family of Lisieux and the suggestion of his working at Geneva or Lyons with a false name or imprint. But all the improbabilities are reconciled when we realise the complexities of Geneva's undercover organisation in France. Abel Clémence is not a false name; he does originate in Lisieux; Rouen may have been a distribution centre only; and the more probable place of printing is Geneva. (Chaix, *Recherches sur l'Imprimerie à Genève de* 1550 *à* 1564, p.161; Geisendorf, *Livre des Habitants*, i, 146. Incidentally the book dated 1567 in the *Library* article reads 1557 in the accompanying plate !)

The case of Clémence, who was at Geneva in 1558, is instructive. He almost certainly brought his press to Geneva and operated from there, using the privy kirks, doubtless, as distributing centres. Other Rouen printers and book-traders were at Geneva: Jean Pautelain, Jean Mutel, Guillaume Henry and Claude Pain (cf. Chaix). But while we have members of a Petit family of Rouen in Geneva (Geisendorf, pp. 41,48), none are printers, but still the career of Jean Petit as a protestant printer in Rouen and Quevilly suggests that he may have been a relative (*Bulletin de la Société du Protestantisme Francais*, xxxvi, 332; a Dieppe printer, Marin Buffe, was at Geneva in 1559). It therefore seems probable to me that someone at Geneva connected with Rouen or someone at Rouen connected with Geneva is responsible not only for the Lindsay but for other works circulating in England and Scotland.

Really the coincidences in Geneva are quite striking. Henry Scrimgeour we have noted. A David Lindsay, a remote relative no doubt of the poet, was at Geneva in 1558 (Geisendorf, p. 139). Along with him was registered Miles Coverdale, an expert in undercover printing, and but lately associated with the Dr. Machabaeus of Copenhagen, stated to have financed the first edition of this very work of Lindsay's. Then there is Knox: had he not been an associate of Sir David in St. Andrews before going to serve in the galleys at Rouen? Did he not himself visit Dieppe in this very year 1558? If Mr. Samuel Jascuy of Paris had relatives anywhere might we not look for them also in Geneva? There can be little doubt that he is of the same ilk as the Dauphiné family of Jacquy, all refugees at Geneva, all members of the book-trade, although not all apparently active as such in Geneva: Francois, Sebastien and Jaulme (Chaix, pp. 196-7). All the pointers indicate Geneva as the real, though unsuspected, source of this master-stroke of Scottish literary propaganda, and Lindsay, even after his death, as still active in the role of impressario for Knox. Moreover, there were those at the receiving end in Scotland who would be grateful to Geneva for circulating such propaganda, including Paul Methven in the privy kirk at Dundee, himself a pupil of Coverdale.

STUDENTS ABROAD

The following Scots are found at Vienna from 1455: Andrew of Scotland (1455); James Frisel of Inverness (1456); Master John Gray of St. Andrews university (1494); Alexander Kymte (1498); Master George Ryethart (1507); Patrick Fort (1515-16); William Barrar of St. Andrews and Dominus Andrew Helm of Glasgow (1516-17); George Barclay of Montrose (1521-22); James Gordon, doctor of theology (1569). *Die Matrikel des Universitat Wien*, ii, 36, 44, 238, 344, 426, 437,; iii, 25, 155.

For Balnavis at Cologne see Calderwood, *History*. Macalpine was incorporated at Wittenberg as a bachelor (in theology) of Cologne (Foerstemann, *Liber Decanorum Facultatis Theol. Academiae Vitebergensis*, p. 29). The following names are taken from the period 1500-60, (Keussen, *Matrikel*, ii):

1500   William of Montrose
       William of Scotland
       Andrew of Scotland
1501   James of St. Mary (Dundee?) of the realm of Scotland
1502   Andrew of Morenia (Moray?)
       Alexander Henderson
1507   David of Angus
1512   James Anderson
       Thomas Tzang
       Henry Anderson
       Thomas Fernus, priest Aberdeen diocese; law
       John Watson, priest St. Andrews diocese; law
       William Phillipson, priest Aberdeen diocese; law
1514   Thomas of Scotland

1515   Thomas of Dundee
      David of Dundee
      John Lyn, acted as cook
      Thomas Forrayt
1516   M. Richard, M. Andrew, M. Ninian Douglas
1519   Thomas of Montrose
      Thomas Clerk
      John de Megloe
1520   Alexander Bar
1521   Robert Kelemuir or Henryson
      Andrew Hunter (Hongter) of Edinburgh, Scot, Glasgow diocese
1522   John Baburne
      William Turner
      Quintin of Lanark
      Thomas of Aberdeen
      William of St. Nicholas, Moray diocese
      Thomas of St. Andrews
1523   D. David Heys, law
      David Thomson (Thome) of Scotland
1527   Andrew Hutten
      John Jameson (Jacobi) of Scotland
1537   Andrew Crawford (Kraeffort) from Scotland
1542   Alexander Snape (Senapius) from Scotland
1546   M. Ninian Templeton, Scot., theology; licentiate theol., 1558
1550   James Panton, Aberdeen . . . and being remote from home, as an
      Irishman, not having, did not give (i.e., made no payment)
1551   Walter (?)Ruthven, Scot (name variously given, " Revignyensis."
      " Riviniensis," " Riveliensis," " Revigutiensis " and " Benig-
      niensis ") Joined the Society of Jesus. (Perhaps Walter *Hay* of
      Rathven ?):

The Wittenberg names, though often printed (incompletely), are worth reprinting: 1519 John " Nutrisen," Scot, St. Andrews diocese; 1528 Nicholas Borthwick; 1533 Alexander Alane (Alesius); 1539 John the Scot; 1540 John Macalpine (Maccabeus); 1544 Walter Spalding (Spalatinus); William Ramsay, M.A., St. Andrews; James Balfour; John Faithus Scot; 1555 John Lyn Scot. In addition, there is 1534 " Rodericus Hector ex Hybernia ", that is Roderick Maclean, son of Hector, later elect of Clonmacnoise and bishop of the Isles; while, 1535 " Johannes Duncan ex hibernia " is most probably a Scot too. At Frankfort, besides Alesius, who soon retired to Leipzig, there were John Fidelis (Fyfe?), professor of theology in 1547; Andrew Lowson Scot, 1549; and John Fidelis, son of the foregoing, 1555. The Marburg names are: 1527 Patrick Hamilton of Linlithgow, M.A., Paris; John Hamilton, Scot; Gilbert Winram of Edinburgh; 1533 Peter " Banckbeus " (?Balnavis); 1537 John Crom " Scotensis " (uncertain). The Greifswald names: 1519, Alexander Russell, cleric Aberdeen diocese; 1545 D. Alexander Dume (for Dunn?), Scot, M.A. pastor of St. James, and later doctor of theology; 1546 Richard Melville; David Peddie; in 1595 this Lutheran centre turned away another Scot for being a Calvinist (Friedlander, *Matrikel*, i, 211).

The following are the Louvain students in this period: (Brussels, Archives du Royaume, Libri Intitulatorum, iii-iv).

1500   Peter Watson (Walteri) of St. Nicholas

PLATE XXV. THE TOMBSTONE OF JOHN WINRAM.

IOANNES CNOXVS.

PLATE XXVI. PUBLICISTS OF THE PROTESTANT PARTY.

William Vain (?Wawane) of St. Nicholas, Aberdeen d., both poor
1501 John of Haddington (addinton)
1502 Simon Simson (Simonis) de " long," St. Andrews d.
1503 Thomas Culross (Chueras), Angus, Brechin d.
Thomas Coutts of Scotland, St. Andrews d., Chateau
Andrew of St. Andrews, St. Andrews d., Chateau
Stephen Yester, St. Andrews d.
Patrick Mure (Moer), of Lindores, St. Andrews d.
William Craik (Creck), of Lothian, same. All poor, Chateau
1504 Robert of St. John (Perth), in Scotland
William Spens of St. Mary (?Dundee)
John of Angus, all poor, Lis
James Clerk of Angus
John Grant of Argyll (Archadia)
John Urie (Vury) of Angus, all poor, Chateau
Thomas Athy, of Lothian, St. Andrews
John Young of Kinnetis (canettis), St. Andrews d. in England
John Weir (Wur) of St. Constantine, Glasgow d., all poor, Chateau
1505 Thomas Crichton of St. John, Glasgow d., rich, Faucon
John Richardson, of Aberdeen, Abd. d., poor, Chateau
Master Robert Blacader, noble, Glasgow d.
Master James Heriot, Glasgow d.
Thomas of Moray
John Elder of Angus (enchusia), poor, Chateau
David Inglis of Moray
D. David Learmouth, St. Andrews d., Faucon
1506 Laurence Thomson (Thome), of Lothian, St. Andrews d., poor Chateau
Thomas Carruthers (carintors), of St. Andrews
Alexander Bisset of Aberdeen
Robert Brown, of Angus, all poor, Lis
John Tervert (?Carver) of St. John (Perth)
John March of St. John, St. Andrews d., rich, both Chateau
Stephen Mure (merra) of St. John, St. Andrews d.
James Ross of Lothian, poor, both Chateau
Andrew Innes of St. John
John Oliver of Angus, both poor, Lis
1508 David White of St. John
Thomas Burns (barnst) of Haddington (adineto) in Scotland
William Black (blaque) of Brechin (bretens) in Scotland, both poor, Lis
Elias of Scotland
John le tasuer (casuer) de ciuitate sancti andree, poor
James Staent of Aberdeen, poor Chateau
James Blackwood of St. John, poor, Lis
William Hay of Aberdeen, poor, Faucon
1509 Andrew Paterson (patricii) of St. John, St. Andrews d. in Scotland
George, son of Andrew de Bunch (bonch), of St. John, St. Andrews d.
D. Alexander Fotheringham, of St. Andrews in Scotland
Thomas Ray of Perth, Scot
Martin Hutchinson of Ireland

James son of Peter Crombie (cramme) de hawane (??), Dunblane d., Lis

1510 James Lin " de carner " (Tarvet?) in Scotland
Peter Hilson of Edinburgh, St. Andrews d.
George Brown (brun) " de sancto briano," St. Andrew d., all poor, Chateau
John of St. John, son of William " huhiptihul " (name indecipherable), St. Andrews d., Scotland, poor, Faucon
William de lauda (?Lauder), St. Andrews d., poor, Faucon
John Mowat of Aberdeen, Glasgow diocese !
The noble lord and master George Ferne archdeacon of the cathedral church of Dunkeld
Laurence Rynd of forgundia (Longforgan?)
Henry Cant of Angus
John Roch of Angus, all poor, Chateau
John Garden of St. Andrews, rich, Lis
Ghysbert of Edinburgh (?), poor, Lis
George Lindsay of Holyrood, of the nation of Scotland, St. Andrews d.

1512 Henry Alan, under the bishop of St. Andrews, Chateau

1513 John of Cupar, son of Thomas Hardie
Nicholas of St. Andrews, son of Alexander Gilmour
Laurence of Forgan (fourcondia), son of John Rentsen, all poor, Faucon
Robert of Dundee (Tonde) of Angus, St. Andrews d., poor, Chateau
Richard of Cupar, St. Andrews d.

1514 John Rent or Reul of " Rossentia," St. Andrews d., poor, Chateau
John, son of William of Robertson, St. Andrews d., poor, Faucon
James Irvine (urwin), of Aberdeen in Scotland

1515 David Arthur of St. Andrews under the bishop of St. Andrews
Walter Matheson (Mathei) of St. John, St. Andrews d.
Charles Henderson of St. John, St. Andrews d., both poor, Chateau
Gavin Pighet of Dickeltmuir (?), St. Andrews d., poor, Lis

1516 John Hay of Dundee, poor, Lis

1517 James of Wittand (or Willand) of Dundee, St. Andrews d. in Scotland, poor, Lis
Peter Ray or Kay, of St. Andrews d., poor, Chateau
William Spinghe (*sic*) of Forgan (virgundia), St. Andrews d., poor, Chateau
John, son of Cuthbert Thomson of Edinburgh, Glasgow diocese (!), poor, chateau

1518 John, son of James Bonkle, of Kelso, St. Andrews d., poor, Chateau
Edward Straton of Edinburgh, St. Andrews, poor, Lis
John of Ellem, Scot, St. Andrews d., Porc
Alexander, son of John Coute (?or Cante) of Edinburgh
James, son of Thomas Paterson of Edinburgh, poor, Chateau
Thomas, son of David Monipenny of St. John
William of Cupar, poor, Porc
Thomas of St. John, Chateau
Andrew Forman of Edinburgh, St. Andrews
George Forman of Edinburgh

Thomas Forman, of St. Andrews, all three rich, Lis

1519   John Sas (?) of St. John under the bishop of St. Andrews, poor, Chateau

Gilbert Robertson (Roberti) of St. Andrews

Laurence Johnson (Johannis) of Dunfermline (sancta margarita) St. Andrews d., poor, Lis

1520   George Clerk of Aberdeen, poor, Lis

1521   Andrew Crom of Moray, poor, Chateau

Robert Gibson of Haddington, under the bishop of St. Andrews

John Adamson of St. Andrews under the bishop of St. Andrews

John Mackoreson (?) of Dumfries, under the bishop of Glasgow all poor, Chateau

Hugh of St. Andrews, Scot

Thomas Duff, poor, Porc

William Davidson, Porc

William son of Patrick Anderson of St. John

John Craig (cracck or craecst) of Aberdeen, both poor, Chateau

John Truson (*sic*) of Archadia, Aberdeen d.

Alexander Spens of St. Andrews, St. Andrews d., both poor, Faucon

John Massie (masse) of Aberdeen, Aberdeen d.

Cornelius Garden (cardine) de Cardinis, St. Andrews d.

James Key of Brechin

Thomas Doutry (?) of Dundee, Brechin d.

David Hill of Dundee, Brechin d.

Alexander Dingwall of Dingwall under the bishop of St. Boniface

Walter de Climner (*or* eltumer?) of St. Andrews, all poor, Chateau

George Johnston, Aberdeen d.

Thomas Wright or Smith (faber), Aberdeen

Gilbert Sinclair, same

Robert Heriot, St. Andrews

John Robertson same

James Pleyrin (?), same, all poor, Lis

1522   Hector Bane of Newbridge (de nouo ponte), Brechin d.

Thomas Davidson of Mar (marouia), Aberdeen d., both poor, Chateau

1523   John de huyo alias Wichart

1524   Alexander, son of John Cochrane (cocherem), of Aberdeen, poor, Chateau

Matthew Paterson of " loundido," St. Andrews, poor, Chateau

1527   Hugh Ryg, Dumfries, Glasgow

David Menzies of Aberdeen under the bishop of Aberdeen, both rich, Chateau

David Forret (foreth) of Cupar, poor, Lis

1528   Mathias Moncur of Dundee (de dono dei), poor, Chateau

Walter Wilson of Dundee, poor, Lis

Alexander, son of John Davidson, of Aberdeen

James, son of David Ferrier, of Dundee under the bishop of Brechin

John Monipenny of Edinburgh, rich, Lis

John Haldane (Holdi) of Brechin

John Joffray of Brechin, both poor, Standonck pedagogy

John of Aberdeen " verberator "

1529 John of Aberdeen, pauper standonicus
John Law, son of Thomas Law, Brechin d. in Scotland
1530 " Georgius filius georgii Wijer de dono dei " (i.e., George Wishart of Dundee), February
Andrew, son of Andrew Finlayson of Whitehill (de albo monte) both poor, Chateau
John Durham (durem), of Edinburgh, St. Andrews d., poor, Chateau
1532 John, son of William of St. Peter (i.e., Montrose), Brechin d.
Walter, son of John Gaw (gol), of St. Peter, Brechin d.
David, son of William Robert of St. Andrews, under the bishop of St. Andrews
1533 John Stewart of St. Michael, Scot, Moray d., rich, Chateau
D. George Liel of Dundee, poor, Chateau
1534 William Blacader, Glasgow d.
Patrick Buchanan, Glasgow d.
1536 Alexander Cock " de bacwuson "
Robert Dunlop of Edinburgh Glasgow diocese (!), poor, Chateau
Alexander Ray of Perth, St. Andrews d., poor, Chateau
John Abercromby, Scot, St. Andrews d.
1542 William Chisholm of Dunblane, Scot, July
John Erskine and William Erskine, both Scots, both Noble
Thomas Strang and Richard Strang, Scots, brothers
1546 Clement Little (parvus), Scot, July
M. William Harvey (herwe), Scot
1549 Domicellus Johannes coluyn scotus minorennis dioecis sancti andree, 17 April
1550 dns. Richardus hilliardus anglus lincolniensis diocesis Jan. 2
1551 The noble and most reverend lord William Gordon, bishop of Aberdeen, August
1552 D. David Brun (?), Scot
1553 Thomas Coyl or Coye, Scot, poor, Faucon
1554 William Chisholm, Scot, rich, Chateau, 27 August
1556 Andrew Galloway, Aberdeen, May
1560 Duncan (Norie), of Aberdeen, poor, Porc
John Melville, 31 May
Gilbert Skein, Scots
M. Robert Hay, Aberdeen, 13 December
1561 D. James Chalmer, Scot, poor, 22nd January
Magister noster Richard Smith " reintitulatus," 15 February
William Crichton (Christon), Scot, 13 November
1562 D. James Gordon, Scot, noble
M. Robert Abercromby, Scot
M. Henry Keyr, Scot
1563 M. Archibald Cumming (Cumineus), Scot
M. Alexander Cheyn, Scot, poor
M. Andrew Middleton, Scot, poor
James (Layne? or) Tayre " parthensis," Scot
William Murdoch, Scot, poor, all January
1564 M. Andrew Ins (Innes?), Scot, 3 May
John Hay, Aberdeen, poor, Porc, August
Archibald Hog, Scot, Aberdeen, 31 October
1565 John Cheyne (Cheesne), Scot, Aberdeen, law
1567 Thomas Schewand (a Scot?), poor, 25 September

James Fraser junior and senior, Aberdeen, rich, Chateau
John Ogilvy, Scot, law
Thomas Ogilvy, Scot, law, 4 October
1568 George Dury, Scot, theology
John Dury, Scot, theology, 26 April

In addition, the following details of graduates in arts are supplied from Reusens, *Promotions*:

1510 (first out of 148) Alexander Ayton, Lis
1523 (second out of 133) Hugh Wishart from St. Andrews
1532 (first out of 118) George Wishart
1563 (Prima linea) no. 11 John Hay, Aberdeen d., Porc
                no. 18 Thomas Low, Mearns, Scot, Porc
  (Postlineales) no. 25 James Tyrie, Scot, Porc

Apart from Louvain, the other successful counter-reforming university was Ingoldstadt, where the familiar of Robert Wauchope, apostolic nuncio, and his nephew were both matriculated in August, 1543: Jean Francois of Arras diocese and Henry Hay, noble of St. Andrews diocese. Other matriculations took place there in 1589 (John Stewart) and 1598 (Archibald Anderson of Culross, student of medicine). John Winzet disputed a thesis there in 1591. (*Die Matrikel der Ludwig-Maximilians Universitat*, i, cols, 597, 1208, 1374.)

DAVID LOWIS AND ROBERTUS BRITANNUS

Britannus was a correspondent also of Gelida and Teyve, two friends of Buchanan. The letters were published in *Roberti Britanni Atrebatis Epistolarum Libri Duo* in 1540 (Paris, Guillaume Bossozel). I have not attempted to date them more precisely. The first is dated from Bordeaux, the second may have been from Paris.

f.28v

" R. Britannus Dauidi Lauxio S.D.

Pudet me diuturni silentii. Quid tu me etiam tui oblitum putas? Non sane id pati unquam possem. Nam et animi vitaeque eleutheriotes tuae, ut tibi faueam compellit: multaque alia: sed inprimis quod te mei studiosum et prae caeteris cupidum semper cognoui. Quare si fui aliquanto tardior ad scribendum, id non humanitati aut negligentiae tribues, sed fortunae, temporumque varietate. Ego enim ex quo a vobis discessi, his sum iactatus fluctibus, ut cum me istis emersisse censerem, tum validius agitari et quasi obrui coeperim. Erimus tamen armati contra omnes procellas, et quicunque erunt venti, nostra ars atque industria non deerit. Commendo tibi Ioannem Tieullanum. Is et eximie diligit bonas literas, et in iure ciuili multum laboris et singularis operae posuit. Huic si quid ad tuam familiaritatem tribueris, magnam non solum ex doctrina capies voluptatem, verumetiam ex moribus et vita. Vale Burdig. iii Id Eeb (*sic*)."

f.35v

" Multa me quotidie hortantur ut me ad meos recipere cupiam: sed tu ipse in primis. Quomodo inquies? Dicam tibi ut res est. Ego cum in te tantum esse eruditionis videam quantum in nullo alio, qui quidem istic agat unquam cognouisse videor; moueor certe, efferorque studio illas sedes visendi, in quibus et doctrina tanta et cum doctrina singularis quaedam comitas et morum suauitas vigeat. De qua cum vellem plura referre, subito tempus angustiae me ista omnia concludere atque in aliud tempus differre coegerunt. Itaque velim ad nos aliquod scribas cum erit ocium. Vale. cal. Nouemb."

ERASMIAN PRAYERS AT ABERDEEN

The two versions of this prayer, one from John Vaus (edition of 1553, editor Theophilus Stewart, successor of Vaus as grammarian at King's College), show a likeness in phrasing that makes it certain that the Aberdeen version is based directly on the other.

Erasmus	*Rules of Aberdeen Grammar Boys*
Gaspar: Mane, simul atque sum experges actus (id fere sit ad sextam, aut quintam) pollice signum crucis pingo in fronte et in pectore. Erasmus: Quid deinde ? Gaspar: Auspicor initium diei, In nomine Patris et Filli et Spiritus Sancti. E: Quid illi narras ? G: Ago gratias, quod eam noctem mihi voluerit esse prosperam, precorque ut diem itidem illum totum mihi bene fortunet, ad ipsius gloriam et animae meae salutem; utque is, qui est vera lux occasum nesciens, sol aeternus omnia vivificans, alens, exhilarans, dignentur illucescere menti meae, ne usquam impingam in ullum peccatum, sed ipsius ductu perveniam ad vitam aeternam. (Colloquia in *Opera Omnia*, Leyden, 1703, i, col. 649).	Inprimis puer ingressus Scholas prosternat se humi genibus flexis, salutet Christum optimum maximum humani generis Authorem et Virginem Deiparam brevi precatiuncula: hoc modo. *Gratias tibi Pater Caelestis ago quod praeteritam noctem mihi volueris esse prosperam: precorque ut diem itidem hunc mihi fortunes, ad tuam gloriam et animae meae salutem: et Tu, qui es Vera Lux, occasum nesciens, Sol eternus, omnia vivificans, alens, exhilarans, digneris illucescere menti meae, ne usquam in ullum impingam peccatum: sed ductu tuo perveniam ad vitam aeternam.* Iesu esto mihi Iesus, et spiritu principali confirma me. (Simpson, *Bon Record*, p. 98).

An address to Jesus, our Lady and certain saints is also in Erasmus.

RICHARD MARSHALL

No doubt several persons were planning catechisms in the first half of the sixteenth century; although shorter tables of confession (like John Ireland's printed in the *Asloan Manuscript*) existed at least in manuscript. It is to such a compendium for the illiterate that Patrick Cockburn refers in his *De Utilitate Verbi Dei* (1551): *quod symbolum et decalogum, alii catechesim seu catechismum vocant* (sig. Eiiiir), and this to be heard in church on the days laid down. After the reformation, in issuing a part of his catechism in London, he implies that lack of subsidy prevented the printing of his catechism entire. (Preface to James White, 1561).

The need for a larger one was obvious. Before Archbishop Hamilton's catechism appeared, with " common placis ordourlie intraittit," (Law, ed., p. 7), two decades had passed in which heretical catechisms circulated: Patrick Hamilton's which treated " exactlie of certane commoun places, which knowne, yee have the pith of all divinitie " (Calderwood, i, 78); Gau's *Richt Way* of 1533; and Thomas Forrett's manuscript catechism (c. 1539; Calderwood, i, 127). Moreover in the text reference is made to the archbishop's request to Richard Smith for a book of commonplaces (*Richt Way*, p. xlviii).

It has been traditional to assign the composition of Hamilton's catechism to John Winram. But clearly Hamilton's and Winram's are two separate entities; the one entry follows the other in the St. Leonard's college inventory printed in *Maitland Miscellany*, i, 319:

> Catechismus D.Jo.Wynrami superintendentis
> Catechismus Jo. Hamiltoun episc.

Fr. Maurice Taylor has already pointed out the anomaly of the description " superintendent." Actually, on checking the manuscript, we find it is an enlargement of " supri.", which more probably means " subprioris." Bale does not record Winram's catechism till 1559; he seems uncertain of his name, though he had seen a copy and calls him " canon regular." Because there was a manuscript catechism in St. Andrews in the late seventeenth century, Mitchell identified this as Winram's, proposing that Winram's catechism was either an unrevised manuscript draft of the printed version or a corrected printed copy (Mitchell, ed., p. cvii). But it might just as well have been something else; for instance, the theological manuscript of one of the early St. Leonard's principals entered in the same inventory (*Ibid.*, p. xi).

However, Mitchell had also noticed in a St. Mary's college inventory a reference to " Some copyes of Freir Maichels Catechisme " (*Maitland, Misc.*, i, 313). This he interpreted as the *Institutio Catholica* of Michael Helding (Mitchell, p. xi). However, once again, on returning to the manuscript we are confronted with something quite different, namely:

> " The Catechisme with uthere certane buikis (*cancelled*)

> Some Copyes of freir marchels Catechismes." (Nat. Lib. of Scotland, Balcarras Papers, vii, 209r).

Now the hand of this inventory is that of John Douglas, provost of St. Mary's (1546-71), who probably compiled it when he handed over his provostship. In a later inventory in Andrew Melville's autograph (but printed in *Maitland Misc.*, i, 307-9 as if it was an earlier inventory) this item disappears. However on a 1598 inventory subscribed by Melville (*Ibid.*, i, 316) the last item is said to be " Catechisme of Johne Archbishop of Sanctandrois 1547." Once again there is a misreading. The original reads 1542 (the 2 has been altered from a 1), an understandable misreading by Melville of 1552, the correct date. Its position on the inventory suggests its identity with Friar Marshall's catechism in the earlier Douglas inventory. (I am indebted to Mr. Cant and Mr. Smart of St. Andrews university archives for invaluable help in tracking down these originals in the vellum-bound " Copies of Bulls, Charters 1413-1672 ").

Who is this " freir marchel ? " Obviously " Friar Richard Marchell " present at the 1549 Scottish provincial council (Patrick, *Statutes of the Scottish Church*, p. 86), a man closely associated with Douglas the compiler of the first inventory.

He was a former Oxford student (Boase, *Register of the Univ. of Oxford*, p. 147), who, as Dominican prior of Newcastle refused to accept Henry's supremacy and fled in 1536 (*Letters and Papers*, x, no. 594). Along with his socius, perhaps Henry Mason or Maxon, Rome transferred him to the Scots province in May, 1539, with permission to reside in Italy and Saxony on his way there (Reichert, *Acta Capitulorum Generalium O.P.*, iv, 283). In 1542 we find him in Edinburgh witnessing a charter with Friars John Grierson and John Rough; Calendar of St. Andrews Charters (G.R.H.), nos. 287, 290. Grierson evidently succeeded John Mair (died 1550) as dean of the theological faculty in St. Andrews. (Patrick, *Statutes* pp. 87 (Mair), 163 (Grierson); Glasgow Univ. Library, Manderston Ms, BE6. b11 f.23r).

In order to live in college outside the Dominican house of study in St. Andrews he had to have the general chapter's licence to be subject to a diocesan bishop, in his instance to the bishop of Brechin, one of the university conservators. He obtained this licence in 1547 (Jarrett-Gumbley, *The English Dominicans*, p. 153), though he was not formally matriculated till three years later (*Early Records*, p. 254).

Under the new dean of theology the St. Mary's set-up, apart from Provost Douglas, was largely Dominican. Douglas himself was required by the foundation to be a doctor of theology and doubtless was. (Quintin Kennedy refers to " Doctor Douglas," Laing's *Knox*, vi, 167; but he had a medical qualification, being recorded as bachelor in medicine, Paris, Univ., Archives, Reg. 15, f.402r). On the eve of the reformation Marshall held the licentiate's post there, i.e., the second mastership (*R.M.S.*, v, 759). John Black probably held the third post (bachelor in theology) as he held the second mastership at his death (" usit to be possessit be ane theolog ", Laing's *Knox*, ii, 504).

But Richard Marshall also held yet another appointment of some interest. The vicarage of Musselburgh was assigned for a preacher (in terms of the provincial council's act of 1549, Patrick, *Statutes*, p. 121) for the abbey church of Dunfermline and churches annexed to it. He had been preaching a good deal in St. Andrews, where he is referred to as " verbi dei preconem egregium " and " ecclesiasten insignem " (Acta Rectorum, ii, 41, 44). He also took part in a famous dispute with a Franciscan, Friar Andrew Cottis, as to whether the Our Father is said to God or also to our Lady and the saints, the latter friar obviously suffering from some over-anxiety because of attacks on prayers to our Lady and the saints: Marshall's sermon, moreover, was given on All Saints day, 1551. (Foxe-Townsend, v, 641). The catechism quite plainly states Marshall's position. (Mitchell, ed., p. xxiv). On the 29th May, 1558, Marshall became official preacher to Dunfermline. (Registrum Assedationum, Dunfermline, G.R.H., f.6r).

The agreement was between George Durie, commendator, and Robert, his successor, and the convent on the one hand and " Rychart marschell doctoure off diuinitie . . . that is to say the said Rychart marschell is bound and oblest to preche and teache in all kyrkis belanging to ye said monestary . . . (quhow) oft and quhensumewir he is commandit yairto be ye said Lorde . . . and conuent, he hawand his heltht and abill to mak travell. S(wa) he sall teache as god gyffis hym grace ane lessone off the script(uris) or sum uyer convenient doctrine to the bretherin of the said abbay thry(ce) in ye owlke and ofter gyf thay requyre hym yairwyth." For which labours and " trawellis yat he is obleist and bound to tak heir," he is to receive £40 usual Scots yearly, entering on his duties from St.

Helen's day, enduring for his life. Moreover he was to have a portion of bread, drink, fish and flesh as much as any other brother of the monastery in hall or at the port, either in his chalmer or elsewhere. He is also to have a chalmer most convenient for his study. He is to be served with his portion with those of his household after the prior, to have two " laid " of coals weekly in winter and a horse with stable room.

PATRICK HAMILTON AT PARIS

Paris, Bibliotheque Nationale
Ms Lat. 9951 (Acta Rectoria)
f.27v
In the rectorate of Nicolas Pastor (10 Oct., 1520-16 Dec., 1520), the following students are among the *iurati*, that is, those who took oath to the rector on incorporation. The entries are slightly out of place, which confused the Paris informant of Peter Lorimer, who gives Nicholas Maillard as Rector, and his date of election as the 8th or 10th August, both dates being erroneous. (*Patrick Hamilton*, pp. 28, 225).

Johannes duncane glasgeuensis (*sic*) diocesis . . .

f.29v
Patricius hamelton glassguensis nobilis . . .

f.19v
(Although on an earlier leaf, this entry refers to the rectorate of Jean le Sieurre, 15 Dec., 1521-24 Mar., 1522).

Sequuntur nomina incipientium in veneranda natione germanie . . .
Dominus Patricius hammeliton sancti Andree diocesis
Incepturus sub magistro Guillermo manderston . . .
Paris, University Archives
Reg. 91 (Liber Receptoris Nationis Alemannie)
f.193r
Anno post virginis puerperium Quingentesimo vigesimo supra Millesimum duodecimo calendis octobris apud diuum Mathurinum Auguste Germanorum Nacionis Comitiis, franciscus Osmanus Alcmaricus ultraiectine diocesis ex Hollandorum principatu per inferioris prouincie Magistros Erarii Quaestor nunc secundum designatus
Acceptorum articulus secundus
Que a baccalaureis
Joanne couden diocesis Sancti Andree
Matheo Nesbet diocesis Glasquensis (*sic*)
Jacobo delpho diocesis Traiectensis
patricio (*followed by blank-Erasure?*) diocesis Sancti Andree bursa 15 solidi parisienses   7 lib. 15 so. par. (Osman was in office from this date, i.e., 20th Sept., 1520, till 20th Sept., 1521, when Blase de Warda, of Hungary, succeeded, as recorded on f.201r)
f.207r
(Warda still receiver)
Recepta post primum compotum . . .
A licenciandis
A Patricio hommoton (*sic*) diocesis Sancti Andree cuius bursa ualet 15 sol. parisienses recepi 3 libras 15 solidos parisienses.
Pro cappa rectoris 2 libras parisienses
Pro iocundo aduentu seu primo uoto 4 solidos par.

f.208v

Et sic receptor facto suo compoto, munimentis et pecuniis nationis in manibus domini decani Magistri Gaspardi pistoris relictis, tum ob pestem que hinc in urbe Parisiensi grassabatur, tum uero quia Hungaria patria eiusdem receptoris ab infidelibus depopulata et pro parte occupata fuit, omnibus Magistris presentibus et futuris animam hilarem, uitam longam, finemque beatum exoptans.

f.209r

New Receiver, William Manderston, elected on the 20th Sept., 1522.

Sudden conversion of John Davidson

The unexpectedness to Archbishop Beaton of Glasgow, his patron, and also their common friend, Giovanni Ferreri, of the conversion to Calvinism of John Davidson, principal in Glasgow university, is well brought out in this excerpt from a letter of Ferreri to Beaton, among the Blairs Archives (Letters), now c/o Rev. W. J. Anderson in Columba House, Edinburgh. It also has an interesting reference to the Hebrew and Greek interests of the dean of Glasgow, later bishop of Ross, Henry Sinclair:

(The first part of the letter, discussing curial matters, is dated " Parisiis. Septemb. 1559.")

. . . Scripseram iam hanc epistolam ad te, cum ad nos uenit 26 Septembris Joannes lewiston qui tuas ad me pertulit. In quibus multa adinueni grauissima et cum summo periculo coniunctissima. Sed fortiter audendum est pro summa omnium, hoc est uera religione Jesu Christi et catholica, contra Sathanicas huius etatis sectariorum opinationes. Deus optimus maximus tibi et tui similibus non deerit in causa sua, sed animos uestros preparabit ad uictoriam. Quod autem insipienter designauit magister Joannes Dauidson olim tuus, nunquam eram crediturus cuiquam, nisi tute ad me de hoc ipso scripsisses. Sed quando ita euenit preter omnium nostram expectationem, Deo sic permittente talia, minus moleste tibi ferendum est. Nam si fuisset in pietate nostra ueteri tam bene confirmatus quantum uideri primum cupiebat, non tam stolide ab Ecclesia catholica discessionem fecisset et ad Congregationem (uerius dixeris dissectionem) quam isti uestri male sani et furiosi uocant, se applicasset. Quid enim audent nomen Ecclesie Sancte proprium, hoc est uere Congregationis et unionis, sibi tribuere, dissipati isti tenebriones, cum scriptum sit, Qui non colligit mecum dispergit ? Que nam potest esse huiusmodi Congregatio, que omnem populi Dei tranquillitatem iam sustulit, humanas uero leges prorsus contemnit, diuinas quoque turbulentissime conculcat ? His igitur tantis malis quis unquam poterit remedium ullum iustum applicare, nisi ferro et flamma uincere ? Quod quidem breui (ut auguror), permittente Deo optimo maximo, consequetur. De bibliis autem nostris in tribus Linguis, quod ad me scribis rogatus, nihil est quod obsit, si tu tamen iusseris. Uerum puto res melius transigetur, si ego hac re una non exuar que est mihi mea uita charior, et alteri uiro optimo nostrique amantissimo de aliis huiusmodi Bibliis prospiciatur alicunde, hic etiam nostra si uolet opera. Ante tres uero menses Triuultius Cardinalis Legatus a Latere Summi Pontificis tunc in Galliis, uoluit mihi pro meis Bibliis scuta 10 annumerare. Sed ego omnino quodcumque precium eo nomine de illo recusaui. Paulo post idem Cardinalis a quodam Bibliopola scutis 17 huiusmodi Biblia me presente redemit. Quod si uolet Dominus Decanus sumptus facere, obseruabo diligenter si quo modo possim Biblia eiusmodi in gratiam illius reperire. Sic illi melius (nisi omnino fallor) et mihi quoque in hac parte fuerit prospectum, quando uterque nostrum uidelicet de amata et sua potietur.

Rursus Uale, 26 Septembris 1559.

T. R. Clientulus,

Jo. ferrerius

Pedemontanus. (Autograph).

Endorsed

Reuerendissimo in Christo patri domino Jacobo Betoun Archiepiscopo Glasquensi, patrono suo singulari

In Scotia.

PATRICK'S PLACES AND OECONOMICA CHRISTIANA

In the *Opera* of Jacobus Latomus, published at Louvain in 1550 is a section from his *De Fide et Operibus*, dated the 6th June, 1530, which makes an interesting comparison between Patrick Hamilton's *Places* and the *Oeconomica Christiana*, anonymously printed, but the work of van Bommel (1523). Latomus replied in 1528, being then in charge of Standonck's foundation for poor students in Louvain:

" . . . Huius secundi generis, nuper prodiit liber quidam sine nomine authoris, impressoris et loci, cui nomen est OEconomica Christiana, liber meo iudicio pestilens, quem tamen cupidissime legere dicuntur Monachi quidam, quos tenet sancti propositi poenitentia, quique tamquam serui fugitiui furtim sui fecerunt, ac circumquaque vagantur, ea ut arbitror ratione quod hic liber eiusmodi homines liberet non seruatae Deo fidei conscientia. Unde sit veresimile authorem huius libri esse unum aliquem ex seruis fugitiuis, qui in qualecunque solatium, afflictae propter sacrilegium conscientiae, undecunque corrasent operimenta propriae turpidinis."

Latomus goes on to say that he replied to it in public in the schools two years ago, but had been advised to publish his reply:

" . . . Sed ut potius ederetur tandem euicerunt amici, praecipue Oliuerius Polus Anglus Eliensis Archidiaconus . . . Alexander Galoai Scotus Abordonensis (*sic*) canonicus, qui eodem ferme tempore alium librum eiusdem generis nobis dedit examinandum . . . "

* * * *

CHURCH COUNCILS IN
SIXTEENTH-CENTURY SCOTLAND

by

THOMAS WINNING

The white banner, which they carried at Pinkie in 1547, depicting a woman weeping before a crucifix with the legend, *Afflictae Sponsae Ne Obliviscaris*,[1] was a stark reminder to the clergy of Scotland of the precarious state of the church in their land, and at the same time an implicit invocation to heaven for the return of Ninian or a second Columba or even for a monarch of the mould of the saintly Margaret. Many of them must have felt that it was now too late to save the Auld Kirk at least from her enemies, for she was entering her last struggle for survival buffeted by the very evils she had for so long dispelled. These last years are pregnant with frustration and tragedy, but are withal not entirely devoid of valiant attempts by the church to set her ideals high once more and save the country for the faith. Those efforts are the councils, which she held and in which she herself laid bare and examined the abuses that had sapped her strength, and for which she herself again prescribed the antidotes.

A council's purpose is to eradicate defects which hinder the church's mission. It is not concerned with recording progress or good behaviour and is therefore not a substitute for a comprehensive survey of the church in any given period. We must be cautious, then, in using this legislation, either as evidence for evils to be remedied or in witness of remedies effected, and must check our findings against more concrete testimony from other sources. Consequently, it would be rash to seek, by these statutes alone, either to conclude immediately to the widespread existence of the abuses they condemn or to infer that everywhere these were being effectively righted. This elementary principle for the student of ecclesiastical legislation is only too often overlooked by our historians.

The bishops of Scotland had to face a situation common to all Europe, and all the provincial councils of this turbulent age follow the same broad pattern and adopt the same technique. Three important issues were before them to be considered and resolved. The *mal du siècle* was undoubtedly the moral laxity of the clergy, which called for immediate remedy, while the laity—from whom or to whom the disease had spread—were in need of systematic instruction to dispel ignorance of the teaching of the church. Lastly, since no one in those days reckoned on more than one true church, that institution was for men as important as the civil authority, for it represented God in the community and was intimately bound into the social system of the day. The church was seen not only as the dispenser of grace but as an owner of property, an endowed institution, where human elements were likely to predominate and where administration was consequently open to abuse. On this side the church was singularly vulnerable and easily discredited by her enemies. New regulations had now to be made to ensure that the church, as a spiritual force, was unhampered by her necessary commitments as an economic

---

1. "Be not unmindful of thy stricken spouse."

entity in society. These three considerations form the basis of all the councils in sixteenth-century Scotland, and it is mainly with these that we are presently concerned. Instead of giving a general conspectus of each item over the last decade before 1560, we have chosen to deal with them all in their proper setting and as they arose in the various councils, for each of these meetings possesses historical features of its own and is for that reason best treated separately. None the less will we observe that the movement for reform from within is one continuous forward action repelled at the last by twin forces from without, lack of time and a powerful minority of antagonists.

The legislative assembly of a bishop and his clergy is a synod, and a council is a meeting, for a like purpose, of two or more bishops. The council is provincial when its membership is restricted to the bishops of an ecclesiastical province, and is national, or plenary, should all the bishops of a nation take part. These episcopal gatherings are empowered to legislate on matters of ecclesiastical discipline but have no power to define doctrine. The latter is possible only at a general council of the whole church under the presidency of the pope, or by the pope himself. Decisions of a provincial council are applied in the whole province, for the legislators are the bench of bishops and not the metropolitan alone, but it is the metropolitan alone who has the right to convoke such a meeting.[2] The first law on provincial councils enjoins that they are to be held twice in the year:[3] but although this regulation was insisted on not a little, by the sixth century we find several canons prescribing an annual meeting of bishops.[4] This law was confirmed at the Fourth Lateran Council,[5] but proved too exacting, and Martin V preferred to give his approbation to a canon of the Council of Constance, which recommended triennial conferences of bishops. This was later incorporated into Session X of the Fifth General Council of the Lateran by Leo X in 1515 and remained in force till Trent. Needless to say, there was nothing to hinder bishops from meeting more frequently if they were so inclined.

It was not until 1472, less than a century before the church was disestablished, that Scotland could boast of a metropolitan, and until that time no bishop had the authority to convoke a provincial council, although provincial or national councils were held in virtue of a papal brief of 1225, which legislated for this defect.[6] Under the arrangement, the Scottish bishops presided in turn at their meetings. Near the end of the fifteenth century, St. Andrews became a metropolitan see with the rest of the dioceses as suffragans,[7] and the status of that bishopric was further enhanced when it received primatial and legatine powers in 1487.[8] From then on the canonist has to tread warily through a maze of exemptions and counter-exemptions as the rival see of Glasgow struggles to free itself from the jurisdiction of St. Andrews. Inevitably, in 1492, Glasgow attained metropolitan rank also,[9] but never became a primatial see, while St. Andrews periodically achieved even greater ascendency

---

2. C.13, D.18.
3. C.2, D.18; c.6, D.18.
4. Cf.c.71. *Concil. Agath.* (506 A.D.); c.18 *Concil. Tolet.*, iii (589 A.D.).
5. C.25, X, *de Accusat.*, V, 1.
6. Robertson, *Statuta Ecclesiae Scoticanae*, ii, p. 3.
7. Theiner, *Vetera Momumenta*, pp. 465-468.
8. Robertson, *op. cit.*, i, pp. cxviii-cxix.
9. *Glasgow*, ii, pp. 470-473; 543-544.

through its archbishop being possessed of the powers of a legate *a latere*. Two types of ecclesiastical council were thus possible in Scotland, a provincial one of either Glasgow or St. Andrews, and a national assembly of all the bishops in the country under the presidency of the primate. To determine who were obliged to attend a national council at a given time, we must take into account the exemption from primatial authority enjoyed from time to time by Glasgow and, at the same time, make certain that this was not cancelled out by the pre-eminent powers of a legate *a latere* in St. Andrews.[10] Unfortunately, many of the Scottish conciliar records of this period have disappeared, but those which have been preserved indicate the custom of holding general provincial councils, that is, national councils, in preference to councils of individual provinces. There is no record of any individual provincial meeting. James Beaton of St. Andrews convoked the first national council of the sixteenth century when he summoned the other bishops in 1536 to discuss the imposition of a clerical tax for James V's College of Justice.[11] Meetings on a national scale were also held in 1543 to raise money for war with England and, in 1546, to meet the expenses of the Scottish bishops who intended to travel to Trent.[12] Although there was also a meeting in 1547, the first council of which we have any acts is that of 1549. Records also exist for the subsequent assemblies of 1552 and 1559 but not for that of 1556. Most of our information, therefore, comes from the councils of 1549, 1552 and, the last one to be held, that of 1559. We have no official minutes of any of the meetings, although for an adequate treatment of any council these are absolutely essential, for they contain the preliminary discussions of the assembly and very often provide the key to the correct interpretation of the statutes.

The Scottish church was in a perilous condition, spiritually and materially, as the sixteenth century approached middle-age, for not only was the whole of Europe in religious turmoil but, nearer home, Henry VIII had abjured the authority of Rome and was doing his best to encourage James V to do the same. Scotland had by then assumed the role of an isolated northern stronghold of catholicism but she was in no fit state to play the part. The innovations of the continental reformers were percolating into the country and finding inevitable acceptance from a few, in spite of an act of parliament which had forbidden the importation of Lutheran literature as far back as 1525. James V was a catholic sovereign, with a clear notion of the disturbing effects a change in the established religion would have on the nation, and like most monarchs of his day he said his prayers and went to mass and the sacraments, but used the church for his own ends, whenever he could, with a selfish disregard for her spiritual mission. For this attitude of mind the bishops must shoulder much of the responsibility, for they had become so secular in their ministry that abuses were allowed to spread unchallenged and suffered to become almost accepted behaviour. To the nobles, the advantages of an ecclesiastical collapse were indeed alluring, for the church possessed much that made her an object of envy, and by the time of Solway Moss, many of the

---

10. The Archbishop of Glasgow was not bound to attend the council of 1547, but was subject to St. Andrews in 1549 and 1552. Although again exempt in 1559, Glasgow was subject to the primate's powers as legate *a latere* and bound to attend. In 1545, Cardinal Beaton summoned Gavin Dunbar, Archbishop of Glasgow, to a national council in virtue of a brief of Paul III, for the exemption which Dunbar had obtained applied even to the powers of a legate *a latere* (cf. Robertson, i, app. xxi).

11. *Ibid.*, app. xvi.

12. *Ibid.*, app. xviii; app. xxi. It was quite common in those days for the crown to call a general convention of the clergy (cf. Wernz-Vidal, *Ius Canonicum*, ii, par. 535).

nobles, not traditionally a pious lot, were already adherents of the reformation doctrines, while James's relations with the more powerful nobility did nothing to encourage the church's attempts to fortify herself against that class. If the Auld Kirk was to survive, she had to save herself, for there were too many vested interests at stake for her to rely on monarch or noble. What she needed was a dose of disciplinary reform from within, not only in Scotland but everywhere in Europe. The dawn of that reform was breaking when, after years of frustrated endeavour to stir up even the will to reform, the pope announced the opening of a general council of the church at Trent in 1545. That event alone was a tremendous boost for the drooping morale of the Scottish church, for in any council her prelates convoked they would have a plan of action already thrashed out for them at Trent.

As far back as 1530 James V had information about the proposed general council and a second intimation was made to him in 1537, when he was in Paris for his marriage to Madeleine. To the papal messengers, James promised that he would do all he could to see that his prelates attended the council.[13] The fact is that no Scottish bishop ever did attend any of the deliberations of the council of Trent, although it seems fairly certain that they did intend at least to be represented, for Cardinal Beaton called a special meeting of the clergy at Edinburgh in 1546 for the specific purpose of raising a clerical tax to defray the expenses of Scotland's representatives at the council.[14] At least on three occasions he himself had been cited by Rome to attend, but he pleaded, and with some justification, the necessity of remaining at his post in Scotland.[15] While we cannot altogether excuse the Scottish bishops for not attending the general council, it would be unfair to attribute their absence to complete indifference, for we have Beaton complaining bitterly at that time that all routes to the continent were virtually closed by the English.[16] Moreover, six months after Trent opened, the cardinal was dead. The extent of the loss the church sustained by Beaton's death would be difficult to exaggerate, for not only was he the ecclesiastical leader of the country, but his influence on the management of state affairs can be gauged by the turn of events following his death. A further ten years of his forceful rule might have averted disaster. As it was, his death made a change in church policy inevitable. The cardinal, in spite of his notorious personal moral failings, was not unconcerned with reform from within: it was at one of his provincial councils that efforts were made to secure theological preaching by providing theologians to suitable benefices. His murder underlined the fact that the church as a spiritual institution must be salvaged in the first instance by spiritual means. Beaton's main policy seems to have been to save the church by saving the country: now there was no alternative to the policy of putting first things first. Unfortunately, any strategy seemed doomed to failure in the chaotic state of the country. Even Beaton's statesmanship had been unable to prevent James V increasing the royal hold on ecclesiastical livings, nor had he personally been a shining light in apportioning these benefices always to worthy candidates. But the disordered state of government after his death, and

---

13. *Concilium Tridentinum, Diariorum Actorum, Epistolarum, Tractatuum Nova Collectio,* iv, pp. xlix & 105.
14. Robertson, *op. cit.,* i, app. xxi–xxii.
15. In 1541, 1542 and 1544. Cf. Theiner, *op. cit.,* pp. 613–614. Beaton was chancellor of the realm at the time.
16. Pollen, *Papal Negotiations,* p. xviii.

the absence of a strong defender of the rights of haly kirk, made the church impotent. Even if she did condemn abuses like abbacies given *in commendam,* what hope had she of effective remedy when those who wielded the only power of redress, the secular arm, coveted the church livings? Moreover, the fact that the metropolitan see was, if not vacant, at least not peaceably possessed for so long after the cardinal's death, did not augur well for the reform of ecclesiastical discipline.

The popular choice for the vacant archbishopric was John Hamilton, bishop of Dunkeld and brother of the Regent Arran. Although Hamilton was not of the same mould or personality as Beaton, there are signs that he was selected for St. Andrews because of his influence over his brother, the regent. In a letter to Paul III, dated 1547, some of the Scottish prelates request Hamiltons' appointment on the grounds that not only is he " . . . *virum doctum, constantem, orthodoxe pietatis studiosum* . . . " but he is well able to manage his brother the regent, and they cite an instance of this in which the bishop was able to win Arran back from some rather heretical leanings.[17] The letter is signed by Gavin Dunbar, archbishop of Glasgow, John of Dunkeld himself and two abbots, Donald of Coupar and Alexander of Cambuskenneth. A similar letter from the nobles, written four days later, was also despatched to Rome.[18] Nothing much had been effected by the church's reform measures and already, by 1547, there is a note of exasperation on the part of some of the clergy, who had held a meeting in Edinburgh under the presidency of Hamilton.[19] As a result of their discussions, John Steinson, provost of the collegiate church of Biggar, wrote on their behalf to the pope, Paul III, to seek his support in their efforts to speed up reform of discipline. From Steinson we learn that it was Beaton who had begun the reform of preaching and instruction in his legislation of 1546, months before Trent issued a very similar instruction at its fifth session. The clergy regret that, so far, many have not accepted these measures and they demand observance of the law in such a way that those who fail to carry out their duties of teaching or preaching should forfeit that day's salary to the church which pays it, and go on to recommend that where there are no vacant livings for professors of theology or preachers, the revenues which are available should be applied to the education of young men or for training teachers of theology. The tone of the letter is even more sternly realistic when it points out that, the greater the authority behind this movement for better ways, the greater will be its acceptance and calls upon the pope to lend his support to their cause by asserting his personal authority with the two archbishops, the abbot of Newbattle and president of the College of Justice, and demanding from them steps to implement the new statute.[20] This may have been the reason for Paul deciding about that time to send a legate to Scotland in the person of Pietro Lippomanno, although the legate did not leave on his mission until 1548.[21] There can be no doubt that he was sowing the seeds of goodwill so necessary before any council could set about effective reform, and there is every reason to believe that it was to Scotland's best interests, even politically, to give the pope

---

17. The letter is dated December 19th, 1546; that is, 1547, by our present reckoning. *Royal Letter Book* (Blairs Archives), p. 106.
18. The date is given as December 23rd of the same year. *Ibid.,* pp. 120-121. Both letters were given at St. Andrews.
19. Robertson cites a meeting of prelates and nobles held about the same time (March 18th, 1547) at which the bishop of Dunkeld seems to have presided (Cf. *op. cit.,* i, p. cxlvi, footnote).
20. *Royal Letter Book,* pp. 104-106. Given at Edinburgh on March 29th, 1547.
21. G. Buschbell, *Concilii Tridentini Epistolarum,* i, p. 803.

do de effectu misericordiæ dei: in præsenti, & de effectu diuini iudicii in futuro, & est sensus, quantò misericordia maior alicui in præsenti impenditur, tantò si ingratus fuerit, grauius in futuro punietur. ¶Nota quod ex quo misericordia superexaltat iudicium, & maior est curia misericordiæ quàm iustitiæ: sicut à minori curia licitum est appellare ad maiorem, ita à ri curia iustitiæ ad curiam misericordiæ Misericordia primo peccata purgat, Prouerb.15, Per misericordiam & fide purgantur peccata. Secundò poenam peccatorum relaxat, Daniel.4. Peccata tua eleemosynis redime, & iniquitates tuas misericordiis pauperum. Tertio custodit à malo, Prouerb. 20, Misericordia & veritas custodiunt regem. Quarto abundare facit in bono, Prouerb. 14, Misericordia & veritas præparauit bona. Quinto hominum benedictionem meretur, Prouerb.22, Qui pronus est ad misericordiam, benedicetur. Sexto dei misericordiam consequitur Matth.5, Beati misericordes, Septimo euadit iudicium, vt hic, Superexaltat misericordia iudicium. Octauo introducit in cælu, Eccle.16, Omnis misericordiæ faciet locum vnicuique secundum meritu suu.

Quid proderit fratres mei si fidem quis dicat se habere, opera autè non habeat ? Nunquid poterit fides saluare eum ? si autem frater & so-

versus misericordiæ dei operibus

Nota

Nota

CONCOR-
DANTIAE BREVIORES
OMNIVM FERME MATERIARVM
ex Sacris Bibliorum libris, non solùm diuini verbi concionatoribus, verumetiam studiosis omnibus summopere vtiles ac necessariæ, Per
V.P. Antonium Konygsteyn, Minoritam,

Ab authore iam postremùm recognitæ, & locupletitæ.

PARISIIS,
Apud Ioannem de Roigny, in via Iacobæa, sub insigni quatuor elementorum.
1551.
Si deus pro nobis quis contra nos?
Rom. 8.31.

PLATE XXVII. PUBLICISTS OF THE OLD ORDER.

PLATE XXVIII. THE SACRAMENT HOUSE AT DESKFORD, BANFFSHIRE.

some sign of confidence in the laws recently issued at Trent. Some success attended the clergy's resolutions, for we have a record of William Gordon, bishop of Aberdeen, appointing, in July of that year, one Master John Watson, a licentiate of theology, to give theological instruction twice a week in the cathedral and to preach there once a month, as well as once in the year in every church attached to the cathedral chapter. This is in terms of a statute passed at a previous provincial council and also prescribed by the Council of Trent and further resolved at a Lenten meeting of clergy in Edinburgh in 1547.[22] The reference to a provincial council would seem to indicate that one held by the late cardinal, while the Edinburgh meeting is obviously the one which was in touch with Rome, and which carried added weight through the recent Tridentine decree which was not in existence when Beaton held his council.

After his enthronement in July, 1549, Archbishop Hamilton lost no time in convening a plenary council at Linlithgow for August of that year. The greatest influence at this council came, as was to be expected, from Trent, which initiated the counter-reformation and which was destined in time to save the church. The bull of convocation was issued by Paul III in May, 1542, although the first session was not held until December, 1545. From that time, until June, 1547, the general council was more or less continuously in session. Then it was prorogued and not reconvened till May, 1551, when the eleventh session opened, but it had only been sitting a few months when, in April of the following year, it was once more prorogued and did not meet again until 1562 under Paul IV. By that time, the church in Scotland had been disestablished and any influence from Trent must therefore come from the first sixteen sessions. The mere convoking of the council had a tonic effect on the church in Europe, even before the canons were solemnly confirmed by the pope. All serious-minded catholics had long realised that only a general council could effectively answer the heretics. It ultimately managed to save the Latin countries for the church but, for most of northern Europe, it was already too late.

The interest of Scots ecclesiastics in continental conciliar legislation is well evidenced from their books, as listed in a recent number of the *Innes Review*.[23] Gavin Dunbar, archbishop of Glasgow, had the decrees of the French council held at Sens in 1528: others had copies of the statutes of the German councils of Mainz and Cologne, and copies of printed *Concilia* were bought up. John Grierson, for instance, had a copy of Carranza's edition of 1550, which included the first decrees of Trent, and as Dominican provincial and professor of theology, he was an influential figure at the provincial councils; his annotated copy of Carranza is now at St. Peter's College, Cardross. The Scots were also abreast of continental controversial theology, for many of those present at the first council of this final decade had, in their libraries, copies of the latest theological works, issued in defence of the church and dealing *ex professo* with the prevalent heresies.

Although none of her bishops attended the general council, Scotland's interests were well represented there, albeit unofficially, by a Scot,

---

22. He is to have a seat and vote in the chapter and succeed to the prebend of Cruden which has been assigned to his office (*Aberdeen*, ii, pp. 317-320).

23. *Innes Review*, ix, *passim.*

Robert Wauchope, archbishop of Armagh.[24] It is to Scotland's credit that this son of hers played a leading part in most of Trent's affairs, heading the committee of theologians which drew up the famous decree on justification at the sixth session. On more than one occasion, Wauchope spoke on Scottish affairs,[25] and it is clear that he had a great deal to do with the prompt transmission of the council's decrees to his native country. When the council was prorogued in 1547, in spite of Wauchope's request to continue discussion, its decisions were printed under the supervision of one of the papal legates, Cervini, the future Pope Marcellus II, who ordered a copy of them to be sent to Wauchope in 1549,[26] and we know that by the end of that year these were used extensively in the Scottish provincial council. Armed with this knowledge of current ecclesiastical trends, the Scots clergy were well equipped to promulgate some much needed legislation when they met in the national council of 1549.[27]

" For the reformation of morals in the Church of Scotland, and for the extirpation of heresyes," so runs the preamble to the decrees, which confesses with frank realism that " whereas there appear to have been mainly two causes and roots of evil which have stirred up among us such great discussions and occasions of heresyes, namely, the corruption of morals and the profane lewdness of life of ecclesiastics of almost every rank, together with the crass ignorance of literature and of the liberal arts, and principally from these two sources many abuses arise, this holy synod and provincial council has determined to apply remedies and check these evils as far as the exigency of the times will permit."[28] Having apportioned the guilt, the bishops proceed with the principal task of correcting the clergy, by introducing a long statute condemning concubinage, which has been taken straight from the council of Basle,[29] and which is followed by another law forbidding the clergy to support their offspring, either by keeping them in their homes, promoting them to their benefices or endowing them at marriage with church revenues.[30] Continuing the reform of the clergy, the council lists several items from which they are barred, such as trading, dressing as laymen and growing beards, and counsels them to live temperately in all things, especially with regard to food and drink, and to keep their domestic staff in order.[31] These laws are evidently based on the council of Trent's rules, laid down at the opening session " concerning the manner of living and matters to be observed during the council." Religious, too, are subject to the rules of the council and the bishop is to visit the various non-exempt monasteries

---

24. Scottish affairs are mentioned at Trent which shows that some kind of contact was possible (*Con. Trid.*, i, pp. 347; 510; 821. Cf. also Dr. Durkan's article " Robert Wauchope, Archbishop of Armagh ", *Innes Review*, i, pp. 48-65).

25. Hefele-Leclercq, *Histoire des Conciles*, x, i, p. 73.

26. Buschbell, *op. cit.*, ii, p. 483.

27. The council first met at Linlithgow in August, 1549, but was apparently adjourned and met again in Edinburgh in November of that year.

28. What these broad phrases in practice mean is a matter for historians to decide (Robertson, *op. cit.*, ii, p. 81).

29. This decree was quoted in many lawful provincial councils on the continent, e.g., the provincial council of Salzburg (1490), and was eventually accepted by Leo X in 1516, who inserted it in session xi of the Fifth Council of the Lateran. One would imagine that the Scottish council would have cited the Fifth Lateran rather than Basle, although in the various editions of *Concilia* in the sixteenth century it is the Basle decree that is given.

30. No. 174. From now on the canons of the Scottish councils will be cited according to their enumeration by Robertson in his *Statuta*, ii. The numbering begins with a document of the thirteenth century and ends with the last act of the 1559 council.

31. Nos. 175-181.

in his diocese and remedy abuses, while the exempt clergy, still outwith the bishop's authority, will be observed also as closely as possible.[32]

In her fifth session on reformation, Trent discussed the low state of theological learning and instruction of the people which, along with the moral laxity of the churchman, were at the root of all the trouble. Edinburgh now leans heavily on this Tridentine support and canons 188 to 194 are word for word with chapters one and two of the fifth session on reform. John Steinson's astute remark, " *duplata cautio . . . non parum momenti* ", is surely the reason behind this obvious repetition, for the Scottish bishops are not content with citing Trent, they also frame their own laws from its context, thereby strengthening their own authority. Trent traced the source of neglected instruction to lack of interest in and knowledge of doctrine. Livings that were originally meant for teachers of theology were mostly occupied by clerics unable to discharge this office. From now on, these benefices must be given only to those capable of the duties, at least through a competent substitute. In cathedrals and other churches where the clergy are numerous, but where there is no benefice reserved for a preacher, the first one that falls vacant (except through resignation) must be allocated to the theologian and, even if this cannot be done, a simple benefice should be erected or the teacher supported from contributions of the other beneficed clergy. In places where the revenues are small or the clergy few, at least a teacher of grammar is to be engaged for young clerics or other poor scholars so that in time these youths may advance to the study of the sacred sciences; at the same time, lectures in doctrine should be given in the grammar schools. The monasteries are to follow suit and provide for a teacher of scripture and the bishops are to see that this is observed by the religious superiors.[33] The primary duty of a bishop is to preach the word of God personally or, if legitimately hindered, to see that others do it for him.[34] So Trent opens her law on preaching. Archpriests (i.e., deans of Christianity) and all others with the care of souls are to preach, on Sundays and solemn feasts, on faith and morals, under threat of censure, if they are foolish enough to neglect this duty for three months. The same applies in monastery churches. From all these decisions, dutifully accepted, Scotland fashions her own additional rules; not only must there be a theologian in every cathedral church but a canonist is also prescribed. The teacher of doctrine will lecture at least once a week and preach in various churches in the presence, if possible, of the bishop and the chapter. Likewise, the canonist must lecture before the canons and clergy of the city.[35] The first livings to fall vacant shall be assigned to these specialists and they shall take up duties by the following Michaelmas (Sept. 29th). If by that time they still have no benefice, the bishop must support them at his own expense.[36] Every monastery shall have a doctrine teacher also, who will lecture and preach in the church.[37] Bishops are let off lightly in 1549 with personal preaching four times a year at the minimum.[38] The same rule applies

---

32. No. 182.
33. Session V, c.1, *de ref.*
34. Session V, c.2, *de ref.*
35. No. 196. The appointment of a canonist is not mentioned by Trent.
36. *Ibid.* Later the council drew up a list of thirty-five benefices, one for each diocese and one each for many of the monasteries. Monasteries without a preaching benefice must give a salary to the preacher: cf. No. 219.
37. No. 197.
38. No. 195. The rubric of this canon is that rectors and bishops are to preach personally four times in the year, but no mention of bishops is made in the body of the statute.

to rectors of parish churches, but vicars and all others in charge of souls are to preach every Sunday and, if possible, on the other greater feasts.[39] If the rector is too young, too old, or otherwise incapable of preaching personally, he is to provide himself with a competent substitute, with this difference, that the young must study to achieve competence, but the elderly must be present at his substitute's sermons.[40]

All preachers will observe a certain order in their discourses: they will begin with an exposition of the epistle and gospel and allot the second half of their time to a short instruction on the rudiments of the faith and the commandments.[41] As for the professors, some are to expound the catholic sense of the scripture, while others, at different times, are to lecture on doctrine from the inspired books, taking as their guides in speculative theology the authors approved by the church, such as Peter Lombard, St. Thomas Aquinas, St. Bonaventure and others. This is the scheme to be followed in universities and in cathedrals.[42] Provision for future specialists in the monasteries is made by ordering members of the more important communities to attend the universities for degrees in theology and scripture, and in this connexion the council actually specifies the number to be sent from the various monasteries.[43]

Without a lead from Trent on the spiritual formation of aspirants to the priesthood, the Scottish canons fall short of anything effective on this important problem, for the general council did not consider this in detail until many years later.[44] The only canon from Edinburgh, dealing with qualifications for orders, is couched in terms too general to be of any consequence, except to indicate that the bishops were conscious of defects in the system.[45] They merely refer to the sacred canons and insist on material provision in the shape of livings. On the other hand, for those already with the care of souls, promotion to benefices is now subject to rigid examination and selection by the ordinary.[46] The vital everyday life of the church, which lay in the administration of the sacraments, the saying of mass and the general spiritual care of the people, was severely handicapped by the conferring of livings on the unworthy and incompetent, and practically everyone of any influence in the country, by canvassing for benefices for his favourites, was responsible for this disastrous practice. Edinburgh is scathing in its denunciation of those who use their position to intrude unsuitable candidates into church livings without a thought for their true purpose and, in addition, it demands proper maintenance for the underpaid vicar pensioners.[47] Absenteeism and the holding of incompatible benefices, both direct consequences of the present iniquitous system of presentation, are proscribed in the words of the third

---

39. *Ibid.* There is a slight discrepancy between the wording of this canon and that of No. 192 which is taken verbatim from Trent: the latter says that " archpriests, curates and all those in places which have care of souls are bound to preach at least on Sundays and solemn feasts," whereas No. 195 relaxes that rule with the words " . . . on every Lord's Day and possibly (*forsan*) on the other greater feasts."

40. *Ibid.*

41. No. 199. The canon calls this " catechism " and says this term means public teaching or instruction: " a short instruction in the rudiments of the faith or an exposition of the articles of the creed, the precepts of the decalogue, the seven deadly sins, the seven sacraments of the church, the Lord's prayer, and the Hail Mary, and the works of mercy."

42. No. 200.

43. No. 198.

44. Session XXIII, *de ref.* (1563).

45. No. 202.

46. Nos. 203; 205.

47. No. 206. Canon 204 directs ordinaries to examine vicars-pensioners and enquire into their fitness from their parishioners.

and fourth chapters of Trent's seventh session on reformation,[48] and the canons on pluralities, annexed benefices and the repair and visitation of churches are likewise borrowed from the general council's decisions.[49] The bishops at this point expressly record their intention of using the canons of Trent as their guide; " the convention or council avails itself of the ordinances that have or shall be made by the Council of Trent, which has not yet been dissolved."[50]

Only when the church itself is healthy can it hope to subdue heresy and here the bishops' plan of campaign is well-conceived. To detect those amongst the clergy who are preaching erroneous doctrines, they establish a group of investigators in each diocese.[51] The court of enquiry is to consist of men of " piety, integrity and learning, experts in theology, of good life, name and of great tact ", for it is recognised that no good will come of extremist measures, which would only serve to alienate those already misled by the novel opinions. Heretical books, published without ecclesiastical approval purposely to destroy the faith, are banned and search is to be made for them. These general investigations are to take place four times in the year, and, when necessity so demands, special enquiries are to be made according to the norms of canon law. Those found preaching heresy will be excommunicated and the like penalty is threatened against those who listen to them.[52] Somewhat pathetically, but in accordance with long-established custom, the council seeks the assistance of the civil authorities in putting down heresy.

In an exhortation addressed primarily by the episcopal lawmakers to themselves, bad example is branded as the ally of error and the bishops seek " to reform their life and morals to better purpose . . . since from this cause arise the greatest scandal to the laity, and the largest proportion of the heresy."[53] It would be difficult to find a more uncompromising confession of guilt. Having put their own souls in order, the bishops are to see that " the Word of God is expounded to their flocks, purely, sincerely and in a catholic sense."[54] The preacher, then, is in the van of the attack and he is to be received with kindly hospitality in the parishes he visits. Books are to be kept in which those who have the care of souls, will note the number of times religious have preached for rectors and vicars, while sermons are to be arranged well in advance to give the people timely notice and ensure a good congregation.[55] A number of articles are drawn up so that the sermons will deal especially with the doctrines then impugned.[56]

In our third category of abuses calling for reform, we link two facets of ecclesiastical activity, the administration of property and the courts of law. The church, as an endowed institution, had titles to ownership as lawful and as ancient as those of the crown. From these endowments,

---

48. Nos. 204; 207; 208; 209.
49. Nos. 207; 208; 209; 216.
50. No. 216.
51. No. 220.
52. No. 221.
53. No. 222.
54. No. 223.
55. No. 224.
56. No. 225. The articles are (1) The mass; sacraments; ceremonies, rites and observances. (2) Church censures. (3) The immortality of the soul. (4) Good works. (5) Purgatory. (6) Prayer and the intercession of the saints. (7) Images. (8) The authority of a general council of the church. (9) Feasts and fasts.

her clergy, secular and regular, drew their livelihood and contributed in no small measure to the economy of the country by working the land, sheep farming, cattle raising, and by meeting the huge tax payments, which were levied on the church in emergencies. Many of these taxes were exacted for some particular project, such as James V's College of Justice, or to meet the expenses of war or the demands of some other national crisis. This meant that the church had to secure ready cash to hand over to the crown, and that could only be done by leasing out church property to nobles who were able to supply the necessary money. One of the most popular means of alienating ecclesiastical goods was *emphyteusis*, which was normally a lease of uncultivated land, granted either in perpetuity or for a long time, on condition that the land was worked and in return for an annual rent or a down payment of a lump sum. Usually the grantee had the right to transfer the contract to others or make it heritable, and the grantor gave a guarantee never to re-acquire possession of the land as long as the rent was being paid or some other suitable arrangement was made. It can be readily seen what detriment this type of contract could cause the church and, although a just reason for entering into such an agreement was always required by canon law, there was no lack of good reasons if one looked for them. Urgent necessity or the evident utility of the church could be read into any crown project or national emergency, to say nothing of the church having to raise money for some purpose of her own. With so many lay influences and acquired rights, it is not surprising that large tracts of church land ceased to be her property, except nominally. It was no longer in many instances administered by ecclesiastics, and consequently any good influence that they may have had on tenants was lost. This applied more so to the monasteries which had done so much for the lower classes. Tithes, the recognised method of church collections, also became negotiable and were leased for a sum of money in a manner reminiscent of the Jewish taxgatherers, and no less obnoxious. Gradually both church lands and teinds drifted farther and farther away from their real owners and, even worse, from their true purpose, as ecclesiastics disengaged themselves from all apparent connexion with them.

The bishops of Scotland, like most of the bishops in Europe at this time, tried to put an end to this damaging practice by forbidding the long lease of glebes, church lands, rectories or vicarages, except for very good reasons approved by the bishops, and not merely for the advantage of private individuals.[57] The leasing of the tithes of important benefices also came under this prohibition.[58]

Although the administration of justice in the church courts was still good and better than anything the civil authorities had to offer, there were many items of procedure open to corruption. In particular, a general speeding up of cases was demanded, for delays spelt further expense for the litigants and some procurators were not above resorting to trifling exceptions, calculated to hold up proceedings, and even to downright unjust practices and exploitation of contestants for mere financial gain. Several statutes of 1549 specify the underhand methods employed. Notaries are to undergo examination by their ordinaries to prove their competence.[59] Procurators are warned not to undertake

---

57. No. 187.
58. These leases are null and void even if made by a bishop or chapter.
59. No. 214.

cases which have no legal basis and must be in complete command of all the facts before accepting an action for the courts.[60] They are not to maintain unjust actions or bring forward irrelevant arguments.[61] Procedure in certain actions is laid down in detail to avoid useless delay and lengthy transactions.[62]

The decisions of this council covered a wide field and at least touched on the evils that were sapping the church of her strength, but they were very clearly only a beginning. No prudent ecclesiastic could have left the council chamber persuaded that the church's troubles were over as a result of the new legislation. The real testing time would come when the bishops enforced the decrees in their own dioceses and the clergy's attitude to their policy became apparent. At best, men could only wait and see. They would not have long to wait for the last decision the council took was to meet again the following year. There is no record of any council in 1550 and it is not until 1552 that the prelates reassemble in the capital for a national council. Everything points to a brief meeting. Nothing is to be gained from a multiplication of precepts which might look well on paper. Rather the policy must be to consolidate what has already been achieved by the earlier directives and to close the ranks for a scrupulous inspection of the situation. Apart from a few important introductions, the bishops confine their discussions to a review of the church's condition. It was far from encouraging, for, on no fewer than four essential issues, the council complains that the previous decrees have as yet not become effective. Just how unsuccessful these laws have been is impossible to say, for we have no means of knowing the extent of their observance. All we can maintain with accuracy is that they were not being obeyed everywhere. The council's survey of the national scene was bound to bring to light many pockets of resistance to reform which could only be broken down by patient endeavour and a show of strength. Neither can we doubt that much of this frustration was caused by weakness in the episcopate, and this seemingly insurmountable obstacle was not to be overcome within a couple of years. The " troublous times and manifold embarrassments ",[63] blamed for the disregard of the decrees, are vague enough to include treason within the camp, as well as opposition from without. The first three canons of this council, in fact, lament the non-observance of decisions which directly concern the bishops. They are accused, along with the rectors of churches, of not obeying the injunction to preach personally at least four times in the year.[64] Some of them at least have not provided their cathedrals with a theologian and canonist, nor seen to it that the monasteries have their theologians and their undergraduates,[65] nor has the proposed examination of curates and vicars been universally enforced.[66] A last warning is issued on all three points and a date fixed by which they must be observed. Even the canon deploring the habit of bringing in a verdict on marriage cases without previous consultation with the bishop, whose exclusive right it is to issue

---

60. No. 228.
61. Nos. 229; 230.
62. No. 236.
63. No. 239.
64. No. 240.
65. No. 241.
66. No. 242.

a decree, is aimed directly at those ordinaries who have allowed this practice to flourish.[67]

The logical consequence of disregard for lawful authority is contempt for its coercive element, namely punishment, which is always despised in an age of anarchy and revolution. The censures of the church fell under this same shadow in the sixteenth century and excommunication, the most feared of all judgments, was mocked the most, precisely because it was so dreaded. To restore some of its effect, the council orders the publication of the names of the excommunicate in the church[68] or public places until they have sought absolution.[69] Moreover, it emphasises that those under this censure should be shunned by the faithful. This was especially important at a time when so many enemies of the church were determined to contaminate their neighbours and sow seeds of doubt and heresy in their minds. Particularly was this true of the cities and townships where already the faith had become weak and " very few indeed out of the most popular parishes deign to be present at the sacrifice of the Holy Mass . . . or to attend the preaching of God's Word." These are the words of a decision ordering mass missers to be noted and investigated at visitation times.[70] Another product of the age was the clandestine marriage, that constant threat to public morality and order which always thrives in an unhealthy society. Condemnations of these secret unions are inevitably found in all the contemporary European councils and more than one form was troubling Scotland. Priests who officiate at them are to be punished with imprisonment and bread and water for a year as well as suspension from the exercise of their orders for three years, and the contracting parties are to be subject to public penances.[71]

In spite of the 1549 decrees on alienation of property, the council has to admit that unlawful leasing has reduced many a parish and its clergy to utter destitution, and even finds it necessary to forbid the leasing of the manses and adjoining crofts. The tone of the law is so stringent that one cannot doubt but that this wholesale spoliation had not been checked by the previous legislation.[72]

The council of 1552 is best remembered for its introduction of the catechism as a complement to the systematic instruction already ordered. Announcing this new medium, the council strikes an unusually optimistic note, " and reflecting meanwhile, how many frightful heresies have, within the last few years, run riot in many diverse parts of this realm, but have now at last been checked by the providence of the all-good and Almighty God, the singular goodwill of princes, and the vigilance and zeal of prelates for the Catholic faith, and seem almost extinguished."[73] If the progress of the lords of the Congregation, some years later, is any indication of the popular trend, this optimism is not only reassuring but well-founded. The purveyors of heresy were many but they found scant

---

67. No. 244.
68. No. 247. Their names are to be kept in a register and read out every Sunday.
69. Nos. 248; 249. They are to be ostracized and their names put up for everyone to see if they remain longer than twenty days without repentance.
70. No. 245.
71. Nos. 251; 252. The former also directs priests to keep registers of banns and of baptisms. The second canon deals with the punishment of offenders. It is extremely severe and the penalties are based on the decree of Innocent III at the Fourth Council of the Lateran: c.3, X *de Cland. Desp.*, IV, 3. The bread and water punishment is a Scottish addition. Contracting parties will be punished with public penances at the discretion of the bishop.
72. No. 250.
73. No. 253.

acceptance amongst the Scots. Unlike so many of the continental councils of this period, we find no doctrinal condemnations of Lutheranism or Calvinism in the canons of Scottish councils, for the simple reason that the church in this country did not regard heresy as its most potent enemy. The sins of the Scottish church were sins of the flesh and not of the spirit. The catechism is described as " a plain and easy statement and explanation of the rudiments of the faith " and is to be published in the name of the primate and the national council. Copies will be distributed by the primate to the other ordinaries for transmission to the rest of their clergy, who will read—" beginning at the very preface or introduction and continuing to the very end of the book "—for half an hour before high mass on Sundays and holidays of obligation. The instructions for the proper reading of the text are so detailed that over the years they have been cited as incontestable evidence of clerical illiteracy; but allowing for the obvious defects of the times and the comparative newness of the printed word it is only to be expected that directives in elocution were necessary. The book has to be read through whole and entire with no allowances for personal taste or discrimination and with no commentaries. Those who transgress are to be fined and the deans are to make diligent enquiry about the use of the catechism.[74]

Another effective method of enforcing legislation was through the rural deans. These deans were delegates of the bishop and were responsible for clerical discipline within their deanery. One example of how the provincial statutes were promulgated to the clergy is given by Sir Hugh Curry, rector of Eassie and dean of christianity of Linlithgow, who summoned the curates of the district to the parish church for the statutory meeting on June 4th, 1555. After calling the roll and noting the absentees, Sir Hugh began to read, " in a loud, clear voice," the provincial synodal statutes for the year, with the most recent additional matter from the synods of St. Andrews. The curates are ordered to copy down statutes that particularly concern them and they are advised to produce copies at the next meeting to be held there on the third holyday after the feast of the Exaltation of the Holy Cross.[75]

There are no acts of the council held in 1556, but we may presume that they merely reiterated the earlier statutes. In the country at large, the position of the church had undoubtedly worsened. The disaffected nobles were gathering in strength and by 1557 they had finally persuaded Knox to abandon his neurotic peregrinations and throw in his lot with them. At the end of that year, the Congregation was officially established and their avowed aim was the overthrow of the ancient faith. Mary of Lorraine was in a compromising mood and was not prepared to alienate anyone. She took her policy from France and the Congregation theirs from England and, between them, they brought about the ruin of the church.

In the midst of this upheaval the church resolved on a last effort to stand firm by calling a national council for March, 1559. Opinions are divided as to when the last council opened and how long it lasted. To seek to resolve this problem would be merely a technical and speculative exercise were it not for the fact that a confusion of dates has been used to sustain a view for which there is no support in reality, namely, that

---

74. *Ibid.*
75. Cf. *The Scottish Historical Review*, xvii, p. 181.

Hamilton's summons to this Edinburgh meeting met with complete indifference from the majority of prelates. Officially, the initial proposal to hold a council came from the primate, Archbishop John Hamilton of St. Andrews. He announced his intention in a letter to the Archbishop of Glasgow, James Beaton, in which he summons the latter to participate.[76] Glasgow was at this time subject to St. Andrews in virtue of Hamilton's possessing the powers of a legate *a latere*. Had this additional authority not been wielded by the eastern metropolitan, Beaton would not have been subject to his jurisdiction for he had obtained perpetual exemption for Glasgow in 1552. In the primate's letter there is more than a hint to Beaton that the time has come for them to stand together under Hamilton's leadership, for he emphasises that the pope has bestowed this pre-eminent authority on him over the holy catholic kirk of Scotland, " or her prelates, ministers and peoples, whatever rights of exemption they may enjoy, and in what way soever they be distinguished," so that the church may triumph over her besetting troubles at a time " when Lutheranism, Calvinism and very many other nefarious heresies are being propagated everywhere in this realm." The primate directs Beaton to inform his suffragans and clergy and to be in Edinburgh for the opening of the council on March 1st, 1559. The only document we have of Beaton summoning his clergy is one dated March 18th, which speaks of " the council now begun,"[77] and six days later we find the vicar-general of the vacant see of Galloway directing his clergy to the council in terms of a letter from his metropolitan, Glasgow.[78] Both documents summon the clergy to Edinburgh on April 6th. Writers have erroneously implied that these two letters were peremptory orders to defaulters who did not appear in response to the appeal to be in Edinburgh for the opening on March 1st. In the first place, we have not sufficient evidence to support this argument, and a simpler explanation is not hard to find. A council such as this one would be very unlikely to last as long as six weeks, continuously meeting in plenary session. Indeed, having regard to the unsettled state of the country, it may have had to be adjourned more than once, either as a matter of policy or through necessity, in which case it would have been sufficient to have had a working committee of theologians and canonists to discuss and prepare outstanding questions for the next full meeting. The date, April 6th, would, therefore, seem to be the date of the re-opening of the plenary sessions. The council had certainly begun when these two letters were issued, for both make express mention of the council as " now begun". Beaton obviously sent two letters on the same day, March 18th, one to his suffragans and the other to his clergy who were to attend the council. The one which has come down to us was given at Edinburgh, which leads us to think that it was written at an adjournment of the council and when the date had already been settled for the re-opening. In Hamilton's letter to Beaton, the writer does not exclude the possibility of an adjournment or prorogation.[79] Even with the inevitable dislocation of ecclesiastical affairs at that time, it is ridiculous to assume that not one suffragan of Glasgow nor one abbot or secular priest obeyed Beaton's original summons to Edinburgh for March 1st.

---

76. No. 255.
77. No. 256: cf. phrasing of the heading.
78. No. 257.
79. The summons is to attend " even to the dissolution, close, end, or prorogation of the said general provincial council inclusively."

Yet this is the insinuation if we assume that these letters of Glasgow and Galloway, written in the second half of that month, were addressed to absentees, for Galloway says that his metropolitan issues the summons " to all and sundry, the ordinaries, his suffragans," and the terms of Beaton's letter to the clergy are equally universal, " to lawfully warn all and sundry, the abbots, priors, etc." Moreover, there is no doubt that many, if not all, of the suffragan bishops were at the opening of the council, for the official acts speak of " convoked and present the venerable lords, the suffragan bishops of both archbishops, also vicars general, abbots," and so on. All this would seem to imply, therefore, that there was at least one adjournment and that March 18th and April 6th are in some way connected with it, and that the letters from Glasgow and Galloway are summonses to a reconvoked meeting on April 6th, addressed to clerics who had no doubt been present at the earlier sessions of the council.

Several times in the course of the preceding decade the church had called for the assistance of the civil authorities in implementing her conciliar decisions, but political expediency or practical impotence had made effective help from that quarter a vain hope. On the other hand, the crown had demanded that the church set about reform of her discipline and this, too, had been thwarted by weak ecclesiastical control. The result was a vicious circle in which both institutions must shoulder the blame, with the heavier load of responsibility in the late fifties falling on the crown, for, by her acquired rights of nomination to bishoprics and other important benefices, she appeared unwilling to release her stranglehold on the church which ostensibly was by this time trying to put matters right. Yet in 1559 it is Mary of Lorraine who initiates the movement for a council.

The primate, in his decree of convocation, twice refers explicitly to the royal request for a council; " and being moved to the foresaid by the pious and gracious request of our most illustrious sovereign Lady, the Queen Regent, seeing, as she does, the exceedingly great and nefarious seditions which prevail among the people "; and again, " furthermore that, in terms of the pious and gracious request of our most illustrious sovereign lady, the Queen Regent." This request took the form of a memorandum drawn up by some of the catholic nobles and presented to the queen regent for transmission to the bishops. It is entitled "Articles proponit to the Quene Regent of Scotland be sum temporall Lordis and Barronis, and sent be hir Grace to the haill Prelatis and principallis of the clargie convenit in thair Provincial Counsall in Edinburgh."[80] The preface to the articles refers to the necessity of reform of discipline in the church and to the attempts already made to bring this about, " of the quhilkis nevertheless thar hes folowit nan or littil fruict as yitt, bot rathare the said Estate (clergy) is deteriorate, nor emends be ony sic persuasion as hes bene hidertills usit." Then follow twelve items of ecclesiastical import containing recommendations and suggesting improvements. Preaching should be the rule at mass in every parish kirk on Sundays and holydays, at least on every third or fourth Sunday and at Christmas, Easter and Whitsunday, with more preaching where it is required. Preachers ought to be examined on doctrine and general competence, while no curate or vicar should receive an appointment, who cannot

---

80. No. 258. The articles have been incorporated into the official acts of the council.

administer the sacraments properly and read the catechism. The lords suggest that exhortations be given before the administration of the sacraments so as to dispel ignorance of these means of grace. They see advantages in having the common prayers and litanies after mass and evening prayers in the vernacular. Stringent measures should be taken against those who foster irreverence against the Blessed Sacrament; the destruction of holy places and the corruption of the rites and ceremonial of the church are deplored. Easter teinds and mortuary fees in their current form are condemned because they are too much bound up with the reception of the sacraments, which are sometimes withheld if the dues are not paid. On the administrative side, benefices reserved to Rome are accounted harmful to the commonweal and this practice should be discontinued. Procedure in consistorial and other cases needs reform.

All of these suggestions embody orthodox catholic teaching and have obviously come from catholics anxious to save the church.[81] The putative authors are some nobles, but the tone of the articles and their doctrinal precision are distinctly clerical. We have already had evidence of an influential body of clerics in the country trying to force the bishops to act, and we do know that outside encouragement, such as came from Wauchope (then dead) and others, carried great weight with the episcopate. It might not be too rash to conjecture, then, that this memorandum was inspired by some such body of priests, who considered that their suggestions would be listened to more readily were they to come from the catholic nobles through the queen regent. It must have been a source of great satisfaction to the authors, whoever they were, to learn that the prelates adopted most of their recommendations.[82]

The text of the decrees of this last council before the reformation is superior to those of the preceding ones and a greater efficiency is unmistakable. The decrees of 1549, a hurried line of defence erected by a rudely awakened church, are recast into a more skilful counter attack, more cogent and less intransigent than before, and more practical. The opening act defines the competence of a provincial council as the correction of abuse, and looks forward to the day when Trent will " provide fitter means of redressing these so great evils." Tribute is paid to Mary of Lorraine, who has assisted the deliberations by her " aid, co-operation

---

81. Even the last item is perfectly catholic in its recommendation that the common prayers with litanies be recited " in our vulgar toung . . . in every peroch kirk upon Sonday and uther holy dayis efter the divine service of the Mess and that the evening prayers be said efternein in likwyse ". Although a preference for the vernacular rather than Latin was the taste of the reformers, there was nothing exclusive about their opinion. Here there is no question of public worship being in the vulgar tongue, but only prayers said in common. Robertson remarks on this point: " It was not for Edinburgh to speak where Trent had as yet been dumb." He is obviously referring to the mass, which is quite another question. The Scottish bishops could have accepted this recommendation if they had so wished, but there were more important considerations up for discussion.

82. Bishop John Leslie of Ross, writing eleven years later, refers to certain articles of reform presented to the council by the regent at the nobles' request. Not only does he cite the items, four in number, but, what is more interesting, he gives the bishops' answers to them. Following a request for prayers and the sacraments in the " Inglis toung ", there is the extraordinary demand that bishoprics and other benefices should be conferred on qualified men elected by the temporal lords and the laity. Residence, competent preaching and suitable *beneficiati* are the other items mentioned by the bishop. The first two points make us doubt that these articles were proposed by catholics, for they have a very protestant tone, although replies from the bishops are perfectly orthodox and expertly phrased. Leslie's version poses a problem: were there two sets of articles for presentation to the council, or only one? Robertson quotes two authors, McCrie and Grub, as holding the former opinion, Leslie's version being those demanded by the reformers, and the series in the acts of the council those submitted by catholic lords. Robertson himself thinks there was only one version, the catholic one. This seems the better solution. We feel that the lapse of time has played havoc with Bishop Leslie's memory, and, having gained knowledge of them from hearsay in the first place, he was setting them down only as he remembered them, and quite possibly he composed the bishops' answers himself. He does not claim that his list is complete, for he concludes, by saying, " with sundrie utheris articles to this effect." These articles are given in Robertson, *op. cit.*, ii, pp. 299-301.

and patronage."[83] In the first place, immorality amongst the clergy is again condemned by a repetition of the decree, *de concubinariis*, of 1549, but this time the emphasis is laid on episcopal offenders, as if to indicate that the previous application of the law was vitiated by lack of good example from the bishops, and a committee of six is established to enquire into their private lives.[84] This court of enquiry is to meet twice yearly and, if necessary, reprimand any offenders personally: if this is of no avail, it shall inform the provincial council, and finally the pope, if need be, so that the transgressors will be competently dealt with.[85]

An attempt was made in 1549 to legislate for clerical children but the decisions were too vague to be applicable. Now these are completely remodelled. On the question of the support of these children, the previous statute laid down that "neither prelates nor their subordinate clergy keep their offspring, born of concubinage, in their company, nor suffer them directly or indirectly to be promoted to their churches, nor under colour of any pretext to marry their daughters to barons or make their sons barons out of the patrimony of Christ."[86] It was more of an exhortation than a law, for no canonist with any knowledge of the prevailing conditions could have held out any hope of such a statute being observed. The evil was too widespread and too deep-rooted, and any remedy, to be effective, would have to take this into account. Three new detailed canons take the place of this mere condemnation, each one three times as long as the original and confining itself to one problem only. The children are not allowed to live in the clerical household, except for a maximum period of four days every three months, and that unobtrusively. Fines are graded according to clerical status.[87] Collation to a father's benefice is *ipso facto* null and void and the superior can freely confer such a benefice on another. The queen is to be asked to petition the pope not to dispense from this statute and any petition to him which fails to mention it will also be void in law.[88] No dowries are to be given from ecclesiastical livings, except a small one, not to exceed one hundred pounds yearly rental. The same applies to the endowment of sons. Similarly, no leases are to be made of church land or tithes to children or mistresses and, if made, they shall be null and void *ipso facto* and *ipso iure*.[89] The small concessions were calculated to make the laws more acceptable to those who found themselves in such circumstances.

Prohibition of clerical trading also comes up for review in a more precise statement providing for a *lacuna legis* in the previous statute, which omitted all mention of the very convenient middle-man.[90] In the employment of servants in clerical homes, prime consideration is given to

---

83. No. 259.
84. No. 261: " to be observed in all its sections, and to be enforced as well upon the archbishops and the bishops their suffragans . . . "
85. "Also that the most reverend lord, John, Archbishop of St. Andrews . . . and the most reverend, James, Archbishop of Glasgow, may not seem to lay grievous burdens on their reverend suffragans and lower clergy, while they perhaps are too freely indulgent to themselves in virtue of their privileges and exemptions, they have spontaneously submitted themselves for the good example of others, to the advice, inquisition, and reproof of the reverend fathers . . . " Here follow the names of the committee of six, three of whom are bishops. From the phrasing of the decree it appears that the archbishops are the main subjects of enquiry, although the rest of the episcopate and even the rest of the clergy are not excluded.
86. No. 174.
87. No. 262.
88. No. 263.
89. No. 264.
90. No. 266. In 1556, Cardinal Sermoneta, in a letter to Paul IV, alludes to the Scottish clergy's addiction to commerce (cf. Pollen, *op. cit.*, pp. 525, ff.).

the observance of religious duties and doctrinal orthodoxy as distinct from the moral considerations of the preceding law, although, of course, these latter are now presumed.[91] The existing law on clerical attire is another example of poor legislation. Undoubtedly the insistance on a priest dressing as such was very important and was a curb on the more secular pursuits of the clergy, but with suspension for priests and excommunication for those in lesser orders the law admitted of no parvity of matter, and canonical censure for a first offence, even although *ferendae sententiae*, was a severe punishment. In the latest enactment, the earlier decree is retained in substance and extended to include abbots, priors and commendators and all others enjoying church livings, but no censures are threatened and the penalty for the first offender is the loss of a quarter of his income.[92]

Spurred on by the memorandum, the council increases the minimum amount of preaching ordered at previous meetings. The bishops must preach personally more than four times in the year and as often, in fact, as they can do this conveniently according to the tenor of church law, that is, they ought to have suitable substitutes ready to take their place in the pulpit, when they are lawfully prevented from personal preaching.[93] Parish priests receive the same counsel and are ordered to preach as often as their ordinary shall think fit and under threat of losing a quarter of their parochial revenue.[94] The rest of the previous statute remains in effect, but some important additions give proof of stricter control: in future no priest will be licensed to preach who has not previously satisfied the ordinary by an examination in doctrine. Those preaching in churches of religious must also undergo this examination and will receive their preaching license from the local ordinary and not from their religious superior.[95] Both secular and regular clergy are to see that their arrangements for substitutes are made and submitted to the bishop before August 1st, 1559; if this is not done and the parish is left without a preacher, a quarter of the income will be forfeited. As before, the discourses will be mainly on controversial doctrine and the council lists eight articles of church teaching on which the people are to be especially instructed.[96]

The legislation demanding the appointment of theological preachers was evidently more widely enforced than has hitherto been suspected. In addition to Master John Watson, already mentioned, who acted as theological preacher in the diocese of Aberdeen, the scanty records disclose a few other names: for example, the provost of the Kirkwall

---

91. No. 265.

92. No. 267.

93. No. 274. Patrick (*op. cit.*, p. 171, footnote no. 2) says that the " general council here quoted is not, as at first might be suspected, the Council of Trent, or a recent council, but the Fourth Lateran of 1215." The latter statute had been incorporated into canon law. This is true but apt to be misleading, for this decree of 1559 was obviously drawn up with Trent in mind and not some previous legislation. In 1546, the general council expressly referred to the Lateran statute (c.15, X, *de Off. jud. ord.*, I, 31) in terms almost identical with the present canon 274: cf. session v, c.2., *de ref.* Moreover, the Tridentine law was quoted in full in the council of 1549; cf. No. 192. Trent did not give a specific ruling on episcopal preaching until 1563, when, in session xxiv, c.4, *de ref.*, it rules that bishops are to preach on Sundays and solemn feasts, and daily, or at least three times a week, during Advent and Lent.

94. No. 275: compare with No. 195. In this latest version of the previous statute, the elderly parson is one who has passed his fiftieth year !

95. The decrees of 1549 did not mention an examination.

96. No. 276. These are: (1) The catholic rule of faith is not sacred scripture alone but catholic tradition also. (2) The veneration and invocation of saints. (3) On the right use of images. (4) On purgatory after this life. (5) On the existence of the body and blood of Christ in the sacrament of the eucharist. (6) On the communion of the laity under one kind. (7) On the benefits from the mass. (8) On the lawful minister of the sacrament of the eucharist.

chapter was appointed by Bishop Reid, and Archbishop Hamilton commissioned Andrew Davidson, bachelor in theology, to preach in his archdiocese and, out of the revenues of Paisley Abbey, he provided pensions for at least two other preachers, John McQuhyn, *concionator Pasletensis*, and Friar James Johnstone, who was probably the Dominican prior of St. Andrews.

For the third time now (or perhaps the fourth) bishops are directed to establish a theologian and canonist in every cathedral, with the added injunction to retain a theologian in the episcopal household.[97] To ensure that the monasteries are complying with the command to send some of their monks to the universities, the superiors are to send a list of their undergraduates to their local ordinary by August 1st, accompanied by certificates from the university authorities. The bishops promise to make diligent enquiries about this law.[98]

Religious feature a great deal in the present legislation and it becomes increasingly evident that the council is gradually relieving the religious orders of their canonical exemption from episcopal jurisdiction or rather interpreting it more strictly. Except for the official visitation of their churches, a bishop has no authority over many of the religious orders, and Trent saw, in the current interpretation of this exemption, the source of much of the corruption of the sixteenth century, not indeed moral corruption, but rather, because it afforded scope for laxity, through the loosening of a bishop's control within his own diocese. The tendency at this juncture was to restrict the privilege of exemption and bring the monasteries under the effective authority of the local ordinary. The decree of 1549 did not go far enough when it merely advised the bishop to report rumours of misconduct or mismanagement of affairs by exempt religious. Now the bishop must see for himself by visiting these monasteries and carrying out the necessary reforms. This was certainly a bold step for the council to take and was not expected to endear the new laws or their observance to the members of the orders.[99]

A quickening of the sacramental life, allied to increased preaching and systematic instruction, is the council's prescription for a healthy laity and they accept the nobles' suggestion that exhortations should be given before the administration of the sacraments. This idea had been introduced on the continent with some success. Witzel, a German theologian, recommends that the priests should preach on the sacraments of the church on certain days, explaining them to the people, taking time also to translate for their benefit the various prayer-formulae connected with the mass, baptism and penance, and to explain the meaning of the gestures and ceremonies and the reason for the clergy doing this or that. All this is to be done in clear, intelligible language so as to satisfy the wishes of the people.[100] In the canons of the provincial council of Cologne

---

97. No. 274. From Patrick's translation (*op. cit.*, pp. 171-172), this would appear to be a part of the earlier decree of 1549, but the Latin version makes it clear that it is an additional point. In any case, there is no mention in the 1549 council of a theologian in the episcopal household.

98. No. 278.

99. No. 269: " Ordinaries . . . shall inspect all the convents, even of exempt monks, situated within their diocese, according to the prescription of the Council of Trent, enquiring into every abuse and making the necessary reforms. That the decree should say that this is in accordance with Tridentine law is puzzling, for, prior to 1559, Trent had not empowered local ordinaries to visit exempt monasteries and correct abuses. It was different with the churches of exempt religious, the bishop could already act there.

100. Some of the Scottish clergy possessed Witzel's writings; cf. *Innes Review*, ix; cf. also *Revue d'Histoire Ecclesiastique*, liv, p. 131: " Witzel et Erasme à propos des Sacraments " by J. P. Dolan.

in 1543 there are directions for exhortations on the proper dispositions for holy communion. The people ought to receive the Blessed Sacrament with true faith, believing the words of Christ at the institution of the sacrament, in which he promised remission of sins to those who receive it worthily. St. Paul is quoted on the need for charity in the approach to holy communion and the people are to be reminded that they must not receive in mortal sin.[101] The Edinburgh council follows this example and promises that short declarations shall be given, according to set formulae, before each sacrament " that the christian people may more easily and profitably understand the purpose, efficacy, and use of the sacraments of the church." A catholic exhortation on the mass will also be composed and read before the celebration of mass on Sundays and the greater feasts.[102] How many of these " catholic exhortations " were actually printed we do not know. Only one—"Ane Godlie Exhortatioun . . . to be red . . . quhen ony ar to resaue the said blyssit sacrament "—has survived in a unique copy.[103] The similarity between this Scottish declaration and that of Cologne is very striking and makes one wonder if the former was not based to a large extent on its German counterpart. After the exhortation is a word of advice to the clergy to administer the Blessed Sacrament " mair godlie, mair honestlie and with gretare reverence than ye war wount to do".

The great majority of the early heretics in Scotland were Lutherans, but Calvinism makes its first appearance in the records of this council and the bishops' apprehension about the validity of some of the sacraments denotes the presence of Zwinglians and their sacramentarian system.[104] A new form of christening has been introduced which seems to have omitted many of the prescribed ceremonies, and children who have been so baptised are to be baptised conditionally. In future no children are to be baptised by anyone, except priests, unless *in articulo mortis*.[105] The sacraments of the Holy Eucharist and matrimony are also to be administered according to the form laid down by the church.[106]

Church livings are dealt with more satisfactorily than before, although the previous decisions are again enforced, but the difference is that they are much more practicable. They set time limits on those who have to show their dispensations for incompatible benefices and order all those with livings to appear before the ordinary before August 1st. If by that time they have not received orders consonant with their spiritual duties, they must resign their livings.[107] Although the council of 1549 prescribed certain rules for the choice of those to be given benefices, these were more a statement of what ought to be rather than what must be. From now on a candidate for a church living is to be examined by the bishop. If he is found unsuitable, he will be rejected and the bishop can appoint whomsoever he wishes so long as he is suitable. This applies to all benefices, even those subject to *ius patronatus* or any other species of provision. The queen, who recommended this in the memorandum, is to be asked

---

101. *Canones Concilii Provincialis Coloniensis*, ff. 47r, 48r. Venice Edition, 1543.
102. No. 277.
103. No. 296.
104. Calvinism as such is mentioned for the first time in the primate's letter to the archbishop of Glasgow, summoning him to this council. Sacramentarians appeared in the 1549 legislation; cf. No. 221.
105. No. 293.
106. No. 294.
107. No. 271.

not to nominate or present or allow to be presented to any benefice, including bishoprics, abbacies and the like, anyone who is in any way unsuitable. Finally, the council resolves in this connexion to inform the pope of its decision and requests him not to promote anyone unqualified in age, learning or morals.[108]

The annual stipend for curates is to be raised from twenty to twenty-four marks in respect of priests in all dioceses, except Aberdeen, Ross, Caithness and Orkney, where living may have been cheaper. These shall continue to receive twenty marks.[109]

As always, the official investigator is a rather unpopular individual and much of the church's efforts at reform were frustrated either by impeded investigations or abuse in the imposition of punishments. Sometimes, these commissaries met with violent resistance, as would appear from the canon on the punishment of offenders and offences.[110] Ordinaries are advised to make certain that reform is not impeded by dishonest officials of the church. To ensure this, three or four canons, " or other good and discreet churchmen ", are to be chosen by each bishop to supervise these investigations.[111] A general revision of the system of appointments of the clergy to committees of episcopal enquiry, on which depended so much of genuine improvement of discipline, was desperately required, and this move to appoint discreet members of the cathedral chapters was only the beginning of a thorough sifting of personnel. Officials and episcopal commissaries are to be priests capable of wielding ecclesiastical jurisdiction. This change is to come into operation by June 1st and is, therefore, more urgent than some of the other laws.[112] Collectors of fines, if not discreetly selected, could also bring opprobrium on the church. These, too, have to be clerics from now on. They will have to be good administrators and organisers and honest enough to be trusted with the disbursement to charity of the fines collected. They will be expected to give an account of their work at the next provincial council.[113] Often that work had been entrusted to laymen who were little more than swindlers and this became increasingly apparent as the anti-catholic faction began their campaign of destruction in the middle fifties and ecclesiastical administration subsequently disintegrated. Tithes were difficult to collect. The spirit of rebellion was being fostered by the Congregation and authority flouted. The church's enemies made the most out of the abuses that did exist. One of these concerned the, to the modern mind, strange custom of handing over to the church a cow or the best garment in the house when someone died. The practice was open to abuse. To silence complaints, the council introduces a scale of offerings based on the dead person's estate, but the ancient usage is retained for barons and burgesses.[114] For the same reason, it is decided that the small teinds and other offerings usually made at Easter should be asked for shortly before Lent. In this way there would be no danger of the Holy Eucharist being withheld from someone who had not paid

---

108. No. 279.
109. No. 272.
110. No. 273.
111. Cf. Nos. 273 and 289.
112. No. 287.
113. No. 289.
114. No. 281. These were called " mortuaries ". The royal articles recommended their abolition.

his dues. Voluntary offerings may still be accepted at the end of the Easter mass.[115]

Great losses had been suffered by the church through the leasing of her land on long-term feus. The same was still happening to the teinds. It was much easier for a priest to lease his teinds for a certain sum than to have to go to all the trouble of collecting them himself or paying men to collect them for him. But a disadvantage of this custom was that the tithes grew to be regarded as an imposition and an unjust demand, for soon they were no longer associated with any spiritual duty to support the clergy. The council now orders that the clergy shall either collect the tithes for their own use or let them out on lease to their tenants.[116] The same tendency to consideration for the poor is evident in the laws on long leases of land. From now on such feuing can be made only to tenants or labourers. The decree is otherwise substantially the same as that of 1549.[117]

Court procedure is to follow the pattern set out in the previous councils. Delays are still deplored.[118] Absolutions from excommunication must be based on genuine repentance and not given to enable someone to be a party in a law suit.[119]

The council was closed on April 10th, 1559. Its last act was to settle the date for the next provincial meeting, which was to be held on February 11th, 1560. By that time the church was too disorganised to insist on the appointment, and the next provincial council of the catholic church in Scotland did not take place until three hundred and twenty-seven years later.[120]

Time was running out. Within nine days of the end of the council, Archbishop Beaton of Glasgow held a diocesan synod at which he promulgated the 1559 decrees and by April 19th he had issued a series of letters, calling for the observance of the newly-promulgated laws.[121] Notice is given to " our rural dean of Teviotdale and to all and sundry other priests with or without cure of souls in the diocese of Glasgow " on the recent decisions about preaching. The archbishop quotes canon 275 of the recent council and ends with a peremptory warning; " and lest the above-written rectors and others should plead ignorance or absence of notification therefore we strictly ordain and command you and each of you, in token of holy obedience and under pain of suspension from divine ordinances, that ye or either of you thereto required lawfully warn by three intimations all of the same tenor, and peremtorily charge all and sundry."[122]

Similar letters are circulated concerning the collection of Easter teinds some time before the beginning of Lent.[123] Two monks from Melrose and one from Jedburgh are to go to the university for a four

115. No. 292.
116. No. 283.
117. No. 282.
118. No. 284.
119. No. 285.
120. In 1886, at the abbey of St. Benedict, Fort Augustus, eight years after Leo XIII restored the hierarchy in Scotland.
121. The letters begin, " whereas by our synodal statutes lately issued within our Catholic Church of Glasgow in accordance with the resolution of the Provincial Council of the prelates of this realm, it hath been decreed . . . ", *Melrose Regality Records*, iii, p. 167.
122. Cn. 275 deals with preaching, *ibid*, pp. 167-168.
123. *Ibid.*, pp. 170-171. Three warnings to be given.

years' course in theology in accordance with the recent statute.[124] Six days' grace are allowed before the law governing clerical servants comes into force.[125] Penalties are threatened for failure to recite the divine office.[126] The metropolitan takes similar action with regard to vicar pensioners who do not observe the laws demanding personal residence in their charges, plurality of benefices and the acceptance of holy orders for the fulfilment of their duties.[127] Investigations are to be made on mass attendance and priests warned that they have to repair their churches as prescribed by the bishops in council.[128] The terms of the statutes on the wearing of clerical dress are to be enforced after three warnings.[129]

On the delicate question of clerical immorality, Beaton admits that several of the clergy are guilty of concubinage and demands their full obedience to the words of the council.[130] The other canons dealing with the support of clerical offspring are also to be enforced, and the sacrament of baptism is to be administered in the see of Glasgow according to the custom of the church.[131]

The commendator of the abbey of Jedburgh, " and likewise a venerable man, Mr. Robert Richartsoun, administrator of the Melrose Abbey", are to be informed by the dean of Teviotdale of the recent decree declaring all monasteries, even those of exempt religious, subject to the visitation and correction of the local ordinary. Beaton diplomatically leaves this investigation to the two deputies mentioned above. They are to carry out his orders " between this and Lammas next " and are to see that there is a sufficient number of religious in their monasteries, that these are competently provided with food and clothing, and that ruined and dilapidated places are repaired. He warns them that they will be excommunicated if they fail to implement his order.[132]

In the eastern metropolitan see, there are also signs that reform is being earnestly tackled, for, in the General Assembly of March, 1569-70, Hamilton is probably the bishop whom the assembly mentions when, in dealing with Adam Bothwell for his neglect of the churches dependent on Holyrood, it recalls that " the bishop of St. Andrews in the time of Papistry sequestrate the whole rents of the said abbacy because only the glassen windows were not holden up and repaired."[133] We know, too, that, as early as August, 1555, the same prelate had made a visitation of the Merse churches and issues a letter on the state of the buildings.[134]

Just before the last council, the bishop of Aberdeen, William Gordon, requested his chapter to draw up a memorandum of their suggestions for reform. In this, the canons exhort their bishop to send monitory letters to all priests in the diocese ordering regular preaching in all churches according to the statutes. The bishop is asked to set a good example

---

124. *Ibid.*, p. 172.
125. *Ibid.*, pp. 177-178. Prelates are to be fined £100 for a first offence. That is half of the amount prescribed by the council.
126. *Ibid.*
127. *Ibid.*, pp. 180; 81.
128. *Ibid.*, pp. 182-183.
129. *Ibid.*, pp. 184-185.
130. *Ibid.*, pp. 185-186.
131. *Ibid.*, pp. 185-186; 170-180.
132. *Ibid.*, pp. 175-176.
133. *The Booke of the Universall Kirk*, i, p. 163.
134. Herkless and Hannay: *Archbishops of St. Andrews*, v, pp. 82-83. Cf. The archbishop's letter on the state of the Merse churches, *Source Book of Scottish History*, ii, pp. 143-144.

to his clergy by putting his own life in order. They also suggest that, where the fabric of a church has been allowed to fall into disrepair, the revenues of the benefice should be sequestrated until the rector agrees to restore the buildings. Absentee clergy should be recalled to their parishes and made to carry out a reform by regular preaching. Persons suspected of heresy should be brought before the bishop, dean and chapter and made to answer the charges against them. The summonses are to be sent to their homes, for such people have stopped going to their parish churches for mass on Sundays and other solemn days.[135]

Theoretically, the laws passed by the councils of Scotland were good enough to salvage the church, for they were basically the same as those framed at Trent. If we are to search for the Achilles' heel, we must surely suspect the episcopate and the system which elected men to this high office. Not a few of the problems in the church's last years before the reformation lend weight to the theory that some of the Scottish bishops were only half-hearted in their desire for reform. For close on a hundred years the nominations to bishoprics and other high ecclesiastical positions had been in the hands of the crown. True, many of the institutions clamouring for reform were outwith the power of the local bishops, but this factor was being remedied near the end, only too late. A bishop's main functions are to teach and visit. Little of either was carried out conscientiously. In particular, visitation could have remedied much that was unseemly in the church, but the importance of this duty seems to have been overlooked in the panic that overtook the prelates of the last decade. On a subject which occupied a great deal of thought and time at Trent, the Scottish councils are singularly silent; only once is episcopal visitation mentioned in the last council, and even then it does not warrant a canon to itself, for it is touched on only obliquely when the assembly is dealing with the neglect of preaching; "And the several bishops shall also in person make a complete visitation throughout their sees at least every two years, and on visitation they themselves and their substitutes shall preach the word of God and they shall reform and rectify whatever they shall find to require reforming."[136] Coming from a council, which spoke boldly to the episcopate on other matters, this feeble and ill-defined order hardly measures up to the danger of the times. It would, perhaps, have been better had the legislation stated in detail what the bishops were to look for and how they were to deal with what they found.[137] At times one feels that in some of these statutes the bishops are being " spoken to " by one or two of their brothers in the episcopate, and it may well have been that conscientious pastors felt impotent in the face of men with authority, who had never been taught how to use it for the good of souls. Many of them were not suited to the mitre and crozier but had been nominated by some ambitious kinsman in search of wealth to augment the family's dwindling fortunes. Often the best and ablest of men were passed over in favour of someone less endowed. One disastrous example of this is worth noting. Robert Wauchope was well-known to Paul III, whom he kept informed of Scottish matters, and on whom he prevailed in 1543 to send Marco Grimani, patriarch of Aquileia, to this country to study the situation. At that time, Paul realised that Wauchope could, no

---

135. *Miscellany Spalding Club*, iv, pp. 57-58.
136. No. 274. The ordinary law was annual visitation, c.10, C.10, q.1.
137. 1563. Session xxiv, c.3, *de ref.* Every two years.

doubt, do for his native Scotland what he had already accomplished with great success for Germany, and that was to inspire the episcopate with a sense of urgency and lead them to a desire for genuine reform. Dunkeld was vacant at the time but Arran nominated his brother, John Hamilton, and wrote indignantly to Paul, resenting the pope's proposal to appoint Wauchope to that see, saying that " such men as the blind theologian who lays blind hands on the rights of the crown ought not to be favoured in Rome." Hamilton succeeded to the bishopric and scant compensation of five hundred ducats was made to Wauchope.[138]

One criticism which cannot be levelled against the Scottish church is that it was not at one with Rome on the ultimate necessity of disciplinary reform and the means to achieve it. The shadow of Trent falls too clearly over the provincial councils to leave us in any doubt about that. It was no mean feat for Scotland to possess the Tridentine decisions months after they were made and to put them into force years before any other country in Europe. With the decree of promulgation of the laws of Trent in 1564, the decisions were immediately accepted in Portugal, Venice, Poland, Spain, all the Italian states and the Duchy of Savoy. Germany did not accept them until 1566 and, although the laws were never officially enrolled in the statute book in France, the French bishops had from early on accepted the dogmatic findings and gradually saw to the enforcement of the disciplinary enactments. Scotland was ahead of them all and, given another ten years, the progressive improvement would have borne fruit. In her 1552 decision to introduce the catechism, Scotland was ahead of Trent by eleven years, while the authorisation of exhortations at mass and the sacraments anticipated the general council by four years.[139]

What, then, emerges from a study of these sixteenth-century councils? In themselves the conciliar decisions measure up well to their continental contemporaries, although the Scottish decrees are not so complete as those of some other provincial councils. This in itself is not a defect, provided the statutes passed meet the needs of the times, but one wonders if the Scottish statutes fulfilled their purpose. For one thing, the range of many of the decrees is too wide: and the subject matter too rambling instead of being precise, brief and direct. This, however, may have been a failing of the sixteenth century, but it is not so apparent in the legislation of other councils. Some aspects of ecclesiastical life are not dealt with sufficiently; canons and chapters, collegiate and cathedral, receive scant attention, although from the general state of affairs we may justly surmise that canons were often a source of trouble, especially with regard to their privileges and their emoluments. Little, too, was done for the candidate for the priesthood. He is seldom mentioned in the decrees and nothing is decided about his spiritual formation. Considering that the future of the church depended on the young clerics, much more stress should have been laid on the necessity to train them well.

Much has been written unfairly about the pre-reformation church in Scotland and the impression is sometimes given that the corruption was part and parcel of the church as such, but the councils themselves are a refutation of that charge. Immorality and abuse were never, and never could have been, officially tolerated by the church. Ever in her human element of membership, she will be the victim of men, and her advance-

---

138. Cf. *Innes Review*, i, p. 61.
139. Session xxiv, c.7, *de ref.* The Tridentine decrees were never officially promulgated in Scotland.

ment will depend on whether her authority at a given time is strong enough to withstand and overcome human weakness. Trent is the finest example of this and the great saints of the sixteenth century, like Inigo Loyola, Girolamo Emiliani or Carlo Borromeo, were the instruments of God, inspiring the church with new life and vigour. Scotland had no such personalities to lead her. Yet, despite this, the church in this country put up a spirited and creditable fight against overwhelming odds, and the greatest feature of the struggle is the unimpeachable teaching she diffused, even in her weakest hour. The statements of doctrine that emerged from her councils are as orthodox and unequivocal today as they were four hundred years ago, equally intelligible to the catholic child of the twentieth century and the pupils of Winzet at the grammar school in Linlithgow. That she should have upheld this teaching and a demand for better living little more than a year before her overthrow, should command respect from the most prejudiced.

The picture sometimes painted of the sixteenth-century Scottish church being so utterly corrupt as to be incapable of engendering even the will to reform is certainly not borne out by the evidence of these councils. One cannot help wondering what might have happened had the programme of reform started sooner, led perhaps by an energetic and papally-appointed bishop like Robert Wauchope. Would the Scottish church have won complete obedience for her laws of reform and survived, or would the political and economic movements within the sixteenth-century revolution still have produced a rebel Congregation, supported by English politicians to destroy her? As it was and in spite of her defects, it would appear, even from the pages of Knox, that many of the ordinary people of Scotland were reluctant to see her pass from their midst.

SOME DOCUMENTS OF THE SCOTTISH REFORMATION

by

WILLIAM JAMES ANDERSON

1. *THE " TWOPENNY FAITH "*

Our knowledge of the last pre-reformation provincial council, which ended on April 10th, 1559, is mainly derived from documents now extant only in copies but probably all once in the archives of James Beaton, Archbishop of Glasgow, and taken by him to Paris. Part are in a paper manuscript of the closing years of the seventeenth century which belonged to Stephen Baluze (1630-1718), a close friend of Thomas Innes, a great book-collector, some of whose books found their way into the Scots College Library: this manuscript, very carelessly written, was copied by M. Alexandre Teulet for Joseph Robertson and is printed in *Statuta Ecclesiae Scoticanae*. Other essential documents were still in the Scots College, Paris, and were copied by Thomas Innes and sent to Archdeacon Wilkins for his great *Concilia*, who also printed the Baluze manuscript from an Innes transcript. The Glasgow archives contained a copy of the mandate sent out by James Beaton to his archdiocese and that sent by the vicar-general of Candida Casa. They also contained an important vernacular document giving articles proposed to the queen regent by some temporal lords and barons and sent on by her to this provincial council. The religious ideas of this group of petitioners deserve study: for a petition of a very different character, sponsored by Sir James Sandilands of Calder, was also presented to the queen regent and can be found in Spottiswood, i, pp. 266 f. and, still another petition, was addressed to the queen regent from parliament, *ibid.* pp. 267 f., (Spottiswoode Society edition, Edinburgh, 1847). The brief account by Knox in his *History*, i, pp. 139 ff. (ed. Croft Dickinson, Edinburgh, 1949) is very unsatisfactory: he can hardly have had access to the acts of the council, and is in error as to the date of its conclusion. Moreover, he says; " The Bishops continued in their Provincial Council even unto that day that John Knox arrived in Scotland. And that they might give some show to the people that they minded Reformation they sparsed abroad a rumour thereof and set forth somewhat in print, which of the people was called ' The Two-penny Faith '." When the document, here reproduced in facsimile, was discovered by Griffin and published by David Laing in the *Bannatyne Miscellany*, iii, pp. 313 ff., in 1855, it was assumed without hesitation that this was the " Two-penny Faith ". Great importance has been attached to this extremely simple document: three times at least it has been printed in type-facsimile (so-called), all different and all highly unsatisfactory, and it can be found in many places, e.g., it is appended to the council by Robertson, in *Statuta Ecclesiae Scoticanae*, and in the version *Statutes of the Scottish Church*, Edinburgh, 1907 (Scottish History Society). It was given by Laing in the "Additions and Corrections " in vol. vi (2) of his edition of the *Works of John Knox*: it was appended to the so-called type-facsimile edition of *Archbishop Hamilton's Catechism* by Dr. Mitchell, Edinburgh, 1882, and again in a re-set, so-called type-facsimile in Gordon's *Scoti-chronicon*. None of these type-facsimiles has much resemblance to the work of John Scot, the original printer: the worst is that in Mitchell, whose initial letters are original, a dog has disappeared from the D and an artistic owl appears in the T.

The known history of the unique copy is as follows. It is one item in a most interesting collection of theses, poems and tracts, some of which bear the ex-libris of John Row, who describes himself in autograph as schoolmaster of Perth, an office he held from 1632 to 1641: it is a reasonable conjecture that the collection was made by Row and bound in limp vellum by him. The book is now in Blairs College Library: the contents, several of which are very rare indeed, will be fully described on some later occasion. The volume was in the possession of the Rev. Henry Small, catholic priest of Dumfries, who died in 1857, from him it passed to the Rev. George Augustine Griffin, a professor at Blairs from 1846 to 1852, and thereafter catholic priest at New Abbey: it was he who noted its interest and lent it to David Laing.

The name " Twopenny Faith " would suggest that it is a short Creed or statement of the catholic faith: what it really is, however, is a simple practical instruction to be given before a priest administers holy communion. The provincial council ordered the preparation of a series of such exhortations or instructions on the sacraments of baptism, holy eucharist, extreme unction and matrimony. Bishops are ordered to give similar instructions before administering confirmation or conferring orders: confessors, too, were to give an instruction before hearing confessions: it is not stated whether that was to be done individually or to a group of penitents awaiting confession: that would seem to be implied by its grouping with the instruction given by a bishop to confirmandi and ordinandi. The section ends; "And the exhortations referred to are recorded in the appendix to this council " (original Latin in Robertson's *Statuta*, in English in Patrick's *Statutes*, paragraph 277). This surely implies that these exhortations were, in fact, drafted and may well have been all printed. One copy of one exhortation has chanced to survive: need we necessarily assume that this is what Knox refers to as the " Twopenny Faith "? Such a name would suit better the short statement on the traditions of the church in eight articles to be found in Latin as no. 276 in the published editions of the statutes of the council. The price of twopence for this four-page leaflet seems high. The idea of affixing a maximum price for propagandist reforming literature was familiar in England. King Henry VIII's *Necessary Doctrine*, London, Barthelet, 1543, has on its last page; " This boke bounde in paper boordes or claspes not to be sold above xvi d." and that is a substantial volume of 228 pages; similarly, the price of the *First Prayer-book* of King Edward VI (Grafton, 1549) was restricted to two shillings and sixpence in sheets, in parchment 3/4, leather 4/-, while in shortened form, without the ordinal, it was to be priced at 2/-, 2/8 and 3/4.

This " Godlie Exhortation " and the others which the council asserts were drafted and appended to its acts was a partial concession of some of the reforms asked for in the articles; but the petitioners wanted much more, in particular they asked that the officiating priest should catechise as well as merely read the exhortation. They also asked " that the common prayers, with litanies in our vulgar tongue, be said in every parish kirk on Sundays and other holy days after the divine service of the mass and that the evening prayers be said afternoon likewise ". The acts of the council, by their grave prohibitions, make it clear that serious innovations in the administration of baptism and marriage existed and the much graver heretical celebration of holy communion by men who were not priests needed condemnation. While this particular group of temporal lords and barons strongly maintain the reverent celebration of mass, it is also manifest that the morning and evening services they asked for had no small resemblance to English practice and, indeed, all that was needed to make the resemblance close was for the priest to omit mass and to begin with the common prayers and litanies in the vulgar tongue. That kind of worship makes the transition from Sunday mass to Sunday matins a good deal easier than it would otherwise have been. And, indeed, worshippers have only to come late to mass, but in time for common prayers, to make the transition quite natural, especially for the large numbers who received holy communion only on very rare occasions, probably only at Easter. It is not surprising that the council gives no approval to this demand for common prayers in the vernacular on Sunday mornings and afternoons. The petitioners clearly wish to remain orthodox catholics, but they also wish to have innovations, and it is to be presumed from the acts of the council that similar and some far graver innovations had already been introduced without any authorization.

What is known of Sir Andrew Oliphant, secretary of the council, who authenticates this " Godlie Exhortation ", will be found in David Laing's notes, in his edition of *Knox*, i, p. 64, and vi (2), p. 666, and in Hay Fleming's notes to the *St. Andrews Kirk Session Register*, i, pp. 90 and 102. He was a permanent curial official in St. Andrews, with much experience of the procedure of Roman appeals, heresy trials and synods and councils, and confidential secretary both to Cardinal Beaton and Archbishop Hamilton.

*   *   *   *   *

2. *THE EXCOMMUNICATION OF EDINBURGH TOWN COUNCIL,* 1558

Hostile criticism of the annual procession of St. Giles on September 1st is expressed in a well-known passage of Sir David Lindsay's *Dialogue between Experience and a Courtier*, lines 2501 ff., supposed to have been finished in 1553 and, wherever printed, available in print about 1554. Our best account of the sacrilegious theft and destruction of the statue in July, 1558, and the only account, apparently, which tries to date it exactly is to be found in a fragment printed by David Laing in the *Wodrow Miscellany*, 1844, pp. 53-85, of which the relevant paragraph is: " It chanced in the said month of July (1558) or a little before that the image of St. Giles was taken out of the High Kirk of Edinburgh privately in the night. And because the wicked custom was that the said idol was borne through the town the first day of September every year, and perceiving the said day approach the Bishop of St. Andrews admonished the magistrates and Council of Edinburgh to cause make a new idol against the said day under pain of his great cursing, and because they obeyed him not, he caused his curate Tod, to curse them as black as coal, from the which they appealed to his unholy father the Pope."

In the council records, as quoted by Dr. Cameron Lees, *St. Giles, Edinburgh, Church, College and Cathedral*, Edinburgh, 1889, p. 357, and cf. references in Dickinson's *Knox*, i, p. 127, we find: " 16th June, 1559; the Baillies and council foresaid ordains Master James Lindsay, to receive from David Somer, burgess of this burgh, the commission impetrated at the instance of the good town in the court of Rome against John, Archbishop of St. Andrews, for non-up-putting of St. Giles and to deliver to the said David the sum of ten crowns of the sun in complete payment of the expenses made upon the impetrating of the said commission."

The document here given from the archives of the Vatican is the brief sent to Archbishop Hamilton in answer to the supplication of the town council of Edinburgh. Notes could be given on many, perhaps most of the Edinburgh burgesses named, but that concerns the history of Edinburgh and it may be sufficient to say that the provost does not come into the matter for a simple reason. In the authoritative book, printed in 1932 for Lord Provost Sir Thomas B. Whitson, *The Lord Provosts of Edinburgh, 1296 to 1932*, Dr. Marguerite Wood, Keeper of the City Records, explains that George, fifth Lord Seton, who was provost from 1557 to 1559, was much absent, for example, on a mission to France for the marriage of Queen Mary (24th April, 1558): and for other services to the queen regent, and " during his absence there were two presidents, first Robert Maitland of Lethington, elder brother of the famous secretary, and, succeeding him, Mr. Thomas McCalyeane, later a Provost ". This explains the prominence of the man, best known later as Lord Cliftonhall, in this document. He appears often in council records simply as "Assessor "; more will be said of him presently.

The account in John Knox (Dickinson's *Knox*, i, p. 127) summarises the Edinburgh reply to the archbishop as if it were a protest against idolatry; but the present document makes it manifest that they did not use that kind of language to the pope, but made a respectful canonical supplication against what they believed to be an injustice. Knox goes on to say " greater things shortly following that passed in oblivion ". We have here, however, manifest proof that the appeal was dealt with at Rome and the brief authorised and, so far as the evidence goes, issued. We do know of its arrival in Scotland, and it is indeed true that " greater things shortly followed ". But the papal reply, while impartial, as one would expect, grants the request of the town council and commands the archbishop to set up a tribunal of enquiry. It can be assumed that the supplication was entirely correct in tone and makes one suspect that the account of the reply given to the archbishop in *Knox* is rhetorical and not historical.

For some reason the provost of the collegiate church of St. Giles does not come into the picture; he was James Chisholm (appointed 5th October, 1557, see *R.P.S.* of that date, and still in possession apparently up to 1566), but apparently he was represented by Laurence Tod, who had the unpleasant task of promulgating the excommunication; of him we know that he was chaplain of St. Margaret's chapel in Edinburgh Castle from 6th July, 1557, but was so no longer 22nd June, 1559 (*R.P.S.* of these dates). Cameron Lees (p. 103) says he presided over the chapter in the absence of the provost.

A full summary of the papal brief can be given rather than a complete literal translation; from a canonical point of view only the Latin is " authentic " and it is highly technical. Anyone interested in the exact powers of the tribunal to be set up must consult it in Latin; our present interest is historical. Pope Paul IV (23/5/1555 - 18/8/1559) writes to Archbishop Hamilton that he has received a supplication from Thomas Macalzean of Cliftonhall, one of the presidents of the town of Edinburgh,

James Lindsay, John Spens, Alexander Aitchison, and William Lawson, bailies; Alexander Baron, Alan Dickson, David Forester, John Preston, William Ker, Alexander Park, Gilbert Balfour, James Curll, Mungo Hunter, and Robert Henryson, councillors; James Adamson, burgh treasurer; Alexander Guthrie, principal town clerk; also James Mure, Michael Gilbert, Andrew Gibson, Alexander Sauchie, Robert Gardner, James Binning, Alexander Durie, David Shank, James Stirk, James Lawson, David Graham, James English, and Andrew Elphinston, masters of the craftsmen and deacons of the trades, narrating that after the theft of the statue of St. Giles from the church the archbishop or his official had ordered them under pain of major excommunication to replace it by having a new statue made, within a time limit; this, they maintained, they were not bound to do. They had been summoned before the procurator-fiscal of the ecclesiastical court and declared to have incurred canonical censures. Against that they had appealed, asserting that the excommunication was null and void and asking for an independent local investigation. The pope commands the archbishop to set up a tribunal consisting of himself and two out of three other bishops, viz., Glasgow, Dunkeld and Dunblane; with very extensive powers to summon evidence, and to compel attendance, and power to prorogue the court as often as might be necessary and, if they saw fit, to quash the sentence of excommunication and, in general, to see that justice was done. This was issued at St. Peter's in Rome on 13th January, 1559.

The actual brief does not exist; what does exist is the minute corrected by several hands from which the brief was drawn up; what is here printed is an attempt to draw it up again from these minutes using all the corrections and including even some errors, not of great moment, but the correctors did not catch all the errors, e.g., " Clistonhall " ought to be " Cliftonhall "; it might be thought that one corrector was possibly even a Scot, but this seems somewhat doubtful, for he corrects " Huntar " into " Hountar ".

A complete photograph is here given, natural size or thereby, but probably some readers would welcome a few words of explanation. Minutes of briefs are written on one side of a long strip of paper: this consists of sheets pasted together to form the strip and it is written on one side only but, on the top of the other side (plate 1), is the docquet used to mark the brief or bundle of brieves when stored away. In this instance one reads: Minute mensis Januarii 1558 (altered to 1559) preceded by a number, perhaps " xlvii ", possibly the number in the bundle. On the other side is a modern number made by an automatic numbering machine, 11,199. In this particular series there are 29,770 minutes made up into 460 bundles with five extra undated bundles. This whole series concerns the years 1523-99. Above it a curial official, apparently one of the correctors, has written his name, " Do. Jo. di Liren ". Apart from the stamp of the Vatican archives, the other marks are traces of the writing on the other side which has soaked through the paper. On the last plate is the name of another official who authenticates it and would sign the actual brief. He is B. Melchiorius. Still another notary, referendary or other official has signed his name on the back, and it can be read (in reverse) just below B. Melchiorius; it is " V. Measuranus ". A referendarius named Melchiori (later bishop of Macerata) is known at this time; but the only point worth stressing is the care with which this brief was checked and corrected.

It is very possible, indeed quite probable, that the petition from the town council of Edinburgh to the pope still exists in its original or in a copy *somewhere* in the Vatican archives; it has not, so far, been found. Only those who have worked there realise the magnitude of these archives. The Register of Briefs alone contains for the period 1490-1800 no less than 852 volumes, each of some 1,000 pages. In addition, unregistered briefs which, like the present, were kept only in the form of minutes and not written up in registers, number, as has been said, 29,770. Work is in progress, but until much more has been done on indexing and calendaring it is impossible to say definitely what does or does not exist. Anyone wishing the latest summary information can find it in the publication of the German Historical Institute in Rome: *Das Vatikanische Archiv*, by Karl August Fink, ed. 2, Rome, 1951.

What is here printed is an attempt to reconstruct the brief sent out; there are a few very minor problems without significance so far as history is concerned; those who wish to check corrections can do so from the complete photograph herewith given.

* * *

PAVLVS PP. IIII
(Breve apertum)

Venerabili fratri Ioanni archiepiscopo Sancti Andreae salutem et apostolicam benedictionem.

Exponi nobis nuper fecerunt dilecti filii Thomas Macalzean a Clistonhall unus ex presidibus urbis Edinburgi regni Scotie regie, Iacobus Lyndesay, Ioannes Spens, Alexander Achisoun, Gulielmus Lauson, ballivi dicte urbis, Alexander Baron, Alanus Dikesoun, David Forester, Ioannes Prestoun, Willelmus Ker, Alexander Park, Gilbertus Balfour, Iacobus Curll, Kintigernus Hountar, et Robertus Henrisoun, consiliarii, Iacobus Adamsoun, questor, Alexander Guthre, dicte urbis scriba precipuus necnon Iacobus Mure, Michael Gilbert, Andreas Gibsoun, Alexander Sauche, Robertus Gardner, Ioannes Bynnyng, Alexander Dure, David Schank, Iacobus Stirk, Iacobus Lausoun, David Grahame, Iacobus Inglische, Andreas Elphinstoun, artium mechanicarum in dicta urbe magistri et artificum decani

QUOD, postquam statua Sancti Egidii que erat in collegiata ecclesia eiusdem Sancti Egidii oppidi Edinburgi Sancti Andreae diocesis fuit ablata,

TU, frater archiepiscopus sive tuus officialis ut dictam statuam de novo facerent seu fieri curarent sub excommunicationis etiam maioris et forsan aliis penis infra certum terminum tunc expressum, et sic inique, cum ad hoc non teneantur; ad tui tamen procuratoris fiscalis curie tue archiepiscopalis monuisti, et deinde Thomam et alios predictos dictas penas incidisse et incurrisse declarasti, et forsan aggravavisti, re-aggravavisti, interdixisti et brachium seculare invocavisti,

QUIBUSQUIDEM monitione, aggravatione, re-aggravatione, interdicto et brachii secularis invocatione fuit infra tempus debitum pro parte Thome et aliorum predictorum ad nos appellatum et de nullitate dictum, ac nobis humiliter supplicatum

QUATENUS aliquibus probis viris in partibus commorantibus ut causam et causas appellationis et appellationum hujusmodi et aliarum quarumcumque pro parte eorundem Thome et aliorum interpositarum nullitatisque et nullitatum iniquitatis et injusticie, tam monitionis declarationis, aggravationis, re-aggravationis, interdicti et brachii secularis invocationis hujusmodi, quam totius processus desuper quomodo-libet habiti et facti, attentatorumque invocationum quorumcumque; necnon quam et quas Thomas et alii prefati habent et monent, habereque et monere volunt et intendunt contra et adversus predictum procuratorem fiscalem omnesque alios et singulos sua communiter vel divisim in premissis interesse putantes, et super omnibus et singulis premissis, rebusque aliis in actis cause et causarum hujusmodi latius deductis et deducendis, et illarum occasione, summarie simpliciter et de plano, sola facti veritate inspecta, unacum omnibus et singulis suis incidentibus, dependentibus, emergentibus, annexis et connexis, audiant, cognoscant, decidant et fine debito terminent;

CUM POTESTATE tam dictum procuratorem fiscalem quam omnes et singulos in decreto vel executione citationis decernen(dos) nominandos etiam per edictum publicum, constato summarie et extra-judicialiter de non tuto accessu, citandi; eisque necnon quibus et quoties opus fuerit, etiam sub excommunicationis, suspensionis et interdicti, aliisque ecclesia-sticis sententiis, censuris et penis, etiam pecuniariis, ex arbitrio imponen-dis, inhibendi; et in eventum non paritionis, sententias censuras et penas hujusmodi rebelles et inobedientes incidisse et incurrisse declarandi, aggravandi, re-aggravandi, interdicendi et auxilium brachii secularis, quatenus opus sit, invocandi; ac Thomam et alios predictos a quibus-cumque censuris et penis in eos premissorum occasione latis, simpliciter vel ad cautelam, prout juris fuerit, absolvendi; ac fatalia toties quoties opus fuerit prorogandi, et de no(vo ... medendi *conj. a word like* instruendi) ac adversus illa in integrum, constato eis de legitimis impedimentis, restituendi; ceteraque faciendi dicendi, gerendi, exercendi, et exequendi in premissis necessaria et opportuna committere et mandare; ac alias eis in premissis de opportuno justicie remedio providere de benignitate apostolica dignaremur.

NOS statum et merita cause et causarum hujusmodi aliorumque forsan de necessitate exprimendorum, tenore-tenus et compendialiter presentibus pro sufficienter expressis habentes, hujusmodi supplicationibus jure moti, FRATERNITATI TUE per presentes committimus et mandamus ut, vocatis vocandis, cum votis venerabilium fratrum archiepiscopi GLAS-GUENSIS et episcoporum DUNKELDENSIS ac DUMBLANENSIS, vel duorum illorum super premissis omnibus et singulis AUCTORITATE NOSTRA procedas, et justiciam facias, non obstantibus premissis constitutionibus et ordinationibus apostolicis ceterisque contrariis quibuscumque.

DATUM Rome apud Sanctum Petrum sub annulo piscatoris, die xiii Januarii 1559, pontificatus nostri anno quarto.

B. MELCHIORIUS.

* * *

(The text has been broken up into paragraphs and some capitals inserted for ease in reading, in such documents one sentence can and does last for a whole page of text.)

We owe the document to the Cistercian scholar, Father Joseph O'Dea of Nunraw, who is at present engaged on research in the Vatican; we owe the photographs to Father Charles Burns, who is also studying in Rome; unfortunately, neither has the leisure to write this notice.

A very brief historical comment will not be out of place. The tribunal envisaged in this document seems actually to have been set up because, in the Edinburgh treasurer's accounts, just about the time when payment was made for the hire of horses to take the town's deputation to Linlithgow to negotiate with the lords of the Congregation, we find the entry: " Item, for taking of twa instrumentis at the presenting of the commissioun direct fra the Pape to my Lord of Sant Androis . . . viijd." Obviously the proceedings could not have gone very far, because on June 29th, 1559, as the Edinburgh burgh records inform us, after long reasoning in the tolbooth, the council, Thomas Macalzean presiding, decided to send a deputation, which included several of the burgesses named in this document to open negotiations with the lords of the Congregation at Linlithgow. The New Order was at hand. But one is tempted to ask what was the religious attitude of these men who were the chief citizens of Edinburgh. Nothing in our records suggest that they underwent what is called evangelical conversion in the period between a respectful petition to the pope and a deputation to the lords of the Congregation. They wanted to save the fabric and treasure of their church of St. Giles, for which they had a sincere affection. Thomas Macalzean was entrusted with the famous relic, the arm-bone of St. Giles. He had a long and somewhat chequered career which can be found in Pitcairn's *Criminal Trials* (i, part iii, pp. 247-8). He had an even more famous daughter, Euphemia, whose fate it was to be bound to a stake and burned quick (that is not previously strangled) on the Castle-hill of Edinburgh on the 24th June, 1591. There were twenty-eight articles in her dittay, all concerning witchcraft. They are very relevant to the enquiries of any one seeking to study post-reformation life in the Canongate. Pitcairn, writing in 1833, comments: " The only reason which can be assigned for such frantic and detestable conduct seems to be that she was devoted to the ancient Roman Catholic faith, and thus bearing personal hatred against the King and the Reformed Religion." This remark tells us more about the religious opinions of Robert Pitcairn, who was secretary of the Calvin Translations Society, than it does about the Macalzean household. There were many in Edinburgh who did not take religious changes tragically: one at least of the clergy of St. Giles, the master of the pre-reformation song school was still at his post in 1577, with a different type of music, leading the praise of the congregation, and " taking up the psalms " instead of rehearsing mass and vespers. In a revolution enthusiasts take sides; others survive; and there were many who survived in Scotland. Thomas Macalzean duly became an elder of the kirk of St. Giles and, on October 20th, 1570, an Ordinary Lord of Session with the title Lord Cliftonhall and he died in 1581 still in possession of the lands of Cliftonhall.

* * * * *

3. A CANON LAW FRAGMENT FROM THE GENERAL REGISTER HOUSE, EDINBURGH

As has been pointed out in the comment on the " Twopenny Faith " almost all our knowledge of the reforming councils in Scotland immediately preceding the reformation of 1560 comes from one manuscript known from its owner as the Baluze manuscript. Indeed we should know very little, and that little none too reliable, from John Knox and other literary sources. Certainly we know very little indeed how far the reforms enacted on paper were made effective in the real world, for there was systematic destruction of canon law manuscripts as of liturgical manuscripts. Such manuscripts were obsolete for two reasons; standard works got into print and canon law ceased to have its original importance in protestant Scotland. Late medieval canon law manuscripts, full of technical contractions and of very numerous references (often very hard to trace) cannot be described as pleasant reading. Scraps of them abound in sixteenth-century bindings and as covers to paper books, manuscript protocol books and so on; indeed a librarian who finds such a scrap of parchment rather expects it to contain canon law or liturgy. The only scraps of a manuscript containing Scottish conciliar matter appear to be those found in the General Register House in bindings and printed by Joseph Robertson, *Concilia Scotiae*, i, p. cciii, and (for text) ii, pp. 251-4; it contains part of an index of contents.

But we can assert with complete confidence that the " officiales " of each diocese must have had contemporary copies of the law they had to administer. All have disappeared. The historian also needs to know what the Canon Law commanded, though he is even more interested in the question how far it was administered. It was subject to many a dispensation and the student of the reformation period in Scotland is familiar with the comment of the *officialis* of Aberdeen (John Leslie, parson of Oyne, later Bishop of Ross) who felt free to act in arbitrary autocratic ways—" I knaw nothing but the cannoun law; and the greatest reasoune that ever I could fynd thair is *Nolumus* and *Volumus* " (Knox, *Reformation*, Laing ii, p. 141).

The manuscript of which this is an index also contained earlier documents, including Bagimond's Roll of which one leaf also survives (printed by Robertson *op. cit.* i, pp. ccciv-cccvi) but that does not belong to reformation legislation.

* * * * *

4. ARCHBISHOP HAMILTON'S CATECHISM

The catechism printed at St. Andrews by the command and at the expense of Archbishop Hamilton and dated 29th August 1552 is quite easily accessible in an excellent edition by Thomas Graves Law, and also in a " type-facsimile edition " by Professor Alexander F. Mitchell; this latter is not entirely accurate and gives a misleading impression of its appearance. Comments on the catechism's doctrinal orthodoxy, on which the theologians are not entirely agreed, will be found elsewhere in this volume. No apology need be given for providing an actual photographic facsimile of a page. The printer's name is not given but the appearance of a device of Hercules and the Centaur make it certain that it is the work of John Scot; we have however no right to assume that the block of Hercules and the Centaur had not a previous history; for we can be very sure that Scot acquired plant from earlier printers. The page here chosen shows three initials; the small " p " and " o " occur also in Bellenden's translation of Boece printed in Edinburgh by Thomas Davidson (undated but possibly 1542) while the capital " P " showing St. Peter and his keys is one of a set of which " H " and " S " were used by Davidson in his *Acts of the Parliament of Scotland*, dated 1541 (Cf. Dickson and Edmond, *Annals of Scottish Printing*, Cambridge, 1890). Scot's supply of type was restricted and second-hand; no doubt the " P " was originally used in some Bible in Latin where it might have been the initial of PETRUS in the first epistle of St. Peter. It has no special significance here, but its use suggests that there was no deliberate exclusion of papal claims, however little the see of Rome may appear in the catechism text.

A remark might be made on the version of the *Pater Noster*. It is said to be " in Inglis " not, be it observed in " Scottis." Nor can we infer that anyone ever used this version when saying their prayers. They said that prayer in Latin. Father Herbert Thurston in *Familiar Prayers* (London 1953), made it clear that there was no standard version in the vernacular until one was imposed on England by King Henry VIII, and it became widely known and used and its use has been continued among catholics to the present day. Indeed the popular superstition that there is a " catholic " form viz. " Our Father who " while the Book of Common Prayer uses " Our Father which " has no historical basis at all. During the Marian reaction, catholics continued to say the *Pater Noster* in Henry VIII's English and did not go back to Latin; no catholic authority imposed " Our Father who;" it appears to have come gradually into use in the seventeenth century as an attempt to get rid of archaic English.

The catechism (like contemporary preachers) quotes the bible in Latin, a preacher then gave his own translation and the version of the *Pater Noster* here is an explanation not a version intended for devotional use. Latin quotations in sermons long continued and were greatly stimulated by the declaration that only the Vulgate Latin was "authentic" and so could alone be used for a logical debating argument.

Typographically the catechism is of great interest as an example of Scottish printing. The standard of paper, type and ink is poor and it is no credit to the University of St. Andrews that better work could not be produced in 1552, for the book is officially sponsored by the Primate of Scotland; no doubt the printer was doing his best. We have no idea of the size of the edition actually printed; it was certainly intended that all parish priests should have a copy (and there were over 1200 parishes in Scotland). It soon became rare. The *Innes Review* printed (viii, p. 44) an interesting comment: in the middle of the seventeenth century, Prefect Ballentine thought there were not many more than the five or six copies he had himself collected and he suggested a modernised reprint for common use. About a dozen copies are now known to exist, many in poor condition; copies are most unlikely to come on the market, and if one did appear a very high price would be asked. Prefect Ballentine's little collection of half a dozen copies, if in good condition, might well be worth, nowadays, at least a thousand pounds.

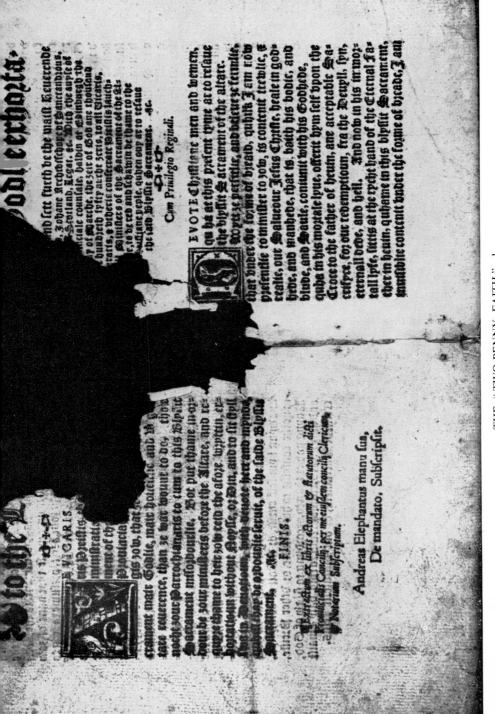

THE "TWO-PENNY FAITH"—1.
PAGES 4 AND 1.

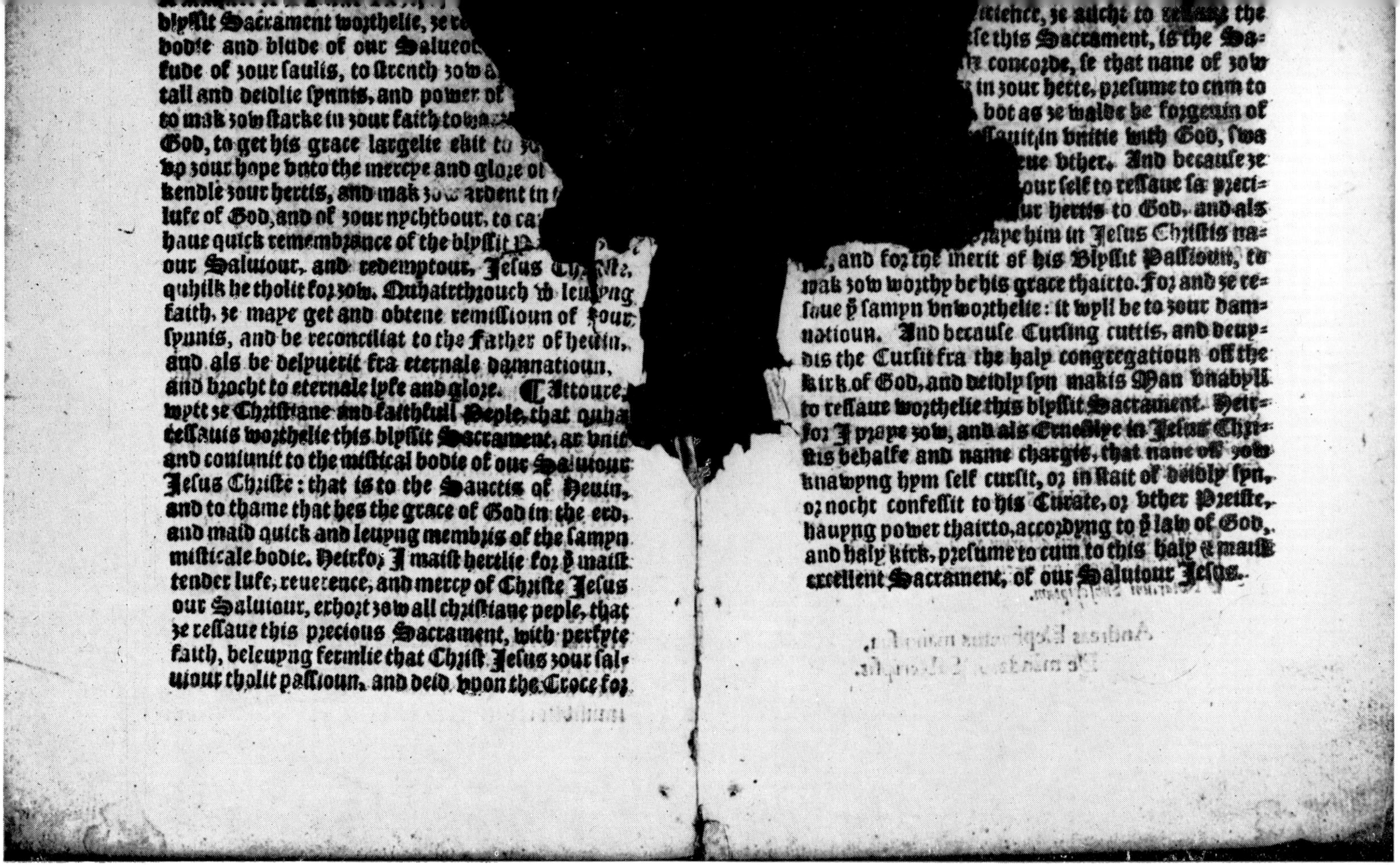

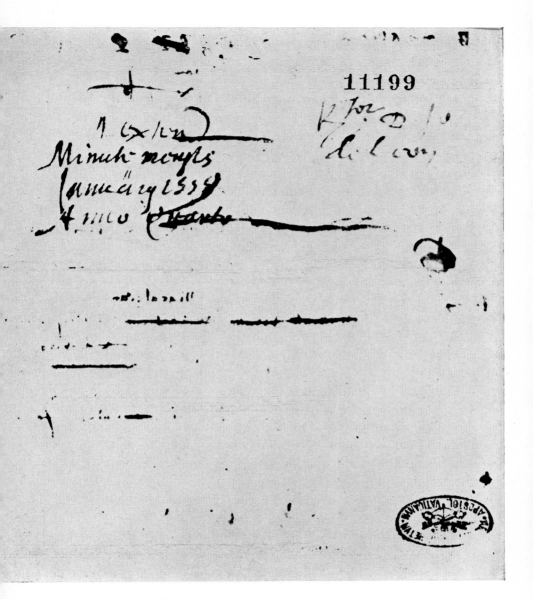

MINUTE OF PAPAL BRIEF—1.

Showing *verso* with docquet and modern serial number.

MINUTE OF PAPAL BRIEF—2.

Beginning to " kintingernus hountar et "

MINUTE OF PAPAL BRIEF—3.

"Robertus Henrisoun" to "seu fieri curarent"

MINUTE OF PAPAL BRIEF—4.

" Sub excommunicationis " to " predictorum ad nos (deletion by corrector) "

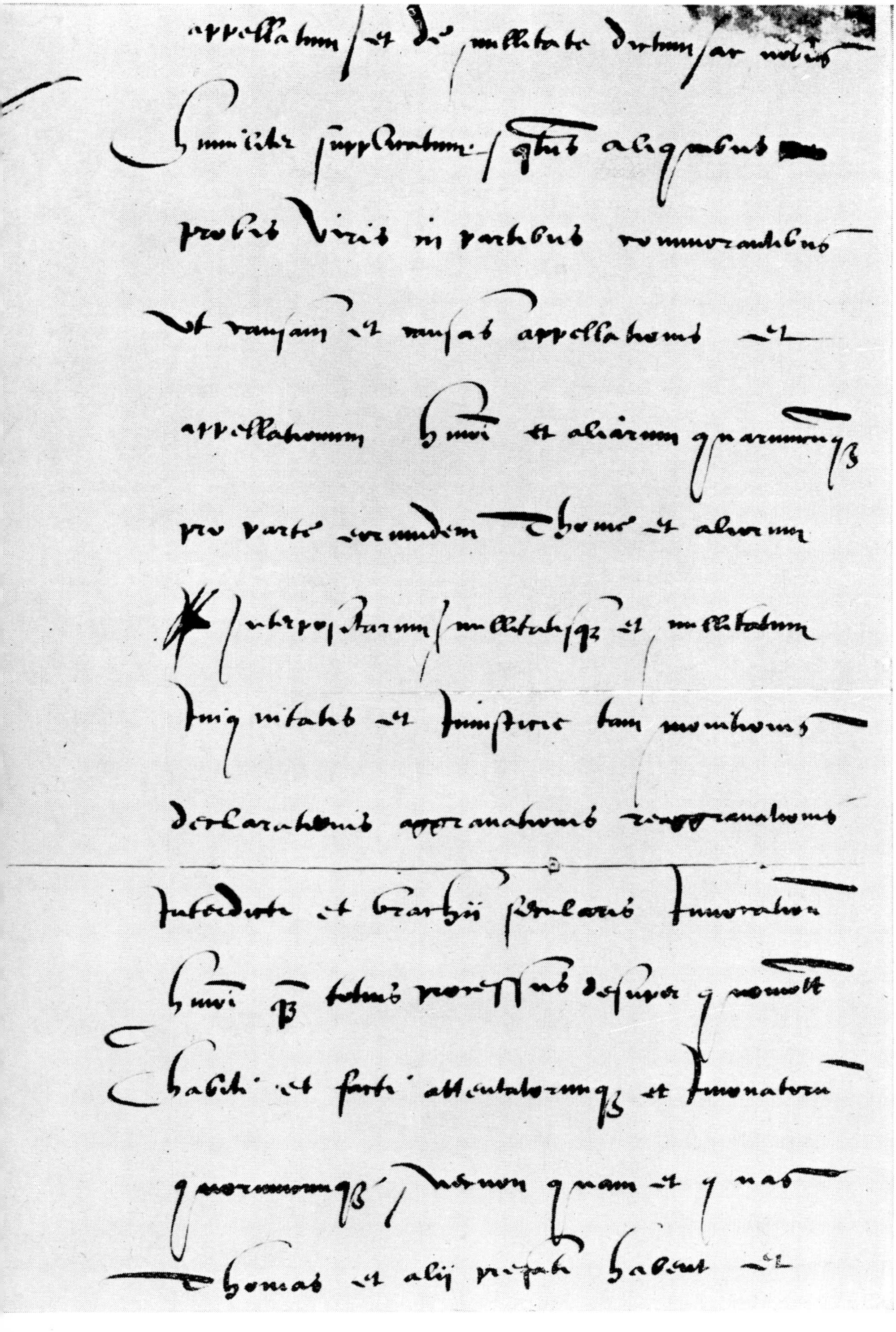

MINUTE OF PAPAL BRIEF—6.

" movere habereque et " to " terminent, cum potestate "

MINUTE OF PAPAL BRIEF—7.

" tam dictum procuratorem " to " quibus opus sit invocandi "

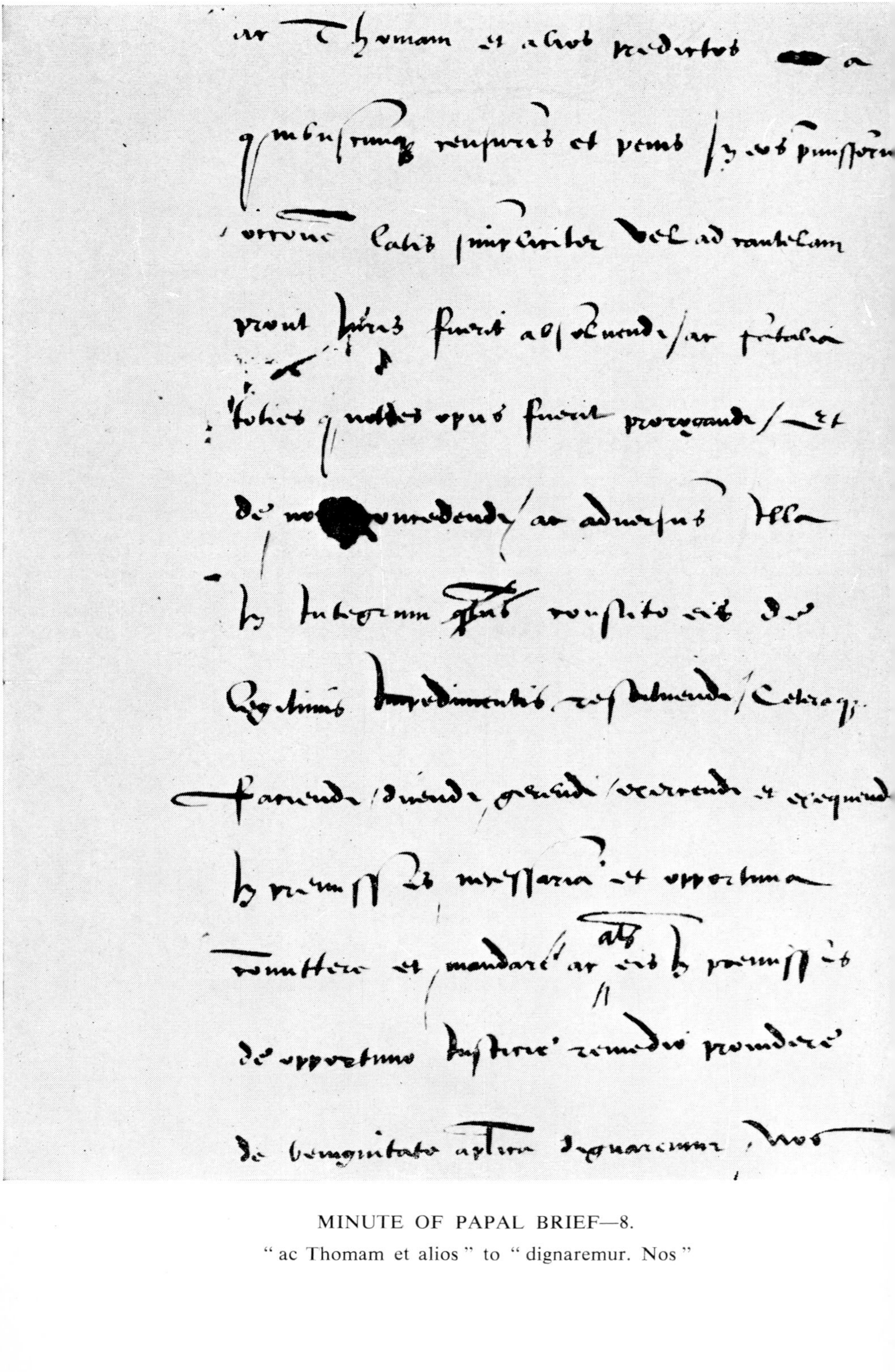

MINUTE OF PAPAL BRIEF—8.

" ac Thomam et alios " to " dignaremur. Nos "

MINUTE OF PAPAL BRIEF—9.

"statum et merita" to "obstantibus premissis"

MINUTE OF PAPAL BRIEF—10.

"(long deletion by corrector) ac constitutionibus" to end.

CANON LAW FRAGMENT FROM THE REGISTER HOUSE, EDINBURGH, *RECTO*.

CANON LAW FRAGMENT FROM THE REGISTER HOUSE. EDINBURGH. *VERSO.*

ATER Noster qui es in cœlis, sanctificatur nomen tuum. Adueniat regnum tuū Fiat voluntas tua, sicut in cœlo & i terra. Panem noſtrum quotidianum, da nobis hodie. Et dimitte nobis debita noſtra, sicut et nos dimittimus debitoribꝰ noſtris. Et ne nos inducas in tentationem. Sed libera nos a malo. Amen.

THE Saine prayer of our LORD
In Inglis.

OVR Father, quhilk is in Heuinis. Thy name mot be hallowit. Thy kyngdome mot cum. Thy wyll mot be done in erd, as it is in heuin. Geue ws this day, our daylie breid. And forgyff ws our dettis, as we forgyfe our dettouris. And lede ws nocht in temptatioun. Bot delyuer ws fra euyl. Sa be it.

The thrid Cheptour.

Sen Christ hes leirit vvs to call god fader vve sulde praye to hym vvith gret confidens,

ATER noster, qui es in cœlis. O our father quhilk is in heuin. We can nocht O christin peple comprehend in our mynd, the gret gudnes of God towart vs, quhilk hes leirit ws, in the beginnyng of our prayar to call God our Father sayand: O our father God. This was nocht vsit to

eidir leis a thuigfin do ghnáith, thú
dó bheith dhathair throcaireach aga,
do bhrídh oibrighthe do Sbiorad na-
omh, do bheith na chroidhe, maras da
chumhachdaibh go madheidir leis thi
ith'antaachtar ar an diabhal, agas bua-
idh do bhreith air fa dheoidh, agas go
ma roil leat fós athogbhail afaoirfe do
Kíoghacha tré chumhachtaibh Iofa
Criofd ar Deighearna.

¶ BIODH AMHLUIDH.

¶ FINID DORDVGH
adh an Bhaifdidh.

❧ FOIRM ❧
TSAGRAMVINTE
Chuirp Chriofd, ré raiter
Suiper an Tighearna, agd
fo fíos.

Tánis bhéas Suiper an Tigheárna aga thoirbhearr don
phobal mar is indeare vair fa mi no gach vair bhios
ail leis an geoimhtionol, labhradh an Mimifder
mar fo fíos.

Vgmaoid dar naire abhraithreacha
ionmhuine, cionnas do ordaigh
Iofa Criofd, Sacramuint naomhtha a
chuirp féin, ré rait ear Suiperan Tighearna, do thoirbheart duinn. Mar a
thrifeas Pól eafbul, fa naonmhadh cai-
bidil dég, don chéd Eibifdil do chuir
fé do chum na Gcóirinteach. Fuair
mife on Tighearna ar fé, an ní tug mé
dhaoibhfe. Anoidhche do braitheadh
Iofa ar Drighearna, do ghabh fé arán
chuige, agas tug buidheachas don A-
thair, agas do bhris an tarfa, agas do
raidh na briathrafa, caithidhfe fo agas
afé fo mo Chorpfa brifidhear par bhr
fonfa, agas denaidhfe fo, mar chuimh-
niughadh oramfa. Mar an geedna. Tu-
reis an Tfuiper do ghabh fé an cup
agas do raidh na briathrafa, afé fo

5. THE GAELIC LITURGY

John Carswell's translation into Gaelic of Knox's *Book of Common Order* is described in Dickson and Edmond's *Annals of Scottish Printing*, there is no need to repeat the details. Archibald, Earl of Argyll, to whom it is dedicated, was the main support of the reformers in the west highlands and whether he or Carswell first planned the translation it was an imaginative bid to secure the Gaelic-speaking districts' adherence to the new order. It should be considered in connection with the whole programme of publications, mainly from the press of Robert Lekprevik in Edinburgh and partly subsidised by the General Assembly from time to time, which provided service-books, catechisms, controversial tracts, broadsheets in prose and verse (Robert Norwell's *The Meroure of an Christiane* was also dedicated to Argyll), for the instruction of the reformed congregations and the confusion of their enemies. The success of Carswell's Gaelic text appears to have been limited, although the sixth Earl of Argyll is said to have insisted on its use in public worship when planting ministers in the main Campbell country in 1574. The west highlands and the isles were probably not amenable to preaching even if there were, which is at least doubtful, ministers to preach to them and attempt to persuade them to accept law and order. As the old clergy died out the greater part of the north-west highlands and the isles became a religious wilderness, parts of which were secured again for their old allegiance by the intermittent efforts of Irish friars in the seventeenth century, while other parts were won for presbyterianism as late as the second half of the eighteenth century. The first effort at printing a Gaelic text was not followed up until long after, it was over two hundred years later that the highlands got a Bible in Gaelic, and Knox's Liturgy was replaced by other forms of worship so that Carswell's translation disappeared from use. Like so many other publications of the time in Scotland it has almost vanished, there are only three known copies, the only perfect one being very appropriately in the possession of the present Earl of Argyll.

*　　*　　*　　*　　*

6. THE APPOINTMENT OF JOHN WATSON AS TRIDENTINE PREACHER, 1548

The instrument by which John Watson was admitted a super-numerary preaching canon of Aberdeen cathedral chapter, without prebend, is now in the Scottish Catholic Archives, Edinburgh, having been previously at Blairs College, Aberdeen and from at least 1834 in the possession of Bishop Kyle at Preshome, by whom it was communicated to the Maitland Club and first edited in their *Miscellaneous Papers principally illustrative of events in the reigns of Queen Mary and King James VI*, by W. J. Duncan, Glasgow, 1834, and again in a rather more accessible volume edited by Cosmo Innes: *Registrum Episcopatus Aberdonensis*, (Spalding Club, 1845 and Maitland Club, 1845) ii, pp. 317-320. It has long kept company with a somewhat mixed collection of parchments, predominantly sasines and similar deeds concerning lands in Moray and the North-East generally, many of which were once in the possession of William Rose of Montcoffer, but the collection includes a few parchments from Archbishop Beaton's Paris archives as well, so we are left in uncertainty as to provenance. Another Aberdeen document, the Bishop's Rental of 1511, described by Cosmo Innes (*loc. cit.* i, p. lxxiii) in 1845 as purchased lately at a London bookseller's sale, and now in the National Library of Scotland, had been in the hands of George Chalmers, and Cosmo Innes suggested that even that had come from the Scots College, Paris. However that may be (and it seems quite unlikely), the present document is probably not from Aberdeen diocesan archives, since it seems obvious that it would be in the possession of Canon John Watson himself for the simple reason that it contains his credentials. Six at least of Watson's books survive, three at Blairs College, two in Aberdeen University Library and his Quignonian Breviary is still at Preshome. On them see the *Innes Review*, ix, p. 157, pl. XL and iii, pp. 33 ff. and plates.

As this document has been already printed twice, it seems to be un-necessary to do so again and the illustration shows its character. The interest of the document is very great as it proves that practical steps were taken at once in Aberdeen diocese to introduce some of the reforms enacted at the Council of Trent in 1546-7. John Watson took his duty seriously, he bought at least three books of model sermons, and as their margins show, he used them; what survive contain sermons on all the Mass Epistles throughout the year, on the Mass Gospels for week-days in Lent, and we have the winter part of a book for the Sunday Gospels, and no doubt there once was and perhaps somewhere there still exists the summer part also. He had them well-bound in leather and two of his books have his name stamped on the covers. Similar volumes to aid busy pastors and curates continue to appear up to the present day.

The document is on parchment about 13 inches square; it once had two seals, no doubt those of the bishop and chapter, both have disappeared. It gives him authority to take the place of the bishop as a preacher, the bishop being prevented by manifold worries and duties and sometimes by disorders; such language is " common form " when a bishop delegates some of his official duties, but William Gordon did really have worries and disorders too. The appointment was made in accordance with the decrees of the Council of Trent, then sitting and also of a provincial council of Edinburgh in 1547, whose decrees are not now extant; for this see Joseph Robertson's note in *Concilia Scotiae* (Bannatyne Club, 1866), i, p. cxlvi where the essential parts of this document are also reprinted with some commentary. John Watson was to preach once a month in the cathedral and once a year in each common church of the chapter and to lecture twice a week on theology.

* * * * *

REFORMATION AND REPRESSION

by

ANTHONY ROSS

This essay is a tentative introduction to the theory and practice of religious discipline in sixteenth-century Scotland. The subject is perhaps not so explosive now as it would have been some fifty or even twenty-five years ago. Our own period has surpassed qualitatively and quantitatively the cruelty and destruction of previous ages in history. After what we have known recently of totalitarian ruthlessness, of gas chambers, the atom bomb, napalm, brainwashing and " double-think ", the actions of sixteenth-century soldiers and statesmen can hardly shock us as they shocked our grandparents. We understand better now, perhaps, the recurrent perversions in human behaviour, and the difficulty men have in dealing justly and humanely with swiftly moving events; the difficulty of knowing what should be tolerated when the safety of the commonweal is threatened; of distinguishing between sin and crime; of remembering the fundamental rights of another person when we are outraged in our own being by his deeds.

Such understanding is needed in discussion of the sixteenth century, especially in Scotland, where so much partisan feeling has been engaged. It is a century with which all of us are inevitably concerned since our deepest religious divisions developed during it, and so much else in our modern life began then. To a modern christian, whatever his ecclesiastical loyalty, there is a great deal in it which is unquestionably alien: the attitude, for example, of Affonso de Albuquerque reporting his crowning victory in India. " In the capture of Goa our Lord did much for us . . . Afterwards I burnt the city and put all to the sword. For four consecutive days your soldiers slaughtered the Moors, not sparing a single one. They herded them into mosques and then set those buildings on fire. We reckoned that six thousand Moors had been slain. Sir, it was a great deed, well fought and well finished, the first time that vengeance has been taken in India for the treacheries and villainies perpetrated by the Moors against your Highness and your people. I am not leaving a single Moorish tomb or building standing, and the Moors captured I have caused to be burned alive . . . "[1]

Behind these words was the struggle of centuries, from the time that the Moslem armies carried fire and sword triumphantly through the Iberian peninsula in the name of Allah and his prophet. The man who wrote them was conscious of leading a bold counter-attack against dangerous odds and an enemy who would show no mercy. He had a firm conviction, inspired partly by his interpretation of Old Testament history, that God was on his side. The slaughter he regarded as a military necessity. The Moslem women were spared, to be the founding mothers of the Goanese race. This was a man of his time, regarded by his contemporaries as a great hero. His methods were not unlike those which Henry VIII adopted, when he sent his armies into Scotland with instructions to spare neither man, woman, nor child from fire and sword.[2] His

---

1. James Brodrick, S.J., *St. Francis Xavier* (1506-1552). London, 1952, p. 100 n.
2. *Hamilton Papers*, ii, no. 207. See Dickinson, Donaldson and Milne, *Source Book of Scottish History* (Edinburgh 1953),ii, p 216, for the key passage.

thankfulness for what had happened was not so different from that of John ab Ulmis, writing cheerfully from London in 1549: " The rebellion of the peasantry has been marvellously subdued; about five thousand papists have been slain."[3]

It is easy, in fact, to paint a sombre picture of the sixteenth century as an age of cruelty and violence, deceit and treachery. Those who urged humane proceedings were few on any side; none had a monopoly in those things which we now generally deplore. Guise and Tudor plotted assassinations as short-cuts to political success. In Spain the agents of the Inquisition secured for the monarchy a firm grip on religious and political affairs alike, their system of espionage and torture well matched by that of Elizabeth's ministers, which established a similar control for the English government. The slaughter of St. Bartholomew's Eve and of the religious wars in France was matched by the atrocities of the Peasants' Revolt in Germany, with an estimated loss of 100,000 lives before it was crushed. Protestant and catholic slew Anabaptists for similar reasons, in England and on the continent. In all these happenings men invoked the name of God as freely as did Albuquerque, sometimes hypocritically and often sincerely. Politics, economics and religion were inextricably mixed, with the responsibility for what happened in all three fields usually very much in the same hands in any country.

At no time in the century was religion free from political and economic issues, nor did the leaders of the reformation or the counter-reformation expect that it should be. The unity of church and state was generally accepted as an axiom. Most catholics and protestants were agreed that religion was " the foundation of the commonwealth ", as Cardinal Pole once said, and that heresy was the most serious crime against the general good. By heresy they did not simply understand error about some point of christian belief, but resistance to the known truth, to propositions which they themselves found so evident that honest denial of any of them seemed impossible. That was why they found it easier to tolerate Jews or pagans than those who fell away from what was considered christian orthodoxy, having once professed it. The majority in the sixteenth century were indeed still at one with the middle ages on the subject of heresy. They accepted the principles stated by St. Thomas Aquinas in the thirteenth century, when he wrote: " He who resists the faith after accepting it, sins more grievously against faith than he who resists it without having accepted it, even as he who fails to fulfil what he has promised sins more grievously than if he had never promised it."[4] And again: " Such should be submitted even to bodily compulsion, that they may fulfil what they have promised, and hold what they have at one time received."[5]

If such compulsion were not applied, there was a grave danger, it was thought, not only for the soul of the heretic, but for the safety of society itself if corruption should spread. Since the roots of heresy were usually taken to be pride or covetousness allied with deliberate malice, it was expected that it should assert itself to the detriment of good order, opening the way to every vice, and the ruin of simple souls. Another

---

3. *Original Letters Relative to the English Reformation* (Parker Society, 1846), ii, p. 394.
4. *Summa Theologica*, IIa.IIae.q.10.a.vi.
5. IIa.IIae.10.viii.

passage of Aquinas expresses the common opinion: " With regard to heretics there are two points to be observed: one on their own side, the other on the side of the Church. On their own side there is the sin whereby they deserve not only to be separated from the Church by excommunication, but also to be severed from the world by death. For it is a much graver matter to corrupt the faith which gives life to the soul, than to forge money, which supports temporal life. Wherefore if forgers of money and other evil-doers are forthwith condemned to death by the secular authority, much more reason is there for heretics, as soon as they are convicted of heresy, to be not only excommunicated but even put to death.

" On the part of the Church, however, there is mercy which looks to the conversion of the wanderer, wherefore she condemns not at once, but after the first and second admonition, as the Apostle directs: after that, if he is yet stubborn, the Church no longer hoping for his conversion, looks to the salvation of others, by excommunicating him and separating him from the church, and furthermore delivers him to the secular tribunal to be exterminated thereby from the world by death. For Jerome, commenting on Galatians, v. 9, *A little leaven*, says: Cut off the decayed flesh, expel the mangy sheep from the fold, lest the whole house, the whole paste, the whole body, the whole flock burn, perish, rot, die. Arius was but one spark in Alexandria, but as that spark was not at once put out, the whole earth was laid waste by its flame."[6]

Illustrations of this position from catholic writers can be easily multiplied, but one more, this time from the sixteenth-century Jesuit theologian, St. Peter Canisius, must suffice to show the continuity of these ideas into the period under discussion. Preaching in 1571, he said: " The secular authorities and ruling princes should remember that the Christian order concerns them, too, and warns them to exercise their functions and administration in a Christian fashion. Since they have received the sword from God in order to protect the devout and to punish the wicked, as St. Paul says, Christ has commanded them to see to it, together with the spiritual leaders, that the sheep of Christ and his Church have nothing to fear from the wolves. That is why the enemies of Christ and the Church should not be borne with and tolerated to the common detriment of the Christian people. Since the true Christian faith is indeed like a mother who protects peace, obedience, unity, discipline, charity and all the good things of the civil as well as the spiritual order, the untrue and anti-Christian faith, on the contrary, is the root from which spring division, disorder, rebellion, insolence and all kinds of excesses. If it is right that the civil authority punishes those that counterfeit money, how can we suffer those that counterfeit the word of God ? Whoever insults and violates authority is guilty of lese-majesty and must be punished in life and limb: what punishment, then, is severe enough for those who scorn, deny and reject the Sacrament of the altar, and who resist God in his bride, the Church, in his holy general Councils, in his divine commandments, those who have no respect for any Christian rule laid down by the Church ? "[7]

Those familiar with the writings of the protestant leaders will recognise the fundamental similarity of outlook between them and the catholic

---

6. IIa.IIae.11.iii.

7. Quoted in Lecler, *Toleration and the Reformation*, trs. by T. L. Westrow (London, 1960), i, p. 280.

writers quoted above. "Whoever shall contend," said Calvin, "that it is unjust to put heretics to death and blasphemers will, knowingly and willingly, incur their very guilt. This is not laid down in human authority: it is God who speaks and prescribes a perpetual rule of his Church."[8] His position was developed fully in the treatise which he published in defence of his action against Servetus, the *Defensio Orthodoxae Fidei*,[9] which belongs so plainly to the century of Albuquerque. There were some already in Europe, protestant and catholic, who found the severity used against religious dissidents excessive. Some had hoped that Servetus might have been spared. For such critics Calvin had no use. "Our sympathy-mongers, who take such great pleasure in leaving heresies unpunished, now see that their fantasy hardly conforms with God's commandment. Afraid lest the Church be blamed for being too severe, they would allow all kinds of errors to spread freely to secure tolerance for one man. But God does not even allow whole towns and populations to be spared, but will have the walls razed and the memory of the inhabitants destroyed and all things frustrated as a sign of his utter detestation, lest the contagion spread. He even gives us to understand that by concealing a crime one becomes an accomplice. Nor is this to be wondered at, since it is here a question of rejecting God and sane doctrine, which perverts and violates every human and divine right."[10]

He was not alone in these views, and he had received solid backing from other protestant leaders in his decision to have Servetus burnt. Bullinger had written to Theodore Beza; "What is your most honourable senate of Geneva going to do with that blasphemous wretch, Servetus? If they are wise, and do their duty, they will put him to death, that all the world may perceive that Geneva desires the glory of Christ to be maintained inviolate."[11] In that summer of 1553, when the fate of Servetus was being discussed, Edward VI was succeeded in England by his sister, Mary Tudor, whose application of the accepted principles was to do something to turn people against burning, at least as a method of repressing heresy. After she had been pilloried in Foxe's *Book of Martyrs*, burning was to become unfashionable, but the principle that heresy deserved capital punishment was still widely accepted, as later reigns would show.[12]

It was, in fact, expected of a christian prince that he should suppress all opposition to the received doctrine, enforce ecclesiastical discipline, even enforce subscription to a creed. The prince was regarded as necessary to the church. Zwingli stated a view common among the reformers, and illustrated long before them in medieval practice—for example, in the letters of caption of Robert II of Scotland[13]—when he wrote; "As the visible Church comprises rebels and criminals who have no faith and could not care less about excommunication, even if launched repeatedly, it needs the magistrate—whether prince or senate—to constrain the impudence of sinners. Since there are shepherds in the Church, by whom

---

8. Quoted Hughes, *The Reformation in England* (London, 1954), ii, p. 278 n.
9. Published in 1554 in Latin, and also in a French version. There is a copy of the Latin edition in Edinburgh University Library, shelfmark Dd.2.19, which belonged to Henry Sinclair, bishop of Ross, and later to Clement Little.
10. Lecler, i, p. 333.
11. *Original Letters*, ii, p. 742.
12. On Mary Tudor's persecution, and the traditional English comment on it, see Hughes, *op. cit.*, ii, pp. 254-304.
13. Cf. Patrick, *Statutes of the Scottish Church* (Scottish History Society, 1907), pp. 225-6.

one should understand ' princes ' according to Jeremias, it is obvious that a Church without a magistrate is a truncated and mutilated Church."[14] The prince or magistrate was to act under the inspiration of the " prophet ", the representative of the Holy Spirit in the community. Their relationship was a delicate one, but there was no doubt as to where priority lay. It belonged to the " prophet ", whose task was to teach, and to show what must be amended. " Thus the prophet will teach religion to all, as he is the pontiff and the initiate. After him the magistrate will undertake the correction of all those who do not practise that teaching or who act in a way which is contrary to the instructions."[15]

Hence the exhortations to rulers to emulate such Old Testament figures as Josias, of whom Calvin wrote to Edward VI that " he performed every duty of an excellent prince, in faith, zeal, and all holiness."[16] Hence, too, the complaint of John ab Ulmis that the Protector Somerset was more gentle in religious matters " than was befitting a nobleman possessed of so much authority."[17] And hence the same writer's remark, prompted by English military activity in Scotland; " We have full confidence respecting Scotland, that when she has been thoroughly subdued, she will embrace the true and wholesome doctrine of Christ with her whole heart."[18] With these passages might be linked the Scottish Lutheran, Alesius, writing to Cranmer in 1536 that no longer truce should be granted to the Lincolnshire " rustics ", but that all impiety and hypocrisy should be torn to pieces at once, even in the teeth of the bishops if necessary.[19]

In Scotland, as elsewhere, there was a basic similarity in theory among catholic and protestant spokesmen; and their continental affinities are obvious. The practical question was: What is the church, and who are its enemies ? That, and not so much what should be done with them when they were identified, was the great question of the day for those who took religion seriously. This is aptly illustrated in a Jesuit's report to Father Parsons in 1581 of a conversation with William Ker of Cessford, the Warden of the Middle March. " He enquired the cause of my arrival, on which I said that I was a refugee for conscience' sake, that protection was not refused even to criminals in distress, and ought still more readily to be conceded to exiles for religion. ' But,' replied the Warden, ' there is no greater criminal than the professor of a false religion, and enemy of the Church of Christ.' This, I replied, was very true, but the question was, who are the enemies of the Church ? He said there

---

14. Lecler, i, p. 315.

15. *Ibid.*, p. 316. The conviction that the spirit of prophecy was among the reformers is evident in Scotland as elsewhere. *Cf.* Knox, *History of the Reformation in Scotland*, ed. W. Croft Dickinson (Edinburgh, 1949), i, pp. 65, 67, 95 and 113; ii, pp. 64-5, 106. It would appear on p. 113 that in the writer's view prophetic cursing by George Wishart was fulfilled by God. See also, as representative of a slightly later generation, Row's *History of the Kirk of Scotland* (Wodrow Society, 1842). On Knox he says, " a verie extraordinarie prophet of God; what ever men, either ignorant or disaffected have spoken to the contrarie " (p. 9). Wishart also " spak many excellent prophesies " (p. 10). An interesting illustration of the prophet and the magistrate at odds is the case of the unfortunate minister who said the Earl of Morton defended an unjust cause. Although so badly tortured, in an effort to disclose a political prompter behind his statement, that he had to be carried to the gallows to be hanged, he claimed steadfastly that he had spoken only by the Holy Spirit. *Cf. Historie of James the Sext* (Edinburgh, 1804), p. 167; *Diurnal of Occurrents* (Bannatyne Club, 1833), p. 293.

16. *Original Letters*, ii, p. 708. The Old Testament illustrations adduced by the reformers constantly illustrate the subordination of the ruler to the prophet as a divinely sent guide to action.

17. *Original Letters*, ii, p. 439.

18. *Op. cit.*, p. 412.

19. *Letters and Papers, Foreign and Domestic, Henry VIII*, xi, 987.

was no doubt whatever that they are the Papists. I smiled at this, and proposed that we should adjourn the controversy until after supper."[20]

We shall return to this interesting conversation later. At a higher level than it represents, the acceptance of the medieval idea of maintenance of ecclesiastical discipline and the suppression of heresy by the secular arm is evident in sixteenth-century Scottish documents. In the *First Book of Discipline*, compiled by an authoritative group of reforming clergy in 1560, it is declared: " Seeing that Christ Jesus is He whom God the Father has commanded only to be heard, and followed of his sheep, we urge it necessary that his Evangel be truly and openly preached in every Kirk and Assembly of this Realm; and that all doctrine repugning to the same be utterly suppressed as damnable to man's salvation." What is understood by " preaching of the Evangel " is explained: then what constitutes the contrary doctrine, " which things, because in God's scriptures they neither have commandment nor assurance, we judge them utterly to be abolished from this realm; affirming, further, that the obstinate maintainers and teachers of such abominations ought not to escape the punishment of the Civil Magistrate." This is in harmony with the words of the Scottish Confession of Faith on the function of civil authority: " To Kings, Princes, Rulers, and Magistrates, we affirm that chiefly and most principally the conservation and purgation of the Religion appertains; so that not only are they appointed for civil policy, but also for maintenance of the true Religion, and for suppressing of idolatry and superstition whatsomever, as in David, Jehoshaphat, Hezekiah, Josiah, and others, highly commended for their zeal in that cause, may be espied. And therefore we confess and avow, that such as resist the supreme power (doing that thing which appertains to his charge), do resist God's ordinance, and therefore cannot be guiltless."[21]

What is implied in the examples from Old Testament history can be seen by reading the accounts of these kings. It is made explicit frequently, notably in the Third Head of the *Book of Discipline*, on the abolishing of idolatry, which runs as follows: "As we require Christ Jesus to be truly preached, and his holy Sacraments to be rightly ministered: so can we not cease to require idolatry, with all monuments and places of the same, as abbeys, monasteries, friaries, nunneries, chapels, chantries, cathedral kirks, canonries, colleges, other than presently are parish Kirks or Schools, to be utterly suppressed in all bounds and places of this Realm (except only the palaces, mansions, and dwelling-places adjacent thereto, with orchards and yards of the same): as also that idolatry may be removed from the presence of all persons, of what estate or condition that ever they be, within this Realm. For let your Honours be assuredly persuaded, that where idolatry is maintained or permitted where it may be suppressed, that there shall God's wrath reign, not only upon the blind and obstinate idolater, but also upon the negligent sufferers of the same; especially if God have armed their hands with power to suppress such abomination. By idolatry we understand, the Mass, invocation of saints,

---

20. Forbes-Leith, *Narratives of Scottish Catholics* (Edinburgh, 1885), p. 169.

21. For the text of the *First Book of Discipline*, see Dickinson's *Knox*, ii, pp. 280 seq. The *Confession of Faith* is given on pp. 257 seq. Knox tells us that from *The Book of Discipline* posterity might " judge as well what the worldlings refused, as what Policy the godly ministers required " (*op. cit.*, i, p. 374). The preachers had " vehemently exhorted " that it should be established by " an Act and public law ", but although a number of influential nobles agreed to this, the majority were against it. It remained, however, a statement of the ideal of those at the centre of the religious revolution.

adoration of images, and the keeping and retaining of the same; and, finally, all honouring of God not contained in his holy Word.''[22]

Stronger language is employed with reference to the use of sacraments, and is directed not only against those still adhering to the mass but also against " despisers " of the sacraments who dared to administer communion to each other privately in their houses, without recognised ministers, and who therefore disturbed that uniformity in practice which was regarded as essential. " Your Honours may clearly see how proudly and stubbornly the most part despise the Evangel of Jesus Christ offered unto you; whom unless that sharply and stoutly ye resist, we mean as well the manifest despiser as the prophaner of the sacraments, ye shall find them pernicious enemies ere it be long. And therefore, in the name of the Eternal God, and of his Son Jesus Christ, we require of your Honours that, without delay, strait laws be made against the one and the other. We dare not prescribe unto you what penalties shall be required of such: But this we fear not to affirm, that the one and the other deserve death; for if he who doth falsify the seal, subscription, or coin of a king is adjudged worthy of death; what shall we think of him who plainly doth falsify the seals of Christ Jesus, Prince of the kings of the earth ? If Darius pronounced that a balk should be taken from the house of that man, and he himself hanged upon it, that durst attempt to hinder the re-edification of the material Temple, what shall we say of those that contemptuously blaspheme God, and manifestly hinder the Temple of God (which is the souls and bodies of the elect) to be purged, by the true preaching of Christ Jesus, from the superstition and damnable idolatry in which they have been of long plunged and held captive ? If ye (as God forbid) declare yourselves careless over the true Religion, God will not suffer your negligence unpunished. And therefore, more earnestly require we, that strait laws may be made against such as dare presume to minister his Sacraments, not orderly called to that office, lest that while there be none found to gainstand impiety, the wrath of God be kindled against the whole.''[23]

It is interesting to see the old argument from the law against forgers, which was used by Aquinas, turning up again; and to note also that the suggested laws were to apply not only to obstinate catholics, but also to unorthodox protestants. There was no place for Anabaptists and such, in Scotland, any more than in Henry VIII's England or Lutheran Germany or Calvinist Geneva. The new inquisition was to penetrate, if all went according to plan, into every home in the country. Although the *First Book of Discipline* was not given force of law, to Knox's disappointment, some of those " strait laws " which it advised were passed in August, 1560, by the " Reformation Parliament ". The key passage runs as follows; " Notwithstanding the reformatioun already made according to Goddis word yit nottheless thair is sum of the same papis kirk that stubburnlie perseveris in thair wickit idolatrie sayand mess and baptizand conforme to the papis kirk prophanand thairthrow the sacramentis foirsaidis in quiet and secreit places regardand thairthrow nather God nor his holie word Thairfoir it is statute and ordanit in this present parliament that na maner of persone or personis in ony tymes cuming administrat ony of the sacramentis foirsaidis secreitlie or in ony uther maner of way bot thai that are admittit and havand power to that effect

---

22. *Op. cit.*, ii, p. 283.
23. *Ibid.*, p. 322.

and that na maner of persone or personis say messe nor yit heir messe nor be present thairat under the pane of confiscatioun of all thair gudis movable and unmovable and puneissing of thair bodeis at the discretioun of the magistrat within quhais jurisdictioun sik personis happynis to be apprehendit for the first falt Banissing of the realme for the secund falt And justifying to the deid for the third falt And ordanis all sereffis stewartis baillies and thair deputis provestis and baillies of burrowis and utheris jugeis quhatsumever within this realme to tak diligent sute and inquisitioun within thair boundis quhair ony sik usurpit ministerie is usit messe saying or thai that beis present at the doing thairof ratifyand and apprevand the samyn and tak and apprehend thame to the effect that the panis abovewrittin may be execute upoun thame."[24]

In these documents it is assumed that there is a duty to God to enforce acceptance of a body of doctrine, a form of ministry and sacraments, and a certain standard of morals in the community. The instrument of excommunication is provided as a principal means of securing the last objective especially, and its application is directed and explained in the Seventh Head of the *Book of Discipline*, on the nature of ecclesiastical discipline. There is provision for a variety of corporal punishments and restraints, economic sanctions and social pressure. The last is well illustrated in the directions for treatment of someone excommunicated as contumacious after three summonses to penitence. "After which sentence may no person (his wife and family only excepted) have any kind of conversation with him, be it in eating and drinking, buying and selling, yea, in saluting and talking with him, except that it be at the commandment or licence of the Ministry for his conversion; that he by such means confounded, seeing himself abhorred of the faithful and godly, may have occasion to repent and so be saved. The sentence of his Excommunication must be published universally throughout the Realm, lest that any man should pretend ignorance."[25] If this treatment did not bring about repentance, the higher penalties of banishment or death could be invoked.

We shall see later something of how these ideas of discipline were put into practice in Scotland. It is plain from their very nature that they would never work without the support of temporal authority in some form. The impossibility of compromise as long as the traditional attitude towards heresy was general is also obvious. The part played by civil authority would be decisive one way or another, and from the reformers' point of view indifference on the part of the secular power was almost as unacceptable as hostility. The religious leaders of the protestant party in Scotland, as distinct from those political and economic interests which used them to their own advantage, were committed to the destruction of " idolatry " and the overthrow of the " high places ". They were opposed inevitably to any civil authority which countenanced, let alone imposed, catholic belief and worship. Their position is shown in the defence of the preachers when Mary of Lorraine complained of their activities: " In open audience they declare the authority of Princes and Magistrates to be of God: and therefore they affirm that they ought to be honoured, feared, obeyed, even for conscience sake: *provided that they command nor require nothing expressly repugning to God's commandment and plain will, revealed*

---

24. *Source Book of Scottish History*, ii, p. 177.

25. Dickinson's *Knox*, ii, p. 307 seq.

in his holy word."[26] But to require that catholic practice should continue freely was to require what expressly repugned to God's commandment and plain will, granted that the mass was idolatry. To support the mass, even in one royal chapel, was to deserve equation with those figures of the Old Testament who defected from the true religion. So the defence of the preachers continued: " Moreover, they affirm, that if wicked persons abusing the authority established by God, command things manifestly wicked, that such as may and do bridle the inordinate appetite of Princes, cannot be accused as resisters of the authority, which is God's good ordinance. To bridle the fury and rage of Princes in free kingdoms and realms, they affirm it appertains to the Nobility, sworn and born Councillors of the same, and also to the Barons and People, whose votes and consent are to be required in all great and weighty matters of the commonwealth. Which, if they do not, they declare themselves criminal with their Princes, and so subject to the same vengeance of God, which they deserve, for that they pollute the seat of justice, and do, as it were, make God the author of iniquity. They proclaim and cry, that the same God who plagued Pharaoh, repulsed Sennacherib, struck Herod with worms, and made the bellies of dogs the grave and sepulchre of despiteful Jezabel, will not spare the cruel Princes, murderers of Christ's members in this our time. On this manner they speak of Princes in general, and of your Grace in particular."[27]

We shall say something later about the reference in this passage to " votes and consent ". The general position may be seen more fully in the discussion between Knox and Lethington reported in the former's *History of the Reformation.* The teaching as to right of rebellion is in line with older views on resistance to tyranny, though not with the new theories of absolute monarchy. What is of special interest is that difference in religion may be an occasion for revolt, even against a prince who is not specifically tyrannical in his method of government. Knox appears to be convinced that " idolatry " in a ruler, however private in practice, could not be allowed because divine vengeance would fall upon the whole people if it were. " What ye may and ought to do by God's express commandment, that I can tell," said Knox; " Idolatry ought not only to be suppressed, but the idolater ought to die the death, unless that we will accuse God."[28] The severity of sentence is to be maintained, in the light of the Old Testament, without respect of persons, and if necessary against whole cities, sparing neither man, woman, nor child. The people is answerable to God for any abomination suffered to exist in its midst, and cannot defend itself against slackness in practice by referring judgment to the hands of God himself. The terrifying principle which underlay the appeal to the Old Testament as a literal guide for christians is laid down in these words of Knox: "*As God of his nature is constant, immutable, so can he not damn in the ages subsequent that which he has approved in his servants before us.* But in his servants before us, He by his own commandment has approved that subjects have not only destroyed their kings for idolatry, but also have rooted out their whole posterity, so that none of

---

26. *Op. cit.,* i, p. 227.

27. *Ibid.* Contrast the tone of this with the regent's letter to her brother, the Cardinal of Lorraine, on January 13th, 1556-57. Text in Pollen, *Papal Negotiations with Queen Mary* (S.H.S., 1901), pp. 423-30. Natural calamities are frequently represented by Knox as divine vengeance on the country for allowing mass to be said at all. *Cf.* Dickinson's *Knox,* ii, pp. 69-70.

28. *Op. cit.,* ii, p. 120. See also p. 123.

that race was left alive after to empire above the people of God."[29] This is in accord with the passage of Calvin quoted above, in defence of the burning of Servetus. It may also be noted in passing that this was the teaching adopted, not invented, by the Covenanters, with their cry of " Jesus and no quarter ! " and their massacre of prisoners and unarmed camp-followers, including children.

Such ideas explain why hatred of heresy could have its roots " not in religious bigotry, but in the fear of sedition, tumult and civil war characteristic of sixteenth-century statesmen."[30] Religion and politics were so closely related, not only for those who may have been more opportunist than enthusiast, but for nearly all who were sincerely devoted to religious causes, that failure to separate them is not surprising. The view that apostate or idolatrous princes might in certain circumstances be opposed by rebellion, with or without the assistance of foreign rulers, was common among catholic and protestant. The Scottish protestant party was understandably in communication with Henry VIII and his representatives, as it was later financed, advised, and given military assistance by Elizabeth's government. It is not necessary for modern Scottish protestants to try to dissociate their forerunners from the idea that the removal of Cardinal Beaton was a deed pleasing to God as well as to the King of England: or to try to dissociate them from some responsibility in the ruthless campaigns in Scotland which were launched, as Henry VIII said, that there might " remayn forever a perpetual memory of the vengeance of God lightened upon (the Scots) for their faulsehode and disloyailtye."[31] A similar spirit was behind plots to assassinate Elizabeth, or to promote a Spanish invasion of Britain. Where a more tolerant spirit appeared in Western Europe, it was likely to be suspected as cover for some deep plot. Only in Poland and Austria were there to appear governments willing to allow religious liberty, and able to defend it.[32] In Scotland there could be no compromise between opposing doctrines, given the views illustrated above.

Passing from theory to practice, however, it is surprising to find how little violence there is in sixteenth-century Scottish religious history compared to that of other Western European countries. There is nothing to match the executions in England under the Tudors, or the bloodshed in France, Spain, the Netherlands and Germany. That is one reason no doubt why the protestant movement took so long to gather strength, the reason perhaps why it triumphed, and the reason why the final shape of Scottish protestantism was so long in crystallizing and in imposing itself upon the country. From the point of view of those who held medieval views on the treatment of religious dissidents there was never at any period in the century a satisfactorily " godly " prince to enforce uniformity of belief and discipline. In the state of society satirised by David Lyndsay and attacked by so many other contemporary writers—for example, the author of *The Complaynt of Scotland* or Archibald Hay— neither the decisions of the provincial councils of 1549, 1552, and 1559,

---

29. *Ibid.*, p. 125. See also the paragraph at the foot of p. 126 containing the statement: " God has promised in his law, that when his people shall exterminate and destroy such as decline from him, that He will bless them and multiply them, as He has promised unto their fathers."

30. *Cf.* Chambers, *Thomas More* (London, 1938), p. 282.

31. *Source Book*, ii, p. 126.

32. On these experiments in limited toleration, see Lecler, *op. cit.*, pp. 266-9 (Austria), and pp. 355 seq. (Poland).

nor the *Book of Discipline*, would have much effect without active support from temporal authority. As Gude Counsall has it:

> Yit, in this realme I wald mak sum repair,
> Gif I beleiffit my name suld nocht forfair,
> For wald this king be gydit yit with resoun,
> And on misdoers mak punitioun;
> Howbeit, I haif lang tyme bene exylit,
> I traist in God my name suld yit be stylit.[33]

In the state of the Scottish monarchy it was on the whole unlikely that any but socially insignificant evildoers would be punished, even were the monarch guided by reason. This weakness of the crown, as well as the character of the monarchs themselves, is relevant to what happened before and after 1560.

Personal devotion to religion would not necessarily have strengthened the secular arm. Yet, given the wealth of the Scottish church before 1560, an alliance between a devout king and a keen metropolitan in St. Andrews could have changed history. An internal reform on an orthodox pattern might then have been brought about through co-operation of the spiritual and temporal power. The church could have financed the forces needed by the crown to assert its authority over the great families, above which the king was so uneasily poised, and in return the king might have suppressed heresy, and enforced discipline upon recalcitrant clerics in accordance with the decrees of the provincial councils and of the Council of Trent. But Flodden left Scotland without an effective king, at a most critical time. The great nobles were to remain powerful throughout the century. There was no parallel in Scotland to the Tudor revolution. Nor were the burghs strong enough to challenge the nobility, although trade was increasing and they were growing in importance. Even in the second half of the century they were still weak enough to be intimidated by powerful clans, as Dundee by the Hays and Aberdeen by the Gordons.[34] Edinburgh, the strongest of the burghs in population and wealth, found it prudent to play neutral when directly faced by the armed nobility. An alliance of king and burghs against the nobles was not feasible as yet. And, indeed, such alliance as there might be between king and church was made less secure by the fact that the great families were so strongly entrenched among the higher clergy, where their private interest took precedence so often over the general good. Above all, the long minorities of James V, Mary, and James VI were decisive in ensuring the position of the great families and the continued weakness of the crown.

It is not surprising, then, if Scottish rulers in the period of religious conflict appear all in some degree *politiques*. They were not alone in that, of course. Mary of Lorraine was typical of her own continental background when she temporised over the settlement of religious difficulties, prepared perhaps to overlook them altogether if she could thereby maintain law and order, balance her budget, and achieve a closer union of France and Scotland. Her husband, James V, had made money out of the religious tensions in the kingdom. His strange character deserves fuller study than it has had so far. How much of a hypocrite was he?

---

33. *The Satyre of the Three Estaitis*, Lyndsay's *Works*, ed. Chalmers (London, 1806), i, p. 392.
34. *Cf. Narratives*, p. 144, and *Extracts from the Burgh Records of Aberdeen*, 1570-1625 (Spalding Club, 1848), p. 92 seq.

Writing to the pope about the need for a higher standard in religion, and especially among prelates, as an accompaniment to attempts to place the offspring of his own incontinence in lucrative benefices; prodding the clergy with literary satires and grim allusions to beheadings in Denmark and burning of bishops in England, but demonstrating his devotion to religion by burning some Lutherans at home; passing on pilgrimage and arranging a trental of masses, but making no noticeable change in his own licentious habits; producing demonstrations towards the establishment of stricter order and justice in the country, but at the expense of less important or more remote offenders whose deaths made little difference to the general condition of things; but always, in one way or another, endeavouring to secure more money, and chiefly from the church which was so open to blackmail owing to the weakness and corruption at Rome, the scandals in Scotland itself, and the threat of heresy everywhere. His interventions against growing heterodoxy were no part of a consistent campaign for the suppression of heresy, or for the reform of religion.[35] Nor is his refusal to follow Henry VIII's advice and enrich himself by the suppression of monasteries strong evidence of orthodoxy. In the state of Scotland he would have gained little by heeding his uncle, but the great families would have done well for themselves, as indeed they were to do later. The Scottish church, intact as an institution, and weakened by the commendatory system and moral failures, was a greater asset to James than a reformed church, catholic or protestant, was likely to be. At his death the nobles were no weaker, clerics no better, than before; and in spite of the laws against heretical books, the exile of Alesius, Maccabaeus, Seton and others, the burning of a few persons at one date or another on charges of heresy, the pro-English and anti-catholic party had increased in strength and religious disaffection had reached serious proportions in some of the ports, notably Dundee.

After James's death, the regency of Arran and the imprisonment of the cardinal sparked off premature action by the protestant party in Dundee, Perth and Edinburgh, with destruction of friaries in Dundee and burning of Lindores Abbey. Attempts upon friaries in Edinburgh were thwarted by the burgesses, whose anger and suspicion as to his part in events caused the English ambassador to leave the town for a while.[36] There was a typical religio-political situation, in fact, with the English government pressing the idea of marriage between the infant queen and the child Prince Edward, at normal diplomatic level, and supporting a strange variety of interests behind the scenes in order to strengthen its position within Scotland. Financial greed or religious zeal were equally welcome allies to Henry VIII: to the Scottish protestants the English alliance gave hopes of solid success.

The collapse of Arran was followed by the most rigorous campaign against heresy in our pre-reformation history, when the cardinal became the effective ruler of the country. Given the circumstances, his action was hardly surprising: a movement involving not simply heresy, but mob violence, arson, sedition and treasonable conspiracy with a foreign government, was reason enough for any government to take strong action. As we have seen earlier, there is no occasion to wonder at the

---

35. *Cf. supra*, pp. 68-70. James's policy should also be related to French proceedings against heresy. He may have disliked heresy hunts personally but have felt compelled by political expediency to engage in them to a limited extent.

36. Thorpe, *Calendar of State Papers*, i, p. 44.

relations between Scottish protestants and the English government, viewed in the light of current theory. Few people at the time would have been outraged by the suggestion that George Wishart was an associate of conspirators who were discussing with a foreign power how much they might expect to be paid for kidnapping or assassinating the chancellor of Scotland. Nor were they outraged by the latter's measures when he succeeded in thwarting the opposition for a time. What is surprising once again, as so often in sixteenth-century Scotland, is not the action taken by Beaton, but the small numbers executed compared to those in similar proceedings elsewhere, for example, in the suppression of risings in England in the previous decade. The measures adopted seemed thoroughly successful against what the cardinal described as " the whole pollution and plague of Anglican impiety."[37] He wrote to the pope afterwards; " By the clemency of Almighty God those differences with regard to the Christian religion and the heretical opinions which formerly flourished have been almost extinguished."[38] After his murder, however, there was to be that series of military efforts by the English government to subdue Scotland which inspired John ab Ulmis' hope of its conversion and which were eventually countered with the help of French forces. After the peace of 1550, it appeared to some that the danger was over, and the provincial council of 1551-52 could reflect with relief that the " frightful heresies " which had within the previous few years " run riot in many diverse parts of this realm have now at last been checked by the providence of All-good and Almighty God, the singular goodwill of princes, and the vigilance and zeal of prelates for the Catholic faith, and seem almost extinguished."[39]

The relief was perhaps understandable, but vain. Beaton had struck at the man who appeared as the ideological leader of the heretical movement, and by his measures in the disaffected towns had struck more severely than anyone before him against heresy. English intervention had failed to secure its end, and the church was giving attention to the problem of setting itself in order. Nevertheless, the optimism, or short-sightedness, of the council is surprising, and we may wonder how it could deceive itself into thinking that heresy was under control. Was it speaking only as a matter of form, with an eye maybe to opinion abroad, especially in Rome ? Was it really unaware that the most important members of the pro-English and heterodox reforming party were still untouched ? It was true of cases of heresy as of other cases, civil or criminal, in Scotland at that time, that the really important people rarely suffered the supreme penalty for anything, unless some deep personal or family antagonism was involved. When examples seemed called for, it was generally the smaller people who suffered. The list of those executed before 1560 is a good illustration of this. Patrick Hamilton is perhaps an exception, although it is possible that his death was brought about more by the political scheming of Angus than by the intention of the clergy, and by his own refusal to find safety in flight with the connivance of Archbishop James Beaton of St. Andrews.[40] Wishart was an important leader,

37. Cardinal Beaton to Pope Paul III: cf. Theiner, *Vetera Monumenta Hibernorum atque Scotorum historiam illustrantia* (Rome, 1864), p. 614. Quoted in MacEwen, *History of the Church in Scotland* (London, 1915), i, p. 438. See MacEwen for fuller details of the cardinal's proceedings against heresy.

38. Theiner, *loc. cit.*

39. *Statutes*, p. 143.

40. *Cf.* Herkless, *Cardinal Beaton* (Edinburgh, 1891), pp. 94-6.

involved at least by personal association with desperate plans. But the others who died were not outstandingly important in church or state; Stratoun, Gourlay, Keillour, Beveridge, Russell, Kennedy, Forret, Henry Forrest, Simson, Roger, some citizens of Perth, Stirling and Cupar, Adam Wallace and Walter Mill. They were members of the lesser clergy, friars, townsfolk, a few minor gentry, executed as a warning to the common people and to the clergy who were in most intimate contact with the people, but leaving untouched the nobles who intrigued with foreign protestantism, the higher clergy, and the unsound members of the universities. The effect of such a policy was to leave the vital problems unsolved, intensified rather by the brave sincerity of those who suffered, whose example made others wonder if perhaps they were right in what they taught. Those who died for their beliefs were an eloquent contrast to many of their judges, whose daily life was a caricature of what they professed. Their sufferings wakened sympathetic interest among a people not generally disposed to suffer much for religion, so greatly had charity decayed; and they provided magnificent material for the new type of eloquence so tremendously exemplified in the written and spoken word of Knox.

Cardinal Beaton could have gone no further than he did, whatever his ideas, without rousing overwhelming opposition among the greater lords. Mary of Lorraine had one advantage, denied to Beaton and to other Scottish rulers in that age; during the short reign of Mary Tudor she was freed from English government interference in support of Scottish protestantism. Had there been the type of ruthless alliance against protestantism which so many imagined to exist, the situation would then have been grim for the protestant party in Scotland, with Tudor and Guise united in a policy of repression of heresy in both countries. But whatever common interest there may, or may not have been, between the two women, it was transcended by the realities of Franco-Spanish political rivalry. In France itself political interest was supreme; (Knox was safe there when he fled from Mary Tudor's England.) In Scotland, even if Mary of Lorraine had been willing to take extreme action against the protestant leaders, her government was never strong enough to do so. The " band " signed by the protestant lords on December 3rd, 1557, has been described as a document than which " nothing could be plainer as a manifesto of revolution ".[41] To anyone acquainted with the teaching of Geneva and Zurich, and its practical effect in Europe, this must have been obvious. But it was followed by a policy of temporising on Mary's part, and talk of liberty of religion, which could lead to no peace, whether she herself was insincere or not in offering some sort of toleration. The Lords of the Congregation had declared: " We shall with all diligence continually apply our whole power, substance, and our very lives, to maintain, set forward, and establish the most blessed word of God and his Congregation; " they had denounced the " Congregation of Sathan, with all the superstitions, abominations and idolatry therof ", promising themselves to be " manifestly enemies thereto ".[42] A resolution adopted immediately afterwards would have imposed their chosen order of worship on every parish church in Scotland.[43] It was the opening of a

41. Law Mathieson, *Politics and Religion in Scotland* (Glasgow, 1902), i, p. 51: *cf.* also the judgment on p. 51 that had the regent at once declared war " her conduct would have been irreproachable ".

42. Dickinson's *Knox*, i, p. 136.

43. *Ibid.*, p. 137 seq.

campaign whose object was the abolition of the mass in Scotland, with all other forms of " impiety, superstition, and idolatry " as defined in Geneva.

The time was propitious. England and France were at war, and the queen-regent in a correspondingly difficult position. It was soon to be even better for the Congregation with the accession of Elizabeth to the throne of England. Fanaticism was now let loose, with the experience of English and continental struggles behind it. It appealed for support to all who were oppressed by the economic difficulties of the time, stressing the part of churchmen in bringing these about, and holding out hopes that the wealth of the church would be applied for relief of the poor. It voiced popular resentment against foreign soldiery, taking advantage of the common ignorance or forgetfulness of its own part in bringing on Scotland much heavier sufferings at the hands of English forces in the previous decade. It appealed also to the nobles who resented foreigners in important offices, and Mary's efforts to enforce civil order with their support. The growth of French influence had given solid reason for alarm. The mob, made up of the " tails " of the nobility and of the " rascal multitude " of strong beggars who would be a problem for a century more, was worked up by inflammatory sermons not primarily against the notorious centres of loose living among the clergy, nor against the centres of greatest wealth, but against the friaries and other orthodox centres which might offer serious opposition.[44]

It was to take over two years, and English intervention, before the Congregation was able to achieve a precarious control of the machinery of government and have the saying and the hearing of mass proscribed, with the penalty of death for the third offence.[45] Nearly four years were to pass from the signing of the " Band " to the return of Mary, Queen of Scots. During that time there was no consistent or powerful opposition to the fierce determination of the preachers, the ferocity of the mob which their demagoguery whipped up, and the diplomatic skill of the small group of politicians who moved at the centre of it all. A foreign commentator would remark: " Even Mohammed never had such arms as the heretics have now with their freedom in printing, licence in promising, their abuse of taxes and imposts as unendurable, and the hopes they hold out of dividing the goods of the Church among the poor."[46] The principles behind the urgent preaching have been noted already, but one more expression of them, written at a later date, may be added, from the *Memoirs* of Knox's secretary: " Howsoever a wicked religion enteris in, as sone as the same is knowin to be wicked, how long continewance, or whatsoever authoritie it hes had, it ought incontinent to be reiected, and the preachoris dewitie is to admonis the people thereof, commanding thame to reiect it and embrace the treuth: and that becaus ane wicked religione tendis directlie to the dishonour of the name of God, which on

---

44. *The Beggars' Summounds*, fixed to the doors of friaries on January 1st, 1558-59, was obviously inspired by Simon Fish's *Supplication of the Beggars* which had been so widely distributed in England over twenty years before. How much sincerity was in it may be guessed by comparing the revenues of the Greyfriars and Blackfriars houses with those of the chief ministers and the superintendents. John Knox was almost certainly wealthier after the reformation than any house of Black or Grey Friars had been in 1558, with one exception.

45. *Cf. Source Book*, ii, pp. 175-8.

46. *Negotiations*, p. 465. The remark was made in 1565 but applies just as well to the years between then and 1560. Skilful use was made of the printing press, specially after 1567. What printing of catholic apologetic there was in Scotland seems to have come to an end with the arrest of John Scot, the printer, in 1562, and the suppression of Ninian Winzet's *Last Blast of the Trompet aganis the usurpit auctoritie of Johne Knox and his Calviniane brether.*

no wayis aucht to be sufferit, yea, not ane hour."[47] Archbishop Hamilton wrote to Mary of Lorraine in September, 1559: " Thay ar heycht in thar wordis—as syndray hes schauin me that hes spokin with tham—and bostis and menasis to bryne and slay tham that will nocht ryd with thame, and now callis all that thai do the defence of the realm and furtht settin of the authorities to the effect that the pepill may haiff that opinion of tham, that the thyngis that thai haiff enterprisit be for the defence and weill of the realm."[48] The whole picture, as can be seen so well in Knox's *History*, is of a highly inflamed situation in which riots were inevitable, if words had any force. Individuals and unarmed communities were helpless before the storm which swept from the Mearns in the north down through Fife and the Lothians to Ayrshire in the south-west. They mostly bowed before it, believing that it was temporary in many cases, and hoping that the government would recover control, with or without foreign assistance.[49] Not for the last time a determined minority with a clear purpose and a command of revolutionary techniques gained the upper hand over a divided, intellectually confused, timid and weakly led majority.

The material damage caused by the supporters of the Congregation has been surveyed elsewhere.[50] It may be wondered whether there was also any loss of life in the course of these proceedings. The Brockie manuscript has some graphic accounts of the rioting, in parts of Fife especially. We read of a friar dying of injuries received when the Dominican house in Perth was destroyed; of others waylaid, beaten and left half-dead; of aged religious dying in the flames of their cloisters. The source is suspect, especially in view of the fact that one of the most eloquent passages describes the death of an otherwise unrecorded Dominican, superior of a priory which quite certainly was not in existence![51] But before the possibility of such incidents is altogether dismissed it is worth remembering the experiences of the papal nuncio De Gouda when he visited Scotland in 1562, and the terror of Henry Sinclair who expected his house to be sacked within twenty-four hours if he received the nuncio. People were afraid for their lives when the mob was loose. They were afraid also of assassination under cover of darkness, the " attempts of secret miscreants ".[52]

To what extent their fears were justified we shall probably never be able to say precisely. Had there been any considerable loss of life, presumably De Gouda would have said something about it, and so would those Scottish Jesuits who wrote later about the state of their native country. On the other hand, there is evidence that such fears were not entirely groundless. The will to slay is plain in the preaching, and in many passages of Knox. But from the beginning the shapers of repression from the protestant side were more subtle than their catholic predecessors in Scotland. They had learned from experience abroad and in England

47. Richard Bannatyne, *Memorials of Transactions in Scotland* (Edinburgh, 1806), p. 162. Bannatyne was Knox's secretary.
48. A. I. Cameron, *Scottish Correspondence of Mary of Lorraine*, 1543-1560 (S.H.S., 1927), p. 427.
49. There were numerous property transactions, entered into by clergy with members of the laity, whose terms suppose a temporary upset.
50. See below, " The Material Destruction caused by the Scottish Reformation."
51. The Dominican Priory of Selkirk was a flourishing house in 1559, according to Brockie's account, but there is no trace of it in any Scottish or Dominican sources known to me, not even in a survey of Dominican houses sent to the Master-General by the last Provincial of the Order in Scotland shortly before their destruction !
52. See De Gouda's letter to Father Laynez, *Negotiations*, pp. 129-39. If Henry Sinclair had read his copy of Calvin's *Defensio Orthodoxae Fidei*, he had good reason to be alarmed.

the value of fostering a legend of catholic cruelty and of playing down anything that might support a *tu quoque*. There was not as yet any significant reaction against cruelty in Scotland, except perhaps on the part of some individuals, whom we shall notice later. Knox had no objection to burning people; he objected to the burning of members of his own party, and saw the tactical importance of not burning catholics; but he personally —and his colleagues then and later—would approve and assist at the burning of people condemned for witchcraft or other crimes.[53] In Scotland before and long after 1560, torture was used to extract confessions; men were broken at the wheel; men and women were burnt alive; there are even cases of children being tortured. Officers of the crown and representative clergy, including some notable ministers in the second part of the century, were involved in such proceedings.[54]

There was disagreement, however, among the protestant leaders themselves on the methods to be adopted in following up the successes of 1559-60. The politically wise restrained the religious zealots who would have adopted more rigorous measures. The position is illustrated in Knox's description of what happened at Holyrood on the first Sunday after Mary's arrival from France.[55] " Preparation began to be made for that idol the Mass to be said in the Chapel; which pierced the hearts of all. The godly began to bolden; and men began openly to speak: ' Shall that idol be suffered again to take place within this realm ? It shall not.' The Lord Lindsay (then but Master), with the gentlemen of Fife, and others, plainly cried in the close, ' The idolater priest should die the death,' according to God's law. One that carried in the candle was evil affrayed; but then began flesh and blood to show itself. There durst no Papist neither yet any that came out of France whisper. But the Lord James (the man whom all the godly did most reverence) took upon him to keep the Chapel door. His best excuse was, that he would stop all Scottish men to enter in to the Mass. But it was, and is, sufficiently known that the door was kept that none should have entry to trouble the priest, who, after the Mass, was committed to the protection of Lord John of Coldingham and Lord Robert of Holyroodhouse, who then were both Protestants, and had communicated at the Table of the Lord. Betwix them two was the priest convoyed to his chamber. And so the godly departed with great grief of heart, and at afternoon repaired to the Abbey in great companies, and gave plain signification that they could not abide that the land which God by his power had purged from idolatry should in their eyes be polluted again." The cry had been: " Let us hang the priest." The Earl of Arran protested against the queen's proclamation to prevent further disturbance in religion, that although

---

53. The first execution which the Rev. James Melvill ever witnessed was that of a witch in St. Andrews " against the quhilk Mr. Knox delt from the pulpet, sche being set upe at a pillar befor him ". *The Diary of Mr. James Melvill*, 1556-1601 (Bannatyne Club, 1829). Was this perhaps the same witch burnt at St. Andrews by the Regent Moray's authority in 1569 ? *Cf. Historie of King James the Sext*, p. 66.

54. See, for example, Pitcairn, *Criminal Trials* (Bannatyne Club, 1833), i, pt. 1, pp. 206-7, 327; pt. 2, pp. 49, 214, 241, 375-7. Those sentenced to be burnt were usually strangled first, as Wishart appears to have been; but Patrick Hamilton was burnt alive, so was Lady Glamis on a rather different charge in 1537, so were two men convicted of sodomy in Edinburgh in 1570. *The Historie of James the Sext* tells us (p. 104): " They were punisht in this maner; first, they were detenit in prisoun for aucht dayes, upoun bread and water, then they were placitt at the market place, with the inscriptioun of thair fault written on thair foirhead. Efter that they were placitt in kirke, to repent befoir the people thrie several Sondayes: forthlie they were dukit in a deep loche, over the head thrie several tymes, and last of all thair bodies were consumit with fire to the death." See also *Diurnal of Occurrents*, pp. 185-6. In 1591 Eufame Makcalzean was burnt alive in Edinburgh. For members of a commission set up in that year to discover witches, see *Register of the Privy Council of Scotland*, iv, p. 680.

55. Dickinson's *Knox*, ii, p. 8. *Cf.* also pp. 25-8, on divisions between the lords and the ministers.

he was obedient to her, and had learned " in Christ's school, to keep peace with all men," nevertheless " Since that God has said, ' The idolater shall die the death,' we protest solemnly, in presence of God and in the ears of the whole people that hear this Proclamation . . . that if any of her servants shall commit idolatry, specially say Mass, participate therewith, or take the defence thereof (which we were loth should be in her Grace's company), in that case, that this Proclamation be not extended to them in that behalf, nor be not a safeguard or gyrth to them in that behalf, no more nor if they commit slaughter or murder, seeing the one is mekle more abominable and odious in the sight of God than is the other: But that it may be lawful to inflict upon them the pains contained in God's word against idolaters, wherever they may be apprehended, but favour."[56] The general assembly had been pressing a few months earlier for the enforcement of the provisions of 1560. The queen's persuasions, and the influence of her half-brothers who feature in the scene described above, brought a slackening for a time of " that fervency that God had kindled in others."[57] It was hoped to bring her to hear sermons and by that means she might be won over to the support of the kirk, a " godly prince " to enforce reformed orthodoxy.

In the meantime, while the position of the supreme civil authority was in such doubt, there were interesting attempts to establish the pattern of " a reformed city " in some of the more important towns where the protestant party was in significant strength. The authority of the burgh magistrates could be a means of strengthening the position of the reformers in key positions in the country; and so it proved. Hence the accusations made from time to time that they caused the burgh officials to exceed their traditional and lawful powers.[58]

The way in which religious and temporal power worked together at municipal level can be illustrated from records of Edinburgh and St. Andrews, but first something should be said about the phrase " votes and consent " quoted above. Such phrases have often been used as evidence that the Scottish reformers were in some way founders of modern democracy. If they were, it was " people's democracy ", and

56. Dickinson's *Knox*, ii, p. 11. This was James Hamilton, third earl, whose father and Archbishop Hamilton were half-brothers. Like other great families, the Hamiltons were divided in religion. It is interesting that Arran perceived, what is sometimes overlooked, that Mary's proclamation, although " penned and put in form by such as before professed Christ Jesus (for in the Council then had Papists neither power nor vote)" (*op. cit.*, p. 10), could be interpreted as allowing catholic practice to continue, for example, in churches not actually occupied by protestants. The vital section stated that until the queen, with advice of the estates of the realm should " have taken a final order . . . which her Majesty hopes shall be to the contentment of the whole, that none of them take upon hand, privately or openly, to make alteration or innovation of the state of religion, or attempt anything against the form which her Majesty found publicly and universally standing at her Majesty's arrival in this her Realm, under the pain of death: With certification, that if any subject of the Realm shall come in the contrary hereof, he shall be esteemed and held a seditious person and raiser of tumult, and the said pain shall be executed upon him with all rigour to the example of others." As Mary had not ratified the enactments of the 1560 parliament, this proclamation could be interpreted as accepting the *status quo* in an attempt to halt further development. On the proceedings of the parliament, see Gordon Donaldson, *The Scottish Reformation* (Cambridge, 1960), p. 67. But on the prosecutions referred to there, see also Dickinson's *Knox*, ii, pp. 70-1.

57. Dickinson's *Knox*, ii, p. 13.

58. *E.g.* Winzet, *The Buke of Four Scoir Thre Questions* (Antwerp, 1563), q. 29, reprinted in *Certane Tractatis* (Scottish Text Society, 1888), p. 94. " Quhy allow ze, and prouokis also, the prouestis and ballies of euiry burgh (quhome we can nocht call magistratis properlie, as ze do, sen thai ar nocht principalis in a fre citie, as wes Rome, to mak lawis, bot suld be subditis to our Souerane Lady) to baneis Christianis and trew Scottismen fra thair roumes and possessiones, confisk thair guidis, put thame to the horne and condemne thame to the dethe, for breking only of thair actis and decreis unknawin to our Souerane Lady, or hir Maiestie's praedecessouris, sen thai haif only pouer to puniss thair awin comburgessis in an viij ss. unlaw or siclyke ? " See also Knox's words, testifying to the effectiveness of the revolution in some of the burghs: " What adulterer, what fornicator, what known mass-monger, or pestilent Papist, durst have been seen in public, within any reformed town within this realm, before that the Queen arrived ? " Dickinson's *Knox*, ii, p. 4. Also to be noted, as throwing further light on the way in which this situation was brought about, are some words in one of his letters, mentioning that priests in Perth were forbidden to say mass there with threats of death. Laing's edition of Knox's *Works*, vi, p. 23.

certainly not majority rule which was their ideal. Given the nature of their religious teaching, it was unlikely that popular voting would give the desired control over the life of the community; as Knox said to Lethington: " Idolatry and a false religion hath ever been, is, and will be, pleasing to the most part of men." [59] This conviction was demonstrated in Edinburgh in July, 1559, when the suggestion was made by Mary of Lorraine that a temporary religious settlement might be arranged by a vote. She left it to the town to decide whether the voting should be by the members of the council and the deacons of the craft guilds, or by all the citizens personally. To this proposal the " faithful brethren of the congregation within Edinburgh " replied; " We for our pairtis knawand the religioun quhilk we hawe presentlie to be of God and conforme to his word, and on the uther pairt knawand the mes and the papis haill religioun to be without the word of God, altogither superstitious damnable idolatrie and of the devill, can nocht consent for our pairtis that Goddis treuthe and that our religioun now establischit conforme to his worde sall be subject to voiting of men, as gif the maist pairt of men allowit it nocht it sould be rejectit, for it is na new thing but mair nor notoir that fra the beginnyng of the world to this day and evin now in all contreyis townis and citeis the maist pairt of men has ever bene aganis God and his treuthe, at the leist hes nocht planlie embraced the samyn." [60] Exactly three years later it would be resolved by the provost and baillies of Edinburgh that there should be religious tests for offices in the burgh, to be accepted not only by office-bearers themselves but by the electors. The resolution was quashed by the queen, but it would reappear in Edinburgh and elsewhere after her downfall, and remains a witness to the type of democracy envisaged by the reformation party. [61] As will be seen from the extract which follows, there were to be penalties for any electors who failed to support the approved type of candidate; an example of what we are now familiar with as " single list " election was designed.

"All in ane voce, votis, grantis, consentis, statutis and ordanis that fra this furth thair sall nane bruke office within this burgh of provest, baillies, dene of gild, thesaurer, dekyn of craft, nor uther office, bot sic as hes adionit thame to the trew kirk of God and congregatioun, and hes communicat with bayth sacramentis, and hes submittit thameselffis under discipline, and gyf ony uther beis chosen, nocht onlie sic to be deprivit bot the electeris and chesaris of thame with thame selffis to be punissit with rigor as manifest contempnaris of all gude and godlie ordour; and this act to be observit in all tymes cuming without the prejudice of the officeris and dekynnis presentlie in office for this instant yeir." [62] The passage reflects an anxiety to tighten effective control over the town, less confidently held since the queen's return, and not so securely even before that, to judge from the fact that soldiers of the Earl of Arran's guard had been hired in July, 1561, for " repressing of the wikit ". [63] The meaning of the term may perhaps be deduced from the proclamations made a short time before, such as that of March 24th, 1560-61, against priests, friars, and other such who were " ganging maist

---

59. Dickinson's *Knox*, ii, p. 110.

60. *Extracts from the Records of the Burgh of Edinburgh*, iii, p. 46.

61. *Op. cit.*, pp. 140-1. See the addition to the burgess oath in 1587, making profession of " the trew relligioun . . . detesting the Romayne relligioun callit papistry ", *ibid.*, p. 497.

62. *Edinburgh Burgh Extracts*, p. 140.

63. *Op. cit.*, pp. 118-9.

bisselie, as is surelie knawin to use, the magistratis of this burgh (into), all the pairtis of the said toun, sawing thair ungodlie opinionis and detestable (workis)".[64] The command of God to root out the wicked and ungodly is recalled in the course of the proclamation. Another shows an association of offenders which was to be almost common form in such documents: " The provest, ballies, counsaill and ane pairt of the dekines of craftis, haveing consideratioun of the grit number of idolatreris quhoremaisteris and harlottis daylie resortand within this burgh, provokand the indignatioun of God upone the samyn ofttymes furtheschawin be the prechouris, ordanis ane proclamatioun to be maid in dew forme and ample that all sic personis cum in presens of the said minister or the elderis to gif testimonie of thair conversioun for the saidis abusis respective betwix [now] and Sonday at none nixttocum, or falyeing thairof the saidis idolatreris to be diffamit be setting thame upone the merkett croce thair to remane for the space of vi houris for thair first falt, carying of the saidis bordelaris houremaisteris and harlottis throw the toun in ane carte for thair first falt, birnying of bayth the kyndis of the saidis personis on the cheik for the second falt, and banisching the toun, and for the thrid falt to be punischit to the deid."[65]

A similar proclamation was made in the beginning of October, 1561, against priests, monks, friars and nuns, that they should leave the burgh and its bounds within twenty-four hours " under the pane of carting through the toun, byrning on the cheik, and banessing the samyn for euir."[66] To some extent words were backed by action against those who opposed, or were indifferent to, the kirk. The obstinate were to be compelled to come to the sermons.[67] There were punishments for those who used injurious or railing words against the ministers or their doctrine; so Ninian M'Crechane, cook to Timothy Bancour (otherwise Timotheo Cagnioli), was scourged and then put in the branks " as ane raillar and sklanderer " who had spoken against John Knox.[68] Master Alexander Skene, advocate, was imprisoned in the Tolbooth at his own expense on May 30th, 1561, for having received " the diabolicall idoll callit the preistis sacrament at Pasche last ". He was freed on June 16th on condition that by July 10th he had made submission to the kirk or else left the burgh himself and his whole family.[69] On the same day Sir George Strachan, priest, was ordered to leave within twenty-four hours.[70] For some reason he escaped more lightly than the priest taken at mass in 1565 and tied three hours together, three successive days, at the mercat cross of Edinburgh with his chalice and vestments, pelted with eggs and rubbish so that he hardly escaped with his life. There are several accounts of this incident.[71] Knox's is especially interesting. The day after his capture the priest " with his assistants, were accused and convicted by an assize according to the Act of Parliament. And albeit for the same offence he deserved death, yet for all punishment he was set upon the Market-Cross for the space of three or four hours, the hangman standing

---

64. *Op. cit.*, p. 101.
65. *Op. cit.*, p. 65.
66. *Op. cit.*, p. 125.
67. *Op. cit.*, p. 107 (April, 1561).
68. *Op. cit.*, p. 132 (April, 1562). See also p. 167.
69. *Op. cit.*, pp. 115, 117. Where could a man and his family hope to live when such " discipline " extended throughout the country ?
70. *Ibid.*
71. Randolph to Leicester, *Calendar of State Papers, Scotland*, ii, 826; *Edinburgh Burgh Extracts*, p. 195; Dickinson's *Knox*, ii, p. 141.

by, and keeping him, the boys and others were busy with eggs casting; and some Papists there were that stopped it as far as they could: and as the press of people increased about the Cross, there appeared to have been some tumult. The Provost, Archibald Douglas, came with some halberdiers, and carried the priest safe again to the Tolbooth." The queen was angry, but the provost and council sent an account of events which satisfied her and she took no action beyond ordering the priest to be set free a few days later, leaving it to the burgh officials to deal with those responsible for the tumult. It gave some idea, remarked Knox, of how angry she would have been if the priest had been used according to his merits.

The affair illustrates the presence in Edinburgh of a still strong catholic opinion, prepared to assert itself on occasion. It also shows the restraining effect of the queen's authority. Both factors limited the protestant party in its efforts to enforce the questionably valid legislation of 1560 and to make capital of the queen's proclamation forbidding any change in the religious situation which existed when she landed. This was shown remarkably in 1563 when the Archbishop of St. Andrews and nearly fifty priests and laymen were arrested on a charge of contravening the law governing religion by saying or hearing mass and hearing confessions in Paisley, Renfrew, Glasgow, and other parts of the west. After a short time in ward, they were released on surety.[72] Knox had been afraid of active interference on their behalf to judge by a letter he sent to Argyll.[73] In their release he saw malice; the fact that arrests had been made at all he attributed to the queen's diplomatic subtlety, as a gesture which would quieten the protestant party before the opening of parliament and so make it more amenable to her wishes.[74] He may well have been right in seeing the arrest as a political move and nothing more; unfortunately, he and many, though not all, in his party, saw in every act of clemency or compromise a step towards fulfilment of a plan to eliminate all protestants in Scotland.

Later in the same year, 1563, twenty-two men and women of Edinburgh were " delatit for arte and parte of the cuming to the Chapell of our soueran ladeis Palice of Halyrudehouse . . . and swa becumyng manifest transgressouris, violatouris, and brekaris of our soueranne ladeis Proclamationis, and as seditious persones, raseris of Tumult and publict uproir aganis the commoun peax and quietnes of the realme: And swa aucht to be adiugit and punesit to the deid with all rigour."[75] The hearing was adjourned, and we have no further notice of it. Presumably once again royal influence may have been responsible for a case being dropped. Another instance is Mary's intervention to remove Father John Black, O.P., from the burgh jurisdiction to her own when an attempt was being made against him under cover of law.[76] She was unable to save him in the end; first, he was set upon and severely wounded by a small group of Edinburgh protestants under cover of darkness in the street, and then killed in Holyrood on the night when Riccio was mur-

---

72. Dickinson's *Knox*, ii, p. 77.
73. *Ibid.*, pp. 74-76.
74. *Ibid.*, p. 77.
75. Pitcairn, i, pt. 1, p. 435.
76. *Edinburgh Burgh Extracts*, iii, p. 133. See also p. 131 where the charge against him is given. The real offence is perhaps indicated in the reference to " the copie of his awin bill writtin be him to be send furth of the realme, contenying the secretis thairof and utheris fals reportis ".

dered.[77] There are other significant incidents in the town during these years, such as the suppression of Ninian Winzet's publication of catholic tractates[78] or the buffetting of a priest at Holyrood,[79] which may leave us wondering how much happened of which we have no record. At any rate, it is clear that there was little hope of setting up a " reformed city " in Edinburgh unless Mary changed her own attitude, or lost what power she had. And whether we accept the figures for Easter communions at Holyrood in 1565 or not, there is sufficient evidence that the preachers who lived in the shelter of the court were having some success, and that there was enough of a catholic revival to alarm not only Knox but also Randolph, who wrote to Cecil that there had been no greater triumph " in any time of most popery " than in the recent celebration of Easter.[80]

In St. Andrews the situation was more favourable to the establishment of " a reformed city ". The court was distant; there was no great and hostile nobleman in the vicinity to trouble the burgh authorities; and there was a strong body of citizens, numbering over three hundred men, joined to the reformed kirk as early as July, 1559.[81] There was some possibility of attempting the necessary instruction of the people and the enforcement of moral discipline. There were double sanctions; offenders were called to submit to ecclesiastical discipline, and were also recommended to the civil magistrates for further correction. The ecclesiastical discipline generally meant some form of public penance, sitting on the stool of penance before the congregation during service or standing at the church door in penitential garments for a stated time on one or more Sundays, with public admission of guilt and submission to public reproof.[82] Repeated faults were visited with excommunication, which became a sentence of terrible effectiveness as the hold of protestantism on the social structure tightened. It appears in St. Andrews that the kirk session could not only call upon the civil magistrates to support it, but had also its own prison and could send its own officers to investigate the private lives of the citizens and call them to account.[83] We can see in the kirk session register the anatomy of a system of surveillance and compulsion designed to produce uniformity of belief, worship, and moral behaviour, and allowing no place in the life of the city to any nonconformist. As the

---

77. *Cf.* Pitcairn, i, pt. 1, p. 475. Bishop Parkhurst of Norwich wrote to Bullinger from Ludham on August 21st, 1566: " In the month of March an Italian called Signor David, skilled in necromancy, and in great favour with the queen of Scots, was forcibly dragged out of her chamber in her presence, and died wretchedly pierced by many stabs. A certain abbot was wounded at the same place, and escaped with difficulty, but died of his wounds shortly after. A monk named Black, a Dominican friar, and a chief man among the papists, was killed in the court at the same time." *Zurich Letters* (Parker Society, 1842), p. 99. The abbot was apparently William Ker of Kelso. *Historie of James the Sext*, p. 7. Laing remarks (Knox's *Works*, ii, p. 594): " It is singular that no notice of this should occur in our own historical writers ". It certainly is singular, especially as other English writers noted his murder with so much interest. Bedford and Randolph both reported it soon after in their letters to England: *cf.* Bain, *Calendar of State Papers, Scotland*, ii, pp. 10, 267. The Spanish ambassador in London reported it to his master: *cf.* Hume, *Spanish State Papers, Calendar of Letters relating to English Affairs*, 23rd March, 1566. The silence of Knox and other Scottish sources about Father Black's murder illustrates their weakness as evidence as to what action may have been taken against defenders of the old religion. Another illustration of how much remains dark is provided by a passage in the *Diurnal of Occurrents*, pp. 340-1, on the suicide of Robert Drummond, alias Dr. Handie, who had been " ane lang servand (of the magistrates) and ane greit seikar and apprehendar of all preistis and papists ". Drummond killed himself in 1574. How long had he been active as a pursuivant ? Where are the official records of his activity ? Were any kept ?

78. *Cf.* Dickson and Edmond, *Annals of Scottish Printing* (Cambridge, 1890), pp. 155-7.

79. Randolph to Cecil. He remarked that " the poor soul (is) much troubled for the preservation of her silly mass ". *Calendar of State Papers, Scotland*, i, p. 186.

80. *Op. cit.*, pp. 207-8: *cf.* also *Negotiations*, pp. 495, 496, 521; Dickinson's *Knox*, ii, p. 185.

81. Hay Fleming, *Register of the Kirk Session of St. Andrews* (S.H.S., 2 volumes, with continuous pagination, 1889, 1890), pp. 6 seq.

82. The number of Sundays might be considerable. Henry Tailyeour, in 1574, after ten Sundays on the penitent stool, had to do ten more and stand in sack-cloth at the kirk door each Sunday before going to the seat. He was the father of an illegitimate child, *op. cit.*, p. 402.

83. *Cf. op. cit.*, pp. 156, 371, 409, 417, 427, 614, among other examples.

sixteenth century went on, the pattern illustrated in St. Andrews was fought for in the country as a whole by the keener members of the reforming party and was at last set up effectively, for a time, in the seventeenth century, in most of Lowland Scotland.

Uniformity of belief was to be advanced mainly by public preaching, at which attendance was obligatory. The *First Book of Discipline* had thought it expedient that in the greater towns there should be a sermon or common prayers or at least " some exercise of reading the Scriptures " every day.[84] In every " notable " town there should be at least one day in the week, in addition to Sunday, with sermon and prayers. In the smaller towns and country places the local congregation would have to decide what was possible, but everywhere there must be strict observation of Sunday, with preaching in the morning and the public exercise of children in the catechism in the afternoon. No work was to be done during the time of sermon during the week. Absence from the preaching was noted, and punished. Proofs of orthodoxy were sought by the session and successful examination was a necessary passport to an untroubled life. By 1570 even the distribution of poor relief was governed by confessional tests. In August of that year it was resolved that there should be no grant of alms to the poor "bot to theis that frequentis and cummis to sermondis, public prayeris, examinatioun and communioun, presenting of thair bairnis to baptisme, and wil gyf compt of thair faitht, and can say the Lordis Prayer, Beleve, and Commandementis of God, or at the least sal learn the sam wythin ane monetht."[85]

Later we find directions that the town should be quartered " to the effect that trial may be takin of the confession of thair faitht befoir the public fasting and communioun nixt to be celebrat And the inhabitantis namis of this citie to be rollit, according to the act statut red and approvit yerlye in this kirk."[86] A little later in the same year, 1572, we read; " The sessioun statut and ordeined the names of them that wilfullie absentit thame fra the last communioun to be presentit to the seat (i.e., the session), and to that effect trial to be takin of everilk quarter be the ministeris and examinatoris thairof: and siclik that inquisitioun be takin be dilatioun of them that ar common bidars from the doctrine and preachingis the dayis appointeid thairto."[87] By this time it was necessary to take proceedings against those who were coming to communion with forged communion tokens[88]; or slipping in without tokens; the system was producing a pretence of religion, although that does not seem to have troubled those who were enforcing it. At any rate, we find them resolving in 1574 that captors should be chosen to visit the whole town on Sundays to apprehend all those absent from the sermon. The party was to consist of a bailie, an elder, two deacons, two officers armed with halberds.[89] In 1581 there was renewed provision for the enrolment of every citizen so that the whole town might be examined as to its orthodoxy.[90] By 1595 it was being resolved that those who refused to communicate with the orthodox brethren were to be esteemed papists and

---

84. Dickinson's *Knox*, ii, pp. 312-315.
85. *Register of the Kirk Session of St. Andrews*, pp. 340-1.
86. *Op. cit.*, p. 371. The small size of the Scottish burghs made such inquisition easy. A man might hide in Paris or London, but hardly in Edinburgh, and certainly not in the other burghs of Scotland for more than a very brief time.
87. *Ibid.*
88. *Op. cit.*, p. 379.
89. *Op. cit.*, p. 394.
90. *Op. cit.*, p. 453.

punished accordingly; the check on sermon attendance was to be weekly, and to cover not only Sundays but also other days appointed for preaching.[91]

Speech had to be guarded under this system of discipline. As early as May 2nd, 1560, a number of men and women were delated for speaking against the reformed doctrine, against the new communion service, and against John Knox.[92] The accused represent the altercations among the common people, " in the oppin fische mercat ", for example. Typical is William Petillok, who said; " The Divell ane kirk will I gang to ! and, The Divell burn up the kirk or I come into it ! and, It wer gude that Knox war kend the gayt quhare fra he come ! "[93] Still more interesting is the case in July, 1561, of a clerical supporter of the reformation who refused obedience to John Winram in his office of superintendent of Fife, saying that he would not obey " ony admonision or command of that fals, dissaitfull, gredy, and dissemblit smayk, for he wes ane of tham that maist oppressed, smored, and held down the Word of God, and now he is cumin to it, and professis the same for grediness of gayr, lurkand and watchand quhill he may se ane other tym."[94] There was here, of course, a question of obedience, but the sentence against the accused refers repeatedly also to his " blasphemy "; for all of which he had to ask forgiveness publicly of God and the superintendent in the kirks of St. Andrews and Balingry. There must have been a good many who secretly sympathised with the remarks about Winram, who had taken part in the trial and burning of more than one protestant, including that of Walter Mill, less than three years before this.[95] But Winram was now administering a more efficient system of discipline than the one with which he had been previously associated, and slanderous remarks were not allowed to pass unpunished; even when not directly associated with disobedience they were likely to diminish respect for an authority which was still insecure and aware of the magnitude of its task. Punishment varied; John Richardson, who had been excommunicated for contempt and disobedience towards his minister, showed signs of repentance in 1564 and in consideration thereof was ordained to appear the next Sunday at the parish church an hour before the sermon and stand there an hour in the jougs with a paper about his head on which was written " Behold the contempnar."[96] In 1584 one John Campbell knelt before the session and asked forgiveness for his " contumelious talk and opprobrius wordis spokin befoir the session ", but was nevertheless sentenced by a majority vote of the same body to eight days' imprisonment and a fine of ten shillings.[97]

---

91. *Op. cit.*, p. 807. Margaret Ogilvy made public penance for saying to the visitors: " Lett thame gang to the kirk that wynnis thair mait in the kirk ": *ibid.*, p. 811.

92. *Op. cit.*, p. 33 seq.

93. *Op. cit.*, p. 36: *cf.* also *Edinburgh Burgh Extracts*, iii, p. 162.

94. *Op. cit.*, p. 86. The offender, Alexander Wardlaw, refused to surrender his church to a new incumbent appointed by Winram. He apparently continued a protestant in spite of his trouble with the superintendent: *cf.* p. 89, n.1.

95. Winram is an outstanding example of how easily some prominent figures were able to pass from one allegiance to another. In spite of his part in heresy trials and executions, he passed from being vicar-general of the archdiocese one year to being superintendent of Fife in the next without any such elaborate public renunciation of past error as some others in St. Andrews had to make. He was undisturbed in his quarters in St. Andrews, increased his personal income handsomely, and acquired a wife. He was able also to provide for some of his old friends and colleagues. The general assembly reproved him in 1562 for laxness in administration, and his appointments were obviously a matter of complaint. *Cf.* Calderwood, *History*, ii, p. 205.

96. *Register of the Kirk Session of St. Andrews*, p. 229.

97. *Op. cit.*, p. 549.

Of still greater interest are the actions to enforce uniformity of belief and of sacramental practice, especially as so many of these concerned individuals who would have been heretics in the eyes of the catholic church as well as of the kirk session. Andrew Hepburn, in July, 1560, was accused of saying that he would make as good a sacrament as the ministers by hallowing a loaf and a pint of ale, but he also asked " vain questions " about the Trinity.[98] John Bickerton, a saddler in the city, was the centre of a lively action in 1564. He had refused to accept the order used in the administration of baptism, on the ground that it was not firmly based on scripture but idolatry invented by the brain of man. The terms of the indictment are so illuminating that it is worth quoting at length. Bickerton was " delated for contempt of the establesched ordor of the Reformed Kirk wythin the citie of Sanctandrois, in procuryng of his barne, laytlie borne wythin this citie, to be presented to baptisme be Mr. Dauid Meldrum, his self being present for the tym wythin the cite wald nocht present his awyn child to baptisme, tharby gevand occasion of offence and sclander to the hoil kyrk. Johane, called befoyr the ministerie to have beyn accused heirof and comperand, prevenit the accusacione, and, all reverence set asyd, stubburnly, wyth pertinacite, affirmit and mantenit his contempt of the said ordor, saying thir wordis in effect following: Quhat is this ye wald wyth me ? I knaw weyll eneuch it is becaus I wald nocht present my awyn barne to baptisme ! I never presented ane of my awyn barnis to baptisme nor never wyll ! I have nothing to do wyth yow nor yowr ordor, it is nocht grundit upon the Scriptur, it is bot idolatrie inventit be the braen of man ! And albeyd the said Johan confessed that he had communicat at the Lordis tabyll wyth the rest of this congregacion, and also that he had assistit the congregacion wyth his body armit in defence aganis the inimeis impugnoris of the trewth; nevertheles, being required be the ministerie to remane and resave ansuer of the foyrsaidis wordis be hym spokyn and to submit hym to disciplyn, he stubburnly departed, refusand to heir the voce of the kyrk, and denyed hym to have ony thing to do wyth the ministerie, or Superintendent, also present for the tym. In respect of the quhilkis premissis, the ministerye ordenis ane supplicacione to be put in dew forme under the sayll of the ministerie, and gevyn up to the magistratis of this cite, requesting thaim of thar dewetie and office to put sic ordor to the said Ihone that be thar autorite he be brocht to obedience of the kyrk: and gyf this sall nocht serve, the ministerie to procead aganis Jhon Bicartoun to excommunicacion, as to the gretast and last punischement belangand to the spirituall ministerie."[99] Bickerton defended his position before the Town Council, and refused to appear again before the ministers for further discussion. The process had begun early in May, and the session took every means to bring about a settlement before proceeding at last, on July 9th, to sentence of excommunication. By terms of this sentence he was cut off from all normal intercourse, talking, buying, selling, eating, drinking, or anything except what the kirk might appoint for his amendment. Bickerton was an important figure among the craftsmen of St. Andrews,[100] but in the end he had to submit, having " sustenit gret dampneg and disays in guddis and body." His public submission was

---

98. *Op. cit.*, p. 43.
99. *Op. cit.*, pp. 194-206.
100. *Cf. op. cit.*, p. 194 n.2; p. 206 n.1, on his position among the hammermen of St. Andrews, whose deacon he was in 1567.

made on February 18th, and in view of a disease which made him unfit to underly such discipline as his demerits were considered justly to deserve, he was let off with acknowledgement of his fault on his knees in the kirk, with a request for forgiveness, and a promise of obedience in the future.

Such internal discipline was a source of strength to the new kirk, but it was not always possible to enforce it, as was shown in the dispute between Knox and Archibald Hamilton, an elder in St. Andrews. This came about after the assassination of the Regent Moray in 1571, by a Hamilton. Knox's fulminations against the Hamiltons from the pulpit in St. Andrews offended protestant members of that family. Robert Hamilton, himself a minister in St. Andrews, was eventually so indignant that he was reported to have said that " Mr. Knox was als grit a murtherer as ony Hamiltoun in Scotland, gif all thingis were well tryed, and therefore suld not cry out so fast against murtherers: for (said Mr. Robert) he had subscryved to the death of the quenis husband, me lord Darnley, with my lord of Murray, quhilk suld have been done in St. Jhonstoune, as said is."[101] (Knox denied that there was any truth in this accusation by a fellow minister.) Meanwhile, Archibald Hamilton was absenting himself from John Knox's preaching " because that he affirmed in his teaching that the Hamiltons were murderers." When summoned to give a reason to the session for his absence, he said he was grieved to see the pulpit " so abused as it was ". On that, " Mr. Knox willed them to tak sic order as they wald answir to God; as one day they suld, gif ordour were not put to his contempt." Many of the Edinburgh congregation had been glad to see Knox leave that city for St. Andrews, and it seems plain that in St. Andrews there were those also who found him too extreme.[102] On the issue of Archibald Hamilton's absence from the sermons the session compromised, receiving protestations from both parties but apparently giving no decision.[103] In fact, there seems to have been a deep disagreement behind the scenes about what was matter for the pulpit, involving prominent members of the university, and behind Knox's letter to the general assembly in August, 1572, in which he wrote: "Above all things preserve the kirk from the bondage of the universities. Perswade them to ruell them selfis peaceablie, and order thair scholes in Christ, but subject never the pulpet to thair iudgement, neather yit exempt them from your iurisdictione."[104] It was such inner conflicts among the reformers which made it advisable to insist as stringently as they did on complete secrecy about what was said in the course of session meetings; a united front had to be presented to the city, but there was tension in the party.[105]

---

101. Bannatyne, *Memorials*, pp. 380-1.

102. On Archibald Hamilton's dispute, see Bannatyne, pp. 383 seq. In a letter of January, 1560, Knox said he had been judged too extreme and had retired from all public assemblies, *Calendar of State Papers*, i, p. 130. When he left St. Andrews for Edinburgh, Bannatyne tells us, it was " not without dolour and displeasour of the few godlie that were in that town but to the greit ioy and pleasour of the rest ", *Memorials*, p. 373. Even Calvin had been bothered by Knox's extremism and in a letter of 1561 referred to the " thoughtless arrogance of one individual ", *Zurich Letters*, ii, pp. 35 and 21. *Cf.* Beza to Bullinger in 1566: *ibid.*, p. 131.

103. Bannatyne, *loc. cit.*

104. Bannatyne, p. 364. To this Hamilton replied that defence of doctrine was the purpose of setting up centres of learning in the reformed kirks. But Knox was not the only reformer at odds with university opinion. Beza's *Traite de L'Authorite du Magistrat en la Punition des Hérétiques* (1560) was directed " contre l'opinion de certains academiques ".

105. *Cf. Register of the Kirk Session of St. Andrews*, pp. 369, 651 seq. Also *Selections from the Ecclesiastical Records of Aberdeen* (Spalding Club, 1846), p. 13.

Discipline was threatened from another quarter than the university, as is shown in the case of Janet Wemyss, Lady Carslogie, who defied the kirk session and the superintendent when told to separate from one John Dalglesh with whom she was living. Her social and economic existence was not so tightly dependent on the city as that of John Bickerton, and she had barons and gentlemen for friends who were prepared to back some rather vigorous action. The superintendent was persuaded to cease proceedings against her. The details of the case are too lengthy to be followed here. Apparently Lady Carslogie was some kind of protestant herself, as at one point serious illness brought a gesture of submission from her. In the end she had her way, with the help of the court of commissary in Edinburgh, whose decision the session accepted. It was easier to discipline the poor than the rich and influential, as an opponent of the kirk pointed out in print.[106]

It would take too much space to follow the efforts of the session in detail as it strove to suppress adultery and fornication, to enforce Sunday observance, to put down swearing and drunkenness and the observance of Christmas and other such feast days. There were penalties for *not* working on Christmas Day. One obstinate mason called James Thomson was bound over to labour on that day and if no man gave him work it was decreed " he sal wirk sum riggen-stanis of his awin ".[107] Plays, games, Robin Hood plays—there were many things which worked against " the cumlye ordour " of the city. One man was sentenced for having baptized a child, affirming " That may be easy done, any man may baptize ane barn if the barn be waik."[108] It was a long time before Mr. Thomas Methven, Commissary of St. Andrews, was brought to accept the " haill articlis of religioun professit within this realme, and promist nevir to use in tymes cuming ony uther religioun, nor yit that kynd of speking to say that he is nather Papist nor Protestane."[109] That was in 1587, but as early as 1561 he had been threatened with prison, having declared to two deacons sent by the superintendent and ministers to summon him to appear before the session: " That he was nether ane Papist nor ane Calwynist, nor of Paul nor of Apollo, bot Jesus Cristis man; he wald nocht cum to tham nor to thar hows; bot gyf the Superintendent or the minister had ocht to do with him, at thar request he wald cum to that chalmer and speik tham." In respect of this answer the superintendent and the ministry directed supplication to be made to the magistrates of the city " ether to caus hym obeye the ordor of the kyrk and subject hym to disciplynn, or ellis to exclud hym this citie, that na perturbacion of the unite and ordor be brokyn by hym."[110] As such cases show, although there were many difficulties in the way of the establishing of unity and order, the intention of the new kirk was plain; the imperfect or slow attainment of the end was not the fault of those who devised the system but of those who temporised in practice about such large matters

---

106. *Catholic Tractates*, p. 63. For this case, which involved questions of ecclesiastical law in matrimonial cases, and which illustrates so many of the difficulties with which the session had to contend, see *Register of the Kirk Session of St. Andrews*, pp. 207-12, 260 seq., 282, 317, 329-334.

107. The fleshers (butchers) were obstinate offenders against Sunday observance: *cf. op. cit.*, pp. 349, 364. For enactments against swearing and drunkenness, see, for example, pp. 343, 409. In Edinburgh, in 1587, one Bartlemo Bell was banished, under pain of death if found again in the burgh, for singing bawdy songs, *Extracts*, iv, p. 508. For suppression of Christmas, *cf. Register of the Kirk Session of St. Andrews*, pp. 387-90, 404 (James Thomson's case), 808. See also *Aberdeen Ecclesiastical Records*, p. 16.

108. *Register of the Kirk Session of St. Andrews*, p. 565 seq.

109. *Op. cit.*, p. 609.

110. *Op. cit.*, pp. 77, 135-139.

as the promulgation of the *Book of Discipline*, or such smaller ones as the restraint of a prominent local personality.

Two anxieties of the authorities in St. Andrews have still to be mentioned. There was the problem of witches, and that of obstinate catholics. The former was not new. In Archbishop Beaton's accounts the expense of burning witches can be compared with that of burning heretics.[111] In the period after 1560 the pursuit of witches was to go to lengths hitherto unheard of in Scotland, as far as we know, and to be accompanied by tortures as revolting as any in Europe. We hear of Knox dealing with a witch at St. Andrews, " sche being sett upe at a pillar befor him ";[112] and of a man and his wife fleeing from the town after being summoned to hear witnesses, in 1575, the woman being under suspicion, and both afraid of what would follow.[113] They had good reason to be afraid, if we may judge by the case of Agnes Melville, whose knowledge of herbs brought her into trouble in 1588.[114] This matter of witches is noticed here, however, simply as a reminder of another element in that grim picture of society discernible in the kirk session register of St. Andrews. We can do no more than note in passing that charges of witchcraft were not only easily made, but may at times have covered some other design.[115] It may also be noted how casually, in many of the extant sources, the execution of witches is referred to;[116] even more casually than the deaths of the soldiers hanged in " the bourd of Brechin ", or the hanging of unnamed common people by Morton during the conflict between the " king's men " and the " queen's men " in 1571-72.[117] It is mistaken to assume that we have full records of all the capital sentences passed by various authorities during this period.[118]

These remarks have some bearing on the question of what was happening to catholics in St. Andrews. Nicol Burne, an ex-Calvinist with personal experience of what happened there and in Edinburgh, wrote in 1581 of " the murther of spiritual magistrats, and pastoris, be felling thame in priuat streittis under silence of nicht, castin of rottin eggis and al kynd of filthe at thame in oppin mercat, be banisin, impresoning, and harling thame on sleddis."[119] He was writing a partisan

---

111. *Cf.* Hannay, *Rentale Sancti Andree* (S.H.S., 1913), pp. 64, 93, 141.

112. Melvill's *Diary*, p. 46.

113. *Register of the Kirk Session of St. Andrews*, p. 414.

114. *Op. cit.*, p. 620 seq.

115. See the accusation of the Master of Orkney in 1596, Pitcairn, i., pt. 2, pp. 375-6. The case of Ewfame Makcalzeane, referred to already, makes one wonder if her real offence was religion, not witchcraft. Some of the material in the witch trials suggests that they served at times to discredit catholicism; *e.g.* the invocation of the saints by familiars.

116. *E.g. Extracts from the Burgh Records of Aberdeen*, 1570-1625 (Spalding Club, 1848), p. 155, where the dean of guild is commended because he " hes extraordinarlie takin panis on the birning of the gryt number of witches brint this yeir " (1597).

117. On the " Bourd of Brechin " (Bourd—joke), when Lennox hanged thirty-two prisoners, see Melvill, *Diary*, p. 27, and also Bannatyne, *Memorials*, p. 34, where we are told that " Captane Couttis and Mure and 30 of thair suddartis dansed thair fill in coardis and therin ended thare miserable lives ". On Morton's actions, see *Diurnal of Occurrents* and *The Historie of James the Sext*, which both give long accounts of the civil war.

118. Quite apart from the fact that formal records suffer in times of revolution and civil war, we have to take into account propagandist action and sometimes actual tampering with material. Pitcairn remarked on the significance of some of the gaps in the criminal records when editing the *Trials*. Row complained of tampering with general assembly records: *History of the Kirk of Scotland*, p. 54. In 1566 James McGill interfered with the edition of the *Acts of Scottish Parliaments* which Lekprevik was completing and suppressed what was obnoxious to the reformers: *cf.* Dickson and Edmond, *op. cit.*, p. 227. For an interesting discussion of propagandist work in connection with Riccio's murder, see Tytler, *History of Scotland* (Edinburgh, 1868), iii, proofs and illustrations, no. xvi, pp. 403-8. See also Pollen, *Negotiations*, p. lix, on the two versions of the campaign against Huntly put out by Moray and Lethington; one for Mary, her relatives in France, and the pope; the other for the Scottish protestants. An illuminating critical study of George Buchanan's official historiography is provided in Dr. Gatherer's *The Tyrannous Reign of Mary Stewart* (Edinburgh, 1958).

119. T. G. Law, *Catholic Tractates* (S.T.S., 1901), p. 167.

pamphlet in which accusations are piled on his opponents with a vehemence and coarseness matching Knox's own flights of personal innuendo and abuse. But he has not been taken so seriously as Knox in the past, when it was tacitly assumed that any such flights from a protestant source were understandable slight exaggerations of reality, while any from a catholic source were lying slanders against men of God. Nevertheless, there is some basis for the charges he makes, as the cases in Edinburgh already mentioned demonstrate, and there is a scatter of fragmentary evidence to suggest that sentence of imprisonment was sometimes the introduction to an experience not unlike our modern brain-washing, even if less advanced in psychological technique.

To appreciate this one has to remember that prisoners in a sixteenth-century Scottish tolbooth did not live as guests of the crown. They were expected to bear their own expenses and sometimes fee the gaoler as well. So it was resolved by the St. Andrews kirk session that its own gaoler should have two shillings from every prisoner, man or woman, before releasing them from prison.[120] The position of somebody without money or friends to maintain him in food could become desperate. There were prisoners in Edinburgh in 1580 described as " poor and like to perish of hunger ".[121] Nicol Burne accused his opponents of having invented a new stratagem, namely, to have tried to starve him to death by refusing his friends all access to him. "And quhen extreme danger of famine constrainit me to hing ouer ane purse at the tolbuith vindo, to craif almous for Christis saik, thay persauing the reuth and compassion of Godlie and cheritable people, quha bestouit thair almous on me maist liberalie, causit cut doun the purse. And althocht thay commandit the Iayvler to impesch my letteris of supplicatione, quhairin I micht haue requirit that quhilk vas conforme to aequitie, yit God sua mouit his hairt, that he praesentit ane requeist of myne to the Prouoste and honorable Concile of Edinburgh for licence to beg almous, quhairbie I micht be sustenit : The quhilk albeit it vas grantit be the discretion of the Prouoste and Honorable Concile, yit the Ministeris obtenit ane discharge forbidding that I sould ask support in the name of ane schollar, or affix onie letter vpon the purse for signification of my indigence : bot nochtwithstanding al thair raige conceaued aganis me, and inuie quhilk thay bure aganis my fauoratis, Cheritabil personis gaif me of thair almous maist largelie, for declaration of the erneast desyre quhilk thay had of the extirpation of thair seditious haeresie, and the imbracement of the treu Catholik religion agane."[122] Nicol Burne was not the only one dependent on alms, nor indeed the only one to be relieved by the pity of the provost and council of Edinburgh, for we find some years later a sum of £5 13s. 4d. paid to the gaoler for the expenses of " ane puir preist callit Sir William Creirie quha wes wairdit be the space of ane moneth ", and also the sum of 20 shillings refunded to the gaoler who had given that amount " at my lord provests command to the said preist ".[123]

These instances draw attention to the importance of hunger as a means of reducing resistance on the part of a prisoner. Insistent questioning of a person in such straits, especially if coupled with threats of torture,

120. *Register of the Kirk Session of St. Andrews*, p. 427.
121. *Edinburgh Burgh Extracts*, iv, p. 195.
122. *Catholic Tractates*, pp. 110-1.
123. *Extracts*, iv, p. 485.

would have some effect also. Before and after 1560 those in prison on charges of heresy were subjected to visits by hectoring inquisitors who tried to trip them into admissions or retractations.[124] There was also the highly efficient method used against Father Ogilvie, S.J., in 1614, keeping him awake eight days and nine nights " with styles, pins, needles, and pinchings ", threatening him in the meantime with " extraordinary tortures " and promising him great rewards.[125] It had been planned " to use his examination with great secrecy, and if he (would) not answer nor confess ingenuously, to give him the Boots or the torture ".[126] The brain-washing technique described above had been used with success in witch trials. Pitcairn commented on it: " Human nature could not long stand so exquisite a torture. The suspected parties were often driven into a state of delirium; and in many instances they must have been glad to confess anything which may have been proposed by their examinators, to escape from a life held by such a miserable tenure."[127] It is with such instances in mind, and the use of torture elsewhere in the sixteenth century, for example, by Calvin in Geneva, that one should look at such cases as that of Sir John Kipper, a priest close on eighty years of age, held, for a length of time not specified, in the castle of St. Andrews " for contempsione and blasphemyng of Cristis religion, Superintendent, and ministeris of Godis Word, and for defending and mantenyng of idolatrie, supersticion, and Papistrie ".[128] His formal submission is a remarkable document, to be compared with those by another very old man, Father John Grierson, O.P., and by John Wilson, canon of Holyrood, and several other priests in St. Andrews.[129] They are in interesting contrast to the simple adhesion to the Congregation of many other clergy, high and low. We are only too familiar now with such confessions, devised to impress a public which is itself receiving constant indoctrination and is being steadily forced by economic and judicial pressure into a new pattern of living. It is worth keeping in mind also that such men in 1560 or 1561 were at a disadvantage which fifty years later no catholic could suffer; they were subjected to questioning and suggestion not simply by manifest antagonists but by such figures as John Winram, for so long familiar to them as vicar-general of the archbishop, or that even more equivocal character the titular Archbishop of Athens, whose peregrinations at this period are so numerous and mysterious.[130] It is surely an over-simplification to suppose that such sources as the St. Andrews kirk session records preserve a full report of what preceded such submissions as they record.

John Wilson's submission appears to have been only for a time, since in 1564 he was one of three priests summoned to undergo discipline " for saying mes and hearyng tharof, and ministracion of sacramentis unadmittit and in privat housis ". All three were at length excommunicated as contumacious offenders who had failed to obey the summons.[131]

---

124. *Cf.* Laing's *Knox*, i, pp. 548-9. As the passage shows, not all visitors were hectoring.

125. *Narratives*, pp. 307-9. Note the use of the irons referred to on p. 304. Text of the *Relatio Incarcerationis et Martyrii* in *Miscellaneous Papers of Q. Mary and K. James* (Maitland Club, 1834).

126. Spottiswood in a letter to the king, *op. cit.*, p. 302, and printed in full in *Miscellaneous Papers*, pp. 165-7.

127. Pitcairn, iii, p. 332, n. 4: *cf.* also iii, pt. 2, p. 50, for some pertinent comment.

128. *Register of the Kirk Session of St. Andrews*, p. 81.

129. *Op. cit.*

130. Alexander Gordon, made titular archbishop of Athens when he failed to get possession of Glasgow after his consecration in 1551, had been nominated to Galloway in 1559, when already associated with the reformers. He may have been useful in persuading lesser clergy to submit to the new order, to judge from the document printed as an appendix to this paper. I am grateful to Dr. Durkan for bringing this document to my notice.

131. *Register of the Kirk Session of St. Andrews*, p. 193. The other two were Nicol Beverage and George Todd.

PLATE XXIX. ABBOT QUINTIN KENNEDY ON THE MASS.

PLATE XXX. BAS-RELIEF IN KINKELL CHURCH, ABERDEENSHIRE.

Earlier, on August 19th, 1562, we find the session concerned by the news that William Cranston, the provost of St. Salvator's College who had refused to join the reformers, was coming to the city. Orders were issued that nobody should have anything to do with him under pain of excommunication.[132] We do not know precisely what happened next, but on September 24th Randolph informed Cecil that Cranston " a great favorer of Papystes, is happelie ded in thys myschevous worlde ".[133]

More trouble was given by Master David Dishington, who over more than three years avoided receiving the protestant communion by a succession of legal shifts, temporary submissions and unfulfilled promises, and excuses of unavoidable absence at the times of communion. Proceedings began in 1568, when the kirk in St. Andrews, " according to the Word of God and practice of utheris reformat citeis and townis wythtin this realme, callit M. Dauid Dischingtoun, M. James Rolland, procuratoris, requiring them of the confessioun of thair faitht ". James Rolland disappears, but the history of David Dishington serves to illustrate the pertinacity of the session and its eventual success in 1571, and the kind of trouble which members of the legal profession appear to have given fairly often. The slowness of the session in proceeding to the extreme of excommunication against him is notable, but so is its refusal to acquiesce in his withdrawal of himself from the communion.[134]

Others appear over the years: Sir Patrick Fergy, a priest excommunicated in 1564 for preaching and administering the sacraments without lawful permission and drawing people to the chapel of Tullibardine from their parish church;[135] Sir John Moreson, who had recanted and become reader in Methil but who seems to have returned to the catholic administration of baptism and marriage and to have been saying mass in private houses, receiving one penny from each communicant;[136] a drunken layman called Robert Braed, termed " ane Papist and mentenar of Papistrie " in 1569;[137] and the " auld ladiis " of Ardre and Culluthy, with their servant, John Lundy, delated in 1573 and again in 1574;[138] with Bessie Brown, servant to Sir George Read, " Papist and nevir cam to the communioun ";[139] in the same year, 1573, " Schir Dauid Mwir, ane of the fundatioun of our Lady alter wythtin the parroche kirk of the cite of Sanctandros, ane Papist unrecantit and obstinet ".[140] A fresh examination of belief and practice was being made just then, part of a new drive to establish discipline. We see in the course of it action against one John Christal, which shows how evasion of the effects of excommunication would become impossible as the framework of ecclesiastical authority grew stronger. He had been excommunicated in Dundee, but was being sheltered in St. Andrews until the kirk session published

---

132. *Op. cit.*, p. 169 seq.
133. *Ibid.*
134. *Op. cit.*, pp. 297, 319, 322, 324, 349, 351 seq. It is obvious from some of the shifts of Lady Carslogie whose case has already been mentioned, that she had some shrewd legal adviser.
135. *Op. cit.*, p. 226.
136. *Ibid.*
137. *Op. cit.*, p. 333: *cf.* also p. 409.
138. *Op. cit.*, p. 376; *cf.* also p. 395.
139. *Ibid.*
140. *Ibid.* The result, presumably of an act of 25th March preceding, which decreed, so " that all suspition of Papistrie in this reformat congregatioun be removit—that the heal preistis that brukis ony fundation wythtin this citie compeir this day xv dayis, of new to gyf confessioun of thair faitht, and to ansueir to sic thingis as sal be sperit and askit of them, concerning the pointis of religion and observance of the preaching and doctrine "(*loc. cit.*).

his excommunication there also and threatened to excommunicate any inhabitants of the city who might receive him into their houses, trade with him, or even frequent his company.[141] There was to be literally no rest or shelter for the excommunicate.

Much the same pattern can be seen in other parts of the country, with fluctuations in the vigour or the success with which it was imposed. We read how in the month of May, 1569, the Regent Moray " maid progress to Sterline, quhair four priestes of Dumblane were condemnit to the death for saying of mes againes the act of parliament; bot he remittit thair lyves, and causit thame be bund to the mercat croce, with thair vestimentis and challices in dirisioun, quhair the people caist eggis and uther villany at thair faces be the space of an hor, and thairefter thair vestimentis and challices were brunt to ashes."[142] In Leith, in June, 1572, Sir William Nickie appears, " accusit for saying of mess, quha was condamnit be ane assyse, and thairefter hangit ".[143] Another priest was hanged in Glasgow in 1574 for saying Mass.[144] In the same year the Regent Morton, in the presence of the Privy Council, admonished the bailies of Aberdeen for not enforcing ecclesiastical discipline.[145] The Aberdeen kirk session itself had gone warily for the first years of its existence, and in its legislation showed a restraint and diplomacy by comparison with St. Andrews;[146] but it had become more active after the fall of Mary and, in 1574, was full of zeal against such offenders as Andrew Philipson, whom it wished to be imprisoned for " blasphemying the doctrine and ministerie of the Kyrk ";[147] Janet Maitland, examined not for the first time but still obstinately refusing to give up " all poynts of papistry ";[148] Gilbert Menzies, junior, who had twice been before the regent and Privy Council in Edinburgh but had not yet fulfilled his promise made to them that he would come to communion;[149] and Marjory Urquhart, who refused to come to communion or submit to the kirk, " allegeand scho had sic ane pyk on her conscience that schow culd nocht be fulle of this present religioune now in Scotland."[150]

However widely such a survey is extended, the picture which emerges is a consistent one. An attempt was being made to enforce religious uniformity in accordance with those theories outlined at the beginning

---

141. *Op. cit.*, p. 379.

142. *Historie of James the Sext*, pp. 65-6.

143. *Diurnal of Occurrents*, p. 301.

144. *Op. cit.*, p. 341.

145. *Selections from Ecclesiastical Records of Aberdeen*, 1562-1681 (Spalding Club, 1846), p. 19 seq.

146. *Op. cit.*, pp. 4-12. There is a remarkable reserve on doctrinal issues, a firm attitude towards adultery and fornication (about which the civil magistrates are judged too lenient), and a ban on personalities in the pulpit which is significant when we recall the trouble caused elsewhere, *e.g.* in St. Andrews and Edinburgh. Adam Heriot, minister in Aberdeen, was one of the moderates in the early kirk.

147. *Aberdeen Ecclesiastical Records*, p. 17.

148. *Ibid.*

149. *Op. cit.*, p. 18.

150. *Op. cit.*, p. 20. Other instances of actions against catholics for religion may be found in Pitcairn, *e.g.* Alexander Crichton of Newhall was in trouble for having mass in his house in 1567 and again in 1572 (i, pt. 2, p. 38). In 1571 Jasper Montgomery and John Mason, dwelling at Eglinton, with Sir John Muir, dwelling at Kilmarnock, were denounced rebels and their goods confiscated " for the abominable and detestable crime of idolatry," *i.e.* celebration of mass at Eglinton (i, pt. 2, p. 30). Was this John Muir the subprior of Crossraguel who died in 1585, and whose will is so catholic in character ? *cf.* *Edinburgh Testaments*, xiv; or one of two other priests of that name ? In July, 1572, three secular priests, two regulars and two laymen, were delated for " contravening the Actis and Ministratioune of Sacramentis in the Papisticall maner " (i, pt. 2, p. 35). In the same year Sir John Johnstone, commendator of Soulseat, was delated for " ministrattioune of the Mass and of the Sacramentis in the Papisticall maner " (i, pt. 2, p. 32). It is notable that in most of these cases we do not know the outcome of the proceedings. Perhaps some of the accused may have taken refuge in England. We read of a Scottish priest who worked in Yorkshire, disguised as a gardener: *cf.* Aveling, *Post Reformation Catholicism in East Yorkshire*, 1558-1790 (East Yorkshire Local History Society, 1960), p. 64. Note also the reference to a Scots priest in 1569, p. 65.

of this essay. The methods used, as illustrated in the examples quoted above, are characteristic of the machinery of repression employed well into the seventeenth century. Their effectiveness was to be increased after 1586, when the presbytery system came into operation and made possible a more extended and continuous inquisition than had been practicable under the simpler structure of general assembly, superintendents and sessions, which existed from 1560. As the sixteenth century advanced, it became clearer how the most efficient use could be made of social and economic sanctions against non-conformists. Serious efforts would be made to prevent catholics owning or even occupying houses in the burghs.[151] Legal disabilities could be used to ruin a family without any process of law in the courts.[152] The ideological pressure grew heavier as more effective control was secured over the system of education, especially in the universities, and as the supply of ministers slowly increased. Before the end of the century it was becoming more feasible to plant ministers on recusant families, to invigilate their lives and press on the indoctrination of themselves and their servants. Scottish catholics would envy the conditions obtaining in England, where it was possible to absent oneself from protestant worship by regular payment of a heavy fine; and where also there was a hope of martyrdom for priests and those who sheltered them.[153] In Scotland there was no such enviable simplicity, but only an endless pressure of interference, abuse, preaching, the pillory, the jail, ostracization, homelessness and economic ruin; a pressure made psychologically more telling because it tightened and slackened unpredictably with the power manoeuvres at the centre of government. Especially under James VI hopes were roused from time to time that there would be a return to the old religion, or that a policy of general toleration might be introduced.[154] But penal legislation remained on the statute book, to be appealed to by the opponents of Jesuit missionaries, to be applied with greater or less severity by the king. The position of the latter was vital, as James VI well knew and so ably demonstrated by a policy which kept all the religious elements in the kingdom in a state of uncertainty until he had secured his own survival and comparative independence of them all on the English throne.[155]

From the viewpoint of the religious leaders of the reformation James's attitude was not satisfactory, and the civil authority as a whole was not zealous enough. There were too many temporisers at the court; too many crypto-catholics who went to sermons so as to be left in peace, but who had no sympathy with the kirk;[156] too many indifferent minds with,

151. *Aberdeen Ecclesiastical Records*, pp. 35, 44; *Edinburgh Burgh Extracts*, iv, pp. 490, 493.

152. See, for example, the letter of William Walcar, April, 1569, to Archbishop Beaton of Glasgow, then in France, in which he says that he " can on na wayis haif justice administrat unto me in quhatsumever action I haif ado befoir the provest and baillies ": *Miscellaneous Papers of Q. Mary and K. James*, p. 24. There are similar complaints to be found in *Narratives*.

153. *Cf. Narratives*, pp. 284, 286, 294.

154. As late as 1598 Father Crichton had described James as " a most indifferent and loving prince to all his subjects, desirous to be resolved of the truth and to knowe the true religion, that he might reforme his countrie and frame his government according to the same ": *An Apologie and Defence of the King of Scotlande*, in *Scottish History Society Miscellany*, i, p. 55.

155. Hence another view of James by the English priest and government agent, John Cecil: "A man who does not trouble himself about any religion . . . an inconstant, fickle, and ill-conditioned person who respects neither law nor promise nor any word whatsoever, unless in so far as his own profit moves him ": *S.H.S. Miscellany*, i, p. 38. Father MacQuhirrie, S.J., writing in 1601, said: " The single object of his ambition is the crown of England, which he would gladly take, to all appearances from the hand of the Devil himself, though Catholics and heretic ministers were all ruined alike, so great is his longing for this regal dignity." *Narratives*, p. 270.

156. Father John Hay, S.J., was invited by a catholic in Edinburgh to accompany him to hear a protestant sermon and replied that he never attended the preaching of the ministers " lest the people should suspect me of favouring their doctrine ": *op. cit.*, p. 159.

at best, a lukewarm, casual interest in religion, subordinated to the interest of the state. From the point of view of Knox, and those who followed in his tradition, indifference was as fatal as direct opposition. Toleration allowed by politicians from motives of expediency would prove fatal to the new religion. Knox was sure of it, and surely he was right. Had there been a monarch strong enough to maintain a policy of general toleration Scotland might have been another Poland, with internecine quarrels sapping the strength of protestantism and creating opportunities readily taken by the apostles of the counter-reformation. As things were, James had no option but to support at least some form of protestantism if he meant to keep his throne. Without greater financial and military strength than Scotland could provide he would have been unable to resist pressure from England, as anxious to prevent the use of Scotland by Spanish forces, as she had been earlier in the century to expel the French. He knew by his own and his ancestors' experience how easy it was to foment rebellion in Scotland from an English base and, however far he might encourage catholics as a useful counterpoise to extreme presbyterian pressure, he would never go so far as to make a serious catholic revival possible. He might dislike theocracy, but such a dislike did not mean a distaste for all protestant religion, still less a leaning towards catholicism. It is likely enough that for James religion was not a matter of great personal concern,[157] but it was a matter of political importance. As so often in that century, it was difficult to avoid confusion of religion and politics. At times the tangle of religious and political issues is reflected in divided opinion even among the Scottish catholic clergy themselves, and still more among the laity. Many, for example, saw the death of Graham of Fintry as martyrdom, and considered that the king's campaign to reduce the catholic earls was an action against religion; but for Father Crichton, a Scottish Jesuit with much experience, Fintry's death and all the rest was simply matter of politics, in which he believed the king justified.[158]

James's influence tended on the whole to mitigate the severity of the laws against catholics; when the latter came into the king's will, the sentence demanded by the letter of the penal laws was usually modified.[159] Even if financial ruin or exile were allowed, the death sentence was rarely carried out. When it was inflicted, it was by insistence of the ecclesiastical authority. This is shown in the case of James Wood of Boniton in 1601, and later, of course, in the case of Blessed John Ogilvie.[160] The impression of judicial murder gained in reading the account of Wood's trial is reinforced by the pages of Calderwood. One of Nicol Burne's accusations against the ministers had been that if anyone opposed them " they travel be al menis to seik his lyf, sua that thay appeir nocht the murtheraris of him: as be experience I knau of myself, aganis quhom thay, lyk fals traitorous learis, as I tak God to vitnes, inuenit thingis

---

157. The story of his comment when he heard of his wife's conversion is in keeping: " Well, wife, if you cannot live without this sort of thing, do your best to keep things as quiet as possible; for, if you don't, our crown is in danger." Father Robert Abercromby, who tells it, and who was Anne's confessor, says that afterwards James always showed him " greater gentleness and kindness ": *op. cit.*, p. 265.

158. *S.H.S. Miscellany*, i, p. 51 seq.

159. To " come into the king's will " meant abandoning any defence against a charge and putting oneself at the king's mercy. It was a useful formula, but might be taken as implying an admission of guilt or recognition of an unjust law. Hence Blessed John Ogilvie's unwillingness to avail himself of it.

160. Spottiswood, the protestant archbishop of Glasgow, was anxious to make a severe example of Father Ogilvie: *cf.* the letter mentioned above. The Boniton case connects with James's unpopularity with the presbyterian leaders after the Gowrie affair; they wanted some convincing evidence that he was a sincere protestant: *cf.* Calderwood, *History*, vi, pp. 104-5.

quhilk I neuer thocht, concerning the honore of the kingis Maiestie, nocht vorthie of rehersal, quhairbie thay laborit my ruine, transferring the caus from professione of religione to lese Maiestie, and treassone as thay vald haue callit it."[161] Wood might have been pardoned, even if the charge of theft had been established, but, we are told, " the ministers were instant with the king to have a proof of his sinceritie. He (Wood) died an obstinat Papist, ever looking for pardoun till the last gaspe. He pretended he suffered for the Catholick Roman religioun, but it was no point of his dittay. Onlie the stealing of his father's evidences and writts was layd to his charge."[162] His catholicism did in fact appear in the ditty, and no answer was made by the prosecution to the point urged by the defence, that the allegedly offended father had brought no accusation himself against his son.[163] Wood may have been sacrificed to appease the ministers, but the extremists among them were far from satisfied. John Davidson complained to the general assembly of 1601 that Wood's religion had not been made the chief issue at the trial, and called for united action to purge the land of idolatry, pointing to the example of the children of Israel " who, hearing but a brute of erectioun of a contrare altar, by their brethrein of Reuben, Gad, and halfe tribe of Manasseh, determined with all speed to have rooted them out with destructioun; if the mater had beene so. The mater with us is out of doubt, and, therefore," he continued, " lett us show our zeale for the Lord and his caus, otherwise we can looke for no blessing at the hands of God." To make the final issue plain he concluded a postscript to his letter with the words: " Finallie, If reasoun be refused, as God forbid, remember, that alwise *melius et optabilius est egregium bellum, pace impia, et a Deo detrahente.*"[164] It is the old cry against the Canaanite, and yet how little response it met with; as Father Crichton wrote only a few years later, the rulers of Scotland prevented the ministers from exercising cruelty and violence even if they would not depose them from authority.[165]

That is, in the last analysis, what is so striking in the Scottish situation. There was a policy of repression of whatever was regarded as heresy before and after 1560. What followed the events of 1560 would have been full-blooded repression had it followed the original design; as it was, considerable restraining influence was brought to bear on the religious leaders. Their machinery would function in a long war of attrition, and so have considerable success in the long run; but for most of half a century they were not able to proceed with the ruthlessness implicit in the letter of the laws against catholicism and demanded from the pulpit. Why not ? There was no lack of ruthlessness in the pursuit of witches, nor for that matter in James VI's punishment of unfortunate wretches who showed disrespect towards himself.[166] But over the sixteenth century as a whole

---

161. *Catholic Tractates*, p. 168.

162. Calderwood, *loc. cit.*

163. Pitcairn, ii, pt. 2, pp. 340-6. See also Francis Shearman, " James Wood of Boniton ", in *Innes Review*, v, pp. 28 seq.

164. See Calderwood, vi, pp. 110-2, for Davidson's letter. John Johnstone, writing to Waser from St. Andrews in August, 1601, said: "A certain notorious papist, son of the laird of Boniton near Montrose, was executed in the month of May for a most notorious crime committed against his parents. Blessed be God, and may he give us grace both to will and to do well ! " *Zurich Letters*, ii, p. 331.

165. *Narratives*, p. 282.

166. See, for example, John Dickson, Englishman in Lyne, hanged although he had come into the king's will, because when drunk he had referred to him as " ane bastard king ": Pitcairn, i, pt. 2, p. 385. Or the even more fantastic case of the man who had *been about* to fix a picture of James, which he was selling at the mercat cross, to the side of the gallows so that it could be seen better: he was hanged for this: *cf. op. cit.*, ii, pt. 2, pp. 349-52.

there is comparatively little in the way of torture for religion,[167] and very few executions for unquestionably religious causes.

The weakness of the secular arm is one important reason for this phenomenon, as has been already suggested, but does not explain it wholly. Had there been a strong majority in the country to support the ministerial demands for the extirpation of idolaters, the secular arm would have been given the necessary strength for the enterprise. Much more serious than the absence of religious zeal on the part of the sovereign was its absence among the great nobility, and even among the barons. Even the Regent Moray was deficient in zeal, judged by the standard of Knox, and still more so was such a man as Mary's secretary, Lethington. Knox's words to Moray are echoed in many judgments in the next fifty years, given by protestant and catholic clergy alike against members of the Scottish ruling class. " I perceive myself," he said, " frustrate of my expectation, which was, that ye should ever have preferred God to your own affection, and the advancement of his truth to your singular commodity."[168] In 1566-67 the papal nuncio described the Earls of Lennox and of Athol as " so lukewarm in the matter of religion, that they have ever preferred their particular interests to the public good ".[169] Jesuit letters refer to the " coldness " of Scottish nobles in matters of religion. One speaks of a baron " who is disposed to favour the Catholic cause in the frigid manner which is customary here ", and names many nobles who were willing to receive English priests, as not amenable to Scots law, but " on condition only that we do not put them to any expense. This is an important point, and Father Persons would do well to take every care to provide for the expenses of the men he sends hither, at any rate for some time; otherwise he will find it very difficult to effect anything, or rather I should say he will do no good whatever."[170] Knox's disappointment in Moray comes to mind as one reads a Jesuit comment on Alexander Seton, Chancellor of Scotland, in 1605: " Lord Seton often said to me in Scotland, when I urged him to support the Catholic cause, ' be not eager to act before the time comes. I have to live in Scotland, and I must give way to circumstances. When the opportunity presents itself, and there is any hope of success, I shall not be sparing of my goods, my blood, or my life, for the restoration of the Catholic religion.' He is now all powerful in Scotland, but he will attempt nothing until he sees a solid foundation for hope. Meanwhile he takes his portion in this life, though at the risk of that which is eternal."[171] Seton is an outstanding example of a type of compromise which really profound religious conviction would have made impossible in conscience. He publicly professed protestantism, went occasionally to sermons and to communion, but two or three times a year went " to Catholic confession and communion, with his mother, brother, sisters, and nephews, who are better Catholics than himself."[172] It would soon be impossible for such a trimmer to receive the catholic sacraments, but the type appears to have been fairly common in Scotland in the later

---

167. What there is comes nearly all after 1560, but even that is restrained compared to what happened elsewhere, and compared to what happened to witches in Scotland. It would seem that while people were desperately afraid of witches they were not so afraid of their religious opponents.

168. Dickinson's *Knox*, ii, pp. 78-9.

169. *Negotiations*, p. 370.

170. *Narratives*, pp. 170-1. See also Father Crichton in 1566: " The Catholics lead licentious lives, and are therefore cold." *Negotiations*, p. 495.

171. *Narratives*, p. 282.

172. *Op. cit.*, p. 279.

sixteenth century. It was not unknown before then, when there was less precision about " communicatio in sacris " than there is now. What is important here is that it indicates a state of mind where religion was governed by expediency, a common enough phenomenon in renaissance Europe and one which would lead eventually to a form of toleration in religion, extended by a fundamentally secularist state.

There may have been more to it than that among some Scots. One of the striking features of Scottish Jesuit reports, borne out by other sources, is the willingness of many in Scotland to discuss religion as a subject of speculative interest. This appears in the meeting of the Jesuit priest and Ker of Cessford already mentioned. After supper, they began a discussion " as to whether it belonged to the Church alone to pronounce judgment on the sense of the Scriptures ". It lasted a considerable time and engaged three ministers who were present. When it concluded, Ker said he would like further discussion and promised kind treatment to anyone else who might come. His Jesuit guest departed with a safe conduct.[173] Such discussions were easily had in private. Father John Hay recounts some with ministers, one with a minister in Leith being notable for the suggestion of scholarly engagement which it conveys. Not every minister would enter into such relations with a Jesuit, and public dispute was something to be avoided, but there appears to have been an element among the protestant clergy possessed of a more eirenic approach than the pages of Knox or the proceedings of general assemblies would suggest. Among the laity there must have been many who were either not wholly committed in religion, like Sir Richard Maitland of Lethington,[174] or who were weary of strife and disorder, like the writers of the *Diurnal of Occurrents* and the *Life of King James the Sext*. There is an awareness of human weakness in such men, and a compassion towards other people's failures and sufferings.

There is, in fact, throughout the history of Scotland at this time, evidence that there were people with a humane outlook on the contemporary world. It is not true to say, as has often been said in partisan apology for violent words and actions, that there was no moderation or charity between members of opposing beliefs or parties. There were catholics and protestants who found the policy of bloody repression, and orthodoxy under terr r, incompatible with the spirit of Christ. Cardinal Beaton and John Knox were representative of much in contemporary life, but there was a more humane and more charitable spirit in sixteenth-century Scotland than either of them represented; we can see indications of it both before and after 1560. It is suggested, for example, in the coldness attributed to Gavin Dunbar, Archbishop of Glasgow, towards heresy trials.[175] Dunbar was a humanist apparently, not the only one among the bishops, and not the only one who was unenthusiastic about the capital punishment of heretics.[176] Erasmian humanism favoured toleration, as

173. *Op. cit.*, pp. 169-70.
174. Maitland, to judge from his poems, could see something to be objected to on both sides. What was said of Bothwell may have been true of others, that he, poised " betuix factiounis of sindrie Religiounis despysing baith sydis, counterfutit ane lufe of thame baith ": *cf. Negotiations*, p. cvi. The charge against the Master of Grey, in 1587, included that he had worked chiefly " to have libertie of conscience to use sic forme of religioun as servit every manis appetyte incontrare the tenore of the Actis of Parliament ": *Reg. of Privy Council*, iv, pp. 166-8.
175. Spottiswoode, *History of the Church of Scotland* (Edinburgh, 1850), i, p. 132.
176. Buchanan is surely sufficient testimony to Dunbar's humanism; *cf.* Hume Brown, *George Buchanan* (Edinburgh, 1890), p. 98. Spottiswoode testifies to the lack of enthusiasm shown by James Beaton of St. Andrews for heresy trials: *op. cit.*, i, p. 124. In connection with Archbishop Hamilton, see Law Mathieson, *op. cit.*, i, pp. 44, 51, 55.

long as there was no danger of revolution. Its influence in Scotland is suggested not only by the libraries of several bishops,[177] but also by the mottoes they adopted: Archbishop Hamilton's *Misericordia et Pax*; the *Moderate* of Bishop Reid; and the stoic phrase of Henry Sinclair, *Sustine et Abstine*.

The last-named, and his brother John, are particularly interesting in this connection. Henry is described in Knox's *History* as " a conjured enemy to Christ Jesus " and as " enemy to all that unfeignedly professed the Lord Jesus, but chiefly to John Knox, for the liberty of his tongue ".[178] Yet, when he was upbraided by Mary for not having voted in condemnation of Knox at a famous meeting of the council, his answer was, according to Knox himself: " Your Grace may consider, that it is neither affection to the man, nor yet love to his profession that moved me to absolve him; but the simple truth, which plainly appears in his defence, draws me after it, albeit that others would have condemned him."[179] The fidelity to legal principle won little gratitude from Knox, but he did admit the learning and the catholic allegiance of the brothers, remarking when they were dead that: " They were both learned in the laws, and given to maintain the Popish religion, and therefore great enemies to the Protestants."[180] Additional testimony to the orthodoxy of John Sinclair may be seen in the fact that his church of Restalrig was singled out for destruction by the first general assembly.[181] But just as his brother appears standing up for justice, on behalf of John Knox, so John appears as a friend to another protestant in even more difficult straits. The account of Adam Wallace's experiences in prison in 1550, just prior to his being burnt for heresy, presents a contrast of clergy who visited him; an English Dominican, holding very strictly to the law and unwilling to discuss doctrine as he had received no commission to do so; a tyrannical, hectoring priest who was in charge of Wallace during his imprisonment; and John Sinclair, then Dean of Restalrig, " who gave him Christian consolation, amongest the which he exhorted him to believe the reality of the sacrament after the consecration ". Sinclair visited him twice, without moving him from his beliefs, but Wallace " confessed himselfe to have receaved good consolation of the said Deane in other behalfes, as becommeth a Christian ".[182]

These glimpses of the Sinclair brothers are tantalising. In Henry's library the importance of Erasmus is striking. So is the appearance of Calvin's *Defensio Orthodoxae Fidei*, written to justify the burning of Servetus. Among John's surviving books is a copy of Castellio's Latin Bible, whose preface contains such a moving protest against the measures taken against heresy: " We are become bloodthirsty killers out of zeal for Christ, who shed his own blood to save that of others . . . Out of zeal for Christ we persecute others, although he told us to offer the left cheek if the right one is struck. Out of zeal for Christ we do wrong to others, although he ordered us to do good for evil."[183] The ideas are those of Erasmus, taken up by a protestant scholar in opposition to such leaders of his own party

---

177 See *Innes Review*, ix.
178. Dickinson's *Knox*, ii, p. 90.
179. *Op. cit.*, ii, pp. 99-100.
180. *Op. cit.*, ii, p. 185.
181. Calderwood, ii, p. 46.
182. The account in Foxe's *Book of Martyrs* is reprinted in Laing's *Knox*, i, pp. 544-50.
183. See Lecler, *op. cit.*, pp. 336-60, for an account of Castellio's views and his disagreement with Calvin and other protestant leaders.

as Calvin and Beza.[184] We have no comment of John Sinclair upon them, but it seems probable from the fragments of evidence we do possess that he and his brother represent that spirit of moderation illustrated abroad, for example, by Cardinal Contarini, and associated with an orthodox stream of renaissance scholarship.

It appears certainly that when religious division became acute in Scotland it sometimes brought an aligning of former friends on opposite sides, with sadness but without bitterness, without the loss of what is referred to as the " auld kindness ". Master John Davidson of Glasgow University, who went over to the reformers, could write of Archbishop James Beaton as having been " my gude Maister and liberall freind, quhowbeit fro Religione we ar now separatit in ane part, (as mony fathers and sonnes is, in thir our dayis), to quhom, I pray God, send the treuth and knawledge of his Worde: at, that may unit us in spirit and mynde againe together that hes separatit us (as apperis) in our warldly kyndenes." He assured Abbot Quintin Kennedy that he wrote against his *Treatise* " for the brotherly luife I beare to all men in Christe, and for the auld Parisiane kyndnes that was betuix us, to bryng your Lordschip, and the people of this countrie, fra the errour and blyndnes that this lytle Buik of yours hes haldin yow and thaim baith in."[185]

How strong that " auld Parisiane kyndnes " could be is movingly illustrated in the relationship of Thomas Smeaton, who was later to become minister of Paisley, and the Scottish Jesuit, Father Edmund Hay, like Smeaton, an alumnus of St. Salvator's College. Smeaton had been expelled from St. Andrews at the reformation and went to France with some idea of becoming a Jesuit. While abroad, he began to have grave doubts about religion, which he communicated to Father Edmund as " a verie lowing frind " in Paris. By the latter's advice and influence he went to stay with the Jesuits in Rome, but, after eighteen months there, was still more disturbed in belief and returned to Paris. There his friend advised him and " nochtwithstanding that he perceavit his mynd turned away from thair ordour and relligion, yit he ceased nocht to counsall him frindlie and fatherlie, and suffered him to want na thing." Father Hay kept him out of danger and, when his mind was at length firmly made up to renounce catholicism, still showed him " na thing bot lowing frindschipe ". So they parted; it was the same Father Hay who thought Mary Stewart too lenient towards heretical leaders, but the ties of friendship were stronger than policy. There is also more than affection in Father Hay's attitude to Smeaton; there is a positive understanding and sympathy for him in his spiritual struggle.[186]

Another Scottish Jesuit, Father John Hay, testifies to kindly treatment during a visit to his native country in 1579, and which, he says, " I aucht iustlie to esteme as lang as I liwe ".[187] He is addressing the nobility of Scotland, and lays the blame for any enmity he experienced upon the protestant ministers, " quhairby I wald hewe hed iuste occasione to lament the great unkyndnes of my natifwe contrie towart me war nocht on the other part I did experiment quhow there proceadings aganest me was on no waye aggreable unto yow perseawand that in yowr hartes the

---

184. Beza thought the preface blasphemous.
185. Laing, *Miscellany of the Wodrow Society*, i, pp. 187, 256-8.
186. Melvill, *Diary*, pp. 56-8.
187. *Catholic Tractates*, p. 33.

awld and accwstomett cowrtesie dois ewir remane."[188] He was writing with an apologetic purpose but his letters to his superiors support the printed statement; they also show him on one occasion having a pleasant dinner with two ministers in Stirling, during which they discussed many subjects, but said nothing about religion.[189] It seems from his experiences that there were varying degrees of hostility, in practice, among the protestant clergy. These were no doubt sometimes due to such personal considerations as have been suggested above, but they were also frequently dictated by prudence. Friendship may have been an important factor in some instances, but kinship was a still stronger reason for mitigation of the severity of the law. Father John Hay's letters show how it operated even in such an old and major centre of the reformed religion as Dundee. The magistrates there were in a dilemma when he landed; if they raised any action against him, " they foresaw that they would expose themselves to great risk from the vengeance of my kinsmen and clansmen; but it was no less evident that they would incur the hostility of their ministers if they allowed me to remain in the town unharmed."[190] Trouble was avoided by the minister secretly warning the landlord of the inn that an arrest was intended, and the landlord warning his guest in good time. When the officers arrived and found the accused gone, they commended the landlord highly. " They quite understood they had gone as far as they durst without offending any of my clansmen; though, in order to avoid incurring suspicion from the chief ministers for neglect of their duty, they summoned into court the master of the vessel which had brought me to Scotland."[191]

The account of events in Dundee and Stirling is too long to be related in full. It does reveal an uneasy balance of strength between the burgh authority, urged on by the kirk, and a powerful local clan. Outside the boundary of the burgh the Jesuit was protected by his kinsmen, and further proceedings against him depended on higher authority, on the Privy Council. At that stage the kinsmen show uneasiness in case the family of the Hays should be too seriously involved; the other side is anxious that there should be no time for the Hays to muster strength in his support when Father Hay comes before the council. In the end, having travelled through most of the clan territory and stayed in Stirling where the court then was (and where he met a minister with whom he had been intimately acquainted in former times), Father Hay was given a fixed time to remain in Scotland, with permission to leave from any port when the time was up. He chose Leith, to avoid further implicating his former host in Dundee with the local authorities. While waiting for departure, he tells us: " I dined almost daily in Edinburgh, the capital, and there no one ever gave me any sort of offence, even by a word, though nearly all knew perfectly well who I was. Not only this, but the minister of Leith very kindly asked me to his house, where we entered on a discussion about the difficulties in Scripture."[192] He visited the castle, whose commander was one of the sermon-going catholics, and talked with a counsellor of D'Aubigny, who was then with the king. It is hardly surprising that Father Hay should have been optimistic about the possibility of a restora-

---

188. *Ibid.*
189. *Narratives*, p. 155 seq.
190. *Op. cit.*, p. 142.
191. *Op. cit.*, p. 144.
192. *Op. cit.*, p. 159. The minister consulted Luther's commentary on Genesis and also Nicholas of Lyra.

tion of catholicism after such experiences, given—but it was a bigger condition than he perhaps realised—a few men of influence with sufficient resolution for the task.

There would always be family assistance for the individual as there had been for him. Hays, Hamiltons, Stewarts, Setons, Gordons, and so many others, had members with differing religious loyalties but with a family loyalty which survived theological disagreement in the majority of cases. The lesser people had no such protection as Father Hay relied upon; no minister or magistrate would connive at their escape from the law to avoid trouble with their clansmen. Knox was right in his appreciation of the importance of the common people. It was they who were to be fashioned by the long pressure of session and presbytery, first in the towns and then in the landward parts, into a protestant people with a growing sense of democracy and an independence of the feudal structure and its endemic anarchy, which the majority of the sixteenth-century nobility, of whatever religion, were so concerned to preserve. The shaping of that people was, however, to be a slow process dependent on the machinery of repression outlined above, on compulsory indoctrination, compulsory reception of the sacraments, religious tests for public office, and the sanctions of public censure, excommunication and the consequent loss of all civil rights, bringing economic ruin, with no escape for the majority except submission, or exile for those few who could hope to survive abroad. The kirk was to fight for a moral standard which the medieval church had defended in its public teaching, but had eventually seemed powerless to enforce in the face of the bad example and practical indifference of prelates and monarchs on whom it had come to depend for the effective backing of its commands. How long and arduous was the struggle of the new kirk can be seen from its own records, and indeed it never had, or could have, the complete victory,[193] but it went a long way towards success, having built up its strength among those whom the nobles, whether clerical or lay, had either failed to appreciate or positively despised. And the strength which it achieved guaranteed that only those christians who felt strongly obliged in conscience would continue to oppose it.

In what has gone before we have noted some of the influences which mitigated the application of the laws against dissenters from the reformed kirk; political expediency, at home and abroad, ties of friendship and of kin, and possibly old academic associations. Was there also any stirring of ideas of religious toleration? We have suggested that possibly even before 1560 there may have been. The question is raised especially, however, in relation to the crucial period from 1560 to 1567, and the key figure of Mary, Queen of Scots. It is not possible to conclude this essay without some discussion of her attitude. From the point of view of leading catholics and protestants at the time her religious policy was vital to their cause; both parties were profoundly dissatisfied with it. She sentenced no one for his religious beliefs; she released catholics when they were summoned for hearing or saying mass; she agreed to the allocation of revenues for support of the new preachers; she would not go to the public sermons but would hear John Knox privately; she must have her mass, but she did not ensure the possibility of other catholics having it,

---

193. There is no difficulty in showing the continuous existence from the reformation period of the kind of opposition to the kirk which was given such powerful expression in eighteenth-century Scots poetry.

in such places as St. Andrews or Dundee; she had priests at Holyrood, but one could find at her court such a person as George Buchanan, and her protestant half-brothers, and Argyll who was married to her half-sister. Even before the death of Darnley and the marriage with Bothwell, her behaviour was bewildering to many. Some of it can be explained in terms of political expediency, and she seems to have been influenced by family ties; the direct personal influence of her half-brother, Moray, affected vitally important decisions.[194] But there is another factor which in justice should be noted; a variety of witnesses suggest that Mary had a regard for other people's consciences which was unusual in Scotland at that time.

Knox is one of the chief witnesses, in several places, of which one must suffice here. He is speaking of the quieting of opposition to the celebration of mass at Holyrood soon after Mary's arrival. " Which thing perceived, a zealous and godly man, Robert Campbell of Kinzeancleuch, said unto the Lord Ochiltree, ' My Lord, now ye are come, and almost the last of all the rest; and I perceive, by your anger, that the fire-edge is not off you yet; but I fear, that after that the holy water of the Court be sprinkled upon you, that ye shall become as temperate as the rest. For I have been here now five days, and at the first I heard every man say, " Let us hang the priest "; but after that they had been twice or thrice in the Abbey, all that fervency was past. I think there be some enchantment whereby men are bewitched.' And in very deed so it came to pass. For the Queen's flattering words upon the one part, ever still crying, *Conscience, conscience; it is a sore thing to constrain the conscience* '; and the subtle persuasions of her supposts (we mean even of such as sometimes were judged most fervent with us) upon the other part, blinded all men, and put them in this opinion: she will be content to hear the preaching, and so no doubt but she may be won."[195] The passage illustrates more than one point already made; what is of interest now is that Mary's words, dismissed by Knox as insincere, may well have expressed a genuine conviction. The English ambassador reported a long interview with her, in the course of which she told him: " You may perceive that I am none of those that will change my religion every year: and as I told you in the beginning, I mean to constrain none of my subjects, but would wish that they were all as I am; and I trust they shall have no support to constrain me."[196]

Evidence from catholic sources indicates that Mary held to this principle, although it appeared madness to many of her friends and supporters and suggestive of unsound faith to some. The papal nuncio wrote from Paris in 1566 that the difficulties in Scotland might be surmounted " if justice were executed against six rebels, who were leaders and originators of the late treason against the queen, and whose deaths would effectually restore peace and obedience in that kingdom. These are the earls of Murray and Argyle, who, now that they are pardoned, as has been said, go on making domestic mischief in the queen's own

---

194. As to whether, for example, she landed at Leith or at Aberdeen, where she would have found military support from Huntly. The overthrow of Huntly so soon afterwards can be attributed largely to Moray's influence on the queen.

195. Dickinson's *Knox*, ii, p. 12. The titular archbishop of Athens, preaching in St. Giles, at the time when so many of his protestant colleagues were refusing even to pray for Mary, said; "Now our ministeris are growne so vantone and ceremonious, that they will not pray for there lauchfull heretrix, wha hes permitted them sic libertie of conscience, that they may use what religione they pleis." Bannatyne, p. 182.

196. See Calderwood, *op. cit.*, ii, p. 136.

household; the Earl of Morton; the Laird of Lethington; Bellenden Justice Clerk; and James MacGyll, Clerk Register, a man of no family, and contriver of all evil."[197] The nuncio was sure that action could be taken and that Darnley could be persuaded to make the necessary moves, but the danger was "that the Cardinal of Lorraine and the queen, in their excessive kindness, would not consent to such an act."[198] He commented again: "The queen could easily have made her position secure by punishing a few ringleaders, but being too prone to pity and clemency she has exposed herself to the risk of being the slave and prey of those heretics, with danger even to her life."[199] Strong efforts were made to persuade Mary to eliminate the leaders of the protestant party, and the Bishop of Dunblane and the Jesuit, Father Edmund Hay, were sent to Scotland to try to convince her to "embrace that most holy enterprise."[200] She would not hear of it, saying she could not stain her hands with her subjects' blood; perhaps she had seen enough of that in France. The baffled nuncio exclaimed: "May God grant that an indulgence so unjust may not bring complete ruin on her Majesty and on her kingdom !"[201] Mary's Tudor relations would not have been so hesitant. There was a better case in law for the execution of Moray and those other five than there ever was against Fisher and More, or the Countess of Salisbury, or Edmund Campion; a better case against some of them than against James Wood of Boniton, to come nearer home. Had Mary been more of a Tudor the reformation in Scotland might have collapsed soon after her marriage with Darnley. As it was, Mary authorised no repression of the Tudor type; Moray, Argyll, Knox and Buchanan, and the rest of her opponents in religion, kept their lives and liberty. The last two used that liberty, among other things, to paint her as the "Jezebel" of Scottish history; a strange irony, if they owed their lives to the inability of Mary's conscience to assent to the liquidation even of those whom she believed to be false prophets.

Scotland was still far from appreciating that cry of "Conscience, conscience; it is a sore thing to constrain the conscience." Nor did she appreciate yet the dangers rising from too close an identification of church and state. The late medieval church had illustrated some of these, particularly the worldliness introduced when the interests of the church were subordinated to those of the state, and benefices awarded for political merit. The new kirk was to illustrate another danger, the growth of hypocrisy which is inevitable when political advancement depends on proofs of religious orthodoxy and an ostentatious practice of religious exercises. The kirk was not alone in that; the same problem would appear in catholic and Lutheran societies on the continent. Not only in Scotland but in most parts of Europe the lesson would be taught, by bitter experience, that the psychology of error in matters of faith is far more complex than the middle ages realised; and that the truth may be better served in the long run by preserving the church in independence of the state. The grace of God which is freely given must be freely received; faith and

---

197. *Negotiations*, p. 278.

198. *Op. cit.*, p. 361.

199. *Op. cit.*, p. 365.

200. *Op. cit.*, p. 370: *cf.* also pp. 314, 323 and p. cxviii.

201. *Op. cit.*, p. 370. A number of people saw that Mary's throne was in danger, before the affair with Bothwell presented a wonderful opportunity of attack for those who, like Knox, wanted her removed because she was not a protestant. On this matter, see Black, *The Reign of Elizabeth*, 2nd edition (*Oxford History of England*, viii, 1959), pp. 102-8.

charity cannot be established in any soul by government enactments and penal laws.

Pressure of time and space have made this study even less adequate as a survey of the subject than I had hoped to make it. A great deal has been taken for granted, for example, the similarity of legislation against heresy in the Scottish parliaments before and after 1560. Something might have been made of delations for heresy before 1560 which were motivated by hope of financial gain from a sentence of escheat. Far more detail of catholic recusancy might have been supplied, even from the printed sources. For the whole period there is still a mass of unprinted material which may supply relevant details as to what went on de facto, as against de jure. The significance of catholic recusancy in south-west Scotland in relation to northern England and events in Ireland must be examined more fully than it has been as yet. But perhaps enough has been written to convince someone of the need for a thorough book on the subject of this essay. And finally, it may be permissible to hope that now, after the passing of four hundred years, we may see the similarity between Patrick Hamilton and John Ogilvie, both so eager for martyrdom, and remember the kindness of Father Edmund Hay to Thomas Smeaton rather than the hatreds of some others at that time.

APPENDIX

The following document (see note 130 *supra*) illuminates a story of intimidation and troubled conscience. Three chaplains, John Bonar, Thomas Lamb, and Robert Christie, have obtained notarial instruments at Abernethy testifying that a certain recantation or renunciation of papal authority and the statutes of the church, which they made before the Archbishop of Athens, was made unwillingly from fear of losing their means of living and even their lives; and they wish that renunciation to be held null and void. The original is in the Protocol Book of John Feyrn, fo. 174 r. in the General Register House.

* * *

" xxiii*o* die mensis februarii anno domini jmvc lix*o* Indictione 3a pontificatus pii pape 3tii anno primo, apud abernethy horam circiter quartam post merediem coram testibus dominis Joanne bonar et Joanne lam capellanis.

Quo die discretus vir dominus Robertus cristie sacellanus quamdam recantacionem sive renunciacionem auctoritatis papalis et statutorum ecclesiasticorum Invitus metu et timore amissionis sue quotidiane sustentationis qua vita sua sustentaretur ac eciam sue vite, coram episcopo atheniensi factam revocavit cassavit et annullavit et pro non factam habere vult pro perpetuo in futurum Super quibus etc ac testes superscripti similiter fecerunt."

MATERIAL DESTRUCTION CAUSED
BY THE SCOTTISH REFORMATION

by

DAVID McROBERTS

Few aspects of the Scottish reformation seem more calculated to rouse partisan spirit than consideration of the material destruction which it occasioned. For a generation or two after the event, most writers, catholics like Father Alexander Baillie or protestants like Archbishop John Spottiswoode, seemed content to attribute all of Scotland's ecclesiastical ruins to protestant hatred of things catholic during the crisis of the reformation struggle[1]. This assumption remained general throughout the seventeenth and eighteenth centuries and it lingers on in some quarters even to the present day. This popular picture of a spontaneous upsurge of Calvinist anger against the trappings of popery is nowhere better described than in the vigorous lines of M. W. Tennant's *Papistry Stormed* (published in 1827);

> " I sing the steir strabush and strife,
> Whan, bickerin' frae the towns o' Fife,
> Great bangs o' bodies, thick and rife
>   Gaed to Sanct Androis town,
> And wi' John Calvin i' their heads,
> And hammers i' their hands and spades,
> Enraged at idols, mass and beads,
>   Dang the Cathedral down;
> I wat the bruilzie then was dour
> Wi' sticks and stanes and bluidy clour,
> Ere Papists unto Calvin's power
>   Gaif up their strangest places;
> And fearfu' the stramash and stour,
> When pinnacle came down and tow'r
> And Virgin Maries in a shower
>   Fell flat and smash't their faces.
> The capper roofs that dazzlit heaven
> Were frae their rafters rent and riven
> The marble altars dash't and driven
>   The cods wi' velvet laces,
> The siller ewers and candlesticks,
> The purple stole and gowden pyx,
> The tunakyls and dalmatyks,
>   Came tumblin' frae their cases;
> The Devil stood bumbazed to see
> The bonny cosy byke, whair he
> Had cuddlit mony a centurie,
>   Ripp't up wi' sic disgraces."

---

1. Not that everyone approved, even among protestants, as witness the well-known story of Archbishop Laud's comment, as he passed the ruined cathedral of Dunblane—" Reformation ! No, Deformation ! " And Archbishop Spottiswoode speaks of it as " a pitiful vastation of churches and churchbuildings throughout all the parts of the realm." *History*, i. p. 372.

This robust and somewhat unapologetic view began to waver in the first breezes of the Romantic Revival. The great Doctor Johnson, visiting Scotland in 1773, felt his piety grow warmer among the ruins of Iona and, " affected with a strong indignation while he beheld the ruins of religious magnificence " at St. Andrews, expressed the hope that John Knox was buried " in the highway ". Through the genius of Sir Walter Scott, the broken ruins of Melrose glimmered in a " pale moonlight " that was ever so romantic and, presently, every ecclesiastical ruin in the land reflected its gleam. Readers were enchanted and there was little need for Scott to add that " the humour of demolishing monuments of ancient piety and munificence, and that in a poor country like Scotland, where there was no chance of their being replaced, was both useless, mischievous and barbarous." Individuals like the Earl of Buchan devoted their energies to the preservation of such ecclesiastical monuments as fell to their care and even the government, following in the wake of public opinion, began to take a practical interest in various ruins, such as Arbroath Abbey (1815) or Elgin Cathedral (1816), tidying up the sites and forbidding any further removal of stones.

This romantic attitude to ecclesiastical ruins became fashionable and placed a valuable weapon in the hands of catholic controversialists, like the Rev. Stephen Keenan of Dundee (1803-62), whose effective use of it roused the ire of protestant protagonists, who saw that a completely new approach to the whole question of the " Knoxian destruction " of religious houses was urgently needed. John Jamieson's *Bell the Cat: or Who Destroyed the Scottish Abbeys* ? (published in 1902) is an attempt at such revision. Those who find such reading congenial will gather that the author is of opinion that the bulk of ecclesiastical ruins in Scotland is due to shoddy building, neglect of maintenance by medieval clergy, and the malevolence of English invaders; the book is unscholarly and, in parts, incredibly naive. A much more scholarly attempt at transferring the blame for Scotland's ruined churches from the " rascal multitude " to medieval negligence and English invasion is Dr. David Hay Fleming's *The Reformation in Scotland* (published in 1910); here is much solid research, but, unfortunately, the author does not approach his subject in that detached frame of mind which is essential for any just appraisement of historical facts. The late Dr. D. E. Easson, in *Medieval Religious Houses; Scotland* (published in 1957) supports this same thesis that, apart from a few friaries and other religious houses actually sacked by the reformers, pre-reformation neglect and English invasion were the main causes of the destruction of Scottish medieval churches.

The whole question has been bedevilled by partisanship and could profitably be lifted out of the arena of religious controversy and examined dispassionately. The religious issues involved in the reformation tend to obscure the fact that the movement was in reality a whole complex of diverse revolutions, political, social, economic, as well as religious. Scotland was no different from the rest of Europe and the incidental destruction of ecclesiastical buildings might originate in any of these simultaneous revolutions and was not always and necessarily done *in odium fidei*. No one, who examines closely the actions of the sixteenth-century Scottish nobility (who were the main supporters of the work of destruction) would credit them, as a body, with any very sincere religious convictions. The author of the *Complaynt of Scotlande*, reproaching the estate of barons and nobles, in 1549, says; "And thou art the special

PLATE XXXI. TOMB OF NINIAN WINZET
AT RATISBON.

PLATE XXXII. FRAGMENTS OF MEDIEVAL GLASS
IN MAGDALENE CHAPEL, EDINBURGH.

cause of (thy country's) ruyne, for thou and thy sect, that professes you to be nobles and gentlemen, there is nocht ane spark of nobleness nor gentrice amang the maist part of you ".[2] As the evidence is sifted, it becomes clear that these were the men responsible for the destruction of a great part of our ancient churches and monuments of religion and art; for, in the final analysis, it was they who gave the necessary backing to the work of destruction and allowed it to go on for their own political and economic advantage, and, for the generality of them, religious considerations scarcely counted at all.

Having stated that, we may now look at the facts of the situation. The medieval church in Scotland, say about the year 1540, was well equipped with buildings of all kinds. There were thirteen cathedrals, ranging in importance from the splendid cathedrals of St. Andrews or Glasgow to the lesser establishments of Dornoch or Iona[3]. There were over one thousand parish churches, some of them extremely wealthy like St. Giles, Edinburgh, or St. Nicholas, Aberdeen, and others, especially in rural districts, desperately poor. Attached to the parochial system was a very great number of chapels maintained by lairds and magnates and a number (not accurately known) of hospitals and bede-houses, which catered for what we would call the social services. Also, linked up with the diocesan system, were roughly forty collegiate churches, some exceedingly rich and important like the Chapel Royal in Stirling or King's College in Old Aberdeen, others were in the country areas were less well endowed. Outside of the diocesan structure, there were over fifty abbeys and priories, some, like Arbroath, Dunfermline, Scone, or Paisley, are an integral part of our history, others were lowly and poor. There were about fifty friaries, chiefly of the orders of St. Dominic and St. Francis, and a dozen nunneries. In each district, these buildings, cathedral, abbey, college kirk or friary were the focal point of social and economic as well as of religious life. In each place, the neighbouring people were proud of their local church " like the bairns of Lasmahagow, who saw never a fairer Abbey nor their owne "[4]. Then, a generation later, say about the year 1580, we find almost all of the larger churches and (especially in the east-central lowlands) a proportion of parish churches in complete or partial ruin, and the spiritual and social life that they had once engendered is proscribed or is in the throes of radical change. And even those churches whose fabric is still intact have been despoiled of their former splendour in furnishing and decoration[5]. One can indicate the agencies by which this fundamental change was effected in the social, economic and religious life of the nation but the motives which inspired the agencies are less easy to determine.

The earliest attacks on the material accessories of catholic worship that we can confidently associate with the Scottish reformation begin a full generation before 1560. The first recorded instance that we have seems to be the case of Walter Stewart, brother of Lord Ochiltree, who was summoned before Archbishop Dunbar of Glasgow, in 1533, to

---

2. *Early English Text Society*, ii, p. 144.
3. The cathedral of Lismore is not given as an example because, even by Scottish medieval standards, it was exceptionally poor.
4. Alexander Baillie, *A True Information*, 1628, p. 31.
5. Cf. Gordon of Rothiemay's description of the nave of Aberdeen Cathedral, still used as a parish church in 1661: "At this day it is bot the carkase of the former church, covered with slates." (*Aberdoniae Vtriusque Descriptio*, Spalding Club, 1842, p. 22.)

answer a charge of malicious damage to a statue of our Lady in the Observant Friars' Kirk at Ayr[6]. Four years later, in 1537, two men were sought for in Dundee and Perth, suspected of " hangeing of the Image of Sanct Francis "[7]. These could not have been isolated instances because among the other enactments for the repression of heresy, parliament, on 14th March, 1540-41, decreed that no one should cast down the images of saints and treat them with dishonour. In the period of unrest and disorder which followed the death of James V, in 1542, and the Regent Arran's brief flirtation with English heresy, Lutheran preachers and their protectors became bolder and the outbreaks of violence increase. In 1545, after Master George Wishart visited Ayr with his friends, Ayr's dean of guild had to pay James Nychole five shillings for taking down the broken images in the parish kirk and much damage to the kirk windows had to be made good[8]. Profiting by such experience, the sheriff of Ayr, Sir Hugh Campbell of Loudon, mounted a guard at the kirk of Mauchline and refused Wishart and his armed supporters entry to the building " for preservation of a tabernacle (an altarpiece) that was there, beautiful to the eye "[9]. The result of Wishart's intensive course of sermons at the mansion house of Barr appears in the activities of John Lockhart of Barr, who with Charles Campbell of Bargour is put to the horn on 16th July, 1550, for not appearing to answer charges of " theftuous and violent carrying off, depredation, stouthreif and spoliation furth of sundry parish churches, religious houses and chapels, within the shires of Lanark, Renfrew, and the stewartries of Kyle, Carrick and Cuninghame, of sundry eucharistic chalices, altars and ornaments of the mass; and also for casting down and breaking choral stalls and other stalls and glazed windows, etc., in the years, 1545, 1546, 1547 and 1548 "[10].

Three of the men hanged at Perth, in January 1543-44, were indicted according to Calderwood " for hanging up the image of Sanct Francis on a cord, nailing of ramme's hornes to his head and a kowe's rumpe to his taile "[11]. The magistrates of Aberdeen, in December 1544, had to deal with two men for " the hinging of the image of Sant Franceis."[12]

These same years saw some mob violence directed against religious houses in some of the towns where Lutheran ideas were now being freely ventilated. These early attacks are directed mainly against the friars, especially the Greyfriars, and there were probably many reasons for this. The friars' houses were in towns, where Lutheran strength was concentrated; they derived their income from tenements in the towns and, in the economic depression of the times, could easily be stigmatized as harsh landlords and have popular indignation stirred up against them; in general, they lacked the protection which the monastic orders may have derived from having kinsfolk of the nobility in their communities; and,

---

6. D. E. Easson, *Gavin Dunbar*, 1947, p. 55.

7. Pitcairn, *Criminal Trials*, i, p. 286.

8. *Ayr Burgh Accounts* (Scottish History Society), 1937, pp. 96-97.

9. Dickinson's *Knox*, i, p. 61.

10. Pitcairn, *Criminal Trials*, i, p. 353. It was probably at this time that the abbey of Kilwinning was threatened. Under date 20th January, 1552, the *R.M.S.* v, 1132, has: " Considering the merits of James, earl of Arran, in past times of the greatest turbulence, because of heretics and raiders and sacrilegious men, who spared neither things sacred nor profane, invading night and day the goods and lands of the said monastery ' ecclesie eiusdem direptionem sunt minati nisi favor et defensio dicti ducis semper adfuissent, sine quibus nihil ab eis fuisset tutum.' "

11. Calderwood: *History of the Kirk of Scotland* (Wodrow Society), i, p. 171.

12. *Extracts from the Council Register of the Burgh of Aberdeen*, 1398-1570 (Spalding Club), 1844, p. 211.

in particular the friars, by their preaching, were in the forefront of the anti-Lutheran campaign and would thus qualify for more than their share of Lutheran violence and obloquy.

One suspects also that the earliest attacks of the revolutionaries were directed against houses where the religious life was being effectively maintained, because such houses were a much greater obstacle to the progress of Lutheran ideas than many a rural abbey where the tempo of religious life was humdrum and harmless. This point might be illustrated from the fate of two nunneries in the later Calvinist attack. The rich Cistercian nunnery of Haddington, where religious life was at a low level and where the interests of the Hepburn and Maitland families were firmly entrenched, seems to have faded out gradually under a succession of prioresses, who disposed of the abbey's possessions to their kinsfolk. Far different was the fate of the " Systeris of the Schenis ", the Dominican nuns of Edinburgh, whose good repute is spoken of by Sir David Lindsay;

> " . . . ane Convent yit unthrall
> To dame Sensuall, nor with ryches abusit,
> So quietlye those ladyis bene inclusit: "[13]

for Lesley, in his history, has to record that, despite its excellent reputation (or perhaps because of it), " that pure and cleine clostir perteining to the sisteris of the Scheines besyd Edinburghe; bot this that quhen of all suspicione it was maist cleine, nochtwithstandeng was the first in the hail Realme eftir the Chartirhous that be the aduersar was wraked and brocht to nocht."[14]

There was an incident in Perth, on the 14th May, 1543, when some citizens of the town invaded the monastery of the Blackfriars and, among other pilfering and damage, stole the " kettle ", containing the friars' dinner, and paraded it about the town. The attackers apparently did not enter the church and there is no mention of any damage to images, so this incident is almost certainly a demonstration of economic, rather than of theological, grievances.[15] About the theological nature of the outbreak of violence in Dundee, that same year, however, there can be little doubt. The thriving port of Dundee imported ideas as well as merchandise and the town became an early stronghold of Lutheranism in Scotland. The motive of the assault on the Dundee friars was theological, though one may question whether it was altogether spontaneous or popular since the shifty Regent Arran later confessed that he had been party to the outrage. The burgh archives still preserve the indictment which, ten years after the event, was preferred against the rioters; " For art and part in the oppression committed on the Friars, Preachers and Minorites of Dundee, by coming to their Places within the said burgh with convocation of the Queen's lieges in great number, armed in warlike manner; and there breaking up the doors and gates of the Places and breaking and destroying the ornaments, vestments, images and candlesticks carrying off the silvering of the altars, and stealing the

13. Laing's *Lindsay*, ii, p. 95.
14. Lesley's *Historie of Scotland* (Scottish Text Society), i, p. 23.
15. What may have been a similar non-theological attack on the Aberdeen Blackfriars was dealt with, by the magistrates, on the 5th September, 1544. *Extracts from the Council Register of the Burgh of Aberdeen, 1398-1570* (Spalding Club), 1844, p. 206.

bed clothes, cowls, etc., victuals, meal, malt, flesh, fish, coals, napery, pewter plates, tin stoups, etc., which were in keeping in the said Places; in company with Mr. Henry Durham and his accomplices—rebels of Our Lady the Queen, and at the horn—on the last day of August, 1543."[16]

The text of this indictment is important because it gives a contemporary and, no doubt, accurate description of what was entailed in the " casting down " of a religious house. The Scottish reformation, like every other revolution, developed its own jargon and the verb " to cast down " is one of its special technical terms. Wherever the phrase " cast down " occurs in the literature of the Scottish reformation it normally means what is described here in this document. The religious house is attacked; its altars, pictures, statues, stalls, vestments, books, the ornamental structure of tombs (and sometimes the actual graves) and also windows (presumably because they displayed images) are destroyed. Doors, screens and wooden furnishings are broken up to provide fuel for the bonfire in the kirkyard. Altar vessels and domestic furnishings are looted. The verb " to cast down ", which is possibly a term translated from some German or Latin original, does not mean the breaking down of the actual structure of the building, though, on occasion (especially if arson is involved or if lead or other materials are stolen from the roofs) the fabric might be more or less severely damaged. In the sixteenth-century documents, the " casting down " of a church is often distinguished from the demolition of the building as, for example, when the provost of Aberdeen, in 1559, says that the Mearns magnates and their retainers are coming " to distroy and cast doune the kirkis and religious places " of Aberdeen: or when the general assembly, of December 1560, decreed that " the Kirk of Restalrig be razed and utterly casten doun " : or when an act of parliament of January, 1572-73, speaks of " divers paroche kirkis within this realme demolischit, cassin doun and destroyit." In this, as in many other features of the Scottish reformation, the pattern of procedure is to be sought on the Continent. Geisberg, *Die Reformation im Einblatt Holzschnitt*, xxvi, 27, gives a contemporary German woodcut of the " casting down " of a church, an operation such as was carried out by Martin Bucer in the convent church of the Dominicanesses at Strasbourg, in February 1529, or by Guillaume Farel in the churches of Geneva, in 1532. The " casting down " of churches is not a Calvinist procedure, for Calvin denounced such behaviour, it is a feature of the Scottish reformation that derives from the earlier Lutheran phase of the movement. The practice of destroying images appears in Scotland with the early Lutheran ideas but the main impetus given to the practice of " casting down " churches came almost certainly from that " innocent lamb ", Master George Wishart.

Sir Ralph Sadler, English envoy in Edinburgh, duly reported the Dundee riots (4th September, 1543) and adds that; " Another company of ' good Christians ' as they call them here have lykewise sacked an abbey in Fyffe and Anguish, called the abbey of Landorse and turned the monkes out of dores; and, if they may be suffered, it is thought they woll procede further to the sackying of the rest of such as they may handsomely com by."[17] The *Diurnal of Occurrents* adds the detail that

---

16. Maxwell's *Old Dundee*, p. 395.
17. The phrase in " in Fyffe and Anguish " is curious: it is meaningless as it stands and suggests that in this, perhaps hurriedly written, letter, Sadler had some religious houses of Angus in his mind possibly Arbroath.

Arbroath was also on the agenda of these rioters but they were prevented from sacking that monastery by Lord Ogilvie; " In this tyme thair was ane greit heresie in Dundie: thair thai distroyit the kirkis and wald have destroyit Abirbrothok Kirk, war not the Lord Ogilbie."[18] A similar attack on the Blackfriars house in Edinburgh (4th September, 1543) was also foiled. This riot, too, originated from the same Arran-Sadler alliance because members of Arran's retinue were among the armed attackers. In this case, the townspeople summoned by the common bell, defended the friary and expelled the would-be pillagers from the town.[19]

To the English envoy, as he sent off reports of these events, the situation must have appeared to be developing nicely. The marriage of Mary Queen of Scots to the English Prince Edward had been agreed to and, in the meantime, the Regent Arran was abetting some useful preliminary destruction of popish strongholds. Then suddenly all was changed. Cardinal Beaton's star was again in the ascendant. Arran abjured his heresy at Stirling on 8th September; the English marriage project was repudiated on 11th December and stern measures were concerted to repress heresy. There now appears the first major agency in the destruction of Scotland's ecclesiastical buildings—the series of English invasions under the Earl of Hertford. Henry VIII, unable to secure the marriage alliance by peaceful means, resorted to intimidation by frightfulness. The instructions given to the Earl of Hertford in 1544, for the " Rough Wooing " are ferocious enough and the other large scale invasions of 1545 and 1547, together with subsidiary raids in the borders, continued in much the same spirit.

These English invasions are probably the decisive factor in the growth and success of the heretical movement in Scotland; here we are concerned with their effect on ecclesiastical buildings, and the destruction caused by them requires very careful consideration, since, in the opinion of many historians, a very high proportion of our ecclesiastical ruins are due to these raids. In any consideration of these English raids, two points must be kept clearly in mind. In the first place, the raids affected only a few limited areas and, secondly, while the damage done to buildings in those areas might, in some instances, be very severe, the devastation in general has been grossly exaggerated. The sources of our information are English war communiqués and propaganda pamphlets and such documents are no more reliable than their modern counterparts.[20]

The first invasion began with the surprise arrival of the English fleet, without any declaration of war, off Leith on 4th May, 1544. For some ten days, the English remained in occupation of Leith, attacked Edinburgh and some towns and villages along the shores of the Firth of Forth. Then, dismissing the fleet, Hertford marched his army home by way of Seton, Haddington, and Dunbar, reaching Berwick on 18th May. Within this

---

18. *A diurnal of remarkable occurrents* (Maitland Club), 1833, p. 29.
19. *Hamilton Papers*, ii, 15.
20. The campaigns of 1544 and 1547 are described in two pamphlets, *The late expedition in Scotland*, published at London, in 1544, and *The Expedition into Scotland, etc.*, published at London, in 1548, by William Patten, who was assisted in his literary work by William Cecil. These pamphlets are printed in A. F. Pollard, *Tudor Tracts*, 1532-1588: they are obviously written as propaganda on behalf of the new regime in England and to curry favour with the " victorious Lord Governor and King, &c.: for whose sake, doubtless, God hath spreaded his blessing over us, in peace to have mirth, and in wars to have victory." There is also a detailed description of the campaign of 1545, written by York Herald, published in *P.S.A.S.*, i, pp. 271-9. The value of these documents and the actual amount of devastation caused by these raids requires careful investigation.

short period a preposterous amount of destruction is claimed by the anonymous pamphleteer who, in 1544, published *The Late Expedition in Scotland*. He would have us believe that all the countryside about Edinburgh " within seven miles every way " and the coastal villages and towns as far as Stirling were ravaged. Seton, Dunbar and Haddington (" with a great nunnery and a house of friars ") were burnt as also were Leith and Edinburgh. Of Edinburgh, he writes; " It was determined by the said Lord Lieutenant utterly to ruinate and destroy the said town with fire; which for that the night drew fast on, we omitted thoroughly to execute on that day: but setting fire in three or four parts of the town, we repaired for that night unto our camp. And the next morning, very early, we began where we left off and continued burning all that day and the two days next ensuing continually, so that neither within the walls nor in the suburbs was left any one house unburnt; besides the innumerable booty, spoil and pillage that our soldiers brought from thence; notwithstanding the abundance which was consumed with fire. Also we burnt the Abbey called Holy Rood House and the Palace adjoining the same."[21]

There was certainly damage done at Holyrood Abbey,[22] the place was also pillaged because its " fair font of solid brasse " was presented by Sir Richard Lee to St. Alban's Abbey and its brass lectern is still to be seen in a village church near St. Albans, but, if the place was burnt, the damage was not extensive.[23] The parish kirk of St. Giles suffered no structural damage and was not pillaged, as we can see from the Hammermen's records.[24] Trinity College Kirk, although outside the walls, seems to have remained intact. The Greyfriars Kirk was undamaged but the Blackfriars suffered considerably and there was a good deal of rebuilding there in the following months.[25] The hospital at Kirk of Field was destroyed,[26] but the rest of the establishment, including the church, survived. It is equally difficult to find corroborative evidence for this extensive devastation outside of Edinburgh. There is a " tradition " at St. Monans that the church there was burnt. The abbey of Newbattle is claimed as burnt both in this raid and in that of 1547,[27]

---

21. Pollard, *Tudor Tracts*, p. 43.

22. Various repairs are mentioned in *R.M.S.*, v, 1242 and 2777 and the English invasions are blamed for the damage.

23. The bells were still in the towers and " the church and much part of the house well covered with lead " when the English next came to the district in 1547.

24. J. Smith, *The Hammermen of Edinburgh*, pp. lxxv-vi. It is true that Bishop Lesley, in his *Historie of Scotland* (Scot. Text Society) ii, p. 279, agrees that Edinburgh was burnt: " Bot the neist day the toune sett in fyr with al diligence it burnte continualie four dayes in a miserable flame." The explanation may lie in the fact that Lesley composed his history in England between 1568 and 1570 and may have made use of *The late expedition in Scotland*. That some of the houses of the city were destroyed by fire is certain (*P.S.A.S.*, v, p. 163) but the wholesale devastation of the town implied by the English pamphleteer and Bishop Lesley is certainly not borne out by the evidence. The picture suggested by some modern writers is of a city, whose houses were all wood, burning from end to end: but unless Alesius is indulging in pure romance, Edinburgh's houses, about 1530, were at least predominantly stone-built. Knox's restrained and almost casual reference to the burning of Edinburgh (Dickinson's *Knox*, i, pp. 57 and 58) does not suggest any large-scale conflagration. However, the whole question needs close examination.

25. W. Moir Bryce, *The Black Friars of Edinburgh*, pp. 51-52.

26. *Collegiate Churches of Midlothian*, p. xxxvii.

27. There is evidence for the rebuilding of certain houses belonging to Newbattle, which had been burnt by the English (*R.M.S.*, v, 2313), which may be all that happened, in spite of the fact that the *Diurnal of Occurrents* (p. 32) says: " Upoun the xv day of Maij (1544), the horsmen raid to Newbottill and brynt it, and owersaw Dalkeith be the moyane of George Dowglas, and brynt many uther tounes thairabout: na skaith was done to any kirkis exceptand thai distroyit the abbay of Newbottill." Part of the difficulty lies in the fact that medieval men liked highly coloured and emphatic expression. It is never enough to say that a building is " in need of repair " or " damaged ": to impress the reader, you must say that it is " utterly ruined " or " made level with the ground." Medieval petitions to Rome from Scotland have many examples of such emphatic expressions. One cannot accept such statements as an accurate description of the condition of a building unless they are corroborated by other evidence.

yet it was still functioning at least a decade later and the same holds good for the nunnery at Haddington.

In June of that same year, 1544, the English wardens of the east and middle marches made a large-scale foray as far as Jedburgh. Here again the town is said to have been burnt, leaving not more than " two howses unbrent in the same " and " the abbey likewise they burned as moche as they might for the stoneworke."[28] The *Late Expedition* adds that " the Grey Friars and divers bastel and fortified houses, whereof there were many in that town " were given to the flames and, on the way home, Morebattle kirk was burned. " Furthermore to the apparent continuance of God's favour unto the purposes of the Englishmen," the abbey of Coldingham was attacked and " it was burnt all saving the church ":[29] the abbey was garrisoned later by the warden of the English east marches. Another report of " Exployts don upon the Scotts " between July and November, 1544, gives as the number of places harried, destroyed and burned during this period; " Towns, towers, stedes, barnekyns, paryshe churches, bastell-houses, 192 "; explicit mention is made of one parish church at the head of "Averdaill ". The church of Eccles was won by assault and the nunnery there was attacked, for they " burnt and spoyled the said abbay and town saving the church ". It is claimed also that they " burnt a market town called Dryburgh, with an abbay in hit, all saving the church ".[30] During the ensuing winter Sir Ralph Eure and Sir Brian Layton attacked Melrose abbey and, among other atrocities, desecrated the Douglas tombs in the abbey kirk.[31]

A detailed account of Hertford's September, 1545, campaign, which was confined to the neighbourhood of Kelso, is supplied by York Herald, who apparently accompanied the expedition.[32] On this occasion, the abbey of Kelso was taken by Hertford's Spanish mercenaries and plundered. It had been intended to convert the abbey buildings into a fortress, but this plan was abandoned in favour of a fortress at Roxburgh, so Kelso abbey was despoiled of its lead roofing and " a Sonday the abbey of Kelse was razed and all put to royen, howsses and towres and stypeles." Other damage claimed in this raid was the razing of the abbeys of Melrose and Dryburgh, as well as the Franciscan friary of Roxburgh, the nunnery of Eccles and, once again, " the abbey of Jedworthe (and) the Freers there ". The list of places " brent, raced and cast doune " in this raid, which lasted some fifteen days (from 8th to 23rd September, 1545), includes sixteen castles, five market towns and 243 villages, which certainly looks as if the reporter has overworked the army.

Two years later, in September, 1547, Hertford, now Lord Protector Somerset, again advanced into Scotland. The story of this invasion is told in *The Expedition into Scotland*, written by William Patten (with the help of William Cecil) and published at London in 1548. The army left Berwick on 4th September, 1547. It marched north by the coast supported by the English fleet, under Admiral Clinton, and the climax of the

28. *Hamilton Papers*, ii, 405, 407.

29. Pollard: *Tudor Tracts*, pp. 49-50.

30. Quoted, from Haynes' *Collection of State Papers*, 1740, in David Hay Fleming's *The Reformation in Scotland*, p. 333. Dr. Hay Fleming suggests, no doubt correctly, that "Averdaill" should read Anerdaill and this he identifies as Annandale. It is much more likely that Anerdaill refers to the valley of the Ale Water, which was anciently known as the Alne Water. This was in the neighbourhood of these military operations, whereas it is a far cry to Annandale from Kelso.

31. This piece of barbarism had the extraordinary result of turning the Earl of Angus into " a good Scotishman " for a brief period.

32. This account is printed in *P.S.A.S.*, i, pp. 271-9.

campaign was the defeat of the Scots army, under Arran, at Pinkie Cleugh, on 10th September. Thereafter, Leith was occupied for a short space and partly burned. Holyrood abbey was despoiled of its lead roofing and two bells. The English retired to the border, garrisoned Roxburgh and this part of the campaign was over by 29th September. In an auxiliary raid on the west marches, Annan kirk is said to have been burned.

In the meantime the English fleet, after occupying Inchcolm,[33] had sailed north to the Firth of Tay, anchored off Dundee and established a bridgehead at Broughty Castle. The town of Dundee suffered badly in this operation and no united effort against the enemy was possible because some of the Lutheran element in the population were working hand in glove with the invaders. The English commander claimed, in one of his reports, that " all the honest and substantial men of the town favoureth the Word of God ".[34] Admiral Wyndham came in December with reinforcements and reported " I trust ere it be long to suppress an abbey or two "[35] and, true to his word, he attacked Balmerino abbey on Christmas night, and advancing to within a few miles of Perth, he raided the Cistercian nunnery of Elcho, carrying off the nuns and many gentlemen's daughters. The damage in both cases was partial, because religious life resumed its accustomed routine after the English and their " fellow travellers " had passed. Before evacuating the town of Dundee in January, 1547-48, the English despoiled the great parish kirk of St. Mary; they " fired the steeple and burned all the idols in the church " and carried off " all the copper and brass that was in the church ". Later that year, after a further brief occupation, they finally left Dundee in November, 1548, and the havoc was completed; St. Mary's Kirk and the lesser churches, the tolbooth with the town muniments and the almshouse " were brunt and cassin down be England ". The former splendour of church worship never returned to Dundee after this devastation. The church plate which had been hidden away was restored to use, but the burgh was too impoverished to restore the smaller churches and it was only after much collecting of funds and through the generosity of the abbey of Lindores that, in 1552, " the reparation and bigging of the queir of the paroch Kirk " was begun and in the re-roofed choir, the more important altars were crowded till such time as the nave could be reconstructed.[36]

An English army returned to the south-east in the spring of 1548 and did much structural damage to the parish kirk and friary kirk in Haddington in their efforts to fortify that town before they were finally expelled in October, 1549. Newbattle abbey was again attacked in the course of these operations and, about the time of the English withdrawal, the town of Peebles was extensively burned and its parish kirk of St. Andrew suffered damage and, although in need of repair, it continued in use till 1560 when the town took over the Cross Kirk for parochial services.

---

33. Whose monks retired to Dunfermline for the duration of the hostilities.
34. Maxwell, *Old Dundee*, p. 99.
35. *Opus cit.*, p. 106.
36. *Opus cit.*, pp. 126 seq.

It is no easy matter to assess the war damage to ecclesiastical buildings in the course of these invasions of the 1540s. While it is clear that there must have been a great deal of pillaging and destruction, it is equally clear that the English war reports are exaggerated and unreliable. It is important to keep in mind that there was nothing like total devastation even in the towns most affected, Dundee, Haddington, Peebles, Leith and Edinburgh, and, apart from one religious house (the friars' house at Jedburgh concerning which no records have survived), the abbeys and churches in the war zone did not suffer final and irreparable destruction. In spite of the scarcity of records, we can see that efforts were made to restore buildings and religious life as far as possible. The nuns of Elcho, for example, borrowed from John Wemyss of that ilk various sums amounting in all to £1,000 Scots to repair their buildings.[37] The Blackfriars of Edinburgh received alms for this purpose and their church and monastery housed the provincial council of 1549.[38] Some references to the repair of Holyrood Abbey and its property survive.[39] There is an allusion in 1565 to the great sums of money that had been spent on repairing the damage of the English raids at Kelso.[40] The nuns at Haddington were engaged on repairs in 1556[41] and, at Newbattle, some of the houses belonging to the abbey, and ruined by the English, were repaired in 1550 and work was in progress on the abbey in 1559.[42] The parish church of Haddington remained a roofless ruin but the Greyfriars church there was partially restored.[43] The abbey kirk at Jedburgh was in sufficiently good condition for the general ordination of Glasgow archdiocese to be held there by Bishop Robert Reid on the Saturday before Passion Sunday (14th March) in the year 1550.[44] The *opus Dei* was maintained at Melrose right up to the proscription of the old faith notwithstanding English claims to have destroyed the abbey and despite the commendator's neglect of badly needed repairs.

The documentation at Melrose is unusually full and gives us a picture of the state of affairs between the English raids and the reformation; these documents, moreover, throw some light on the well-known petition, addressed by Cardinal Sermoneta to Pope Paul IV in December, 1556, which, since its publication by Father Pollen, S.J., in 1901, has been reprinted often as proof of neglect of church buildings by ecclesiastics. The section of the petition which deals with church buildings runs; "Moreover it was declared how, in the said Kingdom, very many churches and monasteries had been established of old in stately buildings, but within the last ten years or thereabouts had been reduced to ruins by hostile inroads or, through the avarice and neglect of those placed in charge, were crumbling to decay and this with their revenues undiminished nay, in some cases, even greater than at the time of their foundation with no one to pity these widowed churches or to take their healing in hand. Wherefore her most serene Majesty made earnest suit to your Holiness

---

37. Fraser. *Memorials of the Family of Wemyss of Wemyss*, ii, 188-192, 294, 295.
38. W. Moir Bryce. *The Blackfriars of Edinburgh*, pp. 52 and 55.
39. *R.M.S.*, v, 1242, 1773, 2777.
40. *R.M.S.*, v, 2440.
41. *R.M.S.*, v, 1753.
42. *R.M.S.*, v, 2313, 1386. Newbattle was in sufficient repair to accommodate a convention of the Queen. Regent's party, preparatory to the declaration of war with England in 1557.
43. W. Moir Bryce. *The Scottish Greyfriars*, i, pp. 172-3.
44. W. Fraser. *Stirlings of Keir*, pp. 399-400.

to appoint prelates of those regions who, by sanction of censure and penalty, might compel the aforesaid rulers, abbots and heads of churches to restore such places as are in need and to spend a fourth part of all and sundry fruits, coming from such benefices as are held by them, on the restoration and repair of the said churches, monasteries and benefices."[45]

This petition is often quoted as if it were an independent and authoritative ecclesiastical statement of conditions in Scotland. Such is not the case. Even though he was cardinal protector of Scotland, Sermoneta had no direct knowledge of the country and, in this petition, he is acting in accordance with his office merely as official spokesman at the Roman court for the Scottish crown and is using information supplied by the crown (in this case by the regent, Mary of Guise). That being so, the most remarkable thing about this part of the petition is its effrontery. It is dishonest in that it conceals all reference to the heavy taxation which had been imposed on the church by James V and by Mary of Guise herself;[46] not to mention the serious drain on the resources of many an abbey, which had to support as lay-abbot some royal bastard or court favourite, whose only aim might be to enrich himself, without any consideration for the monastic community or its property. There is a sad lack of sincerity in asking the pope to appoint worthy prelates, when the papacy, for half a century or more, had been blackmailed by the crown into appointing unprovided, and often unworthy members of royal or noble families to the most important benefices in the realm.[47]

Contemporary with this petition to Pope Paul IV, the Melrose regality records let us see the actual facts of the situation from the point of view of the monks. At Melrose the commendator or titular abbot was James Stewart, one of the several illegitimate sons of James V, who had been provided for, by being appointed to rich abbeys. This particular lay-abbot, by fraud and by bullying the monks, was disposing of the property of the monastic community to his own advantage. He paid no heed to the protests of the monks, who claimed, especially on 19th June, 1556, that their property was being alienated, while the commendator's promises to carry out repair work on several parts of the abbey buildings were unfulfilled. Among other things he had not appointed " ane bruther of the place being maister of werk for reparatioun of the kirk and dortour and uther placis quhair maist neid is and without the kirk be reparit this instant sommer God service will ceise in winter ".[48] On another occasion, when the monks refused to sign and seal a charter alienating property until the promised repairs should be done, my lord commendator " grew crawbit " and (as they declare in an instrument of protest drawn up on 21st August, 1557) they granted the charter only " throcht feyr and dredour of the said conventis leiving to be discharget and tane fra thame be the said commendator conform to his minatorious wordis ". But even long-suffering monks lost patience when they found the " alleget baillie deput of the regalite of Melrose, with thair cumpany

45. Pollen, *Papal Negotiations with Mary Queen of Scots* (Scottish History Society), 1901, pp. 529-530.
46. For an account of the taxation of the church in the thirty years preceding the reformation, see W. Stanford Reid, " Clerical taxation: the Scottish alternative to the dissolution of the monasteries," in the *Catholic Historical Review*, xxxv (1948).
47. Almost at this precise time, Mary of Guise secured the appointment of the Duke of Chatelherault's son, John Hamilton, to the rich abbacy of Arbroath as part of the bribe to persuade the duke to resign from the regency.
48. *Melrose Regality Records* (Scottish History Society), iii, p. 218.

and complicis turweand (removing) the leid of thair closter and causand to cast doune the samyn extending to xj stane of leid or thairby ",[49] especially since they had complained earlier of the commendator " disponing of the placis leid to my Lord of Glasgow quhare our greter neid is of our awin kirk and uther placis ". In the light of such behaviour on the part of her late husband's illegitimate son (appointed abbot both of Melrose and Kelso), Mary of Guise's petition to the pope sounds somewhat hollow.

Further, in the light of such expropriation of monastic capital and revenue by a commendator, one would expect that parish churches dependent on such monasteries would fare ill. One is not surprised to learn then that when Archbishop Hamilton of St. Andrews made his visitation of the Merse churches, in August, 1555, he writes: "We discovered and saw with our own eyes, that a great many of the parish churches—their choirs as well as their naves—were wholly thrown down and as it were levelled to the ground: others were partly ruinous or threatening collapse in respect of their walls and roofs: they were without glazed windows and without a baptismal font and had no vestments for the high altars and no missals or manuals, so that their parishioners could not hear the divine services or masses therein as befits good Christians, neither could masses be celebrated nor the church's sacraments administered; the fault and shortcoming belonging to the parishioners as well as to the parsons." And particular mention is made of the churches of Langton, Simpreme, Fogo, Hume, Greenlaw, and Nenthorn (all of which belonged to Kelso Abbey of which James Stewart was commendator): Stichell, Earlston, Ayton, Lamberton, Edrem, Ednam, Swinton, Auldcambus, and Fishwick (all belonging to Coldingham, of which John Stewart, another of James V's illegitimate sons was commendator): Merton and Smailholm (belonging to Dryburgh Abbey, the commendatorship of which was by now a hereditary perquisite of the Erskines):[50] Duns, Ellem, Whitsome, Foulden and Mordington.[51]

The English invasions are headline news in all the histories of the period and even to-day it is difficult to shake off the effect of the English propaganda and remember that, even in the war zone, the religious houses continued to exist, their routine life was not interrupted for very long and, if other agencies had not intervened, the damage done to buildings would all have been made good in the normal course of events. Further, the war zone was a very restricted area: the greater part of the

49. *Opus cit.*, iii, p. 158.
50. So ingrained was this ruinous practice of using abbeys and bishoprics to provide an income for the offspring of the magnates, who were otherwise unprovided for, that even as late as 1580, when surely anyone in his senses could have seen its disastrous effects, we find Jesuit Abercrombie, writing with obvious approval, that the remaining catholic nobility in Scotland " feel deeply and lament the lack of Bishoprics and catholic abbacies and the bad distribution of church benefices, by means of which, in former times, sons of the nobility were so honourably supported." *Innes Review*, vii, p. 38.
51. *A Source Book of Scottish History*, ii, pp. 143-144. This letter is couched in the usual exaggerated terminology of such documents which makes it difficult to say just how far it represents the actual facts of the situation, but after a decade of unusually bitter border warfare and with self-seeking commendators in charge of the abbeys, the situation in the east marches was probably just as bad as the document states. Archbishop Hamilton, of course, was only putting into effect the decrees of the provincial council of 1549 (Patrick, *Statutes of the Scottish Church*, p. 119). It was probably Archbishop Hamilton who sequestrated the rents of Holyrood Abbey because the windows of its dependent churches were not kept in repair, an action recalled later in the general assembly of March, 1569-70. The general situation of church maintenance throughout the rest of the kingdom (outside of the war zone in the south east), as far as we can judge from contemporary references, and discounting the hyperbolic language, would appear to be the normal mixture of sound and negligent administration with conditions becoming gradually more and more difficult for everyone because of the continuing economic decline.

kingdom was untouched; no cathedral city was affected[52] and in great abbeys like Dunfermline, Scone, Paisley, Kinloss, Cambuskenneth, Arbroath, Coupar Angus or Kilwinning and in important collegiate and parish kirks like St. Nicholas, Aberdeen, St. Giles, Edinburgh, Our Lady and St. Anne, Glasgow, St. Michael, Linlithgow, the Chapel Royal, Stirling, and in many similar establishments the perennial round of mass and divine office continued undisturbed.

What the English invasions did achieve, however, was to intensify the political and economic instability of the kingdom and in the ensuing chaos, the revolutionary elements went from strength to strength. Outbursts of iconoclasm were growing more frequent. On 16th March, 1546-47, Stephen Bell had to find surety for good behaviour after casting down and breaking a statue of St. Mary Magdalene in a chapel at Lany.[53] In the autumn of 1556, some individuals in Edinburgh were accused of taking down images of the Holy Trinity, Our Lady and St. Francis and contemptuously smashing them.[54] Among the points raised by the Chapter of Aberdeen in their advice to the bishop on 5th January, 1558, occurs " the byrnyng of the kirk of Echt or casting doun of ymagis in ony kirkis within the diosie of Abirdene ".[55] In the early summer of 1558, Paul Methven preached " in sundrie gentlemenis places in Angus and also Fyfe, to witt, in Couper, Lundy and at Fawsyd and in sundrie vther places, and ministrat the sacramentis of the communion in Lundie and in Couper of Fyfe, and caused the images thairof to be castin doun and abolished the Popis religion ".[56] And now, according to Knox, " the images were stolen away in all parts of the country; and in Edinburgh was that great idol called Saint Giles, first drowned in the North Loch (and) after burnt, which raised no small trouble in the town ", and for the annual procession in honour of the town's patron, on his feast day that year (1st September, 1558), a statute had to be borrowed from the Greyfriars. Concerning the destruction of this second statue, Knox writes merrily.[57]

These were months of growing unrest: the existing discontent with the state of the church and with the French alliance were sedulously fomented and civil war seemed not far off. Kirkmen, especially the friars in the burghs, took what precautions they could. Property was feued (sometimes conditionally) to local magistrates or to other reliable individuals. The kirk geir, especially the sacred vessels, was distributed for safety in private houses (which was a common precaution in time of war). The prior and brethren of the Dominican house in Inverness handed over their silverwork and vestments to the provost and bailies for safe-keeping, on 24th June, 1559.[58] Three days later the Edinburgh town council took similar measures to ensure the safety of the jewels (sacred vessels and reliquaries) and vestments of St. Giles' Kirk.[59] The

---

52. This statement requires some modification. The city of St. Andrews did indeed escape the English invasions, but it suffered damage at the time of the cardinal's murder, in 1546. Apart from the damage occasioned by the siege of the castle, Norman Leslie is said to have burnt St. Salvator's College, the Blackfriars and the Greyfriars monasteries (*R.S.S.*, iii, 2345, 2363 and 2515).

53. Pitcairn, *Criminal Trials*, i, p. 335.

54. *Extracts from the Burgh Records of Edinburgh*, 1528-57, pp. 251-2.

55. *Miscellany of the Spalding Club*, iv, p. 59.

56. Pitscottie, *Chronicles of Scotland*, 1814, ii, p. 523.

57. Dickinson's *Knox*, i, pp. 125 and 127-9.

58. *The Family of Rose of Kilvarock* (Spalding Club), pp. 226-227.

59. *Extracts from the Records of the Burgh of Edinburgh.* Much interesting information about the kirk geir of St. Giles' Kirk is given *passim*, pp. 27-115, especially pp. 42-44.

major relics of St. Duthac's, at Tain, were placed in the safe keeping of the Laird of Balnagone.[60] On 7th July, 1559, much of the silverwork of Aberdeen Cathedral was distributed among the canons for safety and vestments and treasure were sent to Huntly Castle.[61] The chaplains of St. Nicholas Kirk, Aberdeen, on 16th June, 1559, requested the magistrates to take charge of their vestments and altar-plate till the " uproir and tumilt war put to tranquilite be the antient and wyse counsel of the realme ".[62] This opinion that the crisis was of a temporary nature seems to have been widely held. The regent, Mary of Guise, overlooked what displeased her, " attendant meilleure saison ",[63] and no doubt the vicar of Dowally was not the only one, who would look back on " that tempestuous time when the statutes of the church and of the religious life, as observed for so long, were changed from the original observance by a transformation unexpected by many."[64]

Church leaders were thoroughly alarmed and provincial councils, held in 1549, 1552 and 1559, in the restored Blackfriars convent in Edinburgh, passed salutary decrees for internal reform, decrees which were ineffectual because the church had grown too dependent on the crown and the crown was losing control of the situation. The fortunes of the heretics rose and fell with the political changes of the time. Then, at length the accession of protestant Elizabeth to the English throne gave them such moral and material support as to encourage new boldness in their actions. The " Beggars' Summons " appeared on the gates of friars' houses on 1st January, 1558-59, threatening violence. In May, 1559, John Knox returned finally to Scotland. He had outgrown his Lutheranism and was now a fervent disciple of that " perfect school of Christ ", which John Calvin had set up in Geneva, and when he arrived, he found the protestant lords and their followers facing critical decisions.

In May, 1559, the regent, Mary of Guise, put some of the protestant preachers to the horn and this marks the beginning of the grand assault on the ecclesiastical buildings of the medieval church. In general, we can distinguish two phases in the attack. At first, the altars and furnishings of the churches are destroyed and severe structural damage, except in the case of friaries, is unusual and possibly accidental. Then, in the second phase, after 1560, through public " official " action and through the " unofficial " activity of private persons, the greater buildings, cathedrals, abbeys and priories are unroofed and, in many cases, the actual fabric is extensively damaged until by, say 1580, few, if any, large buildings remain intact and, as we shall see, in the east-central area of the kingdom even parish churches suffered at the hands of " greedy persons ".

We have Knox's own vigorous account of what happened in St. John's Kirk, in Perth, on 11th May, 1559.[65] His followers had apparently come

---

60. Macgill, *Old Ross-shire*, 1909, p. 9.
61. *Registrum Episcopatus Aberdonensis* (Spalding Club), i, pp. lxxxvi-xci.
62. *Extracts from the Council Register of the Burgh of Aberdeen*, 1398-1570 (Spalding Club), 1844, pp. 323-324.
63. Pollen, *opus cit.*, p. 423.
64. *R.M.S.*, v, 211.
65. Dickinson's *Knox*, i, pp. 161-3. In his history, Knox blames the " rascal multitude " for these doings, but in a letter written a week or two later to Mrs. Anna Locke, he gives the credit for them to " the brethren." Andrew Lang, in his *John Knox and the Reformation*, pp. 111-114, discusses this discrepancy and suggests, as the reason, that book ii of the history was intended as a propaganda tract to prove that the movement was not a rebellion and Knox was well aware that Calvin, like Zwingli before him, objected to riotous destruction of churches and images and, for this reason, in the history, " the brethren " on this and other occasions are kept discreetly in the background.

into the church armed with stones to implement their preacher's violent oratory.[66] When the altars, statues, pictures and other furnishings of St. John's Kirk had been " cast down ", the godly then sacked the churches and monasteries of the Blackfriars and Greyfriars. Thereafter they attacked the Carthusian monastery " a building of wondrous cost and greatness ".[67] " These three great places," according to Knox, " were so destroyed that the walls only did remain."[68] A fortnight later, the regent sent Argyll and Lord James to parley and these two took the first opportunity of adhering openly to the rebels. Other religious houses near Perth now suffered a fate similar to those of the town. The Cistercian nuns at Elcho, their buildings now repaired after the English attack of 1547, were now " visited by enemies, their own countrymen, more cruel and more bitter towards their religion, who utterly overthrew their monastery and its buildings so that they had to flee."[69] The Carmelite friars were ejected from Tullilum and both Pitscottie and Bishop Lesley state that that house also was reduced to ruin. Spottiswoode, in his history, adds that " They of Couper in Fife, hearing what was done at Perth, went in like manner to their Church and defaced all the Images, Altars and other instruments of Idolatry; which the Curate took so heavily, as the night following he put violent hands in himself."[70] From such an auspicious beginning, the good work went forward. An early narrative of these events tells us that the lords of the Congregation and their adherents left Perth to make their way to St. Andrews: " The congregation departing everie man to his owne house; and as they past, where they found in their way any kirks or chappells, incontinent they purged them, brekin downe the altars and idolls in all places where they come. And soe praising God continually, in singing of psalmes and spirituall songs, they rejoiced that the Lord wrought thus happily with them."[71]

The vandalism of Perth was continued in Fife. Knox preached at Crail and " by this exhortation the hearers were so moved as they fell immediately to the pulling down of Altars and Images and destroyed all the Monuments which were abused to Idolatry in the Town."[72] Included in this holocaust was the famous Rood of Crail, for Pitscottie adds that they " brunt the rude quhilk was ane great idoll and abussit all men and wemen baitht witht pillgramage." Similar scenes were repeated the following day in Anstruther and, on the Sunday, Knox preached on " our Saviour's purging of the Temple " in the parish kirk of St. Andrews and according to Spottiswoode " he did so incite the

---

66. This seems to be the only reasonable explanation of how the godly found stones so easily to hand.
67. The Perth charterhouse was founded by James I, in 1429, as a royal mausoleum and probably it was a sumptuous building after the fashion of the period. Other contemporary (and very rich) examples of charterhouses, built as burial places for ruling families, include the wonderful Certosa di Pavia (founded in 1396 by the Visconti dukes of Milan), the Chartreuse de Champmol near Dijon (founded in 1383 to house the splendid tombs of the dukes of Burgundy, which are now in the Fine Arts Museum of Dijon) and the superb Cartuja de Miraflores, which was rebuilt in 1454 as the mausoleum of the kings of Castile.
68. Half a century later, Habakkuk Bisset (*Rolment of Courtis*, ii, p. 433) says: " This Charter house is so allutterly decayed now and reywind that the bounds of the Cituatioun is presentli cornefeild land and with(out) an ston theirof left thereupon."
69. Fraser. *Memorials of the Family of Wemyss of Wemyss*, ii, 192-197. The nunnery seems to have remained an unhabited ruin from this time. In *R.M.S.*, v, 1939, it is described, in the year 1570, as " monasterium dirutum et habitantibus vacuum." We must always remember, of course, in dealing with these sixteenth-century documents that their description of dilapidation and ruin are very often exaggerated. The same caveat must be entered regarding the writings of historians like Pitscottie or Lesley.
70. Spottiswoode, *History of the Church of Scotland* (Spottiswoode Society), i, p. 272.
71. " The Historie of the Estate of Scotland " in *Wodrow Miscellany*, pp. 58-59.
72. Spottiswoode, *History of the Church of Scotland* (Spottiswoode Society), i, p. 276.

auditors as, the sermon being ended, they went all and made spoil of the churches, rasing the monasteries of the Black and Gray friers to the ground." Knox, in his history, claims only that the magistrates and townspeople " did agree to remove all monuments of idolatry which also they did with expedition."[73] The metropolitan cathedral, the parish kirk of the Holy Trinity and the college chapels, including Bishop Kennedy's richly furnished chapel of St. Salvator, were all despoiled of their altars, statutes and vestments, their carved woodwork, stained glass and tombs. The " Historie of the Estate of Scotland " says that " before the sunn wes downe there wes never inch standing bot bare walls." Of the Dominican and Franciscan friaries, Bishop Lesley, Buchanan and Spottiswoode state that even the fabric was reduced to ruin, as well as the venerable collegiate church of St. Mary of the Rock, whose traditions and life stretched back into the dim age of Celtic monasticism.[74] The actual fabric of the cathedral probably escaped major structural damage at this point, but the senseless destruction of the furnishings of this, the richest cathedral in the realm, about which medieval chroniclers speak so proudly, was surely a cultural catastrophe of the first magnitude for Scotland. A few broken statues and fragments of bishop's tombs and the remarkable sculptured fragments of the ancient shrine of St. Regulus alone survive to hint at former magnificence.[75]

The godly were now joined by some like-minded spirits from Lothian and the government forces agreed to parley. During the truce, the brethren, contrary to its terms, went to the " Abbey of Lundores, a place of blacke monkes . . . (which) was reformed, their altars overthrowne, their idols, vestments of idolatire and masse bookes were burnt in their owne presence, and they commaunded to cast away their monkish (habits)."[76] The brethren then made a rendezvous at Perth with their friends of Angus, Mearns and Strathearn and having delivered that town from " thraldom upon Sunday the 26 June ", the more " zealous men " decided " that some order should be taken " with the abbey of Scone, which lay near at hand.[77] Knox describes some unavailing efforts to save the buildings and this may well be true because the destruction of this building, which had been a focal point of patriotic pride and sentiment as well as of religion, might well have looked like a serious political blunder. Argyll and Lord James, we are told, " laboured to have saved the Palace and the Kirk. But because the multitude had found, buried in the Kirk, a great number of idols, hid of purpose to have preserved them to a better day (as the Papists speak), the towns of

---

73. Dickinson's *Knox*, i, p. 182. An examination of the chronology suggests that it took three days of sermons to rouse his auditors to action: which is remarkable, considering the position that Lord James held in the city and considering that reinforcements had come in from Dundee and Angus for the express purpose of " reformation to be made there."

74. The Greyfriars monastery was reduced to ruin because it is described in an Instrument of Sasine, dated 21st September, 1559, as " the desolated ground and overthrown buildings of the convent of Friars Minor . . . formerly, before its destruction, inhabited and possessed by . . . the Convent of Friars Minor." W. Moir Bryce, *The Scottish Grey Friars*, ii, p. 202.

75. Presumably the plate and treasures of the cathedral were saved for the time being by being removed to the archbishop's castle. There is a late sixteenth-century note, probably of about this date, which refers to the silver maces of the university and other " geir of St. Salvatoris College " which had been taken into the archbishop's castle for safety. See *P.S.A.S.*, xxvi, p. 468. The university maces survive to give us an inkling of the quality of the silverware that has perished.

76. So Knox writes in a letter to Mrs. Locke from St. Andrews, 23rd June, 1559. (Laing's *Knox*, vi, pp. 21 seq.) but he does not mention this fact in his history. See Dickinson's *Knox*, i, p. 186, n.4.

77. Patrick Hepburn, Bishop of Moray, was Commendator of Scone. The Congregation were simply blackmailing him into joining their party by threatening to wreck his abbey and house. They wrote to him "That unless he would come and assist them, they neither could spare nor save his place" (Dickinson's *Knox*, i, p. 189). The rabble lost patience with these slow negotiations and attacked the abbey.

Dundee and Saint Johnston could not be satisfied till that the whole reparation and ornaments of the Church (as they term it) were destroyed." The following day as the looting proceeded " one of Dundee " was stabbed and Knox again blames " the rascal multitude ", who now, out of control " committed the whole (church and monastery) to the merciment of fire.

The monastic buildings at Scone must have remained partially habitable, since Patrick Hepburn is residing there on 11th June, 1566, when he granted a charter, feuing certain lands for 800 merks, to be expended on the repair of his monastery, which was, at that time, for the greater part, destroyed by fire (*R.M.S.*, v. 681). By 1570, the prior had repaired his own quarters and was residing there (*Liber Ecclesie de Scon*, p. 210). The complete demolition of the ruined walls of the abbey church would take place when the first lay-commendator began building his new palace at the end of the century.

Not many miles away the abbey of Coupar Angus lay exposed to the activities of some of the protestant lairds. Already, in January, 1558, the monastery was complaining about " the insults of many lay magnates and their inferiors of the realm of Scotland opposing in those days the catholic faith and completely destroying many sacred places in diverse neighbouring parts."[78] Now, in June, 1559, (or perhaps a little later) the Congregation opened negotiations with the abbot about reforming his monastery and joining the rebel party. The abbot, Donald Campbell, grand-uncle of the fifth Earl of Argyll (who was one of the leading members of the Congregation at Perth) naturally followed the lead given by the head of his family and one undated document, which is preserved in the Inveraray charter room and which is signed by Abbot Campbell, is of first importance since it sets out the official aims and requirements of the Congregation at this period:

" Thir ar the pointes that the congregatioune desyris of my lord of Cowper.

Imprimis that he incontinent reforme his place of Cowper putting down and birnyng oppinlie all Idolis and Imagis and tubernaculis thairin destroying and putting away the altaris. And that na mess be thair done hereaftir nowther privilie nor opinly. And that the superstitiouse habit of his monkis with their ordour ceremonies and service as you call it be removit. And that na prayeris be usit in the kirk but in the English toung. And thair according to the scriptouris of God.

Item that my lord with all his freindis and folkis at his hale powar assist and mayntein in counsales conventionis and parliament als wele as uther wyse the furth settin of the evangell of cryst and meynteinyng the congregatioune in thair leberte and to the doune putting of all ydolatre abhominationes and papistre. And that his folkis at this present and at all utheris tymis being requirit pass fordwart with thair congregatioune to the forthsetting of the glorie of god. And alswa that my lord in all placis of his dominioune sall endewoyr himself to the forthesattin and executioune of the premissis.

---

78. *R.M.S.*, iv, 1380.

PLATE XXXIII. MELROSE ABBEY. ROXBURGHSHIRE.

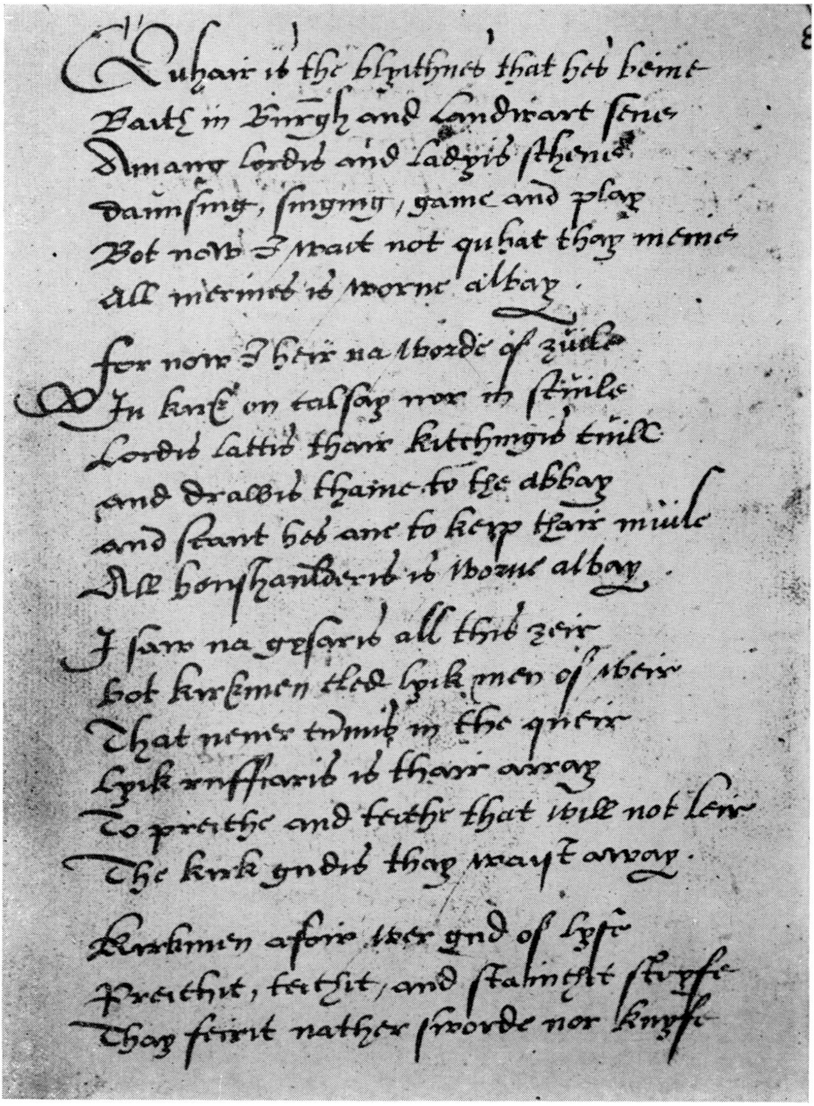

Quhair is the blyithnes that hes beine
Baith in burgh and landwart sene
Amang lordis and ladyis schene
Dansing, singing, game and play
Bot now I wait not quhat thay mene
All mirrines is worne alway.

For now I heir na thordie of zule
In kirk on talfay nor in stule
Lordis lattis thair kitchingis cule
and drawis thaime to the abbay
and scant hes ane to keip thair mule
All hoyshantnis is worne alway.

I saw na gysaris all this zeir
bot kirkmen thed lyik men of weir
That rydis tuinit in the queir
Lyik russaris is thair array
To praithe and feithr that will not leir
The kirk gudis thay wast away.

Kirkmen afoir thair god of lyfe
Praithit, feithit, and stainest stryfe
Thay frint nather sworde nor knyfe

PLATE XXXIV. "QUHAIR IS THE BLYITHNES
THAT HES BEINE."

Item that ane wryting contenyng the heids abufwrittin as thai ar heir contenit subscrivit with my lordis hand be send incontinent to the congregatioune togidder with this samyn tollaratione.

(Signed)   D. Abbot of Cupr "[79]

A letter written to Sir Henry Percy at this time by one of the godly (probably Sir William Kirkcaldy of Grange) gives an eye-witness description of their procedure: "The manour of thair proceidyngis in reformatioun is this. They pull doune all maner of freryes and some abayes which willyngly resavis not ther reformatioun. As to paroys churchis, they cleyns them of ymages and all other monumentis of ydolatrye and commandis that no messis be said in them; in place therof the booke sett fourthe be godlye Kyng Edward is red in the same churches."[80]

In pursuance of their policy Argyll and Lord James marched south and took Stirling before the regent's forces could occupy that town. Here the friaries were destroyed (Knox again blames the "rascal multitude," but Buchanan and Spottiswoode attribute the work to the brethren)[81] and they despoiled the other churches within and about the town, including (according to Spottiswoode) the abbey of Cambuskenneth.[82] Pressing forward towards Edinburgh, they passed through Linlithgow, where again (Lesley tells us) they despoiled the churches and ruined the Carmelite friary. The advance of the army of the Congregation alarmed the town council and the clergy in Edinburgh. The friars tried to disperse their church furnishings among their well-wishers; the town council placed the "altar grayth" of St. Giles in the hands of various trustworthy burghers and they sent a deputation to Linlithgow (29th June, 1559) to treat with the Congregation "for uphald of the ruiffis of the religious placeis and kirkis within this burgh and for sawyng (saving) of the stallis, bakis of aulteris and otheris tymmer werk within

---

79. *Scottish Historical Review*, xxi, pp. 140-143.

80. Laing's *Knox*, vi, p. 34. Cecil's version of this information, written on 9th July, 1559, runs: "They offer no violence, but dissolve relligiose howsees, directing the lands therof to the crowne and to ministery in the chirch. The parish chirchees they delyver of altars and imagees and have receved the service of the Church of England accordyng to King Edward's booke." (Forbes, *Public Transactions*, 1740, i, 155).

81. Dickinson's *Knox*, i, p. 191, note 3.

    There is also what would appear to be an eye-witness account of these proceedings, given in the instructions for Du Fresnoy, when he was sent as envoy to France by Mary of Lorraine in July, 1559. Speaking of the lords of the Congregation the document proceeds: "De là (Perth) se sont acheminez (aprés avoir bruslé une notable et insigne abbaye nommée Scone, voysine dudit St. Jean-Ston, en laquelle les Roys ont accoustumé se faire couronner) vers la ville de Sterling où, de plaine arrivée et à la descente de cheval, les conte d'Arguell et prieur de St. André sont allez en personne aux eglises des Cordelliers et Jacobins qu'ilz ont faict abbattre et myner devant leurs yeulx, sans pardonner aux demeures des moines, et qui est encores plus inhumain, aux arbres fruictiers et jardins. . . ." (Teulet, *Papiers d'Etat relatifs a l'Histoire de l'Ecosse*, i, 320).

    That Argyll's zeal for the new religion was not altogether disinterested is indicated by the fact that when, in 1573, Stirling town council were called upon to submit their accounts, they could only report regarding the site of the Franciscan friary: "my lord of Ergile has the yaird and roume of the place and sua we ressave na proffeit as yit" (Moir Bryce, *Scottish Grey Friars*, i, p. 376).

    The reference to the destruction of trees and plants in the friary at Stirling introduces a curious feature which seems to have recurred a short time later, when the Edinburgh friaries were under attack. In describing the assault on the Edinburgh friaries, Lesley (using a phrase which is surely not to be taken literally) asserts that "hail growing treis (were) plucked up be the ruittis." This would seem to suggest that some of the godly regarded the kailyards and orchards of the friars as equivalent to the groves of Baal and themselves as holding the place of Gideon.

82. The Chapel Royal in Stirling Castle escaped damage at this juncture (the Congregation did not gain control of the castle). The Chapel Royal was later "purgit of all monumentis of ydolatrie" by the Earl of Mar, captain of the castle, in the year 1567, after Queen Mary's abdication. Mar, taking no risks, had his action indemnified by the lords assembled in parliament at Stirling on 28th August, 1571. (C. Rogers, *History of the Chapel Royal of Scotland* (Grampian Club), 1882, pp. lxxv-vii). Later neglect of the structure necessitated the building of a completely new Chapel Royal in 1594.

the said kirkis."[83] The regent withdrew to Dunbar with her forces and Edinburgh fell into the hands of the Congregation: " the Erle of Argyle and all his cumpanie entered in the toune of Edinburgh without anye resistance, quhair they war weill received: and suddantlie the Black and Gray Freris places war spulyeit and cassin doune, the haill growing treis plucked up be the ruitts: the Trinitie College and all the prebendaris houssis thairof lykwyse cassin doun: the altaris and images within Sanc Gelis Kirke and the Kirke of Feild destroyed and brint."[84] Knox adds the further information that the altars were cast down in Holyrood abbey and, in the kirk of Leith, the altars and furnishings were destroyed and " preaching stools " introduced.[85] Like Saul of Israel, the lords of the Congregation seem to have been selective in their destruction of the trappings of idolatry for, at this point they seized the dies of the mint in order (as Mary of Guise believed) to turn their loot into coin of the realm though, as one would expect, Knox vehemently rejects such an interpretation of their action.

Their seizure of Edinburgh exploded the Congregation's claim that their motives were purely religious and, furthermore, they had outrun their own military resources. A truce was agreed to at Leith, on 24th July, 1559: one of its clauses stipulated that the Congregation should refrain from further damage to " kirks, religious places or reparelling thereof, but the same shall stand skaithless of them unto the said tenth day of January."[86] The orgy of destruction went on, nevertheless, during the remainder of that year. Sir James Croft, reporting to England, on 3rd July, 1559, speaks of the concourse of protestants in Edinburgh and says that they intend going to Kelso and so to all the abbeys westward[87] and Cecil re-echoes this information on 9th July, writing to Throck-morton.[88] Bishop Lesley claims that " the Abbacies of Dunfermling, Melrosse, Kelsoe and monie ma miserabillie brokne doune and wasted be thame was."[89] We have notice of one such party, which visited Peebles, late in 1559 or early in 1560: it was led by John, Master of Maxwell, and, acting on behalf of the lords of the Congregation, they bullied the minister (that is, the superior) of the Trinitarians at Peebles, forcing him to change " his white habit for a grey keltour gowne and putting on a how black bonnet " which was meant to symbolise his adoption of the new religion. The minister claims in his public declaration

---

83. *Extracts from the Burgh Records of Edinburgh*, 1557-1571, p. 44. The town council were very proud of their kirk of St. Giles, with all its fine furnishings: at this same time they resolved to hire sixty men to guard St. Giles' Kirk and protect the choir stalls. After the Congregation had been in the city for several days the council had the stalls dismantled and stored for safety in the nether tolbooth.
    The survival of the superb " Beaton Panels " and their carved bosses, which have originally formed part of choir stalls, presumably in Arbroath Abbey, is probably due to the fact that, like the choir stalls of St. Giles, Edinburgh, they were dismantled and stored away for safety.

84. Lesley's *History of Scotland*, (Bannatyne Club), p. 275.

85. Dickinson's *Knox*, i, p. 213. The monks were expelled from Holyrood. Ferreri, writing to Henry Sinclair, 26th January, 1559-60, says: " The Queen Regent of Scotland has restored the monks at Edinburgh, who had previously been cast out. The altars which had been overthrown are again raised in church and upon them sacrifices are offered, according to Christian rite and ancient usage, which are better attended than ever." Pollen, *Papal Negotiations*, pp. 417-18.

86. Dickinson's *Knox*, i, p. 203.

87. Bain, *Calendar of the State papers relating to Scotland*, i, 221.

88. Forbes', *Public Transactions*, i, 155.

89. Lesley's *History* (Scottish Text Society), ii, p. 433. Writers who take the English pamphleteers at their face value and assume that Kelso and other border abbeys remained devastated ruins from the time of the English invasions, must give some explanation of this projected excursion of the godly to Kelso, and the border abbeys. The godly had a good idea of the situation at each religious house. They were, moreover, very busy men at this period and they certainly did not propose a sixty-mile outing for the sole purpose of admiring romantic ruins.

(30th March, 1560) that he did this " for fear of his life and destruction of his place and monastery and not from any hatred of his old religion."[90]

The melancholy trail of destruction spread into the west. On the morning of 29th September, 1559, Alexander Whitlaw was able to tell Sadler, among other things, that the lords of the Congregation " had suppressed the abbeys of Passlow, Kylwynyng and Donfermelying and burned all the ymages, ydolls and popish stuff in the same "[91] and this confirmed an earlier report to the effect that the protestant leaders " have now given in commission to therle of Glencarn and the larde of Down to suppresse thabbey of Paslowe, whereof, the bishop of Saynt Andrewes, the dukis brother, is commendatour."[92]

The altars and statues were still venerated by a very large proportion of the population and it is difficult for us to imagine the profound shock that must have been given by their wholesale destruction. It is reasonable to conjecture that many Scotsmen hesitated to " believe or trow (that the honour of God consisted in demolishing churches), that the glore of the passione of Christ consisted in breking his croce, that the reformatione of his Kirk war in breking Kirkis and altaris and spoiling the Kirk geir."[93] It was, no doubt, evident to more people than Lesley that religion was being made the excuse for some very dubious exploits: " pretending religione for quhat euir vice or crime tha did and al thair wicketnes religioune tha callit " and in particular he mentions the spoliation of the bishops' goods and property; " in quhilk title (religion) fra thair lyuenges, lugengis and Palices tha kaist the Bischopis of Dunkelde, Dunblane, Rosse and al the rest from al thair landis."[94]

A surviving fragment of a process at law illustrates their behaviour at Dunblane. The Congregation, discreetly encouraged by Cecil, had formally declared Mary of Guise deposed from the regency on 21st October, 1559: their subsequent occupation of Edinburgh was followed by a sharp reverse, and, leaving Edinburgh hurriedly, towards midnight on 6th November, 1559, they hastened to Stirling, where Knox addressed them on Wednesday, 8th November, and as a result of his sermon (we have his own word for it) the mind of his hearers " began wondrously to be erected."[95] Results followed speedily. The next day (it is the bishop of Dunblane who now takes up the story) " the Erle of Arrane accumpanit with ane gret nowmer of horsmen and futmen upone the ix day of nouember last bypast come to our said place of Dumblane and enterit thairintill be sik force as we mycht nocht resist quhilk company . . . ." They rifled the place in the courtyard where the bishop, " fering the invasioun of the Congregatioun ", had concealed Lady Fleming's gold chain, which was the subject of the lawsuit. Among other things, the gold chain was stolen and the bishop himself was carried prisoner to Stirling. We can be certain that, on this same occasion, the bishop's cathedral, lying only a

---

90. *Peebles Charters*, p. 259.
91. Sadler's *State Papers*, 1809, ii, p. 6.
92. *Opus cit.*, ii, pp. 2-3. Apparently Paisley had suffered some molestation earlier and £300 had been spent, by January 1557, on repairs (*R.M.S.*, v, 1297).
93. Lesley's *History* (Scottish Text Society), ii, p. 402.
94. *Opus cit.*, ii, p. 443.
95. Dickinson's *Knox*, i, pp. 265-71. It was a notable sermon and " the said John " was evidently rather proud of it for he gives it at length in his history.

stone's throw away, also received attention from these reformers, even though that fact is not mentioned (since it is irrelevant) in the process.[96]

The tide now began to turn finally in favour of the rebel lords. England sent in money, then a fleet, then an army to their aid. The French relieving force was scattered by a storm at sea, and, after the signing of the Treaty of Berwick by the Congregation, on 27th February, 1559-60, England openly took charge of the military operations, which virtually confined the regent's French army to the neighbourhood of Edinburgh and Leith. Shortly after the signing of the Treaty of Berwick, the Duke of Chatelherault, the Earl of Argyll and the Earl of Arran came to Glasgow and caused the altars and images of the churches to be destroyed. Lesley uses the phrase " sacra prius non violata conculcant " —they profane the sacred things hitherto unviolated—referring possibly to an earlier attack on Glasgow churches mentioned in " The Historie of the Estate of Scotland."[97] There is no precise information about three important churches in Glasgow, the Greyfriars, Blackfriars and college kirk of Our Lady and St. Anne: what indications there are suggest that the two last mentioned churches were not only despoiled of their furnishings but were structurally damaged.[98] The cathedral of St. Mungo was certainly in a dismantled condition by 19th July, 1560, when, on the occasion of the institution of Mr. Stephen Betone, as new rector of Govan, the president of the chapter, James, bishop of Lismore, being unable to gain access to the choir and unable to get surplice, cope and the usual ornaments, had to be content with a makeshift ceremony at the door of the church.[99] The damage seems to have gone beyond the mere destruction of internal fittings, because, on 21st August, 1574, we find the town council of Glasgow having consideration " unto the greit dekaye and ruyne that the hie kirk of Glasgw is cum to, throuch taking awaye of the leid, sclait and wther grayth thairof, in this trublus tyme bygane sua that sick ane greit monument will alluterlie fall doun and dekey without it be remedit."[100] Attempts were made here, as elsewhere, by

---

96. This document is given in *P.S.A.S.*, xi, pp. 517-25. The most illuminating passage in the process is the main argument brought against the bishop's case, to the effect that he was manifestly negligent and ought not to have had the gold chain in his house at all " be ressone that he beand had with gret hatrant be the congregatioun and gret men thairof as he grantit yisterday in jugement and haiffand diuers tymes of befoir the allegit spoliatioun of the said chenye distroyit diuers places abbayis kirkmen and places suld nocht (gif he had bene diligent) haif lipnit nor hald in keping in the place of Dumblane sik ane Jowell as the said chenye, lyk as he on nawayis allegis that he had sik vtheris Jowellis into the said place other pertening to himself or to the Kirk of Dumblane, lyk as vtheris prelattis had transportit and lyk as him self did transport ther pretius Jowellis and principall pryssis furth of thair abbayis and duelling places to houssis of strength and sua levand the samin in his said dwelling place at sik trublus tymes fering invasioun of the Congregatioun . . . and haiffing consideration of vtheris trublis and distructionis done to vtheris prelattis and kirkmen apone thair abbayis and places."
Bishop Chisholm was kept prisoner till Christmas and then had to pay the expenses of his captors. (Scot. Hist. Socy. *Miscellany*, ix, p. 103.)
A similar example of a lady's chain girdle (this time of silver), which was apparently buried under the floor of the Franciscan friary of Aberdeen, was unearthed only in 1735. (*P.S.A.S.*, 1872-74, pp. 325-7 and illustration).

97. Lesley's *History* (Scottish Text Society), ii, p. 428 and *Wodrow Miscellany*, p. 62. Part of the cathedral archives and part of the treasure (including a mace of the university) had been removed to safety by Archbishop Beaton: later these things are found at Paris.

98. Moir Bryce, *Scottish Grey Friars*, i, p. 347, note 1, says that the Blackfriars church survived intact till it was struck by lightning in 1670. This is incorrect: the nave at least of the Blackfriars church was ruinous in 1574, when the town council decided to auction the stones of the ruinous western gable and use the proceeds to mend the windows and minister's seat in the church, that is, in the chancel now used as the church (*Glasgow Records*, p. 9). The Blackfriars church of 1574, restored in 1622 and depicted in Slezer's well-known view of Glasgow University was merely the reconditioned chancel of the medieval Blackfriars' Kirk. The comparatively new college church of Our Lady and St. Anne is described as " destructam et dirutam "—destroyed and ruinous, in 1570, when the ground was leased by the town council to James Fleming (*Glasgow Charters*, part ii, p. 142), the phrase is, of course, common form in such documents but it at least indicates that the building was in need of repair.

99. Renwick, *Glasgow Protocols*, v, 1382.

100. *Extract from the Records of the Burgh of Glasgow*, 1573-1642, p. 20.

the still catholic majority to repair the damage caused by the revolutionaries and, on 27th August, 1560, we find the choral vicars of Glasgow paying for some repairs to the said metropolitan church and, in particular, for the restoration of the altar of the Name of Jesus.[101]

The mention of these repairs raises a very pertinent question which must be considered, however briefly. Throughout this whole period we have a very great number of charters (granted mainly by the large ecclesiastical corporations, such as cathedrals and monasteries) alienating church property in return for ready money and the reason given for these transactions is regularly stated to be the repair and upkeep of buildings. This series of charters extends throughout the sixteenth century, both before and after the year 1560. Undoubtedly such charters were, in many instances, simply means of realizing assets and the repair of the ecclesiastical fabric was an obvious fiction. In view of this, are we entitled to use such charters as evidence that repairs were actually carried out ? There is no simple answer to this question but, speaking in general, we would say that, with certain caveats and within certain limitations, one must accept such evidence. The charters under discussion are granted chiefly by the larger ecclesiastical corporations—cathedrals, abbeys, priories, nunneries, collegiate churches, and for such corporations, the events of the year 1560 created a radically new situation. Once it became evident that the revolution was securely in power, say by the year 1561 or 1562, then these large ecclesiastical corporations were doomed to disappear and repairs (to abbey churches for example) were quite pointless. All charters, therefore, granted by such corporations after, say, the year 1561, are almost certainly mere alienations of land in which references to repairs are either purely fictitious or apply to the repair or alteration of the domestic premises of such corporations (as, for example Patrick Hepburn's charter for the repair of Scone Abbey, dated 1566, in *R.M.S.*, v. 681). Before the definite triumph of the revolution, in 1560, however, it was so obviously to the advantage of such corporations to maintain their buildings and equipment that one must accept charter evidence for repairs up to 1560, unless there is some overriding reason to the contrary (as in the case of a commendator like James Stewart of Melrose and Kelso, who is quite recklessly squeezing every possible penny out of his abbeys without any thought for the welfare of the communities of which he is the nominal head).

Within such limits, these charters are valid evidence for repair and maintenance of ecclesiastical property and, more especially, when some specific work is mentioned as for example the west gable of the abbey church of Dundrennan, in 1543,[102] or, even more so, if it is stated that the work is actually in progress, as when, in 1558 and 1559, the abbey of Kilwinning is spending money on repairs and quarrying stone for the work.[103] In such cases one must surely accept the evidence. Normally

---

101. *R.M.S.*, iv, 2911.
102. " Iam in occidentali parte ruinose " *R.M.S.*, iii, 729. This document shows that the threat of destruction by reformers could prove an added incentive to consciencious superiors to put their house in order, for it continues: " Habita consideratione quod status ecclesie in Scotia multum periclitatus est per eos qui hereticam pravitatem insequentes se se obsequium prestare Deo putabant si monasteria claustralia omnino destruerent."
103. *R.M.S.*, v, 858, 1499.

the urge of self-preservation in a community would compel even a lazy or indifferent superior to attend to the fabric of buildings: this is probably the basic reason why, for example, the conscienceless commendator of Scone, Patrick Hepburn, embarked on the extensive repairs to the abbey church of Scone which are detailed in the contract made between himself and " Jhonne Archar " the master mason, on 31st August, 1551.[104]

Some historians, of course, are inclined to go further and ask the question whether Scotland's medieval buildings were kept in repair at all in the generation prior to the reformation. Taking literally the exaggerated language of documents, which frequently describe buildings in need of repair in phrases like " utterly ruinous and levelled with the ground " and taking the evidence of war damage and maladministration in the Merse parish churches and in an important abbey like Melrose, they suggest that this state of affairs might be typical of the whole country at this period. We are prevented by loss of documents from making any categorical statement on this question but, once again we must surely recognize that the situation would vary from one building to another and we cannot take the war zone of the south-east borders, which bore the brunt of the " Rough Wooing ", as characteristic of the entire kingdom and we cannot accept the criminal maladministration of a commendator like James Stewart of Melrose and Kelso as necessarily typical. Those records which have survived, such as the accounts of the collegiate kirk of the Holy Trinity in Edinburgh, the dean of guild accounts relating to the burgh kirks of Edinburgh and Ayr, Ferreri's lives of the abbots of Kinloss, Myln's lives of the bishops of Dunkeld, Boece's lives of the bishops of Aberdeen, the extant rentals of Dunkeld and St. Andrews, all show quite clearly that, during the sixteenth century, a consciencious regard for the fabric of churches of all kinds, cathedral, monastic, collegiate and parochial was certainly not lacking in Scotland. The evidence that there is does suggest that over the country, as a whole, there probably existed that mixture of consciencious and careless administration, which is normal human experience in such a matter.

Towards the close of 1559 the mania for destruction spread north where, so far, no general enthusiasm had been shown in favour of any violent change in religion. Thomas Menzies, provost of Aberdeen, called the citizens together on the forenoon of 29th December, 1559, and asked their assistance in the emergency which had arisen, telling them " quhow he is suirly aduertisit that certane nychtbours of the Mernis men and Angouss men, conuenit in congregatioune, ar to be in this toune this present day to distroy and cast doune the kirkis and religious places thairof, under colour and pretence of godlie reformatioune; and becaus this toune hes no directioune of the authorite of Scotland to assist and concur with thaim in that purpos, bot the same is express contrar the will and mynd of the authorite and thairthrow is manifest tressoun."[105] The first attack of the invaders, directed at the great spire of St. Nicholas, was repelled, but a few days later, 4th January, 1559-60, the townsfolk are told by Bailie David Mar " quhow that certane strangearis and sum nichtbours and induellaris of this burght hes enterit to the blak freiris and quhyt freiris of the town and spulzeit thair places and takin away the

---

104. *Protocol Book of Sir Robert Rollok* (Scottish Record Society), no. 99.
105. *Extracts from the Council Register of the Burgh of Aberdeen*, 1398-1570, p. 326.

gere and gudis of the samen witht the tymmar wark and insicht, togidder with the leid of the kirkis and now ar enterit upoun the ruiffis of the kirkis and biggings and takand away the sklayttis, tymmir and stanis thairof," and it was decided that the burgh treasurer should deal with the disposal of such material and property.[106] The council also agreed unanimously to maintain the buildings of the Greyfriars, who had recently resigned all their property into the hands of the magistrates, with the stipulation that " If it shall happen that our Sovereign Lady, the Queen, shall restore to the rest of the religious brotherhoods their places, churches, or buildings, then similar restitution shall be made to the Friars Minor, without prejudice to them or incurring the wrath of the Queen."[107] The Earl of Huntly intervened at St. Machar's Cathedral, but by that time the place had been pillaged and the chancel wrecked.[108] At the neighbouring King's College, Principal Anderson armed a band of defenders and thus saved that lovely chapel with its fine carved choir stalls and the splendid tomb of its founder.[109]

The cathedral of Brechin was purged about this time and its choir, like that of Aberdeen, reduced to ruin. While we have no documentary proof, we are probably right in assuming that this also was the work of these Mearns magnates and their followers.[110] No record survives either about Arbroath Abbey and modern writers, very often (without any proof), state that this abbey suffered no violence at this time. It seems hardly credible that the zealots of Dundee and Angus left Arbroath Abbey standing unmolested in their midst. From the end of the century Arbroath Abbey kirk was a roofless ruin and we can be fairly certain that it was purged and unroofed about this time. Concerning Dunfermline Abbey, Pitscottie records that; " Vpoun the 28 day thairof (March, 1560), the wholl lordis and barones, that war on this syd of Forth, passed to Stirling and be the way kest doun the abbey of Dumfermling."[111] From a description, a few years later, this casting down of the abbey church seems to have involved not only the destruction of altars, statues, windows, shrines and royal tombs but the choir was apparently unroofed and reduced to ruin. From the Mearns southward, the whole area of Scotland, wherever the wandering bands of Calvinist magnates and their retainers could operate without let or hindrance, the churches, great and small, were despoiled of their furnishings and anything of value, such as roof-lead, was stolen. Naturally, in the resulting disorder, petty thieves and disgruntled people made the most of their opportunities; " In all this

---

106. *Opus cit.*, p. 315.
107. W. Moir Bryce, *Scottish Grey Friars*, i, p. 323.
108. It has been suggested, in Macgibbon and Ross, *Ecclesiastical Architecture of Scotland*, iii, p. 82, that Bishop Elphinstone's new choir of Aberdeen Cathedral may never have been finished. This suggestion is quite improbable in view of the elaborate choir and high altar furnishings provided by Bishop Dunbar, which are apparently in place, when the 1549 inventory was compiled (*Reg. Episcopatus Aberdonensis*, ii, pp. 179-199). Gordon of Rothiemay, who is usually well-informed, writing in 1661 about the impact of the reformation on Aberdeen in 1560, says: " The queere of the church was rased to the very fundatione " (*Description of Both Towns of Aberdeen*, p. 22). Spalding, in *Memorialls of the Trubles in Scotland* (Spalding Club), ii, p. 216, causes confusion by speaking of the demolition, in 1642, of the " hie altar " in Dunbar's Aisle· this surviving altar was, almost certainly, the St. Katherine altar founded by Bishop Dunbar in the south transept.
109. The choir stalls still survive but Elphinstone's tomb fell a victim to seventeenth-century iconoclasts.
110. Once again it is suggested that the building of the choir of Brechin Cathedral had not been completed by the time of the reformation (Hay Fleming, *The Reformation in Scotland*, p. 394). A cursory examination of the *Reg. Ep. Brech.* makes it clear that the choir of the cathedral was complete and furnished from at least a century before the reformation. For example, in 1484, John Spalding, dean of Brechin, left a legacy to ensure that the big brass lectern which he had presented to the choir of Brechin Cathedral, should be thoroughly polished twice a year, before Christmas and before Easter (*Reg. Ep. Brech.*, ii, p. 118-9).
111. Pitscottie, *Chronicles of Scotland*, 1814, p. 555.

tyme (the summer of 1559), all kirkmennis goodis and geir wer spoulyeit and reft frae thame, in everie place quhair the samyne culd be apprehendit; for everie man for the maist part that culd get any thing pertenyng to any Kirkmen thocht the same as wele won geir."[112] Outside of what may be called the epicentre of the explosion (Angus and Mearns, Fife, Strathearn, East Stirlingshire and the Lothians) the traditional way of life continued here and there, albeit fearfully and uneasily.[113]

On the 10th June, 1560, the whole resistance of the catholic and French party collapsed. Mary of Guise died, the French forces withdrew and power automatically fell into the hands of the protestant lords. For a time the protestant party had been aware that the regent was dying and in the *First Book of Discipline*, prepared by the ministers of the New Evangel, in April and May 1560, there is, among much else, a statement of policy regarding the buildings of the medieval church: " As we require Christ Jesus to be truly preached and his holy Sacraments to be rightly ministered; so can we not cease to require idolatry, with all monuments and places of the same, as abbeys, monasteries, friaries, nunneries, chapels, chantries, cathedral kirks, canonries, colleges, other than presently are parish Kirks or Schools, to be utterly suppressed in all bounds and places of this Realm (except only the palaces, mansions and dwelling places adjacent thereto, with orchards and yards of the same): as also that idolatry may be removed from the presence of all persons, of what estate or condition that ever they be, within this Realm."[114]

The " Reformation Parliament " was held in August, 1560. The *First Book of Discipline*, though not approved as far as its financial policy was concerned, became the blue-print for action regarding church buildings. During December, the first general assembly was held in Magdalene Chapel, and among much else, it decreed that " the Kirk of Restalrig be razed and utterly casten down being a monument of idolatry."[115] The next general assembly, held in May, 1561, petitioned the Privy Council to enforce the new enactments against such churches as would now become redundant wherever the new religion was established and the result, in Knox's words, was that " the Lords of Secret Council made an act that all places and monuments of idolatry should be destroyed. And for that purpose was directed to the West the Earl of Arran, having joined with him the Earls of Argyll and Glencairn, together with the Protestants of the West; who burnt Paisley (the Bishop (of Saint Andrews, who was Abbot thereof) narrowly escaped), cast down Failford, Kilwinning and a part of Crossraguel. The Lord

---

112. *Diurnal of Occurrents*, p. 269.

113. This was true for example in the extreme south-west of Scotland and also north of the Mounth where " throuch the authoritie, helpe and supplie of Huntlie and of the Leslies, eftir the vse of the Catholik religione was put from al boundis of Scotland thair in that sam place a lang tyme was keiped vnbrokne, vnuiolat." (Lesley, *History*, ii, p. 430). The penetration of the new fashion in religion beyond the Highland Line and into the western isles was probably not very effective until a later period.

114. Dickinson's *Knox*, ii, p. 283. The excepting clause, of course, was intended to safeguard the property of the protestant commendators who were now in a fair way towards transforming monastic buildings into their own family mansions. As in England, one of the motives for the immediate destruction of the purely ecclesiastical buildings was to ensure the permanence of the new system by making it impossible for the earlier regime to be re-established. For the corresponding English situation, cfr. D. Knowles, *The Religious Orders in England*, iii, pp. 383-8.

115. Restalrig was a parish church and the reason for this attack is obscure. The reason lies either in the fact that the church was a notable place of pilgrimage or in the dislike of Knox for the incumbent, John Sinclair. Sinclair, Dean of Restalrig, if we can judge by Knox's history, was detested by the reformers and, if this were the reason for the decision to destroy his church, it would simply be a continuation of the policy by which some abbeys were attacked to teach the commendator a salutary lesson.

James was appointed to the North, where he made such reformation as nothing contented the Earl of Huntly, and yet seemed he to approve all things. And thus God so potently wrought with us, so long as we depended upon him, that all the world might see his potent hand to maintain us and to fight against our enemies; yea, most to confound them, when that they promised to themselves victory without resistance. Oh! that we should rightly consider the wondrous works of the Lord our God."[116]

These decisions mark the beginning of the second and final phase in the onslaught on the medieval church buildings of Scotland. On paper, a clear distinction had been made; all churches used for parochial and educational purposes were to be maintained. All other ecclesiastical buildings, no matter how valuable artistically or how venerable by reason of their antiquity or associations, were to be classified as " monuments of idolatry " and " utterly suppressed ". No one need be surprised if, in such confused and lawless times, this clear distinction was sometimes lost sight of in practice. Spottiswoode describes, in his history, how " Thereupon insued a pitiful vastation of churches and church-buildings throughout all the parts of the realm: for every one made bold to put their hands, the meaner sort imitating the ensample of the greater and those who were in authority. No difference was made, but all the churches either defaced or pulled to the ground. The holy vessels and whatsoever else men could make gain of, as timber, lead and bells, were put to sale. The very sepulchres of the dead were not spared. The registers of the church and Bibliothekes cast into the fire. In a word, all was ruined and what had escaped in the time of the first tumult did now undergo the common calamity; which was so much the worse that the violences committed at this time were coloured with the warrant of publick authority. Some ill-advised preachers did likewise animate people in these their barbarous proceedings, crying out that the places where idols had been worshipped ought by the Law of God to be destroyed, and that the sparing of them was the reserving of things execrable; as if the commandment given to Israel for destroying the places where the Canaanites did worship their false Gods had been a warrant for them to do the like. The report also went that John Knox (whose sayings were by many esteemed as Oracles) should in one of his sermons say that the sure way to banish the rooks was to pull down their nests: which words (if any such did escape him) were to be understood of the cloisters of monks and friers only, according to the act passed in the council. But popular fury once armed can keep no measure, nor do anything with advice and judgment."[117] Naturally, amid such turmoil and lawlessness, records were not kept of all intromissions with ecclesiastical property, but a certain amount of documentation survives to show the general pattern of events and to show that, as far as the main centre

---

116. Dickinson's *Knox*, i, p. 364. The monks of Kilwinning had been quarrying stones and spending money on repairs in 1558 and 1559 (*R.M.S.*, v, 1499 and 858). The monks of Failford had also, in 1559, been engaged on repair work (*Opus cit.*, v, 1732). At Paisley similar work was in progress in 1557 (*Opus cit.*, v, 1297) and even in 1560, probably as a result of this burning, great sums were expended on repairs (*Opus cit.*, v, 2314). The repairs of 1560 probably included the building of the temporary partition wall to cut off the nave from the burnt-out choir. In a lecture given in 1908, Mr. P. Macgregor Chalmers attributed the burning of the choir and the building of the partition wall to the year 1498, but he admitted that he had no documentary evidence for this assertion (*Trans. Scot. Ecclesiol. Society*, ii, p. 403, and A. R. Howell, *Paisley Abbey*, p. 26). This unfounded assertion must be discarded in face of the fact that the choir of Paisley Abbey was evidently in use in 1551, when the altar of our Lady in the choir received the gift of a missal (*Innes Review*, ix, p. 121).

117. Spottiswoode's *History*, i, pp. 372-3.

of the revolution was concerned, Archbishop Spottiswoode was not indulging in rhetoric or fantasy.

By the proscription of the ancient faith, the larger churches had all become redundant. In the case of cathedrals, collegiate churches and the greater parish churches, only a portion of the building was now needed for the simpler requirements of the new religion. One section, nave or choir as the case might be, was kept in being as the parish church, the remainder was, sooner or later, dismantled.[118] The monastic churches had no longer any useful function since mass and divine office were now illegal: their usual fate was that the abbot's house or other domestic buildings of the abbey were transformed into a new mansion house for the commendator: the abbey kirk was dismantled and left to decay or, in many cases actually demolished, its materials being used to extend the commendator's house or simply sold. Where the magnates led the way, lesser men were not slow to follow: there was much petty thieving and smaller churches, hospitals and bede-houses suffered dilapidation.

We have the actual wording of the commission for the " reforming " of the cathedral of Dunkeld, dated 12th August, 1560, signed by Argyll, Lord James and Ruthven;—" To our Traist friendis, the Lairds of Arntilly and Kinvaid. Traist friendis after maist harty commendacion, we pray yow faill not to pass incontinent to the kyrk of Dunkeld, and tak doun the haill images thereof and bring furth to the kyrk-zayrd and burn thaym oppinly. And siclyk cast down the altaris and purge the kyrk of all kynd of monuments of idolatrye. And this ze fail not to do, as ze will do us singular empleseur; and so committis you to the protection of God. From Edinburgh, the xii of August, 1560. Faill not but ze tak guid heyd that neither the dasks, windocks nor durris be ony ways hurt or broken—eyther glassin wark or iron wark. (Signed) Ar. Ergyll, James Stewart. Ruthven." These instructions may have been faithfully carried out but, either at this time or soon after, the Laird of Cardeny removed the roof of the nave and possibly also that of the chancel which had to be re-roofed in 1600 to serve as a parish church. For the cathedral of Dunblane, documents are lacking, but the roof of the nave was removed and only the choir was maintained as the parish church and there " the original Popish roof . . . very old and not safe was still in place in 1793." At Brechin and at Aberdeen it was the cathedral nave which was kept as the parish church, the choir in each case having been reduced to ruin. Glasgow Cathedral presents a problem, for here the entire fabric survived, despite the fact that, from about 1560 to February, 1596-97, only part of it was used as a parish church. According to the normal procedure the unused portion, nave or choir, should have been unroofed and abandoned. Spottiswoode has a curiously circumstantial story of how, in 1578, the magistrates of Glasgow were prevented from demolishing the cathedral by the crafts of the city[119]. The story is usually rejected because of lack of corroborative evidence in the (incomplete) town records, but Spottiswoode was in a position to know the facts and there was evidently much discussion between the town council and deacons of the

---

118. The poet Burns gives his own impression of this relationship between new and old, during his visit to Linlithgow in 1787: " What a poor pimping business is a Presbyterian place of worship ! dirty, narrow, squalid: stuck in a corner of old popish grandeur such as Linlithgow . " Diary, 25th August, 1787.

119. Spottiswoode's *History*, ii, pp. 258-9.

crafts before the council decided on 27th February, 1582-83, that it was " conwenient and necessar that the *haill* kirk be wphaldin and reparit."[120]

At St. Andrews, the parish kirk of the Holy Trinity sufficed for all needs of the new regime and the great metropolitan cathedral, scheduled for demolition under the Privy Council ordinance of 1561, was unroofed about this time. The claustral buildings continued to house the commendator—Lord James—till 1565. An act of parliament in 1597 speaks of the decay of the monastic buildings.[121] Andrew Melville, writing to his nephew in 1609, speaks of " the rapacious gled (Archbishop Gladstanes) that nestles in the old ruins of the meretricious Babylon."[122] The glory of the metropolitan church was a mere memory for Habakkuk Bisset, writing early in the seventeenth century of how " This Sanct Reulis kirk with the stepill thairof standis (and remainis) zit builded besyde the auld Rewynous wallis of the Cathedrall and sumtyme maist Magnifik kirk of the Archbishoprie of St. Androis."[123] When Charles I, in 1634, considered restoring St. Andrews Cathedral, the master of work was instructed to " survey the vestiges of the sayd church and how the same may best be helped or of new built,"[124] and Gordon of Rothiemay's drawing, dated 1642, shows the cathedral in much the same condition as it stands today : the scene which Arthur Johnstone described in the lines :

" Priscus honor periit : traxerunt templa ruinam,
  Nec superest mystis qui fuit ante nitor."

The fate of the other important monastic cathedral, that of Whithorn, is also poorly documented. On 28th February, 1559-60, Bishop Alexander Gordon acknowledged receipt of 500 merks for the " reparation and bigging of his kirk." Gordon adhered openly to the protestant cause some months later and presumably when Mary Queen of Scots visited Whithorn on 10th August, 1563, the furnishings of the church and the shrine of St. Ninian had disappeared.[125] The church continued for at least a decade (probably partially) in use and, in 1573, we find Bishop Alexander Gordon ordered to do public penance " in the Cathedral kirk of Quhitterne upon a Sunday in the time of public preaching," but, when the nave was re-roofed as a parish church in the early seventeenth century, there had intervened a period during which it had stood roofless and derelict.[126] Far away from the centre of the revolution the cathedral church of Iona, denuded of its altars and images, seems to have remained structurally unharmed (if uncared for) on into the seventeenth century subject only to natural decay and occasional pilfering.[127] No records are available to tell the fate of the little cathedral of Lismore; it was roofless in the mid-seventeenth century and the chancel was re-roofed about 1747 to serve as the parish church: the nave and a western tower have vanished.

120. *Glasgow Records*, p. 100.
121. *Acts of Parliament*, iv, 155.
122. McCrie, *Life of Andrew Melville*, ii, p. 352.
123. *Rolment of Courtis* (Scottish Text Society), ii, p. 345.
124. Hay Fleming, *Reformation in Scotland*, p. 608.
125. A relic of St. Ninian—an arm-bone—was preserved and taken to the Scots College at Douai (*Acta Sanctorum*, Sept. tome v, p. 327) where like the relic of St. Margaret, it was lost at the time of the French Revolution. The sole relic of St. Ninian to survive seems to be the relic preserved in a small twelfth-century reliquary in the British Museum.
126. *P.S.A.S.*, lxxxv, p. 118.
127. As when Bishop Andrew Knox, translated to Raphoe, in 1622, took two bells from Iona Cathedral to his new diocese (*Origines Parochiales*, ii, p. 834.)

In the north also, away from the initial impact of the revolution, the cathedrals survived longer, but all were sooner or later stripped of their decoration, and, except for Kirkwall, reduced at least partially to ruin. At Aberdeen the nave was re-roofed with slates in 1607, and continued in use as the parish church; tombs and carved wood-work seem to have survived in quantity to fall victim to the covenanting iconoclasm of 1640 and 1642. Enough of Bishop Stewart's pulpit has survived to warrant its reconstruction; the noble heraldic ceiling of the nave still survives and an attractive fifteenth-century Madonna of poly-chromed wood was carried overseas and is venerated in the church of Finisterre at Brussels. Vestments and other furnishings of Aberdeen Cathedral survived at Huntly Castle till after the battle of Corrichie.[128] After Queen Mary's abdication, the Regent Moray's Privy Council, in February, 1567-68, commissioned two burgesses of Edinburgh to go to Aberdeen and Elgin to remove the lead roofing of these cathedrals and dispose of it.[129] The central tower at Aberdeen remained standing until the later seventeenth century, when it collapsed: nothing now remains of the central tower or choir. At Elgin the new religious system was sufficiently provided for in the large parish church of St. Giles. The fabric of Elgin Cathedral seems to have stood neglected, and despite the purging of churches which Lord James is said to have carried out in the north, about 1561, and despite the loss of its roof-lead in February, 1567-68, the cathedral remained usable. In 1594, the last recorded mass was celebrated there after the victory of Glenlivet and, as late as the 1640s, it seems to have been used at least occasionally and partially by both catholics and protestants.[130] Incidental damage from natural and human agencies is recorded: on 4th December, 1637, for example, the roof beams of the choir were blown down in a gale and all are familiar with Spalding's account of how, on Monday, 28th December, 1640, Mr. Gilbert Ross, minister at Elgin, with the lairds of Innes and Brodie, without authority, broke up for firewood the rood screen of Elgin Cathedral which, despite the lack of a roof to protect it, still showed, on a background, " illuminat with starris of bright gold, the crucefixing of our blessed Saueour Jesus Christ."[131] By comparing Slezer's view of Elgin Cathedral in 1688 with the view of 1825, we can see the immense structural damage caused by the fall of the neglected tower on Easter Sunday, 1711. We have little information about Fortrose Cathedral, which possibly remained structurally sound until 1572, when William Lord Ruthven received a grant of " the haill leid quhairwith the cathedrall kirk of Ros wes theikit, alsweill principal kirk as queir and ilis

---

128. We find Mary Queen of Scots later refashioning these vestments in strange ways—a bed for the infant James VI and clothes for Bothwell.
129. One of the reasons given for this order was that much of the lead had already been stolen by private individuals. Prefect Ballentine, writing in 1660 (*Innes Review*, viii, p. 109) says: " Elgin is the seat of the Bishopric of Moray, there one can see the ruins of a most magnificent cathedral, built of squared stone and once roofed with lead: the heretics removed the lead and the bells to ship them to Holland, but the vessel, loaded with them, sank with all hands, in clear weather, in Aberdeen harbour." The same story is told of the lead and bells of Aberdeen Cathedral (*Reg. Episc. Aberd.*, i, p. lxvi): possibly the two Edinburgh burgesses loaded all their material from both cathedrals on the same ship. In July, 1569, the Privy Council made a move to have the roof of Elgin recovered, but there are no indications that any work was actually done. Cf. S. G. E. Lythe : *The Economy of Scotland*, 1550-1625, pp. 158-9 : " References to the export of lead appear with ominous frequency in the years just after 1560 : there were protracted proceedings before the Burgh Court at Inverness about shipments to Hamburg by Lewyr Smith and some of the lead certainly came from the Friars' churches . . . what was described as " lead " was still leaving Scotland in quantity in the 1580's." In 1615, it was regarded as a remarkable fact that the abbey of Coldingham still retained its leaden roof. (Forbes-Leith, *Narratives of Scottish Catholics*, p. 306, n.1.)
130. Shaw's *History of the Province of Moray*, pp. 317-8.
131. Spalding's *Memorialls of the Trubles*, i, pp. 83 and 376.

thairof . . . throw being of the said cathedrall kirk na paroch kirk, bot ane monasterie to sustene ydill belleis."[132] The stonework presumably decayed as a result of this and later, in 1653, the Cromwellian soldiers removed the greater part of the stonework (as they did also at Beauly and Kinloss) to build the new citadel at Inverness. Almost complete silence falls also on Dornoch Cathedral in the reformation period. The church apparently escaped the religious vandals only to be burnt down, in 1570, in the course of local clan warfare. On that occasion the shrine of St. Gilbert was desecrated: William Sutherland " burst St. Gilbert his coffin with his foot and threw the ashes of that holy man in the wund, which enormities the almightie God did most justlie punish for that same foot, that burst St. Gilbert his coffin, did afterward rot away and consume to the great terror of all the beholders."[133] What remained of the tower and walls of Dornoch Cathedral was reconstructed as the parish church in 1614. Kirkwall Cathedral was, no doubt, purged of its altars and images in the days of Bishop Adam Bothwell: this purging may have been limited in scope, because the bishop's reforming zeal lacked popular support. St. Magnus' Cathedral still remains structurally complete, its bells survive and some of the carved wood-work remained down to last century.[134]

In regard to the buildings of " religious places ", that is, of friaries, abbeys, priories and nunneries, we can trace the same gradual decrease in iconoclastic violence as we move from the centre of the turmoil into the remoter provinces. The friaries had suffered the first brunt of the attack in the 1540s and they were the especial object of hatred at the peak of the violence in 1559-1560. After Queen Mary's return from France, the Privy Council, on 15th February, 1561-62, ordained that the magistrates of Aberdeen, Elgin, Inverness, Glasgow and other burghs, where the friaries were as yet " undemolissit ", should uphold them that they might serve such godly purposes as schools and hospitals.[135] The Edinburgh Blackfriars and Greyfriars had been, according to Knox, left with " nothing but bare walls, yea, not so much as door or window " on 29th June, 1559,[136] and a couple of years later these buildings were roofless and ruined. In Perth, Stirling,[137] St. Andrews and Dundee was the same state of affairs. In Glasgow, the nave of the Blackfriars Church was a complete ruin and all of their houses in the kingdom (with the possible exceptions of Wigtown and Inverness, of which we have no information) were equally ruinous. John Grierson, provincial of the Scottish Blackfriars, in a letter to the Master General, written almost certainly in 1559, says of the order's Scottish friaries; " many houses were ruined and burnt. The Edinburgh house was burnt in part and sacked completely. That of St. Andrews sacked and completely burnt except for the church. Those of Dundee and Montrose sacked, cast down to the ground and destroyed, and all the others sacked in great part."[138] The solitary remaining fragment of a Dominican friary in Scotland is a

132. *Origines Parochiales*, ii, p. 572.
133. Sir Robert Gordon. *A Genealogical History of the Earldom of Sutherland*, 1813, p. 158.
134. Bishop Adam Bothwell himself, in a letter of 1st February, 1560-61, makes it quite clear that his suppression of catholic practices was meeting with active and determined opposition. Cf. Mark Napier, *Memoirs of John Napier of Merchiston*, 1834, p. 69.
135. *Register of the Privy Council*, i, 202.
136. Dickinson's *Knox*, i, p. 192.
137. *R.M.S.*, iv, 1373.
138. *Innes Review*, ix, pp. 216-217. Grierson's account is corroborated (13th November, 1560) by *R.M.S.*, v, 1790.

broken apse of their church at St. Andrews. The churches of the Grey-friars—Conventual and Observant—fared just as badly; only one or two in the provinces escaped complete ruin. The friars' churches at Elgin and Aberdeen and the friary at Inverkeithing were saved by being handed over to the town councils.[139] At Kirkcudbright the friars' church became, in part at least, the new parish church. At Haddington, the friars' church, restored after the English occupation of the town in 1548, was demolished by the town council in 1572. At Glasgow, Dumfries, Ayr and Jedburgh we have no clear information but, in all of these places, the friars' churches have disappeared before the end of the century. At Roxburgh the friary became a mansion house for Walter Ker of Cesfurd. In the central area, the friaries of Perth, St. Andrews, Stirling and Edinburgh succumbed to the violence of 1559-1560. The Dundee house never recovered from the attack of August, 1543. And, in Dundee, with correct revolutionary technique, the *Gude and Godlie Ballates* blame the friars for bringing disaster upon themselves:

> " Had not zour self begun the weiris
> Zour stepillis had bene standand zit:
> It was the flattering of zour Freiris
> That ever gart Sanct Francis flit."[140]

Of the three or four churches of the Red Friars or Trinitarians, which remained active up to the date of the reformation, the fabric of only two survived, the Trinity Kirk at Aberdeen and the church of the Holy Cross at Peebles. This last church was gifted by the Privy Council to the town as a parish church in place of the dilapidated church of St. Andrew, the town council guaranteeing to " exclude furth of the samin all manner of idolatry."[141] We have little information about the churches of the White Friars, or Carmelites. Fragments of only two of their churches survive—some broken walls at Luffness and the choir and transept of their South Queensferry church (this last escaped because, for a time, it was used as a parish church). The Carmelite churches at Tullilum, Linlithgow and Edinburgh suffered damage in 1559-1560. Of the remainder we have no information except for a document from Banff. On the night of 20th July, 1559, the Banff Carmelites were disturbed by persons unknown " raising of fire in our said place and kyrk under sylens of nicht " and the following morning they discovered that there had been " manifest spuilzie of the insycht of the kirk and place." The friars say they are informed that " syndrie and divers of our wodin places in the Southland had been put to wraik " in the same manner.[142] By about 1570 no friary of any order was inhabited by any friars and for the most part the buildings were in ruin or had been swept away altogether (their stonework being used for other purposes). Writing in the early seventeenth century, about the medieval friaries of Scotland, Habakkuk Bisset says; "All these religius places alluterlie Rewyned and sa demolisched that the partis or places quhere sum of the samyn war

---

139. The Elgin church became a courthouse for a time and now, beautifully restored by the third Marquess of Bute in 1896, and used by the Sisters of Mercy, it is our sole remaining example of a Scottish Grey-friars church. The Aberdeen Greyfriars was demolished in 1903 to make way for the new frontage of Marischal College. The hospitium of the Inverkeithing friary still remains.

140. *A Compendious Book of Godly and Spiritual Songs* (Scottish Text Society), 1897, p. 211.

141. Renwick, *A Peebles Aisle and Monastery*, p. 38.

142. *Notes and Queries*, 1870, p. 521. This document reminds us that part of the domestic buildings of some of the friaries (and, no doubt, of the larger monasteries, too) might be constructed of wood and this possibility has to be kept in mind in dealing with references to the burning down of monasteries.

rycht magnifict and sumptiouslie builded may nocht be knawin in ony wyise."[143]

The churches of abbeys and priories suffered severely in this second phase of the assault on ecclesiastical buildings. For half a century or more the tendency had been for these establishments to fall into the hands of nobles, who taking advantage of the system of commendatory prelates and the extensive feuing of monastic land, necessitated by the heavy taxation, had secured virtual possession of abbey lands and established hereditary claims to official appointments in the monastic administration. A great part of the monastic property of the kingdom was effectively secularized a decade or two before the change of religion and, in many instances, the family hold on abbeys and priories by the nobility was such as to lead almost inevitably to the erection of the ecclesiastical property into a temporal lordship in favour of those who had long since secured such control. Nominal ecclesiastics like Mark Ker, commendator of Newbattle, welcomed the reformation as a means of translating their insecure hold on church property into a regular hereditary tenure. No doubt the schemes of such " abbots " and " priors " inspired the recommendations of the *First Book of Discipline* that the exclusively religious portions of monastic establishments should be " utterly suppressed " but that the " palaces, mansionis and dwelling places adjacent thairto with orchardis and yardis of the samyn " should be preserved intact. Because of such legislation there followed extensive demolition of monastic churches, sometimes by commendators, sometimes by people with less obvious legal title.

Even those monastic churches which served as parish churches were only maintained with difficulty. After the sacking of Dunfermline, in March, 1560, no one seemed anxious to spend money on repairs and the Register of the Privy Council describes a sad state of affairs in September, 1563: the choir which had contained the royal tombs and the shrine of St. Margaret was apparently roofless and dismantled: that was to be expected, but even the nave, which served as the parish church, had been barbarously treated. The walls of the nave were riven in sundry places, the vault parted the one side nearly from the other and the glass windows so decayed that no glass was left in them. The building was so dangerous that parishioners could remain in it only at the risk of their lives.[144] Similar complaints were levelled by the General Assembly of March, 1569-70 against Adam Bothwell, bishop of Orkney, accused of neglecting Holyrood Abbey, the nave of which was used as the Canongate parish church. The solution proposed by Bothwell (and apparently acted upon) was that " the superfluous ruinous parts, to wit the queir and croce kirk (the choir and transepts) might be disponed be faithful men to repair the remanent sufficiently."[145] In other instances, where the abbey church

---

143. *Rolment of Courtis*, ii, p. 126.

144. *Register of the Privy Council* i, 246, 247. At first sight this description looks like a piece of medieval exaggeration, but probably the nave of the church was indeed threatening complete ruin. What presumably happened was that the lean-to roof of the cloister, which had supported the south wall of the nave, was removed either by the original iconoclasts or by subsequent looters and, lacking this support, the wall leaned outwards, breaking the vault. The south aisle vault had eventually to be rebuilt and the enormous buttresses were added about 1620-1625.

145. Alexander Baillie (*A True Information*, 1628, pp. 23-24) claims that: " they at first made stables in Halyrudhous, which was renouned not only for holynes and deuotion wont to be therin, bot also for that it was the Burial-place of our Kings and their royal children. Which surely suld make al true harted countrymen the more to abhorre their abominable and barbarous beastlines: Yea, and their more than turkish ingratitud towards their natiue Princes and Souerains, who sturred not to let horses dung on their moales, without any regard to god or their Kings."

was not claimed for parochial purposes, the commendator or whoever had secured the monastic property simply disposed of the material—timber, lead, iron, stone—as advantageously as possible, if it was not used to transform the abbot's house into a large mansion for the commendator, now become a purely secular lord. At Newbattle, the church disappeared altogether: Scotstarvet describes this transition, where the Ker commendators " did so metamorphose the buildings that it cannot be known that ever it did belong to the church, by reason of the fair new fabric and stately edifices built thereon; except only that the old name and walls of the precinct stands, but instead of the old monks has succeeded the deer."[146] The abbey buildings at Cambuskenneth, which had been purged by the Congregation in June, 1559, were now, in 1570, demolished to provide material for the Earl of Mar's new palace in Stirling. He was in a sufficiently strong position at court to disregard the talk of sacrilege, which his action roused among the common folk, as the insolent inscription on the building made clear:

" Esspy speik furth and spair notht
Considder weil I cair notht."[147]

At Scone, the first lay commendator began building a palace for himself on the ruins of the burnt-out abbey. A later writer blames Lord Stormont for this: " he was vandal enough to raise his palace over the very bones of our ancient kings."[148]

The immemorial round of public monastic prayer ceased in the border abbeys either in July, 1559, or later, as a result of the legislation of August, 1560. At Dryburgh, the conventual buildings became the mansion house of the Erskines and the church became a ruin. At Jedburgh, the nave was fitted up as a parish church and the chancel unroofed and left to decay. At Kelso, which also had recovered in some measure from the devastation of 1547, the visit of the godly brought final ruin and later (after 1580) one of the transepts was fitted up as a parish church, with a gaol on the floor above it. At Melrose the situation is more amply documented: the abbey kirk, though badly needing repair, had remained in use until, at least, 1558. In 1559 or 1560 the *opus Dei* finally ceased and ruin befel. We learn from a decree of the Court of Session, in 1573, that some servants of Sir Walter Scott of Branxholm, during the months of January, February, March and April, 1569, had removed " greit quantities " of stone, timber, lead, ironwork and glasswork from the nave, choir, transepts and tower of the abbey church. They also removed doors, glass, iron and lead from several parts of the conventual buildings.[149] The building of the commendator's new house and the building of the town tolbooth made further dilapidation of the abbey ruins; so much so, that what was practically a new parish church had to be built up in the ruins of the nave in 1618.

Riotous mobs and petty thieves never trouble to leave documentary

146. *Staggering State of Scottish Statesmen*, 1872, pp. 90-91.

147. Reminiscenses of this popular reaction to the spoliation of ecclesiastical buildings occur elsewhere. In the case of the Abbey of Deer and the Earl Marischall, there is the story in *Britane's Distemper* (Spalding Club), p. 113; in *Macfarlane's Geographical Collections* (Scot. Hist. Soc.), iii, 237, there is the legend of the house built with material from the Chapel of Cowie which " rained drops of bloud "; and in Prefect Ballentine's Report of 1660 (*Innes Review*, viii, 44) there are references to similar legends.

148. Prefect Ballentine's Report, *Innes Review*, viii, 105.

149. In other words it was the thieving of Sir Walter Scott of Branxholm which was mainly responsible for the ruin which his namesake and descendant did so much to romanticize. For this interesting document, see *Melrose Regality Records* (Scot. Hist. Soc.) iii, 158-160.

Aprilis florida nutrit.

Aprilis habet dies. xxx. Luna. xxx.
Sol habet horas. r. Dies habet. xiiii.

kł. aprī.
Marie Egyptiace. iii. lec.
Ambrosii epī τ cōfessoris. p. iii. lec. duplex.
None Aprilis.
Dies egr.
Idus Aprilis.

Sol in tauro.

Obitus Reuerendissimi in christo patris Joannis Hamiltoun... ... Archiepiscopi ... abbatis de Paisleto ...

MARTYRIVM V. P. F. IOANNIS GRAY.

Het Martelie van den Eervveer. Pater F. IOANNES GRA[Y]

VENER. P. F. IOANNES GRAY, natione Scotus, ante ingreſſum Ordinis Seraphici Canonicus Andernacéſis, haud procul à Bruxellâ, è patriâ Religionis ergô profligatus, vt Deo quietiùs vacaret, in portum ſancti Franciſci appulit. Cùm Geuſij Bruxellæ in Clerú & Magiſtratum ſeditionem mouentes, omnia cædibus temerarent & rapinis, fugientibus è Monaſterio noſtris FF. P. IOANNEM ſolum in cellulâ reperientes, propter venerandam canitiem putauerunt eſſe Guardianum, pecuniâm ab eo poſcentes. Sed cùm non haberet, iſti ſanguinarij vulneribus duobus cæſum in capite, duobus item punctú in pectore, peremerunt, anno Chriſti 1579. die 5. Iunij.

DEN Eee vveerdig P. Frater Ioa[n]nes Gray, gl[i] boren in Scho[t]landt, vvas o[n] Catholijck gh[e]loof uyt ſijn v[a]derlant verdr[e]uen; vviert ee[n] Canonick van Anderlecht by Bruſſel, daer n[u] hem begeuende tot de Serap[h]ſche Religie d[er] Minderbroede[rs] In den groote[n] oproer binnen Bruſſel hebbe[n] de Geuſen Pat[er] Ioannes allee[n] op ſijn celle[n] ghevonden, ende hem meynende om ſijnen grooten ouderdom Gua[r]diaen te vveſen, vvilden ghel[t] hebben: 't vvelck als hy niet en ha[d]de naer ſijnen ſtaet, hebben de bloe[t]ghe booſvvichten hem tvvee doo[t]lijcke vvonden gheuende in 't hoof[t] ende tvvee in 't herte, het leuen [be]nomen, in het iaer Chriſti duyſen[t] vijf-hondert ſeuentigh neghen, d[en] 5. Iunij.

PLATE XXXVI. A SCOTTISH MARTYR IN BRUSSELS.

proof of their activities, but when we find the chamberlain of Coupar Angus Abbey, in the year 1563, paying " vj⁵ foɪ biggyne wp of twa laicht durris and the vmest dur of the stepill of Cupar, for keping of the tymmer of the kirk and stepill, and v⁵ for gathering of the hail sklatis togydder within the bundis of the clostir for suir keping of thame . . . and xl⁵ giffin to the glassinvrycht for mending of the hail windokis of the abbatis chalmeris quhilk wer all brokin," together with many other sums for miscellaneous repairs,[150] we suspect that a " rascal multitude " has been at work, and we are not surprised to learn that Habakkuk Bisset could only judge the size of Coupar Angus Abbey from " the (auld) Rewynous wallis thairof."[151] The timber roof of Lindores Abbey was removed to serve in the construction of the new tolbooth of Dundee in 1562,[152] and, though there is no record of destruction, the abbey church of Balmerino is described in 1588 as " (locum) super quo ecclesia dicti monasterii prius sita erat."[153] In the same way, apart from the attempted attack on Arbroath by the Dundee mob in 1543, we have no information but, by the end of the century the abbey kirk of Arbroath is a dismantled ruin. Alexander Baillie, who describes the appearance of the place as he saw it, sometime before 1612, attributing its desolation to " the heretical furie of Knox, Methven and the rest," says, "And first as to that of Abbirbroth, surely when before a certaine (number of) years I had first seene it and had stayed a while before the great dore thereof, gazing sadly upon the deplorable state of the defaced and staggering steeples, the battered wals, broken doune pillars and the floore al over-growne with grass and defiled with filth and excrements of unreasonable beasts; and judging of such faire steads and ruines that it hath once bene a most royal braue and gorgious church, I could not but sigh and bewaile it. . . . "[154]

In more remote places, there was no " rascal multitude " and, depending on the goodwill of the local magnate, religious life may even have lingered on for a time. In the south-west, Lord Herries refused to carry out the order of the lords of the Congregation to demolish Dundrennan Abbey and Lord Maxwell refused to obey similar orders concerning Sweetheart Abbey, saying that he was attached to the place " quhair he was maist part brocht up in his youth."[155] The same protection allowed religious life to continue for some years in the college kirk of Lincluden but, further west, the abbot and monks of Glenluce were, in 1560, " driven by force from our said monastery and despoiled of all goods, clothes, utensils and jewels of the said monastery and of our provision and for the reformation, repair and restoration of the altar, choir, dormitory, chapter and other houses thereof utterly and altogether robbed and destroyed," by John Gordon of Lochinvar, in the course of a quarrel with the Earl of Cassillis about securing the heritable bailiary of the abbey estates, in which quarrel theological questions played little or no real part.[156]

150. *Register of Cupar Abbey* (Grampian Club), ii, pp. 279-280.
151. *Rolment of Courtis*, ii, p. 194.
152. Maxwell's *Old Dundee*, pp. 185-186.
153. *R.M.S.*, v, 1608.
154. Alexander Baillie, *A True Information*, 1628, p. 26.
155. *Archaeological Collections of Ayrshire and Galloway*, x, p. 7. Bishop Lesley mentions this group of un-damaged monasteries: " I passe now by the new monasterie or of sweit hartes . . . Drundrennen, Salsiden (Soulseat), our Ladyes Inche, quhais kirkes all and clostiris throuch the wisdome and authoritie of certane illustir and nobill men standis zit haill." (*Historie*, i, p. 13.)
156. Charters published in J. M. Rusk: *The Parish and Abbey of Glen Luce*, pp. 132-139.

In the north, the Cromwellian occupation was the principal period for the demolition of the actual fabric of churches. Pluscarden, in its secluded valley, seems to have suffered mainly from natural decay, but (like Fortrose Cathedral) Beauly Priory and Kinloss Abbey were quarried to build the fort at Inverness. When Prefect Ballentine saw Kinloss Abbey, sometime prior to 1660; only the church lacked its roof.[157] Away in the Western Isles also, a place like Oronsay Priory has evidently suffered more from neglect and natural decay than from the violence of reformers.

The same broad pattern can be discerned even in the ill-documented history of Scotland's few nunneries. Two of the border nunneries, Coldstream and Eccles, together with St. Bothan's, suffered in the English invasions, but survived, to disappear finally with their buildings in the reformation period. Elcho, near Perth, was burned by the English, in December, 1547, and restored only to suffer complete and final ruin at the hands of the godly in 1559. Of the Cistercian house at Manuel we have practically no information. The house of the Dominican nuns of Sciennes had been destroyed and the sisters dispersed before 1567.[158] The nuns of North Berwick apparently escaped the English invasion, but they were scattered and some destruction of their buildings was wrought during the climax of the reformation and, by 1587, we find reference made to " the place where the church and cloister of the said nunnery formerly stood."[159] The buildings of Haddington nunnery, probably the largest in Scotland, escaped destruction in the English invasions: they may also have remained substantially unharmed during the reformation crisis and the reason for this should, no doubt, be sought in the interest of the powerful Hepburn family in its affairs. The buildings were, presumably, dismantled and destroyed piecemeal as the community died out and the property became completely secularized. The only Scottish nunnery of which any substantial fabric remains is the Augustinian nunnery at Iona, which also has some undamaged sepulchral slabs, and this is a sure sign that reverence for the old order lingered here for a long time among the people.

The town councils played a considerable part in this final demolition of ecclesiastical buildings. Some councils took advantage of the unexpected supply of second-hand materials to extend, rebuild or repair their tolbooths. At Dundee, for example, the tolbooth was roofed, in 1562, with timber taken from Lindores Abbey: again, at Musselburgh, the tolbooth was built, in 1590 with material from the ruined Loreto Chapel. The town council of Edinburgh, in 1581, bought ashlar and " thack stanes " of the abbey of Inchcolm for rebuilding their tolbooth.[160] An act of parliament, which in that same year, 1581, ratified the infeftment of the Earl of Moray in possession of Inchcolm, sums up the results of twenty years' policy regarding religious houses: " Forsamekle as be diuerss actis of Parliament maid of befoir concerning the reformatioun of religioun within this realme. The monkreis (monasteries) ar altogidder

---

157. *Innes Review*, viii, p. 109. Ballentine adds the information about Kinloss, that " some of the best ornaments of Kinloss church were carried off by the heretics and put in a chest to be sold overseas, but the ship sank and the chest was washed ashore and the contents were bought back for money by a Catholic gentleman from the finders." As late as 1571, money was being spent at Beauly " pro reparatione templi et reliquorum edificiorum monasterii." (*R.M.S.*, v, 2021.)
158. *R.M.S.*, iv, 1980.
159. *R.M.S.*, v, 1915 and 1493.
160. *Edinburgh Burgh Records*, 1573-89, pp. 204, 210.

abolishit and thair places and abbayis for the maist part left waist."[161]
Apart from possible exceptions, such as Sweetheart, Dundrennan or
Crossraguel, it is safe to say that, by 1581, the churches of all religious
houses were at least partially in ruin and the conventual buildings were
occupied by those who had engineered the revolution or profited by it.
Ninian Winzet commenting, in 1563, on the destruction of the monasteries
and the appropriation of their revenues by the nobles makes the shrewd
observation that the common weal would have been better served by
using such buildings and revenues for educational purposes and, in
questioning the logic which condemns abbey churches as idolatrous,
while deciding that parish churches are not so, he claims that a number
of parish churches have actually been destroyed: "Quhy hef ze wappit
doun the monasteriis and principal policie of this realme and counselis
the rentis thairof iniustlie to be appropriat to wtheris ? Of the quhilkis
monasteriis euery ane be a godly reformatioun, besydes a cumpanie to
waik on prayar, micht haif bene a college of godly leirning to the support
of puir studentis and that to the grete and necessar commoditie of this
realme . . . Gif ze allege the saidis monasteriis to haif bene pollutit with
idolatrie and thairfor suld haif bene destroyit quhy hef ze nocht destroyt
also to the ground (as ze hef done in a part) all paroche kirkis and
bischopes saitis, in the quhilkis the samin thingis wes vseit, haldin be zou
idolatrie ? And quhat pouer haif ze to dispence mair in the ane nor in
the wthir ? "[162]

Winzet's remark about parish churches having been destroyed shows
how difficult it was for the clear distinction of the *First Book of Discipline*
to be maintained in practice. According to the ideas of the Calvinist
faction, large cathedral and monastic churches were quite useless and, as
a matter of course, these were scheduled for demolition, once political
power had been secured. Parish churches were quite a different matter
and, according to their own oft-repeated injunctions, such churches had
to be carefully upheld and maintained. Some writers take for granted
that the new religion, unlike its predecessor, did succeed in maintaining
parish churches in a simple, clean and comely fashion, befitting the new
doctrine. The records of the time, fragmentary though they be, seem to
indicate a less happy state of affairs. The greater burgh kirks were,
of course, too large for the new requirements. One portion, the choir as
at St. Michael's, Linlithgow, St. Mary's, Dundee, or St. Giles', Edinburgh, or the nave in the case of some monastic churches like Dunfermline
or Holyrood, was adapted as a preaching-house and the remainder of
the building allowed to decay or used for secular purposes.[163] Alexander
Baillie of Wurzburg gives a graphic description of St. Giles' Church in
Edinburgh, as he knew it before 1612, the old chancel walled off as a
preaching-house, the remainder divided up into less spiritual resorts:
" bare walls and pillars al cled with dust, sweepings and cobwebs, in
steed of painting and tapestrie: and on every side beholding the restlesse
resorting of people treating of their worldly effaires; some writing and

---

161. *Acts of Parliaments of Scotland*, iii, p. 276a.
162. *Works of Ninian Winzet* (Scot. Text Society), p. 128.
163. Burgh records provide much information about the disposal, by town councils, of stone, timber,
lead and other materials from redundant churches and parts of church buildings, which came within
the jurisdiction of the town authorities. Examples occur regularly: the Peebles bailies selling the bell
of St. Andrew's Kirk to the highest bidder in 1564 (Gunn: *Book of Peebles Church*, p. 188): the Dundee
bailies selling " gutter stanes " from the roofless nave of St. Mary's Church (Maxwell, *Old Dundee*,
p. 172): or the provost of Linlithgow, in the choir of St. Michael's Church, on 19th March, 1560-61,
haggling over the sale price for the whole lead of the church (*Protocol Book of Nicol Thounis*, no. 26).

making obligations, contracts and discharges; other laying countes or telling-over sowmes of money: two and two walking and talking to and fro, some about merchandice or the lawes and too many allas about drinking and courting of woemen, Yea and perhaps about worse nor I can imagine; as is wont to be done al the day long in the common Exchanges of London and Amsterdam and other great cities: And turning him farther towards the west end of the Church which is devided in a high house for the Colledge of Iustice, called the Session or Senat-house, and a low house, called the low Tolbooth, where the Bailiues of the toune use to sit and judge common actions and pleas in the one end therof and a number of harlots and scolds, for flyting and whoredom, inclosed in the other."[164] Some entries in the Edinburgh burgh records make it clear that the condition of St. Giles' church was every bit as bad as Baillie describes.

In the Edinburgh Dean of Guild accounts we can follow the whole, lengthy and expensive process of the reconstruction of St. Giles Kirk, during the years 1560 to 1562, beginning with the demolition of the altars and the rood-screen and the removal of tombstones. It may not be without significance that in the reconstruction of St. Nicholas Kirk, Aberdeen, the town council of Aberdeen, on 7th July, 1596, have to record that their master of works, David Anderson, "refuisit to big the stane wall appoyntit to be biggit betuixt the kirk and the queir for deuyding theirof in tua seuerall kirkis," and another, Andrew Scherar, had to be appointed in his place.

In the instructions anent parish churches, provided in the *First Book of Discipline*, we read: "Lest that the word of God and ministration of the Sacraments, by unseemliness of the place come in contempt, of necessity it is that the churches and places where the people ought publicly to convene be with expedition repaired in doors, windows, thatch and with such preparations within, as appertaineth as well to the majesty of the word of God as unto the ease and commodity of the people."[165] And this insistence on every parish church having "doors, close windows of glass, thatch or slate able to withhold rain" taken together with the instructions for the purging of Dunkeld Cathedral: "tak guid heyd that neither the dasks, windocks nor durris be ony ways hurt or broken" show that the compilers of the *First Book of Discipline* were aware that the casting down of even parish churches had too often involved the smashing of windows and doors and the theft of roofing materials. The state of affairs is illustrated, in 1573, at the college kirk of Crichton (which was also the parish kirk); where "not only were the windows and doors smashed and carried off but even the roof and other parts of it faced ruin."[166] An act of parliament of January, 1572-73 declares that: "thair hes bene divers paroche kirkis within this realme demolischit, cassin doun and destroyit for the maist part" by private persons who appropriated the stones, timber and other material.[167] One of the charges brought against Adam Bothwell, in March 1569-1570, was in regard to twenty-seven parish churches in Lothian and Galloway, which were dependent on Holyrood and "all the said kirks, for the most

---

164. Baillie, *True Information*, pp. 27-28.
165. Dickinson's *Knox*, ii, 320.
166. *R.M.S.*, iv, 2169.
167. *Acts of Parliament*, iii, 76, 77.

part, wherein Christ's Evangell may be preached, are decayed and made, some sheepfolds, and some so ruinous that none darre enter into them for fear of falling; specially Halyrudhouse, although the Bishop of Sanct Andrews in time of Papistry sequestrate the whole rents of the said abbacy, because only the glassen windows were not holden up and repaired." In self defence, Bothwell stated that "he was but of late come to the benefice, and the most part of these kirks were pulled down be some greedy persons, at the first beginning of the Reformatione, which hath never been helped or repaired sensyne, and few of them may be repaired be his small portion of the living."[168]

The parish churches, stripped of their altars, statues, paintings, carved wood and metal work, with windows smashed, doors broken and perhaps with the redundant part of the building in ruin, must have presented a depressing spectacle and especially, when no incumbent had been appointed by the new regime to insist on repairs.[169] It seems clear that, despite the good work achieved by some town councils and the resolutions of successive general assemblies, there were sufficient parish churches in this condition, throughout central Scotland, in the decade or two following the reformation, to create a general impression of devastation. Various writers, Calvinist as well as Catholic, native Scots and foreign observers, are all apparently impressed by this dilapidation and neglect even of parish churches. The Jesuit Goudanus, no doubt, informed to some extent by Hay, for he himself spoke no Scots and travelled little, reporting in 1562, writes: "churches and altars are overthrown, all things holy profaned, the images of Christ and the Saints are broken and cast down."[170] Ten years later, the situation had, if anything, deteriorated: the *Lamentation of Lady Scotland*, published in 1572 and dedicated to the Laird of Dun, Superintendent of Angus and the Mearns, paints a dreary picture:

> " The rowmis appointit pepill to considder,
> To heir Gods word, quhair thay suld pray togidder,
> Ar now conuertit in scheip Coits and Fauldis,
> Or els ar fallin becaus nane thame uphauldis;
> The Parische Kirkis, I mene, thay sa misgyde
> That nane for wynd and rane thairin may byde:
> Thairfor na plesure tak thay of the tempill,
> Nor zit to cum quhair nocht is to contempill (contemplate)
> Bot Crawis and Dowis cryand and makand beir (tumult)
> That nane throuchly the Minister may heir;
> Baith Fedders, Fylth and Doung dois ly abrod
> Quhair folk suld sit to heir the word of God;

---

168. *Book of the Universall Kirk*, i, 163, 167. In these twenty-seven churches of Lothian and Galloway the situation was, no doubt, aggravated by the fact that no minister had ever been appointed, since the parish priests or vicars had been ousted nine or ten years before, and maintenance would accordingly suffer. Conditions would be still worse in places such as Paisley, Aberdeen, Currie, Dupplin, Abergeldie, where there was active opposition to the new regime and parish churches were "steiked" against the entry of the Calvinist ministers.

169. Notaries' protocol books and town records allude regularly to this dismantled condition of churches. We find legal affairs being transacted, for example, in Linlithgow Church, in 1561, at "the site formerly occupied by the high altar"; at Peebles Church, in 1564, "in the place where the altar of St. Andrew the Apostle formerly stood"; or, in St. Giles' Church, Edinburgh, in 1562, at "the pillar where the altar of St. James formerly stood."

170. Pollen, *Papal Negotiations*, p. 135.

Quhilk is occasioun to the adversaryes
To mok and scorne sic things befoir zour eyes."[171]

This might be dismissed as poetic exaggeration, were it not reinforced by a sermon preached, that same year, 1572, by David Ferguson in the kirk of Leith, before the Regent Mar, the general assembly and many of the nobility, where the preacher complains: " For this day Christ is spuilzeit amang vs quhil that quhilk aucht to mantene the Ministerie of the Kirk and the Pure is geuin to prophane men, flattereris in Court, Ruffianes and Hyrelingis. The Pure in the meane tyme oppressit with hounger, the Kirkis and Tempilis decaying for laik of Ministeris and uphalding, and the Schuilis vtterlie neglectit and ouersene. . . . Bot now to speik of zour Tempilis, quhair the word of God suld be preichit and the Sacramentis ministerit, all men seis to quhat miserabill rewyne and decay thay ar cum: zea, thay ar sa prophanit, that in my conscience gif I had bene brocht vp in Germanie or in ony vther countrie, quhair Christ is trewly preichit, and all thingis done decently and in ordour, according to Goddis word, and had hard of that puritie of Religioun that is amang zow and for the lufe thairof had takin trauell to visite this land and then suld haue sene the foull deformitie and desolatioun of zour Kirkis and Tempilis quhilk ar mair like to scheip cottis then the housis of God, I culd not haue judgeit that thair had bene only feir of God or richt Religioune in the maist part of this realme."[172] And Nicol Burne, who had intimate experience of conditions under the Calvinist regime before he returned to the faith of his fathers, has this to add, in 1581: " I desyre that ze schau me of onie ancient historie, that in onie aige the Christian men hes had sik kirkis as ze haue nou in the realme of Scotland. That is the bair vallis destitute of all kynd of ornament, vithout dure, vindo or ruffe."[173]

The state of affairs thus described by writers of different points of view probably prevailed in what we have called the epicentre of the revolution: further afield the medieval buildings and their furnishings would remain relatively immune until Calvinism gradually, over the next decade or two, asserted its control in the outlying provinces.[174]

It is the fashion with some writers to reassure their readers that, while all this work of destruction is regrettable, yet its effect should not be exaggerated: they tell us that it was mainly furnishings and interior decoration that suffered and that the fabric of churches was left unharmed. Now, even if it were true that churches were left structurally sound, it is

---

171. *Satirical Poems of the Time of the Reformation* (Scottish Text Society), p. 232. The same writer (p. 233) refers to colleges, probably collegiate churches, and a university, presumably St. Andrews:
" Ze collegis and Universitie,
That to all vthers suld exempill be,
I se zour tempills cassin downe and reuin;
The maist part are bo theikit with the heuin."

172. *Tracts by David Ferguson, Minister of Dunfermline, MDLXIII—MDLXXII*, (Bannatyne Club), pp. 72-73. John Knox, who had once written merrily about the destruction of churches, now near the end of his days, seems to have realised (like Luther before him) that his success in setting up the New Jerusalem in Scotland had been only partial and, signing the imprimatur of Ferguson's sermon, on 6th August, 1572, he writes: " John Knox with my dead hand but glaid heart praising God that of his mercy he leuis suche light to his Kirk in this desolatioun."

173. Nicol Burne, *Disputation*, 1581, f. 59v.

174. The influence of a local magnate favourable to the old church can be traced here and there in the survival of church furnishing and decoration, even in the area of greatest violence. For example, the survival of altars and carved work in Roslin Chapel must be attributed to the protection of the Sinclairs; or the survival of paintings and woodwork at Foulis Easter results from the protection of Lord Gray. The survival of elaborate Sacrament Houses in parish churches of the north-east shows that the revolution had lost some of its violence before penetrating that area. As late as 1605, for instance, the presbytery of Ellon are still demanding the removal of the " Chancellar Wall " (i.e. the rood screen) in the Kirk of Slains (Thomas Mair, *Records of the Presbytery of Ellon*, 1898, p. 54).

naïve to suggest that comparatively little harm was done. As can be seen in any district of Europe, which has escaped the devastation of the reformation or French Revolution, the greatest beauty and treasure of a medieval church lay more often in its furnishings and decoration than in its architecture: the Sistine Chapel, for example, without its frescoes or renaissance chancel screen would be a barn and the Church of Brou without its marvellous tombs and delicate sculpture would not attract many tourists.

The suggestion may be intended that Scottish medieval churches were poorly furnished and their contents not very valuable in any case. Such an insinuation is easy to make because almost all of the evidence has been destroyed. But we cannot lightly dismiss, as of no consequence whatsoever, the statement of the Spanish ambassador, Don Pedro de Ayala, in 1498, that Scottish " abbeys are very magnificent, the buildings fine and the revenues great," or the statement of the French ecclesiastic, Estienne Perlin, who visited Scotland in 1551 or 1552, that " in this place there are many churches highly ornamented and plenty of monasteries in which there are plenty of religious."[175] Moreover, some inventories and other clues do survive to show that the larger Scottish churches were well furnished. Churches like St. Giles', Edinburgh, St. Nicholas', Aberdeen, St. John's, Perth, were overcrowded with altars, each with its painted or carved altarpiece: they also had embroidered frontals and hangings and vestments: there were carved stalls and screens of wood, and each church had a quantity of metalwork such as lecterns, candelabra, or even a brass font, and there were altar vessels, generally of silver. Some of these furnishings had accumulated over generations and even over centuries. No one would claim that all the altarpieces, tombs, statues, manuscripts, pictures, embroideries, metal work, wood-carving or stained glass of medieval Scottish churches were of a uniformly high quality. The bulk of this material would be mediocre stuff, as in any other country: a proportion of it would, no doubt, be quite wretched: but with equal certainty a proportion of these furnishings, not necessarily in the largest churches, would be of high artistic worth. Much of this material was imported from Flanders or France, Italy or the Empire, but there was also a proportion possibly bigger than we imagine, which displayed the development of native skill and craftsmanship. But, taken all in all, native work and foreign, good, bad and indifferent, it represented practically the whole artistic heritage of the nation and that was what was lost in the tornado of destruction which struck central Scotland in 1559 and 1560 and which spread out into the outlying districts in the next decade or so.

So thoroughgoing has this destruction of liturgical accessories been that it is more difficult to find illustrative material showing the religious ideas and habits prevalent in Scotland five hundred years ago than to illustrate, from material evidence, the customs of ancient Egyptians or Babylonians. Of stained glass, which certainly filled the windows of the greater churches and of many of the lesser churches even in rural districts, there remain a few handfuls of fragmentary quarrels of glass, dug up around some abbey ruins and four roundels, displaying coats of arms,

---

175. Hume Brown, *Early Travellers in Scotland*, pp. 45 and 79.

which have survived in Edinburgh's Magdalene Chapel.[176] Of the eucharistic vessels, chalices, pyxes, ciboria and especially the " eucharists " or monstrances, which every church of any size possessed and which were often examples of the skill of native silversmiths, hardly anything survived the looting and the roups, organised by the town councils in the early 1560s.[177] Apart from reliquaries of St. Margaret and St. Ninian, which were carried overseas to Douay College, nothing seems to have survived of the reliquaries in which pious men had once enshrined the relics of the popular saints of medieval Scotland. A few specimens of Celtic metalwork such as the Brecbennoch of St. Columba, the Quigrich of St. Fillan or the Guthrie Bell-shrine have escaped destruction (probably because their possession gave legal title to property). These pieces, together with the university maces and the splendid thirteenth-century Kennet Ciborium, with its Limousin enamelling, are but tantalizing fragments of vanished splendour.[178] Medieval bells have survived here and there but most of them, like the bells of Elgin and Aberdeen cathedrals, were sold as scrap metal. A brass lectern, from Holyrood Abbey, survives in Hertfordshire, a brass chandelier hanging in St. John's, Perth, an odd candlestick or broken censer, dug up in a country churchyard, are about all that remains of the brazen work of the medieval sanctuary. Apart from a solitary and incomplete brass monument in St. Nicholas' Church, Aberdeen, no pre-reformation brass tomb-cover survives in Scotland. The imposing brass and marble tomb of Bishop Elphinstone, which his scholars saved from the Mearns barons and their followers in 1559, survived only to fall a victim to the vandals of 1642. The tombs of bishops and abbots have all disappeared save for one or two, broken and desecrated, which are mainly at Dunkeld, Aberdeen and Elgin. Not a single royal tomb has survived the reformation attack, not even the elaborate monument which patriotic gratitude had once brought, at great expense, from Paris to Dunfermline, to house the mortal remains of the Bruce.

Little survives of the carved woodwork which adorned the more important churches: the stalls, imported by the Melrose monks from Bruges: the stalls of Glasgow and Dunkeld cathedrals or of St. Nicholas', Aberdeen, product of native craftmanship; or the stalls of St. Giles', which the church-proud bailies of Edinburgh stored for safety in the nether tolbooth; all are gone. Thanks to Elphinstone's regents and scholars, we still have the late fifteenth-century stalls of King's College Chapel, " rycht plesand to the eye." A few stalls survive at Dunblane and fragments of a rood screen at Foulis Easter. And there are the carved panels, made to the order of Cardinal Beaton, possibly for Arbroath Abbey and, whether of foreign or native execution, they are works of superb craftsmanship and stir our imagination regarding what else may have been given over to the " merciment of fire."[179]

---

176. Away from the centre of the revolution, stained glass, like other decoration, would survive for a time, to disappear gradually through decay and theological aversion to its repair. For example, Gordon of Rothiemay, writing about King's College Chapel, Aberdeen, in 1661, says: " all the church windows of old wer of paynted glas and ther remayns as yit a pairt of that ancient braverye."

177. A few stray pieces would, no doubt, survive to be fashioned into other wares at a later date. One chalice from a West Highland provenance survived into the nineteenth century, when it was used in St. Mary's, Calton, Glasgow, but it was stolen on Christmas Day, 1845, and was never seen again.

178. Nicol Burne (*Disputation*, f. 178v.) points out that the poor did not benefit by the expropriation of the sacred vessels: " Zea ze haue fellit en verie deid al the precious ornamentis of the reliques of the Martyris in the Realme of Scotland, but the pure folk ar mair naikit nor ever thay var."

179. In the nineteenth-century restoration of Tain collegiate church, some sections of medieval stalls have been pieced together to form a pulpit which is described as the reconstruction of a pulpit given to Tain by the " good regent Murray." (Taylor, *Researches into the History of Tain*, 1882, pp. 51-52.)

Particularly serious must have been the artistic loss involved in the destruction of tabernacles, those altarpieces, decorated with painted panels, or with niches, containing polychromed statues, adorned with carved and gilded canopies, which formed the most striking feature in the decoration of medieval churches and chapels. A fine example of such a tabernacle, made for a sixteenth-century Scottish confraternity in Denmark still survives at Copenhagen.[180] There were many in medieval Scotland, some, no doubt, painted or carved by native craftsmen, while others were imported from the continent. We can be certain that a proportion of these would rank highly as works of art. One thinks of Abbot Tervas of Paisley who, about 1455, brought home for the adornment of his abbey kirk, from renaissance Italy, " the statliest tabernakle that was in al Skotland and the maist costlie."[181] Some of these leaders in church and state were discriminating patrons of art, like King James III or Archbishop Schevez of St. Andrews, who had his medallion portrait done by no less an artist than Quentin Metsys. One surviving piece gives the lie to any facile assumption that the furnishings of Scottish medieval churches were necessarily unimportant—the panels painted, about 1470, by the great Flemish master Hugo van der Goes for Trinity College Kirk in Edinburgh. These pictures have escaped the general ruin, not because of their great artistic merit, but because they display royal portraits.[182] Most art-historians would probably regard the presence of these Van der Goes pictures in Scotland as a fortuitous and unaccountable phenomenon. It is not generally realised that Hugo van der Goes was related by marriage to the great miniaturist Alexander Bening, who was almost certainly a Scotsman from Edinburgh and that Bening, in his turn, was father-in-law to Andrew Halyburton, the Conservator of the Privileges of the Scottish Nation in the Netherlands.[183] Scots names occur, moreover, in Flemish artists' guilds in the century before the reformation and it is certainly not extravagant to think that, because of such relationships of friendship, marriage and trade, there were among the tabernacles which adorned Scottish churches, other altarpieces, not only by Hugo van der Goes, but also by other equally important Flemish masters. Neither can we exclude the possibility of occasional masterpieces from France, Germany or Italy, or even from the brush or chisel of native Scots artists, but we shall never know, because Moray and Argyll and the other lords of the Congregation, like their predecessors at Lauder Bridge in 1482, were not primarily interested in artistic and spiritual things.

The destruction of archives, manuscripts and printed books was deplorable from many points of view. Recent research has shown that the libraries of printed books possessed by churchmen and ecclesiastical institutions in sixteenth-century Scotland were far more important in size and content than had hitherto been suspected.[184] A strong current of the New Learning was coursing through some sections of the ecclesiastical life of Scotland and the preoccupation with books which this

---

180. Described and illustrated in *Innes Review*, vii, pp. 5-10.
181. *Auchinleck Chronicle*, p. 19.
182. Another example of a panel from a medieval Scottish diptych, preserved because it contains a portrait, is the well-known portrait of Bishop Elphinstone in the possession of the University of Aberdeen.
183. *Innes Review*, x, pp. 94-95.
184. *Innes Review*, ix, pp. 5-167. The survival of over one hundred volumes from the library of Henry Sinclair, Bishop of Ross, seems to be due to the fact that they were stored for safety in Roslin Castle, and even this incomplete list of his books shows the bishop to have been a man of wide culture, interested in contemporary intellectual trends.

research has revealed in some late medieval churchmen makes it credible that there is more than a grain of truth in Marcus Wagner's glowing description of the books he saw in the royal library at Edinburgh and in the monastic libraries of Scone, Cambuskenneth and St. Andrews, when he visited Scotland, in 1553, to collect historical material for Flacius Illyricus.[185] The Book of Hours of King James IV, now in Vienna, was presumably not the only richly illuminated manuscript in the royal collection and the fact that the very important Flemish miniaturists, Alexander and Simon Bening, were probably of Scottish origin and certainly related by marriage to the Scottish Conservator in the Netherlands increases the possibility of some really great artistic treasures among Scottish manuscripts. The twelfth-century glossed psalter which Wagner took away with him from Coupar Angus Abbey, and which is now in the Vatican Library was, according to his own account, far from being the most ancient manuscript he saw in Scottish monastic libraries. We do not know how much may have perished in the senseless attacks on cathedrals, monasteries, friaries and other churches: of several thousand liturgical books which must have existed, less than two hundred have survived. Goudanus with extensive experience of the religious upheaval in northern Europe, was struck by the fact that, in Scotland, "such is the insane fury of these men that they have not only cast away the images of saints but also burnt the writings of the holy fathers of the church."[186] The archives of cathedrals, monasteries and lesser churches have almost entirely disappeared (apart from the few registers and chartularies published by the nineteenth-century historical clubs) with incalculable loss to our knowledge of the ecclesiastical and civil history of Scotland. There is no lack of evidence that books were destroyed wholesale and, when Archbishop Spottiswoode speaks of "Bibliothecks destroied, the volumes of the fathers, councells and other books of humane learning, with the registers of the church, cast into the streets, afterwards gathered in heapes and consumed with fire,"[187] there is no reason why we should doubt his statement. Spottiswoode himself, when in 1609, he removed "a great number of popish books, copes, chalices, pictures, images, and such other popish trash" from Abbot Gilbert Brown's lodging at Sweetheart Abbey and burned them publicly, on a market day, in the High Street of Dumfries, had the grace to spare the books, which he handed over to Maxwell of Kirkconnell. We can only guess at all that perished in that orgy of destruction, but one point is worth making. Modern research has shown that in Scotland, as elsewhere, in late medieval times, love of music was widespread in ecclesiastical and secular life. Ecclesiastical music was composed, we know, by Scotsmen but all that has survived is Carver's book from Scone, an antiphonary from Dunkeld and four other lesser books. It would seem that, in this case, an entire section of medieval cultural achievement has been practically obliterated.

But apart from the probability that important treasures of artistic and historical value were wantonly destroyed in the systematic looting of churches at the peak of the reformation struggle, the sobering fact

---

185. Baxter, *Copiale Prioratus Sanctiandree*, pp. xxviii-xxix.
186. Pollen, *Papal Negotiations*, p. 136.
187. Keith, *Affairs of Church and State* (Spottiswoode Society), iii, p. 37. Gordon of Rothiemay gives the tradition of Aberdeen in his day (1661) about the fate of the Cathedral library: "To this church (St. Machar's Cathedral) lykewayes belonged a bibliotheck, bot about the yeer 1560 all wes taken away or destroyed or embaseled; the bibliothec then burned and no book spared, wher any reid letter wes to be seene."

remains that the furnishings of churches in carved wood and stone, in painting, embroidery and metal-work, whether it was of native or foreign manufacture, represented almost the entire cultural heritage and achievement of the nation. The wilful destruction of all this by mis-guided men was a national calamity of the first magnitude, the effects of which on native artistry and craftsmanship must have been far-reaching indeed. The thoroughness with which all accessories of Scottish medieval church worship were wiped out is unparalleled in Europe. The reformation in Germany or the French Revolution in France never achieved such a complete annihilation of the past, possibly because there was a speedier return to sanity. In Scotland, even after the initial violence had subsided, the process continued and spread into every corner of the land until every object that " smelled of popery " was destroyed or hidden out of sight. A mentality was produced that lasted on into the next century to find expression in acts such as the smashing of the lovely Anglo-Saxon rood at Ruthwell, in 1642, or the desecration of Elphin-stone's tomb, and who will state with certainty that that mentality has entirely disappeared, even yet ?

The evidence for the looting and purging of churches during 1559 and in subsequent years is beyond doubt, and the evidence, during the ensuing decades, for the widespread dismantling of monastic, cathedral, collegiate and even parish churches, which had been made redundant in whole or in part, is also indisputable. Such facts are beyond question, but to fasten the responsibility for all this wanton destruction, or to assign motives for it, is not so simple a matter. To begin with, there were the Calvinist preachers, who were so sure that they were right: then there was the " rascal multitude," part of it, no doubt, genuinely anti-catholic, part of it inspired solely by love of plunder and mischief. Both of these groups were immediately responsible for much of the vandalism. Finally, there were the nobles, a few of them undoubtedly inspired by zeal for " true religion," but most of them, one fears, hankering after security in their monastic acres and seeking additional seats in parliament for their kinsfolk. Without the nobles, the preachers and the mob would have achieved but little; the nobles must therefore bear the ultimate responsibility.[188] As a group, were they sincere? Judging from the record of their breed, it seems hardly likely. Perhaps the key to the whole question lies in a conversation between Arran and Sadler, in April, 1543, in which Arran told Sadler that it would be no easy matter to engineer a reformation in Scotland " for there be so many great men here, that be such papists and pharisees that unless the sin of covetise bring them

188.   The very great dependence of the preachers on the plans of the revolutionary nobles and on the political success or failure of those plans is evident throughout Knox's history and, on occasion, when the tail tries to wag the dog, as in the matter of the ratification of the *First Book of Discipline*, it becomes immediately evident who is really in control. The relationship between the " rascal multitude " and the nobles raises the very pertinent question: " What was the rascal multitude ? " The " rascal multitude " should not be regarded as a new phenomenon thrown up by the reformation—a spon-taneous and popular rising of the citizens of a town clamouring for evangelical religion. In every instance where it appears, its nucleus at least is made up from one of the normal adjuncts of Scottish life—the armed and undisciplined retainers that any Scottish magnate might take with him to burn down a neighbour's castle or intimidate a court of justice. When the " rascal multitude " is first mentioned at Perth, in 1559, it is quite simply the groups of retainers, brought by magnates from Angus and Dundee to overawe justice at the trial of the preachers, which was expected to take place. At Perth they were joined by genuine sympathisers and, no doubt, by riff-raff more interested in loot than in religion. This " rascal multitude " (which may not have been very multitudinous), left at a loose end because the expected trial did not take place and incited by Knox's preaching, proceeded to despoil the religious houses of the town. At Aberdeen, the " rascal multitude " was simply the retainers of the Mearns barons, who were joined by some citizens of the town. At St. Andrews its composition is similar. The " rascal multitude " should be regarded as an extension of the power of the revolutionary nobles, it is certainly not something independent of them.

to it, that is the desire of having the lands of the Abbeys, he knoweth none other mean to win them to his purpose in that behalf."[189] One suspects that the Scottish nobles were, in the main, converted to the principles of the reformation, not by Knox and Calvin, but by Sadler and Cecil.[190]

For Robert Boyd of Trochrig, lecturing to his students in Glasgow in the second decade of the seventeenth century, there was no doubt as to who had benefitted by the destruction of the monasteries. Instead of being made to serve a variety of useful purposes for the common good of the nation, their property had been grabbed by self-seeking men— " in illorum sacrilegorum laicorum manus et possessionem venisse quibus ea nunc in praedam cesserunt." There is scope for sardonic humour when we find this learned protestant divine repeating in elegant Latin precisely the same protestation that Ninian Winzet had expressed in vigorous Scots a full half century before.[191]

Abbot Quintin Kennedy was perhaps too close to the events to see clearly what had happened, and probably too closely related by kinship to the culprits to realise the overweening greed and selfishness of his own social class, when he claims that, if the hearts of the nobles had not been led astray by seditious preachers " than had nocht the policie of this realme bene put to utter confusione and wrakment, as it is, and that nocht without grete calamitie, miserie and hurt of the commoun wele. Than had nocht the antiquiteis andie monumentis of this realme bene schaimfullie distroyit, quhilkis in all uther realmis ar heichly prysit and regardit be all men of godlie leirnyng and jugement."[192]

To assign motives for the destruction of medieval churches and their equipment is even more difficult because the motives stem from every aspect of the complex revolution that was taking place. While we can state that all of the destruction most certainly resulted from the general revolutionary movement that we call the reformation, it is very often impossible to isolate the motive which impelled any particular group or person in each particular instance of vandalism. In the early stages of the revolution theological motives were uppermost: the destruction of

---

189. *Letters and Negotiations of Sir Ralph Sadler*, 1720, p. 148.

190. Knox's own reflections on the sincerity of some of the godly nobles appear when he speaks about the rejection of the *First Book of Discipline* (Dickinson's *Knox*, i, pp. 343-4).

191. Although printed only in 1652, the *Praelectiones in Epistolam ad Ephesios*, were delivered in Glasgow between 1615 and 1621. At page 1199, he comments on the fate of the monasteries: "Quae est sacrilega temporum nostrorum iniquitas, a nobis deflenda ac deploranda summopere ne illa quidem in pietatis usum supersunt loca religiosa, per hoc regnum universum olim commode et copiose constituta ; monasteria, inquam, sive coenobia, quae vel in hominum Christo soli famulantium stativa, vitaeque sanctioris exercitia, pii nostri majores opportune sacraverant, vel per illius aevi caecitatem superstitioni dicata, potuerunt a nobis, immo debuerunt, ad originis suae primaevae puritatem revocari, sublatoque sanctorum et idolorum cultu sacrilego, sublatis votorum laqueis in hominum conscientias temere et fraudulenter injectis, reliquoque fermento papisticae superstitionis expurgato secundum piae veritatis veraeque pietatis normam reformari : quo commodas quoque inter nos stationes et receptus opportunos haberent quicunque rerum secularium et curis et vinculis expediti cuperent vitae strictioris iter amplecti, carni et peccato bellum internecinum indicere, se ad Christi crucem tollendam accingere, se, ut eius decet athletas, per omnia continentes praebere, divinisque se totos obsequiis mancipare : ut his moribus informati, hac imbuti disciplina, hac pietatis palaestra diu multumque subacti et exerciti non sub florem tantum adolescentiae, sed et ad annos usque graviores, Deo post modum evocante, possent ex illis tanquam gazophylaciis, aut vasorum sacrorum armariis et apothecis, in omnes ecclesiae usus et necessitates acciri. Nunquid enim sic fieri, occupari septa illa claustralia praestitisset, quam in illorum sacrilegorum laicorum manus et possessionem venisse quibus ea nunc in praedam cesserunt . . . Et infra, ne quod uspiam piis ac devotis hominibus aut incipientibus aut proficientibus, aut emeritis et rude donatis inter nos receptaculum superesset, ne qua inter nos extaret nel iuventuti palaestra, vel senectuti proseucha, vel orbitati solatium, vel paupertati perfugium, vel virginitati secretum, vel viduitati receptus, vel devotioni secessus . . ."

192. Kennedy, *Ane Oratioune*, 1812, p. 12.

images, the " casting down " of churches by men inflamed by Master George Wishart's preaching; and the early attacks on friaries; all of these were inspired by doctrinal opinion. On the other hand the destruction of ecclesiastical buildings in the war zone of the English invasions is basically political. The vandalism of the years 1559-1560 stems from many sources: for the preachers, theological considerations would be supreme, for many of the nobles, political and economic reasons would urge them to the work; for the camp followers, the " rascal multitude," motives would range from religious convictions to mere rascality and mob hysteria. After 1560, the complete or partial dismantling of the fabric of monastic and other large churches by nobles and by town councils was part of the economic and social aspect of the revolution, and, in general, it had little or no theological significance. The new Calvinist church, while demanding, in its *Book of Discipline*, the demolition of cathedral, monastic, collegiate and other churches as " monuments of idolatry," was equally anxious to maintain the parish churches, but the efforts of their more enthusiastic followers to purge these buildings during 1559-1560 and the more selfish efforts of petty thieves, taking advantage of the lawlessness of the times, had, in many instances in the east-central lowlands, left even these buildings in a dilapidated state. As the new religious system began to organize itself and take effective control, the repair of parish churches was undertaken by town councils and other responsible bodies, beginning in the central area from the first years of the new regime and, as this movement spread out into the provinces, in the next couple of decades, everything that was characteristic of the old religion was rigorously eliminated and the motives, here again, were exclusively religious.

But no matter who was responsible and no matter what their motives were, the fact remains that, when the crisis of the reformation had passed, in Scotland, practically every single one of the larger churches was a complete or partial ruin and the lesser churches were shorn of their glory and very often damaged. For Master Alexander Craig, writing a poetic commendation of Habakkuk Bisset's *Rolment of Courtis*, in the early seventeenth century, the ruins of former ecclesiastical buildings were a conspicuous feature everywhere in the Scottish landscape:

" Tuixt wes, and is, how varius ar the ods:
Quhat one man doeth, an uther doeth ondou:
one consecratis religius workis to Gods:
ane Other leavs sad wrakis and Ruynis now.
Thy book doeth show that suich and suich thingis war,
But wald to god that it culd say they ar.

Quhen I pereir the south, north, east and wast
and mark (alas) each Monument amis:
Then I confer, tyms present with the past
and reid what wes, bot can nocht see what is.
I praise thy book, with woonder but am sorie
To reid old Ruynis in a recent storie."[193]

---

193. *Rolment of Courtis* (Scottish Text Society), i, p. 23.

By that time also the legend, which ascribed the chief part in the work of destruction to John Knox, was firmly established, as seems evident from the statement of that stalwart protestant traveller, William Lithgow who during his occasional wanderings in his native land during the first three decades of the seventeenth century, had apparently been impressed by what " Mr. Knoxe did with our glorious Churches of Abbocies and Monasteries (which were the greatest beauty of the kingdome) knocking all downe to desolation; leaving nought to be seene of admirable Edifices, but like to the Ruines of Troy, Tyrus and Thebes, lumpes of wals and heapes of stones."[194]

---

194.   William Lithgow, *The Totall Discourse*, 1640, p. 507. This popular ascription of the entire work of destruction to John Knox personally is to be found at an even earlier date. Cf., for example, the description of Elgin by John Taylor, the Water-Poet, in 1618: "From thence I went to Elgen in Murray, an ancient citie, where there stood a faire and beautifull church with three steeples, the walls of it and the steeples all yet standing; but the roofes, windowes and many marble monuments and toombes of honourable and worthie personages all broken and defaced: this was done in the time when ruine bare rule and Knox knock'd downe churches." (Hume Brown, *Early Travellers in Scotland*, p. 124).

ROME AND SCOTLAND, 1513-1625

by

WILLIAM JAMES ANDERSON

The year 1513 is chosen because of its importance not only in Scottish history as the date of the Battle of Flodden but also in the story of the papacy as the date of the death of Giuliano della Rovere (Pope Julius II), whose military and political activities form the European background to the attempted Scottish invasion of England, and the date of the election of his successor, Giovanni de' Medici as Pope Leo X. The date 1625 is chosen not only as the date of the death of King James VI and I but also as very close to a date of fundamental importance in the story of the administrative relations between the Holy See and the world. In 1622, Pope Gregory XV established the Congregation *de Propaganda Fide* ; thereafter and, for most purposes, up to 1908, contact between the Holy See and the catholics in Scotland, at that date few in number and wholly lacking church organisation, but presently to be organised into a " mission " with a superior whom we describe first as a prefect-apostolic then as a vicar-apostolic and, from 1878, as a true hierarchy with a diocesan episcopacy, was maintained exclusively through this Roman Congregation and not directly between the Holy See and the civil government and sovereign.

The change is of enormous importance: the vital date in the middle of this period is the recall of the nuncio, Vincenzo Laureo, bishop of Mondovi, in September 1566 by Pope Pius IV, and in particular his message of July 2nd 1567 after the news of the marriage of Mary Queen of Scots to Bothwell: " With regard to the Queen of Scots in particular, it is not His Holiness's intention to have any further communication with her, unless, indeed, in times to come he shall see some better sign of her life and religion than he has witnessed in the past."[1]

The old relations, which we can describe as late medieval, were never thereafter resumed; that did not mean there were not later personal contacts between Mary and the Holy See nor between her son and more than one pope. Some of these are of considerable interest, but they are not of a character which can be described as official relations between the Holy See and any " Ecclesia Scoticana ". For them we have to wait for many years; indeed we have to wait until it was finally realised that the papacy would have to deal for a long time to come with christian countries which were not catholic and with catholic minorities in those countries for whose spiritual welfare provision must be made even in opposition to the determined policy of non-catholic or violently anti-catholic civil governments. In devising a new type of relation the Barberini family and in particular Maffeo Barberini (Pope Urban VIII, 1623-1643) play an important part.

The papacy at the end of the fifteenth century under Pope Julius II was a strong military power, at any rate in Italy; it was also an active political power all over christendom; it was in the third place, spiritually the earthly head of the catholic church. The three activities are hard to harmonise. Loyalty to the pope and devotion to the pope are inculcated

---

1. Pollen, *Papal Negotiations*, pp. 287 ff. and especially page 397.

on every catholic and, in a very special degree, on every catholic bishop in peace and communion with him. There was to be in the sixteenth century a widespread repudiation of that loyalty both by layfolk and by many a bishop. The conflict of duties was obvious. Any armed citizen of Mirandola, in 1511, might have had the duty of sending a cannon-ball to finish the career of Pope Julius II in order to save his own city from pillage, and he would watch the pope climbing a scaling-ladder through the breached city-wall with feelings less than devotion to the shepherd and teacher of all christians. The young man designated to be arch-bishop of St. Andrews and primate of Scotland accompanied his father King James IV to Flodden; he knew well that Pope Julius had organised inside christendom a league against France, partly to drive French influence out of Italy, and that King Henry VIII, then a military defender of the papacy as he was later, under Pope Leo X, its theological defender of the faith, was attacking France at the formal request of the pope, and that Scotland was invading England precisely because of Henry VIII's attack on France, and in military opposition to the papacy. Loyalty to the papacy was being subjected to no small strain in the conscience of Mirandola catholics and of Scottish catholic prelates too. It is difficult to be spiritually loyal when the papacy is in open political alliance and perhaps in open military alliance with a national enemy. The problem re-appears again and again in the period and is a major factor preventing the reconciliation of separated christians.

The primary fact in the relation between the Holy See and the catholic ruler of a country we should describe as " catholic " is that they are in communion with each other, it is also hoped and expected that they are in friendly relations; this hope is an ideal by no means always a reality. But all normal contact between the Holy See and subjects of the catholic ruler are presumed to be with his approval and knowledge. This is of so great importance and is so unfamiliar to us in the modern world that it is really necessary to explain its consequences briefly. We think it of absolute right that the Holy See should have unrestricted and private access to any catholic bishop both by correspondence and by regular visits by bishops to the Holy See; we do not always or often consider that, in what have been called the " Ages of Faith," this free access did not in fact exist and the right was by no means admitted.

Moreover a catholic sovereign, his children and his heir-presumptive have this peculiar status still in modern canon law that they are not in any true sense spiritually subject to the catholic bishop in whose diocese they may be, they are subject to the Holy See alone and can be judged only by the Holy See and spiritual penalties can be inflicted on them only by the Holy See. Royal persons are subject to divine law, and as those who study the matrimonial career of King Henry VIII know well, it is no light matter to determine just what is divine law. " May a man marry his deceased brother's wife ? " is a clear example. If, on the other hand, such a restriction is of ecclesiastical law only, then the question whether a king may do so is entirely different from the question whether a simple lay catholic may do so. It would be exaggeration to say that a ruling sovereign is not subject to canon law; it is no exaggeration to say that only the pope can inflict on him any penalty for breaking it. This is still to be found in the current code of canon law, canon 2227. Dispensations from matrimonial impediments and judgments on the validity of royal marriages bulk largely in our history. Amateur canonists are well advised to refrain from discussing such matters and from applying normal rules to royal marriages whether of Mary Queen of Scots, or of Queen Victoria.

In the late middle ages bishops too and all prelates, that is to say all who had ordinary jurisdiction in the external forum, had frequently if not normally a relation to the state quite distinct from their spiritual status; they were often high officers of state, chancellors, keepers of the Privy Seal, senators or presidents of the College of Justice, and so forth; and they nearly always were land-holders often very extensive land-holders. Appointments to such prelacies, bishoprics or abbacies likely to be combined with high official status could not possibly be in the absolute discretion of the Holy See. In the last resort the Holy See is responsible for the appointment of any bishop, for example, of Thomas Cranmer to Canterbury; in theory a refusal of papal confirmation would deprive any bishop of the right to the obedience of his clergy or faithful, but this weapon could be used only in extreme emergency; in fact the power of the Holy See to appoint medieval bishops was comparatively small; it was very much less than it is when it is a question of an appointment to a bishopric in a modern non-catholic country where the government may well be uninterested, although for important dioceses strong political influences and considerations of prudence may well be brought to the notice of the Holy See and may affect appointments, as anyone can see by reading the life-story of Cardinal Manning.

One of the main topics in any complete account of the relations between Rome and Scotland so long as there were catholic bishops and catholic abbots in Scotland did however concern appointments to these important offices, and negotiations were on occasion long, complicated and disagreeable. Many much lesser benefices too could be filled only after negotiations with the Holy See. As at the present time the appointment may be reserved to the Holy See because of the status of the person to be appointed, for example if he is a member of the papal household; there were many such in the middle ages, the modern lay catholic, who may be inexpert in these matters, describes such men generally as monsignori. No bishop can appoint any such man to a benefice; it is reserved to the pope. In the medieval world, in a catholic country, the catholic king was also involved in every such appointment, not only directly but also indirectly from the fact that *all* communication with the Holy See, not only a personal visit to Rome by a bishop or prelate or their agents, but also correspondence with Rome was presumed to require and did in fact require authorisation from the king. If relations between pope and king were friendly, appointments might be made smoothly and satisfactorily, but the possibilities of obstruction and friction were infinite. Rival candidates for benefices took full advantage of these possibilities.

The relations between a catholic sovereign and the Holy See include what we call diplomatic courtesies: a sovereign on accession announces it to the Holy See and makes a profession of obedience and " adores and venerates " the lawful successor of St. Peter, and receives the papal blessing: so too the pope announces his election to catholic sovereigns and again sends his blessing. No historian takes such diplomatic courtesies at their face value. They prove indeed that so far diplomatic relations have not been broken off; and that is important; for a breaking off of relations may be a prelude to war; they do not necessarily mean much more. One can read in Theiner's *Monumenta*, Document mlxiv, and see in the Vatican archives the document by which the Regent Arran notified Pope Paul III of the death of King James V. It tells us nothing of the religious opinions of the Regent Arran. So too, Document dccccxlvi would be a poor guide to the loyalty of King Henry VIII to Pope Clement VII when he congratulated him on his election. Courtesy *may* be completely insincere. Envoys permanent or temporary for a special occasion may be exchanged. At that period of history it was customary for an envoy to deliver not only his credentials and " ostensible " instructions but also to make a " harangue," a Latin speech in his best rhetorical style. Such speeches are interesting as specimens of humanistic Latin and that is the sum-total of their value. An excellent example was printed by Pollen in *Papal Negotiations* pp. 204-7: it was delivered by William Chisholm, bishop of Dunblane and administrator of Vaison to Pope Pius IV on behalf of Mary Queen of Scots in 1563: but ambassadors then as now had additional instructions, not ostensible, which may modify profoundly or even directly contradict the ostensible instruction they reveal to those to whom they are accredited. The opening of diplomatic archives reveals what ambassadors were told to say and what they wanted others to believe. Even a papal brief of congratulation may prove little more than that the pope may wish to be polite; it does not tell us his opinion of the potentate to whom he writes. Papal diplomacy is no better a guide to historical truth than any other diplomacy.

Papal diplomatic practice has continually changed and was in fact, at the beginning of the sixteenth century, changing rapidly.[2] In modern times we expect to find a papal nuncio in any important country willing to receive one and he is normally an archbishop. In return there will be a permanent ambassador accredited to the Vatican. Smaller countries have diplomats of lesser rank. For various reasons, one of which was certainly its small size and lesser importance, and we may perhaps add, its climate for medieval Scotland was no pleasure resort for any renaissance Italian— Scotland never had a permanent nuncio, even of lesser status. Other methods were used: the papal court may receive, as an ambassador, a cleric or a layman of noble rank, but send no permanent envoy: his place and functions are entrusted to the chief ecclesiastic in the country or even to an ecclesiastic of high but second rank (one thinks of the status of Thomas Wolsey in England, who was Archbishop of York, never of Canterbury) on whom the pope confers ambassadorial functions: if a cardinal he is *legatus a latere*: if not a cardinal he may have similar powers but not necessarily the title.[3] Possibilities are by no means exhausted: certain duties in the Court of Rome might be entrusted to a cardinal " in curia," who is a native of some country but permanently resident in Rome. (One thinks in this period of the peculiar status of Christopher

---

2. On this topic, its background and significance, see Garrett Mattingly, *Renaissance Diplomacy*, London, 1955. Abundant references to the very considerable literature will be found in the notes to that book.

3. Practice varies. The great source for the whole subject of legates in Scotland is still Joseph Robertson, *Concilia Scotiae*, Bannatyne Club, 1866, and its very learned notes throughout: cf. vol. i, p. cxi. He quotes Barbosa and other famous canonists, but seventeenth century practical hand-books of canon law are not necessarily quite a safe guide for practice in sixteenth-century Scotland. We have, too, certain documents, e.g. the legatine faculties granted in 1552 or thereabouts, which are among the Warrender Papers and are summarised as Document xxxi in Cameron and Rait, *Warrender Papers*, vol i (Scottish History Society) Edinburgh, 1931. For such powers there was, no doubt, a standard type, as for episcopal faculties at the present time, yet the powers of a legate *a latere* can be determined only by seeing his faculties, including any private or secret faculties he may have received in any particular instance.

Bainbridge, really an absentee from York). But any cardinal in curia, whether secular or regular, is likely to have special functions in the papal court in dealing with any country of which he is a native. Specialised knowledge was greatly needed: reference books and atlases were so primitive as to be almost non-existent: when the time came to confirm the appointment of a bishop for Caithness, it is difficult to feel any confidence that any very coherent account of the diocese of Caithness was available in Rome. Perhaps even in St. Andrews it was little known. One gets the impression that Scotland and Scottish affairs were none too well-known in Rome in this period: many Scots went to Rome on special business chiefly benefice-hunting, and petitions naturally put forward the point of view of the petitioner: errors exist in the registers, at times incompatible appointments were made by which a benefice is apparently given to two rival petitioners: there were Scottish ecclesiastics in the curia: but large parts of Scotland were imperfectly known even in Scotland.

Papal envoys on special errands arrive from time to time in Scotland, sometimes they are visits of courtesy, sometimes the envoy is correctly described as a tax-collector: a number of them will be mentioned but our knowledge of them and of their work is very far from complete.

Yet only those who have looked into the sources can realise how much Scottish business was transacted in Rome in the period when Scotland was catholic. Much of it was pure routine, but it went on day by day and week by week. It is easy to forget the lesser routine business and to think only of royal letters, and papal briefs and of visits by bishops or prelates and other high ecclesiastics. There were plenty of others. So far little has been published from papal registers of this period: for an earlier period, viz. the ten years 1418-1428, Dr. Dunlop has filled two large volumes of the Scottish History Society with calendared supplications for benefices or dispensations. We can only assume that, for the period 1513-1542, six similar volumes would be required. Week by week appointments were being made to Scottish parishes, whose very names often need research by present-day readers : there was certainly no gazetteer for Scotland in the Vatican in 1520. Moreover the modern work done by Dr. Dunlop was never done when the items were being registered. The Scottish items were never co-ordinated and indexed, they were buried in chronological order in registers dealing with the whole christian world: it is only now that we begin to draw conclusions as to the extent of pluralism and of dispensations from the law preventing the holding of incompatible benefices, or of the number of children of tender age who drew ecclesiastical revenues. We can, by a laborious research, know a great deal more about Scotland than was known in Rome while these records were being compiled. The fees collected from Scotland were duly reckoned up: we can now, if we like to take the trouble, card-index and follow up the career of a successful benefice-hunter all over Scotland. If that had been done one wonders if the formal " Fiat ut petitur " might have been refused if his previous petitions had been collected into a modern office file.

At the beginning of this period Scotland was in unfriendly and equivocal relations with the Holy See and narrowly escaped interdict. The king died while in active military support of France, the political enemy of the pope. King Henry VIII chose to regard King James IV as excommunicated and asked leave to bury the dead king in St. Paul's

Cathedral. He also had a plan for the ecclesiastical re-organisation of Scotland. He asked the pope to suppress the archbishopric of St. Andrews and to bring Scotland under York. He hoped to have a control of the appointments occasioned by the ecclesiastical casualties at Flodden and the fact that some surviving ecclesiastics, who had been active combatants, were certainly under church censures. Scotland was not, however, schismatic; the pope allowed a thanksgiving mass for the English victory in Santa Maria del Popolo in Rome but did not break off relations with Scotland. He did take the opportunity to try and make appointments, e.g. to St. Andrews without any royal approbation.

On the coronation of the young King James V on September 21st 1513, formal letters announcing it were sent to the pope and courteously acknowledged: the tension however continued and formal obedience was not sent till 1517. Just before the news of Flodden reached Rome, Pope Leo X had appointed a nuncio to Scotland, named Balthasar Stuerd " praepositus clavasii, cubicularius et familiaris noster." He is known as the bearer of other papal letters, at this time he had apparently financial duties collecting money, presumably on a commission basis since the appointment was a reward. He did not get to Scotland till 1515, travelling via Brussels, Calais and England, and he had a companion, the secretary of Cardinal Cibo. At the frontier of Scotland the papal nuncio to England, Giovanni Pietro Caraffa (the future Pope Paul IV), was refused admission to Scotland and so was Cardinal Cibo's agent while Stuerd was admitted only on humiliating conditions.[4]

In the *Laing Charters* will be found documents showing the activities of the nuncio, Balthasar Stuerd, convalidating a marriage, inducting a dean of Ross and vicar of Auchtermuchty; no doubt other similar routine business was done but his functions were apparently chiefly financial. He did not leave Scotland till Albany's arrival, which was on 16th May 1515.

Andrew Forman did not succeed in making himself a national figure or ecclesiastical leader. It is supposed that some of his levies on his diocese were made for the purpose of enabling him to attain and maintain his position as a cardinal, and in that ambition he was not successful. He made a praiseworthy attempt to introduce reforming legislation in a synod, but how far that application in Scotland of the Fifth Council of the Lateran was effective we really do not know. Albany had attempted to prevent his getting the powers of a *legatus a latere* and when he did get these powers, which gave him authority to visit exempt houses of religious, we know, for example, that he almost at once conceded immunity from episcopal visitation to the Cluniac houses of Paisley and Crossraguel. It has been suggested that in return he had a financial consideration for so

---

4. Cardinal Cibo, son of Francesco Cibo, who was a son of Pope Innocent VIII by Maddalena de' Medici, sister of Pope Leo X, became cardinal on the accession of Leo X. The pope intended him to be archbishop and, in the first place, administrator of St. Andrews; the idea of appointing an Italian cardinal to a diocesan bishopric is familiar in England, cf. the appointment of Lorenzo Campeggio to Salisbury in 1524. Both King Henry VIII and the Scots had different ideas about St. Andrews, and after complicated negotiations Cibo became Archbishop of Bourges while Andrew Forman resigned Bourges and got St. Andrews; Forman also got the coveted status of *legatus a latere*. It may be worth pointing out that there appears to be a considerable confusion in the text, notes, and especially in the index of Hannay and Hay, *Letters of James V*, Edinburgh, 1954. The " Cardinal of St. Mark " who was protector of Scotland is Domenico Grimani; he was first cardinal deacon of St. Nicholas inter Imagines, then cardinal priest of the title of St. Mark. Cardinal Innocenzo Cibo was cardinal deacon of the title of SS. Cosmas and Damian and then cardinal of Sancta Maria in Domnica, never of St. Mark. Nor was he, apparently, ever cardinal protector of Scotland, though in the index to Hannay and Hay he is listed as such. An opinion on the character of Innocenzo Cibo will be found in Pastor's *History of the Popes* (Eng. trans., vii, pp. 82-3) ; it is completely unfavourable.

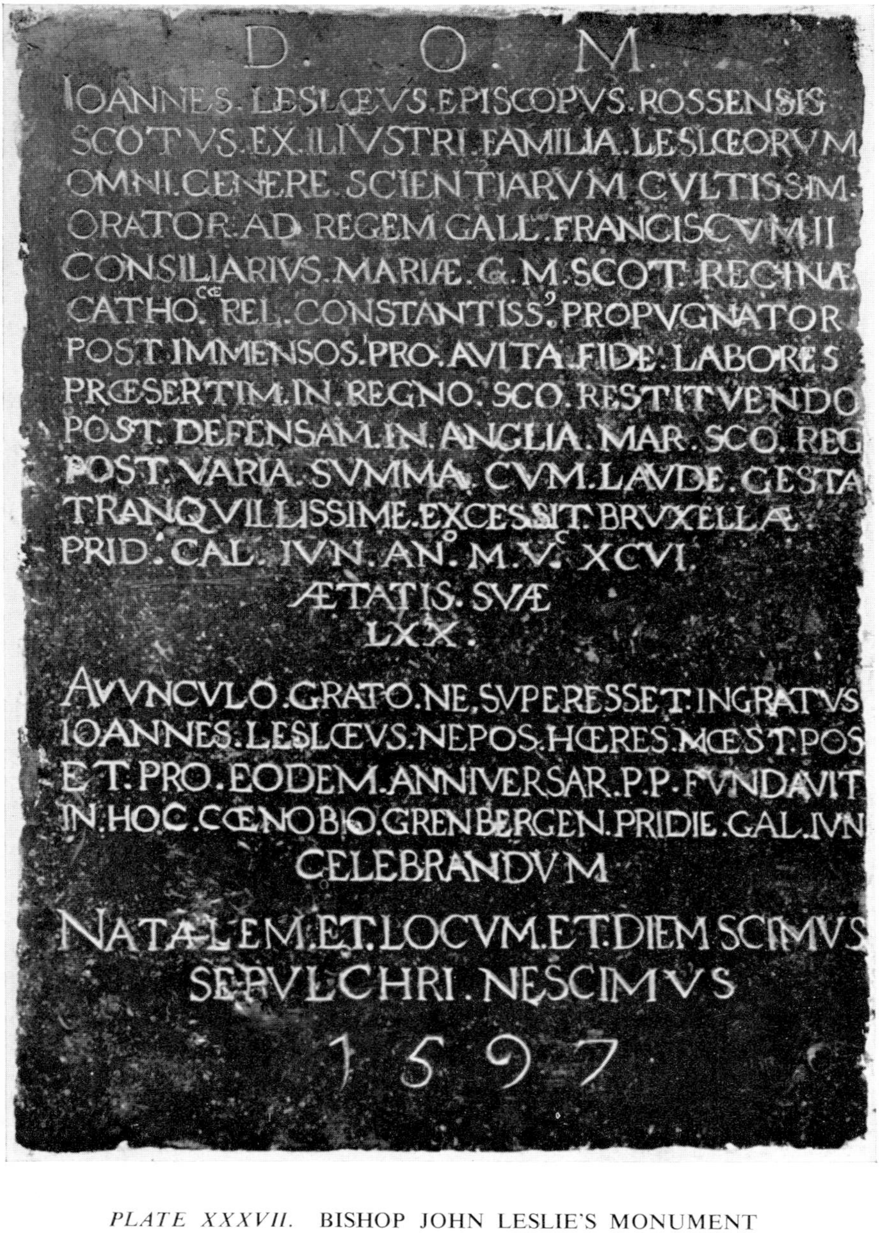

D. O. M.

IOANNES. LESLŒVS. EPISCOPVS. ROSSENSIS
SCOTVS. EX. ILLVSTRI. FAMILIA. LESLŒORVM
OMNI. GENERE. SCIENTIARVM. CVLTISSIM.
ORATOR. AD. REGEM. GALL. FRANCISCVM. II
CONSILIARIVS. MARIÆ. G. M. SCOT. REGINÆ
CATHO.ce REL. CONSTANTISS.9 PROPVGNATOR
POST. IMMENSOS. PRO. AVITA. FIDE. LABORES
PRÆSERTIM. IN. REGNO. SCO. RESTITVENDO
POST. DEFENSAM. IN. ANGLIA. MAR. SCO. REG
POST. VARIA. SVMMA. CVM. LAVDE. GESTA
TRANQVILLISSIME. EXCESSIT. BRVXELLÆ
PRID. CAL. IVN. AN.o M. V.c XCVI.
ÆTATIS. SVÆ
LXX.

AVVNCVLO. GRATO. NE. SVPERESSET. INGRATVS
IOANNES. LESLŒVS. NEPOS. HŒRES. MŒST. POS
ET. PRO. EODEM. ANNIVERSAR. P. P. FVNDAVIT
IN. HOC. CŒNOBIO. GRENBERGEN. PRIDIE. CAL. IVN
CELEBRANDVM

NATALEM. ET. LOCVM. ET. DIEM. SCIMVS
SEPVLCHRI. NESCIMVS
1597

PLATE XXXVII.   BISHOP JOHN LESLIE'S MONUMENT
AT GRIMBERGEN.

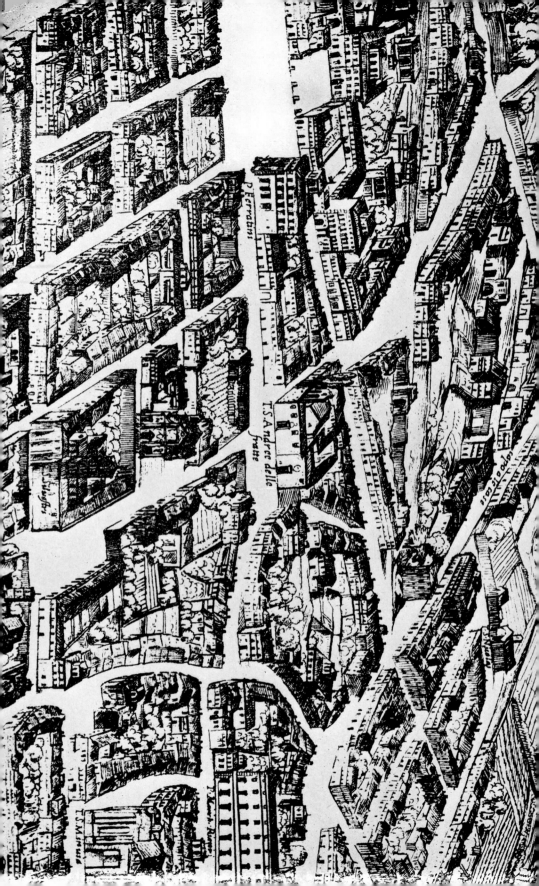

doing. Certainly sometimes his legatine powers were resisted, as in Dunkeld, where he attempted to make an appointment by legatine authority: his messengers were threatened and warned that if they returned they would be thrown over the bridge into the Tay.

It is not easy to judge dispassionately the attitude of King James V to the church and the papacy. A catholic historian like Bellesheim tries to pass a favourable verdict " Notwithstanding his somewhat arbitrary and high-handed dealings with the clergy, James V continued steadfast in his attachment to the Catholic Faith, and in his efforts to promote the best interest of the Scottish Church."

More recent catholic historians tend to accept in large measure the verdict of Professor Hannay who in many writings has discussed his actions rather than his words. It was in this reign that a healthy reform was still possible, no doubt difficult, but there was still time. Church reform was possible only through active co-operation between a determined king and a zealous and competent churchman, both working with papal approval. It is true he resisted the suggestion of King Henry VIII that he might copy the English example and quarrel with the pope and raid monastic wealth: but it can be maintained that he got all he wanted far more easily by *not* copying the English example. In England the suppression of monasteries was very unpopular, and much of their wealth never reached the king. In Scotland we find no need to suppress Kelso or Melrose: one illegitimate son of the king, could, as an infant, become commendatory abbot of both: another son, Robert, could become commendator of Holyrood: another, John, could become prior of Coldingham: and the list is not exhausted. Adam, another of his illegitimate sons appears to have been appointed prior of the Perth Carthusians and to have resigned in favour of a true monastic prior but on consideration of a very substantial pension which was, apparently, being paid to Adam Stewart right up to the end of monastic life in the Perth Charterhouse. For such grave breaches of church order, papal dispensations were necessary and they were available: indeed, the king held a papal permission for three of his illegitimate sons, all born before his own marriage, but one by a married woman, to hold the highest benefices, *including the primacy*, from the age of twenty, suppressing in any bull of provision all mention of irregularity and including in addition the capacity to hold three, four *or more* incompatible benefices. An extensive collection of the letters of King James V is now easily accessible. He received a warning from the pope about Lutheran heresy, sent in a letter by the hands of the Dominican, James Crichton, he replied by the same man and protested to the pope his hatred of all heresy, Lutheranism included, but he added a plain hint that there was still further business to be settled and certain privileges of Scotland which James Crichton will explain. Loyalty on the part of the king deserves concessions in return. Pressure was being put on the papacy to grant some very extraordinary dispensations from most salutary rules of discipline. We find, for example, a certain John Steil being made a cleric at the age of six but, so it is stated, " though youth may be an obstacle to holding a benefice, a father's merits and a sons' promise *often* demand that the rigour of the law should be relaxed." Few royal letters lack a clause asking for some further dispensation from the papacy. Patrick Panter, no doubt an excellent royal secretary and abbot of Cambuskenneth has a series of letters: he had exceptional opportunities but, in addition to

PLATE XXXVIII *Opposite—*

DETAIL FROM TEMPESTA'S PANORAMIC MAP OF ROME, 1593.

his absolution from the censure incurred at the Battle of Flodden, he slips in a clause asking for permission to hold, in addition to what he already held, further incompatible benefices. He keeps on asking for more and more and one cannot avoid the conclusion that he regarded the Holy See primarily as a fount of dispensation from church discipline, as well as of the most generous plenary indulgence to be gained as often as needed in the danger of death, on the most liberal conditions possible. In all such letters expressions of filial loyalty to the Holy See abound and there was, indeed, much politeness. Complimentary regalia give an occasion for more. In 1514, King Henry VIII got a papal sword and cap from Pope Leo X: then, in 1534, King James V got the Garter from King Henry VIII: and on Christmas Night 1536, Pope Paul III blessed a cap and sword for King James V and sent them to Scotland by a papal chamberlain, John Antony Count de Campeggio. On that ceremonial occasion Sir David Lindsay, who was certainly Lyon Herald in 1535, would be on duty: one wonders if his comments on the ecclesiastics present resembled in any way those to be found in the dramatic perform-ance he gave at Linlithgow on Epiphany 1540, which is] the first version of *Ane Satyre of the Thrie Estaitis.*

That work is highly relevant to any consideration of Bellesheim's opinion that King James V " continued steadfast in his efforts to promote the best interests of the Scottish Church." In the introduction to the most recent edition of the Satire (London 1954), Miss Agnes Mure Mackenzie says " Even a fastidious lady of the Renaissance (and Marie had an unblemished reputation and great personal dignity) could take a joke of considerable breadth, while the more cerulean parts would be played in her absence " (p.20). Now the predecessor of Mary of Guise, Madeleine, the first queen of King James V, was a daughter of King Francis I: is it likely she had never met her aunt, Margaret of Navarre, authoress or perhaps only patroness of the authors of the *Heptameron*, which contains at least as coarse and blasphemous lampooning of clergy and especially of Franciscans? There is no sound reason for doubting that both King James and Queen Mary sat through the complete play and enjoyed it. This is not incompatible in any way with the letter of King James V in praise of the Observant Friars and with the assertion that both he and his father held them in veneration. Another letter shows he knew all about the internal dissensions in the Seraphic Order and about a Franciscan, and an Observant Franciscan at that, who had turned Lutheran.   Enough evidence has already been given of the moral character of the king, and, we may add, of the series of ladies of good family who bore his numerous children. He found the papacy useful and had no wish to break with it: he was unfitted to collaborate with it in a serious work of practical re-organisation and reform which were sorely needed in Scotland. Many of his actions speak for themselves: the foundation of the College of Justice was a notable achievement: the bull which established it secured that its cost was largely met from church funds. Again Professor Hannay has pointed out certain aspects of the struggle between the crown and the papacy over episcopal appointments. Delay in presenting a candidate might be made to appear a laudable desire to investigate the merits of several candidates. It has quite another aspect if we remember that the crown drew the revenue from the vacant benefice: there is a financial motive for prolonging a vacancy and seldom any benefit but often great harm to the diocese.

We hear of another papal nuncio who came in 1532, Silvester Dario by name: one of his functions was to confirm and strengthen another privilege by which the first trial of any ecclesiastical cause had to be in Scotland. No doubt the raising of an action at Rome in the first instance might be very burdensome and it is certainly abnormal, nevertheless this privilege is a limitation of the right of access to a Roman court by any catholic and such restrictions are rightly regarded with some suspicion.

In 1536, Pope Paul III sent into Scotland the General of the Servites, Dionisio Loreri, apparently for the sole purpose of announcing the General Council at Mantua, which was one of the first attempts at getting together the Council of Trent. The king was at that time in France for his marriage to Madeleine de Valois on 1st January, 1536-37 and the invitations to the Scottish bishops were entrusted to David Beaton, the future cardinal. This was very welcome news to those anxious for reform, but a great deal had still to be done before the reforming council got to work.[5] One cannot avoid remarking that the Council of Trent began in 1545 and did not end until 1564 with its papal ratification. There were difficulties about the attendance of many bishops, one difficulty however was a lack of desire on the part of many a bishop to go. It is quite true that excuses were made by Queen Mary to the pope and by the Cardinal of Lorraine to the council. It is also true that the absence of bishops too timid to see a papal legate, when he came to Scotland, as Goudanus found them to be, was no great loss to the council. It is quite untrue to suggest they could not get leave to depart from Scotland. In 1563, Henry Sinclair, Bishop of Ross got leave to go to Paris for reasons of health: James Beaton had been there since 1560: once in Paris, a man *can* get to Trent. Anyhow the fact is relevant to any discussion of the relations between Rome and Scotland. No Scottish bishop attended any session of Trent.

The quarrel between Henry VIII and the pope introduces a new complication into the relations between England and Scotland and the political aspects of the relation between Rome and Scotland in any serious study of the reformation. We need not minimise theology or the question whether man is justified by faith alone or whether the mass is a true sacrifice: the answer to neither question is ascertainable by observation or experiment, however important may be the consequences of heretical answers in catholic practice: but anyone can have an opinion whether it was or was not in the interest of Scotland to be in friendly political relations with the papacy. The Three Estates, in August 1560, set down very clearly the opinion that communion with the Holy See, which depended on recognition of papal jurisdiction in spiritual matters had been in the past and was now prejudicial to Scottish interests: this opinion continues to the present day and is the major obstacle to reconciliation between Rome and Scotland. This is what the Estates said; " The thre estaitis then being present understanding that the jurisdictioun and autoritie of the bischops of Rome called the paip usit within this realme in tymes bypast has been verray hurtful and prejudiciall to our soveranis autoritie and commone weill of this realme, thairfor etc., etc." The idea of putting pressure of a political character on England, including even threat of war and actual war, in order to

---

5. References for this will be found in Hubert Jedin, *A History of the Council of Trent*, English translation London, 1957, p. 314.

induce England to return to peace and communion with the Holy See, occurred to many for a lengthy period after the reformation. All catholic countries were at least *possible* political enemies. One of these enemies was catholic Scotland. Scotland was strategically placed as a suitable base for occupation either by France or by Spain, whenever relations between one of these countries and England was bad. England had plenty of motives (quite apart from any apostolic zeal to spread the gospel according to Luther, Calvin or Cranmer) to desire the severance of relations between Rome and Scotland. Few Scots of any standing had not lost relatives at the national disaster of Flodden: one can hardly blame the nobles who were very half-hearted indeed at any policy of political hostility to England, and at any permanent and irrevocable alliance or (as was planned) dynastic union with France. The readiness of Scottish nobles to accept pensions from England has often been commented on: but both sides had financial temptations: Cardinal David Beaton had French citizenship, his name was put forward for the cardinalate by the French king as bishop of Mirepoix. It was a rich diocese. Cardinal David Beaton is certainly the most dramatic and the most picturesque figure in the story of the relations between Rome and Scotland. On the one hand, he can be represented as a patriotic anti-English catholic cardinal archbishop of St. Andrews but those who agree with the opinion of the Three Estates in 1560, will describe him as a French citizen who had attained through French influence the highest but one ecclesiastical dignity and had rich French benefices while at the time he became cardinal he had the confident expectation of becoming the primate of Scotland and occupant of its richest diocese and abbot of its richest abbey. Bishop John Leslie says of his predecessor, James Beaton, " Before his death he had provided successors to all his benefices . . . Mr. David Betoun, then being Cardinal, to the Archbishopric of St. Andrews and the Abbacy of Arbroath." The Scottish patriots on the opposing sides of the debate had, from different sources, powerful incentives to patriotism.[6] The hope of a permanent, if possible dynastic, union between Scotland and England was no new ideal: it had appealed to John Major, whose " Historia Majoris Britanniae tam Angliae quam Scotiae " was dedicated to James V as in the line of descent of both kingdoms. The ideal was that ascribed to Sir David Lindsay, " Habitare fratres in unum / is a blessfull thyng / One God one faith one Baptisme pure / One lawe one land and one kyng / Clappe handes together brethren dere, / unfained truce together make / and like freendes dooe ever accorde / But French and Romaine doe first forsake / You are without the continent / a sole lande of ancient fame / Ab origine a people olde / Bolde Britaines ecleped by name / Sicut erat in principio / Graunt oh God, it maie bee / in saecula seculorum. (Printed by William Bullein in 1564). But its condition was obvious: either England must return to the communion of the Holy See or Scotland must break that union. The desire to be queen of both Scotland and England is the cause of the tragedy of Mary Stuart: her son inherited the ideal and achieved it: if that ideal is put first before peace and communion with the Holy

---

6. In Leslies' Latin: " Hic Antistes, quosdam quos egregie caros habuit, vivus constituebat, ut in beneficia, sibi mortuo, sufficerentur, in Episcopatum Sanctandreapolitanum ac in Abbatiam Arbrothensem, vir summa prudentia et animi magnitudine praestans, David Betonius Cardinalis, ejus ex fratre nepos; in Abbatiam vero Dunfermlingensem Georgius Durius; et in alia denique alii; quam illius voluntatem Rex non impedivit, quominus illi quos Archiepiscopus ante obitum constituerat, beneficiis libere fruerentur, ne cujus vivi mentem semper laudaverat ejus mortui voluntatem malitiose videretur rescidisse." *De Rebus Gestis Scotorum* Lib. ix (page 429 of edition of 1675).

See then its relevance to the relation between Rome and Scotland needs no emphasis.

To the opposite policy of Cardinal Beaton was attributed the next disaster, the rout of Solway Moss. Thereafter followed the Treaty of Greenwich by which, on July 1st 1543, commissioners of Scotland and of England agreed to a marriage between Prince Edward and the infant Queen Mary. On this period amateur moral theologians are well advised to refrain from passing judgment: it would appear that in 1543 England and Scotland were of one religion and that the people of each country could and did receive holy communion side by side at a catholic altar: we are tempted to describe Henry VIII in 1543 as, at least, " schismatic " and to claim that the worship in Holyrood was catholic. Here is Knox's account of the solemn ratification of that treaty; " In the end, so well were all ones content (the Cardinal, the Queen and the faction of France ever excepted) that solemnly in the Abbey of Holyroodhouse, was the contract of marriage betwix the persons foresaid, together with all the clauses and conditions requisite for the faithful observation thereof, read in public audience, subscribed, sealed, approved and allowed of the Governor for his part and the nobility and lords for their parts: and that nothing should lack that might fortify the matter was Christ's body sacred (as Papists term it), broken betwix the said Governor and Master Sadler, Ambassador, and received of them both as a sign and token of the unity of their minds, inviolably to keep that contract, in all points, as they looked of Christ Jesus to be saved, and after to be reputed men worthy of credit before the world." We are tempted to think a general communion of the commissioners as a highly irregular proceeding, but 1543 is not 1959. There could hardly be a more solemn way of showing the unity of their religion (whatever it was) and whatever was the religion of the abbey of the Holy Rood. The Holy See in the person of a cardinal " always excepted."

At this moment there was also in Scotland a representative of the Holy See in the person of Marco Grimani, patriarch of Aquileia. Long afterwards, in 1566, on the occasion of his reception by the Pope, William Chisholm, bishop of Dunblane spoke of the many ambassadors from popes, who had come to Scotland, mentioning inevitably Aeneas Sylvius (Pope Pius II) and he goes on to say" There was also Marco Grimani, a Venetian and patriarch of Aquileia who made himself exceedingly beloved among us as well for his many excellent qualities and especially for his liberality toward the poor. Last of all I will name Petrus Lippo-manus who would have equalled or even surpassed the others if a longer life had been granted to him." The English Privy Council notified Sir Ralph Sadler on May 13th 1543 of the coming of Grimani. He is believed to have stayed until March 1544 and to have been sent to urge co-operation in a crusade against King Henry VIII, with powers to levy contributions from the clergy for that purpose but he was also believed to have brought large sums of money with him for that purpose also. We are, however, inadequately informed about his functions and activities. During that period Cardinal Beaton became legate *a latere*, presumably to continue Grimani's jurisdiction and authority after he left. It is precisely stated in a document quoted in Hume Brown's *Life of Knox*, (ii, p.301) from a private collection, that Pope Paul III sent on two occasions Grimani and Lippomano " with large sums of money " to assist in a reformation, and a setting in order of the church, and its maintenance and defence against the new sects beginning to appear in the kingdom, supported by the neighbouring English sectaries. We hear from French sources that Lippomano had a large sum of money with him when he was in France. In spite of many allusions we seem to be extremely ill-informed about Pietro Lippomano.[7]

The political situation changed rapidly, especially through the disappearance of key-figures. In the first place Cardinal Beaton was murdered on 29th May 1546 at the instigation of King Henry VIII, who himself died in January, 1547. The invasion of Scotland under the Protector Somerset was only partially successful, but the Battle of Pinkie was a further Scottish disaster and a further warning of the political consequences of any quarrel with England.

Only Almighty God knows the hearts of kings, queens and regents, and of a regent's chaplains. It would be hard to describe the religious affiliation of the Regent Arran's two Dominican chaplains one of whom is credited with a translation of the New Testament into the vulgar tongue. We found Arran at his devotions in Holyrood on August 25th 1543: and apparently receiving holy communion side by side with Sir Ralph Sadler. We find him, on September 8th 1543, in the Greyfriars of Stirling and acknowledging that he was responsible for the suppression of sundry abbeys and friaries, and especially that it was by his consent the friaries of Dundee were sacked. For this he received absolution from Cardinal Beaton on promising to defend the profession of monks, friars " and suche other." He then heard mass and received the sacrament, "and the Earls of Argyll and Bothwell held the towel over his head for the time he was receiving of the sacrament." Next day they went on to crown the young queen. One could hardly have a more solemn restoration of good relations between Rome and Scotland. On the murder of the cardinal, Arran announced it to the pope in a fulsome letter containing a panegyric in which he said he had been accustomed to share all his plans and all his thoughts with the cardinal and that he felt his loss like the loss of a father. Official relations with the Holy See could alone secure the appointment of a Hamilton to the see of Glasgow, and on the death of Gavin Dunbar in 1547 the regent commended his illegitimate brother James. (This nomination was unsuccessful but later, in 1553, James Hamilton was provided to Lismore; never consecrated, he, in due course, married, became a protestant and died bishop of Argyll in 1579-1580).

In the absence of suitable terminology one might call the Regent Arran a non-christian catholic. But again we must refer to the Code of Canon Law, canon 1557; " Ipsius Romani Pontificis dumtaxat jus est judicandi eos qui supremum tenent populorum principatum horumque

---

7. Father Pollen, *Papal Negotiations*, summarises references in the Letter-book of Ferreri, and the correction of John Durkan in *Innes Review*, i (1950), p. 61, should be noted as well as further extract from the same source on page 66. There can be no question that he did arrive in Scotland on a ship of the French fleet, the war going on in the summer of 1548 may well explain the little notice taken of him. He carried a letter of recommendation from Ferreri to Bishop William Gordon, bishop of Aberdeen. It is also certain that he died in Scotland and, apparently, in Edinburgh. It does seem odd that allusion to this seems not to be found in the fairly abundant letters and papers concerning Scotland so far published from Scottish sources. But in any case his embassy was too brief to have any result and conditions were far from propitious. There is indeed a letter from Arran to Pope Paul III written from Dunbarton Castle and signed by him at " Haddington, IV Kal. Aug. 1548 " protesting at the pope's failure to accept Arran's nominee, Donald Campbell, abbot of Coupar, for the bishopric of Dunkeld and hostile to the claims of Robert Crichton. In it Peter Lippomano, Bishop of Verona, is mentioned and it can be gathered that part of his instruction had been to look into this matter; Arran assures the pope that the bishop of Verona " si viveret " would have seen his point of view. This letter is in the eighteenth-century transcript of John Leslie's Royal Letter-book in the Blairs Archives now in Edinburgh. (A complete photostat of the book can be consulted in the General Register House).

filios ac filias, eosve quibus jus est proxime succedendi in principatum. (2) Patres Cardinales. (3) Legatos Sedis Apostolicae et, in criminalibus, episcopos, etiam titulares."

Some slight comment must also, however, be made on the Regent Arran's successor the queen-mother, Mary of Guise, and in particular on her suitability to be the intermediary between the Holy See and the Ecclesia Scoticana. In this period there were many strange royal marriages, including the three contracted by and others proposed for Mary Queen of Scots, who could plead maternal example. After three years of marriage to the Duc de Longueville, to whom she bore two children, Mary of Guise became a widow in 1537 at the age of 21. At this moment there was an eligible widower in England. By this time King Henry VIII had already divorced his first wife Catherine, married and beheaded his second wife Anne, Catherine had died in 1536 and, in that same year, he married Jane, who died in 1537. On Henry's somewhat surprising invitation to Mary of Guise to become his fourth wife, she did not indignantly refuse but replied " that he would find her a true and plain gentlewoman in all her proceedings and singularly well affected to all his majesty's desires." Her presence at the performance of the Satire of the Three Estates has also been mentioned. As a widow she paid a visit to King Edward VI at Hampton Court: one could wish to have had her opinions about Bishop Nicholas Ridley whose guest she was in the City of London: did she regard him as the catholic bishop of London? It appears that she came to Hampton Court on 31st October, 1551: and on the 1st of November she " perused the house of Hampton Court and spent some time coursing the deer. " Next morning she went down the Thames in very great state to St. Paul's where the bishop of London (Ridley) received her in his palace. It will have been observed that the days are All Saints and All Souls. Nicholas Ridley disapproved of the mass, and did not keep All Souls' Day.

However the queen-regent was only for a short period the intermediary between the Holy See and the Ecclesia Scoticana: that soon passed to the king of France. It is to be noted that in the large-scale history of the papacy by Pastor, Scotland does not figure at all during the regency of Mary of Guise. Ordinary routine relations continue as before but politically Scotland ceases to exist as an independent nation and becomes a province of France. When the time came to arrange the marriage between the dauphin and Mary the terms of the treaty made it quite clear not only that any heir would unite France and Scotland dynastically, but that in the event of her death without heirs the dauphin would unite both countries. Any papal interest in Scotland was in fact in the hands of the cardinal of Lorraine, the younger brother of the queen regent, he was ten years younger and had been, since the age of nine, archbishop of Reims. France held Scotland by means of a French garrison but the prospect of any serious renovation of religious life in Scotland was not good. It was postponed until such time as a French king would be coming to Scotland to deal with his new province. If we look for political causes of the revolution of 1560 we must include among them dislike of the permanent disappearance of Scotland as an independent country but also the delay in carrying out this change and postponement of problems urgently needing attention. That is one reason for the ineffectiveness of synods and councils, however well-intentioned. The queen-regent's own words are on paper; " I pass over discords as gently as I can, preventing things from getting worse, waiting for a better time." Meanwhile propaganda for a revolutionary change and the overthrow of the old religion continued, and protestant ideas made progress.

A symptom of the new political situation is the appearance of a French bishop, the bishop of Amiens, Nicholas de Pellevé. He was sent by the king of France in June 1559, chosen by the French king, but it was intended by the French king that he should have the powers of a papal legate. The pope, who alone could give the necessary faculties, refused to do so. Doubt was expressed about the bishop's orthodoxy: moreover the relations between Pope Paul IV and France were far from cordial. Pellevé accordingly did arrive in Leith on a ship bringing reinforcements for the French army of garrison, but without papal faculties. However the new pope, Pius IV, did give him ample faculties. But he must still be described not as a papal legate but as a French legate with papal faculties. What is known of his activities does not amount to much: it will be found in Pollen's *Papal Negotiations*. Accounts vary and are rather contradictory: but the French episode was quite unexpectedly short: the treaty had made no provision for the prior death of the dauphin without an heir: in fact King Henry died on June 30th 1559 and Francis II on December 5th 1560. Queen Mary became dowager queen of France the only title she retained all her life: it gave her a large income and the right to have ambassadors. But she had no choice but to return to Scotland of which she was now an independent queen. She was not wanted in France, and, when she was driven from her own country and forced to abdicate it was to England that she turned not to France.

The first papal envoy to Queen Mary was a very different person from Nicholas de Pellevé. He was a Jesuit Father, Nicholas de Gouda, chosen very possibly because he was not a Frenchman, and, strangely enough he seems not to have been able to speak French, nor could he speak Scottish. He had, however competent assistance in Father Rivat but especially in Edmund Hay, later a Jesuit. He arrived in Leith in June 1562, and managed to escape disguised as a sailor, in September. His report is of the highest interest, it reflects the ideas of Edmund Hay: the extreme timidity of the catholic bishops is very notable. This visit achieved little, but it afforded an opportunity for direct news of Scotland in Rome, and for the queen to write to the pope declaring her inability to send bishops to the Council of Trent. It must be added that bishops, too timid to risk even an interview with de Gouda, could have done little for Scotland at Trent. The Tridentine decrees were never promulgated in Scotland and this affected catholic matrimonial law: but Tridentine decrees had an unfavourable reception even in several catholic countries and were, where promulgated, subject to many modifications by concordats, dispensations and in other ways too.

Papal dispensation was required for the marriage between Mary and Darnley, and contact with Rome was allowed for that purpose, the curious story of that dispensation and the embassies of William Chisholm on that errand will be found fully documented in Pollen's *Papal Negotiations*.

Wild rumours about Scotland abounded in Europe, and indeed it is not at all surprising that great ignorance about Scottish affairs prevailed in Rome: what was known concerned almost entirely court circles and certain parts of the lowlands: about the rest of Scotland ignorance was

PLATE XXXIX. ARCHBISHOP JAMES BEATON II
OF GLASGOW.

627

Semin' S'. Andreæ auspiciis Ser.mo Maria Stuarta Scotorum Regina
Parisiis inchoatum, inde beneficio Ser.mi D.N. Gregorÿ XIII tantisper
Nutr. pont. Sustentatum, donec liberalitate Regum Catholicorum
Philippi III et Philippi IV Louanÿ conseruaretur, ac postremo Duaci
stabilem sedem figeret anno Domini 1612.

PLATE XL.

THE
SCOTS
COLLEGE,
AT DOUAY,
IN
1627.

absolute. There begin, however, to be questionings about the loyalty of the queen to the church, and the suggestion is made that she ought to show greater firmness. No doubt normal canon law is silent during a revolution and is inapplicable, but the queen certainly took liberties in bestowing and permitting the alienation of church property, assuming that what she did was as valid as if it had been done by the pope. She bestowed the revenues of benefices on her household and staff: her critics and enemies continually repeat her misuse of church vestments, loot from Huntly Castle, but originally from Aberdeen Cathedral, which she gave from her wardrobe to be made into doublets for Bothwell. This is certainly not in harmony with normal catholic feeling. The culmination of this criticism was the despatch of the bishop of Mondovi, Vincenzo Laureo, as a papal nuncio in June 1566. He got only as far as Paris, and there he learned from Beaton that the cardinal of Lorraine was the real prime mover in sending him. His demand for greater firmness took the form of a suggestion that six leading rebels should be got rid of, beginning with her half-brother, the prior of St. Andrews and earl of Moray. One can find in Pollen a full discussion of the question who was responsible for this suggestion (the method of doing it whether by some kind of state trial or even by assassination does not seem to have greatly troubled Mondovi) and Pollen discusses and compares similar contemporary methods of counter-revolution. It was not, however, Moray who was murdered, it was Darnley. This was news startling enough to interest all Europe in Scotland, above all in the form it circulated from embassy to embassy that the queen was not sorry to lose her husband. Beaton in Paris was greatly perturbed at her failure to punish the murderers, and the pope, on the basis of Mondovi's report on the marriage of Mary to Bothwell, confirmed from other sources, declared he would have no further dealings with her till she showed some better sign of life and religion.

That ends the old, traditional relation between Rome and Scotland by the intermediary of a catholic sovereign: it needs little comment, but one can hardly fail to notice that the bishop of Mondovi thinks politically. His cure for Scotland is in the first place a political counter-revolution, two ways of effecting it were suggested, one was a Spanish invasion or threat of invasion from Flanders, the other was in the nature of what we, who are accustomed to such situations, call a " purge," the forcible " liquidation " of the ring-leaders, of whom he rightly saw the ambitious bastard of Scotland as the chief. Heresiarchs are not mentioned, one can assume he had heard of Knox, he is not on the proscription list. This diagnosis of the Scottish reformation as a political *coup d'état* using (largely insincerely) subversive heretical propaganda as a weapon and Knox as its minister of propaganda (in the modern sense of the word) is worth consideration: Mondovi may have been something of a cynic but he was not a fool.

It is no easy matter to attempt to give any account of the relations between Rome and Scotland during the reign of King James VI, for that is the normal way of thinking of the period 1567-1625. Certain interesting and indeed attractive topics ought to be excluded. Scotland means the people of Scotland and primarily that part of the people who still adhered to the Holy See or, as we should now describe them, Roman Catholics in Scotland. So we leave aside the queen, now deposed and a refugee of her own choice in England. She was a centre of intrigue for others, but no longer any sort of intermediary between the Holy See and Scottish catholics. We leave aside Scots abroad, some of them refugees, even those in Scottish colleges and in Scottish monasteries. More important always are those who, in a revolution do *not* run away: we leave aside Archbishop Beaton too, who lived long enough in comfort in Paris to see King James ascend the throne of England and who threw a party with fireworks to celebrate that event. The only refugee worth consideration is the man or youth who goes overseas for a catholic education he cannot get in Scotland, or for training for the priesthood with the effective intention to return to Scotland on the completion of his studies and to work in Scotland: such deserve our attention, while a man who goes overseas to qualify for a continental benefice and to start life all over again in a new country, deserves no particular notice.

Our main reports about catholics in Scotland come, in the first place, from a small group of young apostolic men, full of patriotic desire to re-convert their own country. A formal request was sent in June 1584 from Beaton in Paris to Pope Gregory XIII, asking him to get the general of the Jesuits to send priests of Scottish birth into Scotland, especially Edmund Hay, James Gordon, James Tyrie and William Crichton. There were others, not Jesuits, notably Dr. James Cheyne, and there were many Scottish priests in Paris, of whom a number professed readiness to go to Scotland if some means of support could be guaranteed. We have letters from these Jesuits, and from others too, for example from the Jesuits Robert Abercrombie, Alexander MacQuhirrie, Patrick Anderson and Blessed John Ogilvie the martyr. This however by no means gives the names of all the Scots who went overseas hoping and praying for the chance to return to Scotland: the sad truth is that they were needed elsewhere, even more than in Scotland and were prevented by religious obedience from returning. They did work for the church in central Europe, in Italy, in France but it was Scotland's loss. The driving of heresy out of the lands we now call Czecho-slovakia and Poland seemed more urgent than work in Scotland. At any rate zeal for the conversion of Scotland is far from prominent in papal councils or even in the central government of the Society of Jesus. The numbers sent were always quite hopelessly inadequate: seldom were there as many as ten or twelve, often far fewer were in Scotland at one time. (Scotland in medieval times had over 1200 parishes.) In 1605, Father Gordon said there was only one priest in all Scotland, and he old and infirm: it was not really quite so bad as that, but we can scarcely speak of the relation of the Holy See to Scotland when we get such statistics.

There was a further complication: one of the ideas then prevalent but rapidly becoming obsolete and old-fashioned was that the best way to convert a country was to begin by converting the king: or failing that by trying to convert his queen. It was not necessarily a bad idea, but it did not succeed. The story of the reconciliation of Anne of Denmark is well-known. Now, in 1603, the king of Scotland had moved permanently to London. The hope was expressed by Father Persons in 1581 to his general that England would be converted by way of Scotland: " Our chief hope is in Scotland, on which depends the conversion not of England only, but of all the North of Europe." But after the king went to London it seemed clear that if England were converted Scotland would follow, and work was concentrated on England. In 1623, Father William Leslie writes to the general to say there are only four Jesuits in all Scotland, two in the north and two in the south. When the English Jesuits were organised into a vice-province in 1619, they numbered 212 in the province and about 100 were in England. Yet in Scotland, Father Patrick Anderson reported that he knew in 1610 over 100 Scottish youths eager to go overseas for training and eager to return. Vocations were not lacking, money was lacking, but above all trained priests were sent elsewhere. We can read Blessed John Ogilvie's pleadings with the general to be sent to Scotland. Then and for a long time to come it was a question of importunate pleading from layfolk, crying out for priests, and for simple clergy pleading to be allowed to go to Scotland and using the impoitunate widow's only weapon, that of making themselves a nuisance until they were heard and till something was done. Indeed the same is true of the secular mission: when it was a question of organising the secular clergy in Scotland we do not find Cardinal Barberini stimulating priests to go to Scotland, we find a group of secular priests, led by William Ballantyne stimulating Cardinal Barberini.

Later on, the Scottish agent in Rome found the same problem and he made himself a very effective nuisance in Rome for fifty years. We have to remember that Scotland was a small and remote country, more than half of it, and the part where priests were most in demand, spoke a strange language: it is certain that, of those who wanted to have priests sent, far more than half were Gaelic-speaking. We can easily find excuses: other countries seemed more important and yet it is impossible to shirk the conclusion that in this period the relation of Rome to Scotland could be summed up in the word " indifference " and one could argue for the more offensive phrase " gross neglect." The penalty of this is far greater than we sometimes think it is. Not only was little or no progress made in recovering Scotland for catholicism: if Scotland had been catholic, the Scottish emigrants to Canada, the United States, to Australia and to New Zealand would not have been so largely protestant. Why are these countries so strongly presbyterian to-day? Mainly because Roman authorities did not take very seriously the problem of converting Scotland until the middle of the seventeenth century.

It is not really to the credit of Roman authorities that Scottish catholics, even if few in number, were left until 1653 without even a rudimentarily organised church at all: nor is it to their credit that so much difficulty was made about providing them with a missionary bishop. The argument was used that a bishop needs to keep up his dignity. In Asiatic missions (from which in fact came the system of vicars-apostolic, under which, from 1694, the church in Scotland was organised until 1878) it did not seem to matter so much, but in Europe, where once there had been magnificent figures like Cardinal Beaton, it seemed to be damaging to prestige if there were bishops walking about the highlands on foot, in a kilt, unaccompanied by monsignori and by canons and escorted by the horsemen expected in books of ceremonial for bishops processing about Italy in state. To some extent the idea that a bishop might himself be a *missionary* had been lost sight of: a country was thought of as ready for bishops only when it could provide means to enable him to officiate at solemn pontifical vespers, surrounded by the canons of his chapter. When, two hundred years later, Bishop Hay visited Rome and said a low mass he found that he had made " a little mistake " and that he did not know, though he had been a bishop for years, that a bishop is expected to give his blessing in the three-fold manner: so far he had been acting in liturgical matters like a simple priest, and had had no occasion to sing a mass at all. A bishop was urgently needed in Scotland and not that he might be a decorative public figure but for spiritual work. It took a little time for the Roman Court to realise that the late middle ages—at least in Scotland—were gone for ever. A sixteenth-century archbishop, like Thomas Wolsey of York, had drawn the revenue of York from 1514 to 1530 without having been once in his archdiocese and he was on his way there for the first time when sent there in political disgrace by his royal master. What Scotland needed and finally got was a man, like James Gordon, who in his forty years' episcopate as vicar-apostolic in Scotland, travelled all over his whole area about thirty times mainly on foot and in appearance as a layman. Even stranger is the further idea that episcopal consecration somehow *incapacitated* a priest for active daily missionary work. He would also, it was thought, need a few chaplains, and there were no priests to spare. The church was only slowly recovering from the evil renaissance days when bishops (unless exceptionally saintly) seldom *said* mass. What, they asked, were chaplains for ?

The new ideas, on which was based the new type of relation between Rome and Scotland and between Rome and any other country, where the catholic church as an organisation had disappeared, come from the foreign missions and from the far east. We have to remember and to be prepared to admit that Scotland is an extreme example of the effects of the reformation, as extreme as Sweden or other Scandinavian countries. In parts of the catholic world the reformation had only gravely damaged the organisation of the church. *There* the problem was how to salvage a wreck, patch it up and get the ship afloat again, and to proceed on the voyage. There were countries, where some bishoprics at least survived, where some religious houses kept together at least a remnant. In Scotland the wreck was total, and it was a total loss: a new ship was needed, there were some materials available, but it was a question of a new ship, and not of a replica of the lost vessel, which had proved unseaworthy.

In the course of human events there came a time when the last pre-reformation priest was dead and the last catholic who had been baptised before 1560 was dead also. When that time had come, the resemblance between the task of converting a pagan country and that of re-converting a protestant country became apparent. Vicars-apostolic seemed a strange invention, and at first they were far from well understood when they were first appointed in England. They were mistaken for bishops, and for bishops of the pre-reformation type. They are indeed in episcopal orders, but they first appear in China, they are adapted to pagan countries. They could also be well adapted to a country, where there could be no question of any use of the sovereign, acting as an intermediary between the Holy See and the organised church of the country, but where the civil government was probably hostile and at best tolerant or indifferent, and where the man in episcopal orders has no sort of special status or dignity.

There are necessarily important differences between a heretical and a pagan country: all, of course in favour of the pagan country. The pagan is a foreigner and stranger who has no duty of allegiance, the heretic is a rebel and a traitor. Personally he may know no better but his status is not improved by invincible ignorance. The church, from the days of St. Peter, had plenty of experience of life under pagan emperors. What had been done in Rome could be tried in China or Japan. But a heretic is not a poor benighted heathen. Can it be right for a catholic to obey a heretic: or, to reverse the terms of the question, can a heretic, and in particular a heretic of the type of King James VI, who never from his tenderest infancy had adhered to the catholic church be the lawful king over catholic subjects? This was a new question. Queen Elizabeth had been, in adult life, a catholic, anyhow had conformed. Henri IV of France, when he faced the question turned catholic. King James VI was very anxious to have the question answered in the affirmative: and he was very sensitive to any hedging or attempted evasion of the question. He wanted to be the first protestant king, clearly acknowledged to be such by catholics: it was for him a matter of prestige. He was in this matter in an entirely different position from Elizabeth who had been a catholic and had abandoned the catholic religion. Time has solved the question and we do not even ask the question whether a protestant king, who has never been a catholic, even if validly baptised, has a right to the obedience of his catholic subjects: he obviously has, the only difficulty concerns directly anti-catholic legislation: he has in fact the same right as a pagan king, or at least his position is very similar. It was entirely suitable that the organisation of missionary work in Great Britain should be modelled on what had been found to work in pagan lands.

By 1622, the whole world had been at least partially explored, it was at least known to be round, and it was somewhat larger than had been expected, but there was no more of it, however little we might know about central Africa or central Australia. The task of the catholic world was to convert it all and a programme of a comprehensive orderly type was for the first time constructed. Those parts of the world which still had catholic rulers remained, as they had been, directly under the pope, with similar relations to what they had before, nuncios, ambassadors and so on. All the rest of the world was entrusted to a new commission or congregation for the spread of the faith (*de Propaganda Fide*). All this vast area got a similar treatment, the only exception, not here relevant, concerned the separated oriental churches, which ultimately came under a special commission of their own. But all pagan or, as we often call them, missionary countries were the chief concern of this congregation, but non-catholic countries revolted from their allegiance to the Holy See also came under Propaganda. This is the reason for the enormous importance of the date 1622 in general catholic history.

The period 1567-1622 may be thought of as a transition period leading up to " Scotland under Propaganda, 1622-1908 " and it is only from that point of view it can be discussed here: but for the sake of completeness some few salient features of this new type of relation between Rome and Scotland ought to be given. It is in the first place a relation between a Roman Congregation and Scottish catholics, not between the pope and a catholic king of Scotland. Missionary priests, working in Scotland, if secular, are organised in a body under a superior who may be at first a simple priest, later he will be in episcopal orders, but not a diocesan bishop: he has a sphere of labours, which is not a diocese, but usually missionary territory, not necessarily with rigid geographical boundaries, for example in Scotland, when it came to be divided first the division was by language, the Gaelic-speakers and the clergy who cared for them were formed into the Highland District, the remainder of the country being the Lowland District, the " Highland Line " roughly dividing the two geographically. Such a missionary bishop is not an " ordinary ": *all* his authority is delegated ultimately from the pope by the intermediary of the Congregation of Propaganda, his exact powers can be ascertained only by inspection of the " faculties " he has received from them. He is easily removable if necessary, while the removal of a diocesan bishop, or the sub-division of his diocese, can indeed be effected by the Holy See but only after a somewhat troublesome process. Such a man, called a vicar-apostolic, need not have, and indeed is not expected to have any relations whatever with a civil government. Normal canon law is profoundly modified in the world under Propaganda. His missionary clergy are indeed his subjects, but they are also directly under Propaganda itself and are expected to send *directly* to Propaganda an annual letter giving an account of their work, and they get a personal subsidy, no doubt distributed by the vicar-apostolic but they are really working under Propaganda quite as much as under a bishop. The bishop and his clergy have an agent in Rome, he is one of the clergy in a most responsible position, with him they correspond and it is his duty to keep the needs of Scotland prominently in the agenda of any meetings of the Congregation of Propaganda to present reports and to report back to Scotland any decisions or comments. Regular priests of all orders except the Society of Jesus also worked under Propaganda: the foreign missions then undertaken by the Society of Jesus were not then and are not now subject to Propaganda. This arrangement caused troubles: but it cannot be said that Propaganda when it took over Scotland in 1622 and began at once to arrange for the missionary work of Irish Franciscans in the islands and highlands was in any way supplanting the Society, which then had no Gaelic-speaking missionaries whatever in Scotland and only four in all Scotland, two in the north and two in the south. Scotland was not in fact being converted at all and it was time to try new methods.

This new type of relation between Rome and Scotland which was begun at the very end of our period was a revolutionary change. Thereafter, Rome knew what was going on in Scotland, especially when the Roman agent was a man of competence, persistence and ability, and we had several such. It would be unfair however not to state that the regime had its critics, and not only from the Society of Jesus. The most famous of all ought to be given. It is Cardinal Newman in a more than usually bad temper. (*Life* i. p. 560). " But now, what do the Bishops do ? All courts are superseded because the whole English-speaking Catholic population all over the world is under Propaganda, an arbitrary military power. Propaganda is our only Court of Appeal, but to it the Bishops go and secure it and commit it before they move one step in the matter which calls for interference. And how is Propaganda to know anything about an English controversy since it talks Italian ? By extempore translation (I do not speak at random) or the *ex parte* assertion of some narrow-minded Bishop, though he may be saintly too. And who is Propaganda ? Virtually one sharp man of business, who works day and night, and despatches his work quick off to the East and the West, a high dignitary, indeed, perhaps an Archbishop but after all little more than a clerk, or (according to his name) a Secretary, and two or three clerks under him. In this age at least *Quantula sapientia regimur* ?" This was written in 1863 or 1864. It tells us a good deal about Cardinal Newman and very little about Propaganda. So far as Scotland was concerned all catholic life and all catholic progress in the conversion of Scotland from 1622, when the congregation took over Scotland, to 1908, when Propaganda finally ceased to control Scottish catholicism, must be ascribed to its work, for which we have every reason to be grateful. Since 1908 the task is in the hands of others.

INDEX

Abercorn, Lord, 231
Abercromby, Andrew, 160, 195, 199, 315n
Abercromby, Robert, S.J., 230, 315, 404, 427, 478
Abernethy, Robert, 290
Abernethy, Walter, 121
Abircrummy, James, 230
Acheson, Robert, 315n
Acts for Repression of Heresy, 68
Act of Restraint of Appeals, 41
Act of Revocation, 67
Act of Supremacy, 44
Adamson, Henry, 204
Adamson, John, 191n, 192-6, 220
Adamson, Patrick, Archbishop of St. Andrews, 30, 161
" Adventure schools," 156
Affleck, John, 230
Aikenhead, Robert, 148
Ainslie, William, 133
Aitken, Thomas, 200, 230
Alane, Alexander, see Alesius
Alane, Thomas, 280
Albany, John, Duke of, 2-4, 37, 44, 48, 222
Albi, Congregation of, 210
Albuquerque, Affonso de, 371
Aleandro, 287
Alesius, 277, 280, 285, 308, 312, 314n, 320, 375, 422n
Alexander VI, Pope, 40-44
Aliases, 134, 228n
Allan, John, 93, 135
Almonries, 118
Amboise, Tumult of, 79
Amyot, Jacques, 291
Ancrum Moor, 11
Anderson, Alexander, 316, 439
Anderson, David, 191n, 192, 203n
Anderson, John, 143
Anderson, Patrick, Schoolmaster in Ayr, 157
Anderson, Patrick, S.J., 273, 478
Anderson, Thomas, 243
Andrew, of Cruden, 191
Anglicisation, 298-302
Anglophobia, 62-3
Angus, Archibald Douglas, 6th Earl of, 2, 4, 11, 27
Angus, Archibald Douglas, 8th Earl of, 28, 30
Angus, John, 149
Annand, John, 190, 195, 224, 283, 307n, 311
Anti-Clericalism, 9, 56, 70, 172
Anti-Humanism, 292
Antinomians, 306
Antiphoners, 101, 216

Antwerp, 170
Appropriations, 74, 86, 129, 138, 215, 355, 427
Aquinas, St. Thomas, 41, 372
Arbuckle, Alexander, 199, 315
Arbuthnot, Alexander, 295
Argyll, Archibald Campbell, 4th Earl of, 5, 14, 15
Argyll, Archibald Campbell (Lord Lorne), 5th Earl of, 15, 21-22, 25-27, 78, 227, 369, 430-436, 440
Argyll, Colin Campbell, 6th Earl of, 27
Ariosto, 287
Arnot, David, Bp. of Galloway, 46, 49
Armada, 30
Arran, James Hamilton, 1st Earl of, 2, 4
Arran, James Hamilton, 2nd Earl of, Duke of Chatelherault, 8n, 9-13, 15, 17, 20, 24-6, 51-3, 75, 78, 171, 205, 287n, 301, 311, 419, 421, 436, 459, 474
Arran, James Hamilton, 3rd Earl of, 18, 20, 78, 387, 388n, 389, 436, 440
Arran, Regent, see Hamilton, James, 2nd Earl of
Arth, Friar, 233
Artillery, 189
Assumption of Thirds of Benefices, 131, 228
Assured Lords, The, 9, 70
Athens, Archbp. of, see Gordon, Alexander
Atholl, John Stewart, 4th Earl of, 23, 25, 27, 406
Auchinleck, John, 140
Augsburg, Interim of, 65-6, 253, 285, 312
Augustinian Canons, 119, 139, 220, 224-7, 230-1, 234-6, 238
Auld Alliance, 3-5, 10, 12-13, 28, 53, 75
Authority, Ecclesiastical and Secular, 312-4
Ayala, Don Pedro de, 455

Babington Plot, 30
Bade, Josse, 276, 285
Balbirny, David, 210
Balcasky, Martin, 299n
Balfour, James, Dean of Glasgow, 288
Balfour, Sir James, of Pittendreich, 22, 297
Ballads, 169-184 passim
Ballantyne, William, 368, 444n, 450, 479

493